Cisco CCNA Exam #640-507 Certification Guide

Wendell Odom, CCIE #1624

CISCO SYSTEMS

CISCO PRESS

Cisco Press
201 W 103rd Street
Indianapolis, IN 46290

Cisco CCNA Exam #640-507 Certification Guide

Wendell Odom

Copyright© 2000 Lacidar Unlimited, Inc.

Cisco Press logo is a trademark of Cisco Systems, Inc.

Published by:
Cisco Press
201 West 103rd Street
Indianapolis, IN 46290 USA

Printed in the United States of America 5 6 7 8 9 0

Library of Congress Cataloging-in-Publication Number: 99-67898

ISBN: 0-7357-0971-8

Warning and Disclaimer

This book is designed to provide information about the Cisco CCNA #640-507 exam. Every effort has been made to make this book as complete and as accurate as possible, but no warranty or fitness is implied.

The information is provided on an "as is" basis. The author, Cisco Press, and Cisco Systems, Inc., shall have neither liability nor responsibility to any person or entity with respect to any loss or damages arising from the information contained in this book or from the use of the discs or programs that may accompany it.

The opinions expressed in this book belong to the author and are not necessarily those of Cisco Systems, Inc.

Trademark Acknowledgments

All terms mentioned in this book that are known to be trademarks or service marks have been appropriately capitalized. Cisco Press or Cisco Systems, Inc., cannot attest to the accuracy of this information. Use of a term in this book should not be regarded as affecting the validity of any trademark or service mark.

Feedback Information

At Cisco Press, our goal is to create in-depth technical books of the highest quality and value. Each book is crafted with care and precision, undergoing rigorous development that involves the unique expertise of members from the professional technical community.

Readers' feedback is a natural continuation of this process. If you have any comments regarding how we could improve the quality of this book, or otherwise alter it to better suit your needs, you can contact us through e-mail at ciscopress@mcp.com. Please make sure to include the book title and ISBN in your message.

We greatly appreciate your assistance.

Publisher	John Wait
Executive Editor	John Kane
Cisco Systems Program Manager	Jim LeValley
Managing Editor	Patrick Kanouse
Development Editor	Christopher Cleveland
Senior Editor	Jennifer Chisholm
Copy Editor	Krista Hansing
Technical Editors	David Barnes
	Tinjin Chang
	Steve Kalman
	Frank Knox
	Barbara Nolley
Team Coordinator	Amy Lewis
Book Designer	Gina Rexrode
Cover Designer	Louisa Klucznik
Production Team	Argosy
Indexer	Christopher Cleveland

CISCO SYSTEMS

CISCO PRESS

Corporate Headquarters
Cisco Systems, Inc.
170 West Tasman Drive
San Jose, CA 95134-1706
USA
http://www.cisco.com
Tel: 408 526-4000
     800 553-NETS (6387)
Fax: 408 526-4100

European Headquarters
Cisco Systems Europe s.a.r.l.
Parc Evolic, Batiment L1/L2
16 Avenue du Quebec
Villebon, BP 706
91961 Courtaboeuf Cedex
France
http://www-europe.cisco.com
Tel: 33 1 69 18 61 00
Fax: 33 1 69 28 83 26

American Headquarters
Cisco Systems, Inc.
170 West Tasman Drive
San Jose, CA 95134-1706
USA
http://www.cisco.com
Tel: 408 526-7660
Fax: 408 527-0883

Asia Headquarters
Nihon Cisco Systems K.K.
Fuji Building, 9th Floor
3-2-3 Marunouchi
Chiyoda-ku, Tokyo 100
Japan
http://www.cisco.com
Tel: 81 3 5219 6250
Fax: 81 3 5219 6001

Cisco Systems has more than 200 offices in the following countries. Addresses, phone numbers, and fax numbers are listed on the Cisco Connection Online Web site at http://www.cisco.com/offices.

Argentina • Australia • Austria • Belgium • Brazil • Canada • Chile • China • Colombia • Costa Rica • Croatia • Czech Republic • Denmark • Dubai, UAE Finland • France • Germany • Greece • Hong Kong • Hungary • India • Indonesia • Ireland • Israel • Italy • Japan • Korea • Luxembourg • Malaysia • Mexico • The Netherlands • New Zealand • Norway • Peru • Philippines • Poland • Portugal • Puerto Rico • Romania • Russia • Saudi Arabia • Singapore • Slovakia • Slovenia • South Africa • Spain • Sweden • Switzerland • Taiwan • Thailand • Turkey • Ukraine • United Kingdom • United States • Venezuela

About the Author

Wendell Odom has worked with networking technology for 15 years. He is currently a Cisco Systems Senior Systems Engineer in the Atlanta, Georgia office, assigned to several large Cisco customers. Prior to joining Cisco in 1999, Wendell provided consulting services on large networks as well as training services. He spent his first eight years in networking working for IBM, helping customers evolve their SNA networks into multiprotocol networks. Wendell is CCIE #1624, is a Certified Cisco Systems Instructor, is Cisco CIP-certified, and is a CCNA-WAN. He has taught various Cisco-certified courses, including Introduction to Cisco Router Configuration (ICRC), Advanced Cisco Router Configuration (ACRC), Cisco SNA for Multiprotocol Administrators (SNAM), Cisco Channel Interface Processor (CIP), MPLS over Cisco WAN Switches, and Cisco ATM (CATM). Wendell is one of the first Cisco instructors certified without a probationary testing period and is the first non-Cisco instructor in the United States to teach Cisco's SNAM, CIP, and DLSw courses.

About the Technical Reviewers

David Barnes is a Network Consulting Engineer for Cisco Systems in Dallas, Texas. He is a Cisco Certified Design Professional, MCSE+Internet, and Master CNE. David specializes in large-scale network design and optimization. He has designed, implemented, and managed networks for numerous Fortune 500 companies over the past 10 years.

Tinjin Chang, CCIE #5137 and CCSI, is an instructor and consultant for Chesapeake Network Solutions, Inc. Tinjin has more than seven years of experience in planning, deploying, and troubleshooting complex and large-scale IP and multiprotocol networks. Prior to joining Chesapeake, he was the lead network engineer at Discover Brokerage, where his design and troubleshooting skills minimized downtime and guaranteed network availability. Discover Brokerage was named the Best Online Broker by *Barron's* magazine for the two years that he worked there.

Steve Kalman is a data communications trainer. He is the author or tech editor of 12 CBT titles and has been the author, tech editor, or trainer for eight instructor-led courses. Steve also is beginning a new distance-learning project as both author and presenter. In addition to those responsibilities, he runs a consulting company, Esquire Micro Consultants, that specializes in data network design.

Frank Knox, CCIE #3698, is a consultant and instructor currently involved in design, implementation, and customer training for mixed SNA-IP networks. He is considered to be an expert in the area of mainframe attached routers. Frank has more than 33 years of networking experience with IBM, GTE, and Skyline Computer Corp.; during that time, he has worked in field service and support, product planning, education, and management. In addition, he has developed and taught several courses for the University of Dallas (Telecommunications MBA program). Frank has a master's degree in telecommunications from Pace University.

Barb Nolley is the president and principal consultant for BJ Consulting, Inc., a small consulting firm that specializes in networking education. Since starting BJ Consulting, Barb has developed and taught training courses for Novell's Master CNE certification, as well as several courses for Cisco System's Engineering Education group. Barb stays current on networking technologies by constantly reading published books and perusing more than 50 industry publications each month. Prior to starting her own company in 1993, Barb worked for Apple Computer, Tandem Computer, and Tymnet (now part of MCI), where she held positions in everything from technical support to project management.

Dedication

My wife, Kris, was a great help to me during this latest writing project. While she took no direct role in the book, everything I do in life is a lot better because the love of my life is with me! Thanks to my parents, Raymond and Fay, who took care of many things during some health problems I had while writing the book. And finally, but most importantly, thanks to Jesus Christ, especially for your joy, peace, and protection in the midst of a tough year.

Acknowledgments

Chris Cleveland, development editor for Cisco Press, is the best in the business! Chris made my job much easier so that I could concentrate totally on the content. I'd probably refuse to write another book if Chris wouldn't be the development editor!

John Kane, executive editor for Cisco Press, provided a great deal of assistance, as usual. John's frequent e-mails and conference calls with Cisco's Worldwide Training organization allowed him to gather the information needed to guide Cisco Press's Cisco certification books, and it also allowed me to focus on writing, instead of sending e-mails and participating in conference calls! Thanks for everything, John.

Many people at Cisco Press have helped make this book a success. Amy Lewis helped greatly by taking care of many details. Many others worked behind the scenes, and although I never met them, they are appreciated! Cisco Press spends much more time producing the book than I do to simply write it—they have the laborious tasks! Thanks to all on the team!

The technical editors deserve most, if not all, of the credit for making the content robust and complete. There is no question that the book is immensely better after the edit process! While all the editors gave a great deal of help, each brought some particular strengths to the task. Tinjin, thanks for pointing out topics for which just a little deeper technical coverage would help to clear up a topic. Steve, thanks for the input relating to points that come up in the many classes you teach. David, thanks for jumping into the fray in the middle of the process and adding some great help. Barb, you get the most credit for removing errors from the book! (Of course, I take full responsibility for any remaining errors.) And, to my old friend Frank, thanks for all the help and the occasional good-bad joke in your editing comments! (An example: "What's a gateway? About 50 pounds!" If you didn't get it, "gateway" sounds like "gate weigh.") All the technical editors were an immense help.

Contents at a Glance

Table of Contents

Figure Icons Used in This Book

Throughout the book, you will see the following icons used for networking devices:

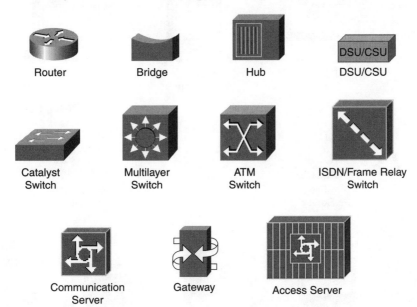

Router   Bridge   Hub   DSU/CSU

Catalyst Switch   Multilayer Switch   ATM Switch   ISDN/Frame Relay Switch

Communication Server   Gateway   Access Server

Throughout the book, you will see the following icons used for peripherals and other devices.

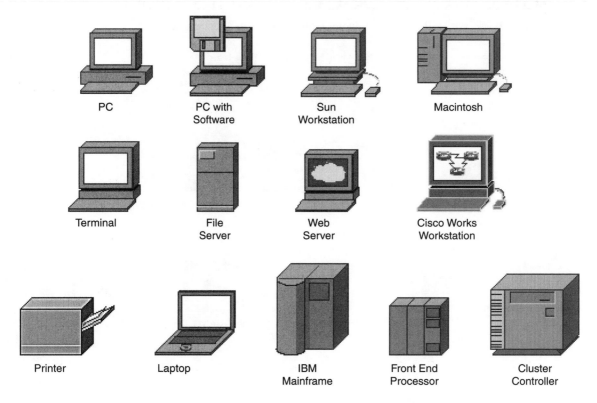

PC

PC with
Software

Sun
Workstation

Macintosh

Terminal

File
Server

Web
Server

Cisco Works
Workstation

Printer

Laptop

IBM
Mainframe

Front End
Processor

Cluster
Controller

Throughout the book, you will see the following icons used for networks and network connections.

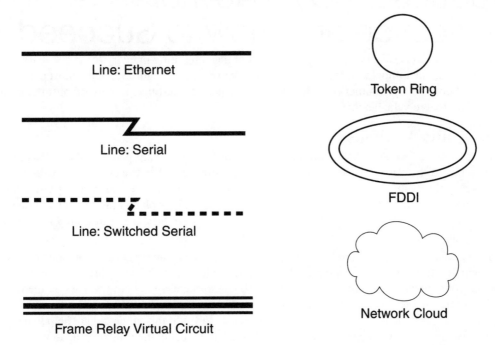

Line: Ethernet

Line: Serial

Line: Switched Serial

Frame Relay Virtual Circuit

Token Ring

FDDI

Network Cloud

Introduction: Overview of Certification and How to Succeed

Professional certifications have been an important part of the computing industry for many years and will continue to become more important. Many reasons exist for these certifications, but the most popularly cited reason is that of credibility. All other considerations held equal, the certified employee/consultant/job candidate is considered more valuable than one who is not.

Objectives and Methods

The most important and somewhat obvious objective of this book is to help you pass the CCNA exam (640-507). In fact, if the primary objective of this book was different, then the book's title would be misleading; however, the methods used in this book to help you pass the CCNA exam are designed to also make you much more knowledgeable about how to do your job. While this book and the accompanying CD together have more than 500 questions, the method in which they are used is not to simply make you memorize as many questions and answers as you possibly can.

One key methodology used in this book is to help you discover the exam topics about which you need more review, to help you fully understand and remember those details, and to help you prove to yourself that you have retained your knowledge of those topics. So, this book does not try to help you pass by memorization, but by helping you truly learn and understand the topics. The CCNA exam is the foundation for many of the Cisco professional certifications, and it would be a disservice to you if this guide did not help you truly learn the material. So, this book will help you pass the CCNA exam by using the following methods:

- Helping you discover which test topics you have not mastered

- Providing explanations and information to fill in your knowledge gaps

- Supplying exercises and scenarios that enhance your ability to recall and deduce the answers to test questions

- Providing practice exercises on the topics and the testing process via test questions on the CD

Who Should Read This Book?

This book is not designed to be a general networking topics book, although it can be used for that purpose. This book is intended to tremendously increase your chances of passing the CCNA exam. Although other objectives can be achieved from using this book, the book is written with one goal in mind: to help you pass the exam.

So why should you want to pass the CCNA exam? To get a raise. To show your manager you are working hard to increase your skills. To fulfill a requirement from your manager before he will spend money on another course. To enhance your résumé. To please your reseller-employer, who needs more certified employees for a higher discount from Cisco. To prove that you know the topic, if you learned via on-the-job training (OJT) rather than from taking the prerequisite classes. Or, one of many other reasons.

Others who might want to use this book are those considering skipping Cisco's Interconnecting Cisco Network Devices (ICND) course to take Cisco's Building Scalable Cisco Networks (BSCN) or Building Cisco

Multilayer Switched Networks (BCMSN) courses. If you can answer a high percentage of the questions in this book, you should be ready for those courses.

Strategies for Exam Preparation

The strategy you use for CCNA preparation might be slightly different than strategies used by other readers, mainly based on the skills, knowledge, and experience you already have obtained. For instance, if you have attended Cisco's Interconnecting Cisco Networking Devices (ICND) course, then you will need to take a slightly different approach compared to someone who has learned Cisco knowledge via on-the-job training. Chapter 1, "All About the Cisco Certified Network Associate Certification," includes a strategy that should closely match your background.

Regardless of the strategy you use or the background you have, the book is designed to help you get to the point where you can pass the exam with the least amount of time required. For instance, there is no need for you to practice or read about IP addressing and subnetting if you fully understand it already. However, many people like to make sure that they truly know a topic and thus read over material that they already know. Several book features will help you gain the confidence that you need to be convinced that you know some material already, and to also help you know what topics you need to study more.

How This Book Is Organized

Although this book could be read cover-to-cover, it is designed to be flexible and allow you to easily move between chapters and sections of chapters to cover just the material that you need more work with. Chapter 1 provides an overview of the CCNA certification, and offers some strategies for how to prepare for the exam. Chapters 2 through 8 are the core chapters and can be covered in any order. If you do intend to read them all, the order in the book is an excellent sequence to use. Chapter 9, "Scenarios for Final Preparation," provides many scenarios that will help you review and refine your knowledge, without giving you a false sense of preparedness that you would get with simply reviewing a set of multiple-choice questions.

The core chapters, Chapters 2 through 8, cover the following topics:

- **Chapter 2, "Cisco Internetwork Operating System (IOS) Fundamentals"**

- The IOS is the software that runs on a variety of Cisco products, particularly in routers and in some LAN switches. This chapter covers many of the features and functions of the IOS, as well as its command-line interface (CLI). Also included in this chapter are details about router hardware.

- **Chapter 3, "OSI Reference Model & Layered Communication"**

- The OSI reference model is mainly used today for comparison to other protocol architectures. The purposes and meanings behind the use of a layered model are discussed in this chapter. The features typically implemented at the various layers also are covered, and example protocols for each layer are given. Much of this information is conceptual and is not necessarily needed in order to implement networks, but it is covered on the exam.

  Also covered in Chapter 3 are the concepts involved in typical operation of the OSI network and data link layers. This conceptual discussion is vital to complete understanding of OSI Layer 2 and Layer 3 operation.

- **Chapter 4, "Bridges/Switches and LAN Design"**

- LANs—in particular, the various forms of Ethernet—are covered in this chapter. The logic behind transparent bridging and LAN switches is also discussed in depth, as is the operation of the Spanning-Tree Protocol. LAN switch configuration on the 1900 series LAN switch, using its IOS CLI, is covered as well.

- **Chapter 5, "Network Protocols"**

- This chapter discusses TCP/IP and NetWare protocols, as well as their configuration on Cisco routers. IP addressing is covered in great depth, with many tools to prepare you for questions on the exam. NetWare initialization flows and encapsulations are detailed as well.

- **Chapter 6, "Routing"**

- Routing protocols are used by routers to dynamically learn routing information. This chapter covers the types of routing protocols, with a detailed look at distance vector routing protocol logic. The implementation of IP RIP and IGRP, and Novell RIP and SAP, is covered here as well.

- **Chapter 7, "Understanding Access List Security"**

- Network security is a very broad subject area. This chapter focuses on the security topics covered on the CCNA exam—namely access lists. IP standard access lists, both numbered and named, are discussed as well. Likewise, numbered and named IPX and SAP access lists are described.

- **Chapter 8, "WAN Protocols and Design"**

- This chapter covers point-to-point serial links as the first type of WAN link and then discusses the various data link protocols used on point-to-point links, both for concepts and configuration. Frame Relay is covered in great detail, largely because point-to-point links and Frame Relay are the two most popular WAN options in routers today. Finally, this chapter covers ISDN protocols and their use in simple dial-on-demand (DDR) environments.

Additional scenarios in Chapter 9 provide a method of final preparation with more questions and exercises. Example test questions and the testing engine on the CD allow simulated exams for final practice.

Each of these chapters uses several features to help you make best use of your time in that chapter. The features are as follows:

- **"Do I Know This Already?" Quiz and Quizlets**—Each chapter begins with a quiz that helps you determine the amount of time you need to spend studying that chapter. The quiz is broken into subdivisions, called "quizlets," that correspond to a section of the chapter. Following the directions at the beginning of each chapter, the "Do I Know This Already?" quiz will direct you to study all or particular parts of the chapter.

- **Foundation**—This is the core section of each chapter that explains the protocols, concepts, and configuration for the topics in the chapter.

- **Foundation Summary**—Near the end of each chapter, a summary collects the most important tables and figures from the chapter. The "Foundation Summary" section is designed to help you review the key concepts in the chapter if you score well on the "Do I Know This Already?" quiz, and they are excellent tools for last-minute review.

- **Scenarios**—Located at the end of most chapters, as well as in Chapter 9, the scenarios allow a much more in-depth examination of a network implementation. Rather than posing a simple question asking for a single fact, the scenarios let you design and build networks (at least on paper) without the clues inherent in a multiple-choice quiz format.

- **CD-based practice exam**—The companion CD contains a large number of questions not included in the text of the book. You can answer these questions by using the simulated exam feature, or by using the topical review feature. This is the best tool for helping you prepare for the test-taking process.

Approach

Retention and recall are the two features of human memory most closely related to performance on tests. This exam preparation guide focuses on increasing both retention and recall of the topics on the exam. The other human characteristic involved in successfully passing the exam is intelligence; this book does not address that issue!

Adult retention is typically less than that of children. For example, it is common for 4-year-olds to pick up basic language skills in a new country faster than their parents. Children retain facts as an end unto itself; adults typically either need a stronger reason to remember a fact or must have a reason to think about that fact several times to retain it in memory. For these reasons, a student who attends a typical Cisco course and retains 50 percent of the material is actually quite an amazing student.

Memory recall is based on connectors to the information that needs to be recalled—the greater the number of connectors to a piece of information, the better chance and better speed of recall. For example, if the exam asks what ARP stands for, you automatically add information to the question. You know the topic is networking because of the nature of the test. You might recall the term "ARP broadcast," which implies that ARP is the name of something that flows in a network. Maybe you do not recall all three words in the acronym, but you recall that it has something to do with addressing. Of course, because the test is multiple-choice, if only one answer begins with "address," you have a pretty good guess. Having read the answer "Address Resolution Protocol," then you might even have the infamous "aha" experience, in which you are then sure that your answer is correct (and possibly a brightly lit light bulb is hovering over your head). All these added facts and assumptions are the connectors that eventually lead your brain to the fact that needs to be recalled. Of course, recall and retention work together. If you do not retain the knowledge, it will be difficult to recall it.

This book is designed with features to help you increase retention and recall. It does this in the following ways:

- By providing succinct and complete methods of helping you decide what you recall easily and what you do not recall at all.

- By giving references to the exact passages in this book that review those concepts you did not recall so that you can quickly be reminded about a fact or concept. Repeating information that connects to another concept helps retention, and describing the same concept in several ways throughout a chapter increases the number of connectors to the same piece of information.

- By including exercise questions that supply fewer connectors than multiple-choice questions. This helps you exercise recall and avoids giving you a false sense of confidence, as an exercise with only multiple-choice questions might do. For example, fill-in-the-blank questions require you to have better recall than a multiple-choice question.

- By pulling the entire breadth of subject matter together. A separate, larger chapter (Chapter 9) contains scenarios and several related questions that cover every topic on the exam and gives you the chance to prove that you have gained mastery over the subject matter. This reduces the connectors implied by questions residing in a particular chapter and requires you to exercise other connectors to remember the details.

- Finally, accompanying this book is a CD-ROM that has exam-like, multiple-choice questions. These are useful for you to practice taking the exam and to get accustomed to the time restrictions imposed during the exam.

CHAPTER 1

All About the Cisco Certified Network Associate Certification

Congratulations! You have made your first step in beginning your journey to joining the Cisco Career Certifications group of certified professionals. CCNA is the first step into your journey.

The Cisco Certified Network Associate (CCNA) certification is the most popular certification among all Cisco certifications. CCNA certification is a prerequisite for several other Cisco Certifications, which of course adds to its popularity.

The exam itself is a computer-based exam, with multiple choice, fill-in-the-blank, and drag-and-drop style questions. The CCNA exam is delivered by our testing vendor, Sylvan Prometric, which you can reach at 1-800-829-NETS, or you may register online at www.2test.com. As we continually update the exams, the duration and number of questions per exam will vary. When you register for your exam, the registrar will reserve the appropriate time. You should check with Sylvan Prometric for the exact length of the exam.

NOTE   Be aware that when you register for the exam, you might be notified of a specific length of time, and when you actually log in to the testing software at the testing center, you might find that the testing time is 15 minutes shorter; that's because Sylvan Prometric expects some time to be required for getting settled and taking the tutorial on the testing engine.

The CCNA exam is not an easy, read the book and you pass kind of exam. It is surprisingly hard, but Cisco's philosophy is that by passing the exam, you fully understand the concepts. More importantly, Cisco wants to be sure that passing the exam proves that you have the skills to actually implement the features, not just talk about them. For instance, you can expect questions that ask for the name of a router command that displays a particular piece of information—most of us don't memorize all the types of things displayed by every **show** command! So, the difficulty helps enhance the value of the CCNA certification, which ultimately is better for those of us who are getting certified.

Also, in order to ensure the exam proves that you know your stuff, the exam does NOT allow you to go back and change an answer, as many other exams allow, and as the original version of the CCNA exam allowed.

Although it is a difficult exam, if your time is spent on training, experience, and study, you are preparing yourself for success. If you don't prepare adequately, it is more than likely that you will not pass the first time. The concepts and commands covered on the exam are not secrets locked in some vault, though—the information is available in many places and forms, including this book. So, while difficult, passing the exam is certainly attainable with proper training and preparation.

How This Book Can Help You Prepare and Pass the CCNA Exam

The first goal for this book came at the request of the Cisco Career Certifications team; they asked that we build a book that didn't just help you pass a test, but also for a book that helped you really understand the concepts and implementation details. (Because Cisco Press is the only Cisco authorized publisher, we tend to listen to Cisco!) A second goal was to make the content of the book the most comprehensive coverage of CCNA-related topics available, but without a lot of coverage of topics not on the exam. The third and ultimate goal is to get you from where you are today to the point where you can confidently pass the CCNA exam. So, all the book features, which are outlined in the Introduction, are geared toward helping you discover what CCNA topics you do know well, what CCNA topics you don't know well, and what information and tools you need to fill in the gaps.

One key assumption this book makes is that the perfect audience is made up of people who either have attended the Interconnecting Cisco Networking Devices class or the Introduction to Cisco Router Configuration class, or have had similar experience with Cisco switches and routers. If you are relatively new to Cisco networking and have not taken any classes, do not despair! You can still use this book, but also should consider either taking the ICND class or buying the book version of the ICND class from Cisco Press—*Interconnecting Cisco Network Devices*. The ICND course, and therefore also the ICND book, are written for an audience of those who are just starting out in the Cisco world.

Overview of Cisco Certifications

Cisco's main motivation behind the current certification program is to provide a means of measuring the skills of people working for Cisco Resellers and Certified Partners. Cisco fulfills only a small portion of its orders via direct sale from Cisco; most times, a Cisco reseller is involved. Also, Cisco has not attempted to become the primary source for consulting and implementation services for network deployment using Cisco products; instead, the company prefers to use partners as much as possible. With that business model, a great need arose to certify the skill levels of the partner companies.

The Cisco Certified Internetworking Expert (CCIE) program was Cisco's first foray into certifications. Introduced in 1994, the CCIE was designed to be one of the most respected, difficult-to-achieve certifications. To certify, a person must pass a written test (also given at

Sylvan Prometric centers) and then pass a 2-day hands-on lab test administered by Cisco. Cisco does not publish numbers on pass/fail rates for CCIE or the other certifications, but rumors have it that the failure rate on all lab test-takers is more than 50 percent, with failure rate for first-time lab-takers at more than 80 percent.

By using the number of employed CCIEs as the gauge, certifying resellers and services partners worked well originally, partly because Cisco had significantly fewer partners than today. Cisco uses the number of CCIEs on staff as part of the criteria in determining the level of partner status for the company, which in turn dictates the discount received by the reseller when buying from Cisco. (If you want a little more insight into reseller certification, look at www.cisco.com/warp/public/767/chan/ptnrcert-matrix.html.) This practice continues to be a good way for Cisco to judge the commitment of resellers to hire people with proven Cisco skills, which in turn improves customer satisfaction—and customer satisfaction is tied to every Cisco executive's bonus plan.

The CCIE certification fell short of the goal to help certify resellers and other partners as the number of partners increased. For instance, there are around 4500 CCIEs worldwide, and about half that many resellers—and not all the CCIEs work for resellers, of course. More importantly, many resellers that did not perform services did not need a CCIE on staff except to get a better discount. Thus, Cisco needed certifications that were less rigorous than CCIE, which would allow Cisco more granularity in judging the skills on staff at a partner company. So, Cisco created several additional certifications, with CCNA included. Figure 1-1 shows the CCIE and career certifications for routing and switching.

Two categories of certifications were developed: one to certify implementation skills, and the other to certify design skills. Resellers working in a presale environment need more design skills, whereas services companies need more implementation skills. So, the CCNA and CCNP provide implementation-oriented certifications, whereas the CCDA and CCDP certifications provide design-oriented certifications.

Rather than instituting just one level of certification besides CCIE, Cisco created two additional levels: an Associate level and a Professional level. CCNA is the more basic, and CCNP is the intermediate level between CCNA and CCIE. Likewise, CCDA is more basic than CCDP. You can view these details at Cisco's Web site, www.cisco.com/warp/public/10/wwtraining/certprog/lan/course.html.

Several of the certifications require other certifications as a prerequisite. For instance, CCNP certification requires CCNA first. Also, CCDP requires both CCDA and CCNA certification. CCIE, however, does not require any other certification prior to the written and lab tests, mainly for historical reasons.

Cisco certifications have taken on a much larger role in the networking industry. From a career standpoint, Cisco certification certainly can be used to help you get a new job. Or, you can add certification to your performance evaluation plan and justify a raise based on passing an exam. If you are looking for a new job, not only might certification help you land the job, but it actually might help you make more money!

Figure 1-1   *Cisco Routing and Switching Certifications*

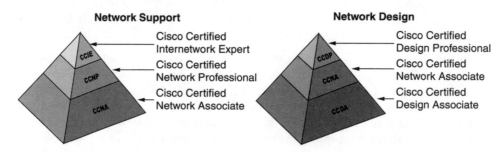

CCNA Proves Implementation Skills for Simple Networks
CCDA Proves Design Skills for Simple Networks
CCNP Proves Implementation Skills for Intermediate Networks
CCDP Proves Design Skills for Intermediate Networks
CCIE   Proves Implementation Skills for Complex Networks

Exams Required for Certification

To certify for CCNA, a single exam is required: Sylvan Prometric exam number 640-507. For CCDA, a single exam is required as well, but multiple exams are required for CCNP and CCDP. The exams generally match the same topics that are covered in one of the official Cisco courses, but in most cases—and certainly on the CCNA exam—more topics are covered on the exam than are in the course. Table 1-1 outlines the exams and the courses with which they are most closely matched.

Table 1-1   *Exam-to-Course Mappings*

Certification	Exam Number	Name	Course Most Closely Matching Exam Requirements
CCNA	640-507	CCNA Exam	Interconnecting Cisco Network Devices (ICND)
CCDA	640-441	DCN Exam	Designing Cisco Networks
CCNP	640-503	Routing Exam	Building Scalable Cisco Networks (BSCN)
	640-504	Switching Exam	Building Cisco Multilayer Switched Networks (BCMSN)
	640-505	Remote Access Exam	Building Cisco Remote Access Networks (BCRAN)
	640-509*	Foundation Exam	BSCN, BCMSN, and BCRAN
	640-506	Support Exam	Cisco Internetwork Troubleshooting (CIT)

Table 1-1   *Exam-to-Course Mappings (Continued)*

Certification	Exam Number	Name	Course Most Closely Matching Exam Requirements
CCDP	640-503	Routing Exam	Building Scalable Cisco Networks (BSCN)
	640-504	Switching Exam	Building Cisco Multilayer Switched Networks (BCMSN)
	640-505	Remote Access Exam	Building Cisco Remote Access Networks (BCRAN)
	640-509*	Foundation Exam	BSCN, BCMSN, and BCRAN
	640-025	CID Exam	Cisco Internetwork Design (CID)

* Exam 640-509 meets the same requirements as passing these three exams: 640-503, 640-504, and 640-505.

Be cautioned that, while the exam coverage and course coverage are similar, there are no guarantees that you will pass the test if you know absolutely everything in the course. Cisco is moving more toward tying the certifications to technology, not to specific courses; note that the exam names do not match the course names, as they previously did. So, a study guide can help you with the other certifications as well as CCNA, with the added guidance of stressing the most important exam items and covering other topics not held in the prerequisite courses.

Other Cisco Certifications

The certifications mentioned so far are oriented toward routing and LAN switching. Cisco has many other certifications as well, as summarized in Table 1-2. Refer to Cisco's Web site at www.cisco.com/warp/public/10/wwtraining/certprog/index.html for the latest information.

Table 1-2   *Additional Cisco Certifications*

Certification	Purpose, Prerequisites
CCNA-WAN	Basic certification for Cisco WAN switches.
CCNP-WAN	Intermediate certification for Cisco WAN switches. Requires CCNA-WAN.
CCDP-WAN	Design certification for Cisco WAN switches. Requires CCNP-WAN.
CCIE-WAN	Expert-level certification for Cisco WAN switches. No prerequisite. Requires exam and lab.
CCIE-ISP Dial	CCIE-level certification for Internet service provider (ISP) and dial network skills. No prerequisite. Requires exam and lab.

continues

Table 1-2   *Additional Cisco Certifications (Continued)*

Certification	Purpose, Prerequisites
CCIE-SNA-IP	Expert-level certification for Cisco products and features used for melding SNA and IP networks. No prerequisite. Requires exam and lab.
CCNP and CCDP specializations	Several specialized certifications are available for CCNP and CCDP (routing/switching); see www.cisco.com/warp/public/10/wwtraining/certprog/special/course.html for more details.

What's on the CCNA Exam

Every test-taker would like to know exactly what is on the CCNA exam, as well as the other Cisco certification exams. Well, to be honest, *exactly* what is on the exam is a very closely guarded secret. Only those who write the questions for Cisco, and who have access to the entire question database, truly know what is really on the exam.

Cisco makes fairly general CCNA exam content available to the public at the Web site www.cisco.com/warp/public/10/wwtraining/certprog/lan/course.html. In fact, two direct quotes from this Web site sumarize the exam:

> CCNA Certification skills: Install, configure, and operate simple-routed LAN, routed WAN, and switched LAN networks.

> What defines "simple" networks: IP, IGRP, IPX, Serial, AppleTalk, Frame Relay, IP RIP, VLANs, IPX RIP, Ethernet, Access Lists.

Frankly, most people could guess more detail about the exam than what these two quotes say about it. As Cisco's authorized external publishing company, Cisco Press provides some additional information, part of which includes some details that are expected to be posted on Cisco's Web site at a later date. At press time, Cisco had not finalized what other details about the exam will be posted on the Web site, so none of those details can be discussed here. Fortunately, you'll have easy access to what Cisco does decide to post. Be sure to check Cisco's Web site for the latest information on the exam.

A couple of comments can be made about the exam in general:

- If we at Cisco Press believe that a topic is definitely on the exam, it is covered in Chapters 2 through 8.

- If we at Cisco Press believe that a topic is simply not in the Cisco CCNA question database, then it is not covered in this book. The only exception would be a topic that is not on the exam that must be explained in order to make a topic that is on the exam more understandable.

Topics on the Exam

The following list outlines the topics that will be the focus of the exam. These topics are shown corresponding to the chapters in which they are covered.

- Chapter 2, "Cisco Internetwork Operating System (IOS) Fundamentals"
    - Router components
    - The IOS CLI
    - Managing configuration files
    - Cisco Discovery Protocol (CDP)
    - Upgrading flash memory
    - IOS initialization
- Chapter 3, "OSI Reference Model & Layered Communication"
    - OSI layers, benefits of layering, interactions of OSI layers
    - TCP/IP and NetWare comparisons with OSI
    - Connectionless and connection-oriented protocols
    - Data link layer functions
    - Network layer functions: addressing and routing
- Chapter 4, "Bridges/Switches and LAN Design"
    - LAN addressing and framing
    - Fast Ethernet and Gigabit Ethernet
    - LAN standards
    - Transparent bridging
    - LAN switching
    - Spanning-Tree Protocol
    - LAN switch configuration (1900 family)
    - VLAN trunking protocol

- Chapter 5, "Network Protocols"
  - TCP/IP
  - IP addressing and subnetting
  - TCP/IP configuration
  - IPX addressing and routing
  - IPX configuration
- Chapter 6, "Routing"
  - Distance vector routing protocols
  - Configuration of IP RIP and IP IGRP
  - Autosummarization and route aggregation
  - IPX RIP, SAP, and GNS concepts
  - IPX configuration
  - Tunneling
  - Integrated routing protocols
- Chapter 7, "Understanding Access List Security"
  - Filtering IP traffic
  - Filtering IPX traffic
- Chapter 8, "WAN Protocols and Design"
  - Frame Relay concepts and configuration
  - Point-to-point concepts and configuration
  - ISDN concepts
  - Dial-on-Demand Routing (DDR)

Recommended Training Path for CCNA

Cisco recommends that you take two courses before you take the CCNA exam. The first, Internetworking Technology Multimedia (ITM), is a CD-based course that you can order directly from Cisco (www.cisco.com/warp/customer/10/wwtraining/cust/course_itm.html) currently for $50. This course covers many of the protocol basics needed for CCNA.

The other suggested course is the instructor-led Interconnecting Cisco Network Devices (ICND) course, which is available from almost every Cisco training partner (for a list of training partners, go to www.cisco.com/warp/public/10/wwtraining/listAllTP.html). The ICND course replaces the old Introduction to Cisco Router Configuration (ICRC) course, as well as the less-popular Cisco Routing and LAN Switching (CRLS) course.

So, if you have taken or will take ICND, that's the best way to prepare for the CCNA exam. Reading the ITM CD will be helpful as well. But what if you took one of the older courses? Or, what if you took the Cisco Networking Academy curriculum? Or, what if you simply choose not to spend the money on an introductory course? The final section of this chapter suggests a strategy for people from each background.

First, an outline of the ICND course, shown in Table 1-3, should be helpful. Remember, although the CCNA exam is not a test on the ICND course, ICND is the course that most closely matches the CCNA topics.

Table 1-3   *ICND Course Summary*

Module Title	Topics in This Module
Interconnecting Cisco Networking Devices Introduction	Typical administrative details.
Internetworking Concepts Overview	OSI model details; common physical and data link specifications; MAC address definition; description of Ethernet, Token Ring, and FDDI operation; a brief explanation of WAN data links.
Assembling and Cabling Cisco Devices	Short chapter on basic physical setup and cabling.
Operating and Configuring a Cisco IOS Device	Logging in, initialization, modes of operation, passwords, help, command editing, and various **show** commands.
Managing Your Network Environment	Telnet, CDP, and managing the IOS and config files.
Catalyst 1900 Switch Operations	LAN switching concepts, spanning tree, and 1900 switch configuration.
Extending Switched Networks with Virtual LANs	Virtual LANs, VLAN trunking, and VLAN configuration on 1900 switches.

continues

Table 1-3   *ICND Course Summary (Continued)*

Module Title	Topics in This Module
Interconnecting Networks with TCP/IP	Protocol stack versus OSI; application layer examples; TCP error recovery; TCP and UDP ports; TCP, UDP, and IP headers; and ICMP. For Class A, B, and C networks: IP addresses, mask subnetting, and planning; configuring IP addresses; configuring host names; configuring DNS; and verifying operation with **ping**, **trace**, and **show** commands.
Determining IP Routes	Configuring static routes; configuring default routes; interior versus exterior routing protocols; configuring RIP; debugging RIP; IGRP configuration; and IGRP **debug** and **show** commands.
Basic IP Traffic Management with Access Lists	The purpose of using access lists, logic diagrams, standard and extended access lists, and TCP/IP access lists; wildcard masks; configuring standard IP access lists; configuring extended access lists; monitoring IP access lists.
Configuring Novell IPX	Protocol versus OSI, IPX addresses, Novell encapsulation options, RIP, SAP, GNS, configuring IPX, displaying IPX, debugging IPX, and IPX access-lists.
Establishing Serial Point-to-point Connections	Telephone company service basics, survey of data link protocols for WANs, SDLC/HDLC/PPP/LAPB framing, PPP functions, PAP and CHAP authentication, and PAP and CHAP configuration.
Completing an ISDN BRI Call	ISDN Protocol basics and dial-on-demand routing (DDR).
Establishing a Frame Relay PVC Connection	Terminology, LMI messages, Inverse ARP, addressing, configuration, monitoring, configuration using subinterfaces, NBMA, and full and partial mesh issues.

How to Use This Book to Pass the Exam

One way to use this book is to start at the beginning and read it cover to cover. Although that certainly would help you prepare, most people would not take that much time, particularly if you already knew a lot about some of the topics in the book.

The rest of you might want to consider a different strategy on how to best use this book, depending on what training you have had. This book is designed to help you get the most out of the time you take to study.

The core material for the CCNA is covered in Chapters 2 through 8. At the beginning of each chapter, you are instructed on how to make the best use of your time reading that chapter, assuming that you are not going to read every detail. The instructions on how to use each chapter are outlined in Figure 1-2.

Figure 1-2   *How to Use Chapters 2 Through 8*

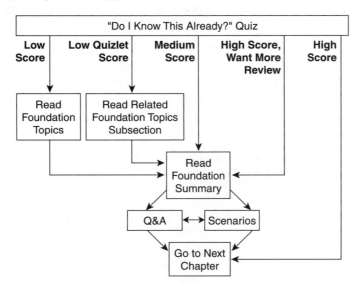

Each of these chapters begins with a quiz, which is broken into subdivisions called "quizlets." If you get a high score, you might simply review the "Foundation Summary" section at the end of the chapter. If you score well on one quizlet but low on another, you are directed to the section of the chapter corresponding to the quizlet on which your score was low. If you score less than 50 percent on the overall quiz, you should read the whole chapter. Of course, these are simply guidelines—if you score well but want more review on that topic, read away!

After completing the core chapters (Chapters 2 through 8), you have several options for your next study activity. Because Chapter 9, "Scenarios for Final Preparation," is the next chapter in succession, it outlines the directions on what to do next. These same directions are repeated here as well. Figure 1-3 outlines your options for final study for the exam.

Figure 1-3   *Final CCNA Exam Preparation Study Strategy*

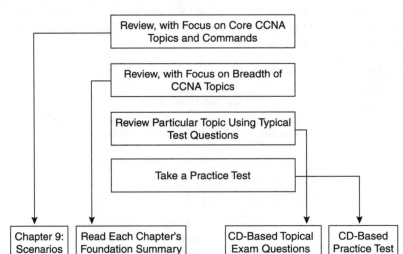

As shown, if you want even more final preparation, you can go over the many practice questions located in each chapter and on the CD. All pre-chapter quiz and chapter-ending questions, with answers, are in Appendix A, "Answers to the 'Do I Know This Already?' Quizzes and Q&A Sections." You can read and review these conveniently located questions and explanations quickly. The CD includes testing software, as well as many additional questions in the format of the CCNA exam. These questions should be a valuable resource when performing final preparations.

Anyone preparing for the CCNA exam can use the guidelines at the beginning of each chapter as a study aid. However, for some additional guidance, the final parts of this chapter give a few strategies for study, based on how you have prepared before buying this book. So, find the section that most closely matches your background in the next few pages, and read about some additional ideas to help you prepare. There is a section for people who have taken ICND, one for those who have taken ICRC, one for those from the Cisco Networking Academies, one for those who will not be taking any classes and have not had much experience, and a final set of strategies for those who will not be taking any classes but who have some experience.

I've Taken ICND—Now What?

For starters, you've taken the best path to prepare yourself. But let me temper that with the fact that if you retain more than 50 percent of what you heard in class, then you are an extraordinary person! That said, you need the following three strategies:

Strategy 1: Use this book exactly as described in the opening pages of Chapters 2 through 8, respectively. Each of the foundational chapters begins with a quiz that helps you assess what you need to study. It then directs you to the appropriate sections in the chapter rather than requiring you to read all of each chapter.

Strategy 2: Make it a point to read the sections of the book that cover topics not found in ICND. These section titles are as follows:

- Chapter 2—"Syslog and Debug"
- Chapter 3—"The OSI, TCP/IP, and NetWare Protocol Architectures"
- Chapter 3—"OSI Transport Layer Functions"
- Chapter 5—"CIDR, Private Addressing, and NAT"
- Chapter 6—"Distance Vector Routing Protocols"
- Chapter 6—"Tunneling"

Strategy 3: Use the directions at the beginning of Chapter 9 to direct your final study before the exam. Chapter 9 is designed to review many concepts, and it outlines a good process for study in the days leading up to your exam.

By using these three strategies, you will fill in the gaps in your knowledge and be confident taking your CCNA exam.

I've Taken ICRC—Now What?

The current version of the exam more closely matches the ICND class. However, if you compared the two course books, you would find much more in common than is different. In fact, more than half of ICND is directly taken from the ICRC course. Of course, if you retain more than 50 percent of what you heard in class, then you are an extraordinary person, so you probably still need to fill in some holes in your knowledge base. For you, the following strategies will be most helpful:

Strategy 1: Begin with a complete study of Chapter 4, which covers LANs and LAN switching. ICRC did not cover LAN switching and Spanning-Tree Protocol, which are covered here in detail. Do not skip the configuration sections, either—they are very important.

Strategy 2: Use this book exactly as described in the opening pages of Chapters 2 through 8. Each of the foundational chapters begins with a quiz that helps you assess what you need to study. It then directs you to the appropriate sections in the chapter rather than requiring you to read all of each chapter. In fact, you probably should use Chapter 4 this way as well, in spite of having read it already, because that will validate what you have learned.

Strategy 3: Make it a point to read the sections of the book that cover topics not found in ICRC. Other than almost all of Chapter 4 of this book, the section titles you will want to be sure to read are as follows:

- Chapter 2—"Syslog and Debug"
- Chapter 3—"The OSI, TCP/IP, and NetWare Protocol Architectures"
- Chapter 3—"OSI Transport Layer Functions"
- Chapter 5—"CIDR, Private Addressing, and NAT"
- Chapter 6—"Distance Vector Routing Protocols"
- Chapter 6—"Tunneling"

Strategy 4: Use the directions at the beginning of Chapter 9 to direct your final study before the exam. Chapter 9 is designed to review many concepts, and it outlines a good process for study in the days leading up to your exam.

So, compared to those who have taken ICND, you should not require a lot of additional study time. The ICRC course did a great job of explaining the basics, and hopefully this book will help you retain enough to confidently pass the exam.

I've Taken the Cisco Networking Academy Courses—Now What?

First of all, congratulations on having the foresight to get into the Cisco Networking Academy program—we need more people who can make this stuff work! (Those of you who didn't take the Cisco Networking Academy track and are wondering what it's all about, check out www.cisco.com/warp/public/779/edu/academy/.) Thankfully, the Networking Academy curriculum actually does a great job of preparing you with the skills and knowledge you need to pass the exam. Unfortunately, your study was probably spread over several semesters, and possibly over a couple of years. So, the details that you do not use frequently may have been forgotten. Now, on to the strategies for success on CCNA:

Strategy 1: Pull out your Networking Academy curriculum and notes, and reread them. Most people's memory is exercised better by seeing familiar material—and even more so when you wrote it down yourself. If you have ever taken a test and pictured in your mind where the answer was on your page of notes, then you can relate.

Strategy 2: Use this book exactly as described in the opening pages of Chapters 2 through 8. Each of the foundational chapters begins with a quiz that helps you assess what you need to study. It then directs you to the appropriate sections in the chapter rather than requiring you to read all of each chapter.

Strategy 3: Make it a point to read the sections that cover some of the theory behind networking and some of the standards. The biggest reason for that is that the Networking Academy is oriented more toward building skills than theoretical knowledge. The suggested sections are listed here:

- Chapter 3—From the beginning of the "Foundation Topics" section up to the beginning of the section "The TCP/IP and NetWare Protocols"

- Chapter 4—"Spanning Tree"
- Chapter 6—"Distance Vector Routing Protocols"

Strategy 4: Use the directions at the beginning of Chapter 9 to direct your final study before the exam. Chapter 9 is designed to review many concepts, and it outlines a good process for study in the days leading up to your exam.

This book should help you sift through the topics and choose the right areas for study, and it also should help you to not waste your time. Congratulations on your Networking Academy work—now add the CCNA certification to take away any doubt in the minds of prospective employers that you know Cisco!

I'm New to Internetworking with Cisco, and I Will Not Be Taking the ICND Course—Now What?

You can pass the CCNA exam without taking any courses. Of course, Cisco wants you to take the recommended courses for all the exams—its motivation is not to make more money, because Cisco does not actually deliver the training; the training partners do. Instead, Cisco truly believes that the more people understand its products, ultimately the happier its customers will be and the more products Cisco will sell. Cisco also believes that the official training is the right way to teach people about Cisco products, so you're encouraged to take the classes.

If you are not taking any course, however, there is no reason to worry. Truthfully, though, you will need more than just this book. Cisco Press publishes the *Interconnecting Cisco Networking Devices* book, which is a book version of the ICND course. The figures look exactly like those in the course book, and the text comes from the course book, expanded and reorganized to work well in book format. So, if you can't get to the course, for not a lot of money you can buy the ICND book.

Of course, this book will be helpful, too. Try these suggestions:

Strategy 1: Buy the ICND book and read it. Although CCNA is not a course-based test, the ICND course is listed as the only leader-led prerequisite course for CCNA.

Strategy 2: After reading ICND, use this book exactly as described in the opening pages of Chapters 2 through 8. Each of the foundational chapters begins with a quiz that helps you assess what you need to study. It then directs you to the appropriate sections in the chapter rather than requiring you to read all of each chapter.

Strategy 3: Make it a point to read the sections of the book that cover topics not found in ICND. These section titles are as follows:

- Chapter 2—"Syslog and Debug"
- Chapter 3—"The OSI, TCP/IP, and NetWare Protocol Architectures"

- Chapter 3—"OSI Transport Layer Functions"
- Chapter 5—"CIDR, Private Addressing, and NAT"
- Chapter 6—"Distance Vector Routing Protocols"
- Chapter 6—"Tunneling"

Strategy 4: Use the directions at the beginning of Chapter 9 to direct your final study before the exam. Chapter 9 is designed to review many concepts, and it outlines a good process for study in the days leading up to your exam.

I've Learned a Lot About CCNA Topics Through Experience, But I Will Not Be Taking the ICND Course—Now What?

If you feel that you know a fair amount about CCNA topics already but are worried about the topics you simply just have not worked with, then this strategy is for you. This book is designed to help you figure out what CCNA topics you need some help with and then help you learn about them. Here's the simple strategy for you:

Strategy 1: Use this book exactly as described in the opening pages of Chapters 2 through 8. Each of the foundational chapters begins with a quiz that helps you assess what you need to study. It then directs you to the appropriate sections in the chapter rather than requiring you to read all of each chapter.

Strategy 2: Use the directions at the beginning of Chapter 9 to direct your final study before the exam. Chapter 9 is designed to review many concepts, and it outlines a good process for study in the days leading up to your exam.

You should be able to fill in the gaps in your knowledge this way and not risk being bored in the ICND class when it covers the topics you already know.

Conclusion

The CCNA certification is arguably the most important Cisco certification. It certainly is the most popular, is required for several other certifications, and is the first step in distinguishing yourself as someone who has proven knowledge of Cisco.

The *CCNA Exam 604-507 Certification Guide* is designed to help you attain CCNA certification. This is the CCNA certification book from the only Cisco-authorized publisher. We at Cisco Press believe that this book certainly can help you achieve CCNA certification—but the real work is up to you! I trust that your time will be well spent.

This chapter covers the following topics that you will need to master as a CCNA:

- **The IOS and Its User Interface**   This section examines the types of memory used by the IOS, in addition to the commands used to examine and change the contents. This section also describes the basic functions and help for the command-line interface (CLI), and discusses how syslog messages are treated.

- **Configuration Processes and the Configuration File**   The configuration file used for a router contains all the configuration for that router. This section covers all commands used to change the configuration and manipulate the configuration file.

- **Managing IOS Images**   This section covers in detail the processes for upgrading the IOS in Flash memory, as well as the commands used to tell the router which IOS image to use. Password recovery is included as well.

CHAPTER 2

Cisco Internetwork Operating System (IOS) Fundamentals

The CCNA exam requires that you understand the basics of the Cisco Internetwork Operating System (IOS). In fact, the only operating system and user interface covered on the CCNA exam is the IOS and its user interface. The omission of other user interfaces, in particular the Catalyst 5000/5500 series user interface, is one of the most important facts to note when determining what to study for the CCNA exam.

The IOS runs on some Cisco switch models and provides the familiar IOS command-line interface (CLI). This chapter is geared toward the IOS CLI on a router. Chapter 4, "Bridges/ Switches and LAN Design," covers some details of IOS CLI on LAN switches. The user interface is the same, but some commands are different.

The exam also includes questions on both router and LAN switch usage of the IOS. No one should be surprised that the CCNA exam covers IOS running on routers. Also covered on the exam is the use of IOS running on Cisco 1900 series switches. User interfaces on other switch platforms might seem to be like IOS and have similar features, but these details are not covered on the exam. That should be particularly helpful for those of you with less hands-on experience.

Cisco requires that CCNAs exhibit a solid recollection of the many details of the CLI. Of course, the best way to learn about any user interface is to use it. If you can spend time using a Cisco router, the knowledge and recall you gain will be of significant value. This chapter is designed to remind you of details you might not notice when practicing and will provide a reference for those of you who do not have access to routers for practice. Still, there is no substitute for hands-on practice.

How to Best Use This Chapter

By taking the following steps, you can make better use of your study time:

- Keep your notes and the answers for all your work with this book in one place, for easy reference.

- Take the "Do I Know This Already?" quiz, and write down your answers. Studies show that retention is significantly increased through writing down facts and concepts, even if you never look at the information again.

- Use the diagram in Figure 2-1 to guide you to the next step.

Figure 2-1   *How to Use This Chapter*

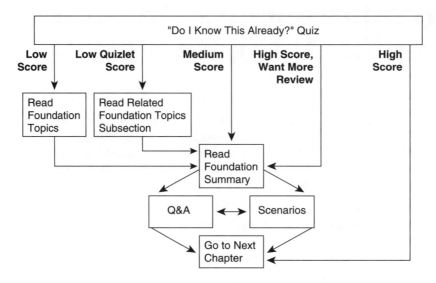

"Do I Know This Already?" Quiz

The purpose of the "Do I Know This Already?" quiz is to help you decide what parts of this chapter to use. If you already intend to read the entire chapter, you do not necessarily need to answer these questions now.

This 12-question quiz helps you determine how to spend your limited study time. The quiz is sectioned into three smaller four-question "quizlets," which correspond to the three major topic headings in the chapter. Figure 2-1 outlines suggestions on how to spend your time in this chapter based on your quiz score. Use Table 2-1 to record your scores.

Table 2-1   *Scoresheet for Quiz and Quizlets*

Quizlet Number	Foundation Topics Section Covering These Questions	Questions	Score
1	The IOS and Its User Interface	1 to 4	
2	Configuration Processes and the Configuration File	5 to 8	
3	Managing IOS Images	9 to 12	
All questions		1 to 12	

1 What are the two different names for the router's mode of operation that, when accessed, enables you to issue commands that could be disruptive to router operations?

_____

_____

_____

2 What command would you use to receive command help if you knew that a **show** command option begins with a **c**, but you cannot recall the option?

_____

_____

_____

3 After typing **show ip route**, which is the only command you issued since logging in to the router, you now want to issue the **show ip arp** command. What steps would you take to execute this command by using command recall keystrokes?

_____

_____

_____

4 What is the name of the user interface mode of operation used when you cannot issue disruptive commands?

_____

_____

_____

5 What configuration command causes the router to require a password from a user at the console? What configuration mode context must you be in—that is, what command(s) must be typed before this command after entering configuration mode? List the commands in the order in which they must be typed while in config mode.

_____

_____

_____

6 What does CDP stand for?

_____

_____

_____

7 What does the NV stand for in NVRAM?

_____

_____

_____

8 Name two commands used to view the configuration that is currently used in a router. Which one is a more recent addition to the IOS?

_____

_____

_____

9 What two methods could a router administrator use to cause a router to load the IOS stored in ROM?

_____

_____

_____

10 What is the process used to update the contents of Flash memory so that a new IOS in a file called c4500-d-mz.120-5.bin, on TFTP server 128.1.1.1, is copied into Flash memory?

_____

_____

_____

11 Two different IOS files are in a router's Flash memory: one called c2500-j-l.111-3.bin and one called c2500-j-l.112-14.bin. Which one does the router use when it boots up? How could you force the other IOS file to be used? Without looking at the router configuration, what command could be used to discover which file was used for the latest boot of the router?

_____

_____

_____

12 What are the primary purposes of Flash memory in a Cisco router?

_____

_____

_____

The answers to the "Do I Know This Already?" quiz are found in Appendix A, "Answers to the 'Do I Know This Already?' Quizzes and Q&A Sections," on page 701. The suggested choices for your next step are as follows:

- **6 or less overall score**—Read the entire chapter. This includes the "Foundation Topics" and "Foundation Summary" sections, the Q&A section, and the scenarios at the end of the chapter.

- **2 or less on any quizlet**—Review the subsection(s) of the "Foundation Topics" part of this chapter, based on Table 2-1. Then move into the "Foundation Summary" section, the Q&A section, and the scenarios at the end of the chapter.

- **7, 8, or 9 overall score**—Begin with the "Foundation Summary" section and then go to the Q&A section and the scenarios at the end of the chapter.

- **10 or more overall score**—If you want more review on these topics, skip to the "Foundation Summary" section and then go to the Q&A section and the scenarios at the end of the chapter. Otherwise, move to the next chapter.

Foundation Topics

The IOS and Its User Interface

IOS, a registered trademark of Cisco Systems, is the name of the operating system found in most of Cisco's routers. The majority of Cisco routers run the IOS, with its familiar command-line interface (CLI). Also, some routing cards in other devices run IOS. For example, the Route/Switch Module (RSM) card for the Catalyst 5000 series LAN switches performs routing functions and executes the IOS.

Fixes and code updates to the IOS can include new features and functions. To learn more about the code release process, features added at particular IOS revision levels, and other terminology that will help you talk to the Cisco Technical Assistance Center (TAC), check out a current Cisco Product Bulletin describing the Software Release Process. One such example is Product Bulletin #537 (http://www.cisco.com/warp/public/cc/cisco/mkt/ios/rel/prodlit/537_pp.htm).

The exam topics covered in this section will become second nature to you as you work with Cisco routers and switches more often. In fact, because this book purposefully was written for an audience that already has some training and experience with Cisco routers, several of the details in this chapter might already be ingrained in your memory. If you would like more review, or if you are still new to the IOS, read on—the details in this section are important to using Cisco routers and switches. This chapter reviews such topics as router components, the CLI, and how to navigate the IOS command set using Help and key sequences for command edit and recall.

Router Components

Before examining the IOS, a review of hardware and hardware terminology is useful. In addition to handling the logic of routing packets, the IOS controls the use of different physical components, which includes memory, processor, and interfaces. This section of the book reviews common hardware details.

All Cisco routers have a console port, and most have an auxiliary port. The console port is intended for local administrative access from an ASCII terminal or a computer using a terminal emulator. The auxiliary port, missing on a few models of Cisco routers, is intended for asynchronous dial access from an ASCII terminal or terminal emulator; the auxiliary port is often used for dial backup.

Each router has different types of memory, as follows:

- **RAM**—Sometimes called DRAM for *dynamic* random-access memory, RAM is used by the router just as it is used by any other computer: for working storage.

- **ROM**—This type of memory (read-only memory) stores a bootable IOS image, which is not typically used for normal operation. ROM contains the code that is used to boot the router until the router knows where to get the full IOS image.

- **Flash memory**—Either an EEPROM or a PCMCIA card, Flash memory stores fully functional IOS images and is the default where the router gets its IOS at boot time. Flash memory also can be used to store configuration files on Cisco 7500 series platforms.

- **NVRAM**—Nonvolatile RAM stores the initial or *startup* configuration file.

All these types of memory are permanent memory except RAM. No hard disk or diskette storage exists on Cisco routers. Figure 2-2 summarizes the use of memory in Cisco routers.

Figure 2-2   *Cisco Router Memory Types*

The processors in the routers vary from model to model. Although they are not specifically listed as requirements for the CCNA exam, some reference to terminology is useful. In most routers, only one processor option is available; thus, you would not order a specific processor type or card. The exception to this is the 7200 and 7500 families of routers. For instance, on the 7500 series, you choose either a Route Switch Processor 1 (RSP-1), RSP-2, or RSP-4 processor. In any case, all 7200 and 7500 routers, as well as most of the other Cisco router families, run IOS. This commonality enables Cisco to formulate exams, such as CCNA, that cover the IOS features without having to cover many hardware details.

Interfaces are used by a router for routing packets and bridging frames through a router. The types of interfaces available change over time due to new technology. For example, packet-over-SONET and voice interfaces are relatively recent additions to the product line. However, some confusion exists about what to call the actual cards that house the physical interfaces. Table 2-2 summarizes the terminology that might be referred to on the test.

Table 2-2   *Samples of Router Interface Terminology*

Model Series	What the IOS Calls Interfaces	What the Product Catalog Calls the Cards with the Interfaces on Them
2500	Interface	Modules and WAN interface cards
3600	Interface	Network modules and WAN interface cards
4500	Interface	Network processor modules
7200	Interface	Port adapters and service adapters
7500	Interface	Interface processors, and versatile interface processors with port adapters

Physical interfaces are referred to as *interfaces* by the IOS commands, as opposed to *ports* or *plugs*. IOS commands familiar on one platform will be familiar on another. Some nuances are involved in numbering the interfaces, however. In some smaller routers, the interface number is a single number. However, with some other families of routers, the interface is numbered first with the slot in which the card resides, followed by a slash and then the port number on that card. For example, port 3 on the card in slot 2 would be interface 2/3. Numbering starts with 0 for card slots and 0 for ports on any card. In some cases, the interface is defined by three numbers: first the card slot, then the daughter card (typically called a port adapter), and then a number for the physical interface on the port adapter. The 2600 and 3600 families also use a slot/port numbering scheme.

In this book, the single-digit interface numbers are used simply for consistency and readability.

If you want to dig deeper, you might want to read about processors and interfaces in the Cisco Product Catalog (http://www.cisco.com/univercd/cc/td/doc/pcat/).

Command-Line Interface

Cisco uses the acronym CLI to refer to the terminal user command-line interface to the IOS. The term CLI implies that the user is typing commands at a terminal, terminal emulator, or Telnet connection. Although you can pass the CCNA exam without ever having used the CLI, actually using the CLI will greatly enhance your chances.

To access the CLI, use one of three methods, as illustrated in Figure 2-3.

Figure 2-3   *CLI Access*

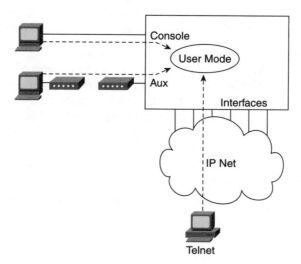

Regardless of which access method is used, a CLI user initially is placed in user mode, or user EXEC mode, after logging in. *EXEC* refers to the fact that the commands typed here are executed, and some response messages are displayed onscreen. The alternative mode is *configuration mode*, which is covered in the next section.

Passwords can be required when accessing the CLI. In fact, the default configuration at IOS 12.x requires a password for Telnet and auxiliary port access, but no password is set—therefore, you must configure passwords from the console first. Table 2-3 reviews the different types of passwords and the configuration for each type.

Table 2-3   *CLI Password Configuration*

Access From . . .	Password Type	Configuration
Console	Console password	**line console** *0* **login** **password** *faith*
Auxiliary	Auxiliary password	**line aux** *0* **login** **password** *hope*
Telnet	vty password	**line vty** *0 4* **login** **password** *love*

The **login** command actually tells the router to display a prompt. The **password** commands specify the text password to be typed by the user to gain access. The first command in each configuration is a context-setting command, as described in the section "Configuration Processes and the Configuration File," later in this chapter. Typically, all three passwords have the same value.

Several concurrent Telnet connections to a router are allowed. The **line vty** *0 4* command signifies that this configuration applies to vtys (virtual teletypes—terminals) 0 through 4. Only these five vtys are allowed by the IOS unless it is an IOS for a dial access server, such as a Cisco AS5300. All five vtys typically have the same password, which is handy because users connecting to the router via a Telnet cannot choose which vty they get.

User EXEC mode is one of two command EXEC modes in the IOS user interface. *Enable* mode (also known as *privileged* mode or *privileged EXEC* mode) is the other. Enable mode is so named because of the command used to reach this mode, as shown in Figure 2-4; privileged mode earns its name because powerful, or privileged, commands can be executed there.

Figure 2-4   *User and Privileged Modes*

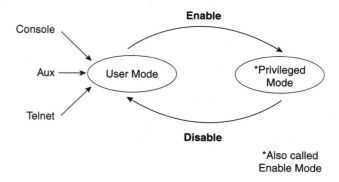

Navigating the IOS CLI

Several references are available for help when you are using the IOS. IOS documentation is available on CD and is free from Cisco if you own one router or switch under a current maintenance agreement. Paper documentation is also available from Cisco. If you prefer, Cisco Press offers the Cisco Documentation series (more information at www.ciscopress.com). In addition, all Cisco documentation is available online at Cisco's Web site (www.cisco.com/univercd/home/home.htm); the IOS command reference is found at www.cisco.com/univercd/cc/td/doc/product/software/ios120/12cgcr/index.htm.

No matter which documentation you use, it is incredibly unlikely that you will remember all IOS commands. (The command reference manuals stack 14 inches high.) Therefore, you will find tools and tricks to recall commands particularly useful. Table 2-4 summarizes command recall help options available at the CLI. Note that in the first column, "Command" represents any command. Likewise, "parm" represents a command's parameter. For instance, the third row lists "command ?," which means that commands such as **show ?** and **copy ?** would list help for the **show** and **copy** commands, respectively.

Table 2-4   *IOS Command Help*

What You Type	The Help You Get
?	Help for all commands available in this mode.
help	Text describing how to get help. No actual command help is given.
command ?	Text help describing all the first parameter options for the command **command**.
com?	A list of commands that start with "com."
command parm?	This style of help lists all parameters beginning with "parm." (Notice, no spaces exist between "parm" and the ?.)

Table 2-4   *IOS Command Help (Continued)*

What You Type	The Help You Get
command parm<Tab>	If the user presses the Tab key midword, the CLI will either spell the rest of this parameter at the command line for the user, or do nothing. If the CLI does nothing, it means that this string of characters represents more than one possible next parameter, so the CLI does not know which to spell out.
command parm1 ?	If a space is inserted before the question mark, the CLI lists all next parameters and gives a brief explanation of each.

*   When you type the **?**, the IOS's CLI reacts immediately; that is, you don't need to press the Enter key or any other keys. The router also redisplays what you typed before the ? to save you some keystrokes. If you press Enter immediately after the ?, the IOS tries to execute the command with only the parameters you have typed so far.

**   "Command" represents any command, not the word "command." Likewise, "parm" represents a command's parameter, not the word "parameter."

The context in which help is requested is also important. For example, when **?** is typed in user mode, the commands allowed only in privileged EXEC mode are not displayed. Also, help is available in configuration mode; only configuration commands are displayed in that mode of operation.

Commands you use at the CLI are stored in a command history buffer that retains the last 10 commands you typed. You can change the history size with the **terminal history size** x command, where x is the number of commands for the CLI to recall; this can be set to a value between 0 and 256.

Of course, most people want to use a previously typed command (perhaps with a different parameter). Commands you have previously used during the current console/aux/Telnet can be retrieved and then edited to save you some time and effort. This is particularly useful when you are typing long configuration commands. Table 2-5 lists the commands used to manipulate previously typed commands.

Table 2-5   *Key Sequences for Command Edit and Recall*

Keyboard Command	What the User Gets
Up-arrow or Ctrl+p	This displays the most recently used command. If pressed again, the next most recent command appears, until the history buffer is exhausted. (The p stands for *previous*.)
Down-arrow or Ctrl+n	If you have gone too far back into the history buffer, these keys will go forward, in order, to the more recently typed commands. (The n is for *next*.)
Left-arrow or Ctrl+b	This moves the cursor backward in the currently displayed command without deleting characters. (The b stands for *back*.)

continues

Table 2-5 *Key Sequences for Command Edit and Recall (Continued)*

Keyboard Command	What the User Gets
Right-arrow or Ctrl+f	This moves the cursor forward in the currently displayed command without deleting characters. (The f stands for *forward*.)
Backspace	This moves the cursor backward in the currently displayed command, deleting characters.
Ctrl+a	This moves the cursor directly to the first character of the currently displayed command.
Ctrl+e	This moves the cursor directly to the end of the currently displayed command.
Esc+b	This moves the cursor back one word in the currently displayed command.
Esc+f	This moves the cursor forward one word in the currently displayed command.
Ctl+r	This creates a new command prompt, followed by all the characters typed since the last command prompt was written. This is particularly useful if system messages confuse the screen and it is unclear what the user has typed so far.

NOTE   One goal of this book is to help you learn more and solidify your understanding of the materials on the CCNA exam. Hopefully, Table 2-5 will further your understanding. Beware—these details are covered on the exam questions.

Syslog and Debug

The IOS creates messages when different events occur and, by default, sends them to the console. These messages are called *syslog* messages. If you have used the console of a router for any length of time, you likely have noticed these messages—and when they are frequent, you probably became a little frustrated.

The **debug** command is one of the key diagnostic tools for troubleshooting difficult problems on a router. **debug** enables monitoring points in the IOS and generates messages that describe what the IOS is doing and seeing. When any debug command option is enabled, the router processes the messages with the same logic as other syslog messages. Beware—some **debug** options create so many messages that the IOS cannot process them all, possibly crashing the IOS.

NOTE   The **no debug all** command disables all debugs. Before enabling an unfamiliar **debug** command option, issue a **no debug all** and then issue the **debug** you want to use; then, quickly retrieve the **no debug all** command. If the messages are voluminous, press Enter immediately to try to prevent the router from crashing by immediately disabling all debugs.

Users might or might not be interested in seeing the messages as they occur. The console port always receives syslog messages. When a user telnets to the router, however, no syslog messages are seen unless the user issues the **terminal monitor** command. This command simply means that this terminal is monitoring syslog messages. Another alternative for viewing syslog messages is to have the IOS record the syslog messages in a buffer in RAM, and then use the **show logging** command to display the messages. For Telnet users, having the messages buffered using the global config command **logging buffered** is particularly useful. Because Telnet users do not get syslog messages by default anyway, these users can wait and look at syslog messages when desired. Finally, the **logging synchronous** line configuration subcommand can be used for the console and vtys to tell the router to wait until the user's last command output is displayed before showing any syslog messages onscreen. That provides a little less interruption for the user.

Syslog messages also can be sent to another device. Two alternatives exist: sending the messages to a syslog server, and sending the messages as SNMP traps to a management station. The **logging** *host* command, where *host* is the IP address or host name of the syslog server, is used to enable sending messages to the external server. After SNMP is configured, the **snmp-server enable trap** tells the IOS to forward traps, including syslog messages.

Figure 2-5 summarizes the flow of syslog messages, including debug messages. For a more detailed view of syslog messages, including restricting messages based on message severity, refer to the IOS documentation CD manual called "Troubleshooting Commands."

Figure 2-5   *Syslog Message Flows*

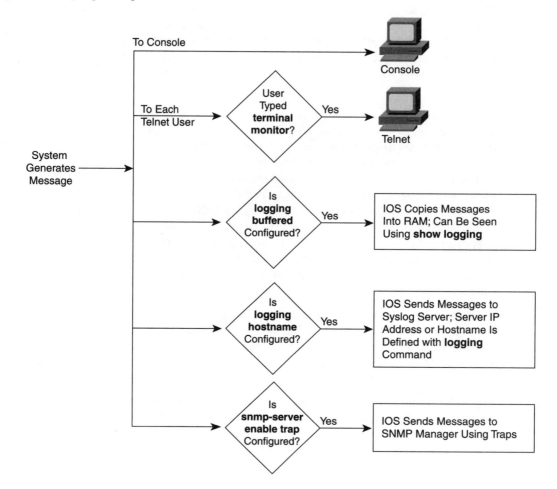

Configuration Processes and the Configuration File

Cisco requires that CCNAs master the process of changing and manipulating the configuration files in the IOS. This includes initially setting up an IOS device, handling ongoing configuration, and moving configuration files.

As mentioned in Chapter 1, "All About the Cisco Certified Network Associate Certification" configuration mode is another mode for the Cisco CLI. Changing the configuration of the router by typing various configuration commands is the purpose of configuration mode. Figure 2-6 illustrates the relationships among configuration mode, user EXEC mode, and priviledged EXEC mode.

Figure 2-6   *CLI Configuration Mode Versus EXEC Modes*

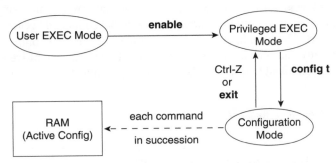

Commands typed in configuration mode update the active configuration file. Changes are moved into the active configuration file each time the user presses the Enter key and are acted upon immediately by the router.

In configuration mode, context-setting commands are used before most configuration commands. These context-setting commands tell the router the topic about which you will type commands. More importantly, they tell the router what commands to list when you ask for help. After all, the whole reason for these contexts is to make online help more convenient and clear for you.

NOTE   *Context setting* is not a Cisco term—it's just a term used here to help make sense of configuration mode.

The **interface** command is the most commonly used context-setting configuration command. As an example, the CLI user could enter interface configuration mode after typing the **interface ethernet 0** configuration command. Command help in Ethernet interface configuration mode displays only commands that are useful when configuring Ethernet interfaces. Commands used in this context are called *subcommands*—or, in this specific case, *interface subcommands*. Figure 2-7 shows several different configuration mode contexts, including *interface configuration mode*, and illustrates the relationships and methods of moving among them.

The labels on the lines in Figure 2-7 represent the action or command that moves the user from one mode to another. For example, from console configuration mode (left box), the **interface ethernet 0** command could move you to the box on the right, which represents interface configuration mode.

If you have significant experience using the CLI in configuration mode, much of this will be second nature. From a CCNA exam perspective, recalling whether popular commands are global commands or subcommands will be useful. No set rules exist for what commands are global or subcommands, but generally, when multiple instances of a parameter can be set in a single router, the command used to set the parameter is likely to be a configuration sub-command. Items that are set once for the entire router are likely to be global commands. For instance, the **hostname** command is a global command because there is only one host name per router. The **interface ethernet 0** command is a global configuration command because there is only one such interface in this router. Finally, the **ip address** command is an interface subcommand that sets the IP address on the interface; each interface will have a different IP address.

Figure 2-7   *Relationships Among Context-Setting Commands*

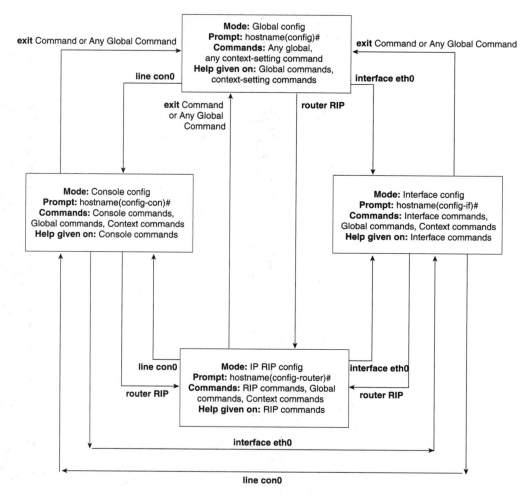

Use Ctrl+z from any part of configuration mode (or use the **exit** command from global configuration mode) to exit configuration mode and return to privileged EXEC mode. The configuration mode **end** command also exits from any point in the configuration mode back to privileged EXEC mode. The **exit** commands from submodes or contexts of configuration mode back up one level toward global configuration mode.

Example Configuration Process

Example 2-1 illustrates how the console password is defined; provides banner, host name, prompt, and interface descriptions; and shows the finished configuration. The lines beginning with "!" are comment lines that highlight significant processes or command lines within the example. The **show running-config** command output also includes comment lines with just a "!" to make the output more readable—many comment lines in the examples in this book were added to explain the meaning of the configuration.

Example 2-1   *Configuration Process Example*

```
This Here's the Rootin-est Tootin-est Router in these here Parts!

User Access Verification

Password:
Yosemite>enable
Password:
Yosemite#configure terminal
Yosemite(config)#enable password lu
Yosemite(config)#line console 0
Yosemite(config-line)#login
Yosemite(config-line)#password cisco
Yosemite(config-line)#hostname Critter
Critter(config)#prompt Emma
Emma(config)#interface serial 1
Emma(config-if)#description this is the link to Albuquerque
Emma(config-if)#exit
Emma(config)#exit
Emma#
 Emma#show running-config
Building configuration...

Current configuration:
!
version 11.2
! Version of IOS on router, automatic command


no service udp-small-servers
no service tcp-small-servers
!
```

continues

Example 2-1   *Configuration Process Example (Continued)*

```
hostname Critter
prompt Emma
! Prompt overrides the use of the hostname as the prompt
!
enable password lu


! This sets the priviledge exec mode password
!
no ip domain-lookup
! Ignores all names resolutions unless locally defined on the router.
!
ipx routing 0000.3089.b170
! Enables IPX rip routing
!
interface Serial0
 ip address 137.11.12.2 255.255.255.0
 ipx network 12
!
interface Serial1
 description this is the link to Albuquerque
 ip address 137.11.23.2 255.255.255.0
 ipx network 23
!
interface TokenRing0
 ip address 137.11.2.2 255.255.255.0
 ipx network CAFE
 ring-speed 16
!
router rip
 network 137.11.0.0
!
no ip classless
!
!
!
banner motd ^C This Here's the Rootin-est Tootin-est Router in these here Parts! ^C
! Any text between the Ctl+C keystrokes is considered part of the banner, including
!the Enter key.!


line con 0
 password cisco
 login
! login tells the router to supply a prompt; password defines what the user must
!type!
!
line aux 0
line vty 0 4
 password cisco
 Login
!
End
```

Managing Configuration Files

The CCNA exam requires that you be able to distinguish between the configuration file used at startup and the active configuration file. The startup configuration file is in NVRAM; the other file, which is in RAM, is the one the router uses during operation. The router copies the stored configuration file from NVRAM into RAM as part of the boot process. Exterior to the router, configuration files can be stored as ASCII text files anywhere using TFTP.

Cisco provides several methods of manipulating configuration files. CiscoWorks and other management products let you create configurations for one or many routers without logging on to those routers. NetSys Connectivity Tools actually check all the configuration files in your network, make suggestions for improvements, and uncover errors. The most basic method for manipulating configuration files and moving them into and out of a router, however, is by using a TFTP server. The **copy** command is used to move configuration files among RAM, NVRAM, and a TFTP server. The files can be copied between any pair, as Figure 2-8 illustrates.

Figure 2-8   *Locations for Copying and Results from Copy Operations*

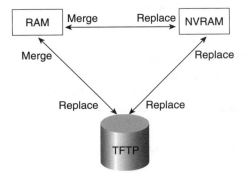

The commands can be summarized as follows:

```
copy {tftp │running-config │startup-config} {tftp │running-config │startup-config}
```

The first parameter is the "from" location; the next one is the "to" location. (Of course, choosing the same option for both parameters is not allowed.)

Confusion about what these commands actually do is pervasive. Any **copy** command option moving a file into NVRAM or a TFTP server replaces the existing file. Any **copy** command option moving the file into RAM, however, is effectively an *add* or *merge* operation. For example, only one host name *Siberia* configuration command is allowed. Therefore, a config file copied into RAM with **hostname *Siberia*** in it replaces the previous **hostname** command (if any). However, if the file being copied has the **access-list *1* permit host *1.1.1.1*** command in it, and if an access list number 1 already exists in the RAM configuration file, then **access-list *1* permit host *1.1.1.1*** is placed at the end of that existing access list (access lists are comprised of a list of configuration commands referencing the same list number or name). The old entries in **access- list** *1* are not deleted. This is because many **access-list** *1* commands are allowed in the same access list. Effectively, any copy into RAM works just as if you typed the commands in the order listed in the config file.

So, why did Cisco not include a replace action, similar to the action used to copy to NVRAM or TFTP? Who knows? A replace action probably would require you to empty all routing tables, which might cause an outage. Possibly, this particular nuance is a result of some Cisco programmer who decided years ago to take the loaded gun out of users' hands. However, advanced users can accomplish the effect of a replace action by entering configuration mode and issuing commands until the running config is changed as desired. This requires that the user know whether each command will replace another that is like it in the RAM configuration file, or whether each command will simply be added to the configuration, as with an **access-list** command.

Two key commands can be used to erase the contents of NVRAM. The **write erase** command is the older command, and the **erase startup-config** command is the newer command. Both simply erase the contents of the NVRAM configuration file. Of course, if the router is reloaded at this point, there will be no initial configuration.

Viewing the Configuration and Old-Style Configuration Commands

Once upon a time, commands that were used to move configuration files among RAM, NVRAM, and TFTP did not use easy-to-recall parameters such as **startup-config** and **running-config**. In fact, most people could not remember the commands or got the different ones confused.

Figure 2-9 shows both the old and new commands used to view configurations.

Figure 2-9   *Configuration show Commands*

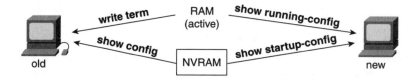

Initial Configuration (Setup Mode)

To pass the CCNA exam, you will need to be familiar with the differences between configuration mode and setup mode. Setup mode is a router configuration mode that prompts the user for basic configuration parameters. A Cisco router can be configured using the CLI in configuration mode without using setup mode. Some users like to use setup mode, however, particularly until they become more familiar with the CLI.

NOTE	If you plan to work with Cisco routers much, you should become accustomed with the CLI configuration mode discussed earlier. Setup mode allows only basic configuration.

Setup mode is a topic covered on the CCNA exam, so regardless of whether you plan to use it, you must remember how it works. Figure 2-10 and Example 2-2 describe the process. Setup mode is most frequently used when the router comes up with no configuration in NVRAM; setup mode can be entered by using the **setup** command from privileged mode.

Figure 2-10   *Getting into Setup Mode*

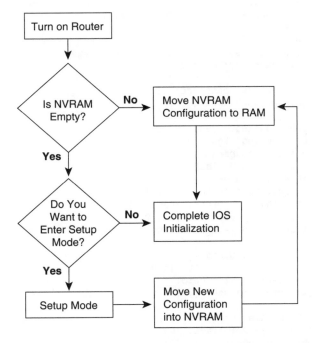

Example 2-2 shows a screen capture of using setup mode after booting a router with no configuration in NVRAM.

Example 2-2   *Router Setup Configuration Mode*

```
Notice: NVRAM invalid, possibly due to write erase.
        --- System Configuration Dialog ---

At any point you may enter a question mark '?' for help.
Use Ctrl+C to abort configuration dialog at any prompt.
Default settings are in square brackets '[]'.Would you
like to enter the initial configuration dialog? [yes]:
```

continues

Example 2-2   *Router Setup Configuration Mode (Continued)*

```
First, would you like to see the current interface summary? [yes]:
Any interface listed with OK? value "NO" does not have a valid configuration

Interface              IP-Address      OK? Method Status              Protocol
Serial0                unassigned      NO  unset  down                down
Serial1                unassigned      NO  unset  down                down

Ethernet0              unassigned      NO  unset  reset               down

Configuring global parameters:

  Enter host name [Router]: fred
The enable secret is a one-way cryptographic secret used
instead of the enable password when it exists.
  Enter enable secret: cisco
The enable password is used when there is no enable secret
and when using older software and some boot images.
  Enter enable password: cisco2

Enter virtual terminal password: cisco
Configure SNMP Network Management? [yes]: n
Configure IP? [yes]:
Configure IGRP routing? [yes]: n
Configure RIP routing? [no]: n
Configuring interface parameters:
Configuring interface Serial0:
  Is this interface in use? [yes]:
Configure IP on this interface? [yes]:
IP address for this interface: 163.4.8.3
Number of bits in subnet field [0]: 0
Class B network is 163.4.0.0, 0 subnet bits; mask is /16

Configuring interface Serial1:
  Is this interface in use? [yes]: n
Configuring interface Ethernet0:
  Is this interface in use? [yes]: y

Configure IP on this interface? [yes]:
IP address for this interface: 163.5.8.3
Number of bits in subnet field [0]: 0
Class B network is 163.5.0.0, 0 subnet bits; mask is /16



The following configuration command script was created:

hostname fred
enable secret 5 $1$aMyk$eUxp9JmrPgK.vQ.nA5Tge.
enable password cisco2
line vty 0 4
password cisco
no snmp-server
!
```

Example 2-2   *Router Setup Configuration Mode (Continued)*

```
ip routing
!
interface Serial0
ip address 163.4.8.3 255.255.0.0
!
interface Serial1
shutdown
no ip address
!
interface Ethernet0
ip address 163.5.8.3 255.255.0.0
!
end

Use this configuration? [yes/no]: y


Building configuration...[OK]
Use the enabled mode 'configure' command to modify this configuration.


Press ENTER to get started!
```

As Example 2-2 illustrates, you can use two methods to get into setup mode. First, if you are at the console and you power up the router, and if there is no configuration file in NVRAM, the router asks whether you want to enter the "initial configuration dialog." Answering **y** or **yes** puts you in setup mode. Alternatively, the **setup** privileged EXEC command puts you in setup mode.

When you are finished with setup, you are asked whether you want to use this configuration. If you answer **yes**, the configuration you created is placed in RAM and NVRAM. This is the only operation in the IOS that changes both files to include the same contents based on a single action.

As of IOS version 12.0, the setup mode prompts no longer ask for the number of subnet bits. Instead, the subnet mask used is requested, which is probably a lot better for most people. Other fine details of the setup mode prompts have changed as well. Example 2-3 shows an example using IOS version 12.0 and is simply shown here for reference.

Example 2-3   *Router Setup Configuration Mode—Version 12.0*

```
         --- System Configuration Dialog ---

Would you like to enter the initial configuration dialog? [yes/no]: yes

At any point you may enter a question mark '?' for help.
Use Ctrl+c to abort configuration dialog at any prompt.
Default settings are in square brackets '[]'.

Basic management setup configures only enough connectivity
for management of the system, extended setup will ask you
to configure each interface on the system
```

continues

Example 2-3   *Router Setup Configuration Mode—Version 12.0 (Continued)*

```
Would you like to enter basic management setup? [yes/no]: no

First, would you like to see the current interface summary? [yes]:

Any interface listed with OK? value "NO" does not have a valid configuration

Interface               IP-Address       OK? Method Status          Protocol
Serial0                 unassigned       NO  unset  down            down
Serial1                 unassigned       NO  unset  down            down
TokenRing0              unassigned       NO  unset  reset           down

Configuring global parameters:

  Enter host name [Router]: fred

  The enable secret is a password used to protect access to
  privileged EXEC and configuration modes. This password, after
  entered, becomes encrypted in the configuration.
  Enter enable secret: cisco

  The enable password is used when you do not specify an
  enable secret password, with some older software versions, and
  some boot images.
  Enter enable password: cisco2

  The virtual terminal password is used to protect
  access to the router over a network interface.
  Enter virtual terminal password: cisco
Configure SNMP Network Management? [yes]: n
Configure DECnet? [no]:
Configure AppleTalk? [no]:
Configure IPX? [no]:
Configure IP? [yes]:
Configure IGRP routing? [yes]: n
Configure RIP routing? [no]:
Configure bridging? [no]:
Configuring interface parameters:
Do you want to configure Serial0  interface? [yes]: y
Configure IP on this interface? [yes]:
IP address for this interface: 163.4.8.3
Subnet mask for this interface [255.255.0.0] : 255.255.255.0
Class B network is 163.4.0.0, 24 subnet bits; mask is /24
Do you want to configure Serial1  interface? [yes]: n
Do you want to configure Ethernet0 interface? [yes]: y
Configure IP on this interface? [yes]:
IP address for this interface: 163.5.8.3
Subnet mask for this interface [255.255.0.0] : 255.255.255.0
Class B network is 163.5.0.0, 24 subnet bits; mask is /24
The following configuration command script was created:

hostname fred
enable secret 5 $1$Qxix$Fi3buBVGTpEig9AIPgzxC.
enable password cisco2
```

Example 2-3 *Router Setup Configuration Mode—Version 12.0 (Continued)*

```
line vty 0 4
password cisco
no snmp-server
!
no decnet routing
no appletalk routing
no ipx routing
ip routing
no bridge 1
!
interface Serial0
ip address 163.4.8.3 255.255.255.0
no mop enabled
!
interface Serial1
shutdown
no ip address
!
interface Ethernet0
ip address 163.5.8.3 255.255.255.0
!
end


[0] Go to the IOS command prompt without saving this config.
[1] Return back to the setup without saving this config.
[2] Save this configuration to nvram and exit.

Enter your selection [2]: 2
Building configuration...
[OK]Use the enabled mode 'configure' command to modify this configuration._


Press ENTER to get started!
```

In the example, notice that an early prompt gives you the choice of performing a simpler configuration for basic management. For instance, you may have the configuration editing in a file on your PC, and all you need is enough IP working so that you can Telnet into the router to copy the configuration. Also note that you have an option to start over after answering the questions, which is very convenient for those of us who are poor typists.

Cisco Discovery Protocol

Cisco Discovery Protocol (CDP) is used by Cisco routers and switches to ascertain basic information about neighboring routers and switches. You can use this information to learn addresses quickly for easier Simple Network Management Protocol (SNMP) management, as well as learn the addresses of other devices when you do not have passwords to log in to the other device.

CDP is a Cisco proprietary protocol; to support forwarding CDP messages over an interface, that interface must support SNAP headers. Any LAN interface, HDLC, Frame Relay, and ATM all support CDP. The router or switch can discover Layer 3 addressing details of neighboring routers—without even configuring that Layer 3 protocol—because CDP is not dependent on any particular Layer 3 protocol.

CDP discovers several useful details from the neighboring device:

- **Device Identifier**—Typically the host name.

- **Address list**—Network and data link addresses.

- **Port Identifier**—Text that identifies the port, which is another name for an interface.

- **Capabilities list**—Information on what the device does—for instance, a router or switch.

- **Platform**—The model and OS level running in the device.

CDP is enabled in the configuration by default. The **no cdp run** global command disables CDP for the entire device, and the **cdp run** global command re-enables CDP. Likewise, the **no cdp enable** interface subcommand disables CDP just on that interface, and the **cdp enable** command switches back to the default state of CDP being enabled.

A variety of **show cdp** command options are available. Example 2-4 lists the output of the commands, with some commentary following.

Example 2-4   *show cdp Command Options*

```
Seville#show cdp neighbor
Capability Codes: R - Router, T - Trans Bridge, B - Source Route Bridge
                  S - Switch, H - Host, I - IGMP, r - Repeater

Device ID          Local Intrfce    Holdtme    Capability  Platform  Port ID
fred               Ser 1            172         R           2500      Ser 1
Yosemite           Ser 0.2          161         R           2500      Ser 0.2

Seville#show cdp entry fred
-------------------------
Device ID: fred
Entry address(es):
   IP address: 163.5.8.3
Platform: cisco 2500,  Capabilities: Router
Interface: Serial1,  Port ID (outgoing port): Serial1
Holdtime : 168 sec

Version :
Cisco Internetwork Operating System Software
IOS (tm) 2500 Software (C2500-D-L), Version 12.0(6), RELEASE SOFTWARE (fc1)
Copyright  1986-1999 by cisco Systems, Inc.
Compiled Tue 10-Aug-99 23:52 by phanguye

Seville#show cdp neighbor detail
-------------------------
Device ID: fred
Entry address(es):
```

Example 2-4 *show cdp Command Options (Continued)*

```
   IP address: 163.5.8.3
Platform: cisco 2500,  Capabilities: Router
Interface: Serial1,  Port ID (outgoing port): Serial1
Holdtime : 164 sec

Version :
Cisco Internetwork Operating System Software
IOS (tm) 2500 Software (C2500-D-L), Version 12.0(6), RELEASE SOFTWARE (fc1)
Copyright  1986-1999 by cisco Systems, Inc.
Compiled Tue 10-Aug-99 23:52 by phanguye

-------------------------
Device ID: Yosemite
Entry address(es):
  IP address: 10.1.5.252
  Novell address: 5.0200.bbbb.bbbb
Platform: cisco 2500,  Capabilities: Router
Interface: Serial0.2,  Port ID (outgoing port): Serial0.2
Holdtime : 146 sec

Version :
Cisco Internetwork Operating System Software
IOS (tm) 2500 Software (C2500-D-L), Version 12.0(6), RELEASE SOFTWARE (fc1)
Copyright  1986-1999 by cisco Systems, Inc.
Compiled Tue 10-Aug-99 23:52 by phanguye

Seville#show cdp interface
Ethernet0 is up, line protocol is down
  Encapsulation ARPA
  Sending CDP packets every 60 seconds
  Holdtime is 180 seconds
Serial0.2 is up, line protocol is up
  Encapsulation FRAME-RELAY
  Sending CDP packets every 60 seconds
  Holdtime is 180 seconds
Serial1 is up, line protocol is up
  Encapsulation HDLC
  Sending CDP packets every 60 seconds
  Holdtime is 180 seconds

Seville#show cdp traffic
CDP counters :
    Packets output: 41, Input: 21
    Hdr syntax: 0, Chksum error: 0, Encaps failed: 0
    No memory: 0, Invalid packet: 0, Fragmented: 0
```

The commands provide information about both the neighbors and the behavior of the CDP protocol itself. In the **show cdp entry** *fred* command in Example 2-4, all the details learned by CDP are shown and highlighted. To know that fred is the device identifier of a neighbor, the **show cdp neighbor** command can be used to summarize the information about each neighbor. **Show cdp neighbor detail** lists the detail of all neighbors, in the same format as **show cdp entry**. In addition, **show cdp traffic** lists the overhead that CDP introduces to perform its functions.

Managing IOS Images

One common task that CCNAs run into is migrating to a new level of IOS. *IOS image* is simply a term referring to the file containing the IOS. Managing image files entails getting new IOS images from Cisco; backing up the currently used, older version from your routers; updating your routers with the new image; and testing. Also included in IOS image management is how to tell a router to use a particular IOS the next time it boots.

IOS files are typically stored in Flash memory. Flash memory is rewritable, permanent storage, which is ideal for storing files that need to be retained when the router loses power. Also, because there are no moving parts, there is a smaller chance of failure as compared with disk drives, which provides better availability.

Upgrading an IOS Image into Flash Memory

As Figure 2-11 illustrates, to upgrade an IOS image into Flash memory, you first must obtain the IOS image from Cisco. Then, you must place the IOS image into the default directory of a TFTP server. Finally, you must issue the **copy** command from the router, copying the file into Flash memory.

Figure 2-11   *Complete IOS Upgrade Process*

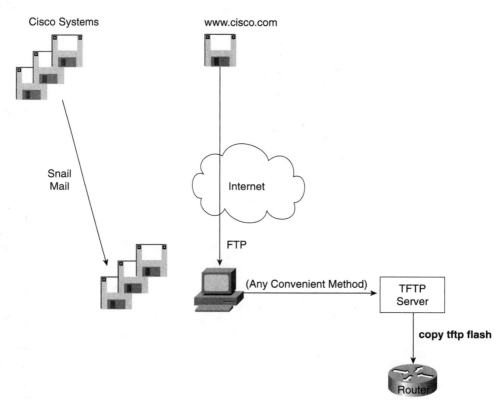

Example 2-5 provides an example of the final step, copying the IOS image into Flash memory.

Example 2-5 *copy tftp flash Command Copies the IOS Image to Flash Memory*

```
R1#copy tftp flash

System flash directory:
File  Length   Name/status
  1   7530760   c4500-d-mz.120-2.bin
[7530824 bytes used, 857784 available, 8388608 total]
Address or name of remote host [255.255.255.255]? 134.141.3.33
Source file name? c4500-d-mz.120-5.bin
Destination file name [c4500-d-mz.120-5.bin]?
Accessing file c4500-d-mz.120-5.bin ' on 134.141.3.33...
Loading c4500-d-mz.120-5.bin from 134.141.3.33 (via TokenRing0): ! [OK]

Erase flash device before writing? [confirm]
Flash contains files. Are you sure you want to erase? [confirm]

Copy 'c4500-d-mz.120-5.bin ' from server
  as 'c4500-d-mz.120-5.bin ' into Flash WITH erase? [yes/no]y
Erasing device... eeeeeeeeeeeeeeeeeeeeeeeeeeeeeeee ...erased
Loading c4500-d-mz.120-5.bin  from 134.141.3.33 (via TokenRing0):
!!!!!!!!!!!!!!!!!!!!!!!!!!!!!!!!!!!!!!!!!!!!!!!!!!!!!!!!!!!!!!!!!!!!!!!!!!!!!
!!!!!!!!!!!!!!!!!!!!!!!!!!!!!!!!!!!!!!!!!!!!!!!!!!!!!!!!!!!!!!!!!!!!!!!!
!!!!!!!!!!!!!!!!!!!!!!!!!!!!!!!!!!!!!!!!!!!!!!!!!!!!!!!!!!!!!!!!!!!!!!!!!!!!!
!!!!!!!!!!!!!!!!!!!!!!!!!!!!!!!!!!!!!!!!!!!!!!!!!!!!!!!!!!!!!!!!!!!!!!!!
!!!!!!!!!!!!!!!!!!!!!!!!!!!!!!!!!!!!!!!!!!!!!!!!!!!!!!!!!!!!!!!!!!!!!!!!!!!!!
!!!!!!!!!!!!!!!!!!!!!!!!!!!!!!!!!!!!!!!!!!!!!!!!!!!!!!!!!!!!!!!!!!!!!!!!
!!!!!!!!!!!!!!!!!!!!!!!!!!!!!!!!!!!!!!!!!!!!!!!!!!!!!!!!!!!!!!!!!!!!!!!!!!!!!
!!!!!!!!!!!!!!!!!!!!!!!!!!!!!!!!!!!!!!!!!!!!!!!!!!!!!!!!!!!!!!!!!!!!!!!!!!!!!
!!!!!!!!!!!!!!!!!!!!!!!!!!!!!!!!!!!!!!!!!!!!!!!!!!!!!!!!!!!!!!!!!!!!!!!!
!!!!!!!!!!!!!!!!!!!!!!!!!!!!!!!!!!!!!!!!!!!!!!!!!!!!!!!!!!!!!!!!!!!!!!!!!!!!!
!!!!!!!!!!!!!!!!!!!!!!!!!!!!!!!!!!!!!!!!!!!!!!!!!!!!!!!!!!!!!!!!!!!!!!!!
!!!!!!!!!!!!!!!!!!!!!!!!!!!!!!!!!!!!!!!!!!!!!!!!!!!!!!!!!!!!!!!!!!!!!!!!!!!!!
!!!!!!!!!!!!!!!!!!!!!!!!!!!!!!!!!!!!!!!!!!!!!!!!!!!!!!!!!!!!!!!!!!!!!!!!
!!!!!!!!!!!!!!!!!!!!!!!!!!!!!!!!!!!!!!!!!!!!!!!!!!!!!!!!!!!!!!!!!!!!!!!!!!!!!
!!!!!!!!!!!!!!!!!!!!!!!!!!!!!!!!!!!!!!!!!!!!!!!!!!!!!!!!!!!!!!!!!!!!!!!!
!!!!!!!!!!!!!!!!!!!!!!!!!!!!!!!!!!!!!!!!!!!!!!!!!!!!!!!!!!!!!!!!!!!!!!!!!!!!!
!!!!!!!!!!!!!!!!!!!!!!!!!!!!!!!!!!!!!!!!!!!!!!!!!!!!!!!!!!!!!!!!!!!!!!!!
!!!!!!!!!!!!!!!!!!!!!!!!!!!!!!!!!!!!!!!!!!!!!!!!!!!!!!!!!!!!!!!!!!!!!!!!!!!!!
!!!!!!!!!!!!!!!!!!!!!!!!!!!!!!!!!!!!!!!!!!!!!!!!!!!!!!!!!!!!!!! !!!!!!!!!!!!
[OK - 7530760/8388608 bytes]

Verifying checksum...  OK (0xA93E)
Flash copy took 0:04:26 [hh:mm:ss]
R1#
```

During this process of copying the IOS image into Flash memory, the router will need to discover several important facts:

1 What is the IP address or host name of the TFTP server?

2 What is the name of the file?

3 Is space available for this file in Flash memory?

4 If not, will you let the router erase the old files?

The router will prompt you for answers, as necessary. Afterward, the router erases Flash memory as needed, copies the file, and then verifies that the checksum for the file shows that no errors occurred in transmission. The **show flash** command then can be used to verify the contents of Flash memory (see Example 2-6). (The **show flash** output can vary between router families.) Before the new IOS is used, however, the router must be reloaded.

Example 2-6 *Verifying Flash Memory Contents with the **show flash** Command*

```
fred#show flash

System flash directory:
File  Length   Name/status
  1    6181132 c4500-d-mz.120-5.bin
[4181196 bytes used, 4207412 available, 8388608 total]
8192K bytes of processor board System flash (Read ONLY)
```

In some cases, Flash memory could be in read-only mode. That is the case when a router loads only part of the IOS into RAM, to conserve RAM. Other parts of the IOS file are kept in Flash memory (Flash memory access time is much slower than RAM). In this case, if Flash memory must be erased to make room for a new image, the IOS could not continue to run. So, if the router is running from a portion of the IOS in Flash memory, the router first must be booted using the IOS in ROM. Then the Flash memory will be in read/write mode, and the erase and copy processes can be accomplished. The **copy tftp flash** command in later releases of the IOS actually performs the entire process for you. In earlier releases, you had to boot the router from ROM and then issue the **copy tftp flash** command.

Choosing Which IOS Image to Load

The CCNA exam requires you to be proficient in configuring a router to load an IOS image from many sources. Two methods are used by a router to determine where it tries to obtain an IOS image to execute. The first is based on the value of the *configuration register*, which is a 16-bit software register in Cisco's more recently developed routers. (Some older routers had a hardware configuration register, with jumpers on the processor card, to set bits to a value of 0 or 1.) The second method used to determine where the router tries to obtain an IOS image is through the use of the **boot system** configuration command. Figure 2-12 shows an example binary breakdown of the default value for the configuration register.

Figure 2-12   *Binary Version of Configuration Register, Value Hex 2102*

15	14	13	12	11	10	9	8	7	6	5	4	3	2	1	0
0	0	1	0	0	0	0	1	0	0	0	0	0	0	1	0

The *boot field* is the name of the low-order 4 bits of the configuration register. This field can be considered a 4-bit value, represented as a single hexadecimal digit. Cisco represents hexadecimal values by preceding the hex digit(s) with *0x*—for example, *0xA* would mean a single hex digit *A*.

The router chooses the IOS image to load based on the boot field and the *boot system* commands in the configuration. Table 2-6 summarizes the use of the configuration register and the **boot system** command at initialization time. (If the files referred to in the boot system commands are not found, then the router will never complete the boot process. The password recovery process must be used to change the config register to 0x2142 so that the NVRAM configuration is ignored and the **boot** commands can be repaired to point to a valid IOS file name. Refer to the section "Password Recovery," later in this chapter, for more details.)

Table 2-6   *boot system Command*

Value of Boot Field	Boot System Commands	Result
0x0	Ignored if present	ROM monitor mode, a low-level problem determination mode, is entered.
0x1	Ignored if present	IOS from ROM is loaded.
0x2-0xF	No **boot** command	The first IOS file in flash is loaded; if that fails, the router broadcasts looking for an IOS on a TFTP server. If that fails, IOS from ROM is loaded.
0x2-0xF	**boot system ROM**	IOS from ROM is loaded.
0x2-0xF	**boot system flash**	The first file from Flash memory is loaded.
0x2-0xF	**boot system flash** *filename*	IOS with name *filename* is loaded from Flash memory.
0x2-0xF	**boot system tftp 10.1.1.1** *filename*	IOS with name *filename* is loaded from TFTP server.
0x2-0xF	Multiple boot system commands, any variety	An attempt occurs to load IOS based on the first boot command in configuration. If that fails, the second boot command is used, and so on, until one is successful.

Password Recovery

Several additional concepts related to loading the IOS must be understood before password recovery can be performed. First, software called the *ROM monitor* (rommon) is held in ROM on all routers and actually provides the code that is first used to boot each router. rommon has a rudimentary command structure that is used as part of the password recovery process. A limited-function IOS is also held in either ROM or in additional Flash memory called *bootflash*; in either case, the IOS in bootflash or ROM is used mainly in cases where the IOS in flash is not available for some reason. Finally, bit 6 of the configuration register set to binary 1 means that the router should ignore the NVRAM configuration when booting.

Password recovery revolves around the process of getting the router to boot while ignoring the NVRAM configuration file. The router will be up, but with a default configuration; this enables a console user to log in, enter privileged mode, and change any encrypted passwords or view any unencrypted passwords. To cause the router to ignore NVRAM at boot time, the configuration register must be changed. To do that, you must be in privileged mode—and if you were already there, you could reset any encrypted passwords or view any unencrypted ones. It seems to be a viscious circle.

The two keys to password recovery are knowing that rommon enables you to reset the configuration register and that a console user can get into rommon mode by pressing the Break key during the first 60 seconds after power-on of the router. Knowing how to reset the config register enables you to boot the router (ignoring NVRAM), allowing the console user to see or change the unencrypted or encrypted passwords, respectively.

The process is slightly different for different models of routers, although the concepts are identical. Table 2-7 outlines the process for each type of router.

Table 2-7   *Password Recovery*

Step	Function	How to Do This for 1600, 2600, 3600, 4500, 7200, 7500	How to Do This for 2000, 2500, 3000, 4000, 7000
1	Turn router off and then back on again.	Use the power switch.	Same as other routers.
2	Press the Break key within the first 60 seconds.	Find the Break key on your console devices keyboard.	Same as other routers.
3	Change the configuration register so that bit 6 is 1.	Use the rommon command **confreg**, and answer the prompts.	Use the rommon command **o/r 0x2142**.
4	Cause the router to load an IOS.	Use the rommon **reload** command or, if unavailable, power off and on.	Use rommon command **initialize**.
5	Avoid using setup mode, which will be prompted for at console.	Just say no.	Same as other routers.

Table 2-7   *Password Recovery (Continued)*

Step	Function	How to Do This for 1600, 2600, 3600, 4500, 7200, 7500	How to Do This for 2000, 2500, 3000, 4000, 7000
6	Enter privileged mode at console.	Press Enter and use **enable** command (no password required).	Same as other routers.
7	View startup config to see unencrypted passwords.	Use exec command **show startup-config**.	Same as other routers.
8	Use appropriate config commands to reset encrypted commands.	For example, use **enable secret xyz123** command to set enable secret password.	Same as other routers.
9	Change config register back to original value.	Use config command **Config-reg 0x2102**.	Same as other routers.
10	Reload the router after saving the configuration.	Use the **copy running-config startup-config** and **reload** commands.	Same as other routers.

A few nuances need further explanation. First, the **confreg** rommon command prompts you with questions that correspond to the functions of the bits in the configuration register. When the prompt asks, "Ignore system config info[y/n]?", it is asking you about bit 6. Entering **yes** sets the bit to 1. The rest of the questions can be defaulted. The last **confreg** question asks, "Change boot characteristics[y/n]?", which asks whether you want to change the boot field of the config register. You don't really need to change it, but the published password recovery algorithm lists that step, which is the only reason that it is mentioned here. Just changing bit 6 to 1 is enough to get the router booted and you into privileged mode to find or change the passwords.

The original configuration is lost through this process, but you can overcome that. When you save the configuration in Step 10, you are overwriting the config in NVRAM. There was no configuration in the running config except default and the few things you configured. So, before Step 8, you might want to perform a **copy startup-config running-config** command and then proceed with the process.

Foundation Summary

The Foundation Summary is a collection of tables and figures that provide a convenient review of many key concepts in this chapter. For those of you already comfortable with the topics in this chapter, this summary could help you recall a few details. For those of you who just read this chapter, this review should help solidify some key facts. For any of you doing your final preparation before the exam, these tables and figures will be a convenient way to review the day before the exam.

Table 2-8 reviews the different types of passwords and the configuration for each type.

Table 2-8   *CLI Password Configuration*

Access from ...	Password Type	Configuration
Console	Console password	**line console** *0* **login** **password** *faith*
Auxiliary	Auxiliary password	**line aux** *0* **login** **password** *hope*
Telnet	vty password	**line vty** *0 4* **login** **password** *love*

Table 2-9 lists the commands used to manipulate previously typed commands.

Table 2-9   *Key Sequences for Command Edit and Recall*

Keyboard Command	What the User Gets
Up-arrow or Ctrl+p	This calls up the most recently used command. If pressed again, the next most recent command appears, until the history buffer is exhausted. (The p stands for *previous*.)
Down-arrow or Ctrl+n	If you have gone too far back into the history buffer, these keys will go forward, in order, to the more recently typed commands. (The n stands for *next*.)
Left-arrow or Ctrl+b	This moves the cursor backward in the currently displayed command without deleting characters. (The b stands for *back*.)
Right-arrow or Ctrl+f	This moves the cursor forward in the currently displayed command without deleting characters. (The f stands for *forward*.)

Table 2-9   *Key Sequences for Command Edit and Recall (Continued)*

Keyboard Command	What the User Gets
Backspace	This moves the cursor backward in the currently displayed command, deleting characters.
Ctrl+a	This moves the cursor directly to the first character of the currently displayed command.
Ctrl+e	This moves the cursor directly to the end of the currently displayed command.
Esc+b	This moves the cursor back one word in the currently displayed command.
Esc+f	This moves the cursor forward one word in the currently displayed command.
Ctrl+r	This creates a new command prompt, followed by all the characters typed since the previous command prompt. This is particularly useful if system messages confuse the screen and it is unclear what the user has typed so far.

Table 2-10 summarizes the use of the configuration register and the **boot system** command at initialization.

Table 2-10   *boot system Command*

Value of Boot Field	Boot System Commands	Result
0x0	Ignored if present	ROM monitor mode, a low-level problem determination mode, is entered.
0x1	Ignored if present	IOS from ROM is loaded.
0x2–0xF	No **boot** command	The first IOS file in flash is loaded; if that fails, IOS from ROM is loaded. If that fails, the router broadcasts looking for an IOS on a TFTP server.
0x2–0xF	**boot system ROM**	IOS from ROM is loaded.
0x2–0xF	**boot system flash**	The first file from Flash memory is loaded.
0x2–0xF	**boot system flash** *filename*	IOS with name *filename* is loaded from Flash memory.
0x2–0xF	**boot system tftp 10.1.1.1** *filename*	IOS with name *filename* is loaded from the TFTP server.
0x2–0xF	Multiple boot system commands, any variety	An attempt occurs to load IOS based on the first boot command in configuration. If that fails, the second boot command is used, and so on, until one is successful.

Figure 2-13 summarizes the use of memory in Cisco routers.

Figure 2-13 *Cisco Router Memory Types*

Figure 2-14 illustrates the relationships among configuration mode, user EXEC mode, and priviledged EXEC mode.

Figure 2-14 *CLI Configuration Mode Versus EXEC Modes*

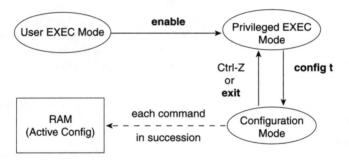

The **copy** command is used to move configuration files among RAM, NVRAM, and a TFTP server. The files can be copied between any pair, as Figure 2-15 illustrates.

Figure 2-15 *Locations for Copying and Results from Copy Operations*

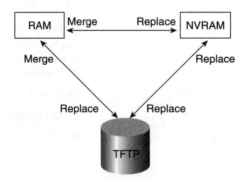

Figure 2-16 shows both the old and new commands used to view configurations.

Figure 2-16   *Configuration show Commands*

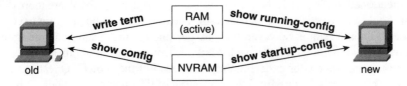

Figure 2-17 summarizes the flow of syslog messages, including debug messages.

Figure 2-17   *Syslog Message Flows*

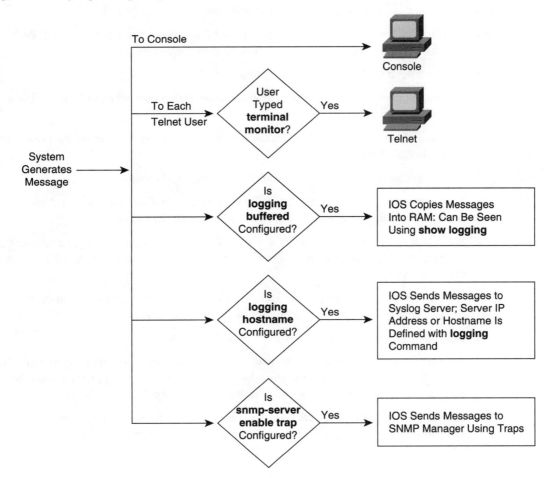

Q&A

As mentioned in Chapter 1, the questions and scenarios in this book are more difficult than what you should experience on the actual exam. The questions do not attempt to cover more breadth or depth than the exam; however, they are designed to make sure that you know the answer. Rather than allowing you to derive the answer from clues hidden inside the question itself, the questions challenge your understanding and recall of the subject. Questions from the "Do I Know This Already?" quiz from the beginning of the chapter are repeated here to ensure that you have mastered the chapter's topic areas. Hopefully, these questions will help limit the number of exam questions on which you narrow your choices to two options and then guess. Make sure to use the CD and take the simulated exams.

The answers to these questions can be found in Appendix A, on page 703.

1 What are the two names for the router's mode of operation that, when accessed, enables you to issue commands that could be disruptive to router operations?

2 What are three methods of logging on to a router?

3 What is the name of the user interface mode of operation used when you cannot issue disruptive commands?

4 Can the auxiliary port be used for anything besides remote modem user access to a router? If so, what other purpose can it serve?

5 How many console ports can be installed on a Cisco 7500 router?

6 What command would you use to receive command help if you knew that a **show** command option begins with a **c**, but you cannot recall the option?

7 While you are logged in to a router, you issue the command **copy ?** and get a response of "Unknown command, computer name, or host." Offer an explanation as to why this error message appears.

8 Is the number of retrievable commands based on the number of characters in each command, or is it simply a number of commands, regardless of their size?

9 How can you retrieve a previously used command? (Name two ways.)

10 After typing **show ip route**, which is the only command you typed since logging in to the router, you now want to issue the **show ip arp** command. What steps would you take to execute this command by using command recall keystrokes?

11 After typing **show ip route 128.1.1.0**, you now want to issue the command **show ip route 128.1.4.0**. What steps would you take to do so, using command recall and command editing keystrokes?

12 What configuration command causes the router to require a password from a user at the console? What configuration mode context must you be in—that is, what command(s) must be typed before this command after entering configuration mode? List the commands in the order in which they must be typed while in config mode.

13 What configuration command is used to tell the router the password that is required at the console? What configuration mode context must you be in—that is, what command(s) must you type before this command after entering configuration mode? List the commands in the order in which they must be typed while in config mode.

14 What are the primary purposes of Flash memory in a Cisco router?

15 What is the intended purpose of NVRAM memory in a Cisco router?

16 What does the NV stand for in NVRAM?

17 What is the intended purpose of RAM in a Cisco router?

18 What is the main purpose of ROM in a Cisco router?

19 What configuration command would be needed to cause a router to use an IOS image named c2500-j-l.112-14.bin on TFTP server 128.1.1.1 when the router is reloaded? If you forgot the first parameter of this command, what steps must you take to learn the correct parameters and add the command to the configuration? (Assume that you are not logged in to the router when you start.)

20 What command sets the password that would be required after typing the **enable** command? Is that password encrypted by default?

21 To have the correct syntax, what must you add to the following configuration command:

```
banner This is Ivan Denisovich's Gorno Router - Do Not Use
```

22 Name two commands that affect the text used as the command prompt.

23 When using setup mode, you are prompted at the end of the process as to whether you want to use the configuration parameters you just typed in. Which type of memory is this configuration stored into if you type yes?

24 What two methods could a router administrator use to cause a router to load the IOS stored in ROM?

25 What could a router administrator do to cause a router to load file xyz123.bin from TFTP server 128.1.1.1 upon the next reload? Is there more than one way to accomplish this?

26 What is the process used to update the contents of Flash memory so that a new IOS in a file called c4500-d-mz.120-5.bin on TFTP server 128.1.1.1 is copied into Flash memory?

27 Name three possible problems that could prevent the command **boot system tftp c2500-j-l.112-14.bin 128.1.1.1** from succeeding.

28 Two different IOS files are in a router's Flash memory: one called c2500-j-l.111-3.bin and one called c2500-j-l.112-14.bin. Which one does the router use when it boots up? How could you force the other IOS file to be used? Without looking at the router configuration, what command could be used to discover which file was used for the latest boot of the router?

29 What does CDP stand for?

30 On what type of interfaces is CDP enabled by default? (Assume IOS versions 11.0 and later.)

31 What command can be used to provide as much detailed information as possible with CDP?

32 Is the password required at the console the same one that is required when Telnet is used to access a router?

33 How could a router administrator disable CDP?

34 Which IP routing protocols could be enabled using setup?

35 Name two commands used to view the configuration to be used at the next reload of the router. Which one is a more recent addition to the IOS?

36 Name two commands used to view the configuration that is currently used in a router. Which one is a more recent addition to the IOS?

37 True or False: The **copy startup-config running-config** command always changes the currently used configuration for this router to exactly match what is in the startup configuration file. Explain.

Scenarios

Scenario 2-1

Compare the following output in Example 2-7 and Example 2-8. Example 2-7 was gathered at 11:00 a.m., 30 minutes earlier than Example 2-8. What can you definitively say happened to this router during the intervening half hour?

Example 2-7 *11:00 a.m. show running-config*

```
hostname Gorno
!
enable password cisco
!
interface Serial0
 ip address 134.141.12.1 255.255.255.0
!
interface Serial1
 ip address 134.141.13.1 255.255.255.0
!
interface Ethernet0
 ip address 134.141.1.1 255.255.255.0
!
router rip
 network 134.141.0.0
!
line con 0
 password cisco
 login
line aux 0
line vty 0 4
 password cisco
 login
```

Example 2-8 *11:30 a.m. show running-config*

```
hostname SouthernSiberia
prompt Gorno
!
enable secret $8df003j56ske92
enable password cisco
!
interface Serial0
 ip address 134.141.12.1 255.255.255.0
!
interface Serial1
 ip address 134.141.13.1 255.255.255.0
!
interface Ethernet0
 ip address 134.141.1.1 255.255.255.0
 no cdp enable
```

continues

Example 2-8 *11:30 a.m.* ***show running-config*** *(Continued)*

```
!
router rip
 network 134.141.0.0
!
line con 0
 password cisco
 login
line aux 0
line vty 0 4
 password cisco
 Login
```

Questions on Scenario 2-1

1 During the process of changing the configuration in Scenario 2-1, the command prompt temporarily was **SouthernSiberia(config)#**. What configuration commands, and in what order, could have changed the configuration as shown and allowed the prompt to temporarily be **SouthernSiberia(config)#**?

2 Assuming that Figure 2-18 is complete, what effect does the **no cdp enable** command have?

Figure 2-18 *Siberian Enterprises' Sample Network*

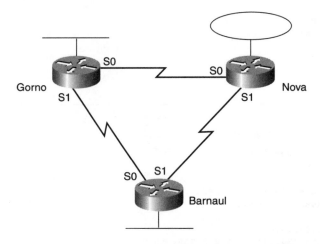

3 What effect would the **no enable password cisco** command have at this point?

Scenario 2-2

Example 2-9 shows that the **running-config** command was executed on the Nova router.

Example 2-9 *Configuration of Router Nova*

```
hostname Nova
banner # This is the router in Nova Sibiersk; Dress warmly before entering! #
!
boot system tftp c2500-js-113.bin 134.141.88.3
boot system flash c2500-j-1.111-9.bin
boot system rom
!
enable password cisco
!
interface Serial0
 ip address 134.141.12.2 255.255.255.0
!
interface Serial1
 ip address 134.141.23.2 255.255.255.0
!
interface TokenRing0
 ip address 134.141.2.2 255.255.255.0
!
router rip
 network 134.141.0.0
!
line con 0
 password cisco
 login
line aux 0
line vty 0 4
 password cisco
 login
```

Questions on Scenario 2-2

1   If this is all the information that you have, what IOS do you expect will be loaded when the user reloads Nova?

2   Examine the following command output in Example 2-10, taken immediately before the user is going to type the **reload** command. What IOS do you expect will be loaded?

Example 2-10 *show ip route on Nova*

```
Nova#show ip route
Codes: C - connected, S - static, I - IGRP, R - RIP, M - mobile, B - BGP
       D - EIGRP, EX - EIGRP external, O - OSPF, IA - OSPF inter area
       N1 - OSPF NSSA external type 1, N2 - OSPF NSSA external type 2
       E1 - OSPF external type 1, E2 - OSPF external type 2, E - EGP
       i - IS-IS, L1 - IS-IS level-1, L2 - IS-IS level-2, * - candidate default
       U - per-user static route, o - ODR

Gateway of last resort is not set
```

continues

Example 2-10 *show ip route* *on Nova (Continued)*

```
         134.141.0.0/24 is subnetted, 6 subnets
C        134.141.2.0 is directly connected, TokenRing0
R        134.141.3.0 [120/1] via 134.141.23.3, 00:00:15, Serial1
R        134.141.1.0 [120/1] via 134.141.12.1, 00:00:20, Serial0
C        134.141.12.0 is directly connected, Serial0
R        134.141.13.0 [120/1] via 134.141.12.1, 00:00:20, Serial0
                      [120/1] via 134.141.23.3, 00:00:15, Serial1
C        134.141.23.0 is directly connected, Serial1
```

3 Now examine the following **show flash** command in Example 2-11, which was issued immediately after the **show ip route** command in Example 2-10, but before the user issued the **reload** command. What IOS do you think would be loaded in this case?

Example 2-11 *show flash* *on Router Nova*

```
Nova#show flash
4096K bytes of flash memory sized on embedded flash.
File    name/status
 0 c2500-j-l.111-3.bin
[682680/4194304 bytes free/total]
```

4 Now examine the configuration in Example 2-12. Assume that there is now a route to 134.141.88.0 and that the file c2500-j-l.111-9.bin is an IOS image in Flash memory. What IOS do you expect will be loaded now?

Example 2-12 *show running-config* *on Router Nova*

```
 hostname Nova
banner # This is the router in Nova Sibiersk; Dress warmly before entering! #
!
boot system tftp c2500-js-113.bin 134.141.88.3
boot system flash c2500-j-l.111-9.bin
!
enable password cisco
!
interface Serial0
 ip address 134.141.12.2 255.255.255.0
!
interface Serial1
 ip address 134.141.23.2 255.255.255.0
!
interface Ethernet0
 ip address 134.141.2.2 255.255.255.0
!
router rip
 network 134.141.0.0
!
line con 0
 password cisco
 login
```

Example 2-12 *show running-config* on *Router Nova (Continued)*

```
line aux 0
line vty 0 4
 password cisco
 login
!
config-register 0x2101
```

Answers to Scenarios

Scenario 2-1 Answers

In Scenario 2-1, the following commands were added to the configuration:

- **enable secret** as a global command.
- **prompt** as a global command.
- **no cdp enable** as an Ethernet0 subcommand.
- The **hostname** command also was changed.

The scenario questions' answers are as follows:

1 If the host name was changed to *SouthSiberia* first and the **prompt** command was added next, the prompt would have temporarily been *SouthSiberia*. Configuration commands are added to the RAM configuration file immediately and are used. In this case, when the **prompt** command was added, it caused the router to use "Gorno," not the then-current host name "SouthernSiberia," as the prompt.

2 No practical effect takes place. Because no other Cisco CDP-enabled devices are on that Ethernet, CDP messages from Gorno are useless. So, the only effect is to lessen the overhead on that Ethernet in a very small way.

3 No effect takes place other than cleaning up the configuration file. The **enable password** is not used if an **enable secret** is configured.

Scenario 2-2 Answers

The answers to the questions in Scenario 2-2 are as follows:

1 The first boot system statement would be used: **boot system tftp c2500-js-113.bin 134.141.88.3**.

2 The **boot system flash** command would be used. The TFTP boot would presumably fail because there is not currently a route to the subnet of which the TFTP server is a part. It is reasonable to assume that a route would not be learned 2 minutes later when the router had reloaded. So, the next **boot system** command (**flash**) would be used.

3 The **boot system ROM** command would be used. Because there is no file in Flash called c2500-j-l.111-9.bin, the boot from Flash memory would fail as well, leaving only one **boot** command.

4 The IOS from ROM would be loaded due to the configuration register. If the configuration register boot field is set to 0x1, **boot system** commands are ignored. So, having a route to the 134.141.88.0/24 subnet and having c2500-j-l.111-9.bin in Flash memory does not help.

This chapter covers the following topics that you will need to master as a CCNA:

- **The OSI, TCP/IP, and NetWare Protocol Architectures** This section describes the history of OSI and its relevance to networking in the new millennium. In addition, this section covers the meaning and usefulness of each layer, the interactions of the layers, and the encapsulation of data.

- **OSI Transport Layer Functions** Routers and switches are mainly concerned with protocols similar to the OSI network and data link layers, and sometimes with the transport layer. This section covers the pertinent details of the transport layer, including connectionless and connection-oriented operation, error recovery, flow control, buffering, and windowing.

- **OSI Data Link Layer Functions** Routers, switches, and bridges use data link layer concepts, both on LAN and WAN connections. This section discusses the data link functions of arbitration, addressing, error detection, and encapsulation.

- **OSI Network Layer Functions** The network layer defines the core concepts used by routers. This section discusses network layer addressing and routing in depth.

CHAPTER 3

OSI Reference Model & Layered Communication

In years past, the need to understand the Open Systems Interconnection (OSI) reference model for networking grew rapidly. The U.S. government passed laws requiring vendors to support OSI software on their systems, or the government would no longer buy the systems. Several vendors even predicted that the global Internet would evolve toward using the OSI protocols instead of TCP/IP. As the century turns, however, OSI has been implemented on a much smaller scale than predicted. Few vendors push their OSI software solutions, if they even have them. However, several components of the OSI model are popularly implemented today. For example, OSI network service access point (NSAP) network layer addresses are often used for signaling in Asynchronous Transfer Mode (ATM) networks. However, full seven-layer OSI implementations are relatively rare today.

So, why have a whole chapter on OSI? As a CCNA, you'll be expected to learn and interpret new technologies and protocols. The OSI seven-layer reference model is an excellent point of reference for describing the concepts and functions behind these new technologies. References to Layer 2 switching and Layer 3 switching, which are popular topics today, refer to the comparison between Layers 2 and 3 of the OSI model. Cisco courses make generous use of the OSI model as reference for comparison with other network protocol implementations. So, this chapter will not actually help you understand OSI fully, but rather it will discuss OSI functions in comparison with popularly implemented protocols.

How to Best Use This Chapter

By taking the following steps, you can make better use of your study time:

- Keep your notes and the answers for all your work with this book in one place, for easy reference.

- Take the "Do I Know This Already?" quiz, and write down your answers. Studies show that retention is significantly increased through writing down facts and concepts, even if you never look at the information again.

- Use the diagram in Figure 3-1 to guide you to the next step.

Figure 3-1 *How to Use This Chapter*

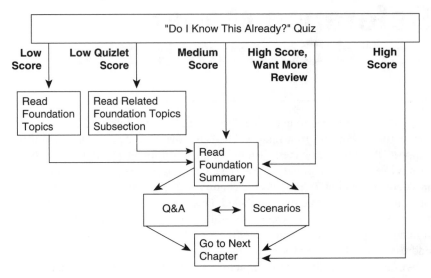

"Do I Know This Already?" Quiz

The purpose of the "Do I Know This Already?" quiz is to help you decide what parts of this chapter to use. If you already intend to read the entire chapter, you do not necessarily need to answer these questions now.

This 12-question quiz helps you determine how to spend your limited study time. The quiz is sectioned into four smaller four-question "quizlets," which correspond to the four major headings in the "Foundation Topics" section of the chapter. Figure 3-1 outlines suggestions on how to spend your time in this chapter. Use Table 3-1 to record your score.

Table 3-1 *Scoresheet for Quiz and Quizlets*

Quizlet Number	Foundation Topics Section Covering These Questions	Questions	Score
1	The OSI, TCP/IP, and NetWare Protocol Architectures	1 to 4	
2	OSI Transport Layer Functions	5 to 8	
3	OSI Data Link Layer Functions	9 to 12	
4	OSI Network Layer Functions	13 to 16	
All questions		1 to 16	

1 Name the seven layers of the OSI model.

_____

_____

_____

2 What is the main purpose(s) of Layer 3?

_____

_____

_____

3 What is the main purpose(s) of Layer 2?

_____

_____

_____

4 What OSI layer typically encapsulates using both a header and a trailer?

_____

_____

_____

5 Describe the features required for a protocol to be considered connectionless.

_____

_____

_____

6 Describe the features required for a protocol to be considered connection-oriented.

_____

_____

_____

7 In a particular error-recovering (reliable) protocol, the sender sends three frames, labeled 2, 3, and 4. On its next sent frame, the receiver of these frames sets an acknowledgment field to 4. What does this typically imply?

_____

_____

_____

8 Name three connection-oriented protocols.

_____

_____

_____

9 Name three terms popularly used as synonyms for MAC address.

_____

_____

_____

10 What portion of a MAC address encodes an identifier representing the manufacturer of the card?

_____

_____

_____

11 Are DLCI addresses defined by a Layer 2 or a Layer 3 protocol?

_____

_____

_____

12 How many bits are present in a MAC address?

_____

_____

_____

13 How many bits are present in an IPX address?

_____

_____

14 Name the two main parts of an IP address. Which part identifies the "group" of which this address is a member?

_____

_____

_____

15 Describe the differences between a routed protocol and a routing protocol.

_____

_____

_____

16 Name at least three routed protocols.

_____

_____

_____

The answers to the "Do I Know This Already?" quiz are found in Appendix A, "Answers to the 'Do I Know This Already?' Quizzes and Q&A Sections," on page 708. The suggested choices for your next step are as follows:

- **8 or less overall score**—Read the entire chapter. This includes the "Foundation Topics" and "Foundation Summary" sections, the Q&A section, and the scenarios at the end of the chapter.

- **2 or less on any quizlet**—Review the subsection(s) of the "Foundation Topics" part of this chapter, based on Table 3-1. Then, move into the "Foundation Summary" section, the quiz, and the scenarios at the end of the chapter.

- **9 to 12 overall score**—Begin with the "Foundation Summary" section, and then go to the Q&A section and the scenarios at the end of the chapter.

- **13 or more overall score**—If you want more review on these topics, skip to the "Foundation Summary" section and then go to the Q&A section and the scenarios at the end of the chapter. Otherwise, move to the next chapter.

Foundation Topics

The OSI, TCP/IP, and NetWare Protocol Architectures

Four topics of particular importance for the CCNA exam are covered in this chapter:

- **The OSI model**—Expect questions on the functions of each layer and examples at each layer in the CCNA exam.

- **Data link protocols**—This section is important to properly understand LAN switching.

- **Network layer protocols**—This section is important to properly understand routing.

- **Transport layer protocols**—This section is important to properly understand end-to-end transport.

The last three sections all use the terminology discussed in the first section.

OSI: Origin and Evolution

To pass the CCNA exam, you must be conversant in a protocol specification with which you are very unlikely to have any hands-on experience. The difficulty these days when using the OSI protocol specifications as a point of reference is that almost no one uses those specifications. You cannot typically walk down the hall and see a computer whose main, or even optional, networking protocols are defined by OSI.

OSI is the Open Systems Interconnection reference model for communications. OSI is a rather well-defined set of protocol specifications with many options for accomplishing similar tasks. Some participants in OSI's creation and development wanted it to become *the* networking protocol used by all applications. The U.S. government went so far as to require OSI support on every computer it would buy (as of a certain date in the early 1990s) via an edict called the Government OSI Profile (GOSIP), which certainly gave vendors some incentive to write OSI code. In fact, in my old IBM days, the company even had charts showing how the TCP/IP installed base would start declining by 1994, how OSI installations would take off, and how OSI would be *the* protocol from which the twenty-first century Internet was built. (In IBM's defense, moving the world to OSI may have been yet another case of "You just can't get there from here.")

What is OSI today? Well, the protocols are still in existence and are used around the world, to some degree. The U.S. government reversed its GOSIP directive officially in May 1994, which was probably the final blow to the possibility of pervasive OSI implementations. Cisco routers will route OSI. OSI NSAP addresses are used in Cisco ATM devices for signaling. Digital Equipment's DECnet Phase V uses several portions of OSI, including the network layer (Layer 3) addressing and routing concepts. More often than not, however, the OSI model now is mainly used as a point of reference for discussing other protocol specifications.

OSI Layers

The OSI model consists of seven layers, each of which can (and typically does) have several sublayers. Cisco requires that CCNAs demonstrate an understanding of each layer as well as the protocols that correspond to each OSI layer. The names of the OSI model layers and their main functions are simply good things to memorize. And frankly, if you want to pursue your Cisco certifications beyond CCNA, these names and functional areas will come up continually.

The upper layers of the OSI model (application, presentation, and session—Layers 7, 6, and 5) are oriented more toward services to the applications. The lower four layers (transport, network, data link, and physical—Layers 4, 3, 2, and 1) are oriented more toward the flows of data from end to end through the network. CCNAs work mostly with issues in the lower layers, in particular with Layer 2, upon which switching is based, and Layer 3, upon which routing is based. Table 3-2 diagrams the seven OSI layers, with a thorough description and a list of example protocols.

Table 3-2   *OSI Reference Model*

Layer Name	Functional Description	Examples
Application (Layer 7)	An application that communicates with other computers is implementing OSI application layer concepts. The application layer refers to communications services to applications. For example, a word processor that lacks communications capabilities would not implement code for communications, and word processor programmers would not be concerned about OSI Layer 7. However, if an option for transferring a file were added, then the word processor would need to implement OSI Layer 7 (or the equivalent layer in another protocol specification).	Telnet, HTTP, FTP, WWW browsers, NFS, SMTP gateways (Eudora, CC:mail), SNMP, X.400 mail, FTAM
Presentation (Layer 6)	This layer's main purpose is defining data formats, such as ASCII text, EBCDIC text, binary, BCD, and JPEG. Encryption is also defined by OSI as a presentation layer service. For example, FTP enables you to choose binary or ASCII transfer. If binary is selected, the sender and receiver do not modify the contents of the file. If ASCII is chosen, the sender translates the text from the sender's character set to a standard ASCII and sends the data. The receiver translates back from the standard ASCII to the character set used on the receiving computer.	JPEG, ASCII, EBCDIC, TIFF, GIF, PICT, encryption, MPEG, MIDI

continues

Table 3-2   *OSI Reference Model (Continued)*

Layer Name	Functional Description	Examples
Session (Layer 5)	The session layer defines how to start, control, and end conversations (called sessions). This includes the control and management of multiple bidirectional messages so that the application can be notified if only some of a series of messages are completed. This allows the presentation layer to have a seamless view of an incoming stream of data. The presentation layer can be presented with data if all flows occur in some cases. For example, an automated teller machine transaction in which you withdraw cash from your checking account should not debit your account, and then fail, before handing you the cash, recording the transaction even though you did not receive money. The session layer creates ways to imply which flows are part of the same session and which flows must complete before any are considered complete.	RPC, SQL, NFS, NetBios names, AppleTalk ASP, DECnet SCP
Transport (Layer 4)	Layer 4 includes the choice of protocols that either do or do not provide error recovery. Multiplexing of incoming data for different flows to applications on the same host (for example, TCP sockets) is also performed. Reordering of the incoming data stream when packets arrive out of order is included.	TCP, UDP, SPX
Network (Layer 3)	This layer defines end-to-end delivery of packets. To accomplish this, the network layer defines logical addressing so that any endpoint can be identified. It also defines how routing works and how routes are learned so that the packets can be delivered. The network layer also defines how to fragment a packet into smaller packets to accommodate media with smaller maximum transmission unit sizes. (Note: Not all Layer 3 protocols use fragmentation.) The network layer of OSI defines most of the details that a Cisco router considers when routing. For example, IP running in a Cisco router is responsible for examining the destination IP address of a packet, comparing that address to the IP routing table, fragmenting the packet if the outgoing interface requires smaller packets, and queuing the packet to be sent out to the interface.	IP, IPX, AppleTalk DDP, ICMP

Table 3-2   *OSI Reference Model (Continued)*

Layer Name	Functional Description	Examples
Data link (Layer 2)	The data link (Layer 2) specifications are concerned with getting data across one particular link or medium. The data link protocols define delivery across an individual link. These protocols are necessarily concerned with the type of media in question; for example, 802.3 and 802.2 are specifications from the IEEE, which are referenced by OSI as valid data link (Layer 2) protocols. These specifications define how Ethernet works. Other protocols, such as High-Level Data Link Control (HDLC) for a point-to-point WAN link, deal with the different details of a WAN link. As with other protocol specifications, OSI often does not create any original specification for the data link layer but instead relies on other standards bodies such as IEEE to create new standards for the data link layer and the physical layer.	IEEE 802.3/802.2, HDLC, Frame Relay, PPP, FDDI, ATM, IEEE 802.5/ 802.2
Physical (Layer 1)	These physical layer (Layer 1) specifications, which are also typically standards from other organizations that are referred to by OSI, deal with the physical characteristics of the transmission medium. Connectors, pins, use of pins, electrical currents, encoding, and light modulation are all part of different physical layer specifications. Multiple specifications are sometimes used to complete all details of the physical layer. For example, RJ-45 defines the shape of the connector and the number of wires or pins in the cable. Ethernet and 802.3 define the use of wires or pins 1, 2, 3, and 6. So, to use a category 5 cable, with an RJ-45 connector for an Ethernet connection, Ethernet and RJ-45 physical layer specifications are used.	EIA/TIA-232, V.35, EIA/TIA- 449, V.24, RJ45, Ethernet, 802.3, 802.5, FDDI, NRZI, NRZ, B8ZS

Some protocols define details of multiple layers. For example, because the TCP/IP application layer correlates to OSI Layers 5 through 7, the Network File System (NFS) implements elements matching all three layers. Likewise, the 802.3, 802.5, and Ethernet standards define details for the data link and physical layers.

CCNAs deal with many aspects of Layers 1 through 4 on a daily basis. However, the upper layers are not as important to CCNAs. In addition, most networking people know what the OSI model is but do not need to memorize everything about it. Table 3-2 shows plenty of detail and explanation for a more in-depth idea of the OSI model components. If you are daunted by the task of memorizing all the examples in Table 3-2, you can refer to Table 3-3, which offers a more condensed description of the layer characteristics and examples. This table is taken directly from Cisco's ICND course, so if you are just not willing to try and remember all of Table 3-2, the information in Table 3-3 is a good compromise. (ICND is the instructor-led course in the official CCNA training path.)

Table 3-3   *OSI Reference Model (Condensed Information)*

OSI Layer Name	Functional Description	Examples
Application (Layer 7)	User interface	Telnet, HTTP
Presentation (Layer 6)	How data is presented Special processing, such as encryption	JPEG, ASCII, EBCDIC
Session (Layer 5)	Keeping data separate from different applications	Operating systems and application access scheduling
Transport (Layer 4)	Reliable or unreliable delivery Multiplexing	TCP, UDP, SPX
Network (Layer 3)	Logical addressing, which routers use for path determination	IP, IPX
Data link (Layer 2)	Combination of bits into bytes, and bytes into frames Access to the media using MAC address Error detection and error recovery	802.3/802.2, HDLC
Physical (Layer 1)	Moving of bits between devices Specification of voltage, wire speed, and cable pin-outs	EIA/TIA-232, V.35

Layering Benefits and Concepts

Many benefits can be gained from the process of breaking up the functions or tasks of networking into smaller chunks, called layers, and defining standard interfaces between these layers. One obvious benefit is that the individual protocols or layers are less complex and therefore can be defined in great detail. The following list summarizes the benefits of layered protocol specifications:

- Humans can discuss and learn about the many details of a protocol specification easier.

- Standardized interfaces among layers facilitates modular engineering. Different products can provide functions of only some layers (such as a router with Layers 1 to 3), or some products could supply parts of the functions of the protocol (such as Microsoft TCP/IP built into Win95, or the Eudora e-mail application providing TCP/IP application layer support).

- A better environment for interoperability is created.

- Reduced complexity allows easier program changes and faster product evolution.

- Each layer can define headers and trailers around the user data. Anyone examining these headers or trailers for troubleshooting can find the header or trailer for Layer X and know what type of information should be found.

- One layer uses the services of the layer immediately below it. Therefore, remembering what each layer does is easier. (For example, the network layer needs to deliver data from end to end. To do this, it uses data links to forward data to the next successive device along that end-to-end path.)

Interaction Between OSI Layers

CCNAs frequently deal with the concepts of layer interaction and encapsulation, particularly because routers build new data link headers and trailers to encapsulate the packets they route. The process of how layers interact on the same computer, as well as how the same layer processes on different computers communicate with each other, is all interrelated. The software or hardware products implementing the logic of some of the OSI protocol layers provide two general functions:

- Each layer provides a service to the layer above it in the protocol specification.

- Each layer communicates some information with the same layer's software or hardware on other computers. In some cases, the other computer is connected to the same media; in other cases, the other computer is on the other end of the network.

In the coming pages, you will learn more about each of these two functions.

Interactions Between Adjacent Layers on the Same Computer

To provide services to the next higher layer, a layer must know about the standard interfaces defined between layers. These interfaces include definitions of what Layer $N+1$ must provide to Layer N to get services, as well as what information Layer N must provide back to Layer $N+1$.

Figure 3-2 presents a graphical representation of two computers and provides an excellent backdrop for a discussion of interactions between layers on the same computer.

Figure 3-2 *Example for Discussion of Adjacent-Layer Interactions*

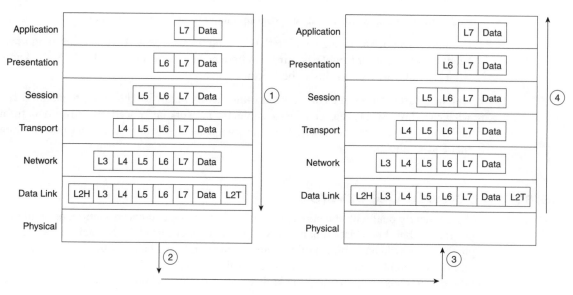

L# – Layer # Header   L#H – Layer # Header   L#T – Layer # Trailer

The data is created by some application on Host A. For example, an e-mail message is typed by the user. Each layer creates a header and passes the data down to the next layer. (The arrows in Figure 3-2, Step 1, denote the passing of data between layers.) Passing the data down to the next layer implies that the lower layer needs to perform some services for the higher layer; to perform these services, the lower layer adds some information in a header or trailer. For example, the transport layer hands off its data and header; the network layer adds a header with the correct destination network layer address so that the packet can be delivered to the other computer.

From each layer's perspective, the bits after that layer's header are considered to be data. For instance, Layer 4 considers the Layer 5, 6, and 7 headers, along with the original user data, to be one large data field.

After the application creates the data, the software and hardware implementing each layer perform their work, adding the appropriate header and trailer. The physical layer can use the media to send a signal for physical transmission, as shown in Step 2 in Figure 3-2.

Upon receipt (Step 3), Host B begins the adjacent layer interactions on Host B. The right side of Figure 3-2 shows an arrow pointing next to the computer (Step 4), signifying that the received data is being processed as it goes up the protocol stack. In fact, thinking about what each layer does in the OSI model can help you decide what information could be in each header.

The following sequence outlines the basics of processing at each layer and shows how each lower layer provides a service to the next higher layer. Consider the receipt of data by the host on the right side of Figure 3-2:

Step 1   The physical layer (Layer 1) ensures bit synchronization and places the received binary pattern into a buffer. It notifies the data link layer that a frame has been received after decoding the incoming signal into a bit stream. Therefore, Layer 1 has provided delivery of a stream of bits across the medium.

Step 2   The data link layer examines the frame check sequence (FCS) in the trailer to determine whether errors occurred in transmission (error detection). If an error has occurred, the frame is discarded. (Some data link protocols perform error *recovery*, and some do not.) The data link address(es) are examined so that Host B can decide whether to process the data further. If the data is addressed to host B, the data between the Layer 2 header and trailer is given to the Layer 3 software. The data link has delivered the data across that link.

Step 3   The network layer (Layer 3) destination address is examined. If the address is Host B's address, processing continues (logical addressing) and the data after the Layer 3 header is given to the transport layer (Layer 4) software. Layer 3 has provided the service of end-to-end delivery.

Step 4   If error recovery was an option chosen for the transport layer (Layer 4), the counters identifying this piece of data are encoded in the Layer 4 header along with acknowledgment information (error recovery). After error recovery and reordering of the incoming data, the data is given to the session layer.

Step 5   The session layer (Layer 5) can be used to ensure that a series of messages is completed. For example, this data could be meaningless if the next four exchanges are not completed. The Layer 5 header could include fields signifying that this is a middle flow in a chain, not an ending flow. After the session layer ensures that all flows are completed, it passes the data after the Layer 5 header to the Layer 6 software.

Step 6   The presentation layer (Layer 6) defines and manipulates data formats. For example, if the data is binary instead of character data, the header denotes that fact. The receiver does not attempt to convert the data using the default ASCII character set of Host B. Typically, this type of header is included only for initialization flows, not with every message being transmitted (data formats).

After the data formats have been converted, the data (after the Layer 6 header) is then passed to the application layer (Layer 7) software.

Step 7 The application layer (Layer 7) processes the final header and then can examine the true end-user data. This header signifies agreement to operating parameters by the applications on Host A and Host B. The headers are used to signal the values for all parameters; therefore, the header typically is sent and received at application initialization time only. For example, for file transfer, the size of the file to be transferred and the file formats used would be communicated (application parameters).

Interactions Between the Same Layers on Different Computers

Layer N must interact with Layer N on another computer to successfully implement its functions. For example, the transport layer (Layer 4) can send data, but if another computer does not acknowledge that the data was received, the sender will not know when to perform error recovery. Likewise, the sending computer encodes a destination network layer address (Layer 3) in the network layer header. If the intervening routers do not cooperate by performing their network layer tasks, the packet will not be delivered to the true destination.

To interact with the same layer on another computer, each layer defines a header and, in some cases, a trailer. Headers and trailers are additional data bits, created by the sending computer's software or hardware, that are placed before or after the data given to Layer N by Layer $N+1$. The information needed for this layer to communicate with the same layer process on the other computer is encoded in the header and trailer. The receiving computer's Layer N software or hardware interprets the headers and trailers created by the sending computer's Layer N, learning how Layer N's processing is being handled, in this case.

Figure 3-3 provides a conceptual perspective on the same-layer interactions. The application layer on Host A communicates with the application layer on Host B. Likewise, the transport, session, and presentation layers on Host A and Host B also communicate. The bottom three layers of the OSI model have to do with delivery of the data; Router 1 is involved in that process. Host A's network, physical, and data link layers communicate with Router 1; likewise, Router 1 communicates with Host B's physical, data link, and network layers. Figure 3-3 provides a visual representation of the same-layer interaction concepts.

Figure 3-3   *Same-Layer Interactions on Different Computers*

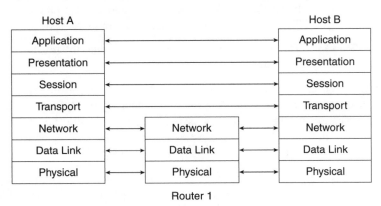

Data Encapsulation

The concept of placing data behind headers (and before trailers) for each layer is typically called *encapsulation* by Cisco documentation. As seen previously in Figure 3-2, when each layer creates its header, it places the data given to it by the next-higher layer behind its own header, thereby encapsulating the higher layer's data. In the case of a data link (Layer 2) protocol, the Layer 3 header and data are placed between the Layer 2 header and the Layer 2 trailer. The physical layer does not use encapsulation because it does not use headers or trailers.

Again referring to Figure 3-2, Step 1, the following list describes the encapsulation process from user creation of the data until the physical signal is encoded at Step 2:

Step 1   The application has already created the data. The application layer creates the application header and places the data behind it. This data structure is passed to the presentation layer.

Step 2   The presentation layer creates the presentation header and places the data behind it. This data structure is passed to the session layer.

Step 3   The session layer creates the session header and places the data behind it. This data structure is passed to the transport layer.

Step 4   The transport layer creates the transport header and places the data behind it. This data structure is passed to the network layer.

Step 5   The network layer creates the network header and places the data behind it. This data structure is passed to the data link layer.

Step 6 The data link layer creates the data link header and places the data behind it. The data link trailer is added to the end of the structure. This data structure is passed to the physical layer.

Step 7 The physical layer encodes a signal onto the medium to transmit the frame.

The previous seven-step process is accurate and meaningful for the seven-layer OSI model. However, encapsulation by each layer does not happen (typically) for each transmission of data by the application. Normally, Layers 5 through 7 use headers during initialization (and on occasion after initialization), but in most flows, there is no Layer 5, 6, or 7 header. This is because there is no new information to exchange for every flow of data.

An analogy can help in this case. A friend of mine from church spent several summers teaching English in a communist country. When I wrote to her, she assumed that I would write in English, but I could not write about "church" without the sensors tossing the letter. So, we agreed on encryption before she left. Under our code, God was called "Phil," and I could write things such as, "I saw Fred at Phil's house yesterday, and he said hi." I still had to address the letters before I mailed them, just like the lower OSI layers need to exchange some information for every piece of data sent. I didn't need to repeat what "Phil" really meant in each letter, just like the upper layers do not need to repeat encryption rules.

Previous CCNA exams referred to a five-step process for encapsulation. This included the typical encapsulation by the transport, network, and data link layers as steps 2 through 4 in the process. The first step was the application's creation of the data, and the last step was the physical layer's transmission of the bit stream. In case any questions remain in the CCNA question database referring to a five-step encapsulation process, the following list provides the details and explanation.

NOTE The term L*x*PDU, where *x* represents the number of one of the layers, is used to represent the bits that include the headers and trailers for that layer, as well as the encapsulated data. For instance, an IP packet is an L3PDU, which includes the IP header and any encapsulated data.

Step 1 **Create the data**—This simply means that the application has data to send.

Step 2 **Package the data for transport**—In other words, the transport layer creates the transport header and places the data behind it. The L4PDU is created here.

Step 3   **Add the destination network layer address to the data**—The network layer creates the network header, which includes the network layer address, and places the data (L4PDU) behind it. In other words, the L3PDU is created here.

Step 4   **Add the destination data link address to the data**—The data link layer creates the data link header, places the data (L3PDU) behind it, and places the data link trailer at the end. In other words, the L2PDU is created here.

Step 5   **Transmit the bits**—The physical layer encodes a signal onto the medium to transmit the frame.

This five-step process happens to match the TCP/IP network model very well. Figure 3-4 depicts the concept; the numbers shown represent each of the five steps.

Figure 3-4   *Five Steps of Data Encapsulation*

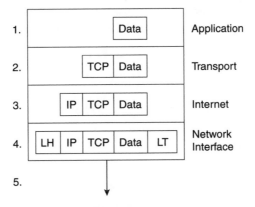

Sifting through terminology is a frequent task for CCNAs. Some common terminology is needed to discuss the data that a particular layer is processing. *Layer N PDU* (protocol data unit) is a term used to describe a set of bytes that includes the Layer *N* header and trailer, all headers encapsulated, and the user data. From Layer *N*'s perspective, the higher-layer headers and the user data form one large *data* or *information* field. A few other terms also describe some of these PDUs. The Layer 2 PDU (including the data link header and trailer) is called a *frame*. Similarly, the Layer 3 PDU is called a *packet*, or sometimes a *datagram*. Finally, the Layer 4 PDU is called a *segment*. Figure 3-5 illustrates the construction of frames, packets, and segments and the different layers' perspectives on what is considered to be *data*.

Figure 3-5   *Frames, Packets, and Segments*

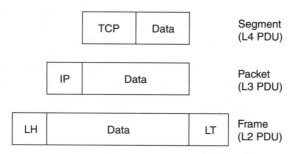

The TCP/IP and NetWare Protocols

Two of the most pervasively deployed protocols are TCP/IP and Novell NetWare; these also are the two key protocol architectures covered on the CCNA exam. TCP/IP and NetWare are covered in much more detail in the upcoming chapters.

This short section compares TCP/IP, Novell, and OSI. The goal is to provide some insight into what some popularly used terminology really means. In particular, routing is defined as a *Layer 3 process*; this section reviews how that term relates to TCP/IP and NetWare.

For perspective, Figure 3-6 shows the layers of these two protocols as compared with OSI.

Figure 3-6   *OSI, TCP/IP, and NetWare Protocols*

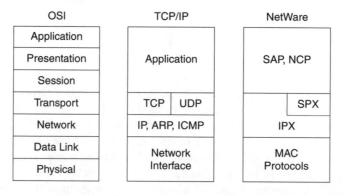

As Figure 3-6 illustrates, the IP and IPX protocols most closely match the OSI network layer—Layer 3. Many times, even on the CCNA exam, IP and IPX will be called *Layer 3 protocols*. Clearly, IP is in TCP/IP's Layer 2, but for consistent use of terminology, it is commonly called a Layer 3 protocol because its functions most closely match OSI's Layer 3. Both IP and IPX define logical addressing, routing, the learning of routing information, and end-to-end delivery rules.

As with OSI Layers 1 and 2 (physical and data link, respectively), the lower layers of each stack simply refer to other well-known specifications. For example, the lower layers all support the IEEE standards for Ethernet and Token Ring, the ANSI standard for FDDI, the ITU standard for ISDN, and the Frame Relay protocols specified by the Frame Relay Forum, ANSI, and the ITU. The protocol stacks can accommodate other evolving Layer 1 and Layer 2 specifications more easily by referring to emerging international standards rather than trying to evolve these standards themselves.

OSI Transport Layer Functions

The transport layer (Layer 4) defines several functions. Two important features covered in this chapter are error recovery and flow control. Routers discard packets for many reasons, including bit errors, congestion that has caused a lack of buffer space, and instances in which no correct routes are known. The transport layer can provide for retransmission (error recovery) and can help avoid congestion (flow control).

Transport layer protocols are typically categorized as either connectionless or connection-oriented, so CCNAs deal with the concepts of connectionless and connection-oriented protocols on a regular basis. This next section compares the two and provides some explanation for the functions of each. Error recovery and flow control are covered in the section "How Error Recovery Is Accomplished."

Connection-Oriented Versus Connectionless Protocols

The terms *connection-oriented* and *connectionless* have some relatively well-known connotations inside the world of networking protocols. However, the typical connotation can be a bit misleading. For instance, most people correlate connection-oriented protocols with reliable or error-recovering protocols because the two features are often implemented by a single protocol. However, connection-oriented protocols do not have to provide error recovery, and error-recovering protocols do not have to be connection-oriented.

First, some basic definitions are in order:

Connection-oriented protocol: A protocol that either requires an exchange of messages before data transfer begins or has a required pre-established correlation between two endpoints.

Connectionless protocol: A protocol that does not require an exchange of messages and that does not require a pre-established correlation between two endpoints.

The definitions are sufficiently general so that all cases can be covered. TCP is connection-oriented because a set of three messages must be completed before data is exchanged. Likewise, SPX is connection-oriented. Frame Relay, when using PVCs, does not require any messages be sent ahead of time, but it does require predefinition in the Frame Relay switches, establishing a connection between two Frame Relay attached devices. ATM PVCs are also connection-oriented, for similar reasons.

As mentioned earlier, connection-oriented protocols are often assumed to also perform error recovery. However, Frame Relay and ATM are two examples in which the protocols are connection-oriented but the protocol does not provide error recovery. Table 3-4 provides some example protocols and tells whether they are connection-oriented and error-recovering.

Table 3-4   *Protocol Characteristics: Recovery and Connections*

Connected?	Reliable?	Examples
Connection-oriented	Yes	LLC type 2 (802.2), TCP (TCP/IP), SPX (NetWare), X.25
Connection-oriented	No	Frame Relay virtual circuits, ATM virtual connections, PPP
Connectionless	Yes	TFTP, NetWare NCP (without Packet Burst)
Connectionless	No	UDP, IP, IPX, AppleTalk DDP, most Layer 3 protocols, 802.3, 802.5

The most typical option is for a protocol to be connectionless and not perform error recovery, or to be connection-oriented and to also perform error recovery. In fact, many connection-oriented protocols exchange information important to error recovery when the connection is established.

Cisco expects CCNAs to be able to distinguish between *error detection* and *error recovery.* Any header or trailer with a frame check sequence (FCS) or similar field can be used to detect bit errors in the PDU. Error detection uses the FCS to detect the error, which results in discarding the PDU. However, error recovery implies that the protocol reacts to the lost data and somehow causes the data to be retransmitted. An example of error recovery is shown later in this section.

NOTE   Some documentation refers to the terms *connected* or *connection-oriented.* These terms are used synonymously. You will most likely see the use of the term *connection-oriented* in Cisco documentation.

In the context of previous Cisco official courses, reliable, error-recovering protocols were always defined as also being connection-oriented. In the current ICND course, part of the official Cisco CCNA training path, those references have been removed. If you are studying using an older ICRC or CRLS course book, pay particular attention to the comparisons made about connection orientation and error recovery in this book.

The following litany describes the attitude of the current Cisco course books on error recovery:

- The protocol implementing the connection defines headers and uses part of these headers to number and acknowledge the data. For example, TCP provides error recovery and defines a TCP header. The headers used by that protocol have some numbering and acknowledgment fields to both acknowledge data and notice when it has been lost in transmission. The endpoints that are sending and receiving data use the fields in this header to identify that data was sent and to signify that data was received.

- A sender of data will want an acknowledgment of the data. When an error occurs, many error-recovery algorithms require the sender to send all data, starting with the lost data. To limit the negative effect of having to resend lots of data, a window of unacknowledged data, which can be dynamic in size, is defined. This window defines the maximum amount of data that can be sent without getting an acknowledgment.

How Error Recovery Is Accomplished

Regardless of which protocol specification performs the error recovery, all work in basically the same way. Generically, the transmitted data is labeled or numbered. After receipt, the receiver signals back to the sender that the data was received, using the same label or number to identify the data. Figure 3-7 summarizes the operation.

Figure 3-7   *Forward Acknowledgment*

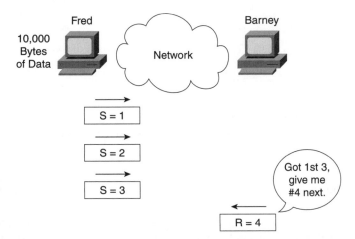

As Figure 3-7 illustrates, the data is numbered, as shown with the numbers 1, 2, and 3. These numbers are placed into the header used by that particular protocol; for example, the TCP header contains similar numbering fields. When Barney sends his next frame to Fred, Barney acknowledges that all three frames were received by setting his acknowledgment field to 4. The number 4 refers to the next data to be received, which is called *forward acknowledgment*. This means that the acknowledgment number in the header identifies the next data that is to be received, not the last one received. (In this case, 4 is next to be received.)

In some protocols, such as LLC2, the numbering always starts with zero. In other protocols, such as TCP, the number is stated during initialization by the sending machine. Also, some protocols count the frame/packet/segment as 1; others count the number of bytes sent. In any case, the basic idea is the same.

Of course, error recovery has not been covered yet. Take the case of Fred and Barney again, but notice Barney's reply in Figure 3-8.

Figure 3-8   *Recovery Example*

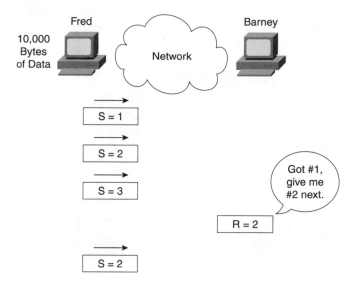

Because Barney is expecting packet number 2 next, what could Fred do? Two choices exist. Fred could send numbers 2 and 3 again, or Fred could send number 2 and wait, hoping that Barney's next acknowledgment will say 4, indicating that Barney just got number 2 and already had number 3 from earlier.

Finally, error recovery typically uses two sets of counters: one to count data in one direction, and one to count data in the opposite direction. So, when Barney acknowledges packet number 2 with the *number acknowledged* field in the header, the header would also have a *number sent* field that identifies the data in Barney's packet. For instance, assume in Figure 3-8 that the previous packet Barney had sent was number 5. The packet shown in the figure would be labeled 6.

Table 3-5 summarizes the concepts behind error recovery and lists the behavior of three popular error-recovery protocols.

Table 3-5   *Examples of Error-Recovery Protocols and Their Features*

Feature	TCP	SPX	LLC2
Acknowledges data in both directions?	Yes	Yes	Yes
Uses forward acknowledgment?	Yes	Yes	Yes
Counts bytes or frame/packets?	Bytes	Packets	Frames
Necessitates resending of all data, or just one part and wait when resending?	One and wait	Resend all	Resend all

Flow Control

Flow control is the process of controlling the rate at which a computer sends data. Depending on the particular protocol, both the sender and the receiver of the data (as well as any intermediate routers, bridges, or switches) might participate in the process of controlling the flow from sender to receiver.

Flow control is needed because data is discarded when congestion occurs. A sender of data might be sending the data faster than the receiver can receive the data, so the receiver discards the data. Also, the sender might be sending the data faster than the intermediate switching devices (switches and routers) can forward the data, also causing discards. Packets can be lost due to transmission errors as well. This happens in every network, sometimes temporarily and sometimes regularly, depending on the network and the traffic patterns. The receiving computer can have insufficient buffer space to receive the next incoming frame, or possibly the CPU is too busy to process the incoming frame. Intermediate routers might need to discard the packets based on temporary lack of buffers or processing as well.

Flow control attempts to reduce unnecessary discarding of data. Comparing flows when flow control is used, and when it is not used, is helpful for understanding why flow control can be useful. Without flow control, some PDUs are discarded. If some reliable protocol in use happens to implement error recovery, then the data is re-sent. The sender keeps sending as fast as possible. With flow control, the sender can be slowed down enough that the original PDU can be forwarded to the receiving computer, and the receiving computer can process the PDU. Flow-control protocols do not prevent the loss of data due to congestion; these protocols simply reduce the amount of lost data, which in turn reduces the amount of retransmitted traffic, which hopefully reduces overall congestion. However, with flow control, the sender is artificially slowed or throttled so that it sends data less quickly than it could without flow control.

The CCNA exam requires that you be familiar with three features, or methods, of implementing flow control:

- Buffering
- Congestion avoidance
- Windowing

Buffering

Buffering simply means that the computers reserve enough buffer space that bursts of incoming data can be held until processed. No attempt is made to actually slow the transmission rate of the sender of the data. In fact, buffering is such a common method of dealing with changes in the rate of arrival of data that most of us would probably just assume that it is happening. However, some older documentation refers to "three methods of flow control," of which buffering is one of the methods, so be sure to remember it as a separate function.

Congestion Avoidance

Congestion avoidance is the second method of flow control covered here. The computer receiving the data notices that its buffers are filling. This causes either a separate PDU, or field in a header, to be sent toward the sender, signaling the sender to stop transmitting. Figure 3-9 shows an example.

Figure 3-9   *Congestion Avoidance Flow Control*

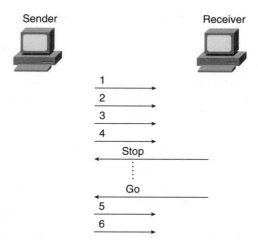

"Hurry up and wait" is a popular expression used to describe the process used in this congestion avoidance example. This process is used by Synchronous Data Link Control (SDLC) and Link Access Procedure, Balanced (LAPB) serial data link protocols.

A preferred method might be to get the sender to simply slow down instead of stopping altogether. This method would still be considered congestion avoidance, but instead of signaling the sender to stop, the signal would mean to slow down. One example is the TCP/IP Internet Control Message Protocol (ICMP) message "Source Quench." This message is sent by the receiver or some intermediate router to slow the sender. The sender can slow down gradually until "Source Quench" messages are no longer received.

Windowing

The third category of flow-control methods is called *windowing*. A window is the maximum amount of data the sender can send without getting an acknowledgment. If no acknowledgment is received by the time the window is filled, then the sender must wait for acknowledgment. Figure 3-10 shows an example. The slanted lines indicate the time difference between sending a PDU and its receipt.

Figure 3-10   *Windowing Flow Control*

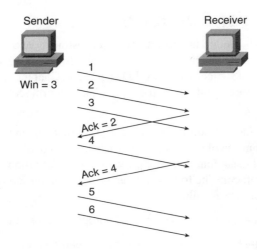

In this example, the sender has a window of three frames. After the receiver acknowledges the receipt of frame 1, frame 4 can be sent. After a time lapse, the acknowledgment for frames 2 and 3 are received, which is signified by the frame sent by the receiver with the acknowledgment field equal to 4. So, the sender is free to send two more frames—frames 5 and 6—before another acknowledgment is received.

Flow Control Summary

One of Cisco's goals for CCNA and its other certifications is to ensure that passing means that you really understand the technology rather than simply understanding how to pass a particular exam. Focusing on understanding the concepts, as always, gives you a chance to get the exam questions correct. Table 3-6 summarizes the flow control terms and provides examples of each type. Memorizing these terms should help trigger your memory of flow-control concepts.

Table 3-6   *Flow-Control Methods—Summary*

Name Used in This Book	Other Names	Example Protocols
Buffering	N/A	N/A
Congestion Avoidance	Stop/Start, RNR, Source Quench	SDLC, LAPB, LLC2
Windowing	N/A	TCP, SPX, LLC2

OSI Data Link Layer Functions

As a CCNA, you'll need to understand both the abstract concepts about the OSI layers and particular instances of such protocols. This section focuses on more of the abstract concepts. Chapter 4, "Bridges/Switches and LAN Design," and Chapter 8, "WAN Protocols and Design," provide more details about particular data link protocols, as well as their configuration in the IOS.

This section examines four different protocols: Ethernet, Token Ring, HDLC, and Frame Relay. A generalized definition of the function of a data link protocol will be used to guide you through the comparison of these four data link protocols. This definition could be used to examine any other data link protocol. The four components of this definition of the functions of data link (Layer 2) protocols are as follows:

- **Arbitration**—Determines when it is appropriate to use the physical medium.

- **Addressing**—Ensures that the correct recipient(s) receives and processes the data that is sent.

- **Error detection**—Determines whether the data made the trip across the medium successfully.

- **Identifying the encapsulated data**—Determines the type of header that follows the data link header. This feature is included in a subset of data link protocols.

Ethernet and Token Ring are two popular LAN Layer 2 protocols. These protocols are defined by the IEEE in specifications 802.3 and 802.5, respectively. Because 802.3 and 802.5 define how a station accesses the media, the IEEE calls these protocols Media Access Control (MAC) protocols. Also, both 802.3 and 802.5 call for the use of another IEEE specification as a separate part of the data link layer, namely 802.2 Logical Link Control (LLC). 802.2 is purposefully designed to provide functions common to both Ethernet and Token Ring, whereas 802.3 and 802.5 were designed specifically for data link functions pertinent to either Ethernet or Token Ring topologies, respectively.

The Ethernet standards before the IEEE created 802.3 have been called *DIX Ethernet* for quite a while (the letters DIX represent Digital, Intel, and Xerox). DIX Version 2 defines similar functions to both the 802.3 and 802.2 specifications.

HDLC is the default data link protocol (encapsulation) on Cisco routers serial interfaces. Frame Relay headers are coincidentally based on the HDLC specification, but Frame Relay was created for multiaccess networks (with more than two devices). The clear differences between Frame Relay and HDLC provide a good backdrop to examine the functions of the data link layer (Layer 2).

Data Link Function 1: Arbitration

Arbitration is needed only when there are instants in time during which it is not appropriate to send data across the media. LANs were originally defined as a shared media on which each device must wait until the appropriate time to send data. The specifications for these data link protocols define how to arbitrate the use of the physical medium.

Ethernet uses the carrier sense multiple access collision detect (CSMA/CD) algorithm for arbitration. The basic algorithm for using an Ethernet when there is data to be sent consists of the following steps:

Step 1   Listen to find out whether a frame is currently being received.

Step 2   If no other frame is on the Ethernet, send.

Step 3   If another frame is on the Ethernet, wait and then listen again.

Step 4   While sending, if a collision occurs, stop, wait, and listen again.

With Token Ring, a totally different mechanism is used. A free-token frame rotates around the ring while no device has data to send. When sending, a device claims the free token, which really means changing bits in the 802.5 header to signify "token busy." The data is then placed onto the ring after the Token Ring header. The basic algorithm for using a Token Ring when there is data to be sent consists of the following steps:

Step 1   Listen for the passing token.

Step 2   If token is *busy*, listen for the next token.

Step 3   If the token is *free*, mark the token as a *busy* token, append the data, and send the data onto the ring.

Step 4   When the header with the busy token returns to the sender of that frame, after completing a full revolution around the ring, the sender removes the data from the ring.

Step 5   The device sends a free token to allow another station to send a frame.

The algorithm for Token Ring does have other rules and variations, but these are beyond the depth of what is needed for the CCNA exam. Network Associates (the "Sniffer" people) have an excellent class covering Token Ring in detail. To find out more about these classes, go to www.nai.com.

With HDLC, arbitration is a nonissue today. HDLC is used on point-to-point links, which are typically full-duplex (four-wire) circuits. In other words, either endpoint can send at any time.

From a physical perspective, Frame Relay is comprised of a leased line between a router and the Frame Relay switch. These links are also typically full-duplex links, so no arbitration is needed. The Frame Relay network is shared among many data terminal equipment (DTE) devices, whereas the access link is not shared, so arbitration of the medium is not an issue.

CAUTION   **A Word About Frames**

As used in this book and in the ICND course, the word *frame* refers to particular parts of the data as sent on a link. In particular, *frame* implies that the data link header and trailer are part of the bits being examined and discussed. Figure 3-11 shows frames for the four data link protocols.

Figure 3-11   *Popular Frame Formats*

802.3	802.2	Data	802.3

HDLC	Data	HDLC

802.5	802.2	Data	802.5

F.R.	Data	F.R.

Data Link Function 2: Addressing

Cisco requires that CCNAs master the formats and meanings of data link and network layer addresses. Addressing is needed on LANs because there can be many possible recipients of data—that is, there could be more than two devices on the link. Because LANs are *broadcast media*—a term signifying that all devices on the media receive the same data—each recipient must ask the question, "Is this frame meant for me?"

With Ethernet and Token Ring, the addresses are very similar. Each uses Media Access Control (MAC) addresses, which are 6 bytes long and are represented as a 12-digit hexadecimal number. Table 3-7 summarizes most of the details about MAC addresses.

Table 3-7   *LAN MAC Address Terminology and Features*

LAN Addressing Terms and Features	Description
MAC	Media Access Control. 802.3 (Ethernet) and 802.5 (Token Ring) are the MAC sublayers of these two LAN data link protocols.

Table 3-7   *LAN MAC Address Terminology and Features (Continued)*

LAN Addressing Terms and Features	Description
Ethernet address, NIC address, LAN address, Token Ring address, card address	Other names often used instead of MAC address. These terms describe the 6-byte address of the LAN interface card.
Burned-in address	The 6-byte address assigned by the vendor making the card. It is usually burned in to a ROM or EEPROM on the LAN card and begins with a 3-byte Organizationally Unique Identifier (OUI) assigned by the IEEE.
Locally administered address	Via configuration, an address that is used instead of the burned-in address.
Unicast address	Fancy term for a MAC that represents a single LAN interface.
Broadcast address	An address that means "all devices that reside on this LAN right now."
Multicast address	Not valid on Token Ring. On Ethernet, a multicast address implies some subset of all devices currently on the LAN.
Functional address	Not valid on Ethernet. On Token Ring, these addresses are reserved to represent the device(s) on the ring performing a particular function. For example, all source-route bridges supply the ring number to other devices; to do so, they each listen for the Ring Parameter Server (RPS) functional address.

HDLC includes a meaningless address field because it is used only on point-to-point serial links. The recipient is implied; if one device sent a frame, the other device is the only possible intended recipient.

With Frame Relay, there is one physical link that has many logical circuits called *virtual circuits (VCs)*. (See Chapter 8 for more background on Frame Relay.) The address field in Frame Relay defines a data-link connection identifier (DLCI), which identifies each VC. For example, in Figure 3-12, the Frame Relay switch to which router Timbuktu is connected receives frames; the switch forwards the frame to either Kalamazoo or East Egypt based on the DLCI, which identifies each VC. So, Timbuktu has one physical connection but multiple logical connections.

Figure 3-12 *Frame Relay Network*

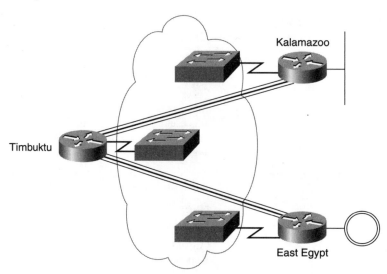

Data Link Function 3: Error Detection

Error detection is simply the process of learning whether bit errors occurred during the transmission of the frame. To do this, most data links include a *frame check sequence (FCS)* or *cyclical redundancy check (CRC)* field in the data link trailer. This field contains a value that is the result of a mathematical formula applied to the data in the frame. The FCS value calculated and sent by the sender should match the value calculated by the receiver. All four data links discussed in this section contain an FCS field in the frame trailer.

Error detection does not imply recovery; most data links, including 802.5 Token Ring and 802.3 Ethernet, do not provide error recovery. In these two cases, however, an option in the 802.2 protocol, called LLC type 2, does perform error recovery. (SNA and NetBIOS are the typical higher-layer protocols in use that request the services of LLC2.)

Data Link Function 4: Identifying the Encapsulated Data

Finally, the fourth part of a data link identifies the contents of the data field in the frame. Figure 3-13 helps make the usefulness of this feature apparent.

Figure 3-13   *Multiplexing Using Data Link Type and Protocol Fields*

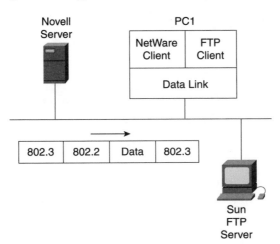

When PC1 receives data, does it give the data to the TCP/IP software or the NetWare client software? Of course, that depends on what is inside the data field. If the data came from the Novell server, then PC1 hands the data off to the NetWare client code. If the data comes from the Sun FTP server, PC1 hands it off to the TCP/IP code.

Ethernet and Token Ring 802.2 LLC provide a field in its header to identify the type of data in the data field.

PC1 receives frames that basically look like the two shown in Figure 3-14. Each data link header has a field with a code that means IP, or IPX, or some other designation defining the type of protocol header that follows. The first item to examine in the header is the 802.2 DSAP field. In the first frame in Figure 3-14, the destination service access point (DSAP) field has a value of E0, which means that the next header is a Novell IPX header. In the second frame, the DSAP field is AA, which implies that a SNAP header follows. Next, the type field in the Subnetwork Access Protocol (SNAP) header, which has a value of 0800, signifies that the next header is an IP header. RFC 1700, the "Assigned Numbers" RFC (http://www.isi.edu/in-notes/rfc1700.txt), lists the SAP and SNAP Type field values and the protocol types they imply.

Similarly, HDLC and Frame Relay need to identify the contents of the data field. Of course, it is atypical to have end-user devices attached to either of these types of data links. In this case, routers provide an example more typically found in most WAN environments, as shown in Figure 3-15.

Figure 3-14   *802.2 SAP and SNAP Type Fields*

14	1	1	1		4		
802.3	E0 DSAP	E0 SSAP	CTL	IPX Data	802.3		

			802.5		**SNAP**		
802.3	AA DSAP	AA SSAP	03 CTL	OUI	0800 Type	IP Data	802.3
14	1	1	1	3	2		4

Figure 3-15   *Identifying Protocols over HDLC and Frame Relay*

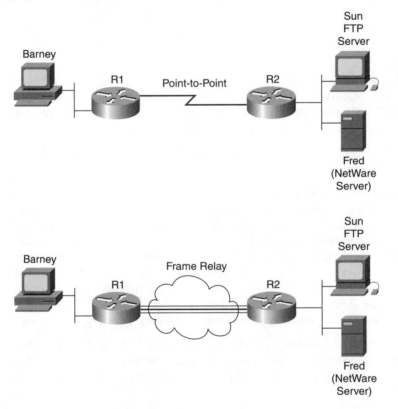

Referring to the top part of Figure 3-15, if Barney is using FTP to transfer files to the Sun system and is also connected to the NetWare server (Fred) using IPX, then Barney will generate both TCP/IP and NetWare IPX traffic. As this traffic passes over the HDLC controlled link, R2 will need to know whether an IP or IPX packet follows the HDLC header. Mainly, this is so that the router can find the Layer 3 destination address, assume its length (32 bits or 80 bits), perform table lookup in the correct routing table (IP or IPX), and make the correct routing decision.

HDLC does not provide a mechanism to identify the type of packet in the data field. IOS adds a proprietary 2-byte field immediately after the HDLC header that identifies the contents of the data. As shown in the bottom of Figure 3-15, the intervening Frame Relay switches do not care what is inside the data field. The receiving router, R2, does care for the same reasons that R2 cares when using HDLC—that is, the receiving router needs to know whether an IP or IPX packet follows the Frame Relay header. Frame Relay headers originally did not address this issue, either, because the headers were based on HDLC. However, the IETF created a specification called RFC 1490 that defined additional headers that followed the standard Frame Relay header. These headers include several fields that can be used to identify the data so that the receiving device knows what type is hidden inside.

The ITU and ANSI picked up the specifications of RFC 1490 and added it to their official Frame Relay standards: ITU T1.617 Annex F and ANSI Q.933 Annex E, respectively.

Figure 3-16 shows the fields that identify the type of protocol found in the data field.

Figure 3-16 *HDLC and Frame Relay Protocol Type Fields*

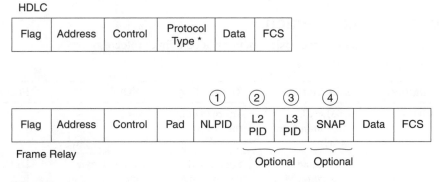

As seen in Figure 3-16, a protocol type field comes after the HDLC control field. In the Frame Relay example, four different options exist for identifying the type of data inside the frame. RFC 2427, which obsoletes RFC 1490, provides a complete reference and is useful reading for those of you moving on to CCNP certification (www.isi.edu/in-notes/rfc2427.txt). ("Obsoletes" in the RFC world implies that a newer document has superceded it but does not necessarily mean that all or most of the original RFC has been changed.)

Table 3-8 summarizes the different choices for encoding protocol types for each of the four data link protocols. Notice that the length of some of these fields is only 1 byte, which historically has led to the addition of other headers. For example, the SNAP header contains a 2-byte type field because a 1-byte DSAP field is not big enough to number all the available options for what type of protocol is inside the data.

Table 3-8   *Different Choices for Encoding Protocol Types for Each of the Four Example Data Link Protocols*

Data Link Protocol	Field	Header in Which It Is Found	Size
802.3 Ethernet and 802.5 Token Ring	DSAP	802.2 header	1 byte
802.3 Ethernet and 802.5 Token Ring	SSAP	802.2 header	1 byte
802.3 Ethernet and 802.5 Token Ring	Protocol Type	SNAP header	2 bytes
Ethernet (DIX)	Ethertype	Ethernet header	2 bytes
HDLC	Cisco proprietary protocol id field	Extra Cisco header	2 bytes
Frame Relay RFC 2427	NLPID	RFC 1490	1 byte
Frame Relay RFC 2427	L2 or L3 Protocol ID	Q.933	2 bytes each
Frame Relay RFC 2427	SNAP Protocol Type	SNAP Header	2 bytes

Summary: Data Link Functions

Table 3-9 summarizes the basic functions of data link protocols:

Table 3-9   *Data link Protocol Functions*

Function	Ethernet	Token Ring	HDLC	Frame Relay
Arbitration	CSMA/CD Algorithm (part of MAC)	Token passing (part of MAC)	—	—
Addressing	Source and destination MAC addresses	Source and destination MAC addresses	Single 1-byte address; unimportant on point-to-point links	DLCI used to identify virtual circuits
Error Detection	FCS in trailer	FCS in trailer	FCS in trailer	FCS in trailer
Identifying contents of data	802.2 DSAP, SNAP header, or Ethertype, as needed	802.2 DSAP or SNAP header, as needed	Proprietary Type field	RFC 1490/2427 headers, with NLPID, L2 and L3 protocol IDs, or SNAP header

OSI Network Layer Functions

On the CCNA exam, the two key functions for any Layer 3 protocol are *routing* and *addressing*. These two functions are intertwined and are best understood by considering both at the same time.

Network layer (Layer 3) addressing will be covered in enough depth to describe IP, IPX, and AppleTalk addresses. Also, now that data link and network layer addresses have been covered in this chapter, this section undertakes a comparison of the two as well.

Routing

Routing can be thought of as a three-step process, as seen in Figure 3-17. Thinking about routing in these three separate steps helps make some of the details more obvious. However, most people will not think of routing as a three-step process when going about their normal jobs—this is just a tool to make a few points more clearly.

Figure 3-17   *Three Steps of Routing*

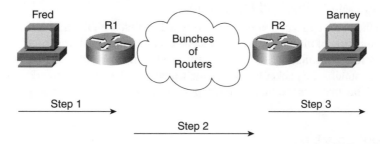

As illustrated in Figure 3-17, the three steps of routing include the following:

Step 1   Sending the data from the source computer to some nearby router

Step 2   Delivering the data from the router near the source to a router near the destination

Step 3   Delivering the data from the router near the destination to the end destination computer

Step 1: Sending Data to a Nearby Router

The creator of the data, who is also the sender of the data, decides to send data to a device in another group. A mechanism must be in place so that the sender knows of some router on a *common data link with the sender* to ensure that data can be sent to that router. The sender sends a data link frame across the medium to the nearby router; this frame includes the packet in the data portion of the frame. That frame uses data link (Layer 2) addressing in the data link header to ensure that the nearby router receives the frame.

Step 2: Routing Data Across the Network

The routing table for that particular network layer protocol type is nothing more than a list of network layer address groupings. As shown in Table 3-10 later in this section, these groupings vary based on the network layer protocol type. The router compares the destination network layer address in the packet to the entries in the routing table in memory, and a match is made. This matching entry in the routing table tells this router where to forward the packet next.

Any intervening routers repeat the same process. The destination network layer (Layer 3) address in the packet identifies the group in which the destination resides. The routing table is searched for a matching entry, which tells this router where to forward the packet next. Eventually, the packet is delivered to the router connected to the network or subnet of the destination host, as previously shown in Figure 3-17.

Step 3: Delivering Data to the End Destination

When the packet arrives at a router sharing a data link with the true destination, the router and the destination of the packet are in the same L3 grouping. That final router can forward the data directly to the destination. As usual, a new data link header and trailer are created before a frame (which contains the packet that made the trip across the entire network) can be sent on to the media. This matches the final step (Step 3), as previously shown in Figure 3-17.

A Comment About Data Links

Because the routers build new data link headers and trailers, and because the new headers contain data link addresses, the routers must have some way to decide what data link addresses to use. An example of how the router determines which data link address to use is the IP Address Resolution Protocol (ARP) protocol. ARP is used to dynamically learn the data link address of some IP host.

An example specific to TCP/IP will be useful to solidify the concepts behind routing. Imagine that PC1 is sending packets to PC2. (If you do not understand the basics of IP addressing already, you may want to bookmark this page and refer to it after you have reviewed Chapter 5, which covers IP addressing.) Figure 3-18 provides an example network so that you can review the routing process.

Figure 3-18   *Routing Logic and Encapsulation—PC1 Sending to PC2*

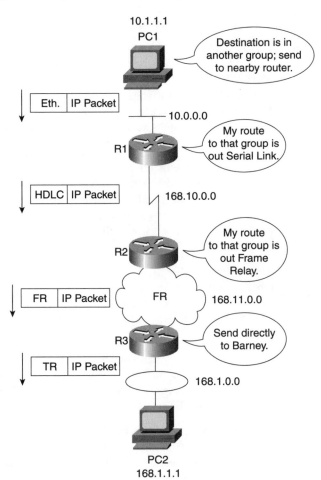

The logic behind the earlier three-step routing process is described in the following steps. Steps A and B that follow describe the first of the three routing steps in this example. Steps C, D, E, F, and G correspond to Step 2. Finally, Step H corresponds to routing Step 3.

Step A   PC1 needs to know its nearby router. PC1 first knows of R1's IP address by having either a *default router* or a *default gateway* configured. The default router defined on some host is the router to which that host forwards packets that are destined for subnets other than the directly attached subnet. Alternatively, PC1 can learn of R1's IP address using Dynamic Host Configuration

Protocol (DHCP). Because DHCP is not mentioned for the CCNA exam, you can assume that a default router of 10.1.1.100 is configured on PC1 and that it is R1's Ethernet IP address.

Step B   PC1 needs to know R1's Ethernet MAC address before PC1 can finish building the Ethernet header (see Figure 3-18). In the case of TCP/IP, the ARP process is used to dynamically learn R1's MAC address. (See Chapter 5 for a discussion of ARP.) When R1's MAC address is known, PC1 completes the Ethernet header with the destination MAC address being R1's MAC address.

Step C   At Step 2 of the routing process, the router has many items to consider. First, the incoming frame (Ethernet interface) is processed only if the Ethernet FCS is passed and the router's MAC address is in the destination address field. Then, the appropriate *protocol type* field is examined so that R1 knows what type of packet is in the data portion of the frame. At this point, R1 discards the Ethernet header and trailer.

Step D   The next part of Step 2 involves finding an entry in the routing table for network 168.1.0.0, the network of which PC2 is a member. In this case, the route in R1 references 168.1.0.0 and lists R1's serial interface as the interface by which to forward the packet.

Step E   To complete Step 2, R2 builds an HDLC header and trailer to place around the IP packet. Because HDLC data link uses the same address field every time, no process like ARP is needed to allow R1 to build the HDLC header.

Step F   Routing Step 2 is repeated by R2 when it receives the HDLC frame. The HDLC FCS is checked; the type field is examined to learn that the packet inside the frame is an IP packet, and then the HDLC header and trailer are discarded. The IP routing table in R2 is examined for network 168.1.0.0, and a match is made. The entry directs R2 to forward the packet to its Frame Relay serial interface. The routing entry also identifies the next router's IP address—namely R3's IP address on the other end of the Frame Relay VC.

Step G   Before R2 can complete its Step 2 of this end-to-end routing algorithm, R2 must build a Frame Relay header and trailer. Before it can complete the task, the correct DLCI for the VC to R3 must be decided. In most cases today, the dynamic Inverse ARP process will have associated R3's IP address with the DLCI R2 uses to send frames to R3. (See Chapter 8 for more details on Inverse ARP and Frame Relay mapping.) With that mapping information, R2 can complete the Frame Relay header and send the frame to R3.

Step H   Step 3 of the original algorithm is performed by R3. Like R1 and R2 before it, R3 checks the FCS in the data link trailer, looks at the type field to decide whether the packet inside the frame is an IP packet, and then discards the Frame Relay header and trailer. The routing table entry for 168.1.0.0 shows that the outgoing interface is R3's Token Ring interface. However, there is no next router IP address because there is no need to forward the packet to another router. R3 simply needs to build a Token Ring header and trailer and forward the frame that contains the original packet to PC2. Before R3 can finish building the Token Ring header, an IP ARP must be used to find PC2's MAC address (assuming that R3 doesn't already have that information in its IP ARP cache).

Network Layer (Layer 3) Addressing

Cisco requires that CCNAs master the details of Layer 3 addressing, both the concepts and the particulars of IP and IPX. One key feature of network layer addresses is that they were designed to allow logical grouping of addresses. In other words, something about the numeric value of an address implies a group or set of addresses, all of which are considered to be in the same grouping. In TCP/IP, this group is called a *network* or a *subnet*. In IPX, it is called a *network*. In AppleTalk, the grouping is called a *cable range*.

Network layer addresses are also grouped based on physical location in a network. The rules differ for some network layer protocols, but the grouping concept is identical for IP, IPX, and AppleTalk. In each of these network layer protocols, all devices with addresses in the same group cannot be separated from each other by a router that is configured to route that protocol, respectively. Stated differently, all devices in the same group (subnet/network/cable range) must be connected to the same data link; for example, all devices must be connected to the same Ethernet.

Routing relies on the fact that Layer 3 addresses are grouped together. The routing tables for each network layer protocol can reference the group, not each individual address. Imagine an Ethernet with 100 Novell clients. A router needing to forward packets to any of those clients needs only one entry in its IPX routing table. If those clients were not required to be attached to the same data link, and if there was no way to encode the IPX network number in the IPX address of the client, routing would not be capable of using just one entry in the table. This basic fact is one of the key reasons that routers, using routing as defined by a network layer (Layer 3), can scale to allow tens and hundreds of thousands of devices.

With that in mind, most network layer (Layer 3) addressing schemes were created with the following goals:

- The address space should be large enough to accommodate the largest network for which the designers imagined the protocol would be used.

- The addresses should allow for unique assignment so that little or no chance of address duplication exists.

- The address structure should have some grouping implied so that many addresses are considered to be in the same group.

- In some cases, dynamic address assignment is desired.

A great analogy for this concept of network addressing is the addressing scheme used by the U.S. Postal Service. Instead of getting involved with every small community's plans for what to name new streets, the Post Office simply has a nearby office with a ZIP code. The rest of the post offices in the country are already prepared to send mail to new businesses and residences on the new streets; they care only about the ZIP code, which they already know. It is the local postmaster's job to assign a mail carrier to deliver and pick up mail on those new streets. There may be hundreds of Main Streets in different ZIP codes, but as long as there is just one per ZIP code, the address is unique—and with an amazing percentage of success, the U.S. Postal Service delivers the mail to the correct address.

Example Layer 3 Address Structures

Each Layer 3 address structure contains at least two parts. One (or more) part at the beginning of the address works like the ZIP code and essentially identifies the grouping. All instances of addresses with the same value in these first bits of the address are considered to be in the same group—for example, the same IP subnet or IPX network or AppleTalk cable range. The last part of the address acts as a local address, uniquely identifying that device in that particular group. Table 3-10 outlines several Layer 3 address structures.

Table 3-10   *Layer 3 Address Structures*

Protocol	Size of Address (Bits)	Name and Size of Grouping Field	Name and Size of Local Address Field
IP	32	Network or subnet (variable, between 8 and 30 bits)	Host (variable, between 2 and 24 bits)
IPX	80	Network (32)	Node (48)

Table 3-10 *Layer 3 Address Structures (Continued)*

Protocol	Size of Address (Bits)	Name and Size of Grouping Field	Name and Size of Local Address Field
AppleTalk	24	Network (16) (Consecutively numbered values in this field can be combined into one group, called a cable range.)	Node (8)
OSI	Variable	Many formats, many sizes	Domain Specific Part (DSP) (typically 56, including NSAP)

For more information about IP and IPX addresses, refer to Chapter 5.

Routing Protocols

Conveniently, the routing tables in the example based on Figure 3-18 all had the correct routing information already in their routing tables. In most cases, these entries are built dynamically by use of a *routing protocol*. Routing protocols define message formats and procedures, just like any other protocol. With routing protocols, however, the goal is not to help with end-user data delivery—the end goal is to fill the routing table with all known destination groups and with the best route to reach each group.

A technical description of the logic behind two underlying routing protocol algorithms, *distance vector* and *link-state*, is found in Chapter 5. Specific routing protocols for TCP/IP and IPX are listed in Chapter 6, "Routing."

Nonroutable Protocols

In the early and mid-1990s, one of the reasons that Cisco sold a lot of routers is that the IOS could route more Layer 3 protocols than most—if not all—competitors. However, some protocols are not routable. To support those, Cisco supported and evolved variations of bridging to support nonroutable protocols.

What makes a protocol nonroutable? Basically, a protocol stack that does not define an OSI Layer 3 equivalent, including a logical Layer 3 address structure, cannot be routed. To be fair, because the answer to the question "Is a protocol routable?" for any particular protocol is more of a geek-party discussion, there are no hard and fast rules that govern what has to be true for a protocol to be considered routable. As this chapter shows, however, forwarding packets (L3PDUs) based on a destination Layer 3 equivalent address involves routing; a protocol stack with no Layer 3 is considered nonroutable.

If a protocol is not routable, then bridging must be enabled to support those protocols. (Bridging concepts are covered in Chapter 4.) To support nonroutable protocols over WAN links, some other protocol must be used, such as encapsulated transparent bridging and data link switching (a form of remote bridging for SNA and NetBIOS).

The details of how to support nonroutable protocols is beyond the scope of CCNA. What is reasonably expected to be in the scope of CCNA is to know the most popular nonroutable protocols. Consider Table 3-11, which lists protocols that some people consider to be nonroutable:

Table 3-11 *Purported Nonroutable Protocols*

Protocol	Do Protocol Specifications Allow Routing?	Does IOS Support Routing This Protocol?
DEC Local Area Transport (LAT)	No	No
NetBIOS	No	No
SNA (Traditional Subarea SNA)	Yes; routed by IBM products running VTAM and NCP	No
SNA (APPN)	Yes	Yes

DEC LAT and NetBIOS (sometimes referred to as NetBEUI, for NetBIOS End User Interface) are definitely nonroutable. IBM's SNA has two general categories: Subarea SNA is the traditional Mainframe DataCenter SNA, and Advanced Peer-to-Peer Networking (APPN) is a newer, more easily routable variation. Both are routable, have Layer 3 addressing, and can be routed by products you can purchase today. However, be careful—Cisco folklore has it that SNA is not routable. If CCNA exam questions touch on this topic, focus on the context and be sure to remember that LAT and NetBIOS are truly nonroutable.

This section, however, presents an anecdote that may help you remember the difference between the terms *routing*, *routed protocols*, and *routing protocols*.

NOTE This somewhat silly story is the result of the Cisco World Wide Training division's proctors for the instructor certification process, who emphasize that the instructors should be creative in the use of tools to help students remember important details. After I tried this story during certification, it was propagated by other instructors. I am curious—if you have heard this story or a variation, please let me know when you heard it and from whom (wendell@lacidar.com).

The Story of Ted and Ting

Ted and Ting both work for the same company at a facility in Snellville, Georgia. They work in the same department; their job is to make lots of widgets. (Widgets are imaginary products; the term *widget* is used in the United States often to represent a product when the actual product is not the topic of discussion.)

Ted worked quickly and was a hard worker. In fact, because he was a very intense person, Ted tended to make more widgets than anyone else in Snellville, including Ting. Ted also liked to have everything he needed instantly available when and where he wanted it so that he could make the widgets more quickly.

Ting, on the other hand, also worked very hard but was much more of a planner. He tended to think first and then act. Ting planned very well and had all supplies well stocked, including all the instructions needed to make the different kinds of widgets. In fact, all the information about how to build each type of widget was on a table by his door. He had a problem with the table getting "reallocated" (that is, stolen), so he applied a nonremovable label with the words "Ting's Table" to the surface so that he could find the table in case someone stole it.

It turns out that Ted's productivity was in part a result of sitting next to Ting. In fact, Ted often was ready to make the next widget but needed something, such as the instruction sheet for a particular unique widget. By swinging into Ting's office, Ted could be back at it in just a few seconds. In fact, part of the reason Ting kept the instruction sheets on Ting's Table by the door was that he was tired of Ted always interrupting him looking for something.

Well, Ted got lots of bonuses for being the most productive worker, and Ting did not. Being fair, though, Ted realized that he would not be as successful without Ting, so Ted shared his bonuses with Ting. (Hey, it's an imaginary story!)

Then one day the president decided to franchise the company because it was the best widget-making company in the world. The president, Dr. Rou, decided to make a manual to be used by all the franchisees to build their business. So, Dr. Rou went to the most productive widget-maker, Ted, and asked him what he did every day. Along the way, Dr. Rou noticed that Ted went next door a lot. So, being the bright guy that he was, Dr. Rou visited Ting next and asked him what he did.

The next day Dr. Rou emerged with the franchise manual. Being an ex-computer networking professional, he had called the manual "Protocols for Making Widgets." One part of the protocol defined how Ted made widgets very fast. Another part described how Ting kept everything needed by Ted at arm's length, including all the instructions Ted needed. It even mentioned Ting's Table as the place to store the instruction sheets. To give credit where credit was due—but not too much credit—the names of these protocols were:

- **The "Rou-Ted Protocol"**—How to make widgets really fast
- **The "Rou-Ting Protocol"**—How to plan so that the other guy can make widgets fast
- **The "Rou-Ting Table"**—The place to store your widget-making instruction sheets

Similarly, with networking, the *routed protocol* is the one being routed, such as IP, IPX, OSI, DECnet, and so forth. The *routing protocol* is the one preparing the information needed to perform the routing process quickly, such as RIP, IGRP, OSPF, NLSP, and so forth. The *routing table* is where the information needed to perform routing is held, as built by the routing protocol and used by the routing process to forward the packets of the routed protocol.

That's all just to distinguish among the terms *routed protocol*, *routing protocol*, and *routing table*.

Foundation Summary

The Foudation Summary is a collection of tables and figures that provide a convenient review of many key concepts in this chapter. For those of you already comfortable with the topics in this chapter, this summary could help you recall a few details. For those of you who just read this chapter, this review should help solidify some key facts. For any of you doing your final prep before the exam, these tables and figures will be a convenient way to review the day before the exam.

Table 3-12 lists the OSI layer functions and provides examples for each layer, taken directly from the ICND course.

Table 3-12   *OSI Reference Model (Condensed Information)*

Layer Name	Functional Description	Examples
Application (Layer 7)	User interface	Telnet, HTTP
Presentation (Layer 6)	How data is presented	JPEG, ASCII, EBCDIC
	Special processing, such as encryption	
Session (Layer 5)	Keeping data from different applications separate	Operating systems and application access scheduling
Transport (Layer 4)	Reliable or unreliable delivery	TCP, UDP, SPX
	Error correction before retransmit	
Network (Layer 3)	Logical addressing, which routers use for path determination	IP, IPX
Data link (Layer 2)	Combination of bits into bytes, and bytes into frames	802.3/802.2, HDLC
	Access to the media using MAC address	
	Error detection, not correction	
Physical (Layer 1)	Moving of bits between devices	EIA/TIA-232, V.35
	Specification of voltage, wire speed, and cable pin-outs	

Table 3-13 provides some example protocols and shows whether they are connection-oriented and error-recovering.

Table 3-13 *Protocol Characteristics: Recovery and Connections*

Connected?	Reliable?	Examples
Connection-oriented	Yes	LLC type 2 (802.2), TCP (TCP/IP), SPX (NetWare), X.25
Connection-oriented	No	Frame Relay virtual circuits, ATM virtual connections, PPP
Connectionless	Yes	TFTP, NetWare NCP (without Packet Burst)
Connectionless	No	UDP, IP, IPX, AppleTalk DDP, most Layer 3 protocols, 802.3, 802.5

Figure 3-19 provides a visual representation of the same-layer interaction concepts.

Figure 3-19 *Same-Layer Interactions on Different Computers*

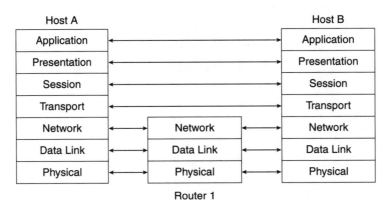

Table 3-14 summarizes the concepts behind error recovery and lists the behavior of three popular error-recovery protocols.

Table 3-14 *Examples of Error-Recovery Protocols and Their Features*

Feature	TCP	SPX	LLC2
Acknowledges data in both directions?	Yes	Yes	Yes
Provides forward acknowledgment?	Yes	Yes	Yes
Counts bytes or frame/packets?	Bytes	Packets	Frames
Necessitates resending of all data, or just one part and wait when resending?	One and wait	Resend all	Resend all

Table 3-15 summarizes the flow control terms and provides examples of each of the three types of flow control.

Table 3-15   *Flow-Control Methods—Summary*

Name Used in This Book	Other Names	Example Protocols
Buffering	—	—
Congestion avoidance	Stop/Start, RNR, Source Quench	SDLC, LAPB, LLC2
Windowing	—	TCP, SPX, LLC2

Table 3-16 summarizes most of the details about MAC addresses.

Table 3-16   *LAN MAC Address Terminology and Features*

LAN Addressing Terms and Features	Description
MAC	Media Access Control. 802.3 (Ethernet) and 802.5 (Token Ring) are the MAC sublayers of these two LAN data link protocols.
Ethernet address, NIC address, LAN address, Token Ring address, card address	Other names often used instead of MAC address. These terms describe the 6-byte address of the LAN interface card.
Burned-in address	The 6-byte address assigned by the vendor making the card. It is usually burned in to a ROM or EEPROM on the LAN card, and it begins with a 3-byte Organizationally Unique Identifier (OUI) assigned by the IEEE.
Locally administered address	Via configuration, an address that is used instead of the burned-in address.
Unicast address	Fancy term for a MAC that represents a single LAN interface.
Broadcast address	An address that means "all devices that reside on this LAN right now."
Multicast address	Not valid on Token Ring. On Ethernet, a multicast address implies some subset of all devices currently on the LAN.
Functional address	Not valid on Ethernet. On Token Ring, these addresses are reserved to represent the device(s) on the ring performing a particular function. For example, all source-route bridges supply the ring number to other devices. To do so, they each listen for the Ring Parameter Server (RPS) functional address.

Table 3-17 summarizes the different choices for encoding protocol types for each of the four data link protocols covered in this chapter.

Table 3-17 *Different Choices for Encoding Protocol Types for Each of the Four Data Link Protocols*

Data Link Protocol	Field	Header in Which It Is Found	Size
Ethernet and Token Ring	DSAP	802.2 header	1 byte
Ethernet and Token Ring	SSAP	802.2 header	1 byte
Ethernet and Token Ring	Protocol Type	SNAP header	2 bytes
Ethernet (DIX)	Ethertype	Ethernet header	2 bytes
HDLC	Cisco proprietary protocol id field	Extra Cisco header	2 bytes
Frame Relay RFC 1490	NLPID	RFC1490	1 byte
Frame Relay RFC 1490	L2 or L3 Protocol ID	Q.933	2 bytes each
Frame Relay RFC 1490	SNAP Protocol Type	SNAP header	2 bytes

Table 3-18 summarizes the basic functions of data link protocols.

Table 3-18 *Data Link Protocol Functions*

Function	Ethernet	Token Ring	HDLC	Frame Relay
Arbitration	CSMA/CD algorithm (part of MAC)	Token passing (part of MAC)	—	—
Addressing	Source and destination MAC addresses	Source and Destination MAC addresses	Single 1-byte address; unimportant on point-to-point links	DLCI used to identify virtual circuits
Error detection	FCS in trailer	FCS in trailer	FCS in trailer	FCS in trailer
Identifying contents of "data"	802.2 DSAP, SNAP header, or Ethertype, as needed	802.2 DSAP, or SNAP header, as needed	Proprietary Type field	RFC 1490 headers, with NLPID, L2 and L3 protocol IDs, or SNAP header

Table 3-19 outlines several Layer 3 address structures.

Table 3-19   *Layer 3 Address Structures*

Protocol	Size of Address (Bits)	Name and Size of Grouping Field	Name and Size of Local Address Field
IP	32	Network or subnet (variable, between 8 and 30 bits)	Host (variable, between 2 and 24 bits)
IPX	80	Network (32)	Node (48)
AppleTalk	24	Network (16) (Consecutively numbered values in this field can be combined into one group, called a cable range.)	Node (8)
OSI	Variable	Many formats, many sizes	DSP (typically 56, including NSAP)

Figure 3-20 illustrates the construction of frames, packets, and segments and shows the different layers' perspectives on what is considered to be the data.

Figure 3-20   *Frames, Packets, and Segments*

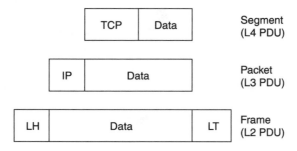

Figure 3-21 provides an example network by which to review the routing process.

Figure 3-21 *Routing Logic and Encapsulation—PC1 Sending to PC2*

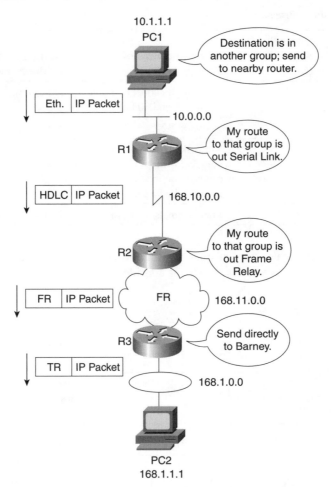

Q&A

As mentioned in Chapter 1, "All About the Cisco Certified Network Associate Certification," the questions and scenarios in this book are more difficult than what you should experience on the actual exam. The questions do not attempt to cover more breadth or depth than the exam; however, they are designed to make sure that you know the answer. Rather than allowing you to derive the answer from clues hidden inside the question itself, the questions challenge your understanding and recall of the subject. Questions from the "Do I Know This Already?" quiz from the beginning of the chapter are repeated here to ensure that you have mastered the chapter's topic areas. Hopefully, these questions will help limit the number of exam questions on which you narrow your choices to two options and then guess.

The answers to these questions can be found in Appendix A, on page 710.

1 Name the seven layers of the OSI model.

2 What is the main purpose(s) of Layer 7?

3 What is the main purpose(s) of Layer 6?

4 What is the main purpose(s) of Layer 5?

5 What is the main purpose(s) of Layer 4?

6 What is the main purpose(s) of Layer 3?

7 What is the main purpose(s) of Layer 2?

8 What is the main purpose(s) of Layer 1?

9 Describe the process of data encapsulation as data is processed from creation until it exits a physical interface to a network. Use the OSI model as an example.

10 Describe the features required for a protocol to be considered connectionless.

11 Name at least three connectionless protocols.

12 Describe the features required for a protocol to be considered connection-oriented.

13 In a particular error-recovering protocol, the sender sends three frames, labeled 2, 3, and 4. On its next sent frame, the receiver of these frames sets an acknowledgment field to 4. What does this typically imply?

14 Name three connection-oriented protocols.

15 What does MAC stand for?

16 Name three terms popularly used as a synonym for MAC address.

17 Are IP addresses defined by a Layer 2 or Layer 3 protocol?

18 Are IPX addresses defined by a Layer 2 or Layer 3 protocol?

19 Are OSI NSAP addresses defined by a Layer 2 or Layer 3 protocol?

20 What portion of a MAC address encodes an identifier representing the manufacturer of the card?

21 Are MAC addresses defined by a Layer 2 or Layer 3 protocol?

22 Are DLCI addresses defined by a Layer 2 or Layer 3 protocol?

23 Name two differences between Layer 3 addresses and Layer 2 addresses.

24 How many bits are present in an IP address?

25 How many bits are present in an IPX address?

26 How many bits are present in a MAC address?

27 Name the two main parts of an IPX address. Which part identifies which "group" this address is a member of?

28 Name the two main parts of an IP address. Which part identifies which "group" this address is a member of?

29 Name the two main parts of a MAC address. Which part identifies which "group" this address is a member of?

30 Name three benefits to layering networking protocol specifications.

31 What header and/or trailer does a router discard as a side effect of routing?

32 Describe the differences between a routed protocol and a routing protocol.

33 Name at least three routed protocols.

34 Name at least three routing protocols.

35 How does an IP host know what router to send a packet to? In which cases does an IP host choose to send a packet to this router instead of directly to the destination host?

36 How does an IPX host know which router to send a packet to? In which case does an IPX host choose to send a packet to this router instead of directly to the destination host?

37 Name three items in an entry in any routing table.

38 What OSI layer typically encapsulates using both a header and a trailer?

Scenarios

Scenario 3-1

Given the network in Figure 3-22 and the address table in Table 3-20, perform the tasks that follow. This scenario uses an imaginary Layer 3 addressing structure as a method to review concepts. When in doubt, concentrate on the concepts. Also, the imaginary Layer 3 used in this example is here only to allow you to concentrate on the concepts instead of a particular protocol; there is no need to memorize this scheme or expect questions like this on the exam.

Figure 3-22 *Musketeer Network for Scenario*

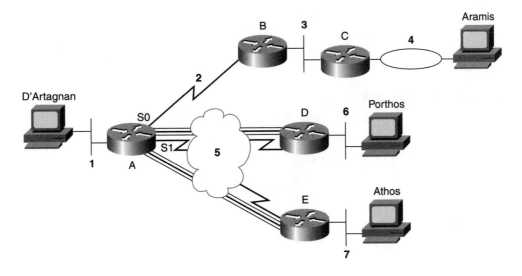

Table 3-20 provides the routing table for the network setup in Figure 3-22.

Table 3-20 *Layer 3 Address Table for Network in Figure 3-22*

Router	Interface	Address
A	E0	group-1.local-A
A	S0	group-2.local-A
A	S1	group-5.local-A
B	S0	group-2.local-B
B	E0	group-3.local-B

continues

Table 3-20 *Layer 3 Address Table for Network in Figure 3-22 (Continued)*

Router	Interface	Address
C	E0	group-3.local-C
C	T0	group-4.local-C
D	S0	group-5.local-D
D	E0	group-6.local-D
E	S0	group-5.local-E
E	E0	group-7.local-E
D'Artagnan		group-1.local-M
Aramis		group-4.local-M
Porthos		group-6.local-M
Athos		group-7.local-M

Task 1 for Scenario 3-1

Create the routing table in Router A; assume that all parts of the network are up and working properly. Table 3-21 provides an empty routing table to record your answers.

Table 3-21 *Scenario 3-1 Task 1 Routing Table Answer Form*

Group	Outgoing Interface	Next Router

Task 2 for Scenario 3-1

D'Artagnan sends a packet to Aramis (source group-1.local-M, destination group-4.local-M). D'Artagnan sends this packet inside an Ethernet frame to Router A. Given this information, determine the following:

1 List the routing table entries in each router that are necessary for the packet to be delivered to Aramis.

2 What type of data link header or trailer is discarded by each router in that route?

3 What destination data link addresses are placed into the new data link headers by each router?

4 What routes must be in which routers to ensure that Aramis can send a return packet to D'Artagnan?

Task 3 for Scenario 3-1

D'Artagnan sends a packet to Porthos (source group-1.local-M, destination group-6.local-M). D'Artagnan sends this packet inside an Ethernet frame to Router A. Given this information, determine the following:

1 List the routing table entries in each router that are necessary for the packet to be delivered to Porthos.

2 What type of data link header or trailer is discarded by each router in that route?

3 What destination data link addresses are placed into the new data link headers by each router?

4 What routes must be in which routers to ensure that Porthos can send a return packet to D'Artagnan?

Scenario Answers

Answers to Task 1 for Scenario 3-1

Based on the network design illustrated in Figure 3-22, Task 1 for Scenario 3-1 asks you to create the routing table in Router A; assume that all parts of the network are up and working properly. The routing table for Router A is as follows:

Group	Outgoing Interface	Next Router
group-1	Ethernet 0	—
group-2	serial 0	—
group-3	serial 0	group-2.local-B
group-4	serial 0	group-2.local-B
group-5	serial 1	—
group-6	serial 1	group-5.local-D
group-7	serial 1	group-5.local-E

Answers to Task 2 for Scenario 3-1

Based on the network design illustrated in Figure 3-22, Task 2 for Scenario 3-1 states that D'Artagnan sends a packet to Aramis (source group-1.local-M, destination group-4.local-M). D'Artagnan sends this packet inside an Ethernet frame to Router A. The following are the solutions to exercises 1 through 4 for Task 2.

1 The routing tables are as follows:

In Router A:

Group	Outgoing Interface	Next Router
group-2	serial 0	—
group-4	serial 0	group-2.local-B

In Router B:

Group	Outgoing Interface	Next Router
group-3	Ethernet 0	—
group-4	Ethernet 0	group-3.local-C

In Router C:

Group	Outgoing Interface	Next Router
group-4	Token Ring 0	—

2 Router A discards the Ethernet header and adds an HDLC header. Router B discards the HDLC header and adds an Ethernet header. Router C discards the Ethernet header and adds a Token Ring header.

3 Router A places the never-changing HDLC address (Hex 03) into the header. Router B places Router C's Ethernet MAC address into the destination address field. Router C places Aramis's Token Ring MAC address into the destination address field.

4 This is all noise if Aramis cannot get a packet back to D'Artagnan. The following routing tables show the routes needed for both directions; the routes with asterisks signify routes required for the routes back to D'Artagnan.

In Router A:

Group	Outgoing Interface	Next Router
group-1*	Ethernet 0	—
group-2	serial 0	—
group-4	serial 0	group-2.local-B

In Router B:

Group	Outgoing Interface	Next Router
group-1*	serial 0	group-2.local-A
group-2*	serial 0	—
group-3	Ethernet 0	—
group-4	Ethernet 0	group-3.local-C

In Router C:

Group	Outgoing Interface	Next Router
group-1*	Ethernet 0	group-3.local-B
group-3*	Ethernet 0	—
group-4	Token ring 0	—

Answers to Task 3 for Scenario 3-1

Based on the network design illustrated in Figure 3-22, Task 3 for Scenario 3-1 states that D'Artagnan sends a packet to Porthos (source group-1.local-M, destination group-6.local-M). D'Artagnan sends this packet inside an Ethernet frame to Router A. The following are the solutions to exercises 1 through 4 for Task 3.

1 The routing tables are as follows:

In Router A:

Group	Outgoing Interface	Next Router
group-5	serial 1	—
group-6	serial 1	group-5.local-D

In Router D:

Group	Outgoing Interface	Next Router
group-6	Ethernet 0	—

2 Router A discards the Ethernet header and adds a Frame Relay header. Router D discards the Frame Relay header and adds an Ethernet header.

3 Router A places the Frame Relay DLCI for the VC connecting it to Router D into the address field in the header. Router D places Porthos's Ethernet MAC address into the destination address field.

4 This is all noise if Porthos cannot get a packet back to D'Artagnan. The following routing tables show the routes needed for both directions; the routes with asterisks signify routes required for the routes back to D'Artagnan.

In Router A:

Group	Outgoing Interface	Next Router
group-1*	Ethernet 0	—
group-5	serial 1	—
group-6	serial 1	group-5.local-D

In Router D:

Group	Outgoing Interface	Next Router
group-1*	serial 0	group-5.local-A
group-5*	serial 0	—
group-6	Ethernet 0	—

This chapter covers the following topics that you will need to master as a CCNA:

- **LAN Overview**   A review of the basics of LAN terminology and operation is covered here. Details on the different types of Ethernet, Fast Ethernet, and Gigabit Ethernet are included as well.

- **Bridging, Switching, and Spanning Tree**   The logic behind bridging, switching, and Spanning Tree is important to almost all campus networks today. This section covers the basic logic and also compares the forwarding process with bridges, switches, and routers. Spanning-Tree Protocol (STP) is covered as well.

- **Virtual LANs**   The terms and concepts relating to virtual LANs are covered here. Basic design choices are also discussed.

- **LAN Switch Configuration**   Cisco actually has several variations of user interfaces for its LAN switch products. This section covers the IOS-like CLI of the Cisco 1900 switches, which is the only LAN switch user interface tested for on the CCNA exam.

CHAPTER 4

Bridges/Switches and LAN Design

Cisco folklore tells of the day in 1998 when Cisco's revenues from LAN switching and hub products exceeded router revenues. That event in Cisco's history was significant because most people in the marketplace thought of Cisco as "that router company" for a long time. In fact, Cisco would prefer to even shake the reputation as a great router/switch/hub company and instead be known for empowering the Internet generation, a catch-phrase from the company's television ads.

So, if switches and hubs drive more revenue for Cisco, why is most of the popular Cisco certification about routers and routing issues? One issue is that LAN (Layer 2) issues are inherently less complicated than Layer 3 issues. However, that in no way means that LAN issues are not complicated; there are simply fewer concepts and issues to consider. Furthermore, because Layer 3-aware devices, such as routers, make extensive use of Layer 2 features to forward packets, the routing-centric topics can never totally ignore LAN and WAN Layer 2 concepts. So, this book includes one LAN-specific chapter and one WAN-specific chapter (Chapter 8, "WAN Protocols and Design"), in addition to the more lengthy coverage of routing.

This single chapter devoted totally to LANs reviews LAN basics, with a concentration on Ethernet. This chapter explains bridging and switching, along with some comparisons of bridging, switching, and routing. This chapter also covers Spanning Tree to a depth beyond what is probably needed for the exam, but understanding Spanning Tree is very important to the typical jobs performed by CCNAs. This chapter also covers virtual local-area networks (VLANs) and offers some switch configuration examples.

Cisco expects CCNAs to remember the names and functions of the LAN standards, not just the concepts behind them. So, while the concepts in this chapter might in part be review and in part be new information or a reminder of something you have forgotten, do not neglect to memorize the LAN standard's names, at least. The concepts are very important to your success in your job; knowing the names of standards is very important to being able to communicate about your networks, which is one of Cisco's expectations for CCNAs.

How to Best Use This Chapter

By taking the following steps, you can make better use of your study time:

- Keep your notes and the answers for all your work with this book in one place, for easy reference.

- Take the "Do I Know This Already?" quiz, and write down your answers. Studies show that retention is significantly increased through writing down facts and concepts, even if you never look at the information again.

- Use the diagram in Figure 4-1 to guide you to the next step.

Figure 4-1   *How to Use This Chapter*

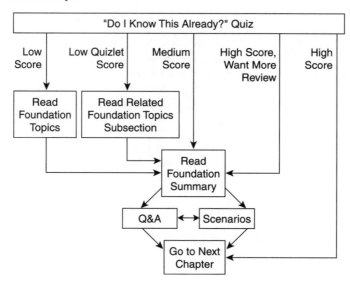

"Do I Know This Already?" Quiz

The purpose of the "Do I Know This Already?" quiz is to help you decide what parts of this chapter to use. If you already intend to read the entire chapter, you do not necessarily need to answer these questions now.

This 16-question quiz helps you determine how to spend your limited study time. The quiz is sectioned into four smaller four-question "quizlets," which correspond to the three major headings in the chapter. Suggestions on how to spend your time in this chapter, based on your quiz scores, are outlined in Figure 4-1. Use Table 4-1 to record your score.

Table 4-1   *Scoresheet for Quiz and Quizlets*

Quizlet Number	Foundation Topics Section Covering These Questions	Questions	Score
1	LAN Overview	1 to 4	
2	Bridging, Switching, and Spanning Tree	5 to 8	
3	Virtual LANs	9 to 12	

Table 4-1   *Scoresheet for Quiz and Quizlets (Continued)*

Quizlet Number	Foundation Topics Section Covering These Questions	Questions	Score
4	LAN Switch Configuration	13 to 16	
All questions		1 to 16	

1 What do the letters MAC stand for? What other terms have you heard to describe the same or similar concept?

_____

_____

_____

2 What standards body owns the process of ensuring unique MAC addresses worldwide?

_____

_____

_____

3 What is the distance limitation of 10BaseT? 100BaseTX?

_____

_____

_____

4 How fast is Fast Ethernet?

_____

_____

_____

5 What routing protocol does a transparent bridge use to learn about Layer 3 addressing groupings?

_____

_____

_____

6 Name two of the methods of internal switching on typical switches today. Which provides less latency for an individual frame?

_____

_____

_____

7 If a switch hears three different configuration BPDUs from three different neighbors on three different interfaces, and if all three specify that Bridge 1 is the root, how does it choose which interface is its root port?

_____

_____

_____

8 Assume that a building has 100 devices attached to the same Ethernet. These users then are migrated onto two separate shared Ethernet segments, each with 50 devices, with a transparent bridge in between. List two benefits that would be derived for a typical user.

_____

_____

_____

9 Define the term _broadcast domain_.

_____

_____

_____

10 Describe the benefits of creating three VLANs of 25 ports each, versus a single VLAN of 75 ports, in each case using a single switch. Assume that all ports are switched ports (each port is a different collision domain).

_____

_____

_____

11 If two Cisco LAN switches are connected using Fast Ethernet, what VLAN trunking
protocols could be used? If only one VLAN spanned both switches, is a VLAN trunking
protocol needed?

_____

_____

_____

12 Define the term *VLAN*.

_____

_____

_____

13 How many IP addresses must be configured for network management on a Cisco Catalyst
1900 switch if eight ports are to be used with three VLANs?

_____

_____

_____

14 What Catalyst 1900 switch command displays the version of IOS running in the switch?

_____

_____

_____

15 Configuration is added to the running configuration in RAM when commands are typed
in Catalyst 1900 configuration mode. What causes these commands to be saved into
NVRAM?

_____

_____

_____

16 Name the three VTP modes. Which of these does not allow VLANs to be added or
modified?

_____

_____

_____

The answers to the quiz are found in Appendix A, "Answers to the 'Do I Know This Already?' Quizzes and Q&A Sections," on page 715. The suggested choices for your next step are as follows:

- **8 or less overall score**—Read the entire chapter. This includes the "Foundation Topics" and "Foundation Summary" sections and the Q&A section at the end of the chapter.

- **2 or less on any quizlet**—Review the subsection(s) of the "Foundation Topics" part of this chapter, based on Table 4-1. Then move into the "Foundation Summary" section and the Q&A section at the end of the chapter.

- **9 to 12 overall score**—Begin with the "Foundation Summary" section, and then go to the Q&A section and the scenarios at the end of the chapter.

- **13 or more overall score**—If you want more review on these topics, skip to the "Foundation Summary" section, and then go to the Q&A section at the end of the chapter. Otherwise, move to the next chapter.

Foundation Topics

LAN Overview

Cisco expects CCNAs to be familiar with the three types of LANs: Ethernet, Token Ring, and FDDI. There is a bias toward questions about Ethernet, which is reasonable given the installed base in the marketplace. For this reason, this chapter concentrates on Ethernet, with some comments on FDDI and Token Ring, as appropriate.

Ethernet is best understood by considering the early 10Base5 and 10Base2 specifications. With these two specifications, a bus is shared among all devices on the Ethernet, using the carrier sense multiple access with collision detection (CSMA/CD) algorithm for accessing the bus. The CSMA/CD algorithm works like this: The sender is ready to send a frame. The device listens to detect whether any frame is currently being received. When the Ethernet is silent, the device begins sending the frame. During this time, the sending device listens to ensure that the frame it is sending does not collide with a frame that another station is sending. If no collisions occur, the bits of the sent frame are received back successfully. If a collision has occurred, the device sends a jam signal and then waits a random amount of time before repeating the process, again listening to hear whether another frame is currently being received.

Because of the CSMA/CD algorithm, Ethernet 10Base5 and 10Base2 become more inefficient under higher loads. In fact, two particular negative features of the CSMA/CD algorithm are as follows:

- All collided frames sent are not received correctly, so each sending station must resend the frames. This wastes time on the bus and increases the latency for delivering the collided frames.

- Latency can increase for stations waiting for the Ethernet to be silent before sending their frames. Devices must wait before sending a frame if another frame is already being sent by another station. This increases latency while waiting for the incoming frame to complete.

Ethernet hubs were created with the advent of 10BaseT. These hubs are essentially multiport repeaters; they extend the bus concept of 10Base2 and 10Base5 by regenerating the same electrical signal sent by the original sender of a frame out every other port. Therefore, collisions can still occur, so CSMA/CD access rules continue to be used. (This is true of shared Ethernet— switched Ethernet is covered later.) Knowledge of the operation of Ethernet cards and the attached hub is important to have a complete understanding of the congestion problems and the need for full-duplex Ethernet. Figure 4-2 outlines the operation of half-duplex 10BaseT with hubs.

Figure 4-2   *10BaseT Half-Duplex Operation*

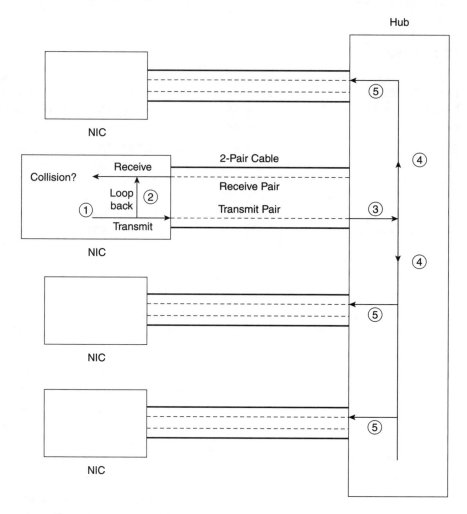

The chronological steps illustrated in Figure 4-2 are as follows:

Step 1   The network interface card (NIC) sends a frame.

Step 2   The NIC loops the sent frame onto its receive pair.

Step 3   The hub receives the frame.

Step 4   The hub sends the frame across an internal bus so that all *other* NICs can receive the electrical signal.

Step 5   The hub repeats the signal from each receive pair to all other devices. In other words, the hub sends so that the attached stations receive on their receive pair. (Similarly, the hub listens on the transmit pair because that is the pair used by the station for transmissions.)

Half-duplex behavior is required of all attached stations when using a shared 10BaseT Ethernet hub, as shown in Figure 4-2. The hub has created the electrical equivalent of a bus, so CSMA/CD rules are still in effect. Essentially, if the topology allows collisions, then CSMA/CD is used to react to the collisions. Because CSMA/CD rules are used when collisions could occur and half-duplex operation is required for CSMA/CD, full-duplex operation is not possible with a shared 10BaseT hub. With a shared 10BaseT hub, if a station is receiving a frame, it would not choose to also start sending another frame because that would cause a collision.

Full-duplex behavior is allowed when the possibility of collisions is removed. Consider the use of Ethernet between a pair of NICs, instead of cabling the NIC to a hub. Figure 4-3 shows the full-duplex circuitry.

Figure 4-3   *10BaseT Full-Duplex Operation*

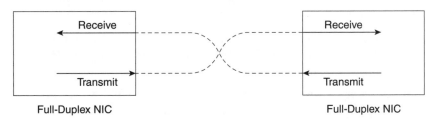

Full-Duplex NIC   Full-Duplex NIC

Because no collisions are possible, the NICs disable their loopback circuitry. Both ends can send and receive simultaneously. This reduces Ethernet congestion and provides the following advantages, as compared to half-duplex 10BaseT operation:

- Collisions do not occur; therefore, time is not wasted retransmitting frames.

- There is no latency waiting for others to send their frames.

- There are 10 Mbps in each direction, doubling the available capacity (bandwidth).

Of course, if full duplex was useful only when two NICs were cabled directly to each other, as shown in Figure 4-3, then the full duplex would not be very useful. However, full duplex is also an option when using switches. When a single device is connected to the switch port, the switch can ensure that there is no collision, which allows full duplex to work. If a shared hub is connected to a switch port rather than a single device, then full duplex is not allowed because collisions could still occur.

LAN Addressing

As a CCNA, you'll be expected to confidently understand and interpret LAN addresses. One important function of MAC addresses is to identify or address the LAN interface cards on Ethernet, Token Ring, and FDDI LANs. Frames between a pair of LAN stations use a source and destination address field to identify each other. These addresses are called *unicast addresses*, or *individual addresses*, because they identify an individual LAN interface card. (The term *unicast* was chosen mainly for contrast with the terms *broadcast*, *multicast*, and *group addresses*.)

Having globally unique unicast MAC addresses on all LAN cards is a goal of the IEEE, so the organization administers a program in which manufacturers encode the MAC address onto the LAN card, usually in a ROM chip. The first half of the address is a code that identifies the vendor; this code is sometimes called the *Organizationally Unique Identifier*. The second part is simply a unique number among cards that the vendor has manufactured. These addresses are called *burned-in addresses (BIAs)*, sometimes called *Universally Administered Addresses (UAA)*. The address used by the card can be overridden via configuration; the overriding address is called a *Locally Administered Address (LAA)*.

Another important function of IEEE MAC addresses is to address more than one LAN card. *Group* addresses (as opposed to unicast addresses) can address more than one device on a LAN. This function is satisfied by three types of IEEE group MAC addresses:

- **Broadcast addresses**—The most popular type of IEEE MAC address, the broadcast address, has a value of FFFF.FFFF.FFFF (hexadecimal notation). The broadcast address implies that all devices on the LAN should process the frame.

- **Multicast addresses**—Used by Ethernet and FDDI, multicast addresses fulfill the requirement to address a subset of all the devices on a LAN. A station processes a received frame with a particular multicast destination address only if configured to do so for that multicast address. An example of multicast addresses is a range of addresses— 0100.5exx.xxxx—where different values are assigned in the last 3 bytes; these MAC addresses are used in conjunction with Internet Group Multicast Protocol (IGMP) and IP multicast. IP hosts on an Ethernet that want to receive IP packets to a particular IP multicast address all use the same Ethernet MAC address, which begins with 0100.5E.

- **Functional addresses**—Valid only on Token Ring, functional addresses identify one or more interfaces that provide a particular function. For example, c000.0000.0001 is used by the device on a Token Ring that is currently implementing the Active Monitor function.

A subtle quirk about LAN addressing is that the order of bits in each byte of the addresses is different between Ethernet and the other LAN types. As Figure 4-4 illustrates, the bytes are listed in the same order; however, the bit order in each byte is opposite.

Figure 4-4   *MAC Address Format*

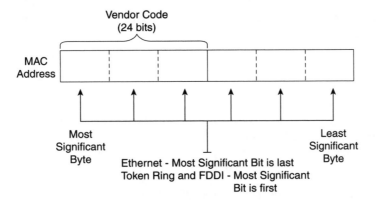

The bit order in Ethernet is called little-endian; on FDDI and Token Ring, it is called big-endian. Let's examine the meaning of these terms: On Ethernet, the most significant bit in a byte is listed last in the byte. For example, assume that the binary string 01010101 is the value in a byte of an Ethernet address. The right-most bit is considered to be the most significant bit in this byte. However, if writing the same value in a byte of a Token Ring address, the value written would be 10101010, so that the most significant bit is on the left. When bridging between Ethernet and another type of LAN, the bit order in each byte of the MAC addresses must be inverted. For example, the Token Ring address 4000.3745.0001 would be converted to 0200.ECA2.0080 before being sent onto an Ethernet.

The following list summarizes many of the key features of MAC addresses:

- Unicast MAC addresses address an individual LAN interface card.

- Broadcast MAC addresses address all devices on a LAN.

- Multicast MAC addresses address a subset of the devices on an Ethernet or FDDI LAN.

- Functional MAC addresses identify devices performing a specific IEEE-defined function, on Token Ring only.

- Ethernet orders the bits in each byte of the MAC address with the least significant bit first; this convention is called *little-endian*.

- Token Ring and FDDI order the bits in each byte of the MAC address with the most significant bit first; this convention is called *big-endian*.

- The most significant bit on the first byte of an address must have a value of binary 0 for unicast addresses and 1 for broadcast, multicast, and functional addresses. This bit is called the *broadcast bit*.

- The second most significant bit in the first byte of the MAC address is called the local/ universal bit. A binary value of 0 implies that a burned-in or Universally Administered Address (UAA) is being used; a binary 1 implies that a Locally Administered Address (LAA) is being used.

LAN Framing

Figure 4-5 shows the details of LAN frames. You should remember some details about the contents of the headers and trailers for each LAN type—in particular, the addresses and their location in the headers. Also, the name of the field that identifies the type of header that follows the LAN headers is important. Finally, the fact that a frame check sequence (FCS) is in the trailer for each protocol is also vital. Figure 4-5 summarizes the various header formats.

The 802.3 specification limits the data portion of the 802.3 frame to a maximum of 1500 bytes. The data was designed to hold some Layer 3 packets. The term *maximum transmission unit (MTU)* is used to define the maximum Layer 3 packet that can be sent over a medium; hence, with 802.3 Ethernet, 1500 is the largest MTU allowed.

The function of identifying the header that follows the LAN header (what's in the data in Figure 4-5) is covered rather extensively in Chapter 3, "OSI Reference Model & Layered Communication." Any computer receiving a LAN frame needs to know what is in the data portion of the frame. Table 4-2 summarizes the fields that are used for identifying the types of data contained in a frame.

Table 4-2   *Protocol Type Fields in LAN Headers*

Field Name	Length	LAN Type	Comments
Ethernet Type	2 bytes	Ethernet	RFC 1700 (Assigned Numbers RFC) lists the values. Xerox owns the assignment process.
802.2 DSAP and SSAP	1 byte each	IEEE Ethernet, IEEE Token Ring, ANSI FDDI	The IEEE Registration Authority controls the assignment of valid values. The source SAP (SSAP) and destination SAP (DSAP) do not have to be equal, so 802.2 calls for the sender's protocol type (SSAP) and the destination's type (DSAP).
SNAP Protocol	2 bytes	IEEE Ethernet, IEEE Token Ring, ANSI FDDI	Uses EtherType values. Used only when DSAP is hex AA. It is needed because the DSAP and SSAP fields are only 1 byte in length.

Figure 4-5   *LAN Header Formats*

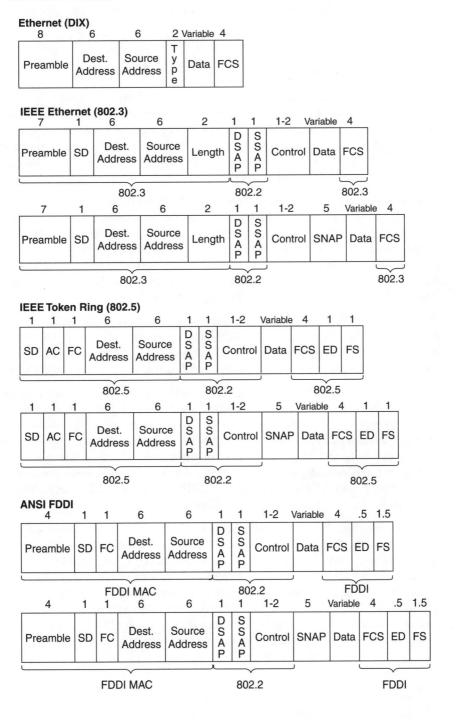

Some examples of values in the Ethernet Type and SNAP Protocol fields are: 0800 for IP and 8137 for NetWare. Examples of IEEE SAP values are: E0 for NetWare, 04 for SNA, and AA for SNAP.

Fast Ethernet and Gigabit Ethernet

The two key additional features of Fast Ethernet, as compared to 10-Mbps Ethernet, are higher bandwidth and autonegotiation. Autonegotiation allows an Ethernet card, hub, or switch to determine which type of 100-Mbps Ethernet is supported by the device, hub, or switch on the other end of the cable. Also, support for half duplex or full duplex is negotiated. If the other device, such as a 10BaseT NIC, does not support autonegotiation, then autonegotiation will settle for half-duplex 10BaseT.

Fast Ethernet retains many familiar features of 10-Mbps Ethernet variants. The age-old CSMA/CD logic still exists and can be disabled for full-duplex point-to-point topologies in which no collisions can occur. A variety of cabling options is allowed—unshielded and shielded copper cabling, as well as multimode and single-mode fiber. Both Fast Ethernet shared hubs and switches can be deployed. However, because Fast Ethernet gained market acceptance around the same time that LAN switching became popular, most Fast Ethernet cards either are connected to a switch or are directly cabled to another device.

Gigabit Ethernet also retains many familiar features of slower Ethernet variants. CSMA/CD is still used and can still be disabled for full-duplex support. Although gigabit hubs are allowed, it is more likely that Gigabit Ethernet switch ports will be the most popular use for Gigabit Ethernet, along with use as a trunk between high-throughput switches and routers.

The biggest differences between Gigabit Ethernet and its slower cousins are the obvious speed difference and the use of a different physical layer. The physical layer differences are truly beyond the scope of the CCNA exam, but the history is interesting. To improve speed to market, the specifications call for the use of a slightly changed FibreChannel physical layer (ANSI X3T11) to operate at 1.25 gigabaud. An 8B/10B encoding scheme, which transmits a 10-bit energy signal (baud) that represents an 8-bit value, is used. (The concept of the 8B/10B encoding is not terribly different from FDDI's 4B/5B encoding.) The net result is that 8 bits are exchanged per baud; at 1.25 gigabaud, 1 Gbps is achieved.

Both Fast Ethernet (FE) and Gigabit Ethernet (GE) relieve congestion in some fairly obvious ways. Collisions and wait time are decreased when compared to 10-Mbps Ethernet, simply because it takes 90 percent (FE) or 99 percent (GE) less time to transmit the same frame on the faster LANs. Capacity is greatly increased as well: If all frames were 1250 bytes long, a 10,000 frames per second theoretical maximum could be reached on Fast Ethernet, and a 100,000 frames per second theoretical maximum could be reached on Gigabit Ethernet. (Of course, this little math problem ignores such details as interframe gaps and the unlikely case of identical length frames; they're listed here for perspective.)

Autonegotiation uses a priority scheme to define the more preferred options for Fast and 10-Mbps Ethernet. The lower the priority value, the more preferred the specification. The names of these standards are listed in Table 4-3, along with the priority used by the autonegotiation process.

Table 4-3   *100Bx Standards and Autonegotiation Priority*

Standard	Full or Half Duplex	Autonegotiation Priority
100BaseT2	Full	1
100BaseT2	Half	2
100BaseTX	Full	3
100BaseTX	Half	4
100BaseT4	Half	5
10BaseT	Full	6
10BaseT	Half	7

Autonegotiation uses a series of Fast Link Pulses (FLPs) to communicate with the device on the other end of the cable. An exchange takes place as to what each endpoint is capable of supporting. The Autonegotiation Priority in Table 4-3 shows the choice that the process would make if more than one option was supported—of the supported options, the one with the lowest autonegotiation priority is the option chosen.

The autonegotiation process has been known to fail. Cisco recommends that for more important devices, you should configure the LAN switch to the correct setting rather than depend on autonegotiation.

LAN Standards

Cisco expects CCNAs to be very familiar with Ethernet specifications, as well as be familiar with the basics of FDDI and Token Ring standards. The IEEE defines most of the standards for Ethernet and Token Ring, with ANSI defining standards for FDDI. Table 4-4 lists the specification that defines the Media Access Control (MAC) and Logical Link Control (LLC) sublayers of the three LAN types for comparison.

Table 4-4   *MAC and LLC Details for Three Types of LANs*

Name	MAC Sublayer Spec	LLC Sublayer Spec	Other Comments
Ethernet Version 2 (DIX Ethernet)	Ethernet	Not applicable	This spec is owned by Digital, Intel, and Xerox.
IEEE Ethernet	IEEE 802.3	IEEE 802.2	This is also popularly called 802.3 Ethernet.

continues

Table 4-4 *MAC and LLC Details for Three Types of LANs (Continued)*

Name	MAC Sublayer Spec	LLC Sublayer Spec	Other Comments
Token Ring	IEEE 802.5	IEEE 802.2	IBM helped with development before the IEEE took over.
FDDI	ANSI X3T9.5	IEEE 802.2	ANSI liked 802.2, so it just refers to the IEEE spec.

With the advent of Fast Ethernet and Gigabit Ethernet, the variety of Ethernet standards has increased to the point that most networking personnel do not memorize all the standards. However, the CCNA exam will require you to be very familiar with Ethernet standards, or at least the standards for 10- and 100-Mbps Ethernet. Table 4-5 lists the key Ethernet specifications and several related details about the operation of each.

Table 4-5 *Ethernet Standards*

Standard	MAC Sublayer Specification	Maximum Cable Length	Cable Type	Pairs Required
10Base5	802.3	500 m[1]	50-Ohm thick coaxial cable	—
10Base2	802.3	185 m[1]	50-Ohm thin coaxial cable	—
10BaseT	802.3	100 m[1]	Category 3, 4, or 5 UTP	2
10BaseFL	802.3	2000 m[2]	Fiber	1
100BaseTx	802.3u	100 m[2]	Category 5 UTP	2
100BaseT4	802.3u	100 m[2]	Category 3 UTP	4
100BaseT2	802.3u	100 m[2]	Category 3, 4, or 5 UTP	2
100BaseFx	802.3u	400/2000 m[3]	Multimode fiber	1
100BaseFx	802.3u	10,000m	Single-mode fiber	1
1000BaseSx	802.3z	220-550m	Multimode fiber	1
1000BaseLx	802.3z	3000m	Single-mode or multimode fiber	1
1000BaseCx	802.3z	25m	Shielded copper	2
1000BaseT	802.3ab	100m	Category 5 UTP	2

1. For entire bus, without using a repeater
2. From device to hub/switch
3. Numbers shown are for half or full duplex

For more information on Fast Ethernet and information on Gigabit Ethernet, try the following Web pages:

- wwwhost.ots.utexas.edu/ethernet/ethernet-home.html
- www.ots.utexas.edu/ethernet/descript-100quickref.html
- www.iol.unh.edu/training
- www.cisco.com/warp/customer/cc/cisco/mkt/switch/fasteth/tech/feth_tc.htm
- www.cisco.com/warp/customer/cc/cisco/mkt/switch/gig/tech/index.shtml
- www.gigabit-ethernet.org

NOTE   A cco login is required for the Cisco URLs above.

Bridging, Switching, and Spanning Tree

Transparent bridging and LAN switching are two topics you must understand to succeed on the CCNA exam. The underlying logic between the two is very similar, so both are described in this section. The Spanning-Tree Protocol, which prevents loops from occuring in a bridged/switched network, is described after bridging and switching basics are completed. Finally, a comparison of what happens when a single Ethernet is migrated to a pair of Ethernets—separated by a bridge in one case, a switch in another case, and a router in the third case—serves as a good review of the concepts behind all three types of campus forwarding devices.

The IOS also supports other types of bridging, namely source-route bridging (SRB), source-route transparent bridging (SRT), and source-route translational bridging (SR/TLB). Cisco expects CCNAs to be familiar with transparent bridging.

Transparent Bridging

Transparent bridging is called transparent because the endpoint devices do not need to know that the bridge(s) exists. In other words, the computers attached to the LAN do not behave any differently in the presence or absence of transparent bridges.

Transparent bridging is the process of forwarding frames, when appropriate. To accomplish this, transparent bridges perform three key functions:

- Learning MAC addresses by examining the source MAC addresses of each frame received by the bridge
- Deciding when to forward a frame and when to filter a frame, based on the destination MAC address
- Creating a loop-free environment with other bridges using the Spanning-Tree Protocol

To fully understand transparent bridging logic, consider Figure 4-6. A client first asks for a DNS name resolution and then connects to a Web server. All three devices are on the same LAN segment. ARP requests are used to find the MAC addresses of the DNS and the Web server.

Figure 4-6 *Example Protocol Flows—Single Ethernet Segment*

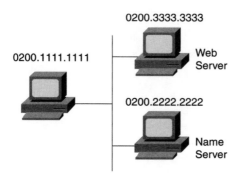

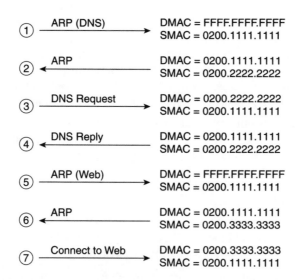

①	ARP (DNS) →	DMAC = FFFF.FFFF.FFFF SMAC = 0200.1111.1111
②	← ARP	DMAC = 0200.1111.1111 SMAC = 0200.2222.2222
③	DNS Request →	DMAC = 0200.2222.2222 SMAC = 0200.1111.1111
④	← DNS Reply	DMAC = 0200.1111.1111 SMAC = 0200.2222.2222
⑤	ARP (Web) →	DMAC = FFFF.FFFF.FFFF SMAC = 0200.1111.1111
⑥	← ARP	DMAC = 0200.1111.1111 SMAC = 0200.3333.3333
⑦	Connect to Web →	DMAC = 0200.3333.3333 SMAC = 0200.1111.1111

The following list provides some additional text relating the steps shown in Figure 4-6:

Step 1   The PC is preconfigured with the IP address of the DNS; it must use ARP to find the DNS's MAC address.

Step 2   The DNS replies to the ARP request with its MAC address, 0200.2222.2222.

Step 3   The PC requests name resolution by the DNS for the Web server's name.

Step 4   The DNS returns the IP address of the Web server to the PC.

Step 5   The PC does not know the Web server's MAC address, but it does know its IP address, so the PC sends an ARP broadcast to learn the MAC address of the Web server.

Step 6   The Web server replies to the ARP, stating that its MAC address is 0200.3333.3333.

Step 7   The PC can now send frames directly to the Web server.

Now consider the same protocol flow, but with the DNS on a separate segment and a transparent bridge separating the segments, as shown in Figure 4-7. The computers act no differently, sending the same frames and packets. The transparent bridge forwards all broadcasts, all unicast destination frames not in its bridge table, and multicasts.

Figure 4-7 illustrates several important ideas related to segmentation. The ARP requests in Steps 1 and 5 are forwarded by the bridge because they are broadcasts. Likewise, requests from the client to and from the DNS are forwarded. However, the rest of the frames from the client to the Web server and back are not forwarded by the bridge because the bridge knows that both MAC addresses (client and Web server MACs) are on the same Ethernet as its E0 interface. Also, because there is no redundant path through other bridges, there is no need to use the Spanning-Tree Protocol to block interfaces and limit the flow of frames.

Some characterizations of transparent bridge behavior, as compared to a single segment with no bridges, are listed here:

- Broadcasts and multicast frames are forwarded by a bridge.

- Transparent bridges perform switching of frames using Layer 2 headers and Layer 2 logic and are Layer 3 protocol-independent. This means that installation is simple because no Layer 3 address group planning or address changes are necessary. For example, because the bridge retains a single broadcast domain, all devices on all segments attached to the bridge look like a single subnet.

- Store-and-forward operation is typical in transparent bridging devices. Because an entire frame is received before being forwarded, additional latency is introduced (as compared to a single LAN segment).

- The transparent bridge must perform processing on the frame, which also can increase latency (as compared to a single LAN segment).

Figure 4-7 *Example Protocol Flows—Using a Transparent Bridge*

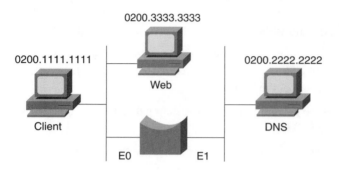

Address Table After Step 1

0200.1111.1111	E0

Address Table After Step 2

0200.1111.1111	E0
0200.2222.2222	E1

Address Table After Step 3

0200.1111.1111	E0
0200.2222.2222	E1

Address Table After Step 6

0200.1111.1111	E0
0200.2222.2222	E1
0200.3333.3333	E0

(1) ARP (DNS) →
DMAC = FFFF.FFFF.FFFF
SMAC = 0200.1111.1111

(2) ← ARP
DMAC = 0200.1111.1111
SMAC = 0200.2222.2222

(3) DNS Request →
DMAC = 0200.2222.2222
SMAC = 0200.1111.1111

(4) ← DNS Reply
DMAC = 0200.1111.1111
SMAC = 0200.2222.2222

(5) ARP (Web) →
DMAC = FFFF.FFFF.FFFF
SMAC = 0200.1111.1111

(6) ← ARP
DMAC = 0200.1111.1111
SMAC = 0200.3333.3333

(7) Connect to Web →
DMAC = 0200.3333.3333
SMAC = 0200.1111.1111

LAN Switching

An Ethernet switch appears to use the same logic as a transparent bridge. However, the internal logic of the switch is optimized for performing the basic function of choosing when to forward and when to filter a frame. Just as with a transparent bridge, the basic logic of a LAN switch is as follows:

Step 1   A frame is received.

Step 2   If the destination is a broadcast or multicast, forward on all ports.

Step 3   If the destination is a unicast and the address is not in the address table, forward on all ports.

Step 4   If the destination is a unicast and the address is in the address table, forward the frame out the associated port, unless the MAC address is associated with the incoming port.

Consider Figure 4-8, which separates LANs with a switch.

Figure 4-8   *Example Protocol Flows—Using a Switch*

		Address Table After Step 1
①	ARP (DNS) DMAC = FFFF.FFFF.FFFF SMAC = 0200.1111.1111	0200.1111.1111 E0

		Address Table After Step 2
②	ARP DMAC = 0200.1111.1111 SMAC = 0200.2222.2222	0200.1111.1111 E0 0200.2222.2222 E2

		Address Table After Step 3
③	DNS Request DMAC = 0200.2222.2222 SMAC = 0200.1111.1111	0200.1111.1111 E0 0200.2222.2222 E2

④ DNS Reply
DMAC = 0200.1111.1111
SMAC = 0200.2222.2222

⑤ ARP (Web)   DMAC = FFFF.FFFF.FFFF
SMAC = 0200.1111.1111

		Address Table After Step 6
⑥	ARP DMAC = 0200.1111.1111 SMAC = 0200.3333.3333	0200.1111.1111 E0 0200.2222.2222 E2 0200.3333.3333 E1

⑦ Connect to Web   DMAC = 0200.3333.3333
SMAC = 0200.1111.1111

The following list provides some additional insights relating to the steps shown in Figure 4-8:

Step 1   The PC is preconfigured with the IP address of the DNS. The PC notices that the DNS IP address is in the same subnet as its own IP address; therefore, the PC sends an ARP broadcast hoping to learn the DNS's MAC address.

Step 2   The DNS replies to the ARP request with its MAC address, 0200.2222.2222.

Step 3   The PC requests name resolution for the Web server by sending a packet with the destination IP address of the DNS.

Step 4   The DNS returns the IP address of the Web server to the PC in the DNS reply.

Step 5   The PC does not know the Web server's MAC address, so it sends an ARP broadcast to learn the MAC address. Because it is a MAC broadcast, the switch forwards the frame on all ports.

Step 6   The Web server replies to the ARP, stating that its MAC address is 0200.3333.3333.

Step 7   The PC can now connect to the Web server.

The two ARP broadcasts (Steps 1 and 5) are sent out all switch ports because switches and bridges do not perform the *broadcast firewall* function that a router performs. After the switching table (often called the address table) is built, the switch forwards unicasts only out of the appropriate ports. In other words, frames sent from the client to the Web server, and vice versa (which are unicasts), are never sent out port E2.

The switch network has created three separate Ethernet segments, as compared to the transparent bridge network in Figure 4-7, which creates two LAN segments. Each segment is called a *collision domain* because frames sent by any device on that segment could collide with other frames on the segment. Switches can be used to create many collision domains.

Another feature of switches is that they forward broadcasts and multicasts on all ports. However, they reduce the impact of collisions because devices on separate switch ports are on separate Ethernet segments (which are separate collision domains). This behavior of switches resulted in the creation of the terms *collision domain* and *broadcast domain*. Figure 4-9 shows a network with six collision domains—six sets of interface cards for which CSMA/CD logic is used to share the LAN segment.

Each collision domain is separated by either a transparent bridge, a switch, or a router. The figure suggests that the segments on either side of the bridge could be 10Base2, 10Base5, or any shared hub. The segment between the router and switch, and between the switch and the PCs on the right, can be a single cable, as shown. In either case, if a bridge (transparent bridge or switch) or routing function separates devices, the devices are in separate collision domains.

Figure 4-9   *Collision Domains*

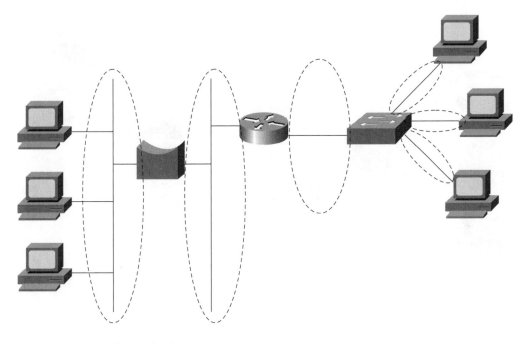

The broadcast domain concept is similar to the concept of collision domains; however, only routers stop the flow of broadcasts. Figure 4-10 provides the broadcast domains for the same network depicted in Figure 4-9.

The broadcast domain is not affected by the inclusion or exclusion of switches or bridges. The router creates its own broadcasts (RIP, IGRP, SAP, and so on), but the router does not forward broadcasts received in the left-side interface out the right-side interface. In other words, broadcasts created and sent by a device in one broadcast domain are not sent to devices in another broadcast domain.

Figure 4-10 *Broadcast Domains*

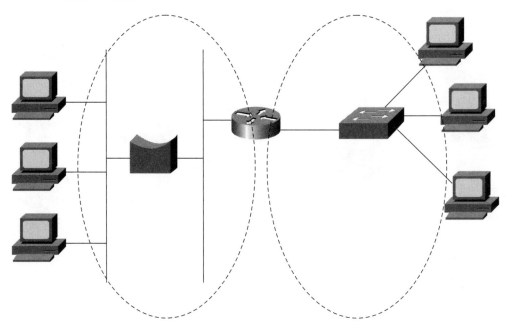

General definitions for collision domain and broadcast domain are as follows:

> A *collision domain* is a set of interface cards (NICs) for which a frame sent by one NIC could result in a collision with a frame sent by any other NIC in the collision domain.

> A *broadcast domain* is a set of NICs for which a broadcast frame sent by one NIC will be received by all other NICs in the broadcast domain.

Layer 3 addressing is affected whenever a router is added to a network. For example, if only bridges and switches had existed in the network in Figure 4-10, and if the router was later added, Layer 3 IP and IPX addresses would have changed. To use the terminology in Chapter 3, two separate address groupings (for example, IP subnets) would be used for IP—one for the devices to the left of the router and another for devices to the right of the router. A definition of Layer 3 address groupings on LANs will help you understand VLANs better:

NOTE   All devices in the same broadcast domain (Layer 2) will be in the same Layer 3 address grouping—in other words, the same IP subnet or same IPX network.

The internal processing on the switch can decrease latency for frames. Transparent bridges use store-and-forward processing, meaning that the entire frame is received before the first bit of the frame is forwarded. Switches can use store-and-forward as well as cut-through processing logic. With cut-through processing, the first bits of the frame are sent out the outbound port before the last bit of the incoming frame is received instead of waiting for the entire frame to be received. In other words, as soon as the switching port receives enough of the frame to see the destination MAC address, the frame is transmitted out the appropriate outgoing port to the destination device. The unfortunate side effect is that because the frame check sequence (FCS) is in the Ethernet trailer, the forwarded frame may have bit errors that the switch would have noticed with store-and-forward logic. And, of course, if the outbound port is busy, the switch will store the frame until the port is available.

The internal processing algorithms used by switches vary among models and vendors; regardless, the internal processing can be categorized as one of the methods listed in Table 4-6.

Table 4-6   *Switch Internal Processing*

Switching Method	Description
Store-and-forward	The switch fully receives all bits in the frame (store) before forwarding the frame (forward). This allows the switch to check the FCS before forwarding the frame. (FCS is in the Ethernet trailer.)
Cut-through	The switch performs the address table lookup as soon as the destination address field in the header is received. The first bits in the frame can be sent out the outbound port before the final bits in the incoming frame are received. This does not allow the switch to discard frames that fail the FCS check. (FCS is in the Ethernet trailer.)
FragmentFree	This performs like cut-through, but the switch waits for 64 bytes to be received before forwarding the first bytes of the outgoing frame. According to Ethernet specifications, collisions should be detected during the first 64 bytes of the frame; frames in error due to collision will not be forwarded. The FCS still cannot be checked.

Full Duplex and Switches

Frames can be forwarded concurrently through a switch. Consider Figure 4-11, with Fred sending a frame to Wilma, and Barney sending a frame to Betty.

In this figure, the switch forwards the frame coming in Port 1 out Port 3 and does the same for the frame coming in Port 2 and out Port 4. These frames also are in four different collision domains. For these reasons, no collision occurs. A four-port transparent bridge would behave the same way, but switches are optimized for concurrent frame forwarding, so latency is likely to be less with a switch.

In conjunction with switches, full-duplex Ethernet can add other benefits. Figure 4-12 shows a server (Pebbles) that is both sending and receiving a frame at the same time. Betty and Wilma are in different collision domains, so Pebbles cannot undergo a collision due to the nature of full-duplex Ethernet.

Figure 4-11 *Concurrently Switching Frames in a Switch*

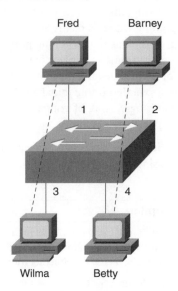

Figure 4-12 *Full-Duplex Ethernet and Switches*

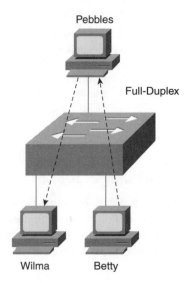

Comparison of LAN Segmentation Using Bridges, Switches, and Routers

Cisco expects CCNAs to have command of the tradeoffs involved when designing campus LANs. One key consideration is to understand the different behavior when separating, or segmenting, LAN segments with some switching device. All the concepts related to LAN segmentation using bridges, switches, and routers are included in other parts of this chapter or in other chapters. However, the comparisons made in this section are important and would be missed if this book simply covered the technical content when covering bridging, switching, and routing.

The basic workings of a bridge and a switch have already been covered in this chapter. For review, routing logic is covered first, followed by a comparison of segmentation using the three different device options.

Routing is covered more fully in other chapters. For comparison, the same example flow of a client connecting to a Web server is shown, this time with a router separating two Ethernet segments. This same example is shown for bridging and switching earlier in this chapter. Figure 4-13 illustrates a couple of key features of routing.

The flows in the figure match the numbers in this list, which explains the meaning and implications of the flows in the figure:

Step 1   The PC is preconfigured with the IP address of the DNS. The PC notices that the IP address is on a different subnet, so the PC wants to forward the packet to its default router. However, the PC does not know its default router's MAC address yet, so it must use ARP to find that router's MAC address.

Step 2   The router replies to the ARP request with its MAC address, 0200.4444.4444.

Step 3   The PC requests name resolution for the Web server by sending a packet with the destination IP address of the DNS. The destination MAC address in the frame sent by the PC is the router's E0 MAC address. The router receives the frame, extracts the packet, and forwards it.

Step 4   The DNS returns the IP address of the Web server to the PC in the DNS reply.

Step 5   The PC does not know the Web server's MAC address, so it sends an ARP broadcast to learn the MAC address. The router has no need to forward the ARP broadcast.

Step 6   The Web server replies to the ARP, stating that its MAC address is 0200.3333.3333.

Step 7   The PC can now connect to the Web server.

Figure 4-13 *Example Protocol Flows—Using a Router*

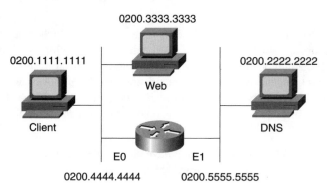

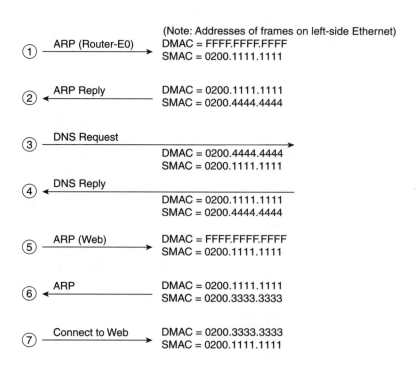

The ARP broadcasts are not forwarded by the router. In fact, the logic in Step 1 begins with an ARP looking for the MAC address of the client's default router—namely, the router's E0 MAC address. This broadcast was not forwarded by the router, a fact that causes a router to be called a *broadcast firewall*. Comparing this to a transparent bridge or a LAN switch, this difference in broadcast treatment is the biggest advantage of routers.

Table 4-7 lists several features relating to segmenting LANs with bridges, switches, and routers. Essentially, this chart summarizes features that could differ among the three devices. Table 4-8 lists features that describe how each device performs when compared to using a single Ethernet segment with no bridge, switch, or router. The two tables together provide the necessary details when comparing the three types of devices.

Table 4-7   *Comparison of Segmentation Options*

Feature	Bridging	Switching	Routing
Forwards LAN broadcasts?	Yes	Yes	No
Forwards LAN multicasts?	Yes	Yes; can be optimized with CGMP	No[1]
OSI layer used when making forwarding decision	Layer 2	Layer 2	Layer 3
Internal processing variants	Store-and-forward	Store-and-forward, cut-through, FragmentFree	Store-and-forward
Frame/packet fragmentation allowed?	No	No	Yes
Multiple concurrent equal-cost paths to same destination allowed?	No	No	Yes

1. Routers can forward IP multicast packets, if configured to do so. However, this does not mean that the LAN multicast frame is forwarded.

Table 4-8 lists features that should be interpreted within the following context: "If I migrated from a single Ethernet segment to a network with two segments separated by a bridge/switch/router, and if traffic loads and destinations stayed constant, the result would be _____."

Table 4-8   *Comparison of a Single Segment to Multiple Segments*

Feature	Bridging	Switching	Routing
Greater cabling distances allowed	Yes	Yes	Yes
Decrease in collisions, assuming equal traffic loads	Yes	Yes	Yes
Decreased adverse impact of broadcasts	No	No	Yes
Decreased adverse impact of multicasts	No	Yes, with CGMP	Yes
Increase in bandwidth	Yes	Yes	Yes
Filtering on Layer 2 header allowed	Yes	Yes	Yes
Filtering on Layer 3 header allowed	No	No	Yes

Certainly, the most important distinction among the three segmentation methods is their treatment of broadcasts and multicasts. Remembering the concepts of collision domains, broadcast domains, and how each device separates LANs into different domains is one key to understanding campus LAN design and troubleshooting.

Spanning Tree

The Spanning-Tree Protocol is an important topic for a true understanding of bridged and switched networks. A thorough understanding of Spanning Tree also is important for CCNP and CCIE certification; the basics are required for CCNA certification.

NOTE	Two wonderful sources of information can help you learn more about the Spanning-Tree Protocol. One is a book by Radia Perlman called *Interconnections: Bridges, Switches, and Routers*. The other is the Cisco Press book *Cisco LAN Switching*, by Kennedy Clark and Kevin Hamilton. Both books cover Spanning Tree in a clear and detailed manner; the Cisco Press book also covers implementation details on Cisco's LAN switching products. Perlman's book has been a long-time favorite of mine, but the Clark and Hamilton book has recently been added to my list of top five favorite (computer) books.

The purpose of the Spanning-Tree Protocol is to dynamically create a bridged/switched network in which only one active path exists between any pair of LAN segments (collision domains). To accomplish this task, all bridging devices, including switches, use a dynamic protocol. The result of the protocol is that each interface on a bridging device will settle into a *blocking* state or a *forwarding* state. Blocking means that the interface cannot forward or receive data frames, but it can send and receive Configuration Bridge Protocol Data Units (CBPDUs); forwarding means the interface can both send and receive data frames. By having a correct subset of the interface's block, a single currently active logical path will exist between each pair of LANs.

NOTE	For the rest of this chapter, the terms *bridge* and *bridging device* refer to a device that can be a transparent bridge or a LAN switch. If a distinction between the two needs to be made, the terms *transparent bridge* or *switch* will be used.

Figure 4-14 demonstrates the obvious need for a loop-free path between segments. Frames destined for unknown MAC addresses, or broadcasts, will be forwarded infinitely by the bridges.

Figure 4-14   *Looping Without the Spanning-Tree Protocol*

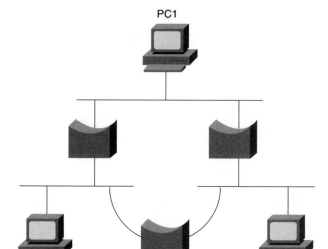

Frames addressed to PC3's MAC address will loop forever—or at least until time is no more! No mechanism defined in Ethernet marks the frame to be thrown away by a bridge, similar to the way an IP router uses the time-to-live field. The frame destined to PC3 would be forwarded because the bridges do not have PC3's MAC address in their bridge tables. Similarly, bridges forward broadcasts on all interfaces, so if PC1 or PC2 sent a broadcast, the broadcast would loop for a long time.

Of course, having only one physical path between segments is a poor design for availability. If any part of that one path failed, the network would be broken into separate parts whose devices could not communicate. So, there is a need for physical redundancy, but with only one active path because transparent bridging logic will not tolerate multiple active paths. The solution is to build bridged networks with physical redundancy and to use Spanning Tree to dynamically block some interface(s) so that *only one active path exists at any instant in time*.

Finally, any possibility of loops occurring during the process of converging to a new Spanning Tree must be avoided. Consider Figure 4-15, particularly Bridges 4 and 5. If a loop occurred in this network, frames would rotate forever and the number of frames would grow. A frame on either segment that both Bridges 4 and 5 are attached to would be forwarded by both bridges, duplicating the frames. In a few short seconds, all LAN segments would be filled with copies of the frames that occurred during the loop, possibly preventing the Spanning-Tree Protocol from completing its task of re-creating the loop-free environment.

Figure 4-15   *Looping and Frame Replication*

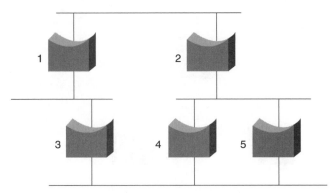

To sum up, the benefits of the Spanning-Tree Protocol are as follows:

• Physically redundant paths in the network are allowed to exist and be used when other paths fail.

• Bridging logic is confused by multiple active paths to the same MAC address; Spanning-Tree Protocol avoids this by creating only one path.

• Loops in the bridged network are avoided.

How the Spanning-Tree Protocol Works

The Spanning-Tree Algorithm results in each bridge interface being placed into either a forwarding state or a blocking state. Interfaces in forwarding state are considered to be in the current Spanning Tree; those in blocking state are not considered to be in the tree. The algorithm is elegant but basic. Figure 4-16 illustrates a network with physical redundancy, which will need to use STP.

The setup in Figure 4-16 uses four switches (B1, B2, B3, and B5) and one transparent bridge. A variety of bridges and switches are shown to make the point that both Ethernet switches and transparent bridges use Spanning Tree.

The key to the algorithm is that the set of all forwarding interfaces (those in the tree) form one path through the LAN segments (collision domains), assuming that at least one physical path is available. Three criteria are used to place an interface into forwarding mode:

• All interfaces on the root bridge are in forwarding state.

• Each nonroot bridge considers one of its ports to have the least administrative cost between itself and the root bridge. This interface, called that bridge's *root port*, is placed into a forwarding state.

• Many bridges can attach to the same segment. These bridges advertise Configuration Bridge Protocol Data Units (CBPDUs) declaring their administrative cost to the root bridge. The bridge with the lowest such cost of all bridges on that segment is called the *designated bridge*. The interface on the *designated bridge* on that segment is placed in a forwarding state.

Figure 4-16   *Sample Bridged Network in Need of STP*

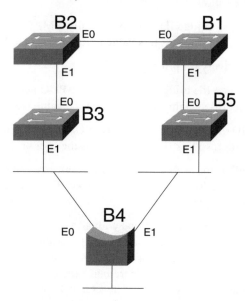

All other interfaces are placed in a blocking state. Table 4-9 summarizes the reasons why Spanning Tree places a port in forwarding or blocking state:

Table 4-9   *Spanning Tree: Reasons for Forwarding or Blocking*

Characterization of Port	Spanning Tree State	Explanation
All root bridge's ports	Forwarding	The root bridge is always the designated bridge on all connected segments.
Each nonroot bridge's root port	Forwarding	The root port is the port receiving the lowest-cost CBPDU from the root.
Each LAN's designated bridge	Forwarding	The bridge forwarding the lowest-cost CBPDU onto the segment is the designated bridge.
All other ports	Blocking	The port is not used for forwarding frames, nor are any frames received on these interfaces considered for forwarding.

Building an Initial Spanning Tree

Each bridge begins by claiming to be the root bridge. The Spanning-Tree Protocol defines messages used to exchange information with other bridges. These messages are called *Configuration Bridge Protocol Data Units (CBPDUs)*. Each bridge begins by sending a CBPDU stating the following:

- The root bridge's bridge ID. This is typically a MAC address on one of the bridge's interfaces. Each bridge sets this value to its own bridge ID.

- An administratively set priority.

- The cost between the bridge sending this CBPDU and the root. At the beginning of the process, each bridge claims to be root, so the value is set to 0.

- The bridge ID of the sender of this CBDPU. At the beginning of the process, each bridge claims to be root, so this ID is the same as the root bridge's ID.

The root bridge will be the bridge with the lowest priority value. If a tie occurs based on priority, the root bridge with the lowest ID will be the root. The bridge IDs should be unique because MAC addresses are supposed to be unique.

The process of choosing the root begins with all bridges claiming to be the root by sending CBPDUs with their bridge IDs and priorities. If a bridge hears of a better candidate, it stops advertising itself as root and starts forwarding the CBPDUs sent by the better candidate. Before forwarding that CBPDU, the bridge increments the cost by a value based on a cost setting of the interface on which the better candidate's CBPDU was received. It's almost like a political race, with candidates dropping out once they cannot win and throwing their support behind the best candidate. At the end of the election, the best candidate wins. Figure 4-17 outlines what the bridges do after the process has settled. Table 4-10 lists the different costs used on each interface.

Given the scenario in Figure 4-17, Bridge 2 adds its E0 cost (100) to the cost of the CBPDU from Bridge 1 (root = Bridge 1, cost = 0), so Bridge 2 considers its cost to the root to be 100. However, Bridge 2 does not send a CBPDU out its E0 port because that is the port in which the CBPDU about the best root candidate entered. Instead, Bridge 2 advertises a CBPDU only out its other ports. Bridge 3 receives the CBPDU from Bridge 2 and adds the port cost of the incoming port, its E0 port, to the cost. Bridge 3 considers its cost to the root to be 200, as reflected in its CBPDU.

Consider the steady-state CBPDU messages from Bridge 4's perspective. This bridge receives a CBPDU about Bridge 1 as root from both Bridge 3 and Bridge 5. The cost in the CBPDU from Bridge 5 is lower; therefore, that is the message to which Bridge 4 reacts. Following the same logic, Bridge 4 adds its E1 port cost to the cost learned from Bridge 5, leaving a total of 110. Bridge 4 sends a CBPDU out all other ports besides its E1 port.

Figure 4-17   *Root Bridge Election—Bridge 1 Wins*

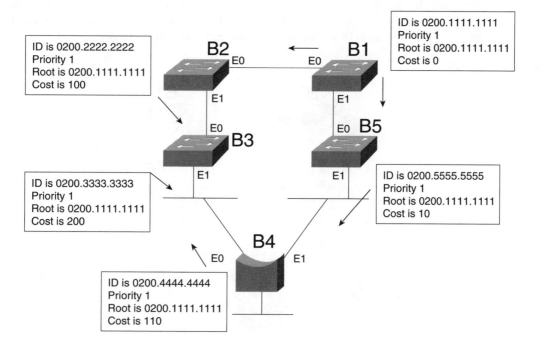

Table 4-10   *Bridge Cost Values*

Bridge Interface	Cost
Bridge 1, E0	100
Bridge 1, E1	10
Bridge 2, E0 *	100
Bridge 2, E1	100
Bridge 3, E0 *	100
Bridge 3, E1	10
Bridge 4, E0	10
Bridge 4, E1 *	100
Bridge 5, E0 *	10
Bridge 5, E1	100

*   Signifies the values that affected the cost values in the CBPDUs

Of course, the creation of the Spanning Tree causes some interfaces to forward and others to block, which is the goal. Both ports on Bridge 1 will be in a forwarding state. The interface in which the other bridges receive their lowest-cost CBPDU about the root is considered to be their root port. Figure 4-18 shows the root ports with a simple designation of RP.

Figure 4-18   *Root Ports*

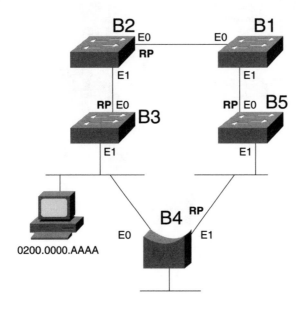

RP= Root Port

The final step in the process is for each bridge to decide whether to forward or block on its nonroot ports. Each LAN has one bridge that is sending the CBPDU about the root with the least cost. Referring to Figure 4-17, the segment to which Bridge 3 and Bridge 4 are attached shows Bridge 4 advertising the lower cost (110). Bridge 4 is then considered to be the *designated bridge* on that LAN segment, so Bridge 4 places its E0 port into forwarding state. On the other LAN segments, only one bridge is sending CBPDUs, so it is obvious which bridge will be designated bridge on each of those segments—Bridge 2's E1 port and Bridge 5's E1 port will be placed into forwarding state as well.

The process is now complete, with all ports in forwarding state except for Bridge 3's E1 interface. Table 4-11 outlines the state of each port and shows why it is in that state.

Table 4-11   *The State of Each Interface*

Bridge Interface	State	Reason Interface Is in Forwarding State
Bridge 1, E0	Forwarding	Interface is on root bridge
Bridge 1, E1	Forwarding	Interface is on root bridge
Bridge 2, E0	Forwarding	Root port
Bridge 2, E1	Forwarding	Designated bridge
Bridge 3, E0	Forwarding	Root port
Bridge 3, E1	Blocking	Not root bridge, not root port, no designated bridge
Bridge 4, E0	Forwarding	Designated bridge
Bridge 4, E1	Forwarding	Root port
Bridge 5, E0	Forwarding	Root port
Bridge 5, E1	Forwarding	Designated bridge

Noticing and Reacting to Changes in Network Topology

A periodic notice is sent to tell all bridges that nothing has changed in the network. The protocol mechanism begins when the root sends CBPDUs on all its interfaces with the same information in it as before: its bridge ID, priority, cost (0), and the root bridge ID, which is itself. As seen in Figure 4-17, the bridges receive the CBPDUs, adjust the cost, and send the CBPDUs on all interfaces except their root ports.

The CBPDU created by the root also includes some important timers:

- **Hello time**—The time that the root waits before resending the periodic CBPDUs, which are then forwarded by successive bridges.

- **MaxAge**—The time any bridge should wait before deciding that the topology has changed.

- **Forward Delay**—Delay that affects the time involved when an interface changes from a blocking state to a forwarding state; this timer will be covered in more depth shortly.

The MaxAge timer is typically a multiple of Hello. This allows some CBPDUs to be lost, without the bridges reacting and changing the Spanning Tree. The MaxAge setting should also consider the variations in how long it takes the CBPDUs to traverse the network. In a local environment, these variations should be minimal unless severe congestion causes a large number of frames to be discarded.

When the network is up and no problems are occurring, the process works like this:

Step 1   The root sends a CBPDU, cost 0, out all its interfaces.

Step 2   The neighboring bridges send CBPDUs out their nonroot port interfaces referring to the root, but with their cost added.

Step 3   Step 2 is repeated by each bridge in the network as it receives these CBPDUs, as long as the CBPDU is received on a bridge's root port.

Step 4   The root repeats Step 1 every Hello time.

Step 5   If a bridge does not get a CBPDU in Hello time, it continues as normal, unless the larger MaxAge timer is passed.

Reacting to Changes in the Spanning Tree

The process used to react to changes in topology varies depending on the situation. This section describes two instances, one briefly and the other in detail. Other variations than the two instances covered here do occur. Regardless of the details, the process always begins when a bridge does not receive a CBPDU on its root port in MaxAge time.

No CBPDUs Received on Any Ports

If the bridge whose MaxAge parameter expires is also not receiving any other CBPDUs on ports that are not the root port, that bridge reacts by claiming to be the root bridge and begins sending CBPDUs describing itself. This process reduces to the same logic as described earlier in the section "Building an Initial Spanning Tree."

For instance, imagine that the root bridge failed in the network in Figure 4-17. Each bridge would have MaxAge expire at about the same time. Each would claim to be the root; one would be elected. A different Spanning Tree would result, but the process is the same as described earlier.

CBPDUs Received on Some Ports

The process of recalculating the Spanning Tree occurs only if CBPDUs are no longer received on the root port. However, a bridge can still be receiving CBPDUs on other ports. Consider the familiar diagram shown in Figure 4-19. Bridge 5's E1 port has failed, preventing Bridge 4 from receiving CBPDUs on its root port (E1) interface.

Figure 4-19   *CBPDUs While Bridge 4's MaxAge Expires*

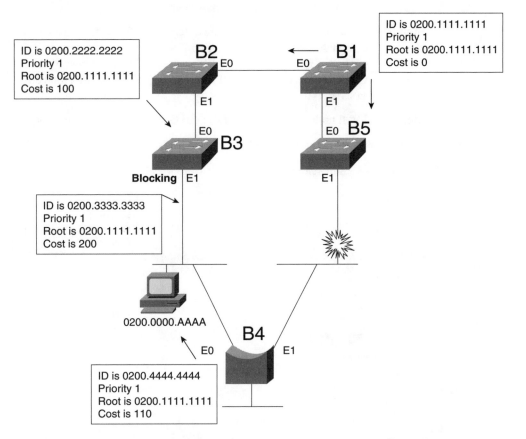

ID is 0200.2222.2222
Priority 1
Root is 0200.1111.1111
Cost is 100

ID is 0200.1111.1111
Priority 1
Root is 0200.1111.1111
Cost is 0

ID is 0200.3333.3333
Priority 1
Root is 0200.1111.1111
Cost is 200

ID is 0200.4444.4444
Priority 1
Root is 0200.1111.1111
Cost is 110

A review of the behavior of this network is useful before seeing how it is about to change. For example, the frame on the Ethernet between Bridges 3 and 4 cannot be forwarded by Bridge 3 because it is blocking on its E1 interface. The instant Bridge 5's E1 port fails, frames can no longer be forwarded or received on that interface. So, during the period that MaxAge is expiring on Bridge 4, frames can be sent by hosts on the segment between B4 and B3; then, B4 can forward the frames, but B5 cannot. If the destination of such frames is on the opposite side of Bridge 5, the frames are not delivered.

Only Bridge 4's MaxAge expires. The other bridges are still receiving CBPDUs on their root ports. After MaxAge expires, Bridge 4 will decide the following:

Step 1   My E1 port is no longer my root port.

Step 2   The same root bridge is being advertised in a CBPDU on my E0 port.

Step 3   No other CBPDUs are being received.

Step 4 My best path (and the only path, in this case) to the root is out my E0 port; therefore, my root port is now E0.

Step 5 Because no other CBPDUs are entering my E1 port, I must be the designated bridge on that segment. So, I will start sending CBPDUs on E1, adding my E0 port cost (10) to the cost of the CBPDU received in the CBPDU entering E0 (200), for a total cost of 210.

Step 6 I will no longer send CBPDUs out E0 because it is my root port.

Figure 4-20 illustrates the result of Bridge 4's reaction.

Figure 4-20 *CBPDUs After Bridge 4's MaxAge Expires*

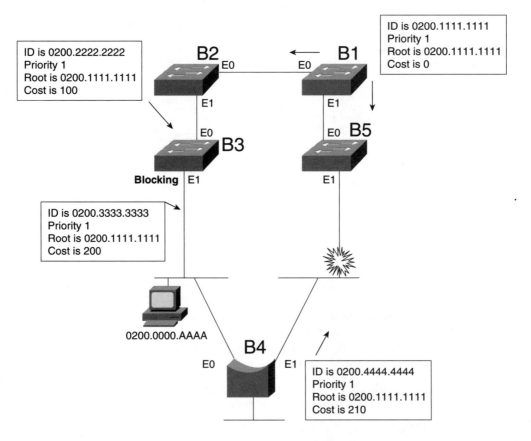

The logic used by Bridge 4 seems relatively straightforward, albeit detailed. There is a subtle but important occurrence in this case: Both of Bridge 4's interfaces were forwarding before the change, and both are still forwarding. In other words, neither interface has changed state. But the process is not finished because some change to the Spanning Tree must take place for new paths to be available. In this case, Bridge 3's E1 will need to change from a blocking to forwarding state, which has not occurred yet. The key part of the upcoming logic is based on this corollary of Spanning Tree:

> A change that affects the Spanning Tree results in at least one bridge interface changing from blocking to forwarding, or vice versa.

At this point in the process, no changes to the Spanning Tree have been made, and many address table entries refer to the path that has failed. Table 4-12 refers to the address table entries for 0200.0000.AAAA in all five bridges, showing that four of the five bridge address tables refer to the failed path. Use Table 4-12 in conjunction with Figure 4-20 to verify that the path to this MAC address is still invalid.

Table 4-12   *Address Table Entries for 0200.0000.AAAA, Before Spanning Tree Has Been Changed*

Bridge	MAC	Outgoing Interface
Bridge 1	0200.0000.AAAA	E1
Bridge 2	0200.0000.AAAA	E0
Bridge 3	0200.0000.AAAA	E0
Bridge 4	0200.0000.AAAA	E0
Bridge 5	0200.0000.AAAA	E1

The Spanning Tree change needed is for Bridge 3 to change from blocking state to forwarding state on its E1 interface. Bridge 3's reaction to the lack of CBPDUs from Bridge 4 causes this change to occur. Consider the logic that Bridge 3 uses in this case:

Step 1   I am no longer receiving any CBPDUs on my E1 interface.

Step 2   After Step 1 has occurred for MaxAge time, I assume that the designated bridge has failed. I will become the designated bridge on the LAN segment to which E1 is attached because no other bridges are forwarding CBPDUs onto that segment.

Step 3   I will immediately change E1's status from blocking to *listening*. That means that I will not learn addresses based on frames entering E1. I will not forward frames entering E1, nor will I forward frames out E1.

Step 4   I will clear entries in my address table using a short timer (typically a few seconds).

Step 5   I will send a message out my root port signifying that a topology change is being made. (The root will eventually receive the message.)

Step 6   A Forward Delay timer is started at Step 3. When it expires, I will change my E1 status to *learning* and will begin to add address table entries learned from frames entering my E1 interface. I will not forward frames out my E1 interface yet, nor will I forward frames that enter E1 yet.

Step 7   Another Forward Delay timer was started after Step 6. When that timer expires, I will change my E1 status to *forwarding*.

The Spanning Tree has now changed so that a single active path exists among all LAN segments. The intermediate states are used in an effort to reduce the possibility of temporary loops. Table 4-13 summarizes the intermediate states of the Spanning Tree.

Table 4-13   *Spanning Tree Interface States*

State	Forward Data Frames?	Learn MACs Based on Received Frames?	Transitory or Stable State?
Blocking	No	No	Stable
Listening	No	No	Transitory
Learning	No	Yes	Transitory
Forwarding	Yes	Yes	Stable

The listening and learning states are intermediate states as a bridge makes a new choice about which bridge is root. In listening state, all that matters is listening for CBPDUs so that a new choice for root and designated bridge can be made. In learning state, MAC addresses can be learned based on incoming frames.

One last step is necessary to complete the logic. The address table entries might not have timed out yet (see Table 4-12). The Spanning-Tree Protocol includes the concept of notifying all bridges that a tree change has occurred, allowing the bridges to quickly time out address table entries. By doing so, the new path can be used very quickly.

The notification of a changing Spanning Tree is begun by Bridge 3 in Figure 4-20, in Step 5 of its logic (shown in the list following Figure 4-20). The topology change message is received by the root because each intervening bridge is tasked with forwarding the message. The root reacts by setting a topology change flag in its CBPDUs for a period of time. Because all bridges propagate these messages, all bridges will notice the *topology change flag* in the CBPDU. Each bridge can then choose to use a shorter time (for example, 2 seconds) to time out address table entries.

Spanning-Tree Protocol Summary

Spanning Trees accomplish the goals of allowing physical redundancy, but with only one currently active path through a bridged network. Spanning Tree uses the following features to accomplish the goal:

- All bridge interfaces eventually stabilize at either a forwarding state or a blocking state. The forwarding interfaces are considered to be a part of the Spanning Tree.

- One of the bridges is elected as root. The process includes all bridges claiming to be root, until one is considered best by all. All root bridge interfaces are in forwarding state.

- Each bridge receives CBPDUs from the root, either directly or forwarded by some other bridge. Each bridge can receive more than one such message on its interfaces, but the port in which the least-cost CBPDU is received is called the root port of a bridge, and that port is placed in forwarding state.

- For each LAN segment, one bridge sends the forwarded CBPDU with the lowest cost. That bridge is the designated bridge for that segment. That bridge's interface on that segment is placed in forwarding state.

- All other interfaces are placed in blocking state.

- The root sends CBPDUs every Hello time seconds. The other bridges expect to receive copies of these CBPDUs so that they know that nothing has changed. Hello time is defined in the CBPDU itself, so all bridges use the same value.

- If a bridge does not receive a CBPDU for MaxAge time, it begins the process of causing the Spanning Tree to change. The reaction can vary from topology to topology. (MaxAge is defined in the CBPDU itself, so all bridges use the same value.)

- One or more bridges decide to change interfaces from blocking to forwarding or vice versa, depending on the change in the network. If moving from blocking to forwarding, the interim listening state is entered first. After Forward Delay time (another timer defined in the root CBPDU), the state is changed to learning. After another Forward Delay time, the interface is placed in forwarding state.

- The Spanning-Tree Protocol includes these delays to help ensure that no temporary loops occur.

Virtual LANs

A virtual LAN (VLAN) is a broadcast domain created by one or more switches. (Cisco expects CCNAs to have a solid command of VLAN concepts.) The VLAN is created via configuration in the switch, or possibly configuration referred to by the switch but residing in some external server (for example, using VLAN Membership Policy Server [VMPS]). If a design calls for three separate broadcast domains, three switches could be used—one for each broadcast domain. Each switch would also be connected to a router so that packets could be routed between broadcast domains. Instead, using VLANs, one switch could be used and the switch would treat three different sets of ports as three different broadcast domains.

Figures 4-21 and 4-22 offer a comparison of two networks, each with three broadcasts domains. In the first case, three switches are used and no VLANs are required. Each switch treats all ports as members of one broadcast domain. In Figure 4-22, one switch is used; the switch is configured so that the ports are considered to be in three different broadcast domains. In both cases, separate broadcast domains imply separate Layer 3 groupings; a router is needed for forwarding traffic among the different Layer 3 groups.

Figure 4-21   *Example with Three Broadcast Domains, No VLANs*

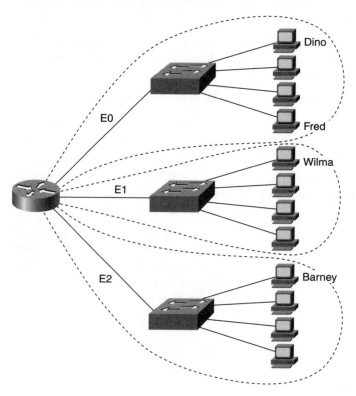

Figure 4-22   *Example with Three Broadcast Domains, Three VLANs*

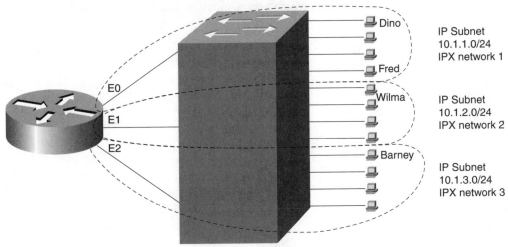

The switch in Figure 4-22 forwards frames to the router interfaces only if the frame is a broadcast or is destined for one of the MAC addresses of the router. For example, Fred sends frames to the router's E0 MAC address when trying to communicate with Barney; this is because Fred's default router should be the router's E0 interface's IP address. However, when Fred sends frames to Dino, the destination MAC address of the frame is Dino's MAC address, and there is no need for the switch to get the router involved. Broadcasts sent by Fred do not go to the other VLANs because each VLAN is a separate broadcast domain.

VLANs allow easy moves, additions, and changes. For example, if Barney moved to a different office, which was cabled to a different port on the switch, he can still be configured to be in VLAN 3. No Layer 3 address changes are necessary, which means that no changes need be made on Barney.

To implement VLANs in one switch, a separate address (bridging) table is used for each VLAN. If a frame is received on a port in VLAN 2, the VLAN 2 address table will be searched. When a frame is received, the source address is checked against the address table so that it can be added if the address is currently unknown. Also, the destination address is checked so that a forwarding decision can be made. For both learning and forwarding, the search is made against the address table for that VLAN only.

Implementing VLANs with multiple switches adds more complexity that is not necessarily obvious. Consider Figure 4-23, which uses two switches connected with a Fast Ethernet. Two VLANs are configured.

Figure 4-23 *Two Switches, Two VLANs*

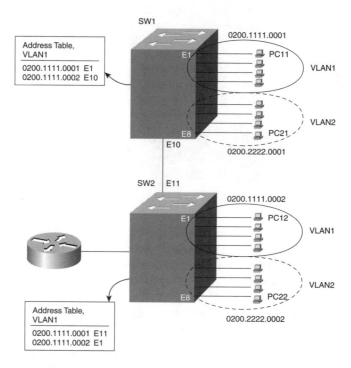

The address table for VLAN1 lists the only two MAC addresses being used in VLAN1. Consider a frame sent from PC11 to PC12:

Step 1 PC11 generates the frame, with destination MAC 0200.1111.0002.

Step 2 Switch 1 receives the frame on port E1.

Step 3 Switch 1 performs address table lookup in VLAN1's address table because incoming port E1 is in VLAN1.

Step 4 Switch 1 forwards the frame out its E10 port.

Step 5 Switch 2 receives the frame in its E11 port.

At this point in the logic, everything seems straightforward. In the next step, however, several choices could have been made by those who created the protocols used for LAN switching. The choices for how Switch 2 could react to the incoming frame are as follows:

Step 6 Switch 2 considers port E11 to be in VLAN1, so it performs table lookup for 0200.1111.0002 in that address table.

Or . . .

Step 7 Switch 2 does not consider port E11 to be in any particular VLAN, so it does table lookup in all tables and forwards out all ports matched.

Or . . .

Step 8 Before Switch 1 forwards the frame in Step 4, it adds a header that identifies the VLAN. Then, Switch 2 can look at the frame header to identify the VLAN number and can do table lookup just in that VLAN's address table.

The third option for Step 6 is the one that actually was implemented. The first option would work fine for one VLAN and is used when connecting multiple switches without using VLANs. However, the logic in this first option fails when devices in VLAN2 send frames because their addresses would never be found in VLAN1's address table. The second option would work well for unicasts, particularly because a unicast address should be found in only a single address table. However, broadcasts would be sent on all interfaces, regardless of VLAN, which would cause horrendous side effects for OSI Layer 3 processes. So, the third option, called *VLAN tagging*, is used.

ISL (Inter-Switch Link) is one of the tagging options used in switches; Figure 4-24 shows ISL framing details. Understanding all the values in the ISL header fields is not vital. However, there are two very important features. First, the ISL header encapsulates the LAN frame, which lengthens the frame. 802.1Q, the IEEE-defined Ethernet VLAN protocol, actually modifies the existing header to accomplish the same tagging goal. The second important feature is the VLAN ID field, which identifies the VLAN to which the encapsulated frame belongs. The source address field in the ISL header is the address of the sending switch, and the destination address is a special multicast address, whose first 5 bytes are 0100.0C00.00 and whose last byte is actually comprised of the values shown in the type and user fields of Figure 4-24. The two ISL features most important for CCNAs, however, are that ISL encapsulates the orignal frame and that there is a VLAN-ID field in the ISL header.

Figure 4-24 *ISL Framing*

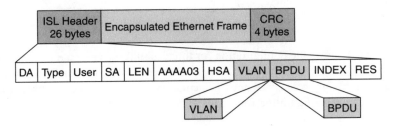

Tagging also can be used to reduce the number of router ports that are needed. Figure 4-23 shows the router with a single interface and a single connection to Switch 2. The same tagging method used between switches is used for frames sent to the router so that the router knows from which VLAN the frame originated. For frames that the router routes between the two VLANs, the incoming frame is tagged with one VLAN ID, and the outgoing frame is tagged with the other VLAN ID by the router before sending the frame back to the switch. Figure 4-25 shows an example network, with flows from VLAN 1 to VLAN 2. The BPDU field also is used to identify whether the encapsulated frame is a CBPDU. Example 4-1 shows the router configuration required to support ISL encapsulation and forwarding between these VLANs.

Figure 4-25 *Example of Router Forwarding Between VLANs*

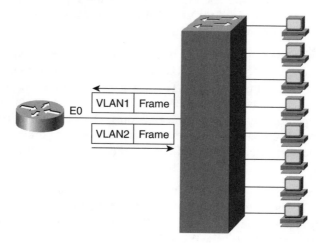

Example 4-1 *Router Configuration for ISL Encapsulation in Figure 4-25*

```
interface ethernet 0.1
ip address 10.1.1.1 255.255.255.0
encapsulation isl 1
!
interface ethernet 0.2
ip address 10.1.2.1 255.255.255.0
encapsulation isl 2
!
interface ethernet 0.3
ip address 10.1.3.1 255.255.255.0
encapsulation isl 3
```

Example 4-1 shows the configuration for three subinterfaces of the Ethernet interface on the router. Each is assigned an IP address because the interface is actually a part of three broadcast domains, implying three IP subnets. The **encapsulation** command numbers the VLANs, which must match the configuration for VLAN IDs in the switch.

Table 4-14 lists the various types of tagging used by Cisco and the types of interfaces on which they are used:

Table 4-14   *Frame Trunking/Tagging Protocols*

Tagging Method	Media
Inter-Switch Link (ISL)	Fast Ethernet
802.1Q	Fast Ethernet
802.10	FDDI
LAN Emulation (LANE)	ATM

The first three options in Table 4-14 are much easier to conceptualize. The frame headers are encapsulated or modified to reflect a VLAN ID before the frame is sent onto the link between switches. Before forwarding to the endpoint device, the frame header is changed back to the original format. With LANE, there is an ATM network between switches. (LANE is a way to make the ATM network behave like an Ethernet in some ways.) There is no tagging in LANE, but instead, a different ATM virtual connection is used between the switches for each VLAN. The virtual connection used implies the VLAN ID.

VLAN Summary

Many benefits can be gained from VLANs, including these:

- With VLANs, moves, additions, and changes to device connections are easier.

- By forcing a Layer 3 routing device to be involved between VLANs, greater administrative control can be used (better accounting, access lists, and so on).

- Unnecessary LAN bandwidth consumption is reduced compared to a single broadcast domain.

- Unnecessary CPU usage is reduced by the resulting reduction in broadcast forwarding.

LAN Switch Configuration

Cisco expects CCNAs to master the concepts behind LAN switching and VLANs. This mastery includes the ability to configure IOS-based LAN switches using the IOS CLI. This section outlines the similarities of the switch IOS CLI to the router IOS CLI, as well as contrasting the commands, syntax, and required configuration elements unique to switches.

Not all Cisco LAN switches provide an IOS CLI interface to the network engineer. Cisco wants its certifications to prove that the candidate knows the technology and can implement it; that proof would be onerous if all switch families' user interfaces were required on the CCNA exam.

This book covers some implemetation details and examples on the 1900 series switch, which is the same (and only) switch user interface covered by the CCNA Training Path ICND course.

The similarities with the router IOS CLI far outnumber the differences. In fact, most of the differences relate to the commands needed on a switch, which are simply not needed on a router. The up-arrow retrieves the previous command. The ? key requests help. The Tab key completes a parameter after you have typed in a unique set of beginning characters. The **configure terminal** command takes you from privleged EXEC mode to configuration mode. The **show running-config** lists the currently used configuration. In fact, when in doubt, you can assume that the switch and router IOS CLIs are identical. The important differences will be mentioned as appropriate in this section.

Basic 1900 Switch Configuration

On the Catalyst 1900 switch, three different configuration methods exist:

- Menu-driven interface from the console port

- Web-based Visual Switch Manager (VSM)

- IOS command-line interface (CLI)

As mentioned earlier, this book focuses on using the CLI to configure the switch. Table 4-15 lists the switch commands referred to in this section.

Table 4-15   *Commands for Catalyst 1900 Switch Configuration*

Command	Description
ip address *address subnet-mask*	Sets the IP address for in-band management of the switch
ip default-gateway	Sets the default gateway so that the management interface can be reached from a remote network
show ip	Displays IP address configuration
show interfaces	Displays interface information
mac-address-table permanent *mac address type module/port*	Sets a permanent MAC address
mac-address-table restricted static *mac address type module/port src-if-list*	Sets a restricted static MAC address
port secure [max-mac-count *count*]	Sets port security
show mac-address-table {security}	Displays the MAC address table; the security option displays information about the restricted or static settings
**address-violation {suspend	disable	ignore}**	Sets the action to be taken by the switch if there is a security address violation
show version	Displays version information

Table 4-15   *Commands for Catalyst 1900 Switch Configuration (Continued)*

Command	Description
copy tftp://10.1.1.1/config.cfg nvram	Copies a configuration file from the TFTP server at IP address 10.1.1.1.
copy nvram tftp://10.1.1.1/config.cfg	Saves a configuration file to the TFTP server at IP address 10.1.1.1.
delete nvram	Removes all configuration parameters and returns the switch to factory default settings

Default 1900 Configuration

The default values vary depending on the features of the switch. The following list provides some of the default settings for the Catalyst 1900 switch. (Not all the defaults are shown in this example.)

- IP address: 0.0.0.0
- CDP: Enabled
- Switching mode: FragmentFree
- 100BaseT port: Auto-negotiate duplex mode
- 10BaseT port: Half duplex
- Spanning Tree: Enabled
- Console password: None

Numbering Ports (Interfaces)

The terms *interface* and *port* both are used to describe the physical connectors on the switch hardware. For instance, the **show running-config** command uses the term *interface*; the **show spantree** command uses the term *port*. The numbering of the interfaces is relatively straightforward; the interface numbering convention for the 1912 and 1924 switches is shown in Table 4-16. Example 4-2 shows three EXEC commands and highlights the use of the terms interface and port.

Table 4-16   *Catalyst 1912 and 1924 Interface/Port Numbering*

	Catalyst 1912	**Catalyst 1924**
10BaseT Ports	12 total (e0/1 to e0/12)	24 total (e0/1 to e0/24)
AUI Port	e0/25	e0/25
100BaseT Uplink Ports	fa0/26 (port A)	fa0/26 (port A)
	fa0/27 (port B)	fa0/27 (port B)

Example 4-2 *show run Output Refers to Port e0/1 as Interface Ethernet 0/1*

```
wg_sw_d#show running-config

Building configuration...
Current configuration:
!
!
interface Ethernet 0/1
!
interface Ethernet 0/2
! Portions omitted for brevity...

wg_sw_d#show spantree

Port Ethernet 0/1 of VLAN1 is Forwarding
    Port path cost 100, Port priority 128
    Designated root has priority 32768, address 0090.8673.3340
    Designated bridge has priority 32768, address 0090.8673.3340
    Designated port is Ethernet 0/1, path cost 0
    Timers: message age 20, forward delay 15, hold 1
! Portions omitted for brevity...
wg_sw_a#show vlan-membership

Port  VLAN   Membership Type    Port  VLAN   Membership Type
- - - - - - - - - - - - - - - - - - - - - - - - - - - - - - - - - - -
1      5       Static           13     1        Static
2      1       Static           14     1        Static
3      1       Static           15     1        Static
```

Basic IP and Port Duplex Configuration

Two features commonly configured immediately during switch installation are TCP/IP support and the setting of duplex on key switch ports. Switches support IP, but in a very different way than with a router. The switch acts more like a normal IP host, with a single address/mask for the switch and a default router. Each port/interface does not need an IP address because the switch is not performing Layer 3 routing. In fact, if there were no need to manage the switch, IP would not be needed on the switch at all.

The second feature typically configured at installation time is to preconfigure some ports to always use half or full duplex rather than allow negotiation. At times, autonegotiation can produce unpredictable results. For instance, if a device attached to the switch does not support autonegotiation, the Catalyst switch sets the corresponding switch port to half-duplex mode by default. If the attached device is configured for full duplex, late collision errors will occur at the full-duplex end. To avoid this situation, manually set the duplex parameters of the switch to match the attached device when support for autonegotiation is in question.

Similar to the router IOS, the Catalyst 1900 switch has various configuration modes. Example 4-3 shows the initial configuration of IP and duplex, with the actual prompts showing the very familiar EXEC and configuration modes.

Example 4-3   *Configuration Modes for Configuring IP and Duplex*

```
wg_sw_a# configure terminal
wg_sw_a(config)#ip address 10.5.5.11 255.255.255.0
wg_sw_a(config)#ip default-gateway 10.5.5.3
wg_sw_a(config)# interface e0/1
wg_sw_a(config-if)#duplex  half
wg_sw_a(config-if)#end
wg_sw_a
```

In the example, the duplex could have been set to one of the following modes:

- **auto**—Sets autonegotiation of duplex mode. This is the default option for 100 Mbps TX ports.

- **full**—Sets full-duplex mode.

- **full-flow-control**—Sets full-duplex mode with flow control.

- **half**—Sets half-duplex mode. This is the default option for 10 Mbps TX ports.

To verify the IP configuration and duplex settings on a given interface, use the **show ip** and **show interface** commands, as seen in Example 4-4.

Example 4-4   *show ip and show interfaces Output*

```
wg_sw_a#show ip
IP address: 10.5.5.11
Subnet mask: 255.255.255.0
Default gateway: 10.5.5.3
Management VLAN:   1
Domain name:
Name server 1: 0.0.0.0
Name server 2: 0.0.0.0
HTTP server: Enabled
HTTP port:  80
RIP: Enabled
wg_sw_a#
wg_sw_a#sh interfaces

Ethernet 0/1 is Enabled
Hardware is Built-in 10Base-T
Address is 0090.8673.3341
MTU 1500 bytes, BW 10000 Kbits
802.1d STP State:  Forwarding      Forward Transitions:  1
Port monitoring: Disabled
Unknown unicast flooding: Enabled
Unregistered multicast flooding:  Enabled
```

continues

Example 4-4 *show ip* and *show interfaces* Output (Continued)

```
Description:
Duplex setting: Half duplex
Back pressure: Disabled

      Receive Statistics                      Transmit Statistics
---------------------------------       ---------------------------------
Total good frames           44841       Total frames                404502
Total octets              4944550       Total octets              29591574
Broadcast/multicast frames  31011       Broadcast/multicast frames  390913
Broadcast/multicast octets 3865029      Broadcast/multicast octets 28478154
Good frames forwarded       44832       Deferrals                        0
Frames filtered                 9       Single collisions                0
Runt frames                     0       Multiple collisions              0
No buffer discards              0       Excessive collisions             0
                                        Queue full discards              0
Errors:                                 Errors:
  FCS errors                    0         Late collisions                0
  Alignment errors              0         Excessive deferrals            0
  Giant frames                  0         Jabber errors                  0
  Address violations            0         Other transmit errors          0
```

Notice that there is no IP address in the **show interface** output because the IP address is associated with the entire switch, not just a single interface. The Spanning Tree state of the interface is shown, as is the duplex setting. If duplex was mismatched with the device on the other end, the later collisions counter would most likely increment rapidly.

Viewing and Configuring Entries in the MAC Address Table

The switching/bridging table concept discussed earlier in this chapter is called the *MAC address table* on the 1900 family of switches. The MAC address table contains dynamic entries, which are learned when the switch receives frames and examines the source MAC address. Two other variations of entries in the MAC address table are important to switch configuration and are outlined along with dynamic entries in the following list:

- **Dynamic addresses**—MAC addresses added to the MAC address table via normal bridge/switch processing. In other words, when a frame is received, the source MAC of the frame is associated with the incoming port/interface. These entries in the table time out with disuse and are cleared whenever the entire table is cleared.

- **Permanent MAC addresses**—Via configuration, a MAC address is associated with a port, just as it would have been associated as a dynamic address. However, permanent entries in the table never time out.

- **Restricted-static entries**—Via configuration, a MAC address is configured to be associated only with a particular port, with an additional restriction: Frames destined to that MAC address must have entered via a particular set of incoming ports.

Figure 4-26 provides a simple example to show the use of permanent and restricted-static addresses. A popular server (Server 1) is on port E0/3, and there is never a case when its MAC address should not be in the table. So, just in case the 1024 entries in the MAC address table are filled, which causes the switch to flush and relearn the entries, the server will remain in the table. The payroll server is also on this switch, and only the company comptroller is allowed access. The configuration and resulting MAC address table are shown in Example 4-5, which follows the figure.

Figure 4-26   *MAC Address Table Manipulation—Sample Network*

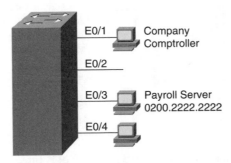

Example 4-5   *The MAC Address Table, with Dynamic, Permanent, and Restricted-Static entries*

```
wg_sw_a(config)#mac-address-table permanent 0200.2222.2222 ethernet 0/3
wg_sw_a(config)#mac-address-table restricted static 0200.1111.1111 e0/4 e0/1
wg_sw_a(config)#End
wg_sw_a#
wg_sw_a#sh mac-address-table
Number of permanent addresses : 1
Number of restricted static addresses : 1
Number of dynamic addresses : 5

Address              Dest Interface      Type        Source Interface List
---------------------------------------------------------------------------
0200.4444.4444       Ethernet 0/1        Dynamic     All
00E0.1E5D.AE2F       Ethernet 0/2        Dynamic     All
0200.2222.2222       Ethernet 0/3        Permanent   All
0200.1111.1111       Ethernet 0/4        Static      Et0/1
00D0.588F.B604       FastEthernet 0/26   Dynamic     All
00E0.1E5D.AE2B       FastEthernet 0/26   Dynamic     All
00D0.5892.38C4       FastEthernet 0/27   Dynamic     All
```

Another feature affecting the MAC address table is called *port security*. Port security is a feature that, when enabled, limits the number of MAC addresses associated with a port in the MAC address table. In other words, there is a preset limit to the number of sources that can forward frames into that switch port.

An example is particularly useful for understanding the concept; the configuration is very straightforward. Consider Figure 4-27, which shows a similar configuration to Figure 4-26, except that the finance department has increased to three employees. These three employees are on the same shared hub, which is then cabled to switch port 0/1.

Figure 4-27   *Sample Network with Port Security*

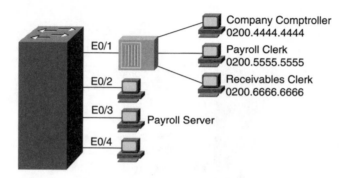

Port security can be used to restrict port 0/1 so that only three MAC addresses can source frames that enter port 0/1—this is because only the finance department is expected to use the shared hub. Any permanent or restricted-static MAC addresses count against this total of three. Example 4-6 shows a sample configuration, with **show** commands:

Example 4-6   *Port Security Example*

```
wg_sw_a(config)#mac-address-table permanent 0200.2222.2222 ethernet 0/3
wg_sw_a(config)#mac-address-table permanent 0200.4444.4444 ethernet 0/1
wg_sw_a(config)#mac-address-table restricted static 0200.1111.1111 e0/4 e0/1
wg_sw_a(config)#interface ethernet 0/1
wg_sw_a(config-if)#port secure max-mac-count 3
wg_sw_a(config-if)#End
wg_sw_a#
wg_sw_a#sh mac-address-table
Number of permanent addresses : 2
Number of restricted static addresses : 1
Number of dynamic addresses : 6

Address              Dest Interface      Type        Source Interface List
-----------------------------------------------------------------------------
0200.4444.4444       Ethernet 0/1        Permanent   All
0200.5555.5555       Ethernet 0/1        Dynamic     All
0200.6666.6666       Ethernet 0/1        Dynamic     All
00E0.1E5D.AE2F       Ethernet 0/2        Dynamic     All
0200.2222.2222       Ethernet 0/3        Permanent   All
0200.1111.1111       Ethernet 0/4        Static      Et0/1
00D0.588F.B604       FastEthernet 0/26   Dynamic     All
00E0.1E5D.AE2B       FastEthernet 0/26   Dynamic     All
00D0.5892.38C4       FastEthernet 0/27   Dynamic     All
```

Example 4-6 *Port Security Example (Continued)*

```
wg_sw_a#show mac-address-table security
Action upon address violation : Suspend

Interface        Addressing Security     Address Table Size
---------------------------------------------------------------
Ethernet 0/1     Enabled                 3
Ethernet 0/2     Disabled                N/A
Ethernet 0/3     Disabled                N/A
Ethernet 0/4     Disabled                N/A
Ethernet 0/5     Disabled                N/A
Ethernet 0/6     Disabled                N/A
Ethernet 0/7     Disabled                N/A
Ethernet 0/8     Disabled                N/A
Ethernet 0/9     Disabled                N/A
Ethernet 0/10    Disabled                N/A
Ethernet 0/11    Disabled                N/A
Ethernet 0/12    Disabled                N/A
```

In this example, the permanently defined MAC address of 0200.4444.444, the comptroller's MAC address, is always associated with port e0/1. Notice that the two new employees' MAC addresses are also in the MAC address table.

The **port secure max-mac-count 3** command means that a total of three addresses can be learned on this port. So, the first two addresses learned, in addition to the permanent address that is configured, are considered to be *sticky-learned*. These two addresses are considered to be static, so that if someone came along and plugged into the finance hub, the switch would not add that hacker's MAC address to the MAC address table.

So what should the switch do when a fourth MAC address sources a frame that enters E0/1? An address violation occurs when a secured port receives a frame from a new source address that, if added to the MAC table, would cause the switch to exceed its address table size limit for that port. When a port security address violation occurs, the options for action to be taken on a port include suspending, ignoring, or disabling the port. When a port is suspended, it is re-enabled when a frame containing a valid address is received. When a port is disabled, it must be manually re-enabled. If the action is ignored, the switch ignores the security violation and keeps the port enabled.

Use the **address-violation** global configuration command to specify the action for a port address violation. The syntax for this command is as follows:

```
address-violation {suspend | disable | ignore}
```

Use the **no address-violation** command to set the switch to its default value, which is suspend.

Managing Configuration and System Files

Commands used to manage and control the configuration and system software files are slightly different on the 1900 switch family than on IOS-based routers. One of the reasons for the difference is that the switch does not actually run IOS—it has many features like IOS, including the IOS CLI, but there are and probably always will be some differences. For instance, in Example 4-7, the familiar **show version** command is used to display uptime and software levels, but it does not show the IOS level because IOS is not running.

Example 4-7 *show version Output Displays Switch Hardware and IOS Information*

```
wg_sw_a#show version
Cisco Catalyst 1900/2820 Enterprise Edition Software
Version V9.00.00(12) written from 171.071.114.222
Copyright  Cisco Systems, Inc.  1993-1999
DS2820-1 uptime is 2day(s) 19hour(s) 34minute(s) 41second(s)
cisco Catalyst 2820 (486sxl) processor with 2048K/1024K bytes of memory
Hardware board revision is 1
Upgrade Status: No upgrade currently in progress.
Config File Status: No configuration upload/download is in progress
25 Fixed Ethernet/IEEE 802.3 interface(s)
SLOT A:
 FDDI (Fiber DAS Model), Version 00
  v1.14 written from 172.031.004.151: valid
SLOT B:
 100Base-TX(1 Port UTP Model), Version 0
Base Ethernet Address: 00-E0-1E-87-21-40
```

Another difference is that when the configuration is changed, running-config is modified, but the startup-config file in NVRAM is automatically updated. In other words, there is no need for a **copy running-config startup-config** command on the 1900 family of switches. Configuration files can be copied to an external TFTP server, but instead of the keyword **startup-config**, **NVRAM** is used.

The syntax of the **copy** command is slightly different than what was covered in Chapter 2, "Cisco Internetwork Operating System (IOS) Fundamentals," relating to the router IOS **copy** command. The syntax of the command used to copy the NVRAM configuration file to host 10.1.1.1, into file mybackup.cfg is **copy nvram tftp://10.1.1.1/mybackup.cfg**.

Unlike the router IOS, the switch IOS CLI will not prompt for the server name or IP address or the name of the file. Instead, the address or server host name and the file name are entered at the command line. The fact that the command will not prompt you is certainly different than with the router IOS. However, the same general syntax is available on the router IOS as of IOS 12.0. For instance, a similar, valid router IOS command would be **copy startup-config tftp:// 10.1.1.1/myrouter.cfg**.

Table 4-17 summarizes some of the key differences between the router IOS CLI and the 1900 IOS CLI:

Table 4-17   *IOS CLI Differences: Router Versus 1900 Switch*

Function	Router Command, Features	Switch Command, Features
Finding software version	**show version** command; shows IOS version	**show version** command; shows switch software version
Copying configuration files to TFTP server	**copy startup-config tftp** command; router IOS prompts for TFTP parameters	**copy nvram tftp//server/file** command; switch IOS CLI does not prompt for TFTP parameters
Updating the config file used at reload time	**copy running-config startup-config** command	Changes to running configuration using config mode are automatically reflected in NVRAM config file
Erasing the config file used at reload time	**write erase** or **erase startup-config** command	**delete nvram** command

Basic VLAN Configuration

This section discusses the guidelines for configuring VLANs on the Cisco 1900 switch. You should remember several items before you begin VLAN configuration:

- The maximum number of VLANs is switch-dependent. The Catalyst 1900 supports 64 VLANs with a separate Spanning Tree per VLAN.

- VLAN1 is one of the factory-default VLANs.

- CDP and VTP advertisements are sent on VLAN1.

- Catalyst 1900 IP address is in the VLAN1 broadcast domain.

- The switch must be in VTP server mode to create, add, or delete VLANs.

One term not covered yet in this list is VLAN Trunking Protocol (VTP). VTP is a Layer 2 messaging protocol that maintains VLAN configuration consistency throughout a common administration domain. VTP accomplishes this goal by managing the additions, deletions, and name changes of VLANs across networks. VTP minimizes misconfigurations and configuration inconsistencies that can cause problems, such as duplicate VLAN names or incorrect VLAN-type specifications.

VTP will be covered in the next section of this chapter; to configure the VLAN features in this section, the switches will need to be configured in VTP transparent mode.

Table 4-18 represents the commands covered in this section and gives a brief description of each command's function.

Table 4-18   *VLAN Command List*

Command	Description
delete vtp	Resets all VTP parameters to defaults and resets the configuration revision number to 1
vtp [**server** | **transparent** | **client**] [**domain** *domain-name*] [**trap** {**enable** | **disable**}] [**password** *password*] [**pruning** {**enable** | **disable**}]	Defines VTP parameters
vtp trunk pruning-disable *vlan-list*	Disables pruning for specified VLANs on a particular trunk interface (interface subcommand)
show vtp	Displays VTP status
trunk [**on** | **off** | **desirable** | **auto** | **nonegotiate**]	Configures a trunk interface
show trunk	Displays trunk status
vlan *vlan#* **name** *vlanname*	Defines a VLAN and its name
show vlan	Displays VLAN information
vlan-membership static *vlan#*	Assigns a port to a VLAN
show vlan-membership	Displays VLAN membership
show spantree *vlan#*	Displays Spanning Tree information for a VLAN

Sample Configuration for a Single Switch

When VTP is not in use (in other words, when VTP transparent mode is in use), VLAN configuration consists of three primary tasks:

1   Enabling VTP transparent mode

2   Creating the VLAN numbers and names

3   Configuring each port's assigned VLAN

First, use the **vtp** global configuration command to configure VTP transparent mode. Use the **vlan** global command to define each VLAN number (required) and associated name (optional). Then assign each port to its associated VLAN using the **vlan-membership** interface subcommand. Example 4-8 shows an example, based on Figure 4-28.

Figure 4-28   *Sample Network, One Switch, Three VLANs*

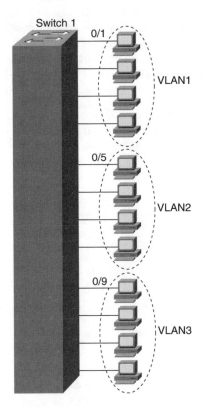

Example 4-8   *Single-Switch VLAN Configuration Matching Figure 4-28*

```
switch(config)# vtp transparent domain dummy
switch(config)# vlan 2 name VLAN2
switch1(config)# vlan 3 name VLAN3
switch1(config)# interface e 0/5
switch1(config-if)# vlan-membership static 2
switch1(config-if)# interface e 0/6
switch1(config-if)# vlan-membership static 2
switch1(config-if)# interface e 0/7
switch1(config-if)# vlan-membership static 2
switch1(config-if)# interface e 0/8
switch1(config-if)# vlan-membership static 2
switch1(config-if)# interface e 0/9
switch1(config-if)# vlan-membership static 3
switch1(config-if)# interface e 0/10
switch1(config-if)# vlan-membership static 3
switch1(config-if)# interface e 0/11
switch1(config-if)# vlan-membership static 3
switch1(config-if)# interface e 0/12
switch1(config-if)# vlan-membership static 3
```

Notice that some configuration seems to be missing. VLAN 1, with name VLAN1, is not configured because it is configured automatically. In fact, the name cannot be changed. Also, any ports without a specific static VLAN configuration are considered to be in VLAN1. Also, the IP address of the switch is considered to be in VLAN1's broadcast domain. Ports 5 through 8 are statically configured for VLAN2; similarly, VLAN3 comprises ports 9 through 12. In addition, the yet-unexplained VTP is set to transparent mode, with a meaningless domain name of *dummy*—this setting is not important (yet); it simply must be set.

After the VLAN is configured, the parameters for that VLAN should be confirmed to assure validity. To verify the parameters of a VLAN, use the **show vlan** *vlan#* privileged EXEC command to display information about a particular VLAN. Use **show vlan** to show all configured VLANs. Example 4-9 demonstrates the **show** command output, which shows the switch ports assigned to the VLAN.

Example 4-9 *show vlan Output*

```
Switch1#sh vlan 3

VLAN Name              Status     Ports
- - - - - - - - - - - - - - - - - - - - - - - - - - - - - - - - - - - - - -
3   VLAN3              Enabled    9-12
- - - - - - - - - - - - - - - - - - - - - - - - - - - - - - - - - - - - - -

VLAN Type         SAID    MTU    Parent RingNo BridgeNo Stp  Trans1 Trans2
- - - - - - - - - - - - - - - - - - - - - - - - - - - - - - - - - - - - - - - -
3   Ethernet      100003 1500       0     1       1    Unkn    0      0
- - - - - - - - - - - - - - - - - - - - - - - - - - - - - - - - - - - - - - - -
```

Other VLAN parameters shown in Example 4-9 include the type (default is Ethernet), SAID (used for FDDI trunk), MTU (default is 1500 for Ethernet VLAN), Spanning-Tree Protocol (the 1900 supports only the 802.1D Spanning-Tree Protocol standard), and other parameters used for Token Ring or FDDI VLANs.

Sample Configuration for Multiple Switches

To allow VLANs to span multiple switches, you must configure *trunks* to interconnect the switches. Trunks are simply LANs connecting switches. Cisco calls the use of a trunking protocol such as ISL over such a link trunking, so the command to enable these protocols is called **trunk**.

Use the **trunk** interface configuration command to set a Fast Ethernet port to trunk mode. On the Catalyst 1900, the two Fast Ethernet ports are interfaces fa0/26 and fa0/27. Enabling and defining the type of trunking protocol can be done statically, or dynamically for ISL using the

Dynamic Inter-Switch Link (DISL) protocol. DISL manages automatic ISL trunk negotiation. The syntax for the **trunk** fast Ethernet interface configuration subcommand is as follows:

```
switch(config)# trunk [on | off | desirable | auto | nonnegotiate]
```

The options for the **trunk** command function are as follows:

- **on**—Configures the port into permanent ISL trunk mode and negotiates with the connected device to convert the link to trunk mode.

- **off**—Disables port trunk mode and negotiates with the connected device to convert the link to nontrunk.

- **desirable**—Triggers the port to negotiate the link from nontrunking to trunk mode. The port negotiates to a trunk port if the connected device is either in the **on**, **desirable**, or **auto** state. Otherwise, the port becomes a nontrunk port.

- **auto**—Enables a port to become a trunk only if the connected device has the state set to **on** or **desirable**.

- **nonegotiate**—Configures a port to permanent ISL trunk mode, and no negotiation takes place with the partner.

As seen in the list, many options exist. Choices for these options are mostly personal preference. Because trunks seldom change, my preference is to configure either **on** or **off**.

Figure 4-29 and Example 4-10 provide an expanded sample network, along with the additional configuration required.

Notice that not only was trunking enabled on both Fast Ethernet ports, but each of the three VLANs was statically configured on those ports. By also configuring the VLANs, the switch treats the trunk ports as part of those VLANs. The router also must be configured to support ISL, as seen earlier in this chapter.

To verify a trunk configuration, use the **show trunk** privileged EXEC command to display the trunk parameters, as demonstrated in Example 4-10. The syntax is as follows:

```
Switch1(config)# show trunk [a | b]
```

The parameters a and b represent the Fast Ethernet ports:

- Port a represents Fast Ethernet 0/26.

- Port b represents Fast Ethernet 0/27.

Figure 4-29 *Sample Network, Two Switches, Three VLANs*

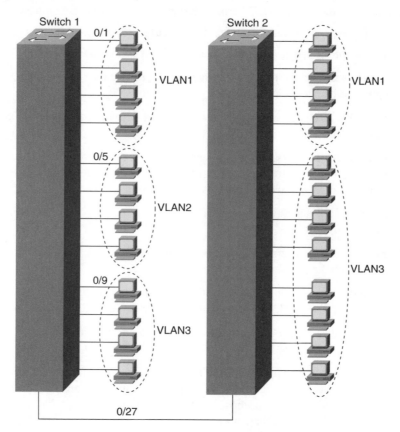

Example 4-10 *Two Switch VLAN Configurations Matching Figure 4-29*

```
Switch1(config)# interface fa 0/26
switch1(config-if)# trunk on
switch1(config-if)# vlan-membership static 1
switch1(config-if)# vlan-membership static 2
switch1(config-if)# vlan-membership static 3
switch1(config-if)# interface fa 0/27
switch1(config-if)# trunk on
switch1(config-if)# vlan-membership static 1
switch1(config-if)# vlan-membership static 2
switch1(config-if)# vlan-membership static 3
```

Example 4-11 shows a sample of the **show trunk** command, as well as the **show vlan-membership** command:

Example 4-11 *show trunk Output*

```
Switch1# show trunk a
DISL state: Off, Trunking: On, Encapsulation type: ISL

Switch1#show vlan-membership

   Port  VLAN  Membership Type       Port   VLAN  Membership Type
   --------------------------------------------------------------------------
     1     1   Static                 14     1    Static
     2     1   Static                 15     1    Static
     3     1   Static                 16     1    Static
     4     1   Static                 17     1    Static
     5     2   Static                 18     1    Static
     6     2   Static                 19     1    Static
     7     2   Static                 20     1    Static
     8     2   Static                 21     1    Static
     9     3   Static                 22     1    Static
    10     3   Static                 23     1    Static
    11     3   Static                 24     1    Static
    12     3   Static                AUI     1    Static
    13     1   Static
     A    1-3  Static
     B    1-3  Static
```

Use the **show spantree** privileged EXEC command to display the Spanning-Tree Protocol configuration status of the switch, as demonstrated in Example 4-12.

Example 4-12 *show spantree Output*

```
Switch1# show spantree 1
VLAN1 is executing the IEEE compatible Spanning-Tree Protocol
    Bridge Identifier has priority 32768, address 0050.F037.DA00
    Configured hello time 2, max age 20, forward delay 15
    Current root has priority 0, address 00D0.588F.B600
    Root port is FastEthernet 0/27, cost of root path is 10
    Topology change flag not set, detected flag not set
    Topology changes 53, last topology change occurred 0d00h17m14s ago
    Times:  hold 1, topology change 8960
            hello 2, max age 20, forward delay 15
    Timers: hello 2, topology change 35, notification 2
Port Ethernet 0/1 of VLAN1 is Forwarding
    Port path cost 100, Port priority 128
    Designated root has priority 0, address 00D0.588F.B600
    Designated bridge has priority 32768, address 0050.F037.DA00
    Designated port is Ethernet 0/1, path cost 10
    Timers: message age 20, forward delay 15, hold 1
```

Example 4-12 displays various Spanning Tree information for VLAN1, including the following:

- Port e0/1 is in the forwarding state for VLAN1.

- The root bridge for VLAN1 has a bridge priority of 0, with a MAC address of 00D0.588F.B600.

- The switch is running the IEEE 802.1d Spanning-Tree Protocol.

VLAN Trunking Protocol (VTP)

VTP is a Layer 2 messaging protocol that maintains VLAN configuration consistency throughout a common administration domain. VTP manages the additions, deletions, and name changes of VLANs across multiple switches. VTP minimizes misconfigurations and configuration inconsistencies that can cause problems, such as duplicate VLAN names or incorrect VLAN-type specifications.

VTP distributes and synchronizes identifying information about VLANs configured throughout a switched network. Configurations made to a single switch, which is called the VTP server, are propagated across trunk links to all switches in the same VTP domain. VTP allows switched network solutions to scale to large sizes by reducing the manual configuration needs in the network.

The VTP domain is created by having each switch in the domain configure the same domain name. The network administrator chooses which switches are in the same domain by deciding which switches share common VLANs. One switch is chosen and then configured as the VTP server; then, the others are configured as clients for full VTP operation. (VTP transparent mode, a third option, will be covered shortly.)

How VTP Works

VTP advertisements are flooded throughout the management domain every 5 minutes, or whenever there is a change in VLAN configurations. Included in a VTP advertisement is a configuration revision number, as well as VLAN names and numbers, and information about which switches have ports assigned to each VLAN. By configuring the details on one server and propagating the information via advertisements, all switches know the names and numbers of all VLANs.

One of the most important components of the VTP advertisements is the *configuration revision number*. Each time a VTP server modifies its VLAN information, it increments the configuration revision number by one. The VTP server then sends out a VTP advertisement that includes the new configuration revision number. When a switch receives a VTP advertisement with a larger configuration revision number, it updates its VLAN configuration. Figure 4-30 illustrates how VTP operates in a switched network.

Figure 4-30   *VTP Operation*

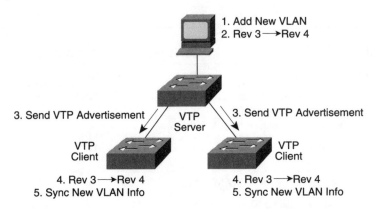

1. Add New VLAN
2. Rev 3 ⟶ Rev 4

VTP Server

3. Send VTP Advertisement   3. Send VTP Advertisement

VTP Client   VTP Client

4. Rev 3 ⟶ Rev 4   4. Rev 3 ⟶ Rev 4
5. Sync New VLAN Info   5. Sync New VLAN Info

VTP operates in one of three modes: server mode, client mode, or transparent mode. VTP servers can create, modify, and delete VLANs and other configuration parameters for the entire VTP domain; this information in turn is propagated to the VTP clients in that same domain. VTP servers save VLAN configurations in the Catalyst NVRAM, whereas in clients, the VLAN configuration is not stored. When you make a change to the VLAN configuration on a VTP server, the change is dynamically propagated to all switches in the VTP domain. VTP messages are transmitted by the server out all trunk connections.

A VTP client cannot create, change, or delete VLANs, nor can it save VLAN configurations in nonvolatile memory. So, why be a VTP client? Well, if one person or department is in control of several switches, then using VTP can save configuration time and effort. The VTP-learned configuration information is kept in the running configuration on each client switch, so even if the server fails, VLAN configuration information is still available to the clients.

VTP transparent mode is used when a switch does not need or want to participate in VTP, but is willing to pass VTP advertisements to other switches. A switch in transparent mode forwards VTP advertisements received from other switches that are part of the same management domain. A switch configured in VTP transparent mode can create, delete, and modify VLANs, but the changes are not transmitted to other switches in the domain; they affect only the local switch. Choosing to use transparent mode is typical when there is a need for distributed administrative control of the switches, in spite of the fact that they each control parts of the same VLANs. That administrative need is relatively rare. Also, VTP pruning, a topic covered later in this chapter, is available only to VTP servers and clients, which is another compelling reason to not use VTP transparent mode.

Table 4-19 offers a comparative overview of the three VTP modes.

Table 4-19   *VTP Modes*

Function	Server Mode	Client Mode	Transparent Mode
Originates VTP advertisements	Yes	No	No
Processes received advertisements and synchronizes VLAN configuration information with other switches	No	Yes	No
Forwards VTP advertisements received in a trunk	No	Yes	Yes
Saves VLAN configuration in NVRAM	Yes	No	Yes
Can create, modify, or delete VLANs using configuration commands	Yes	No	Yes

VTP Pruning

Because ISL trunk lines carry VLAN traffic for all VLANs, some traffic might be needlessly broadcast across links that do not need to carry that traffic. VTP pruning uses VLAN advertisements to determine when a trunk connection is flooding traffic needlessly. By default, a trunk connection carries traffic for all VLANs in the VTP management domain. Commonly, some switches in an enterprise network do not have local ports configured in each VLAN. In Figure 4-31, Switches 1 and 4 support ports statically configured in VLAN 10. As illustrated, with VTP pruning enabled, when Station A sends a broadcast, the broadcast is flooded only toward any switch with ports assigned to VLAN 10. As a result, broadcast traffic from Station A is not forwarded to Switches 3, 5, and 6 because traffic for VLAN 10 has been pruned on the links indicated on Switches 2 and 4.

VTP pruning increases available bandwidth by restricting flooded traffic to those trunk links that the traffic must use to access the appropriate network devices. VTP pruning is one of the two most compelling reasons to use VTP—the other is to make VLAN configuration easier and more consistent.

VLAN Configuration Using VTP

Basic VLAN configuration, with the switch in VTP transparent mode, has already been covered. This section focuses on VTP configuration for client and server and shows an example configuration for two switches: one the VTP server and one a VTP client.

Figure 4-31   *VTP Pruning*

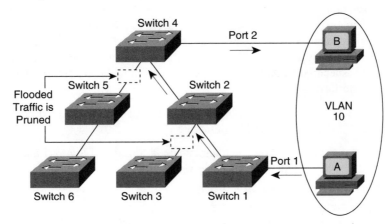

Several parameters can be set for VTP operation on a switch. The server, client, and transparent mode options have already been discussed. Several other important parameters are allowed. The default VTP configuration parameters for the Catalyst 1900 switch are as follows:

- VTP domain name: None

- VTP mode: Server

- VTP password: None

- VTP pruning: Disabled

- VTP trap: Enabled

The VTP domain name can be specified or learned. By default, the domain name is not set, and the switch is set to the VTP server mode. If a switch using the defaults receives a VTP advertisement with a domain name, then that switch assumes the use of that domain name. However, if a switch is configured with one domain name and it receives an advertisement that includes a different domain name, the advertisement is ignored. One advantage of this process is that with default configuration on all switches, VTP will be enabled, all switches will be in server mode, but all will be listening for advertisements—thus, VTP will still work. If one switch is configured with the domain name, then it will propagate to the other switches. Or, if multiple domains are in use, simply configure each switch with the correct name, and the other domains' VTP updates will be ignored.

A password can be set for the VTP management domain. The password entered must be the same for all switches in the domain. If you configure a VTP password, VTP does not function properly unless you assign the same password to each switch in the domain.

VTP pruning eligibility defines where VTP pruning is enabled for *the entire management domain*. Enabling or disabling VTP pruning on a VTP server propagates the change throughout the management domain. If pruning is enabled, all VLANs are pruned *except* VLAN1; VLAN1 is used for propagating VTP advertisements, so any pruning would make it difficult to graft the branches back into the tree. Pruning can be globally enabled in the domain and then selectively disabled for specified VLANs on specified trunks using the **vtp trunk pruning-disable** *vlan-list* trunk interface subcommand.

Enabling a VTP trap causes an SNMP message to be generated every time a new VTP message is sent out. VTP trap is enabled by default.

Examples 4-13 and 4-14 show the complete configuration of Switch1 and Switch2 from Figure 4-29. Switch1 will be the VTP server.

Example 4-13 *Switch1 Complete Configuration as VTP Server*

```
Switch1# configure terminal
Switch1(config)#ip address 10.5.5.11 255.255.255.0
Switch1(config)#ip default-gateway 10.5.5.3
Switch1(config)# vtp server domain Hartsfield pruning enable
Switch1(config)# vlan 2 name VLAN2
switch1(config)# vlan 3 name VLAN3
switch1(config)# interface e 0/5
switch1(config-if)# vlan-membership static 2
switch1(config-if)# interface e 0/6
switch1(config-if)# vlan-membership static 2
switch1(config-if)# interface e 0/7
switch1(config-if)# vlan-membership static 2
switch1(config-if)# interface e 0/8
switch1(config-if)# vlan-membership static 2
switch1(config-if)# interface e 0/9
switch1(config-if)# vlan-membership static 3
switch1(config-if)# interface e 0/10
switch1(config-if)# vlan-membership static 3
switch1(config-if)# interface e 0/11
switch1(config-if)# vlan-membership static 3
switch1(config-if)# interface e 0/12
switch1(config-if)# vlan-membership static 3
Switch1(config)# interface fa 0/26
switch1(config-if)# trunk on
switch1(config-if)# vlan-membership static 1
switch1(config-if)# vlan-membership static 2
switch1(config-if)# vlan-membership static 3
switch1(config-if)# interface fa 0/27
switch1(config-if)# trunk on
switch1(config-if)# vlan-membership static 1
switch1(config-if)# vlan-membership static 2
switch1(config-if)# vlan-membership static 3
```

Example 4-14 *Switch2 Complete Configuration as VTP Client*

```
Switch2# configure terminal
Switch2(config)#ip address 10.5.5.12 255.255.255.0
Switch2(config)#ip default-gateway 10.5.5.3
Switch2(config)# vtp client
switch2(config)# interface e 0/5
switch2(config-if)# vlan-membership static 2
switch2(config-if)# interface e 0/6
switch2(config-if)# vlan-membership static 2
switch2(config-if)# interface e 0/7
switch2(config-if)# vlan-membership static 2
switch2(config-if)# interface e 0/8
switch2(config-if)# vlan-membership static 2
switch2(config-if)# interface e 0/9
switch2(config-if)# vlan-membership static 2
switch2(config-if)# interface e 0/10
switch2(config-if)# vlan-membership static 2
switch2(config-if)# interface e 0/11
switch2(config-if)# vlan-membership static 2
switch2(config-if)# interface e 0/12
switch2(config-if)# vlan-membership static 2
switch2(config-if)# interface fa 0/27
switch2(config-if)# trunk on
switch2(config-if)# vlan-membership static 1
switch2(config-if)# vlan-membership static 2
```

Several items are particularly important in these configurations. The **vtp** global command in Example 4-13 shows Switch1 as the server, with domain *Hartsfield*. No password is used in this case. Switch2 is not configured with the domain name but will learn it with the first advertisement. Missing from Example 4-14 is the definition of the VLANs, which is not only unnecessary but also is not allowed when in VTP client mode. And, because pruning was enabled in the **vtp** command on Switch1, VTP prunes VLAN2 from Switch2 because Switch2 has no ports in VLAN3. VLAN3 broadcasts received by Switch1 are not forwarded to Switch2.

To verify a recent configuration change, or to just view the VTP configuration information, use the **show vtp** privileged EXEC command, as demonstrated in Example 4-15. Also displayed is the IP address of the device that last modified the configuration and a time stamp of the time the modification was made. VTP has two versions: VTP Version 1 supports only Ethernet; VTP Version 2 supports Ethernet and Token Ring.

Example 4-15 *show vtp Output*

```
Switch1# show vtp
VTP version: 1
Configuration revision: 4
Maximum VLANs supported locally: 1005
Number of existing VLANs: 3
VTP domain name:Hartsfield
VTP password:
VTP operating mode: Server
VTP pruning mode: Enabled
VTP traps generation: Enabled
Configuration last modified by: 10.5.5.3 at 00-00-0000 00:00:00
```

Foundation Summary

The Foundation Summary is a collection of tables and figures that provide a convenient review of many key concepts in this chapter. For those of you already comfortable with the topics in this chapter, this summary could help you recall a few details. For those of you who just read this chapter, this review should help solidify some key facts. For any of you doing your final prep before the exam, these tables and figures will be a convenient way to review the day before the exam.

Figure 4-32 summarizes the various LAN header formats.

Table 4-20 summarizes the fields used for identifying the types of data contained in a frame.

Table 4-20   *Protocol Type Fields in LAN Headers*

Field Name	Length	LAN Type	Comments
Ethernet Type	2 bytes	Ethernet	RFC 1700 (Assigned Numbers RFC) lists the values. Xerox owns the assignment process.
802.2 DSAP and SSAP	1 byte each	IEEE Ethernet, IEEE Token Ring, ANSI FDDI	The IEEE Registration Authority controls the assignment of valid values. The source SAP (SSAP) and destination SAP (DSAP) do not have to be equal, so 802.2 calls for the sender's protocol type (SSAP) and the destination's type (DSAP).
SNAP Protocol	2 bytes	IEEE Ethernet, IEEE Token Ring, ANSI FDDI	Uses EtherType values. Used only when DSAP is hex AA. It is needed because the DSAP and SSAP fields are only 1 byte in length.

Figure 4-32   *LAN Header Formats*

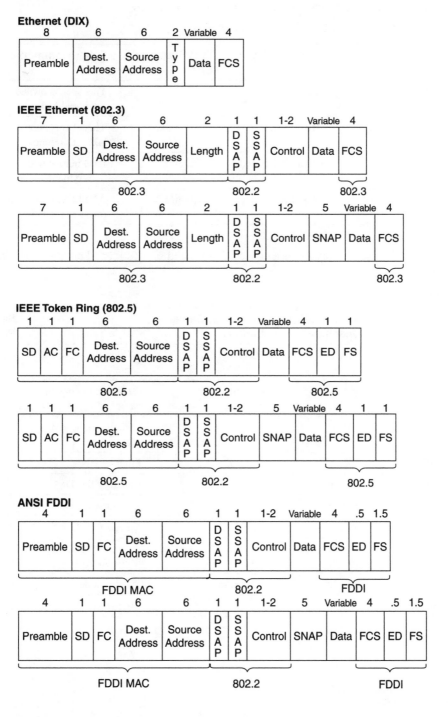

Table 4-21 lists the specification that defines the Media Access Control (MAC) and Logical Link Control (LLC) sublayers of the three LAN types, for comparison.

Table 4-21 *MAC and LLC Details for Three Types of LANs*

Name	MAC Sublayer Spec	LLC Sublayer Spec	Other Comments
Ethernet Version 2 (DIX Ethernet)	Ethernet	—	This spec is owned by Digital, Intel, and Xerox.
IEEE Ethernet	IEEE 802.3	IEEE 802.2	This also is popularly called 802.3 Ethernet.
Token Ring	IEEE 802.5	IEEE 802.2	IBM helped with development before the IEEE took over.
FDDI	ANSI X3T9.5	IEEE 802.2	ANSI liked 802.2, so it just refers to the IEEE spec.

Table 4-22 lists the key Ethernet specifications and several related details about the operation of each.

Table 4-22 *Ethernet Standards*

Standard	MAC Sublayer Specification	Maximum Cable Length	Cable Type	Pairs Required
10Base5	802.3	500 m[1]	50 ohm thick coaxial cable	—
10Base2	802.3	185 m[1]	50 ohm thin coaxial cable	—
10BaseT	802.3	100 m[1]	Category 3, 4, or 5 UTP	2
10BaseFL	802.3	2000 m[2]	Fiber	1
100BaseTx	802.3u	100 m[2]	Category 5 UTP	2
100BaseT4	802.3u	100 m[2]	Category 3 UTP	4
100BaseT2	802.3u	100 m[2]	Category 3, 4, or 5 UTP	2
100BaseFx	802.3u	400/2000 m[3]	Multimode fiber	1
100BaseFx	802.3u	10,000 m	Single-mode fiber	1
1000BaseSx	802.3z	220-550 m	Multimode fiber	1

Table 4-22   *Ethernet Standards (Continued)*

Standard	MAC Sublayer Specification	Maximum Cable Length	Cable Type	Pairs Required
1000BaseLx	802.3z	3000 m	Single-mode or multimode fiber	1
1000BaseCx	802.3z	25 m	Shielded copper	2
1000BaseT	802.3ab	100 m	Category 5 UTP	2

1. For entire bus
2. From device to hub/switch
3. Numbers shown are for half/full duplex

The internal processing methods of LAN switches are listed in Table 4-23.

Table 4-23   *Switch Internal Processing*

Switching Method	Description
Store-and-forward	The switch fully receives all bits in the frame (store) before forwarding the frame (forward). This allows the switch to check the FCS before forwarding the frame. (FCS is in the Ethernet trailer.)
Cut-through	The switch performs the address table lookup as soon as the destination address field in the header is received. The first bits in the frame can be sent out the outbound port before the final bits in the incoming frame are received. This does not allow the switch to discard frames that fail the FCS check. (FCS is in the Ethernet trailer.)
FragmentFree	This performs like cut-through, but the switch waits for 64 bytes to be received before forwarding the first bytes of the outgoing frame. According to Ethernet specifications, collisions should be detected during the first 64 bytes of the frame; frames in error due to collision are not forwarded. The FCS still cannot be checked.

Table 4-24 lists several features relating to segmenting LANs with bridges, switches, and routers.

Table 4-24   *Comparison of Segmentation Options*

Feature	Bridging	Switching	Routing
Forwards LAN broadcasts?	Yes	Yes	No
Forwards LAN multicasts?	Yes	Yes; can be optimized with CGMP	No[1]

continues

Table 4-24   *Comparison of Segmentation Options (Continued)*

Feature	Bridging	Switching	Routing
OSI layer used when making forwarding decision	Layer 2	Layer 2	Layer 3
Internal processing variants	Store-and-forward	Store-and-forward, cut-through, FragmentFree	Store-and-forward
Frame/packet fragmentation allowed?	No	No	Yes
Multiple concurrent equal-cost paths to same destination allowed?	No	No	Yes

1. Routers can forward IP multicast packets, if configured to do so. However, this does not mean that the LAN multicast frame is forwarded.

Table 4-25 lists features that must be interpreted within the following context: "If I migrated from a single Ethernet segment to a network with two segments separated by a bridge/switch/router, and if traffic loads and destinations stayed constant, the result would be _____."

Table 4-25   *Comparison of a Single Segment to Multiple Segments*

Feature	Bridging	Switching	Routing
Greater cabling distances allowed	Yes	Yes	Yes
Decrease in collisions, assuming equal traffic loads	Yes	Yes	Yes
Decreased adverse impact of broadcasts	No	No	Yes
Decreased adverse impact of multicasts	No	Yes, with CGMP	Yes
Increase in bandwidth	Yes	Yes	Yes
Filtering on Layer 2 header allowed	Yes	Yes	Yes
Filtering on Layer 3 header allowed	No	No	Yes

Table 4-26 summarizes the reasons why Spanning Tree places a port into forwarding or blocking state:

Table 4-26   *Spanning Tree—Reasons for Forwarding or Blocking*

Characterization of Port	Spanning Tree State	Explanation
All root bridge's ports	Forwarding	The root bridge is always the designated bridge on all connected segments.
Each nonroot bridge's root port	Forwarding	The root port is the port receiving the lowest-cost CBPDU from the root.

Table 4-26   *Spanning Tree—Reasons for Forwarding or Blocking (Continued)*

Characterization of Port	Spanning Tree State	Explanation
Each LAN's designated bridge	Forwarding	The bridge forwarding the lowest-cost CBPDU onto the segment is the designated bridge.
All other ports	Blocking	The port is not used for forwarding frames, nor are any frames received on these interfaces considered for forwarding.

Table 4-27 summarizes the intermediate states of the Spanning Tree.

Table 4-27   *Spanning Tree Interface States*

State	Forward Data Frames?	Learn MACs Based on Received Frames?	Transitory or Stable State?
Blocking	No	No	Stable
Listening	No	No	Transitory
Learning	No	Yes	Transitory
Forwarding	Yes	Yes	Stable

Table 4-28 lists the various types of tagging used by Cisco and the types of interfaces on which they are used.

Table 4-28   *Frame Trunking/Tagging Protocols*

Tagging Method	Media
Inter-Switch Link (ISL)	Fast Ethernet
802.1Q	Fast Ethernet
802.10	FDDI
LAN Emulation (LANE)	ATM

Q&A

As mentioned in Chapter 1, "All About the Cisco Certified Network Associate Certification," the questions and scenarios in this book are more difficult than what you should experience on the actual exam. The questions do not attempt to cover more breadth or depth than the exam; however, they are designed to make sure that you know the answer. Rather than allowing you to derive the answer from clues hidden inside the question itself, the questions challenge your understanding and recall of the subject. Questions from the "Do I Know This Already?" quiz from the beginning of the chapter are repeated here to ensure that you have mastered the chapter's topic areas. Hopefully, these questions will help limit the number of exam questions on which you narrow your choices to two options and then guess.

The answers to these questions can be found in Appendix A, on page 718.

  1 What do the letters MAC stand for? What other terms have you heard to describe the same or similar concept?

  2 Name two benefits of LAN segmentation using transparent bridges.

  3 What routing protocol does a transparent bridge use to learn about Layer 3 addressing groupings?

  4 What settings are examined by a bridge or switch to determine which should be elected as root of the Spanning Tree?

  5 Define the term *VLAN*.

  6 Assume that a building has 100 devices attached to the same Ethernet. These users then are migrated onto two separate shared Ethernet segments, each with 50 devices, with a transparent bridge in between. List two benefits that would be derived for a typical user.

  7 What standards body owns the process of ensuring unique MAC addresses worldwide?

  8 Assume that a building has 100 devices attached to the same Ethernet. These devices are migrated to two different shared Ethernet segments, each with 50 devices. The two segments are connected to a Cisco LAN switch to allow communication between the two sets of users. List two benefits that would be derived for a typical user.

  9 Name two of the methods of internal switching on typical switches today. Which provides less latency for an individual frame?

 10 What is the distance limitation of 10BaseT? 100BaseTX?

 11 Describe how a transparent bridge decides whether it should forward a frame, and tell how it chooses the interface out which to forward the frame.

 12 How fast is Fast Ethernet?

 13 Describe the benefit of the Spanning-Tree Protocol as used by transparent bridges and switches.

14 If a switch hears three different configuration BPDUs from three different neighbors on three different interfaces, and if all three specify that Bridge 1 is the root, how does the switch choose which interface is its root port?

15 How does a transparent bridge build its address table?

16 How many bytes long is a MAC address?

17 Assume that a building has 100 devices attached to the same Ethernet. These users then are migrated onto two separate Ethernet segments, each with 50 devices and separated by a router. List two benefits that would be derived for a typical user.

18 Does a bridge/switch examine just the incoming frame's source MAC, destination MAC, or both? Why does it examine the one(s) it examines?

19 Define the term *collision domain*.

20 When a bridge or switch using Spanning-Tree Protocol first initializes, who does it assert should be the root of the tree?

21 Name the three reasons why a port is placed in forwarding state as a result of Spanning Tree.

22 Define the difference between broadcast and multicast MAC addresses.

23 Excluding the preamble and starting delimiter fields, but including all other Ethernet headers and trailers, what is the maximum number of bytes in an Ethernet frame?

24 Define the term *broadcast domain*.

25 Describe the benefits of creating three VLANs of 25 ports each, versus a single VLAN of 75 ports, in each case using a single switch. Assume that all ports are switched ports (each port is a different collision domain).

26 If two Cisco LAN switches are connected using Fast Ethernet, what VLAN trunking protocols could be used? If only one VLAN spanned both switches, is a VLAN trunking protocol needed?

27 Explain the function of the loopback and collision detection features of an Ethernet NIC in relation to half-duplex and full-duplex operation.

28 Name the three interface states that the Spanning-Tree Protocol uses, other than forwarding. Which of these states is transitory?

29 What are the two reasons that a nonroot bridge/switch places a port in forwarding state?

30 Can the root bridge/switch ports be placed in blocking state?

31 How many IP addresses must be configured for network management on a Cisco Catalyst 1900 switch if eight ports are to be used and with three VLANs?

32 What command on a 1900 series switch would cause the switch to block frames destined to 0200.7777.7777, entering interface 0/5, from going out port 0/6?

33 What Catalyst 1900 switch command displays the version of IOS running in the switch?

34 What does the Catalyst 1900 switch command **address violation disable** do?

35 What command erases the startup config in a Catalyst 1900 switch?

36 Configuration is added to the running configuration in RAM when commands are typed in Catalyst 1900 configuration mode. What causes these commands to be saved into NVRAM?

37 How do EXEC and configuration commands refer to the two Fast Ethernet ports on a Catalyst 1912 switch?

38 What Catalyst 1900 switch command displays the switching table?

39 What does VTP do, and what does the abbreviation stand for?

40 Name the three VTP modes. Which of these does not allow VLANs to be added or modified?

41 What Catalyst 1900 switch command assigns a port to a particular VLAN?

42 What Catalyst 1900 switch command creates VLAN 10 and assigns it a name of bigbadvlan?

43 What Catalyst 1900 switch command lists the details about VLAN number 10?

44 What Catalyst 1900 switch command configures ISL trunking on fastethernet port 26 so that as long as the switch port on the other end of the trunk is not disabled (off) or configured to not negotiate to become a trunk, the trunk will definitely be placed in trunking mode?

45 What type of VTP mode allows a switch to create VTP advertisements?

This chapter covers the following topics that you will need to master as a CCNA:

- **TCP/IP Protocols** The TCP/IP protocol suite is very important in networks today. This section covers several portions of the protocol suite, including TCP, UDP, ARP, ICMP, FTP, and TFTP.

- **IP Addressing and Subnetting** IP addressing is absolutely the most important topic on the CCNA exam. This section takes a detailed look at IP addressing and outlines five different types of questions the CCNA exam uses to test your knowledge.

- **IP Configuration** This section covers the configuration commands required for IP addressing and name resolution on a Cisco router.

- **IPX Addressing and Routing** The Novell NetWare protocol suite is the other major protocol suite covered in detail on the CCNA exam. This section covers IPX addressing and routing and also discusses the concepts and parameters used for the varied IPX encapsulation options.

- **IPX Configuration** This section covers the IOS commands used for configuration of IPX features.

CHAPTER 5

Network Protocols

TCP/IP is the most important protocol covered on the CCNA exam and is the protocol used most often in networks today. This chapter covers the TCP/IP protocols as well as IP addressing and subnetting. Cisco expects CCNAs not just to know IP addressing and routing, but also to know the concepts behind many other TCP/IP protocols. In addition, CCNAs should be able to easily recall the commands used to examine the details of IP processing in a router. Of course, Cisco also requires you to continually prove your understanding of IP subnetting on the CCNA exam and on almost all other Cisco exams.

This chapter also covers Novell's NetWare protocols. NetWare protocols have been well established and widely implemented for more than a decade. Very few changes that affect the router's role in forwarding NetWare traffic have been made in the last four years. Routing is straightforward; if you understand IP routing, then you likely will find IPX routing easy to grasp. Of course, this book also assumes that you have completed the ICND course or have logged equivalent experience, so the text is written under the assumption that NetWare protocols are not new to you. This chapter briefly reviews the main concepts, clarifies the trickiest details, and helps you refine your retention and recall with questions and scenarios.

How to Best Use This Chapter

By taking the following steps, you can make better use of your study time:

- Keep your notes and the answers for all your work with this book in one place, for easy reference.

- Take the "Do I Know This Already?" quiz, and write down your answers. Studies show that retention is significantly increased through writing down facts and concepts, even if you never look at the information again.

- Use the diagram in Figure 5-1 to guide you to the next step.

Figure 5-1 *How to Use This Chapter*

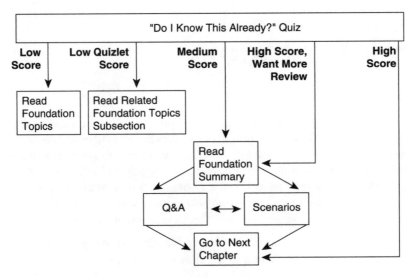

"Do I Know This Already?" Quiz

The purpose of the "Do I Know This Already?" quiz is to help you decide what parts of this chapter to use. If you already intend to read the entire chapter, you do not necessarily need to answer these questions now.

This 16-question quiz helps you determine how to spend your limited study time. The quiz is sectioned into four smaller four-question "quizlets," which correspond to the four major headings in the chapter. Figure 5-1 outlines suggestions on how to spend your time in this chapter. Use Table 5-1 to record your score.

Table 5-1 *Scoresheet for Quiz and Quizlets*

Quizlet Number	Foundation Topics Section Covering These Questions	Questions	Score
1	TCP/IP Protocols	1 to 4	
2	IP Addressing and Subnetting	5 to 8	
3	IP Configuration	9 to 12	
4	IPX Addressing and Routing IPX Configuration	13 to 16	
All questions		1 to 16	

1 What do TCP, UDP, IP, and ICMP stand for? Which protocol is considered to be
Layer 3-equivalent when comparing TCP/IP to the OSI protocols?

_____

_____

_____

2 Describe how TCP performs error recovery. What role do the routers play?

_____

_____

_____

3 Does FTP or TFTP perform error recovery? If so, describe the basics of how error
recovery is performed.

_____

_____

_____

4 How many TCP segments are exchanged to establish a TCP connection? How many
are required to terminate a TCP connection?

_____

_____

_____

5 Given the IP address 134.141.7.11 and the mask 255.255.255.0, what is the subnet
number?

_____

_____

_____

6 Given the IP address 134.141.7.11 and the mask 255.255.255.0, what is the subnet broadcast address?

_____

_____

_____

7 Given the IP address 200.1.1.130 and the mask 255.255.255.224, what are the assignable IP addresses in this subnet?

_____

_____

_____

8 Given the IP address 220.8.7.100 and the mask 255.255.255.240, what are all the subnet numbers if the same (static) mask is used for all subnets in this network?

_____

_____

_____

9 Create a minimal configuration enabling IP on each interface on a 2501 router (two serial, one Ethernet). The NIC assigned you network 8.0.0.0. Your boss says that you need, at most, 200 hosts per subnet. You decide against using VLSM. Your boss says to plan your subnets so that you can have as many subnets as possible, rather than allow for larger subnets later. You decide to start with the lowest numerical values for the subnet number you will use. Assume that point-to-point serial links will be attached to this router and that RIP is the routing protocol.

_____

_____

_____

10 Describe the question and possible responses in setup mode when a router wants to know the mask used on an interface. How can the router derive the correct mask from the information supplied by the user?

_____

_____

_____

11 Define the purpose of the **trace** command. What type of messages does it send, and what type of ICMP messages does it receive?

_____

_____

_____

12 What causes the output from an IOS **ping** command to display "UUUUU?"

_____

_____

_____

13 How many bytes comprise an IPX address?

_____

_____

_____

14 Give an example of an IPX network mask used when subnetting.

_____

_____

_____

15 Create a configuration enabling IPX on each interface, with RIP and SAP enabled on each as well, for a 2501 (two serial, one Ethernet) router. Use networks 100, 200, and 300 for interfaces S0, S1, and E0, respectively. Choose any node values.

_____

_____

_____

16 What **show** command lists the IPX address(es) of interfaces in a Cisco router?

_____

_____

_____

The answers to this quiz are found in Appendix A, "Answers to the 'Do I Know This Already?' Quizzes and Q&A Sections," on page 724. The suggested choices for your next step are as follows:

- **8 or less overall score**—Read the entire chapter. This includes the "Foundation Topics" and "Foundation Summary" sections, the Q&A section, and the scenarios at the end of the chapter.

- **2 or less on any quizlet**—Review the subsection(s) of the "Foundation Topics" part of this chapter, based on Table 5-1. Then move into the "Foundation Summary" section, the Q&A section, and the scenarios at the end of the chapter.

- **9 to 12 overall score**—Begin with the "Foundation Summary" section, and then go to the Q&A section and the scenarios at the end of the chapter.

- **13 or more overall score**—If you want more review on these topics, skip to the "Foundation Summary" section, and then go to the Q&A section and the scenarios at the end of the chapter. Otherwise, move to the next chapter.

Foundation Topics

TCP/IP Protocols

CCNAs work with multiple protocols on a daily basis; none of these is more important than TCP/IP. This section examines the TCP, UDP, ICMP, and ARP protocols in detail. TCP and UDP are the two transport layer (Layer 4) protocols most often used by applications in a TCP/IP network. ICMP and ARP are actually parts of the network layer (Layer 3) of TCP/IP and are used in conjunction with IP. As you'll see on the exam, IP addressing is something that all CCNAs must master to confidently pass the exam. Due to the importance of IP, IP addressing will be covered in great detail in the next section of this chapter.

Transmission Control Protocol

One common feature of routing is to discard packets for a variety of reasons. For instance, no route might match the packet, or there may not be enough buffer space in the router to store the packet until the next link is available. Layer 3 protocols do not typically provide for retransmission; a typical commentary is, "That's done by some higher-layer protocol."

To pass the CCNA exam, you must understand how one popular "higher-layer" protocol does error recovery—namely, the Transmission Control Protocol (TCP). Defined in RFC 793, TCP performs error recovery as well as other features, including these:

- Data transfer
- Multiplexing
- Error recovery (reliability)
- Flow control using windowing
- Connection establishment and termination

TCP accomplishes these goals via mechanisms at the endpoint computers. TCP relies on IP for end-to-end deliveries of the data, including routing issues. In other words, TCP performs only part of the functions necessary to deliver the data between applications.

Figure 5-2 shows the fields in the TCP header. Not all the fields will be described in this text, but several fields will be referred to in this section. The Internetworking Technologies Multimedia (ITM) CD, which is a suggested prerequisite for the exam, lists the fields with a brief explanation, as does the Cisco Press book on which ITM is based: *Internetworking Technologies Handbook*.

Figure 5-2   *TCP Header Fields*

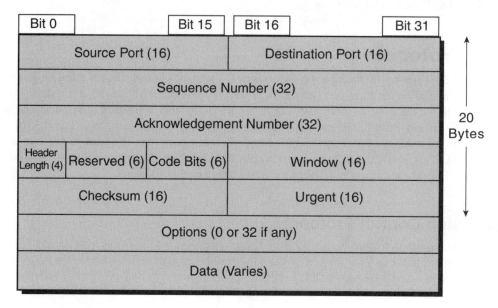

Ordered Data Transfer

As with other functions in any protocol stack, TCP provides service for the next-higher layer. The TCP/IP protocol stack has only four layers, so TCP's next-higher layer is the application layer. Therefore, TCP data transfer implies delivering data from one application to another. (The TCP/IP application layer performs functions similar to the upper three layers of the OSI model.) Applications use TCP services by issuing programmatic calls to TCP, supplying the data to be sent, the destination IP address, and a port number that identifies the application that should receive the data. The port number, along with the destination IP address and the name of the transport layer protocol (TCP), form a socket.

TCP accomplishes data transfer by establishing a connection between a socket on each of the endpoint computers. *Applications use TCP services by opening a socket; TCP manages the delivery of the data to the other socket.* A socket source/destination pair uniquely identifies a relationship between two applications in a network. TCP manages the ordered transfer of data between these two sockets, using IP services to deliver the data.

Multiplexing

In this context, multiplexing refers to the choices made upon receipt of data. TCP's multiplexing task is to decide which application layer process to give the data to, after the data is received. For example, in Figure 5-3, Larry is a multiuser system in which two users have telnetted to Curly. The socket used by the Telnet server on Curly consists of an IP address, the transport layer protocol in use, and a port number—in this case, 10.1.1.3, TCP, 23. Because data coming from both Telnet clients is sent to that socket, Curly cannot distinguish which client has sent data to the Telnet server based on only Curly's socket. For the Telnet server to know which connection the data is coming over, the combination of the socket at the server and the socket at the client is used to uniquely identify connection. For example, Client 1 uses socket 10.1.1.1, TCP, 1027; Client 2 uses socket 10.1.1.1, TCP, 1028. Now Curly can distinguish between the two clients. So, TCP uses the socket connection between the two sockets to perform multiplexing.

Figure 5-3   *Connections Between Sockets*

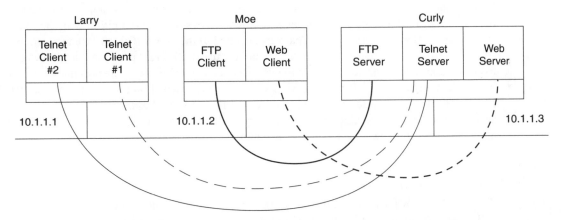

Port numbers are a vital part of the socket concept. Well-known port numbers are used by servers; other port numbers are used by clients. Applications that provide a service, such as FTP, Telnet, and Web servers, open a socket using a well-known port and listen for connection requests. Because these connection requests from clients are required to include both the source and the destination port numbers, the port numbers used by the servers must be well known. Therefore, each server has a hard-coded well-known port number, as defined in the well-known numbers RFC. On client machines, where the requests originate, any unused port number can be allocated. The result is that each client on the same host uses a different port number, but a server uses the same port number for all connections. For example, 100 Telnet clients on the same host would each use a different port number, but the Telnet server, with 100 clients connected to it, would have only one socket and therefore only one port number. The combination of source and destination sockets allows all participating hosts to distinguish the source and destination of the data. (Look to www.rfc-editor.org to find RFCs such as the well-known numbers RFC 1700.)

Table 5-2 summarizes the socket connections as shown in Figure 5-3.

Table 5-2   *TCP Connections from Figure 5-3*

Connection	Client Socket	Server Socket
Telnet client 1 to server	(10.1.1.1, TCP, 1027)	(10.1.1.3, TCP, 23)
Telnet client 2 to server	(10.1.1.1, TCP, 1028)	(10.1.1.3, TCP, 23)
FTP client to FTP server	(10.1.1.2, TCP, 1027)	(10.1.1.3, TCP, 21)
Web client to Web server	(10.1.1.2, TCP, 1029)	(10.1.1.3, TCP, 80)

In this context, multiplexing is defined as the process of choosing which application receives the data after it is received by lower-layer protocols. Consider that definition with the four socket connections in Table 5-2, for packets destined to the server (Curly). All destination socket information is for 10.1.1.3, with TCP, but the use of different port numbers allows Curly to choose the correct service to which to pass the data. Also notice that the port numbers do not have to be unique. The FTP client on Moe and the Telnet Client 1 on Larry both use port 1027, but their sockets are unique because each uses a different IP address. Also, when the Telnet servers send data back to Clients 1 and 2, Larry knows how to multiplex to the correct client application because each uses a unique port number on Larry.

Error Recovery (Reliability)

Reliable data transfer is one of the most important and most typically remembered features of TCP. To accomplish reliability, data bytes are numbered using the sequence and acknowledgment fields in the TCP header. TCP achieves reliability in both directions, using the sequence number field of one direction combined with the acknowledgment field in the opposite direction. Figure 5-4 shows the basic operation.

Figure 5-4   *TCP Acknowledgment Without Errors*

In Figure 5-4, the acknowledgment field in the TCP header sent by the Web server implies the next byte to be received; this is called *forward acknowledgment*. The sequence number reflects the number of the first byte in the segment. In this case, each TCP segment is 1000 bytes in length; the sequence and acknowledgment fields count the number of bytes.

Figure 5-5 depicts the same scenario, but the second TCP segment was lost or in error. The Web server's reply has an ACK field equal to 2000, implying that the Web server is expecting byte number 2000 next. The TCP function at the Web client could then recover lost data by resending the second TCP segment. The TCP protocol allows for resending just that segment and then waits, hoping that the Web server will reply with an acknowledgment that equals 4000. TCP also allows the resending host to begin with a segment in error and resend all TCP segments.

Figure 5-5   *TCP Acknowledgment with Errors*

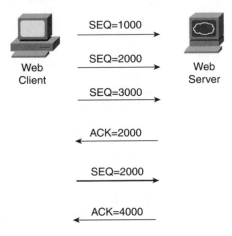

Flow Control Using Windowing

TCP implements flow control by taking advantage of the sequence and acknowledgment fields in the TCP header, along with another field called the *window* field. This window field implies the maximum number of unacknowledged bytes outstanding at any instant in time. The window starts small and then grows until errors occur. The window then "slides" up and down based on network performance. When the window is full, the sender will not send, which controls the flow of data. Figure 5-6 shows windowing, with a current window size of 3000. Each TCP segment has 1000 bytes of data.

Notice that the Web client must wait after sending the third segment because the window is exhausted. When the acknowledgment has been received, another window can be sent. Because there have been no errors, the Web server grants a larger window to the client, so now 4000 bytes can be sent before an acknowledgment is received by the client. In other words, the window field is used by the receiver to tell the sender how much data it can send before the next acknowledgment. As with other TCP features, windowing is symmetrical—both sides send and receive, and in each case the receiver grants a window to the sender using the window field.

Figure 5-6   *TCP Windowing*

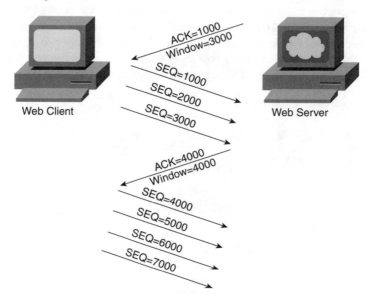

Windowing does not require that the sender stop sending in all cases, as is shown in Figure 5-6. If an acknowledgment is received before the window is exhausted, the sender continues to send data until the current window is exhausted. With no errors or congestion, the sender can send continually after the initially small window has been increased.

Connection Establishment and Termination

Connection establishment is the last TCP function reviewed in this section, but it occurs before any of the other TCP features can begin their work. Connection establishment refers to the process of initializing sequence and acknowledgment fields and agreeing to the port numbers used. Figure 5-7 shows an example of connection establishment flow.

Figure 5-7   *TCP Connection Establishment*

This three-way connection establishment flow must complete before data transfer can begin. The connection exists between the two sockets, although there is no single socket field in the TCP header. Of the three parts of a socket, the IP addresses are implied based on the source and destination IP addresses in the IP header. TCP is implied because a TCP header is in use, as implied by the protocol field value in the IP header. Therefore, the only parts of the socket that need to be encoded in the TCP header are the port numbers.

Two single-bit portions of the flags field of the TCP header are used to signal the three-step process for connection establishment. Called the SYN and ACK flags, these bits have a particularly interesting meaning. SYN means, "Synchronize the sequence numbers," which is one necessary component in initialization for TCP. The ACK field means "the acknowledgment field is valid in this header." Until the sequence numbers are initialized, the acknowledgment field cannot be very useful. Also notice that in the initial flow in Figure 5-7, no acknowledgment number is shown—this is because that number is not valid yet. Because the ACK field must be present in all the ensuing segments, the ACK bit will continue to be set until the connection is terminated.

The sequence and acknowledgment number fields are initialized to any number that fits into the 4-byte fields; the actual values shown in Figure 5-7 are simply example values. The initialization flows are each considered to have a single byte of data, as reflected in the acknowledgment number fields in the example.

Figure 5-8 shows TCP connection termination.

Figure 5-8   *TCP Connection Termination*

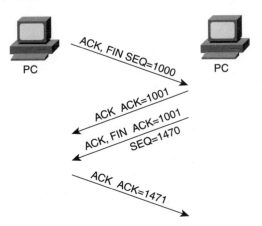

This four-way termination sequence is straightforward and uses an additional flag, called the FIN bit. (FIN is short for "finished," as you might guess.) One interesting note: Before the device receiving the first FIN segment sends the third flow in the sequence, TCP notifies the application that the connection is coming down. TCP waits on an acknowledgment from the application before sending the segment. That's why the second flow is required: To acknowledge the first so that the side taking down the connection doesn't start resending the first TCP segment.

TCP Function Summary

Table 5-3 summarizes TCP functions.

Table 5-3   *TCP Function Summary*

Function	Description
Data transfer	Continuous stream of ordered data.
Multiplexing	Function that allows receiving hosts to decide the correct application for which the data is destined, based on the port number.
Error recovery (reliability)	Process of numbering and acknowledging data with sequence and acknowledgment header fields.
Flow control using windowing	Process that uses window sizes to protect buffer space and routing devices.
Connection establishment and termination	Process used to initialize port numbers and sequence and acknowledgement fields.

User Datagram Protocol

The CCNA exam requires that you be able to compare and contrast the User Datagram Protocol (UDP) with TCP. UDP was designed to provide a service for applications in which messages could be exchanged. Unlike TCP, UDP provides no reliability, no windowing, and no function to ensure that the data is received in the order in which it was sent. However, UDP provides some functions of TCP, such as data transfer and multiplexing, and it does so with fewer bytes of overhead in the UDP header.

UDP multiplexes use port numbers in an identical fashion to TCP. The only difference in UDP (compared to TCP) sockets is that instead of designating TCP as the transport protocol, the transport protocol is UDP. An application could open identical port numbers on the same host but use TCP in one case and UDP in the other. This is not typical but certainly is allowed. Servers that allow use of TCP and UDP reserve the use of the same port number for each, as shown in the assigned numbers RFC (currently RFC 1700—www.isi.edu/in-notes/rfc1700.txt).

UDP data transfer differs from TCP in that no reordering or recovery is accomplished. Applications using UDP are tolerant of the lost data, or they have some application mechanism to recover lost data. For example, Domain Name System (DNS) requests use UDP because the user will retry an operation if the DNS resolution fails. The Network File System (NFS) performs recovery with application layer code, so UDP features are acceptable to NFS.

Table 5-4 contrasts typical transport layer functions as performed (or not performed) by UDP or TCP.

Table 5-4   *TCP and UDP Functional Comparison*

Function	Description (TCP)	Description (UDP)
Data transfer	Continuous stream of ordered data	Message (datagram) delivery
Multiplexing	Receiving hosts decide the correct application for which the data is destined, based on port number	Receiving hosts decide the correct application for which the data is destined, based on port number
Reliable transfer	Acknowledgment of data using the sequence and acknowledgment fields in the TCP header	Not a feature of UDP
Flow control	Process used to protect buffer space and routing devices	Not a feature of UDP
Connections	Process used to initialize port numbers and other TCP header fields	UDP is connectionless

Figure 5-9 shows TCP and UDP header formats. Note the existence of both source and destination port number fields in the TCP and UDP headers, but the absence of sequence acknowledgment fields in the UDP header, as shown in Figure 5-9. UDP does not need these fields because it makes no attempt to number the data for acknowledgments or resequencing.

Figure 5-9   *TCP and UDP Headers*

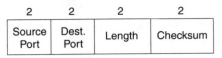

2	2	4	4	4 bits	6 bits	6 bits	2	2	2	3	1
Source Port	Dest. Port	Sequence Number	Ack. Number	Offset	Reserved	Flags	Window size	Checksum	Urgent	Options	PAD

TCP Header

2	2	2	2
Source Port	Dest. Port	Length	Checksum

UDP Header

* Unless specified, lengths shown
  are the numbers of bytes

UDP gains some advantages over TCP by not using the sequence and acknowledgment fields. The most obvious advantage of UDP over TCP is that there are fewer bytes of overhead. Not as obvious is the fact that UDP does not require waiting on acknowledgments or holding the data in memory until it is acknowledged. This means that UDP applications are not artificially slowed by the acknowledgment process, and memory is freed more quickly.

Address Resolution Protocol

One common problem that CCNAs deal with on a regular basis is this: Given some Layer 3 address, what is its corresponding Layer 2 address? Address Resolution Protocol (ARP) is the process by which this question is answered for an IP host on a LAN.

ARP is needed because to send an IP packet across some LAN, the data link header and trailer (which encapsulate the packet) must first be created. The source MAC address in this new header is known, but the destination MAC is not known in advance; ARP is the method IP uses to discover the destination MAC address. Figure 5-10 shows an example of the ARP process.

Figure 5-10   *The ARP Process*

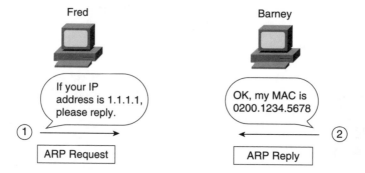

The ARP reply includes Barney's MAC address in this example. An ARP cache holds the ARP entries (IP address and MAC address in each entry) for each interface. If packets are flowing in and out the interface from and to the IP address, the cache entry stays fresh. After a period of disuse for an entry, the entry in the table is removed. Any need to send packets to that IP address out that same interface after the ARP entry times out will require another ARP exchange.

From an architecture perspective, ARP is a Layer 3 function and is defined in RFC 826. From a programming perspective, ARP calls the LAN data link layer code, which is indicative of a Layer 3 protocol. Note the location of ARP in the architectural model in Figure 5-11.

Figure 5-11 *TCP/IP Architectural Model*

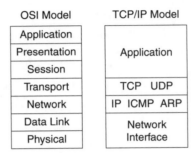

Internet Control Message Protocol

The CCNA exam requires that you know both the general concepts and several specifics about the Internet Control Message Protocol (ICMP). *Control Message* is the most descriptive part of the name—ICMP helps control and manage the work of IP and therefore is considered to be part of TCP/IP's network layer. RFC 792 defines ICMP and includes the following excerpt, which describes the protocol well:

> Occasionally a gateway or destination host will communicate with a source host, for example, to report an error in datagram processing. For such purposes this protocol, the Internet Control Message Protocol (ICMP), is used. ICMP uses the basic support of IP as if it were a higher level protocol; however, ICMP is actually an integral part of IP, and must be implemented by every IP module.

Several ICMP messages are in use in even the smallest IP network, so Cisco requires CCNAs to be familiar with several of these messages. Table 5-5 lists several ICMP messages, with the ones most likely to be on the exam noted with an asterisk. Not surprisingly, these are the same messages used most often. The Destination Unreachable, Time Exceeded, and Redirect messages will be described in more detail following Table 5-5.

Table 5-5 *ICMP Message Types*

Message	Purpose
*Destination Unreachable	This tells the source host that there is a problem delivering a packet.
*Time Exceeded	The time it takes a packet to be delivered has become too long; the packet has been discarded.
Source Quench	The source is sending data faster than it can be forwarded; this message requests that the sender slow down.

continues

Table 5-5   *ICMP Message Types (Continued)*

Message	Purpose
*Redirect	The router sending this message has received some packet for which another router would have had a better route; the message tells the sender to use the better router.
*Echo	This is used by the **ping** command to verify connectivity.
Parameter Problem	This is used to identify a parameter that is incorrect.
Timestamp	This is used to measure roundtrip time to particular hosts.
Address Mask Request/Reply	This is used to inquire about and learn the correct subnet mask to be used.
Router Advertisement and Selection	This is used to allow hosts to dynamically learn the IP addresses of the routers attached to the subnet.

*   More likely to be on the CCNA exam.

Each ICMP message contains a Type field and a Code field, as shown in Figure 5-12. The Type field implies the message types from Table 5-5. The Code field implies a subtype; several subtypes will be shown in the following examples.

Figure 5-12   *ICMP Header Formats*

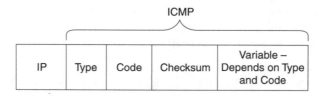

Destination Unreachable ICMP Message

The five separate *unreachable* functions (codes) are accomplished using this single ICMP unreachable message. All five code types pertain directly to some IP, TCP, or UDP feature and are better described by using Figure 5-13 as an example network.

Assume that Fred is trying to connect to the Web server, which uses TCP as the transport layer protocol. Three of the ICMP unreachable codes would possibly be used by Routers A and B. The other two codes would be used by the Web server. These ICMP codes would be sent to Fred as a result of the packet originally sent by Fred.

A code meaning "Network Unreachable" would be used by Router A if Router A did not have a route to 10.1.2.0/24. The message would be sent by Router A to Fred, in response to Fred's packet destined to 10.1.2.14.

Figure 5-13   *Sample Network for Discussing ICMP Unreachable*

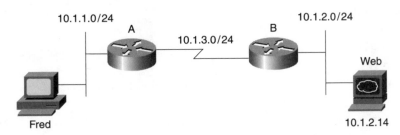

Host Unreachable is a code used if that single host is unavailable. If Router A had a route to 10.1.2.0/24, the packet would get to Router B. However, if the Web server is down, Router B will not get an ARP reply from Web; Router B will send an unreachable back to Fred, with the Host Unreachable code field.

Can't Fragment is the third unreachable code that is likely to be sent by a router. If Router A or Router B needed to fragment the packet, but the Do Not Fragment bit was set in the IP header, the router would send an unreachable back to Fred with the Can't Fragment value in the code field.

If the packet successfully arrives at the Web server, two other unreachable codes are possible. One implies that the protocol above IP, typically TCP or UDP, is not running on that host. This is highly unlikely today. If true, this host would reply with an unreachable with the code field value implying Protocol Unavailable. The final code field value is more likely today. If the server was up but the Web server software was not running, the TCP/IP code on the server would reply with an unreachable with the code field implying Port Unavailable. In other words, the Web server software has not opened a listening socket connection using the Web server well-known port of 80.

Cisco IOS documentation and configuration commands sometimes treat each different code value as a separate message. For example, the documentation lists **ping** responses, stating something like an "ICMP host unreachable" message. There is no such message, but there is a "destination unreachable" with the Host Unreachable code set. The exam probably will not expect you to know that there is no Host Unreachable message, though.

Table 5-6 summarizes the ICMP unreachable codes.

Table 5-6   *ICMP Unreachable Codes*

Unreachable Code	When Used	Typically Sent By...
Network Unreachable	There is no match in a routing table for the destination of the packet.	Router
Host Unreachable	The packet can be routed to a router connected to the destination subnet, but the host is not responding.	Router

continues

Table 5-6   *ICMP Unreachable Codes (Continued)*

Unreachable Code	When Used	Typically Sent By...
Can't Fragment	The packet has the Don't Fragment bit set, and a router must fragment to forward the packet.	Router
Protocol Unreachable	The packet is delivered to the destination host, but the transport layer protocol is not available on that host.	Endpoint host
Port Unreachable	The packet is delivered to the destination host, but the destination port has not been opened by an application.	Endpoint host

Time Exceeded ICMP Message

The CCNA exam requires that you understand how routing protocols avoid creating routing loops. However, if a loop occurs, the Time To Live (TTL) field in the IP header is used to time out looping packets so that the packets do not loop forever.

The Time Exceeded ICMP message is used in conjunction with the IP TTL header field. One of the two codes for Time Exceeded will be described here—namely, the Time To Live (TTL) code option.

An analogy for Time Exceeded may help. In the 1970s, a science fiction movie called *Logan's Run* was created. When they turned 30, citizens on this planet participated in a religious ceremony in which they were cremated; the reason was for population control. Logan turned 30 and decided that he did not like the rules—so he ran.

The TTL field in the IP header is like the counter used for citizens in *Logan's Run*. When the counter expires, so does the packet. Each router decrements the TTL field in each packet header. (The router does not actually calculate a time that should be decremented; it just decrements by 1.) However, if TTL decrements to 0, the packet is discarded. (For those who remember *Logan's Run*, you can think of TTL as the Logan's Run field.)

The TTL exceeded option is used in a message generated by the router that discards the packet when TTL expires. The router sends the "ICMP Time Exceeded, code Time To Live Exceeded" message to the originator of the discarded packet. TTL is used to ensure that packets that are looping do not do so forever. TTL exceeded lets the originating host know that a routing loop may be occurring.

The **trace** command uses the "TTL exceeded" message to its advantage. By purposefully sending IP packets (with a UDP transport layer) with TTL set to 1, an "ICMP Time Exceeded" message is returned by the first router in the route. That's because that router decrements TTL to 0, causing it to discard the packet, and also sends the "TTL exceeded" message. The **trace** command learns the IP address of the first router by receiving the "TTL exceeded" message from that router. (The **trace** command actually sends three successive packets with TTL=1.) Another set of three IP packets, this time with TTL=2, is sent by the **trace** command. The first router forwards these packets, but the second router discards it and sends a "TTL exceeded" message as well. Eventually, a set of packets is delivered to the destination, which sends back an "ICMP port unreachable" message. The original packets sent by the host **trace** command use a destination port number that is very unlikely to be used so that the destination host will return the "port unreachable" message. The "ICMP port unreachable" message signifies that the packets reached the true destination host, without having TTL exceeded. Example 5-1 shows a **trace** command from a router (Router A) that is one hop away from a host; another router (Router B) has **debug ip icmp** enabled, which shows the resulting TTL exceeded messages. The commands were performed in the network in Figure 5-13.

Example 5-1   *ICMP* **debug** *on Router B, When Running* **trace** *Command on Router A*

```
RouterA#trace 10.1.2.14

Type escape sequence to abort.
Tracing the route to 10.1.2.14

  1 10.1.3.253 8 msec 4 msec 4 msec
  2 10.1.2.14 12 msec 8 msec 4 msec
RouterA#
```
```
RouterB#
ICMP: time exceeded (time to live) sent to 10.1.3.251 (dest was 10.1.2.14)
ICMP: time exceeded (time to live) sent to 10.1.3.251 (dest was 10.1.2.14)
ICMP: time exceeded (time to live) sent to 10.1.3.251 (dest was 10.1.2.14)
```

Redirect ICMP Message

ICMP redirect messages provide a very important element in routed IP networks. Many hosts are preconfigured with a default router IP address. When sending packets destined to subnets other than the one to which they are directly connected, these hosts send the packets to their default router. If there is a better local router to which the host should send the packets, an ICMP redirect can be used to tell the host to send the packets to this different router.

For example, in Figure 5-14, the PC uses Router B as its default router. However, Router A's route to subnet 10.1.4.0 is a better route. (Assume use of mask 255.255.255.0 in each subnet in Figure 5-14.) The PC sends a packet to Router B (Step 1 in Figure 5-14). Router B then forwards the packet based on its own routing table (Step 2); that route points through A, which has a better route. Finally, Router B sends the ICMP redirect message to the PC (Step 3), telling it to forward future packets destined for 10.1.4.0 to Router A instead. Ironically, the host can ignore the redirect and keep sending the packets to Router B.

In summary, ICMP defines several message types and several subtypes, called codes. Popular use of terminology treats each differing code as a different message; the exam is likely to treat these codes as different messages as well, although it is unlikely that the level of granularity will be important toward getting the right answer. Pay particular attention to the messages denoted with asterisks in Table 5-5. Finally, RFC 792 is a short and straightforward RFC to read if you want more information.

Figure 5-14   *Example of an ICMP Redirect*

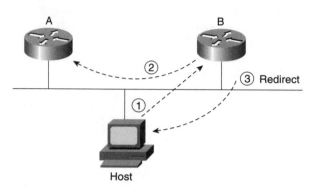

ICMP Echo Request and Echo Reply

The ICMP Echo and Echo Reply messages are sent and received by the **ping** command. In fact, when people say that they sent a ping packet, they really mean that they sent an ICMP Echo Request. These two messages are very much self-explanatory. The Echo Request simply means that the host to which it is addressed should reply to the packet. The Echo Reply is the ICMP message type that should be used in the reply. The Request includes some data, which can be specified by the **ping** command; whatever data is sent in the Echo Request is sent back in the Echo Reply.

The **ping** command itself supplies many creative ways to use Echo Requests and Replies. For instance, the **ping** command enables you to specify the length as well as the source and destination address, and it also enables you to set other fields in the IP header. Example 5-6, later in this chapter, shows a good example of the capabilities of the **ping** command.

FTP and TFTP

File Transfer Protocol (FTP) and Trivial File Transfer Protocol (TFTP) are two popularly used file transfer protocols in a typical IP network. Most users use FTP, whereas router and switch administrators use TFTP. Which is "better" depends partially on what is being done. A more important question may typically be, "Which is supported on the devices that need to transfer the file?" Given a choice today, most users will choose FTP because it has many more robust features. TFTP is a favorite of router administrators, however, because the IOS does not support FTP as an application.

FTP

FTP is a TCP-based application that has many options and features, including the capabilities to change directories, list files using wildcard characters, transfer multiple files with a single command, and use a variety of character sets or file formats. More important in this context is the basic operation of FTP. Figures 5-15 and 5-16 show a typical FTP connection—or, better stated, connections:

Figure 5-15   *FTP Control Connections*

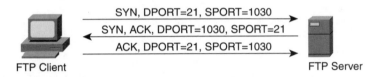

The connection shown in Figure 5-15 is called an *FTP control connection*. When a user (FTP client) asks to connect to an FTP server, a TCP connection is established to the FTP server's well-known port (21). The connection is established like any other TCP connection. The user is typically required to enter a user name and password, which the server uses to authenticate the files available to that user for read and write permissions. This security is based on the file security on the server's platform. Access to files on the client side is implied by the environment from which the client created the FTP connection; again, this is dependent on the operating system on the client platform. All the commands used to control the transfer of a file are sent across this connection—hence the name FTP control connection.

At this point, the user has a variety of commands available to enable settings for transfer, change directories, list files, and so forth. However whenever a **get** or a **put** command is entered (or **mget** or **mput**—m is for *multiple*) or the equivalent button is clicked, then a file is transferred. The data is transferred over a separate *TCP data connection*. Figure 5-16 outlines the FTP data connection process.

Figure 5-16   *FTP Data Connection*

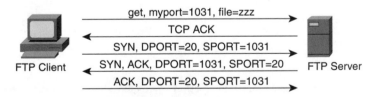

As shown in Figure 5-16, another TCP connection is established, this time to well-known port 20. Using this convention, a file can be transferred without getting in the way of the control connection. If many files are to be transferred rather than make a single control/data connection for each file, the control connection is made once. The environment is defined using the control connection, and these settings affect the functioning of the data connection. For instance, the default directory to use in future transfers can be defined using commands on the control connection, as well as the type of data (binary or ASCII). The control connection stays up until the user breaks it. While the control connection is up, a separate data connection is established for each file transfer.

An additional step helps prevent hackers from breaking in and transferring files, as shown in Figure 5-16. Rather than just creating a new connection, the client tells the server with an application layer message what port number will be used for the new connection. The server will not transfer the file (zzz, in this case) over any other data connection except the one to the correct socket—the one with the client's IP address, TCP, and the port number declared to the server (1031, in this case).

TFTP

Trivial File Transfer Protocol (TFTP) is a UDP-based application with very basic features. One of the reasons that such an application is needed (when the more robust FTP is available) is that TFTP takes little memory to load and takes little time to program. With the advent of extremely low-cost memory and processing, such advantages seem trivial. Practically speaking, if you intend to transfer files frequently from your PC, FTP is probably what you will use. However, to transfer files into and out of IOS-based routers and switches, Cisco supports TFTP, not FTP.

TFTP uses UDP, so there is no connection establishment and no error recovery by the transport layer. However, TFTP uses application layer recovery by embedding a small header between the UDP header and the data. This header includes codes—for instance, read, write, and acknowledgment—along with a numbering scheme that numbers 512-byte blocks of data. These block numbers are used to acknowledge receipt and resend the data. TFTP sends one block and waits on an acknowledgment before sending another block—essentially, the equivalent of a window size of 1.

Table 5-7 summarizes some features of TFTP and FTP.

Table 5-7   *Comparison of FTP and TFTP*

FTP	TFTP
Uses TCP	Uses UDP
Uses robust control commands	Uses simple control commands
Sends data over a separate TCP connection from control commands	Uses no connections, due to UDP
Requires more memory and programming effort	Requires less memory and programming effort
Is not supported as an application in IOS	Is supported as an application in IOS

IP Addressing and Subnetting

Probably no one reading this would be shocked to hear that IP addressing is one of the most important topics on the CCNA exam. A comfortable, confident understanding of IP addressing and subnetting is required for success on any Cisco certification. For CCNA, questions directly ask for your interpretation of an address, its network number, its subnet number, the other IP addresses in the same subnet, the broadcast address, and the other subnets that could be used if the same mask were in use. In other words, you had better know subnetting!

This section of the book provides two key functions. First, you will find an extensive review of IP addressing and subnetting. Second, this section takes a structured look at how to answer CCNA IP addressing questions. No other topic will be covered as extensively as IP addressing and subnetting on the exam. This section helps you prepare for answering those questions confidently and quickly.

IP Addressing Review

To pass the CCNA exam, you *must* have complete familiarity with the terminology used with IP addressing. This terminology can sometimes get in the way of a good understanding of IP addressing. Table 5-8 lists the IP terms used in the upcoming sections.

Table 5-8   *IP Addressing Terminology*

Term	Definition
IP address	32-bit number, usually written in dotted decimal form, that uniquely identifies an interface of some computer.
Host address	Another term for IP address.
Network	The concept of a group of hosts.
Network number	A 32-bit number, usually written in dotted decimal form, that represents a network. This number cannot be assigned as an IP address to an interface of some computer. The host portion of the network number has a value of all binary 0s.
Network address	Another name for network number.
Broadcast address	A 32-bit number, usually written in dotted decimal form, that is used to address all hosts in the network. The host portion of the broadcast address has a value of all binary 1s. Broadcast addresses cannot be assigned as an IP address.
Subnet	The concept of a group of hosts, which is a subdivision of a network.
Subnet number	A 32-bit number, usually written in dotted decimal form, that represents all hosts in a subnet. This number cannot be used as an IP address for some computer's interface.
Subnet address	Another term for subnet number.

continues

Table 5-8   *IP Addressing Terminology (Continued)*

Term	Definition
Subnetting	The process of subdividing networks into smaller subnets. This is jargon—for example, "Are you subnetting your network?"
Network mask	A 32-bit number, usually written in dotted decimal form. The mask is used by computers to calculate the network number of a given IP address by performing a Boolean AND of the address and mask. The mask also defines the number of host bits in an address.
Mask	A generic term for a mask, whether it is a default mask or a subnet mask.
Address mask	Another term for a mask.
Default Class A mask	The mask used for Class A networks when no subnetting is used. The value is 255.0.0.0.
Default Class B mask	The mask used for Class B networks when no subnetting is used. The value is 255.255.0.0.
Default Class C mask	The mask used for Class C networks when no subnetting is used. The value is 255.255.255.0.
Subnet mask	A non-default mask used when subnetting.
Network part or network field	Term used to describe the first part of an IP address. The network part is 8, 16, or 24 bits for Class A, B, and C networks, respectively.
Host part or host field	Term used to describe the last part of an IP address. The host part is 24, 16, or 8 bits for Class A, B, and C networks, respectively, when subnetting is not used. When subnetting, the size of the host part depends on the subnet mask chosen for that network.
Subnet part of subnet field	Term used to describe the middle part of an IP address. The subnet part is variable in size, based on how subnetting is implemented.

Classes of Networks

Class A, B, and C networks provide three network sizes. By definition, all addresses in the same network have the same numeric value network portion of the addresses. The rest of the address is called the host portion of the address. Individual addresses in the same network all have a different value in the host parts of the addresses but have identical values in the network part.

Class A networks have a 1-byte-long network part. That leaves 24 bits for the rest of the address, or the host part. That means that 2^{24} addresses are numerically possible in a Class A network. Similarly, Class B networks have a 2-byte-long network part, leaving 16 bits for the host portion of the address. So, 2^{16} possible addresses exist in a single Class B network. Finally, Class C networks have a 3-byte-long network part, leaving only 8 bits for the host part, which implies only 2^8 addresses in a Class C network. Table 5-9 summarizes the characteristics of Class A, B, and C networks.

Table 5-9   *Sizes of Network and Host Parts of IP Addresses with No Subnetting*

Any Network of This Class	Number of Network Bytes (Bits)	Number of Host Bytes (Bits)	Number of Addresses per Network*
A	1 (8)	3 (24)	2^{24} minus two special cases
B	2 (16)	2 (16)	2^{16} minus two special cases
C	3 (24)	1 (8)	2^8 minus two special cases

*   There are two reserved host addresses per network.

For example, Figure 5-17 shows a small network with addresses filled in. Network 8.0.0.0 is a Class A network; Network 130.4.0.0 is a Class B network; Network 199.1.1.0 is a Class C network.

Figure 5-17   *Sample Network Using Class A, B, and C Network Numbers*

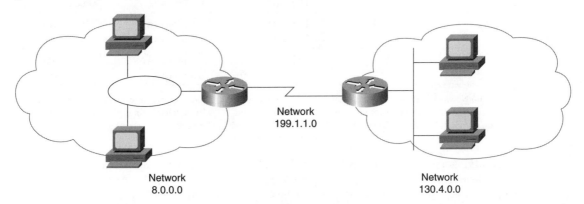

Network 199.1.1.0

Network 8.0.0.0

Network 130.4.0.0

Network numbers look like addresses (in dotted decimal format), but they are not assignable to any interface as an IP address. Conceptually, network numbers represent the group of all IP addresses in the network. Numerically, the network number is built with a nonzero value in the network part but with all 0s in the host part of the network number. Given the three examples from Figure 5-17, Table 5-10 provides a closer look at the numerical version of the three network numbers: 8.0.0.0, 199.1.1.0, and 130.4.0.0.

Table 5-10   *Example Network Numbers, Decimal and Binary*

Network Number	Binary Representation, with Host Part Bold
8.0.0.0	0000 1000 **0000 0000 0000 0000 0000 0000**
130.4.0.0	1000 0010 0000 0100 **0000 0000 0000 0000**
199.1.1.0	1100 0111 0000 0001 0000 0001 **0000 0000**

Many different Class A, B, and C networks exist. If connecting to the Internet without using a form of Address Translating Gateway (such as the Cisco PIX), then your firm must use registered, unique network numbers. To that end, the Network Information Center (NIC) assigns networks so that uniqueness is achieved. Table 5-11 summarizes the possible network numbers, the total number of each type, and the number of hosts in each Class A, B, and C network.

Table 5-11   *List of All Possible Valid Network Numbers**

Class	First Octet Range	Valid Network Numbers	Total Number of This Class of Network	Number of Hosts per Network
A	1 to 126	1.0.0.0 to 126.0.0.0	2^7 minus two special cases	2^{24} minus two special cases
B	128 to 191	128.1.0.0 to 191.254.0.0	2^{14} minus two special cases	2^{16} minus two special cases
C	192 to 223	192.0.1.0 to 223.255.254.0	2^{21} minus two special cases	2^8 minus two special cases

*   Valid Network Numbers column shows actual network numbers. There are several reserved cases. For example, network 0.0.0.0 (available for use as a broadcast address) and 127.0.0.0 (available for use as the loopback address) are reserved. Networks 128.0.0.0, 191.255.0.0, 192.0.0.0, and 223.255.255.0 are also reserved.

Classifying a network as Class A, B, or C should become an instantaneous process before you take the test. Memorize the ranges in the second column of Table 5-11. Also memorize the number of octets in the network part of Class A, B, and C addresses, as shown in Table 5-9.

Masks and IP Address Formats

One common task that CCNAs run into is the interpretation of a network or subnet mask. This mask is used for several purposes. One key purpose is to define the number of host bits in an address. This mask also is used by computers when calculating the network or subnet number of which that address is a member.

To fully appreciate what the mask is used for, you must understand the format of an IP address. Consider Figure 5-18, which shows the format of Class A, B, and C addresses when no subnetting is used.

Figure 5-18 *Address Formats, When No Subnetting Is Used*

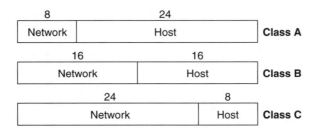

Notice that there are only two portions of the address—namely, the network part and the host part. The only variable is whether the address in question is in a Class A, B, or C network.

The default mask used with each class of network defines the number of host bits. The mask has binary 0 for each corresponding bit position in the address that is considered to be part of the host portion of the address. Similarly, it appears that the mask implies the size and position of the network part of the address; however, the network part is actually already implied by the class of network. Table 5-12 summarizes the default masks and reflects the sizes of the two parts of an IP address.

Table 5-12 *Class A, B, and C Networks—Network and Host Parts and Default Masks*

Class of Address	Size of Network Part of Address, in Bits	Size of Host Part of Address, in Bits	Default Mask for Each Class of Network
A	8	24	255.0.0.0
B	16	16	255.255.0.0
C	24	8	255.255.255.0

When subnetting, a third part of an IP address appears—namely, the subnet part of the address. This field is created by "stealing" bits from the host part of the address. Figure 5-19 shows the format of addresses when subnetting.

Three portions of the address now exist: network, subnet, and host. The network part size is determined by the class (A, B, or C). The host part is determined by the subnet mask in use—the number of bits of value 0 in the subnet mask define the number of host bits. The remaining bits define the size of the subnet part of the address. For instance, a mask of 255.255.255.240, used with a Class C network, implies four host bits. As shown in Figure 5-19, a Class C network has 24 network bits. (The mask can be more easily converted to decimal using the table in Appendix B.) The mask has four binary 0s at the end, implying 4 host bits.

Figure 5-19   *Address Formats, When Subnetting Is Used*

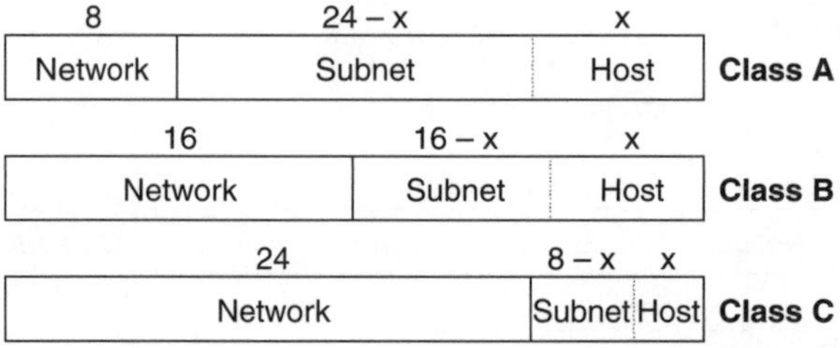

The number of hosts per network or subnet is defined by the number of host bits; $2^{hostbits}$ minus two special reserved cases, is the number of assignable IP addresses in a network or subnet. Similarly, the number of subnets of a network, assuming that the same mask is used on all subnets, is defined by the number of subnet bits; $2^{subnetbits}$ is the number of usable IP subnets of that network. Two special cases, the "zero subnet" and "broadcast subnet," were reserved in years past but are now usable.

Some definitions help summarize the concepts behind the address formats:

- Two unique IP addresses in the same network have identical values in the network part of their address and have different values in their host parts.

- Two unique IP addresses in the same subnet have identical values in the network part of their address, identical values in the subnet part of their address, and different values in their host parts.

- Two unique IP addresses in different subnets of the same Class A, B, or C network have identical values in the network part of their address and have different values in the subnet part of their address.

- Without subnetting, the network number, the network broadcast address, and all assignable IP addresses in the network have the same value in the network part of their addresses.

- With subnetting, the subnet number, the subnet broadcast address, and all assignable IP addresses in the subnet have the same value in the network *and* subnet parts of their addresses.

- Most people treat the combined network and subnet parts of addresses as one part of the address and call it the subnet part of the address, or simply the *subnet*.

IP Grouping Concepts and Subnetting

Cisco requires that CCNAs exhibit a thorough understanding of IP subnetting. Almost every organization with a network uses IP, and almost every one of these organizations uses subnetting. Subnetting is simply the process of treating subdivisions of a single Class A, B, or

C network as if it were a network itself. By doing so, a single Class A, B, or C network can be subdivided into many nonoverlapping subnets.

The needs for subnetting are both technical and administrative, as documented in the following list:

- All organizations connected to the Internet (and not using IP address translation) are required to use IP networks registered with the NIC.

- IP protocols enforce the following grouping concept: All hosts in the same group must not be separated by an IP router.

- A corollary to the grouping concept is this: Hosts separated by an IP router must be in separate groups.

- Without subnetting, the smallest group is a single, entire Class A, B, or C network number.

- Without subnetting, the NIC would be woefully short of assignable networks.

- With subnetting, the NIC can assign one or a few network numbers to an organization, and then the organization can subdivide those networks into subnets of more usable sizes.

An example drives these points home. Consider all network interfaces in Figure 5-20, and note which ones are not separated by a router.

In Figure 5-20, six groupings exist, each of which is a Class B network. Four networks are more obvious, those being the set of all interfaces attached to each of the four LANs. In other words, the LANs attached to Routers A, B, C, and D are each a separate network. Additionally, the two serial interfaces composing the point-to-point serial link between Routers C and D are both in the same network because they are not separated by a router. Finally, the three router interfaces composing the Frame Relay network with Routers A, B, and C would not be separated by an IP router and would compose the sixth network.

If building this network today, the NIC would not assign six separate Class B network numbers, as shown in Figure 5-20. Instead, you might get one or two Class C networks assigned by the NIC, with the expectation that you would use subnetting.

Figure 5-21 illustrates a basic subnetting example. (*Basic* is a term used for purposes in this book to denote subnetting examples for which the math is easy. More advanced subnetting is covered later in this section.)

Figure 5-20   *Backdrop for Discussing Numbers of Different Networks/Subnets*

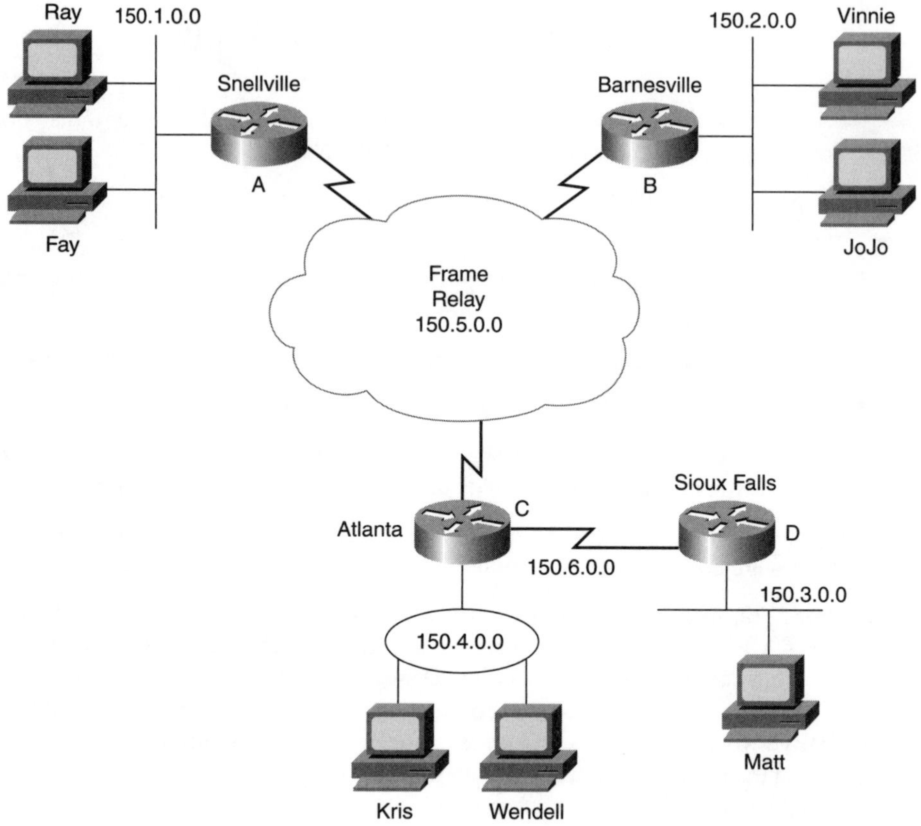

In the example in Figure 5-21, Class B network 150.150.0.0 is used (possibly assigned by the NIC). The IP network designer has chosen a mask of 255.255.255.0, the last octet of which implies 8 host bits. Because it is a Class B network, there are 16 network bits. Therefore, there are 8 subnet bits, which happen to be bits 17 through 24—in other words, the third octet. Notice that each subnet number in the figure shows a different value in the third octet, representing each different subnet number.

Binary View of Subnetting

The benefit of a binary definition of subnetting is that it is exact. For a full understanding of subnetting—particularly more advanced subnetting topics—as well as other IP addressing and routing topics beyond the scope of this book, an exact definition is required. If your job will include planning subnet number assignment or troubleshooting, this binary understanding will be useful.

Figure 5-21   *Using Subnets*

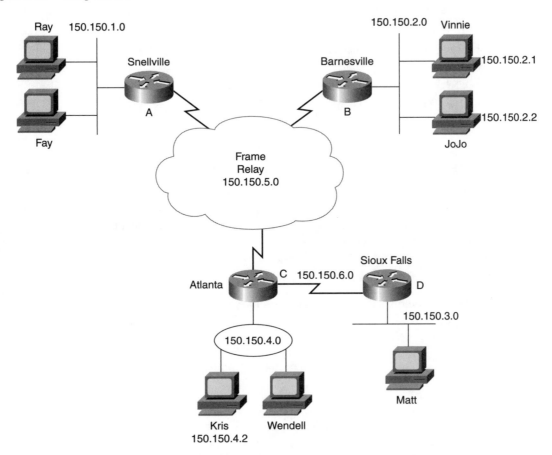

A review of some basic concepts relating to networks without subnetting can be used as a comparison to networks with subnetting. When not subnetting, the default mask defines the number of host bits. The mask accomplishes this by simply using binary 0 for each bit position in the mask that corresponds to the host part of the address in question. For example, the mask 255.255.0.0 (Class B) has a value of all binary 0s in the last 16 bits. This implies 16 host bits at the end of the address. The following list summarizes basic concepts when not using subnetting:

- The mask defines the number of host bits in the host part of an address.

- Class A, B, and C rules define the number of network bits in the network part of the address.

- Without subnetting, these two fields (network and host) compose the entire 32-bit address.

- Each host address in the network has the same value in the network part of the address.

- Each host address in the network has a unique value in the host part of the address. (For example, 130.1.1.1 and 130.1.1.2 are in the same network but can be assigned to two different network interfaces.)

Subnetting creates a third part of the address, called the *subnet field* or *subnet part*. For example, using network 150.150.0.0 again, assume that you want a third field called the subnet field. Several assertions are true in this case:

- The Class A, B, and C network field sizes cannot be changed; they remain as 8, 16, and 24 bits, respectively.

- The IP address must still be 32 bits in length.

- Therefore, to create a third field called the subnet part of the address, *some of the bits previously in the host part of the address are used.*

The subnet part of an address identifies the different subdivisions of this network. An address with a different value in the subnet field, as compared with a second address, is considered to be in a different subnet. For example, examine the following three IP addresses that are part of Table 5-13 and are valid addresses in Figure 5-21:

Table 5-13   *Subnet Part of Sample Addresses*

Address in Decimal	Address in Binary
150.150.2.1	1001 0110 1001 0110 **0000 0010** 0000 0001
150.150.2.2	1001 0110 1001 0110 **0000 0010** 0000 0010
150.150.4.2	1001 0110 1001 0110 **0000 0100** 0000 0010

The example shows that the subnet field consists of bits 17 through 24 (the entire third byte). 150.150.2.1 and 150.150.2.2 are in the same subnet because they are in the same Class B network and because *their subnet fields have the same value* (0000 0010). 150.150.4.2 is in a different subnet of the same Class B network because the subnet field has a different value than the first two addresses (0000 0100). 150.150.4.2 must be physically located with at least one IP router between itself and 150.150.2.1 and 150.150.2.2.

Five Ways the Exam Will Test Your IP Addressing Knowledge

CCNAs deal with IP addressing concepts from many different perspectives every day. To pass the CCNA exam, you'll need to demonstrate the ability to think about IP addressing from each of the following perspectives:

1 Given an IP address and mask, what is the network/subnet number?

2 Given an IP address and mask, what is the network/subnet broadcast address?

3 Given an IP address and mask, what are the assignable IP addresses in that network/subnet?

4 Given a network number and a static subnet mask, what are the valid subnet numbers?

5 Given a network number and a static subnet mask, how many hosts per subnet, and how many subnets?

This section provides both a decimal and a binary algorithm for each perspective on IP addressing. The decimal processes will help you find the answers more quickly; the binary algorithms will help you more fully understand IP addressing.

Given an IP Address and Mask, What Is the Network/Subnet Number?

Both people and computers need to think about the question, "Which network is a particular address a member of?" Humans care because it is useful in troubleshooting, planning, and address assignment; computers need to know because the answer is a vital part of routing.

Decimal Algorithm for Deriving the Network Number, No Subnetting in Use

When no subnetting is in use, the decimal algorithm is as follows:

Step 1   Write down the IP address in decimal.

Step 2   Copy below the IP address either the first one, two, or three dotted decimal numbers of the address, based on whether the address is a Class A, B, or C address, respectively.

Step 3   For the remaining dotted decimal numbers, record decimal value 0.

Table 5-14 shows some examples for deriving the network number (no subnetting in use) based on the steps in the preceding list.

Table 5-14   *Example Dissections of IP Addresses, No Subnetting*

IP Address (Step 1)	Network Part (Step 2)	Network Number (Step 3)
8.1.4.5	8	8.0.0.0
130.4.100.1	130.4	130.4.0.0
199.1.1.4	199.1.1	199.1.1.0
172.100.2.2	172.100	172.100.0.0

Binary Algorithm for Deriving the Network Number, No Subnetting in Use

When a computer needs to answer this same question, it performs a Boolean math operation called AND between the address in question and the mask. The result of the AND operation is that the host bits are masked out—that is, changed to binary 0s. The binary process, with no subnetting, is as follows:

Step 1   Write down the IP address in binary.

Step 2   Write down the default mask appropriate for the class of address, in binary, beneath the binary IP address from Step 1.

Step 3   Record the results of the Boolean AND below the two numbers.

Step 4   Convert the result of Step 3 back into decimal, 8 bits at a time.

To perform the Boolean AND, each bit is examined in the address and is compared to the corresponding bit in the mask. The AND operation results in a binary 1 if both the address and the mask bits are also 1; otherwise, the result is 0. The Boolean AND for the addresses in Table 5-14 is shown in the following IP address table examples.

Address (Step 1)	8.1.4.5	0000 1000 0000 0001 0000 0100 0000 0101
Mask (Step 2)	255.0.0.0	1111 1111 **0000 0000 0000 0000 0000 0000**
Result (Steps 3 and 4)	8.0.0.0	0000 1000 0000 0000 0000 0000 0000 0000

Address (Step 1)	130.4.100.1	1000 0010 0000 0100 0110 0100 0000 0001
Mask (Step 2)	255.255.0.0	1111 1111 1111 1111 **0000 0000 0000 0000**
Result (Steps 3 and 4)	130.4.0.0	1000 0010 0000 0100 0000 0000 0000 0000

Address (Step 1)	199.1.1.4	1100 0111 0000 0001 0000 0001 0000 0100
Mask (Step 2)	255.255.255.0	1111 1111 1111 1111 1111 1111 **0000 0000**
Result (Steps 3 and 4)	199.1.1.0	1100 0111 0000 0001 0000 0001 0000 0000

Address (Step 1)	172.100.2.2	1010 1100 0110 0100 0000 0010 0000 0010
Mask (Step 2)	255.255.0.0	1111 1111 1111 1111 **0000 0000 0000 0000**
Result (Steps 3 and 4)	172.100.0.0	1010 1100 0110 0100 0000 0000 0000 0000

Consider the second example using address 130.4.100.1, mask 255.255.0.0. The binary mask shows 16 binary 1s; any other binary value ANDed with binary 1 yields the original binary value. In other words, any 16-bit number ANDed with 16 binary 1s yields the same number you started with. So, the result shows 1000 0010 0000 0100 for the first 16 bits, which literally could be copied from the binary version of the address. The last 16 bits of the mask are all binary 0s; any value ANDed with a binary 0 yields a 0. So, no matter what value is in the last 16 bits of the address, once ANDed with the mask, the result will be all binary 0s, as shown in the example result. The result is called the *network number* when no subnetting is used; the result is the *subnet number* when subnetting is used.

Decimal Algorithm for Deriving the Subnet Number, Basic Subnetting

The decimal algorithm, when basic subnetting is in use, is as follows:

Step 1   Write down the IP address in decimal.

Step 2   Copy below the IP address either the first one, two, or three dotted decimal numbers of the address, based on whether the subnet mask is 255.0.0.0, 255.255.0.0, or 255.255.255.0, respectively.

Step 3   For the remaining dotted decimal numbers, record decimal value 0.

This algorithm is very similar to the algorithm that is used when there is no subnetting. The only difference is in Step 2. In fact, this later version of the algorithm would work fine when there is no subnetting in use. Table 5-15 lists several examples.

Table 5-15   *Subnetting Examples*

IP Address	Subnet Mask	Network and Subnet Part*	Full Subnet Number
8.1.4.5	255.255.0.0	8.1	8.1.0.0
130.4.100.1	255.255.255.0	130.4.100	130.4.100.0
199.1.1.4	255.255.255.0	199.1.1	199.1.1.0**
172.100.2.2	255.255.255.0	172.100.2	172.100.2.0
17.9.44.3	255.255.255.0	17.9.44	17.9.44.0

*   The third column of Table 5-15 can be thought of as Step 2 in the decimal algorithm.
**   This example shows a Class C address, with default mask. No subnetting is in use in this case.

Binary Algorithm for Deriving the Subnet Number, Basic Subnetting

The binary algorithm to determine the subnet number, when using basic subnetting, is practically identical to the algorithm used when there is no subnetting. Again, the key is in knowing what subnet mask is in use. The binary process, with basic subnetting, is as follows:

Step 1   Write down the IP address in binary.

Step 2   Write down the subnet mask used in this network, in binary, beneath the binary IP address from Step 1.

Step 3   Record the results of the Boolean AND below the two numbers.

Step 4   Convert the result of Step 3 back into decimal, 8 bits at a time.

Repeating the same samples from Table 5-15, using the Boolean AND delivers the following results:

Address (Step 1)	8.1.4.5	0000 1000 0000 0001 0000 0100 0000 0101
Mask (Step 2)	255.255.0.0	1111 1111 1111 1111 **0000 0000 0000 0000**
Result (Steps 3 and 4)	8.1.0.0	0000 1000 0000 0001 0000 0000 0000 0000

Address (Step 1)	130.4.100.1	1000 0010 0000 0100 0110 0100 0000 0001
Mask (Step 2)	255.255.255.0	1111 1111 1111 1111 1111 1111 **0000 0000**
Result (Steps 3 and 4)	130.4.100.0	1000 0010 0000 0100 0110 0100 0000 0000

Address (Step 1)	199.1.1.4	1100 0111 0000 0001 0000 0001 0000 0100
Mask (Step 2)	255.255.255.0	1111 1111 1111 1111 1111 1111 **0000 0000**
Result (Steps 3 and 4)	199.1.1.0	1100 0111 0000 0001 0000 0001 0000 0000

Address (Step 1)	172.100.2.2	1010 1100 0110 0100 0000 0010 0000 0010
Mask (Step 2)	255.255.255.0	1111 1111 1111 1111 1111 1111 **0000 0000**
Result (Steps 3 and 4)	172.100.2.0	1010 1100 0110 0100 0000 0010 0000 0000

Address (Step 1)	17.9.44.3	0001 0001 0000 1001 0010 1100 0000 0011
Mask (Step 2)	255.255.255.0	1111 1111 1111 1111 1111 1111 **0000 0000**
Result (Steps 3 and 4)	17.9.44.0	0001 0001 0000 1001 0010 1100 0000 0000

An example network will be used as a backdrop to discuss this binary view of subnetting.

Figure 5-22 illustrates six different subnets. Table 5-16 provides the list of subnet numbers.

Figure 5-22 *Siberian CCNA Sample Network*

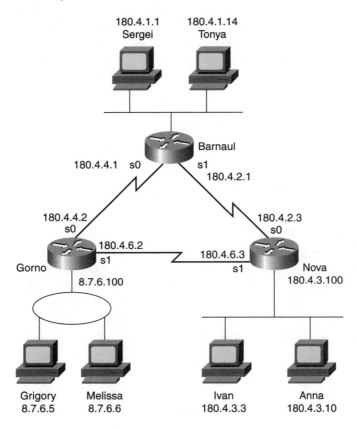

Table 5-16 *Siberian Subnets*

Location of Subnet Geographically	Subnet Mask	Subnet Number
Ethernet off router in Barnaul	255.255.255.0	180.4.1.0
Ethernet off router in Nova	255.255.255.0	180.4.3.0
Token Ring off router in Gorno	255.255.0.0	8.7.0.0
Serial link between Barnaul and Nova	255.255.255.0	180.4.2.0
Serial link between Barnaul and Gorno	255.255.255.0	180.4.4.0
Serial link between Nova and Gorno	255.255.255.0	180.4.6.0

Keep in mind that all the addresses on the same data link must be in the same subnet. For example, Ivan and Anna must be in the same subnet, so performing either the easy decimal algorithm or the more involved binary algorithm on either address will yield the same subnet number, 180.4.3.0. If the answers are unclear, do several of these using the algorithm used by computers. For example, using Ivan, the results will be as follows:

Address (Step 1)	180.4.3.3	1011 0100 0000 0100 0000 0011 0000 0011
Mask (Step 2)	255.255.255.0	1111 1111 1111 1111 1111 1111 **0000 0000**
Result (Steps 3 and 4)	180.4.3.0	1011 0100 0000 0100 0000 0011 0000 0000

For additional practice, you may want to go to the scenarios section at the end of the chapter, specifically to Scenarios 5-2 and 5-3.

Binary Algorithm for Deriving the Subnet Number, Difficult Subnetting

Difficult subnetting is a term used in this book to denote subnetting when the mask is not all 255s and 0s. The decimal algorithm for calculating the subnet, when basic subnetting is in use, is more challenging. In fact, several math tricks come in handy so that the result can be calculated without thinking about binary math. However, starting with the binary algorithm is helpful.

These *difficult* masks typically contain one of the values shown in Table 5-17. To speed up the process of examining these addresses (in case you are taking a timed test), memorizing the decimal and binary numbers in Table 5-17 will be useful.

Table 5-17 *Typical Difficult Mask Values*

Decimal	Binary
0	0000 0000
128	1000 0000
192	1100 0000
224	1110 0000
240	1111 0000
248	1111 1000
252	1111 1100
254	1111 1110
255	1111 1111

The binary algorithm to determine the subnet number, when using difficult subnetting, is identical to the algorithm used when there is no subnetting or basic subnetting. Again, the key is in knowing what subnet mask is in use. The binary algorithm is as follows:

Step 1   Write down the IP address in binary.

Step 2   Write down the subnet mask used in this network, in binary, beneath the binary IP address from Step 1.

Step 3   Record the results of the Boolean AND below the two numbers.

Step 4   Convert the result of Step 3 back into decimal, 8 bits at a time.

The biggest obstacle to understanding this algorithm is failing to realize this one fact: Binary-decimal-binary conversion is independent of the size of the network, subnet, and host fields. Conversion always is from one decimal number to eight binary digits, and vice versa.

Typically, an example usually helps. Consider the following binary example:

Address	8.1.100.5	0000 1000 0000 0001 0110 0100 0000 0101
Mask	255.255.240.0	1111 1111 1111 1111 1111 0000 0000 0000
Result	8.1.96.0	0000 1000 0000 0001 0110 0000 0000 0000

Ignoring the decimal numbers on the left, a slow examination of the binary address, mask, and Boolean AND result shows that the conversion to binary and AND are correct as shown. The typical difficulty is the step of conversion. Many people want to convert the 12-bit host field to a decimal number and the 4-bit subnet field to a decimal number. Instead, for the last step (conversion to decimal), convert the first 8-bit set to decimal (0000 1000 converted to decimal 8). Likewise, convert the second 8-bit set (the second byte) to decimal (0000 0001 converted to decimal 1). Then convert the entire third byte to decimal (0110 0000 converted to decimal 96). Finally, convert the entire last byte to decimal (0000 0000 converted to decimal 0). The third byte contains the entire subnet field and part of the host field; the binary-to-decimal conversion ignores the subnet/host boundaries, always using byte boundaries.

The following examples are shown as additional examples of deriving the subnet number when a more difficult mask is used:

Address (Step 1)	130.4.100.129	1000 0010 0000 0100 0110 0100 1000 0001
Mask (Step 2)	255.255.255.128	1111 1111 1111 1111 1111 1111 1000 0000
Result (Steps 3 and 4)	130.4.100.128	1000 0010 0000 0100 0110 0100 1000 0000

Address (Step 1)	199.1.1.4	1100 0111 0000 0001 0000 0001 0000 0100
Mask (Step 2)	255.255.255.224	1111 1111 1111 1111 1111 1111 1110 0000
Result (Steps 3 and 4)	199.1.1.0	1100 0111 0000 0001 0000 0001 0000 0000

Address (Step 1)	172.100.201.2	1010 1100 0110 0100 1100 1001 0000 0010
Mask (Step 2)	255.255.254.0	1111 1111 1111 1111 1111 1110 0000 0000
Result (Steps 3 and 4)	172.100.200.0	1010 1100 0110 0100 1100 1000 0000 0000

Address (Step 1)	17.9.44.70	0001 0001 0000 1001 0010 1100 0100 0110
Mask (Step 2)	255.255.255.192	1111 1111 1111 1111 1111 1111 1100 0000
Result (Steps 3 and 4)	17.9.44.64	0001 0001 0000 1001 0010 1100 0100 0000

Decimal Algorithm for Deriving the Subnet Number, Difficult Subnetting

The decimal algorithm that I like best for difficult subnetting works well. However, this algorithm is not very helpful for understanding subnetting. So, if you understand subnetting and are willing to use the more time-consuming binary algorithm on the exam for the difficult cases, you may want to skip this section to avoid getting confused. The algorithm is as follows:

Step 1   Write down the IP address in decimal.

Step 2   Write down the mask in decimal.

Step 3   Examine the mask. One of the four octets will have a value besides 255 or 0; otherwise, this would not be considered to be a difficult case. The octet with the non-255, non-0 value is considered to be the "interesting" octet. The other three are considered "boring." Write down the number (1, 2, 3, or 4) of the interesting octet. (For example, mask 255.255.240.0 has an interesting third octet.)

Step 4   Subtract the mask's interesting octet value from 256. Call that value the *multiplier*. Write it down.

Step 5   For any boring octets to the left of the interesting octet, copy those octets' values onto your paper, leaving space for the remaining octets. This will be where you record your subnet number.

Step 6   For any boring octets to the right of the interesting octet, record a value 0 in your subnet number. One of the four octets should still be empty—the interesting octet.

Step 7   Examine the interesting octet of the original IP address. Discover the multiple of the *multiplier* closest to this number, but less than the number. Write down this interesting multiple of the multiplier into the interesting octet of the subnet number.

For those of you in doubt, examine the examples that follow. In each case, the steps in the algorithm are shown. The crux of the algorithm is to search for the integer multiple of the *multiplier* that is close to, but less than, the value in the interesting octet of the IP address.

Address (Step 1)	130.4.101.129
Mask (Step 2)	255.255.252.0
Interesting octet (Step 3)	3
Multiplier (Step 4)	256 – 252 = 4
Subnet (boring octets to the left) (Step 5)	130.4.____.____
Subnet (boring octets to the right) (Step 6)	130.4.____.0
Subnet (Step 7)	130.4.100.0

Address (Step 1)	199.1.1.4
Mask (Step 2)	255.255.255.224
Interesting octet (Step 3)	4
Multiplier (Step 4)	256 – 224 = 32
Subnet (boring octets to the left) (Step 5)	199.1.1.____
Subnet (boring octets to the right) (Step 6)	199.1.1.____
Subnet (Step 7)	199.1.1.0

Address (Step 1)	172.100.201.2
Mask (Step 2)	255.255.254.0
Interesting octet (Step 3)	3
Multiplier (Step 4)	256 – 254 = 2
Subnet (boring octets to the left) (Step 5)	172.100.____.____
Subnet (boring octets to the right) (Step 6)	172.100.____.0
Subnet (Step 7)	172.100.200.0

Address (Step 1)	17.9.44.70
Mask (Step 2)	255.255.255.192
Interesting octet (Step 3)	4
Multiplier (Step 4)	256 – 192 = 64
Subnet (boring octets to the left) (Step 5)	17.9.44.____
Subnet (boring octets to the right) (Step 6)	17.9.44.____
Subnet (Step 7)	17.9.44.64

Given an IP Address and Mask, What Is the Network/Subnet Broadcast Address?

CCNAs are expected to be able to derive the valid, assignable addresses in any subnet; calculation of the broadcast address of the subnet is a vital part of the process. As mentioned earlier, there are two reserved numbers in each network or subnet. One number is the network number or subnet number, which is used to represent the entire network or subnet. The other reserved number is called the *broadcast address*. This number is used to represent all IP addresses in the network or subnet. The broadcast address is used when a packet must be sent to all hosts in a network or subnet. All hosts receiving the packet should notice that the packet is destined for their own network or subnet broadcast address and then process the packet.

The broadcast address for a network is particularly important when planning an IP addressing structure for a network. Take a look at the following definition:

> The network/subnet number is the lowest value numerically in that network/subnet. The broadcast address is the *largest* value numerically in that network/subnet. The valid, assignable addresses in that network are the numbers between the network/subnet number and the broadcast address.

Decimal Algorithm for Deriving the Broadcast Address, No Subnetting or Basic Subnetting

The algorithms, both binary and decimal, for deriving the broadcast addresses are similar to the same algorithms for deriving the subnet numbers. The algorithms used for basic subnetting are used as a basis for the following algorithms for deriving the broadcast addresses. First, the decimal algorithm is as follows:

Step 1   Write down the IP address in decimal.

Step 2   Copy below the IP address either the first one, two, or three dotted decimal numbers of the address, based on whether the subnet mask is 255.0.0.0, 255.255.0.0, or 255.255.255.0, respectively.

Step 3   For the remaining dotted decimal numbers, record decimal value 255.

The only difference between this algorithm and the one to derive the subnet number is that Step 3 directs you to plug in 255 instead of 0. Some examples follow in Table 5-18.

Table 5-18   *Subnetting Examples*

IP Address (Step 1)	Subnet Mask	Network and Subnet Part (Step 2)	Broadcast Address (Step 3)
8.1.4.5	255.255.0.0	8.1	8.1.255.255
130.4.100.1	255.255.255.0	130.4.100	130.4.100.255
199.1.1.4	255.255.255.0	199.1.1	199.1.1.255*

Table 5-18   *Subnetting Examples (Continued)*

IP Address (Step 1)	Subnet Mask	Network and Subnet Part (Step 2)	Broadcast Address (Step 3)
172.100.2.2	255.255.255.0	172.100.2	172.100.2.255
17.9.44.3	255.255.255.0	17.9.44	17.9.44.255

*   This example shows a Class C address, with default mask. The broadcast address in that case is a network broadcast, not a subnet broadcast address.

Binary Algorithm for Deriving the Broadcast Address

The binary algorithm to determine the broadcast address when using no subnetting or basic subnetting is a little trickier than the similar algorithm for finding the subnet number. The algorithm shown here is not really what computers use, but it is more instructive about how broadcast addresses are structured. It starts by repeating the binary algorithm for computing the subnet number and then adding two short steps. The algorithm is as follows:

Step 1   Write down the IP address in binary.

Step 2   Write down the subnet mask used in this network, in binary, beneath the binary IP address from Step 1.

Step 3   Record the results of the Boolean AND below the two numbers. (This is the subnet number.)

Step 4   Copy down the network and subnet bits of the subnet number onto the next line. This is the beginning of the broadcast address.

Step 5   Fill in the host bit values with all binary 1s. This is the broadcast address.

Step 6   Convert the result of Step 5 back into decimal, 8 bits at a time.

As usual, a few examples will help:

Address (Step 1)	8.1.4.5	0000 1000 0000 0001 0000 0100 0000 0101
Mask (Step 2)	255.255.0.0	1111 1111 1111 1111 **0000 0000 0000 0000**
Boolean AND (Step 3)	8.1.0.0	0000 1000 0000 0001 0000 0000 0000 0000
Broadcast address (Steps 4 to 6)	8.1.255.255	0000 1000 0000 0001 **1111 1111 1111 1111**

Address (Step 1)	130.4.100.1	1000 0010 0000 0100 0110 0100 0000 0001
Mask (Step 2)	255.255.255.0	1111 1111 1111 1111 1111 1111 **0000 0000**
Boolean AND (Step 3)	130.4.100.0	1000 0010 0000 0100 0110 0100 0000 0000
Broadcast address (Steps 4 to 6)	130.4.100.255	1000 0010 0000 0100 0110 0100 **1111 1111**

Address (Step 1)	199.1.1.4	1100 0111 0000 0001 0000 0001 0000 0100
Mask (Step 2)	255.255.255.0	1111 1111 1111 1111 1111 1111 **0000 0000**
Boolean AND (Step 3)	199.1.1.0	1100 0111 0000 0001 0000 0001 0000 0000
Broadcast address (Steps 4 to 6)	199.1.1.255	1100 0111 0000 0001 0000 0001 **1111 1111**

Address (Step 1)	172.100.2.2	1010 1100 0110 0100 0000 0010 0000 0010
Mask (Step 2)	255.255.255.0	1111 1111 1111 1111 1111 1111 **0000 0000**
Boolean AND (Step 3)	172.100.2.0	1010 1100 0110 0100 0000 0010 0000 0000
Broadcast address (Steps 4 to 6)	172.100.2.255	1010 1100 0110 0100 0000 0010 **1111 1111**

Address (Step 1)	17.9.44.3	0001 0001 0000 1001 0010 1100 0000 0011
Mask (Step 2)	255.255.255.0	1111 1111 1111 1111 1111 1111 **0000 0000**
Boolean AND (Step 3)	17.9.44.0	0001 0001 0000 1001 0010 1100 0000 0000
Broadcast address (Steps 4 to 6)	17.9.44.255	0001 0001 0000 1001 0010 1100 **1111 1111**

Decimal Algorithm for Deriving the Broadcast Address, Difficult Subnetting

The decimal algorithm for deriving the broadcast address when difficult subnetting is used is shown next. When in doubt, use the binary algorithm. However, the following decimal algorithm will yield the correct results:

Step 1   Write down the IP address in decimal.

Step 2   Write down the mask in decimal.

Step 3   Examine the mask. One of the four octets will have a value besides 255 or 0; otherwise, this would not be considered to be a "difficult" case. The octet with the non-255, non-0 value is considered to be the "interesting" octet. The other three are considered "boring." Write down the number (1, 2, 3, or 4) of the interesting octet. (For example, mask 255.255.240.0 has an interesting third octet.)

Step 4   Subtract the mask's interesting octet's value from 256. Call that value the *multiplier*. Write it down.

Step 5   For any boring octets to the left of the interesting octet, copy those octets from the subnet onto a new line on your paper, leaving space for the remaining octets. This line will be where you record the broadcast address.

Step 6   For any boring octets to the right of the interesting octet, record a value of 255 in the broadcast address (the same number as in Step 5.) One of the four octets should still be empty—the interesting octet.

Step 7   Examine the interesting octet of the original IP address. Discover the multiple of the *multiplier* closest to this number but *greater* than the number. Subtract 1 from this multiple. Write down this value (1 less than the integer multiple of the multiplier) in the interesting octet of the broadcast address.

For those of you in doubt, examine the examples that follow. In each case, the steps in the algorithm are shown. The crux of the algorithm is to search for the integer multiple of the *multiplier* that is close to but greater than the value in the interesting octet of the IP address.

2	130.4.101.129
Mask (Step 2)	255.255.252.0
Interesting octet (Step 3)	3
Multiplier (Step 4)	256 – 252 = 4
Broadcast address (boring octets to the left) (Step 5)	130.4.____.____
Broadcast address (boring octets to the right) (Step 6)	130.4.____.255
Broadcast address (104 is the closest multiple of 4 and is greater than 101; 104 – 1 = 103) (Step 7)	120.4.103.255

Address (Step 1)	199.1.1.5
Mask (Step 2)	255.255.255.224
Interesting octet (Step 3)	4
Multiplier (Step 4)	256 – 224 = 32
Broadcast address (boring octets to the left) (Step 5)	199.1.1.____
Broadcast address (boring octets to the right) (Step 6)	199.1.1.____
Broadcast address (32 is the closest multiple of 32 and is greater than 4; 32 – 1 = 31) (Step 7)	199.1.1.31

Address (Step 1)	172.100.201.2
Mask (Step 2)	255.255.254.0
Interesting octet (Step 3)	3
Multiplier (Step 4)	256 – 254 = 2

Broadcast address (boring octets to the left) (Step 5)	172.100.____.____
Broadcast address (boring octets to the right) (Step 6)	172.100.____.255
Broadcast address (202 is the closest multiple of 2 and is greater than 201; 202 − 1 = 201) (Step 7)	172.100.201.255

Address (Step 1)	17.9.44.70
Mask (Step 2)	255.255.255.192
Interesting octet (Step 3)	4
Multiplier (Step 4)	256 − 192 = 64
Broadcast address (boring octets to the left) (Step 5)	17.9.44.____
Broadcast address (boring octets to the right) (Step 6)	17.9.44.____
Broadcast address (128 is the closest multiple of 64 and is greater than 70; 128 − 1 = 127) (Step 7)	17.9.44.127

Given an IP Address and Mask, What Are the Assignable IP Addresses in That Network/Subnet?

CCNAs deal with the question, "What IP addresses are in this subnet?" on a regular basis. This section describes how to answer this question if you know how to derive the subnet and broadcast addresses. Simply put, the valid IP addresses that are available for assignment in a subnet are those numerically between the subnet number and the broadcast address.

There is little else to be considered. Certainly, no decimal or binary algorithm needs to be considered for such a simple concept, right? Table 5-19 shows some familiar IP addresses and the corresponding IP addresses in the same subnet.

Table 5-19   *Assignable Addresses*

Subnet Number	Subnet Mask	Broadcast Address	Range of Assignable Addresses
130.4.100.0	255.255.252.0	130.4.103.255	130.4.100.1 to 130.4.103.254
199.1.1.0	255.255.255.224	199.1.1.31	199.1.1.1 to 199.1.1.30
172.100.200.0	255.255.254.0	172.100.201.255	172.100.200.1 to 172.100.201.254
17.9.44.64	255.255.255.192	17.9.44.127	17.9.44.65 to 17.9.44.126

The ranges seem obvious. However, look at the 172.100.200.0 subnet. How many assignable IP addresses are in that subnet, and what are those addresses? Is 172.100.200.255 valid? What about 172.100.201.0? In fact, both are valid IP addresses when using 255.255.254.0 as the mask. The rule is that the subnet numbers (and also the broadcast addresses) are not usable as an IP address. Otherwise, the addresses are assignable to an interface.

Given a Network Number and a Static Subnet Mask, What Are the Valid Subnet Numbers?

One of the reasons you find so many different slants on IP addressing in this chapter is that the CCNA exam questions you about IP in many different ways. The question in the heading of this section is unlikely to be the exact question, however. You should expect to see something like, "Which of the following are valid subnets of network X, using mask Y?," followed by the suggested answers. If you can figure out all the subnets of that network, you should be able to answer the multiple-choice exam question easily.

A few additional facts will help you in thinking about the possible subnet numbers:

- All subnet numbers have all binary 0s in the host part of the subnet number.

- All subnet numbers of the same Class A, B, or C network have identical values in the network part of the subnet numbers.

- All subnet numbers of the same Class A, B, or C network have different values in the subnet part of the subnet numbers.

In other words, the only thing that is different about two different subnets of the same network is the subnet part of the subnet number. The network and host parts are identical. An example helps in this case. Examine Figure 5-23, which shows a familiar network with six subnets.

Figure 5-23 shows six subnets of network 150.150.0.0. Subnet mask 255.255.255.0 is used, implying two network octets, one subnet octet, and one host octet. The subnets already used in this example are as follows:

- 150.150.1.0

- 150.150.2.0

- 150.150.3.0

- 150.150.4.0

- 150.150.5.0

- 150.150.6.0

As long as you can find another value not already used in the third byte, you can find another subnet number. In fact, simply counting sequentially, subnet numbers continue—150.150.7.0, 150.150.8.0, and so on, up through 150.150.254.0. That gives a total of 254 subnets, assuming that the zero and broadcast subnets are not used.

Figure 5-23   *Sample Network Using Class A, B, and C Network Numbers*

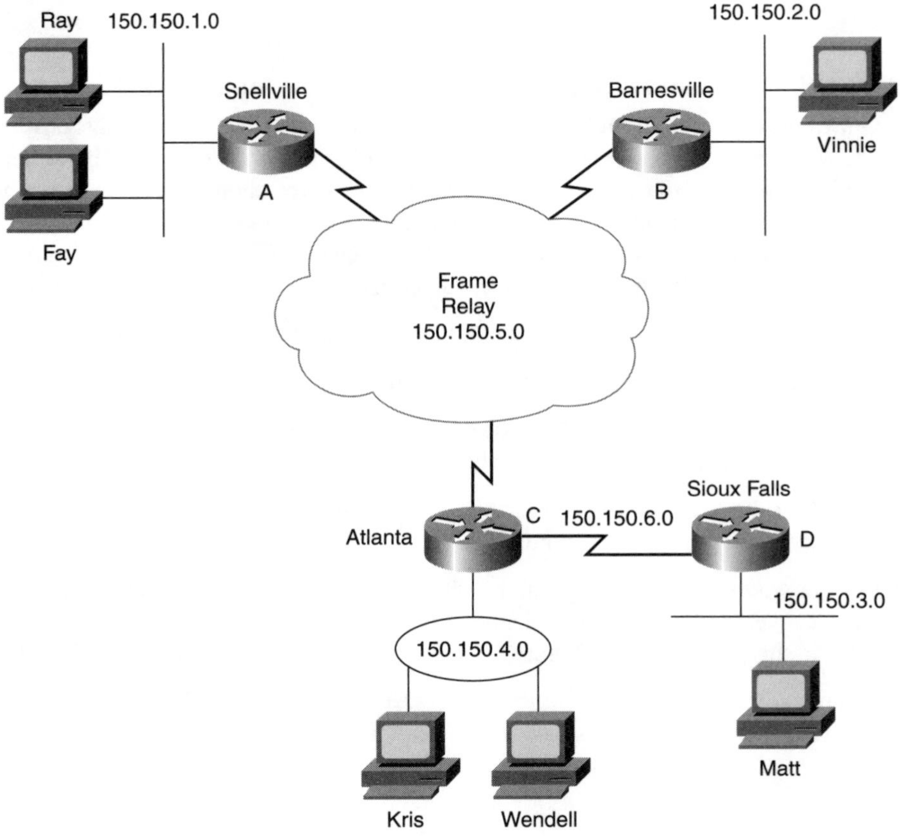

Decimal Algorithm for Deriving the Valid Subnets with Basic Subnetting

Time counts when taking the CCNA exam, so it's a good idea to take advantage of the easier decimal algorithms to derive facts about subnetting. The algorithm for deriving the subnet numbers of a network, given a static, basic mask, is extremely intuitive. Two cases for the decimal algorithm will be examined here: a Class A network subnetted using mask 255.255.0.0, and a Class B network subnetted using mask 255.255.255.0:

Step 1   Write down the 1 or 2 bytes of the network number.

Step 2   Leave a space immediately to the right to add a value in the next octet.

Step 3   Write down two octets (in the case of Class A) or one octet (in the case of Class B) of 0 after the one-octet space left in Step 2, leaving a number with three octets written and an open space in the subnet part of the number.

Step 4   Write down a 1 in the open octet.

Step 5   Repeat Steps 1 through 4, but in Step 4 add 1 to the number. Continue repeating these steps until you reach 254.

A similar algorithm is used when a Class A network is subnetted, using mask 255.255.255.0, although that is not shown here.

The number of valid subnets is an important concept when deriving the actual subnet numbers. How many should you expect to find? The formula is very straightforward, with a few twists on the real answer. First, the formula:

$$2^{\text{number-of-subnet-bits}}$$

The previous example in Figure 5-23 provides a good context in which to consider the formula. A Class B network 150.150.0.0 is used, so there are 16 network bits. The mask is 255.255.255.0, so there are 8 host bits. That leaves 8 subnet bits—$2^8 = 256$, for 256 subnets. From the previous example, 150.150.0.0 is the first subnet, and 150.150.255.0 was the last, which is consistent with the formula.

Two previously reserved cases, 150.150.0.0 and 150.150.255.0, were not used in the example. The first of these, which is called the *zero subnet* because the subnet value is all binary 0s, is usable only if the **ip subnet-zero** global command is configured. The other subnet, called the *broadcast subnet* because it looks like a typical broadcast address, is usable without any special configuration.

NOTE   Do not confuse the *zero subnet* and *broadcast subnet* with the two reserved IP addresses in each subnet. There are still two reserved addresses in each subnet that cannot be assigned to any interface as an IP address. Those two numbers are the numbers used for the subnet number itself and the broadcast address for the subnet.

Binary Algorithm for Deriving the Valid Subnets with Basic and Difficult Subnetting

This section details a binary algorithm you can use to derive the subnet numbers. With basic subnetting, you probably would not want to go through this much trouble. However, with difficult subnetting, the binary algorithm will be useful, at least until you become comfortable with the decimal algorithm. The following binary algorithm is valid for basic subnetting as well.

Step 1   Reserve space to record a series of 32-bit numbers, one over the other. Also leave space between each nibble and byte on each line for better readability.

Step 2   Write down the 8, 16, or 24 bits of the network part of the address, in binary, on each line.

Step 3   Write down binary 0s in the host field on each line. This should result in a long list of binary numbers, with the subnet bits unrecorded at this point.

Step 4   Write down all binary 0s in the subnet bit positions of the first number in the list. This is the first subnet number, in binary. This is also the *zero subnet*.

Step 5   Add binary 1 to the subnet field in the previous line, and record the result in the subnet field of the next line.

Step 6   Repeat Step 5 until the subnet field is all binary 1s. That is the last subnet number, which is also the broadcast subnet.

Step 7   Convert any of these 32-bit numbers back to decimal, 8 bits at a time. IGNORE THE BOUNDARIES BETWEEN THE SUBNET AND HOST FIELDS—do the conversion 8 bits at a time.

As usual, an example is better than a generic algorithm. First, a repeat of the 150.150.0.0, 255.255.255.0 example will be shown. Then network 150.150.0.0, with a different mask of 255.255.248.0, will be shown. Table 5-20 shows the first several iterations of 150.150.0.0, mask 255.255.255.0, but with a few of the intermediate subnet numbers not shown.

Table 5-20   *Valid Subnet Numbers*

Step 2 (only one line shown)	1001 0110 1001 0110		
Step 3 (only one line shown)	1001 0110 1001 0110	0000 0000	
Step 4	1001 0110 1001 0110 **0000 0000** 0000 0000		150.150.0.0
Step 5	1001 0110 1001 0110 **0000 0001** 0000 0000		150.150.1.0
Step 6	1001 0110 1001 0110 **0000 0010** 0000 0000		150.150.2.0
Step 6	1001 0110 1001 0110 **0000 0011** 0000 0000		150.150.3.0
Step 6	1001 0110 1001 0110 **0000 0100** 0000 0000		150.150.4.0
Step 6	1001 0110 1001 0110 **0000 0101** 0000 0000		150.150.5.0
	Skipped a few for brevity		
Step 6	1001 0110 1001 0110 **1111 1111** 0000 0000		150.150.255.0

As Table 5-20 shows, the same 256 subnet numbers are derived with the binary algorithm as with the decimal algorithm. The second example shows one not-so-obvious (at least in decimal) case with difficult subnetting (Table 5-21).

Table 5-21   *Valid Subnet Numbers, 150.150.0.0, Mask 255.255.248.0*

Step 2 (only one line shown)	1001 0110 1001 0110		
Step 3 (only one line shown)	1001 0110 1001 0110	000 0000 0000	
Step 4	1001 0110 1001 0110 **0000 0**000 0000 0000	150.150.0.0	
Step 5	1001 0110 1001 0110 **0000 1**000 0000 0000	150.150.8.0	
Step 6	1001 0110 1001 0110 **0001 0**000 0000 0000	150.150.16.0	
Step 6	1001 0110 1001 0110 **0001 1**000 0000 0000	150.150.24.0	
Step 6	1001 0110 1001 0110 **0010 0**000 0000 0000	150.150.32.0	
Step 6	1001 0110 1001 0110 **0010 1**000 0000 0000	150.150.40.0	
	Skipped a few for brevity		
Step 6	1001 0110 1001 0110 **1111 1**111 0000 0000	150.150.248.0	

So, with 5 subnet bits, there should be 2^5 or 32 subnets, including the zero and broadcast subnets. Examining the third octet of the decimal subnet numbers, with a little imagination, the 32 subnet numbers are 150.150.*x*.0, where *x* is an integer multiple of 8. The zero subnet is 150.150.0.0, and 150.150.248.0 is the broadcast subnet.

Decimal Algorithm for Deriving the Valid Subnets with Basic and Difficult Subnetting

CCNAs will need to derive the valid subnets of a network on a regular basis, so a decimal algorithm to derive the valid subnets—even when difficult subnetting is used—proves invaluable. With some practice, you can use the following algorithm without pen and paper or a calculator. This algorithm works only if the subnet field is less than 8 bits. If the subnet field is larger, you can use a similar algorithm (which is not shown) once you understand this specific algorithm. The algorithm is as follows:

Step 1   Based on the network number and mask, all subnet bits are in 1 byte. (Having all subnet bits in 1 byte is an assumption used for this algorithm.) This is the "interesting" byte. Write down which byte is the interesting byte. The other 3 octets/bytes are considered "boring."

Step 2   Find the number of host bits in the interesting octet, and call that number N. 2^N is called the *increment*. Record that number.

Step 3   Create a list, one entry above the other, that contains repeated copies of the decimal network number. However, leave the interesting octet blank. This will become the list of subnet numbers.

Step 4   In the first number in the list, in the interesting octet, write a decimal 0. This is the first (zero) subnet.

Step 5   For each successive entry in your list of subnets, add the increment to the previous entry's interesting octet value, and record that value in the interesting octet.

Step 6   When 256 is the value to be recorded in Step 5, you have completed the list of subnet numbers.

Two examples of the nonbinary algorithm will be shown. First, Table 5-22 shows the familiar 150.150.0.0, mask 255.255.248.0

Table 5-22   *Valid Subnet Numbers, 150.150.0.0, Mask 255.255.248.0*

Step 1	Interesting byte is 3
Step 2	Increment $2^3 = 8$
Step 3	150.150.____.0
	150.150.____.0
	150.150.____.0
	150.150.____.0
	150.150.____.0 and so forth
Step 4	150.150.**0**.0
Step 5	150.150.**8**.0
	150.150.**16**.0
	150.150.**24**.0
	Skipped a few for brevity
	150.150.**248**.0 (This is the last one)
Step 6	150.150.256.0 (This one is invalid)

For one other example, Table 5-23 shows network 128.1.0.0, with mask 255.255.252.0.

Table 5-23   *Valid Subnet Numbers, 128.1.0.0, Mask 255.255.252.0*

Step 1	Interesting byte is 3
Step 2	Increment $2^2 = 4$
Step 3	128.1.____.0
	128.1.____.0
	128.1.____.0
	128.1.____.0
	128.1.____.0 and so forth
Step 4	128.1.**0**.0
Step 5	128.1.**4**.0
	128.1.**8**.0
	128.1.**12**.0
	Skipped a few for brevity
	128.1.**252**.0 (This is the last one)
Step 6	128.1.256.0 (This one is invalid)

Given a Network Number and a Static Subnet Mask, How Many Hosts per Subnet, and How Many Subnets?

Finally, one more way the exam is likely to test your knowledge of IP addressing and subnetting is to ask which subnet masks will meet a set of requirements. This last type of question would be phrased as something like, "If you need at least 30 hosts in each subnet and only 4 subnets, and if you are using network 192.1.1.0, which of the following masks meet your requirements?"

To answer these types of questions confidently, you must have a good understanding of the three parts of an IP address. Figure 5-19 earlier in the chapter shows the network, subnet, and host parts of an address. These fields and their sizes are important because they identify the number of subnets possible and the number of hosts per subnet.

The number of hosts per subnet is defined by this formula:

$$2^{\text{number of host bits}} - 2$$

The number of host bits in an address is equal to the number of binary 0s in the subnet mask.

The number of subnets per network is defined by this formula:

$2^{\text{number of subnet bits}}$

The number of subnet bits is based on the mask and class of address. The number of subnet bits is:

32 – (number of network bits) – (number of host bits)

NOTE   In some documents, the number of subnets is shown as 2 less than $2^{\text{number of subnet bits}}$, implying two reserved cases. These two cases are no longer reserved, however, and can be used.

An algorithm may help, along with some samples.

Step 1   Write down the network number and mask in question.

Step 2   Write down the number of network bits based on Class A, B, and C rules.

Step 3   Write down the number of host bits, which is equal to the number of binary 0s in the mask.

Step 4   Write down the number of subnet bits. The network, host, and subnet bits should total 32.

Step 5   Calculate $2^{\text{host bits}}$ minus 2, and record this as the number of hosts per subnet.

Step 6   Calculate $2^{\text{subnet bits}}$, and record this as the number of subnets in this network.

Table 5-24 lists several examples. If the choices for the number of host and subnet bits is confusing, convert the mask to binary and mark off the network bits based on class rules. Then mark off the 0s at the end of the mask. The bits in between are the subnet bits.

Table 5-24   *Examples of Number of Hosts per Subnet, and Number of Subnets*

Network and Mask	Number of Network Bits	Number of Host Bits	Number of Subnet Bits	Number of Hosts per Subnet	Number of Subnets
10.0.0.0, 255.255.240.0	8	12	12	4094	4096
150.150.0.0, 255.255.248.0	16	11	5	2046	32

Table 5-24 *Examples of Number of Hosts per Subnet, and Number of Subnets (Continued)*

Network and Mask	Number of Network Bits	Number of Host Bits	Number of Subnet Bits	Number of Hosts per Subnet	Number of Subnets
192.1.1.0, 255.255.225.224	24	5	3	30	8
128.1.0.0, 255.255.255.252	16	2	14	2	16384

CIDR, Private Addressing, and NAT

When connecting to the Internet, using a registered network number or several registered network numbers is a very straightforward and obvious convention. With registered network numbers, no other organization connected to the Internet will have conflicting IP addresses. In fact, this convention is part of the reason the global Internet functions well.

In the early and mid-1990s, concern arose that the available networks would be completely assigned so that some organizations would not be capable of connecting to the Internet. This one fact was the most compelling reason for the advent of IP Version 6 (IPv6). (The version discussed in this book is Version 4. Version 5 was defined for experimental reasons and was never deployed.) Version 6 calls for a much larger address structure so that the convention of all organizations using unique groupings (networks) of IP addresses would still be reasonable—the numbers of IPv6-style networks would reach into the trillions and beyond. That solution is still technically viable and possibly one day will be used because IPv6 is still evolving in the marketplace.

Three other functions of IP have been used to reduce the need for IP Version 4 (IPv4) registered network numbers. Network Address Translation (NAT), often used in conjunction with Private Addressing, allows organizations to use unregistered IP network numbers and still communicate well with the Internet. Classless interdomain routing (CIDR) is a feature used by Internet service providers (ISPs) to reduce the waste of IP addresses in networks so that more organizations can be serviced by a single registered network number.

CIDR

CIDR is a convention, defined in RFC 1817 (www.ietf.org/rfc/rfc1817.txt), that calls for aggregating multiple network numbers into a single routing entity. CIDR was actually created to help the scalability of Internet routers—imagine a router in the Internet with a route to every Class A, B, and C network on the planet! By aggregating the routes, fewer routes would need to exist in the routing table. For instance, consider Figure 5-24. Class C networks 198.0.0.0 through 198.255.255.0 (they may look funny, but they are valid Class C network numbers) are registered networks for an ISP. All other ISPs' routing tables would have a separate route to each of the 2^{16} networks without CIDR. However, as seen in Figure 5-24, now the other ISPs' routers will have a single route to 198.0.0.0/8—in other words, a route to all hosts whose IP address begins with 198. More than 2 million Class C networks alone exist, but CIDR has helped Internet routers reduce their routing tables to a more manageable size, in the range of 70,000 routes at the end of 1999.

Figure 5-24 *Typical Use of CIDR*

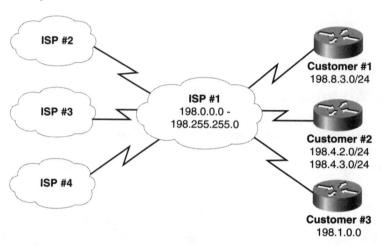

By using a routing protocol that exchanges the mask as well as the subnet/network number, a "classless" view of the number can be attained. In other words, treat the grouping as a math problem, ignoring the bourgeois Class A, B, and C rules. For instance, 198.0.0.0/8 (198.0.0.0, mask 255.0.0.0) defines a set of addresses whose first 8 bits are equal. This route is advertised by ISP #1 to the other ISPs, who need a route only to 198.0.0.0/8. In its routers, ISP #1 knows which Class C networks are at which customer sites. This is how CIDR gives Internet routers a much more scalable routing table, by reducing the number of entries in the tables.

Historically speaking, ISPs then found ways to use CIDR to allow better use of the IP Version 4 address space. Imagine that Customer #1 and Customer #3 need 10 and 20 IP addresses— ever. Each customer has only a router and a single Ethernet. Each customer could register its own Class C network, but if both did so, it would not be in the range already registered to the ISP.

So, to help CIDR work in the Internet, ISP #1 wants its customers to use IP addresses in the 198.*x.x.x* range. As a service, the ISP suggests to Customer #1 something like this: Use IP subnet 198.8.3.16/28, with assignable addresses 198.8.17 to 198.8.30. To Customer #3, who needs 20 addresses, ISP #1 suggests 198.8.3.32/27, with 30 assignable addresses (198.8.3.33 to 198.8.3.62). (Feel free to check the math with the IP addressing algorithms listed earlier.)

NOTE	The notation with the / followed by the number is a common designation on Cisco routers meaning that the mask has that number of 1 bit. This number of 1 bit is called the *prefix*. In this case, the mask implied with prefix /27 would be 255.255.255.224.)

The need for registered IP network numbers is reduced through CIDR. Instead of the two customers consuming two whole Class C networks, each consumes a small portion of a single network. The ISP gets customers to use its IP addresses in a convenient range of values, so CIDR works well and enables the Internet to grow.

Private Addressing

A legitimate need exists for IP addresses that will never be used in the interconnected IP networks called the Internet. So, when designing the IP addressing convention for such a network, an organization could pick any network number(s) it wanted and use it, and all would be well. Of course, that's true until the organization decides to connect to the Internet—but that will be covered later.

When IP addresses that aren't connected to the Internet are needed, they can also be pulled from a set of IP networks called private Internets, as defined in RFC 1918, "Address Allocation for Private Internets" (www.ietf.org/rfc/rfc1918.txt). This RFC defines a set of networks that will never be assigned to any organization as a registered network number. Table 5-25 shows the private address space defined by RFC 1918.

Table 5-25 *RFC 1918 Private Address Space*

Range of IP Addresses	Class of Networks	Number of Networks
10.0.0.0 to 10.255.255.255	A	1
172.16.0.0 to 172.31.255.255	B	16
192.168.0.0 to 192.168.255.255	C	256

In other words, any organization can use these network numbers. However, no organization is allowed to advertise these networks as routes into the Internet.

The IP Version 4 address space is conserved if all organizations use private addresses in cases for which there will never be a need for Internet connectivity. So, the dreaded day of exhausting the registered IP Version 4 network numbers has been delayed again, in part by CIDR and in part by private addressing.

Private addressing's requirement that the privately addressed hosts cannot communicate with others through the Internet can be a particularly onerous restriction. The solution: private addressing with the use of Network Address Translation (NAT).

Network Address Translation

Network Address Translation (NAT) is an RFC-defined function implemented in IOS that allows a host that does not have a valid registered IP address to communicate with other hosts through the Internet. The hosts may be using private addresses or addresses assigned to another organization; in either case, NAT allows these addresses that are not Internet-ready to continue to be used but still allow communication with hosts across the Internet.

NAT achieves its goal by using a valid address in some registered IP network to represent the invalid address to the rest of the Internet. The NAT function changes the IP addresses as necessary inside each IP packet, as shown in Figure 5-25.

Figure 5-25   *NAT IP Address Swapping—Private Addressing*

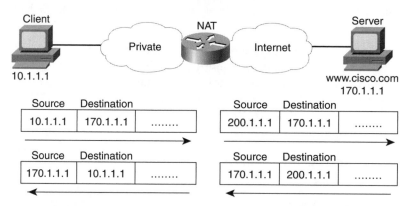

Notice that the packet's source IP address is changed when leaving the private organization, and the destination address is changed each time a packet is forwarded back into the private network. Network 200.1.1.0 has been registered as a network owned by Cisco in Figure 5-25, with address 200.1.1.1 configured as part of the NAT configuration. The NAT feature, configured in the router labeled NAT, performs the translation. As you might expect, NAT certainly requires more processing than simply routing the packet. Cisco does not recommend using NAT for a large volume of different hosts.

NAT also can be used when the private organization is not using private addressing but is instead using a network number registered to another company. (A client company of mine had originally done just that—ironically, the company was using a network number registered to Cabletron, which my client saw used in a presentation by an ex-Cabletron employee who then worked at 3COM. The 3COM SE explained IP addressing using the Cabletron registered network number; my client liked the design and took him at his word—exactly.) If one company inappropriately uses the same network number that is registered appropriately to a different company, NAT can be used, but both the source and the destination IP addresses will need to be translated. For instance, consider Figure 5-26, with Company A using a network that is registered to Cisco (170.1.0.0):

Figure 5-26   *NAT IP Address Swapping—Unregistered Networks*

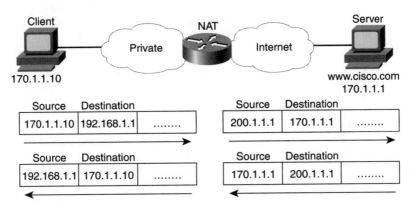

In this case, the client in Company A couldn't send a packet to 170.1.1.1—or, at least, if it did, the packet would never get to the real 170.1.1.1 in Cisco's network. That is because there is a very reasonable possibility that the private network has a route matching 170.1.1.1 in its routing table that points to some subnet inside the private company. So, when the DNS reply comes back past the NAT router, the DNS reply is changed by NAT so that the client in Company A thinks www.cisco.com's IP address is 192.168.1.1. NAT not only translates the source IP address in outgoing packets, but it also translates the destination. Likewise, packets returning to Company A have both the source and the destination IP addresses changed.

NAT uses terminology to define the various IP addresses used for translation. Table 5-26 summarizes the terminology and meaning.

Table 5-26   *NAT Addressing Terms*

Term	Meaning	Value in Figure 5-26
Inside local	Address of the host in the private network. When NAT is needed, this address is typically a private address or an address in a network registered to another organization.	170.1.1.10
Inside global	The Internet (global network) view of the inside local address. This address is in a network registered to the company responsible for the NAT router.	200.1.1.1
Outside global	The Internet (global network) view of the address of the host correctly attached to the Internet.	170.1.1.1

continues

Table 5-26   *NAT Addressing Terms (Continued)*

Term	Meaning	Value in Figure 5-26
Outside local	When the private company reuses a network number registered to someone else, the outside local address represents the outside global address in the local (private) network. Because this address is used only in the private organization, it can be any IP address.	192.168.1.1

IP Configuration

Configuration of TCP/IP in a Cisco router is straightforward. Table 5-27 and Table 5-28 summarize many of the most common commands used for IP configuration and verification. Two sample network configurations, with both configuration and EXEC command output, follow. The Cisco IOS documentation is an excellent reference for additional IP commands; the Cisco Press book *Installing Cisco Network Devices* is an excellent reference, particularly if you are not able to attend the instructor-led version of the class.

Table 5-27   *IP Configuration Commands*

Command	Configuration Mode
ip address *ip-address mask* **[secondary]**	Interface mode
ip host *name* [*tcp-port-number*] *address1* [*address2...address8*]	Global
ip route *prefix mask* {*next-hop-router\output-interface*}	Global
ip name-server *server-address1* [[*server-address2*]...*server-address6*]	Global
ip domain-lookup	Global
ip routing	Global
ip netmask-format {**bitcount | decimal | hexadecimal**}	Interface mode
ip default-network *network*	Global
ip classless	Global
ip host *name* [*tcp-port-number*] *address1* [*address2...address8*]	Global

Table 5-28 *IP EXEC Commands*

Command	Function
show hosts	Lists all hostnames and corresponding IP addresses
show interfaces [*type number*]	Lists interface statistics, including IP address
show ip interface [*type number*]	Provides a detailed view of IP parameter settings, per interface
show ip interface brief	Provides a summary of all interfaces and their IP addresses
show ip route [*subnet*]	Shows entire routing table, or one entry if **subnet** is entered
show ip arp	Displays IP ARP cache
debug ip packet	Issues log messages for each IP packet
terminal ip netmask-format {**bitcount** I **decimal** I **hexadecimal**}	Sets type of display for subnet masks in **show** commands
ping	Sends and receives ICMP echo messages to verify connectivity
trace	Sends series of UDP packets with increasing TTL values, to verify the current route to a host

Collectively, Figure 5-27 and Example 5-2, Example 5-3, and Example 5-4 show three sites, each with two serial links and one Ethernet. The following site guidelines were used when choosing configuration details:

- Use name servers at 10.1.1.100 and 10.1.2.100.

- Use host names from Figure 5-27.

- The router's IP addresses are to be assigned from the last few valid IP addresses in their attached subnets; use a mask of 255.255.255.0.

Figure 5-27 *TCP/IP Configuration and Verifications*

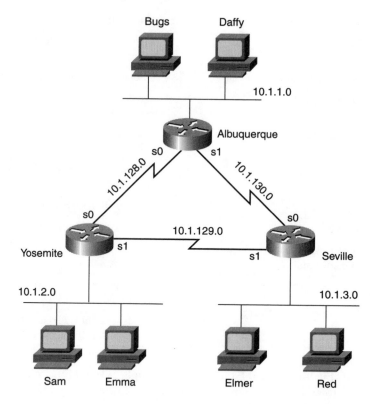

Example 5-2 *Albuquerque Router Configuration and EXEC Commands*

```
Albuquerque#show running-config
Building configuration...

Current configuration:
!
version 11.2

hostname Albuquerque
!
enable secret 5 $1$skrN$z4oq6OHfB6zu1WG4P/6ZY0
!
ip name-server 10.1.1.100
ip name-server 10.1.2.100
!
interface Serial0
 ip address 10.1.128.251 255.255.255.0
!
interface Serial1
 ip address 10.1.130.251 255.255.255.0
```

Example 5-2 *Albuquerque Router Configuration and EXEC Commands (Continued)*

```
!
interface Ethernet0
 ip address 10.1.1.251 255.255.255.0
!
no ip classless
banner motd ^C
   Should've taken a left turn here! This is Albuquerque...   ^C
!
line con 0
 password cisco
 login
line aux 0
line vty 0 4
 password cisco
 login
!
end

Albuquerque#show ip route
Codes: C - connected, S - static, I - IGRP, R - RIP, M - mobile, B - BGP
       D - EIGRP, EX - EIGRP external, O - OSPF, IA - OSPF inter area
       N1 - OSPF NSSA external type 1, N2 - OSPF NSSA external type 2
       E1 - OSPF external type 1, E2 - OSPF external type 2, E - EGP
       i - IS-IS, L1 - IS-IS level-1, L2 - IS-IS level-2, * - candidate default
       U - per-user static route, o - ODR
Gateway of last resort is not set

     10.0.0.0/24 is subnetted, 3 subnets
C       10.1.1.0 is directly connected, Ethernet0
C       10.1.130.0 is directly connected, Serial1
C       10.1.128.0 is directly connected, Serial0

Albuquerque#terminal ip netmask-format decimal
Albuquerque#show ip route
Codes: C - connected, S - static, I - IGRP, R - RIP, M - mobile, B - BGP
       D - EIGRP, EX - EIGRP external, O - OSPF, IA - OSPF inter area
       N1 - OSPF NSSA external type 1, N2 - OSPF NSSA external type 2
       E1 - OSPF external type 1, E2 - OSPF external type 2, E - EGP
       i - IS-IS, L1 - IS-IS level-1, L2 - IS-IS level-2, * - candidate default
       U - per-user static route, o - ODR

Gateway of last resort is not set

     10.0.0.0 255.255.255.0 is subnetted, 3 subnets
C       10.1.1.0 is directly connected, Ethernet0
C       10.1.130.0 is directly connected, Serial1

C       10.1.128.0 is directly connected, Serial0
Albuquerque#
```

Example 5-3 *Yosemite Router Configuration and EXEC Commands*

```
Yosemite#show running-config
Building configuration...

Current configuration:
!
version 11.2
!
hostname Yosemite
!
enable secret 5 $1$.Iud$7uHqWzDYgvJN09V7HSkLZ/
!
ip name-server 10.1.1.100
ip name-server 10.1.2.100
!
interface Serial0
 ip address 10.1.128.252 255.255.255.0
 no fair-queue
!
interface Serial1
 ip address 10.1.129.252 255.255.255.0
!
interface Ethernet0
 ip address 10.1.2.252 255.255.255.0
!
no ip classless
banner motd ^C
   This is the Rootin-est Tootin-est Router in these here parts!  ^C
!
line con 0
 password cisco
 login
line aux 0
line vty 0 4
 password cisco
 login
!
end

Yosemite#show ip interface brief
Interface              IP-Address      OK? Method Status                Protocol
Serial0                10.1.128.252    YES manual up                    up
Serial1                10.1.129.252    YES manual up                    up
Ethernet0              10.1.2.252      YES manual up                    up
Yosemite#
```

Example 5-4 *Seville Router Configuration and EXEC Commands*

```
Seville#show running-config
Building configuration...

Current configuration:
!
version 11.2

!
hostname Seville
!
enable secret 5 $1$ZvR/$Gpk5a5K5vTVpotd3KUygA1
!
ip name-server 10.1.1.100
ip name-server 10.1.2.100
!
interface Serial0
 ip address 10.1.130.253 255.255.255.0
 no fair-queue
!
interface Serial1
 ip address 10.1.129.253 255.255.255.0
!
Ethernet0
 ip address 10.1.3.253 255.255.255.0
!
no ip classless
banner motd ^C
  Take a little off the top, Wabbit!  (Elmer)    ^C
!
line con 0
 password cisco
 login
line aux 0
line vty 0 4
 password cisco
 login
!
end

Seville#show ip route
Codes: C - connected, S - static, I - IGRP, R - RIP, M - mobile, B - BGP
       D - EIGRP, EX - EIGRP external, O - OSPF, IA - OSPF inter area
       N1 - OSPF NSSA external type 1, N2 - OSPF NSSA external type 2
       E1 - OSPF external type 1, E2 - OSPF external type 2, E - EGP
       i - IS-IS, L1 - IS-IS level-1, L2 - IS-IS level-2, * - candidate default
       U - per-user static route, o - ODR

Gateway of last resort is not set


10.0.0.0/24 is subnetted, 3 subnets
C        10.1.3.0 is directly connected, Ethernet0
```

continues

Example 5-4 *Seville Router Configuration and EXEC Commands (Continued)*

```
C       10.1.130.0 is directly connected, Serial0
C       10.1.129.0 is directly connected, Serial1


Seville#show ip interface serial 1
Serial1 is up, line protocol is up
  Internet address is 10.1.129.253/24
  Broadcast address is 255.255.255.255
  Address determined by nonvolatile memory
  MTU is 1500 bytes
  Helper address is not set
  Directed broadcast forwarding is disabled
  Outgoing access list is not set
  Inbound  access list is not set
  Proxy ARP is enabled
  Security level is default
  Split horizon is enabled
  ICMP redirects are always sent
  ICMP unreachables are always sent
  ICMP mask replies are never sent
  IP fast switching is enabled
  IP fast switching on the same interface is enabled
  IP Fast switching turbo vector
  IP multicast fast switching is enabled
  IP multicast distributed fast switching is disabled
  Router Discovery is disabled
  IP output packet accounting is disabled
  IP access violation accounting is disabled
 TCP/IP header compression is disabled
  RTP/IP header compression is disabled
  Probe proxy name replies are disabled
  Policy routing is disabled
  Network address translation is disabled
  Web Cache Redirect is disabled
  BGP Policy Mapping is disabled

Seville#show interface serial 0
Serial0 is up, line protocol is up
  Hardware is HD64570
  Internet address is 10.1.130.253/24
  MTU 1500 bytes, BW 1544 Kbit, DLY 20000 usec, rely 255/255, load 1/255
  Encapsulation HDLC, loopback not set, keepalive set (10 sec)
  Last input 00:00:05, output 00:00:04, output hang never
  Last clearing of "show interface" counters never
  Queuing strategy: fifo
  Output queue 0/40, 0 drops; input queue 0/75, 0 drops
  5 minute input rate 0 bits/sec, 0 packets/sec
  5 minute output rate 0 bits/sec, 0 packets/sec
     273 packets input, 18621 bytes, 0 no buffer
     Received 215 broadcasts, 0 runts, 0 giants, 0 throttles
     0 input errors, 0 CRC, 0 frame, 0 overrun, 0 ignored, 0 abort
     309 packets output, 20175 bytes, 0 underruns
     0 output errors, 0 collisions, 23 interface resets
```

Example 5-4 *Seville Router Configuration and EXEC Commands (Continued)*

```
       0 output buffer failures, 0 output buffers swapped out
       0 carrier transitions
       DCD=up  DSR=up  DTR=up  RTS=up  CTS=up

Seville#show ip arp
Protocol  Address          Age (min)  Hardware Addr  Type   Interface
Internet  10.1.3.102              0    0060.978b.1301  ARPA   Ethernet0
Internet  10.1.3.253              -    0000.0c3e.5183  ARPA   Ethernet0

Seville#debug ip packet
IP packet debugging is on
Seville#ping 10.1.130.251
Type escape sequence to abort.
Sending 5, 100-byte ICMP Echos to 10.1.130.251, timeout is 2 seconds:
!!!!!
Success rate is 100 percent (5/5), round-trip min/avg/max = 80/81/84 ms
Seville#
00:09:38: IP: s=10.1.130.251 (local), d=10.1.130.251 (Serial1), len 100, sending
00:09:38: IP: s=10.1.130.251 (Serial1), d=10.1.130.253 (Serial1), len 100, rcvd 3
00:09:38: IP: s=10.1.130.253 (local), d=10.1.130.251 (Serial1), len 100, sending
00:09:38: IP: s=10.1.130.251 (Serial1), d=10.1.130.253 (Serial1), len 100, rcvd 3
00:09:38: IP: s=10.1.130.253 (local), d=10.1.130.251 (Serial1), len 100, sending
00:09:38: IP: s=10.1.130.251 (Serial1), d=10.1.130.253 (Serial1), len 100, rcvd 3
00:09:38: IP: s=10.1.130.253 (local), d=10.1.130.251 (Serial1), len 100, sending
00:09:38: IP: s=10.1.130.251 (Serial1), d=10.1.130.253 (Serial1), len 100, rcvd 3
00:09:38: IP: s=10.1.130.253 (local), d=10.1.130.251 (Serial1), len 100, sending
00:09:38: IP: s=10.1.130.251 (Serial1), d=10.1.130.253 (Serial1), len 100, rcvd 3
Seville#
```

Notice that the configuration matches the output of the **show interface**, **show ip interface**, and **show interface ip brief** commands. For instance, in Example 5-3, the IP addresses in the configuration match the output of **show ip interface brief**. If these details did not match, one common oversight is that you are looking at the configuration in NVRAM, not in RAM. Make sure to use the **show running-config** or **write terminal** commands to see the active configuration.

The subnet mask in the output of **show** commands is encoded by numbering the network and subnet bits. For example, 10.1.4.0/24 means 24 network and subnet bits, leaving 8 host bits with this subnetting scheme. The **terminal ip netmask** command can be used to change this formatting, as seen in Example 5-2.

Example 5-4 shows the ARP cache generated by the **show ip arp** output. The first entry shows the IP address and MAC address of another host on the Ethernet. The timer value of 0 implies that the entry is very fresh—the value grows with disuse. One entry is shown for the router's Ethernet interface itself, which never times out of the ARP table.

The **debug ip packet** output in Example 5-4 lists one entry per IP packet sent and received. This command is a very dangerous command—it could crash almost any production router due to the added overhead of processing the debug messages. Notice that the output shows both the source and destination IP addresses.

The routing table in Example 5-4 does not list all subnets because the routing protocol configuration has not been added. Notice that the **show ip route** commands list routes to the directly attached subnets, but no others. The **ip route** commands in Example 5-5 have been added to Albuquerque. Example 5-6 and Example 5-7 contain **show** commands executed after the new configuration was added.

Example 5-5   *Static Routes Added to Albuquerque*

```
ip route 10.1.2.0 255.255.255.0 10.1.128.252
ip route 10.1.3.0 255.255.255.0 10.1.130.253
```

Example 5-6   *Albuquerque Router EXEC Commands, After Adding Static Routes for 10.1.2.0 and 10.1.3.0*

```
Albuquerque#show ip route
Codes: C - connected, S - static, I - IGRP, R - RIP, M - mobile, B - BGP
       D - EIGRP, EX - EIGRP external, O - OSPF, IA - OSPF inter area
       N1 - OSPF NSSA external type 1, N2 - OSPF NSSA external type 2
       E1 - OSPF external type 1, E2 - OSPF external type 2, E - EGP
       i - IS-IS, L1 - IS-IS level-1, L2 - IS-IS level-2, * - candidate default
       U - per-user static route, o - ODR

Gateway of last resort is not set

     10.0.0.0/24 is subnetted, 5 subnets
S       10.1.3.0 [1/0] via 10.1.130.253
S       10.1.2.0 [1/0] via 10.1.128.252
C       10.1.1.0 is directly connected, Ethernet0
C       10.1.130.0 is directly connected, Serial1
C       10.1.128.0 is directly connected, Serial0
Albuquerque#ping 10.1.128.252

Type escape sequence to abort.
Sending 5, 100-byte ICMP Echos to 10.1.128.252, timeout is 2 seconds:
!!!!!
Success rate is 100 percent (5/5), round-trip min/avg/max = 4/4/8 ms

! Note: the following extended ping command will result in some debug messages
! on Yosemite in Example 5-7.

Albuquerque#ping
Protocol [ip]:
Target IP address: 10.1.2.252
Repeat count [5]:
Datagram size [100]:
Timeout in seconds [2]:
Extended commands [n]: y
Source address or interface: 10.1.1.251
Type of service [0]:
Set DF bit in IP header? [no]:
Validate reply data? [no]:
Data pattern [0xABCD]:
Loose, Strict, Record, Timestamp, Verbose[none]:
Sweep range of sizes [n]:
Type escape sequence to abort.
```

Example 5-6   *Albuquerque Router EXEC Commands, After Adding Static Routes for 10.1.2.0 and 10.1.3.0 (Continued)*

```
Sending 5, 100-byte ICMP Echos to 10.1.2.252, timeout is 2 seconds:
. . . . .
Success rate is 0 percent (0/5)
Albuquerque#
```

Example 5-7   *show ip route on Yosemite, After Adding Static Routes to Albuquerque*

```
Yosemite#show ip route
Codes: C - connected, S - static, I - IGRP, R - RIP, M - mobile, B - BGP
       D - EIGRP, EX - EIGRP external, O - OSPF, IA - OSPF inter area
       N1 - OSPF NSSA external type 1, N2 - OSPF NSSA external type 2
       E1 - OSPF external type 1, E2 - OSPF external type 2, E - EGP
       i - IS-IS, L1 - IS-IS level-1, L2 - IS-IS level-2, * - candidate default
       U - per-user static route, o - ODR

Gateway of last resort is not set

     10.0.0.0/24 is subnetted, 3 subnets
C       10.1.2.0 is directly connected, Ethernet0
C       10.1.129.0 is directly connected, Serial1
C       10.1.128.0 is directly connected, Serial0
Yosemite#ping 10.1.128.251

Type escape sequence to abort.
Sending 5, 100-byte ICMP Echos to 10.1.128.251, timeout is 2 seconds:
!!!!!
Success rate is 100 percent (5/5), round-trip min/avg/max = 4/4/8 ms
Yosemite#ping 10.1.1.251

Type escape sequence to abort.
Sending 5, 100-byte ICMP Echos to 10.1.1.251, timeout is 2 seconds:
.....
Success rate is 0 percent (0/5)
Yosemite#debug ip icmp
ICMP packet debugging is on
Yosemite#
Yosemite#show debug
Generic IP:
  ICMP packet debugging is on
Yosemite#

!NOTE: the following debug messages are a result of the extended ping
!command issued on Albuquerque in Example 5-6;
!these messages are generated by Yosemite!

ICMP: echo reply sent, src 10.1.2.252, dst 10.1.1.251
ICMP: echo reply sent, src 10.1.2.252, dst 10.1.1.251
ICMP: echo reply sent, src 10.1.2.252, dst 10.1.1.251
ICMP: echo reply sent, src 10.1.2.252, dst 10.1.1.251
ICMP: echo reply sent, src 10.1.2.252, dst 10.1.1.251
```

Two subtleties of the **ping** command are used in these two example console dialogs of Examples 5-6 and 5-7:

- Cisco **ping** commands use the output interface's IP address as the source address of the packet, unless otherwise specified in an extended **ping**. The first **ping** in Example 5-6 uses a source of 10.1.128.251; the extended **ping** uses the source address shown (10.1.1.251).

- ICMP Echo Reply messages (ping responses) reverse the IP addresses used in the ICMP Echo Request to which it is responding.

The extended version of the **ping** command can be used to more fully refine the underlying cause of the problem. In fact, when a **ping** from a router works but a **ping** from a host does not, the extended **ping** could help in re-creating the problem without needing to work with the end user on the phone. For instance, the extended **ping** command on Albuquerque sent an Echo Request from 10.1.1.251 (Albuquerque's Ethernet) to 10.1.2.252 (Yosemite's Ethernet); no response was received by Albuquerque. Normally, the echoes are sourced from the IP address of the outgoing interface; with the use of the extended **ping** source address option, the source IP address of the echo packet can be changed. It appears that the ICMP Echo Requests were received by Yosemite because the debug messages on Yosemite imply that it sent ICMP Echo Replies back to 10.1.1.251. Somewhere between Yosemite creating the ICMP echo replies and Albuquerque receiving them, a problem occurred.

An examination of the steps after the echo replies were created by Yosemite is needed to understand the problem in this example. ICMP asks the IP software in Yosemite to deliver the packets. The IP code performs IP routing table lookup to find the correct route for these packets, whose destination is 10.1.1.251. However, the **show ip route** command output in Example 5-7 shows that Yosemite has no route to subnet 10.1.1.0. It seems that Yosemite created the Echo Reply messages but failed to send them because it has no route to 10.1.1.0/24. This is just one example in which the route in one direction is working fine, but the route in the reverse direction is not.

Other options for extended **ping** are also quite useful. The Don't Fragment (DF) bit can be set, along with the amount of data to send in the echo, so that the MTU for the entire route can be discovered through experimentation. Echo packets that are too large to pass over a link due to MTU restrictions will be discarded because the DF bit is set. The timeout value can be set so that the **ping** command will wait longer than the default 2 seconds before thinking that an echo will receive a reply. Furthermore, not only can a single size for the ICMP Echo be set, but a range of sizes can be used to give a more realistic set of packets.

One key to troubleshooting with the **ping** command is understanding the various codes the command uses to signify the various responses it can receive. Table 5-29 lists the various codes that the Cisco IOS **ping** command can supply.

Table 5-29   *Explanation of the Codes the **ping** Command Receives in Response to Its ICMP Echo Request*

ping Command Code	Explanation
!	ICMP Echo Reply received
.	Nothing received
U	ICMP unreachable (destination) received
N	ICMP unreachable (network) received
P	ICMP unreachable (port) received
Q	ICMP source quench received
M	ICMP can't fragment message received
?	Unknown packet received

Using Secondary Addresses

As a CCNA, Cisco expects you to be comfortable and familiar with IP address planning issues. One such issue involves what to do when there are no more unassigned IP addresses in a subnet. One alternative solution is to change the mask used on that subnet, making the existing subnet larger. However, changing the mask could cause an overlap. For example, if 10.1.4.0/24 is running out of addresses and you make a change to mask 255.255.254.0 (9 host bits, 23 network/subnet bits), an overlap can occur. 10.1.4.0/23 includes addresses 10.1.4.0 to 10.1.5.255; this is indeed an overlap with subnet 10.1.5.0/24. If subnet 10.1.5.0/24 already exists, using 10.1.4.0/23 would not work. Another alternative for continued growth is to place all the existing addresses in the mostly full subnet in another larger subnet. There must be a valid subnet number that is unassigned, that does not create an overlap, and that is larger than the old subnet. However, this solution causes administrative effort to change the IP addresses. In either case, both solutions that do not use secondary addressing imply a strategy of using different masks in different parts of the network. Use of these different masks is called variable-length subnet masking (VLSM), which brings up another set of complex routing protocol issues.

This same issue can be solved by the use of IP secondary addressing. Secondary addressing uses multiple subnets on the same data link. Secondary IP addressing is simple in concept. Because more than one subnet is used on the same medium, the router needs to have more than one IP address on the interface attached to that medium. For example, Figure 5-27 has subnet 10.1.2.0/24; assume that the subnet has all IP addresses assigned. Assuming secondary addressing to be the chosen solution, subnet 10.1.7.0/24 could also be used on the same Ethernet. Example 5-8 shows the configuration for secondary IP addressing on Yosemite.

Example 5-8 *Secondary IP Addressing Configuration and* **show ip route** *Command on Yosemite*

```
! Excerpt from show running-config follows...
Hostname Yosemite
ip domain-lookup
ip name-server 10.1.1.100 10.1.2.100
interface ethernet 0
ip address 10.1.7.252   255.255.255.0 secondary
ip address 10.1.2.252   255.255.255.0
interface serial 0
ip address 10.1.128.252   255.255.255.0
interface serial 1
ip address 10.1.129.252   255.255.255.0

Yosemite#show ip route
Codes: C - connected, S - static, I - IGRP, R - RIP, M - mobile, B - BGP
       D - EIGRP, EX - EIGRP external, O - OSPF, IA - OSPF inter area
       N1 - OSPF NSSA external type 1, N2 - OSPF NSSA external type 2
       E1 - OSPF external type 1, E2 - OSPF external type 2, E - EGP
       i - IS-IS, L1 - IS-IS level-1, L2 - IS-IS level-2, * - candidate default
       U - per-user static route, o - ODR

Gateway of last resort is not set

     10.0.0.0/24 is subnetted, 4 subnets
C       10.1.2.0 is directly connected, Ethernet0
C       10.1.7.0 is directly connected, Ethernet0
C       10.1.129.0 is directly connected, Serial1
C       10.1.128.0 is directly connected, Serial0
Yosemite#
```

The router has routes to subnets 10.1.2.0/24 and 10.1.7.0/24, so it can forward packets to each subnet. The router also can receive packets from hosts in one subnet and can forward the packets to the other subnet using the same interface.

IP Addressing with Frame Relay Subinterfaces

Frame Relay configuration can be accomplished with or without the use of subinterfaces. If subinterfaces are not used, then all router interfaces attached to this same Frame Relay cloud should be configured with IP addresses in the same subnet. In other words, treat the Frame Relay cloud as any other multiaccess medium (such as a LAN). However, Frame Relay configuration without subinterfaces introduces some routing protocol issues when there is not a full mesh of virtual circuits (VCs) between each pair of routers. Subinterfaces allow distance vector routing protocols to work well because individual VCs can be considered as separate interfaces. This allows the routing protocol to maintain its split-horizon feature to defeat routing loops.

Chapter 8, "WAN Protocols and Design," covers issues relating to the design choices of when to use subinterfaces and what type to use. This current section discusses how to assign IP addresses after those choices are made.

The use of subinterfaces and the type of subinterface implies the number of subnets used for Frame Relay. A point-to-point subinterface terminates one VC and has an IP address assigned to it; the router on the other end of the VC uses an IP address in the same subnet. These two IP addresses are the only two addresses in the subnet. Each separate instance of a pair of routers on opposing ends of a VC, each with a point-to-point subinterface configuration, implies the use of yet another subnet, with only two host addresses in the subnet.

The use of no subinterfaces and the use of multipoint subinterfaces are identical from the perspective of how to assign IP addresses. Multipoint subinterfaces are used when multiple VCs terminate at the subinterface; this subinterface, along with all subinterfaces on other routers at the other end of these VCs, are configured to be in the same subnet. With no subinterfaces used, all the routers attached to the Frame Relay network are also considered to be in the same subnet.

Most often, point-to-point subinterfaces are used when a partial mesh of VCs is used. Conversely, multipoint subnets are used when a full mesh is used. However, both types of subinterface are allowed in the same router. Figure 5-28 shows a Frame Relay configuration requiring three different subnets over a Frame Relay cloud.

Figure 5-28   *Frame Relay Subnets with Point-to-Point and Multipoint Subinterfaces*

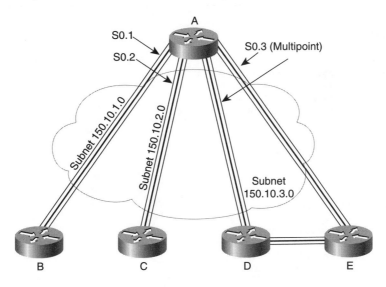

Example 5-9, Example 5-10, and Example 5-11 show the configurations on Routers A, B, and E, respectively.

Example 5-9 *Router A Configuration*

```
hostname routerA
interface serial 0
encapsulation frame-relay
!
interface serial 0.1 point-to-point
ip address 150.10.1.250    255.255.255.0
frame-relay interface-dlci 40
description this is for the VC to site B
!
interface serial 0.2 point-to-point
ip address 150.10.2.250    255.255.255.0
frame-relay interface-dlci 41
description this is for the VC to site C
!
interface serial 0.3 multipoint
ip address 150.10.3.250    255.255.255.0
interface-dlci 42
interface-dlci 43
description this is for the VC's to sites D and E
```

Example 5-10 *Router B Configuration*

```
hostname routerB
!
interface serial 0
encapsulation frame-relay
!
interface serial 0.1 point-to-point
ip address 150.10.1.251    255.255.255.0
frame-relay interface-dlci 44
description this is for the VC to site A
```

Example 5-11 *Router E Configuration*

```
hostname routerE
!
interface serial 0
encapsulation frame-relay
!
interface serial 0.3 multipoint
ip address 150.10.3.254    255.255.255.0
frame-relay interface-dlci 44
description this is for the VC to site A
```

For a more complete review of the concepts behind IP addressing over Frame Relay, refer to Chapter 8.

MTU and Fragmentation

The maximum transmission unit (MTU) is a concept that implies the largest Layer 3 packet that can be forwarded out an interface. The maximum MTU value allowed is based on the data link protocol; essentially, the maximum size of the data portion of the data link frame (where the packet is placed) is the maximum setting for the MTU on an interface. The default MTU value is 1500.

If an interface's MTU is smaller than a packet that must be forwarded, fragmentation is performed by the router. Fragmentation is the process of simply breaking the packet into smaller packets, each of which is less than or equal to the MTU value. For instance, consider Figure 5-29, with a point-to-point serial link whose MTU has been lowered to 1000.

Figure 5-29   *IP Fragmentation*

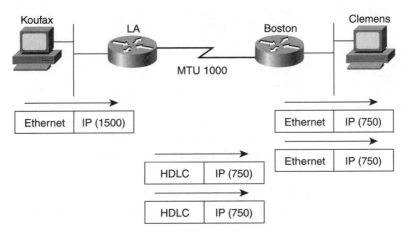

As Figure 5-29 illustrates, Koufax threw a 1500-byte packet toward Router LA. LA removed the Ethernet header but could not forward the packet because it was 1500 bytes and the HDLC link supported only an MTU of 1000. So, LA fragmented the original packet into two packets. After forwarding the two packets, Boston receives the packets and does not reassemble them—reassembly is done by the endpoint host, which in this case is Clemens.

The IP header contains fields useful for reassembly to the fragments into the original packet. The IP header includes an ID value that is the same in each fragmented packet, as well as an offset value that defines which part of the original packet is held in each fragment. So, fragmented packets arriving out of order can be identified as part of the same original packet and can be reassembled into the correct order using the offset field in each fragment.

Two configuration commands can be used to change the IP MTU size on an interface: the **mtu** interface subcommand and the **ip mtu** interface subcommand. The **mtu** command sets the MTU for all Layer 3 protocols; unless there is a need to vary the setting per Layer 3 protocol, this command is preferred. If a different setting is desired for IP, the **ip mtu** command sets the value used for IP.

A few nuances relate to the two MTU-setting commands. If both are configured on an interface, then the IP MTU setting takes precedence on the interface. However, if the **mtu** command is configured after the **ip mtu** is configured, the **ip mtu** value is reset to the same value as that of the **mtu** command. So, care must be taken when changing these values.

IP Naming Commands and Telnet

Names are never important to the process of routing IP packets. However, most human users prefer to use names instead of IP addresses, for obvious reasons. So, the process of using names—and, most frequently, using a Domain Name System (DNS) to identify the IP address that corresponds to a name—is important for end users.

Router and switch administrators like to use names in many cases, for the same reason that end users like to use names. When the administrator uses a PC or workstation, that person can open up a variety of windows and Telnet to various routers and switches. This short section is not concerned with naming in that case.

When a router or switch administrator is logged in to the router or switch, a variety of commands are available. Particularly for the **trace**, **ping**, and **telnet** commands, one key parameter is the IP address or host name of that with which you want to trace, ping, or telnet. This section describes the use of host names on an IOS-based device. Along the way, some nuances of the use of Telnet are covered.

The IOS can use statically configured names as well as refer to one or more DNSs. Example 5-12 shows some names statically configured, with configuration pointing to two different DNSs.

Example 5-12 *IP Naming Configuration and* **show ip host** *Command*

```
hostname Cooperstown
!
ip host Mays 10.1.1.1
ip host Aaron 10.2.2.2
ip host Mantle 10.3.3.3
!
ip domain-name lacidar.com
ip name-server 10.1.1.200  10.2.2.200
ip domain-lookup

Seville#show hosts
Default domain is lacidar.com
Name/address lookup uses static mappings

Host                    Flags       Age Type   Address(es)
Mays                    (perm, OK)  0   IP     10.1.1.1
Aaron                   (perm, OK)  0   IP     10.2.2.2
Mantle                  (perm, OK)  0   IP     10.3.3.3
Seville#
```

Three names are statically configured in this case—Mays, Aaron, and Mantle. When logged into Cooperstown, any command referring to Mays, Aaron, or Mantle will resolve into the IP addresses shown in the **ip host** command.

DNS configuration is shown toward the end of the configuration. For names that do not include the full domain name, the **ip domain-name** command defines the domain name that should be assumed by the router. The IP addresses of the name servers are shown in the **ip name-server** command. Up to six DNSs can be listed; they are searched for each request sequentially based on the order in the command. Finally, the **ip domain-lookup** command enables the IOS to ask a name-server. IP domain-lookup is the default; **no ip domain-lookup** disables the DNS client function.

The name Cooperstown in the **hostname** command is shown to make a point that it is not a definition that creates a correlation between a name and an IP address. The **hostname** command tells this device what its own name is; any command referring to a host name and with Cooperstown typed as the host name would need either an **ip host** command or a DNS resolution for Cooperstown for the command to work.

The **show ip host** command lists the static entries, in addition to any entries learned from a DNS request. Only the three static entries were in the table, in this case. The term *perm* in the output implies that the entry is static.

Telnet on the IOS

The **telnet** IOS EXEC command can be particularly useful when working with more than one router or switch at the same time. If you prefer, you could open more windows on your desktop and Telnet to the various routers and switches. However, if you log in to one router and then want to Telnet to others, this subsection provides you with some interesting capabilities of the IOS Telnet client and server.

Each IOS runs a Telnet server automatically. Just like other Telnet servers, it listens on port 23. The **telnet** EXEC command is a Telnet client, which can be used to Telnet to many other devices, not just another router or switch. So, many of the same assumptions you make about Telnet are true for the IOS-based Telnet client and server.

The convenient use of the suspend function of the Telnet client is one of the best features of the Telnet client. For this discussion, you will need to refer to the network diagram in Figure 5-30.

Figure 5-30 *Telnet Suspension*

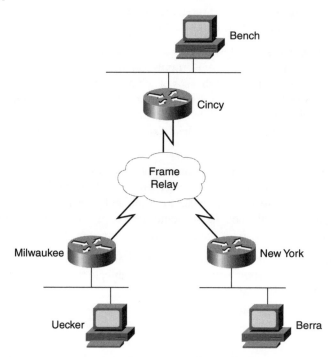

In the figure, the router administrator is using Bench to Telnet into the Cincy router. Once in Cincy, the user Telnets to Milwaukee. Once in Milwaukee, the user suspends the Telnet by pressing Ctrl+Shift+6, followed by pressing the letter x. The user then Telnets to New York and again suspends the connection. Example 5-13 shows an example output:

Example 5-13 *Telnet Suspensions*

```
Cincy#telnet milwaukee
Trying Milwaukee (10.1.4.252)... Open


User Access Verification

Password:
Milwaukee>
Milwaukee>
Milwaukee>
(Note: User pressed CTL-SHIFT-6, then x)
Cincy#telnet NewYork
Trying NewYork (10.1.6.253)... Open


User Access Verification
```

Example 5-13 *Telnet Suspensions (Continued)*

```
Password:
NewYork>
NewYork>
NewYork>
NewYork>
(Note: User pressed CTL-SHIFT-6, then x)

Cincy#show sessions
Conn Host              Address            Byte  Idle Conn Name
    1 milwaukee        10.1.4.252            0     0 milwaukee
*   2 NewYork          10.1.6.253            0     0 NewYork

Cincy#where
Conn Host              Address            Byte  Idle Conn Name
    1 milwaukee        10.1.4.252            0     0 milwaukee
*   2 NewYork          10.1.6.253            0     0 NewYork

Cincy#resume 1
[Resuming connection 1 to milwaukee ... ]

Milwaukee>
Milwaukee>
Milwaukee>
(Note: User pressed CTL-SHIFT-6, then x)
Cincy#
[Resuming connection 1 to milwaukee ... ]
(Note: User, when at Cincy, just pressed return)
Milwaukee>
Milwaukee>
Milwaukee>
(Note: User pressed CTL-SHIFT-6, then x)
Cincy#disconnect 1
Closing connection to milwaukee [confirm]
Cincy#
[Resuming connection 2 to NewYork ... ]
(Note: User, when at Cincy, just pressed return)
NewYork>
NewYork>
NewYork>
(Note: User pressed CTL-SHIFT-6, then x)
Cincy#disconnect 2
Closing connection to NewYork [confirm]
Cincy#
```

Example 5-13 begins with the Cincy command prompt that would be seen in Bench's Telnet window because the user at Bench Telnetted into Cincy first. After Telnetting to Milwaukee, the Telnet connection was suspended. Then, after Telnetting to NewYork, that connection was suspended. The two connections can be suspended or resumed easily. The **resume** command can be used to resume the connections; however, the **resume** command requires a connection ID, which is shown in the **show connections** command. (The **where** command provides the same output.)

The interesting and potentially dangerous nuance here is that if a Telnet session is suspended and you simply press **Enter**, *the IOS resumes the connection to the most recently suspended Telnet connection.* That is fine, until you realize how much you tend to press the **Enter** key occasionally to clear some of the clutter from the screen. With a suspended Telnet connection, you also just happened to reconnect to another router. This is particularly dangerous when you are changing the configuration or using potentially damaging EXEC commands—be careful about what router you are actually using when you type the command.

Default Routes and the ip classless Command

Default route processing can be useful in several situations. Default route processing is a general term that refers to the choices that the router can make when no match exists between the routing table and the destination address of a packet. Without any default routes, a packet whose destination is not matched in the routing table is discarded.

Figure 5-31 shows a typical case in which some form of default route would be useful. R1, R2, and R3 are connected to the rest of this network only via R1's Token Ring interface. If R2 and R3 could forward packets meant for unknown destinations to R1, and if R1 knew to send them to router Dist1, then all three routers could deliver packets to the rest of the network without actually needing to route to all the other networks subnets in their routing tables.

Figure 5-31 *Example Static Default Network*

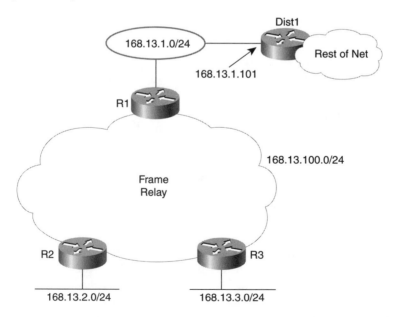

By coding a default route on R1 that points to router Dist1 in Figure 5-31, the default routing can be accomplished. R1 advertises the default route to R2 and R3. Examples 5-14 and 5-15, along with Figure 5-31, show an example of a default route on R1.

Example 5-14 *R1 Static Default Route Configuration and Routing Table*

```
R1(config)#ip route 0.0.0.0 0.0.0.0 168.13.1.101

R1#show ip route
Codes: C - connected, S - static, I - IGRP, R - RIP, M - mobile, B - BGP
       D - EIGRP, EX - EIGRP external, O - OSPF, IA - OSPF inter area
       N1 - OSPF NSSA external type 1, N2 - OSPF NSSA external type 2
       E1 - OSPF external type 1, E2 - OSPF external type 2, E - EGP
       i - IS-IS, L1 - IS-IS level-1, L2 - IS-IS level-2, * - candidate default
       U - per-user static route, o - ODR

Gateway of last resort is 168.13.1.101 to network 0.0.0.0

     168.13.0.0/24 is subnetted, 4 subnets
C       168.13.1.0 is directly connected, TokenRing0
R       168.13.3.0 [120/1] via 168.13.100.3, 00:00:05, Serial0.1
R       168.13.2.0 [120/1] via 168.13.100.2, 00:00:21, Serial0.1
C       168.13.100.0 is directly connected, Serial0.1
S*   0.0.0.0/0 [1/0] via 168.13.1.101
R1#
```

Example 5-15 *R3—Nuances with Successful Use of Static Route on R1*

```
R3#show ip route
Codes: C - connected, S - static, I - IGRP, R - RIP, M - mobile, B - BGP
       D - EIGRP, EX - EIGRP external, O - OSPF, IA - OSPF inter area
       N1 - OSPF NSSA external type 1, N2 - OSPF NSSA external type 2
       E1 - OSPF external type 1, E2 - OSPF external type 2, E - EGP
       i - IS-IS, L1 - IS-IS level-1, L2 - IS-IS level-2, * - candidate default
       U - per-user static route, o - ODR

Gateway of last resort is 168.13.100.1 to network 0.0.0.0

     168.13.0.0/24 is subnetted, 4 subnets
R       168.13.1.0 [120/1] via 168.13.100.1, 00:00:13, Serial0.1
C       168.13.3.0 is directly connected, Ethernet0
R       168.13.2.0 [120/1] via 168.13.100.2, 00:00:06, Serial0.1
C       168.13.100.0 is directly connected, Serial0.1
R*   0.0.0.0/0 [120/1] via 168.13.100.1, 00:00:14, Serial0.1
R3#ping 168.13.200.1

Type escape sequence to abort.
Sending 5, 100-byte ICMP Echos to 168.13.200.1, timeout is 2 seconds:
.....
Success rate is 0 percent (0/5)
R3#
R3#conf t
Enter configuration commands, one per line.  End with CNTL/Z.
```

continues

Example 5-15 *R3—Nuances with Successful Use of Static Route on R1 (Continued)*

```
R3(config)#ip classless
R3(config)#^Z
R3#ping 168.13.200.1

Type escape sequence to abort.
Sending 5, 100-byte ICMP Echos to 168.13.200.1, timeout is 2 seconds:
!!!!!
Success rate is 100 percent (5/5), round-trip min/avg/max = 80/88/112 ms
R3#
```

The default route shows up in the routing tables in R1, R2, and R3. The default route is defined with a static **ip route** command, with destination 0.0.0.0, mask 0.0.0.0. This route matches all destinations.

The default route on R3 is not used, however, in the first **ping** on R3. This is because the **no ip classless** command was configured on R3 (not shown). This causes R3's matching logic to mean "best match in the same network as the destination of the packet." In other words, the destination (168.13.200.1) is in Class B network 168.13.0.0. Because there is no match between 168.13.200.1 and the known subnets of 168.13.0.0, then the destination is not matched by R3 and the packet is not forwarded. When **ip classless** is added to R3 (it was already configured on R1), the routing logic is changed to "best match in the entire routing table." In other words, the router ignores class rules when routing. Because the route to 0.0.0.0 is a match for any destination, that route is used and the second **ping** in Example 5-15 succeeds.

The gateway of last resort, highlighted in the **show ip route** command output, sounds like a pretty desperate feature. There are worse things than having to discard a packet in a router, but this phrase simply references the current default route. It is possible that several default routes have been configured and then distributed with a routing protocol; the Gateway of last resort is the currently used default on a particular router. Be careful—multiple defaults can cause a routing loop.

Another style of configuration for the default route uses the **ip default-network** command. This command is used most typically when you want to reach other Class A, B, or C networks by default, but all the subnets of your own network are expected to be in your own routing tables. For instance, imagine that the cloud next to Dist1 in Figure 5-31 has subnets of network 10.0.0.0 in it, as well as other networks. (Dist1 could be an ISP router.) The network in Figure 5-31 is still in use, but instead of the **ip route 0.0.0.0 0.0.0.0 168.13.1.101** command, the **ip default-network 10.0.0.0** command is used on R1. R1 uses its route to network 10.0.0.0 as its default and advertises this route as a default route to other routers. Examples 5-16 and 5-17 show several details on R1 and R3.

Example 5-16 *R1's Use of the* **ip default-network** *Command*

```
R1#show ip route
Codes: C - connected, S - static, I - IGRP, R - RIP, M - mobile, B - BGP
       D - EIGRP, EX - EIGRP external, O - OSPF, IA - OSPF inter area
       N1 - OSPF NSSA external type 1, N2 - OSPF NSSA external type 2
       E1 - OSPF external type 1, E2 - OSPF external type 2, E - EGP
       i - IS-IS, L1 - IS-IS level-1, L2 - IS-IS level-2, * - candidate default
       U - per-user static route, o - ODR

Gateway of last resort is 168.13.1.101 to network 10.0.0.0

     168.13.0.0/24 is subnetted, 5 subnets
R       168.13.200.0 [120/1] via 168.13.1.101, 00:00:12, TokenRing0
C       168.13.1.0 is directly connected, TokenRing0
R       168.13.3.0 [120/1] via 168.13.100.3, 00:00:00, Serial0.1
R       168.13.2.0 [120/1] via 168.13.100.2, 00:00:00, Serial0.1
C       168.13.100.0 is directly connected, Serial0.1
R*   10.0.0.0/8 [120/1] via 168.13.1.101, 00:00:12, TokenRing0
R1#
```

Example 5-17 *R3 Routing Table and* **trace** *Command Samples*

```
R3#show ip route
Codes: C - connected, S - static, I - IGRP, R - RIP, M - mobile, B - BGP
       D - EIGRP, EX - EIGRP external, O - OSPF, IA - OSPF inter area
       N1 - OSPF NSSA external type 1, N2 - OSPF NSSA external type 2
       E1 - OSPF external type 1, E2 - OSPF external type 2, E - EGP
       i - IS-IS, L1 - IS-IS level-1, L2 - IS-IS level-2, * - candidate default
       U - per-user static route, o - ODR

Gateway of last resort is 168.13.100.1 to network 0.0.0.0

     168.13.0.0/24 is subnetted, 5 subnets
R       168.13.200.0 [120/2] via 168.13.100.1, 00:00:26, Serial0.1
R       168.13.1.0 [120/1] via 168.13.100.1, 00:00:26, Serial0.1
C       168.13.3.0 is directly connected, Ethernet0
R       168.13.2.0 [120/1] via 168.13.100.2, 00:00:18, Serial0.1
C       168.13.100.0 is directly connected, Serial0.1
R    10.0.0.0/8 [120/2] via 168.13.100.1, 00:00:26, Serial0.1
R*   0.0.0.0/0 [120/2] via 168.13.100.1, 00:00:26, Serial0.1
R3#trace 168.13.222.2

Type escape sequence to abort.
Tracing the route to 168.13.222.2

  1 168.13.100.1 68 msec 56 msec 52 msec
  2 168.13.1.101 52 msec 56 msec 52 msec
R3#trace 10.1.222.2

Type escape sequence to abort.
Tracing the route to 10.1.222.2
```

continues

Example 5-17 *R3 Routing Table and* **trace** *Command Samples (Continued)*

```
  1 168.13.100.1 68 msec 56 msec 52 msec
  2 168.13.1.101 48 msec 56 msec 52 msec
R3#trace 1.1.222.2

Type escape sequence to abort.
Tracing the route to 1.1.222.2

  1 168.13.100.1 68 msec 56 msec 52 msec
  2 168.13.1.101 48 msec 56 msec 52 msec
R3#
```

Both R1 and R3 have default routes, but they are shown differently in their respective routing tables. R1 shows a route to network 10.0.0.0 with an *, meaning that it is a candidate to be the default route. In R3, 0.0.0.0 shows up in the routing table as the candidate default route. The reason that R3 shows this information differently is that RIP advertises default routes using network number 0.0.0.0. If IGRP or EIGRP were in use, there would be no route to 0.0.0.0 on R3, and network 10.0.0.0 would be the candidate default route. That's because IGRP and EIGRP would flag 10.0.0.0 as a candidate default route in their routing updates rather than advertise the special case of 0.0.0.0.

The default route on R3 is used for destinations in network 168.13.0.0, 10.0.0.0, or any other network because **ip classless** is still configured. The **trace** commands in Example 5-17, which show destinations in three different networks, all succeed. The **trace** commands each show that the first router in the route was R1, then Dist1, and then the command finished. If *n* many other routers had been present in the network of Figure 5-31, then these routers could have shown up in the **trace** output as well. (In each case, the destination address was the address of some loopback interface in Dist1, so there were no routers beyond Dist1.) **ip classless** was still configured; it is recommended to configure **ip classless** if using any form of default routes.

IPX Addressing and Routing

Cisco requires a thorough knowledge of two protocol stacks for the CCNA exam—TCP/IP and Novell NetWare. Novell's NetWare protocol stack defines Internetwork Packet Exchange (IPX) as a network layer equivalent protocol, as seen in Figure 5-32. IPX will be the focus of this initial section.

IPX defines the 80-bit address structure, which uses a 32-bit network part and a 48-bit node part. As with IP and AppleTalk, all interfaces attached to the same data link use addresses in the same network. Table 5-30 lists four features of IPX addressing. The features listed in Table 5-30 are the same features used to generically describe a well-designed Layer 3 addressing scheme in Chapter 3, "OSI Reference Model & Layered Communication."

Figure 5-32   *Novell NetWare Protocols*

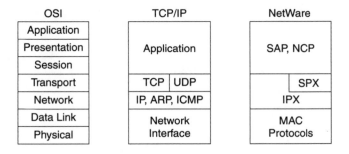

Table 5-30   *IPX Addressing Details*

Feature	Description
Size of a group	IPX addresses use a 48-bit node part of the address, giving 2^{48} possible addresses per network (minus a few reserved values), which should be big enough.
Unique addresses	IPX calls for the LAN MAC address to be used as the node part of the IPX address. This allows for easy assignment and little chance of duplication. Ensuring that no duplicates of the network numbers are made is the biggest concern because the network numbers are configured.
Grouping	The grouping concept is identical to IP, with all interfaces attached to the same medium using the same network number. There is no equivalent of IP subnetting.
Dynamic address assignment	Client IPX addresses are dynamically assigned as part of the protocol specifications. Servers and routers are configured with the network number(s) on their physical interfaces. Servers can choose to automatically generate an internal network number at installation time.

IPX routing works just like routing, as described in the section "Routing" in Chapter 3. The logic from the routing algorithm in Chapter 3 is shown here in Figure 5-33 for reference, with changes made to reflect IPX terminology.

Figure 5-33 *IPX Routing Algorithm*

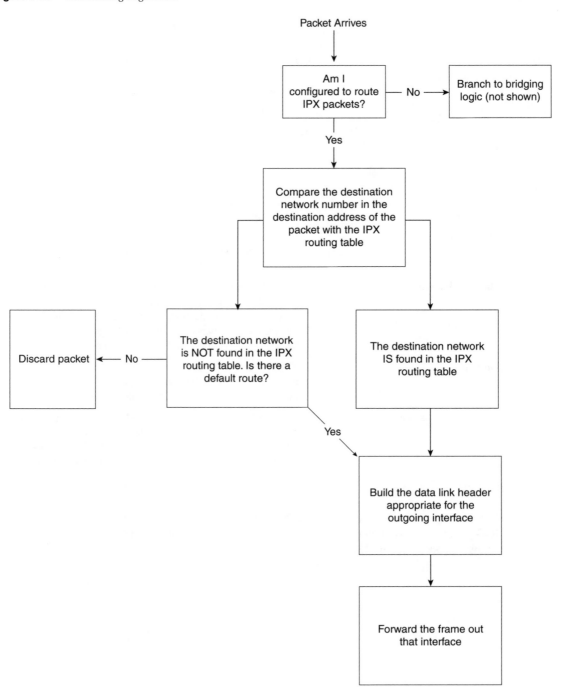

Internal Networks and Encapsulation Types

Cisco requires that CCNAs understand encapsulation, particularly with IPX. It is always Cisco's desire that the professional certifications prove that the candidate knows how to make networks that work rather than to certify individuals who are willing to memorize just for the sake of passing the test. However, IPX encapsulation is one area in which memorization is important once the base concepts are understood. Table 5-32, later in this section, lists several terms you should remember.

Encapsulation is best understood in the context of two additional and important concepts related to routing, as seen using Figure 5-34. NetWare servers use internal network numbers. Also, clients, servers, and routers all must be configured to use the correct encapsulation. Routing will also be reviewed using the same figure.

Figure 5-34   *Sample IPX Network 1*

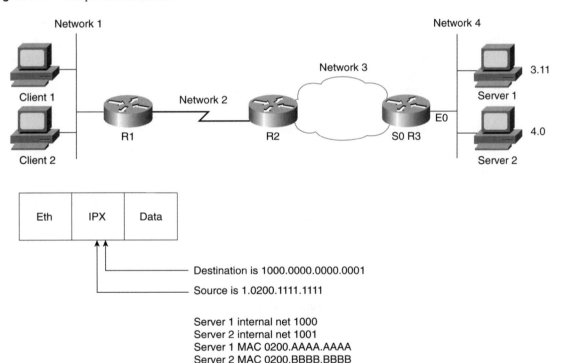

Client 1 has already logged in to Server 1 and is busily sending packets. Because NetWare servers use an internal network number, the destination of packets from Client 1 to Server 1 is 1000.0000.0000.0001. The source address of these packets is Client 1's IPX address

(1.0200.1111.1111, in this case). Of course, the routers need network 1000 in their IPX routing tables. For example, Table 5-31 shows the contents of the IPX routing table of R3:

Table 5-31   *IPX Routing Table, R3*

Network	Outgoing Interface	Next Router
1	s0	3.0200.0000.2222
2	s0	3.0200.0000.2222
3	s0	—
4	E0	—
1000	E0	4.0200.AAAA.AAAA
1001	E0	4.0200.BBBB.BBBB

R3 learned the routes to Network 3 and Network 4 because they are directly attached. The other four routes were learned via a routing protocol, which can be RIP, EIGRP, or NLSP. (NLSP is not covered on the CCNA exam.) Server 1 and Server 2 send RIP updates advertising networks 1000 and 1001, respectively. That is one reason why NetWare servers send RIP updates even if they have only one interface, as is the case with Server 1.

So, servers' internal network numbers must be in the routing tables of the routers because their internal addresses are used as the destination address of packets.

Encapsulation is the term used by Cisco to describe the type of data link header built in the routing algorithm illustrated in Figure 5-33. Encapsulation is also a source of confusion for many people when considering IPX, particularly when Ethernet is in use. Consider the IPX packet sent by Client 1 to Server 1 in Figure 5-34. Each successive router discards the data link header of the incoming frame and builds a new data link header according to the type of interface. However, Novell supports four different styles of Ethernet header that can be built at R3. The types of encapsulating Ethernet headers are shown in Figure 5-35 and are listed in Table 5-32. First, here's a brief summary of encapsulation:

> Data link encapsulation defines the details of data link headers and trailers created by a router and placed around a packet, before completing the routing process by forwarding the frame out an interface.

Figure 5-35   *IPX Ethernet Encapsulations*

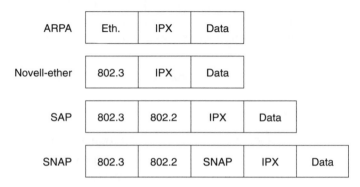

Table 5-32   *IPX Ethernet Encapsulations*

Novell's Name	Cisco IOS's Name	Hints for Remembering the Names and Meanings
Ethernet_II	ARPA	One way to help correlate the two names is to remember that ARPA was the original agency that created TCP/IP and that Ethernet_II is the older version of Ethernet; remember that the "old" names go together.
Ethernet_802.3	Novell-ether	Novell's name refers to the final header before the IPX header, in this case. There are no suggestions on easier ways to recall the IOS name Novell-ether. This setting is Novell's default on NetWare 3.11 and prior releases.
Ethernet_802.2	SAP	Novell's name refers to the final header before the IPX header, in this case. Novell's name refers to the committee and complete header that defines the SAP field; Cisco's name refers to the SAP part of the 802.2 header. (The SAP field denotes that an IPX packet follows the 802.2 header.) This setting is Novell's default on NetWare 3.12 and later releases.
Ethernet_SNAP	SNAP	Novell's name refers to the final header before the IPX header, in this case. Cisco's name refers to this same header.

The key for remembering the Novell encapsulation names is that each name refers to the header that directly precedes the IPX packet. This can help you recall header formats as well. Remembering the names in the order in this book can also help because the size of the headers increases with the third and fourth options, as compared with the first two options (see Figure 5-35).

The same encapsulation issue exists on Token Ring and FDDI interfaces. Table 5-33 outlines the options.

Table 5-33   *IPX Token Ring and FDDI Encapsulations*

Novell's Name	Cisco IOS's Name	Description and Hints for Remembering
FDDI_Raw	Novell-fddi	The IPX packet follows directly after the FDDI header. No Type field of any kind is used.
FDDI_802.2	SAP	The IPX packet follows the 802.2 header. Novell's name refers to the committee and complete header that defines the SAP field; Cisco's name refers to the SAP part of the 802.2 header.
FDDI_SNAP	SNAP	Novell's name refers to the final header before the IPX header, in this case. Cisco's name refers to this same header.
Token-Ring	SAP	The IPX packet follows the 802.2 header. Novell's name refers to the committee and complete header that defines the SAP field; Cisco's name refers to the SAP part of the 802.2 header.
Token-Ring_SNAP	SNAP	Novell's name refers to the final header before the IPX header. Cisco's name refers to this same header.

One or more encapsulations are needed per Ethernet interface. If all NetWare clients/servers on the Ethernet use the same encapsulation, just that single encapsulation is needed. However, if more than one encapsulation is used, then multiple encapsulations are needed on the router. To configure multiple encapsulations in the IOS, multiple IPX network numbers must be used on the same Ethernet, one per encapsulation.

Two methods of configuration can be used to create two IPX networks on the same link. The first method uses IPX secondary addresses, and the other uses subinterfaces. Both require one IPX network number per encapsulation type per physical interface. Both methods cause the same protocol flows to occur. The subinterface style of configuration allows the use of NLSP, whereas secondary interface configuration does not. (Sample configurations are shown in the next section of this chapter.)

Figure 5-36 illustrates the concept of IPX secondary addressing. Server 1 uses Novell-ether, and Server 2 uses SAP encapsulation. Network 4 devices use Novell-ether, and Network 5 devices use SAP.

Figure 5-36   *Multiple IPX Encapsulations on One Ethernet*

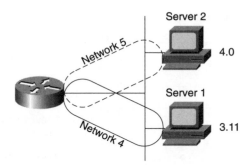

The router's choice of encapsulation for forwarding packets is relatively straightforward. If the route refers to a next router in Network 4, the router uses Novell-ether encapsulation. If the route refers to a next router in Network 5, the router uses SAP encapsulation. For RIP and SAP updates, the router sends updates on to both IPX networks, using the two different encapsulations, respectively. This is also true if the subinterface style of supporting multiple encapsulations is used instead of secondary addressing.

Troubleshooting can be more challenging because clients or servers using only a single encapsulation cannot communicate directly if they are using different encapsulations. Also, clients and servers on the same LAN that happen to use different encapsulations will require that their packets be routed by the router so that the encapsulation is changed. Therefore, there are many advantages to not using multiple encapsulations.

IPX Configuration

Configuration of IPX and IPX RIP on a Cisco router is relatively straightforward. Hands-on experience is the best way to fully learn the details of configuration. In lieu of that, this section lists commands, provides examples, and points out any tricky features. Table 5-34 and Table 5-35 summarize the more popular commands used for IPX configuration and verification. Two configuration samples follow. The Cisco IOS documentation serves as an excellent reference for additional IPX commands; the Cisco Press book *Installing Cisco Network Devices* also is an excellent reference, particularly if you are not able to attend the instructor-led version of the class.

Table 5-34   *IPX and IPX RIP Configuration Commands*

Command	Configuration Mode
ipx routing [*node*]	Global
ipx maximum-paths *paths*	Global
ipx network *network* [**encapsulation** *type*] [**secondary**]	Interface mode

Table 5-35   *IPX EXEC Commands*

Command	Function
show ipx interface	Gives detailed view of IPX parameter settings, per interface
show ipx route [*network*]	Shows entire routing table, or one entry if **network** is entered
show ipx servers	Shows SAP table
show ipx traffic	Shows IPX traffic statistics
debug ipx routing [*events*	*activity*]	Gives messages describing each routing update
debug ipx sap [*events*	*activity*]	Gives messages describing each SAP update
ping *ipx-address*	Sends IPX packets to verify connectivity

The first sample is a basic configuration for the network in Figure 5-37. Example 5-18, Example 5-19, and Example 5-20 provide the configuration.

NOTE

The IPX samples also contain IP configuration. This is not required for correct operation of IPX. However, to Telnet to the routers to issue commands, IP must be configured. In fact, in almost every network with Cisco routers, IP is indeed configured. Therefore, the IPX examples generally include IP configuration.

Figure 5-37   *IPX Network with Point-to-Point Serial Links*

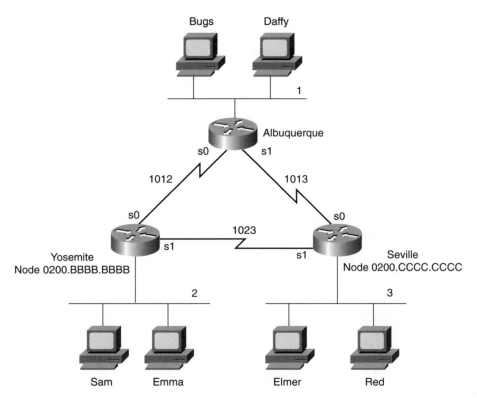

Example 5-18 *Albuquerque Configuration for IPX, Sample 1*

```
ipx routing
!
interface serial0
ip address 10.1.12.1 255.255.255.0
ipx network 1012
bandwidth 56
!
interface serial1
ip address 10.1.13.1 255.255.255.0
ipx network 1013
!
interface ethernet 0
ip address 10.1.1.1 255.255.255.0
ipx network 1
```

Example 5-19 *Yosemite Configuration for IPX, Sample 1*

```
ipx routing 0200.bbbb.bbbb
!
interface serial0
ip address 10.1.12.2 255.255.255.0
ipx network 1012
bandwidth 56
!
interface serial1
ip address 10.1.23.2 255.255.255.0
ipx network 1023
!
interface ethernet 0
ip address 10.1.2.2 255.255.255.0
ipx network 2
```

Example 5-20 *Seville Configuration for IPX, Sample 1*

```
ipx routing 0200.cccc.cccc
!
interface serial0
ip address 10.1.13.3 255.255.255.0
ipx network 1013
!
interface serial1
ip address 10.1.23.3 255.255.255.0
ipx network 1023
!
interface ethernet 0
ip address 10.1.3.3 255.255.255.0
ipx network 3
```

Enabling IPX routing globally as well as on each interface is all that is required to route IPX in a Cisco router. The **ipx routing** command enables IPX in this router and initializes the RIP and SAP processes. The individual **ipx network** commands on each interface enable IPX routing into and out of each interface and enable RIP and SAP on each interface, respectively.

The IPX addresses are not completely defined, however. Only the network number is configured. The full IPX network number is created by adding the MAC address of each interface to the configured IPX network number. For non-LAN interfaces, the MAC address of a LAN interface is used by default. However, for easier troubleshooting, a MAC address to be used as the node part of the IPX address on non-LAN interfaces can be configured. Notice the difference in the two commands in Example 5-21. The first is on Albuquerque, and the second is on Seville:

Example 5-21 *show ipx interface serial 0 on Albuquerque and Seville*

```
Albuquerque#show ipx interface serial 0
Serial0 is up, line protocol is up
  IPX address is 1012.0000.0ccf.21cd [up]
  Delay of this IPX network, in ticks is 6 throughput 0 link delay 0
  IPXWAN processing not enabled on this interface.
  IPX SAP update interval is 1 minute(s)
  IPX type 20 propagation packet forwarding is disabled
  Incoming access list is not set
  Outgoing access list is not set
  IPX helper access list is not set
  SAP GNS processing enabled, delay 0 ms, output filter list is not set
  SAP Input filter list is not set
  SAP Output filter list is not set
  SAP Router filter list is not set
  Input filter list is not set
  Output filter list is not set
  Router filter list is not set
  Netbios Input host access list is not set
  Netbios Input bytes access list is not set
  Netbios Output host access list is not set
  Netbios Output bytes access list is not set
  Updates each 60 seconds, aging multiples RIP: 3 SAP: 3
  SAP interpacket delay is 55 ms, maximum size is 480 bytes
  RIP interpacket delay is 55 ms, maximum size is 432 bytes
  Watchdog processing is disabled, SPX spoofing is disabled, idle time 60
  IPX accounting is disabled
  IPX fast switching is configured (enabled)
  RIP packets received 39, RIP packets sent 44
  SAP packets received 27, SAP packets sent 29
Albuquerque#


Seville#show ipx interface serial 0
Serial0 is up, line protocol is up
  IPX address is 1013.0200.cccc.cccc [up]
  Delay of this IPX network, in ticks is 6 throughput 0 link delay 0
  IPXWAN processing not enabled on this interface.
  IPX SAP update interval is 1 minute(s)
  IPX type 20 propagation packet forwarding is disabled
  Incoming access list is not set
  Outgoing access list is not set
  IPX helper access list is not set
  SAP GNS processing enabled, delay 0 ms, output filter list is not set
  SAP Input filter list is not set
  SAP Output filter list is not set
  SAP Router filter list is not set
  Input filter list is not set
  Output filter list is not set
  Router filter list is not set
```

continues

Example 5-21 *show ipx interface serial 0 on Albuquerque and Seville (Continued)*

```
  Netbios Input host access list is not set
  Netbios Input bytes access list is not set
  Netbios Output host access list is not set
  Netbios Output bytes access list is not set
  Updates each 60 seconds, aging multiples RIP: 3 SAP: 3
  SAP interpacket delay is 55 ms, maximum size is 480 bytes
  RIP interpacket delay is 55 ms, maximum size is 432 bytes
  Watchdog processing is disabled, SPX spoofing is disabled, idle time 60
  IPX accounting is disabled
  IPX fast switching is configured (enabled)
  RIP packets received 51, RIP packets sent 51
  SAP packets received 2, SAP packets sent 28
Seville#
```

The **show ipx interface** command provides a lot of information about IPX, including the complete IPX address. In this case, you can see that the node part of Seville's IPX address is easily recognizable, whereas Albuquerque's is not. Seville's node address is 0200.cccc.cccc based on its **ipx routing 0200.cccc.cccc** configuration command (refer to Example 5-20). However, because the node parameter was omitted from the **ipx routing** command on Albuquerque (refer to Example 5-18), the router chooses a MAC on one of the LAN interfaces to use as the node portion of the IPX addresses on non-LAN interfaces.

NOTE   After the **ipx routing** command is entered, the router saves the command with the node value. In other words, even if Albuquerque's configuration were typed as in Example 5-18, the node number chosen from a LAN interface would be shown at the end of the **ipx routing** command when viewing the configuration in the future.

Several nuances are involved in how the node parts of the addresses are assigned. The first is that if the node part of the IPX address on WAN interfaces is derived from the MAC of a LAN interface, and if there is more than one LAN interface, then the IOS must choose one MAC address to use. The algorithm uses the MAC address of the "first" Ethernet interface—or the first Token Ring interface, if no Ethernet exists, or the first FDDI interface, if no Ethernet or Token Ring exists. The lowest numbered interface number is considered to be "first." The next nuance is that if no LAN interfaces exist, the node parameter on the **ipx routing** command *must* be configured, or IPX routing will not work on a WAN interface. The final nuance is that the node part of IPX addresses on router LAN interfaces ignores the node parameter of the **ipx routing** command, and uses its specific MAC address as the node part of the address.

The second sample network (illustrated in Figure 5-38) uses Frame Relay with point-to-point subinterfaces. Example 5-22, Example 5-23, Example 5-24, and Example 5-25 show the configuration for this network.

Figure 5-38   *IPX Network with Frame Relay and Point-to-Point Subinterfaces*

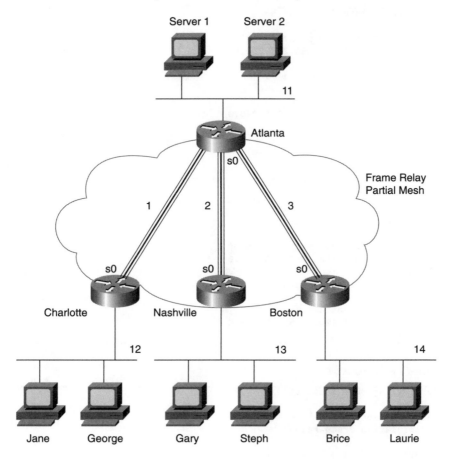

Example 5-22 *Atlanta Configuration*

```
ipx routing 0200.aaaa.aaaa
!
interface serial0
encapsulation frame-relay
!
interface serial 0.1 point-to-point
ip address 140.1.1.1   255.255.255.0
ipx network 1
frame-relay interface-dlci 52
!
interface serial 0.2 point-to-point
ip address 140.1.2.1 255.255.255.0
ipx network 2
```

continues

Example 5-22 *Atlanta Configuration (Continued)*

```
frame-relay interface-dlci 53
!
interface serial 0.3 point-to-point
ip address 140.1.3.1 255.255.255.0
ipx network 3
frame-relay interface-dlci 54
!
interface ethernet 0
ip address 140.1.11.1 255.255.255.0
ipx network 11
```

Example 5-23 *Charlotte Configuration*

```
ipx routing 0200.bbbb.bbbb
!
interface serial0
encapsulation frame-relay
!
interface serial 0.1 point-to-point
ip address 140.1.1.2  255.255.255.0
ipx network 1
frame-relay interface-dlci 51
!
interface ethernet 0
ip address 140.1.12.2 255.255.255.0
ipx network 12
```

Example 5-24 *Nashville Configuration*

```
ipx routing 0200.cccc.cccc
!
interface serial0
encapsulation frame-relay
!
interface serial 0.2 point-to-point
ip address 140.1.2.3 255.255.255.0
ipx network 2
frame-relay interface-dlci 51
!
interface ethernet 0
ip address 140.1.13.3 255.255.255.0
ipx network 13
```

Example 5-25 *Boston Configuration*

```
ipx routing 0200.dddd.dddd
!
interface serial0
encapsulation frame-relay
!
interface serial 0.3 point-to-point
```

Example 5-25 *Boston Configuration (Continued)*

```
ip address 140.1.3.4 255.255.255.0
ipx network 3
frame-relay interface-dlci 51
!
interface ethernet 0
ip address 140.1.14.4  255.255.255.0
ipx network 14
```

The configuration is very similar to the point-to-point network of Figure 5-37. The biggest difference is that each point-to-point subinterface is a different IPX network, as seen in Figure 5-38. Otherwise, SAP and RIP are enabled globally with the **ipx routing** command; each is allowed to be broadcast on interfaces (or subinterfaces) with the **ipx network** interface subcommand. SAP and RIP updates are sent out each subinterface—this means that Atlanta will replicate and send three copies of the RIP update and three copies of the SAP update on its serial0 interface, one per subinterface, every 60 seconds.

Configuration when using multiple Ethernet encapsulations is the final configuration option to be reviewed. In Figure 5-38, assume that Gary is an old NetWare client running NetWare version 3.11 client software and using the Ethernet_802.3 Novell encapsulation. Stephanie is newer and uses the Ethernet_802.2 encapsulation. Two IPX networks are used on Nashville's Ethernet 0 interface in this case.

Gary will be in Network 13, and Stephanie will be in Network 23. Example 5-26 shows just the Ethernet configuration for the Nashville network, with a secondary IPX network on Ethernet 0. Example 5-26 also shows an alternative configuration using subinterfaces.

Example 5-26 *Nashville Configuration with Secondary IPX Network on Ethernet 0*

```
ipx routing 0200.cccc.cccc

!
interface ethernet 0

ipx network 13 encapsulation novell-ether
ipx network 23 encapsulation sap secondary
! Or instead of the previous 3 lines, use the following 4 lines:
interface ethernet 0.1
ipx network 13 encapsulation novell-ether
interface ethernet 0.2
ipx network 23 encapsulation sap
```

Example 5-27 shows the output of the **debug ipx sap events** and **debug ipx routing events** commands. The network in Figure 5-39 was used to gather the sample output.

Figure 5-39   *Sample Network Used for IPX debug Commands*

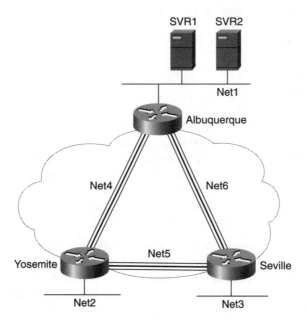

Example 5-27 *IPX **debug** Commands*

```
Seville#show ipx route
Codes: C - Connected primary network,   c - Connected secondary network
       S - Static, F - Floating static, L - Local (internal), W - IPXWAN
       R - RIP, E - EIGRP, N - NLSP, X - External, A - Aggregate
       s - seconds, u - uses, U - Per-user static

9 Total IPX routes. Up to 1 parallel paths and 16 hops allowed.

No default route known.

C         3 (NOVELL-ETHER),   Et0
C         5 (FRAME-RELAY),    Se0.2
C         6 (FRAME-RELAY),    Se0.1
R         1 [07/01] via       6.0200.aaaa.aaaa,   51s, Se0.1
R         2 [07/01] via       5.0200.bbbb.bbbb,   40s, Se0.2
R         4 [07/01] via       5.0200.bbbb.bbbb,   40s, Se0.2
R        11 [08/03] via       6.0200.aaaa.aaaa,   51s, Se0.1
R        22 [08/03] via       6.0200.aaaa.aaaa,   51s, Se0.1
R       200 [08/02] via       6.0200.aaaa.aaaa,   51s, Se0.1
Seville#
Seville#debug ipx routing events
IPX routing events debugging is on

01:04:03: IPXRIP: 5 FFFFFFFF not added, entry in table is static/connected/internal
01:04:12: IPXRIP: positing full update to 6.ffff.ffff.ffff via Serial0.1
(broadcast)
```

Example 5-27 *IPX debug Commands (Continued)*

```
01:04:14: IPXRIP: 6 FFFFFFFF not added, entry in table is static/connected/internal
01:04:14: IPXRIP: positing full update to 5.ffff.ffff.ffff via Serial0.2
(broadcast)
01:04:20: IPXRIP: positing full update to 3.ffff.ffff.ffff via Ethernet0
(broadcast)
01:05:03: IPXRIP: 5 FFFFFFFF not added, entry in table is static/connected/internal
01:05:11: IPXRIP: positing full update to 6.ffff.ffff.ffff via Serial0.1
(broadcast)
01:05:14: IPXRIP: 6 FFFFFFFF not added, entry in table is static/connected/internal
01:05:14: IPXRIP: positing full update to 5.ffff.ffff.ffff via Serial0.2
(broadcast)
01:05:20: IPXRIP: positing full update to 3.ffff.ffff.ffff via Ethernet0
(broadcast)
Seville#debug ipx routing activity
IPX routing debugging is on
Seville#
01:07:02: IPXRIP: update from 6.0200.aaaa.aaaa
01:07:02: IPXRIP: 5 FFFFFFFF not added, entry in table is static/connected/internal
01:07:02:     5 in 2 hops, delay 13
01:07:02:     200 in 2 hops, delay 8
01:07:02:     11 in 3 hops, delay 8
01:07:02:     22 in 3 hops, delay 8
01:07:02:     1 in 1 hops, delay 7
01:07:02:     2 in 2 hops, delay 13
01:07:02:     4 in 1 hops, delay 7
01:07:10: IPXRIP: positing full update to 6.ffff.ffff.ffff via Serial0.1
(broadcast)
01:07:10: IPXRIP: Update len 64 src=6.0200.cccc.cccc, dst=6.ffff.ffff.ffff(453)
01:07:10:     network 3, hops 1,  delay 7
01:07:10:     network 4, hops 2,  delay 13
01:07:10:     network 2, hops 2,  delay 13
01:07:10:     network 5, hops 1,  delay 7
01:07:13: IPXRIP: positing full update to 5.ffff.ffff.ffff via Serial0.2
(broadcast)
01:07:13: IPXRIP: Update len 80 src=5.0200.cccc.cccc, dst=5.ffff.ffff.ffff(453)
01:07:13:     network 1, hops 2,  delay 13
01:07:13:     network 22, hops 4,  delay 14
01:07:13:     network 11, hops 4,  delay 14
01:07:13:     network 200, hops 3,  delay 14
01:07:13:     network 3, hops 1,  delay 7
01:07:13:     network 6, hops 1,  delay 7
01:07:13: IPXRIP: update from 5.0200.bbbb.bbbb
01:07:13: IPXRIP: 6 FFFFFFFF not added, entry in table is static/connected/internal
01:07:13:     6 in 2 hops, delay 13
01:07:13:     22 in 4 hops, delay 14
01:07:13:     11 in 4 hops, delay 14
01:07:13:     200 in 3 hops, delay 14
01:07:13:     1 in 2 hops, delay 13
01:07:13:     2 in 1 hops, delay 7
01:07:13:     4 in 1 hops, delay 7
```

continues

Example 5-27 *IPX **debug** Commands (Continued)*

```
Seville#undebug all
All possible debugging has been turned off

Seville#show ipx servers
Codes: S - Static, P - Periodic, E - EIGRP, N - NLSP, H - Holddown, + = detail
U - Per-user static
4 Total IPX Servers

Table ordering is based on routing and server info

     Type Name                      Net      Address      Port    Route Hops Itf
P    4    SVR1                      200.0000.0000.0001:0452        8/02    3  Se0.1
P    4    SVR2                      200.0000.0000.0001:0452        8/02    3  Se0.1
P    7    SVR1                      200.0000.0000.0001:0452        8/02    3  Se0.1
P    7    SVR2                      200.0000.0000.0001:0452        8/02    3  Se0.1
Seville#debug ipx sap activity
IPX service debugging is on
Seville#
00:13:21: IPXSAP: Response (in) type 0x2 len 288 src:6.0200.aaaa.aaaa
dest:6.ffff.ffff.ffff(452)
00:13:21:    type 0x4, "SVR2", 200.0000.0000.0001(452), 3 hops
00:13:21:    type 0x4, "SVR1", 200.0000.0000.0001(452), 3 hops
00:13:21:    type 0x7, "SVR2", 200.0000.0000.0001(452), 3 hops
00:13:21:    type 0x7, "SVR1", 200.0000.0000.0001(452), 3 hops
00:13:27: IPXSAP: positing update to 6.ffff.ffff.ffff via Serial0.1 (broadcast)
(full)
00:13:27: IPXSAP: suppressing null update to 6.ffff.ffff.ffff
Seville#
Seville#
00:13:30: IPXSAP: Response (in) type 0x2 len 288 src:5.0200.bbbb.bbbb
dest:5.ffff.ffff.ffff(452)
00:13:30:    type 0x7, "SVR1", 200.0000.0000.0001(452), 4 hops
00:13:30:    type 0x7, "SVR2", 200.0000.0000.0001(452), 4 hops
00:13:30:    type 0x4, "SVR1", 200.0000.0000.0001(452), 4 hops
00:13:30:    type 0x4, "SVR2", 200.0000.0000.0001(452), 4 hops
undebug all
All possible debugging has been turned off
Seville#
```

The **debug ipx SAP events** command lists the details of each sent and received SAP update. Notice that the number of hops to the server is shown, as is the type of service and the server name. The source and destination of the update packets are also listed. The **debug ipx routing events** command lists just summary information about routing updates, whereas the **debug ipx routing activity** command gives the details.

Foundation Summary

The Foundation Summary is a collection of tables and figures that provides a convenient review of many key concepts in this chapter. For those of you already comfortable with the topics in this chapter, this summary could help you recall a few details. For those of you who just read this chapter, this review should help solidify some key facts. For any of you doing your final prep before the exam, these tables and figures will hopefully be a convenient way to review the day before the exam.

Table 5-36 lists the IP addressing terms used in this chapter.

Table 5-36   *IP Addressing Terminology*

Term	Definition
IP address	32-bit number, usually written in dotted decimal form, that uniquely identifies an interface of some computer.
Host address	Another term for IP address.
Network	The concept of a group of hosts.
Network number	A 32-bit number, usually written in dotted decimal form, that represents a network. This number cannot be assigned as an IP address to an interface of some computer. The host portion of the network number has a value of all binary 0s.
Network address	Another name for network number.
Broadcast address	A 32-bit number, usually written in dotted decimal form, that is used to address all hosts in the network. The host portion of the broadcast address has a value of all binary 1s. Broadcast addresses cannot be assigned as an IP address.
Subnet	The concept of a group of hosts, which is a subdivision of a network.
Subnet number	A 32-bit number, usually written in dotted decimal form, that represents all hosts in a subnet. This number cannot be used as an IP address for some computer's interface.
Subnet address	Another term for subnet number.
Subnetting	The process of subdividing networks into smaller subnets. This is jargon—for example, "Are you subnetting your network?"
Network mask	A 32-bit number, usually written in dotted decimal form. The mask is used by computers to calculate the network number of a given IP address by performing a Boolean AND of the address and mask. The mask also defines the number of host bits in an address.

continues

Table 5-36   *IP Addressing Terminology (Continued)*

Term	Definition
Mask	A generic term for a mask, whether it is a default mask or a subnet mask.
Address mask	Another term for a mask.
Default Class A mask	The mask used for Class A networks when no subnetting is used. The value is 255.0.0.0.
Default Class B mask	The mask used for Class B networks when no subnetting is used. The value is 255.255.0.0.
Default Class C mask	The mask used for Class C networks when no subnetting is used. The value is 255.255.255.0.
Subnet mask	A nondefault mask used when subnetting.
Network part or network field	Term used to describe the first part of an IP address. The host part is 8, 16, or 24 bits for Class A, B, and C networks, respectively.
Host part or host field	Term used to describe the last part of an IP address. The network part is 24, 16, or 8 bits for Class A, B, and C networks, respectively, when subnetting is not used. When subnetting, the size of the host part depends on the subnet mask chosen for that network.
Subnet part of subnet field	Term used to describe the middle part of an IP address. The subnet part is variable in size, based on how subnetting is implemented.

Table 5-37 summarizes NAT terminology.

Table 5-37   *NAT Addressing Terms*

Term	Meaning	Value in Figure 5-26
Inside local	Address of the host in the private network. When NAT is needed, this address is typically a private address or an address in a network registered to another organization.	170.1.1.10
Inside global	The Internet (global network) view of the inside local address. This address is in a network registered to the company responsible for the NAT router.	200.1.1.1
Outside global	The Internet (global network) view of the address of the host correctly attached to the Internet.	170.1.1.1
Outside local	When the private company reuses a network number registered to someone else, the outside local address represents the outside global address in the local (private) network. Because this address is used only in the private organization, it can be any IP address.	192.168.1.1

Table 5-38 contrasts typical transport layer functions as performed (or not performed) by UDP or TCP.

Table 5-38 *TCP and UDP Functional Comparison*

Function	Description (TCP)	Description (UDP)
Data transfer	Continuous stream of ordered data	Message (datagram) delivery
Multiplexing	Process that allows receiving hosts to decide the correct application for which the data is destined, based on port number	Process that allows receiving hosts to decide the correct application for which the data is destined, based on port number
Reliable transfer	Acknowledgment of data using the sequence and acknowledgment fields in the TCP header	Not a feature of UDP
Flow control	Process used to protect buffer space and routing devices	Not a feature of UDP
Connections	Process used to initialize port numbers and other TCP header fields	UDP is connectionless

Table 5-39 summarizes the ICMP unreachable codes.

Table 5-39 *ICMP Unreachable Codes*

Unreachable Code	When Used	Typically Sent By
Network Unreachable	No match exists in a routing table for the destination of the packet.	Router
Host Unreachable	The packet can be routed to a router connected to the destination subnet, but the host is not responding.	Router
Can't Fragment	The packet has the Don't Fragment bit set, and a router must fragment to forward the packet.	Router
Protocol Unreachable	The packet is delivered to the destination host, but the transport layer protocol is not available on that host.	Endpoint host
Port Unreachable	The packet is delivered to the destination host, but the destination port has not been opened by an application.	Endpoint host

Table 5-40 summarizes some of the features of TFTP and FTP.

Table 5-40 *Comparison of FTP and TFTP*

FTP	TFTP
Uses TCP	Uses UDP
Uses robust control commands	Uses simple control commands
Sends data over a separate connection than control commands	Uses no connections, since UDP
Requires more memory and programming effort	Requires less memory and programming effort
Is not supported as an application in IOS	Is supported as an application in IOS

Table 5-41 lists the various codes that the Cisco IOS **ping** command can supply.

Table 5-41 *Explanation of the Codes the **ping** Command Receives in Response to Its ICMP Echo Request*

ping Command Code	Explanation
!	ICMP Echo Reply received
.	Nothing received
U	ICMP unreachable (destination) received
N	ICMP unreachable (network) received
P	ICMP unreachable (port) received
Q	ICMP Source Quench received
M	ICMP "can't fragment" message received
?	Unknown packet received

Figure 5-40 shows the types of encapsulating Ethernet headers that are listed and described in Table 5-42.

Figure 5-40   *IPX Ethernet Encapsulations*

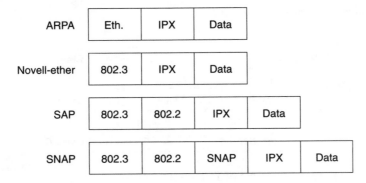

Table 5-42   *IPX Ethernet Encapsulations*

Novell's Name	Cisco IOS's Name	Hints for Remembering the Names and Meanings
Ethernet_II	ARPA	One way to help correlate the two names is to remember that ARPA was the original agency that created TCP/IP and that Ethernet_II is the older version of Ethernet; remember that the old names go together.
Ethernet_802.3	Novell-ether	Novell's name refers to the final header before the IPX header, in this case. There are no suggestions on easier ways to recall the IOS name Novell-ether. This setting is Novell's default on NetWare 3.11 and prior releases.
Ethernet_802.2	SAP	Novell's name refers to the final header before the IPX header, in this case. Novell's name refers to the committee and complete header that defines the SAP field; Cisco's name refers to the SAP part of the 802.2 header. (The SAP field denotes that an IPX packet follows the 802.2 header.) This setting is Novell's default on NetWare 3.12 and later releases.
Ethernet_SNAP	SNAP	Novell's name refers to the final header before the IPX header, in this case. Cisco's name refers to this same header.

Figure 5-41 shows the format of addresses when subnetting.

Figure 5-41   *Address Formats, When Subnetting Is Used*

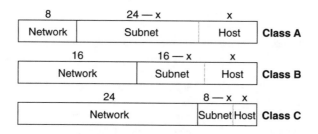

Figure 5-42 shows an example of TCP error recovery.

Figure 5-42   *TCP Acknowledgment with Errors*

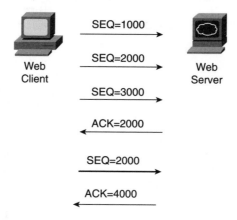

Figure 5-43 shows a TCP connection establishment flow, which in this case is for an FTP control connection to well-known port 21.

Figure 5-43   *FTP Control Connections*

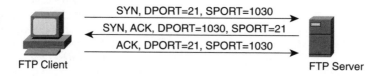

Table 5-43 summarizes many of the most common configuration commands used for IP.

Table 5-43   *IP Configuration Commands*

Command	Configuration Mode
ip address *ip-address mask* [**secondary**]	Interface mode
ip host *name* [*tcp-port-number*] *address1* [*address2...address8*]	Global
ip route *prefix mask* {*next-hop-router* I *output-interface*}	Global
ip name-server *server-address1* [[*server-address2*]...*server-address6*]	Global
ip domain-lookup	Global
ip routing	Global
ip netmask-format {**bitcount** I **decimal** I **hexadecimal**}	Interface mode
ip default-network *network*	Global
ip classless	Global
ip host *name* [*tcp-port-number*] *address1* [*address2...address8*]	Global

Table 5-44 summarizes the more popular commands used for IPX configuration.

Table 5-44   *IPX and IPX RIP Configuration Commands*

Command	Configuration Mode
ipx routing [*node*]	Global
ipx maximum-paths *paths*	Global
ipx network *network* [**encapsulation** *type*] [**secondary**]	Interface mode

Table 5-45 summarizes the **show** and **debug** commands in this chapter and lists the examples in the chapter in which a sample can be found.

Table 5-45   *EXEC Command Summary for Chapter 5*

Command	Information Supplied
show hosts	Lists all host names and corresponding IP addresses
show interface [*type number*]	Shows interface statistics, including IP address
show ip interface [*type number*]	Gives a detailed view of IP parameter settings, per interface
show ip interface brief	Shows a summary of all interfaces and their IP addresses
show ip route [*subnet*]	Shows the entire routing table, or one entry if **subnet** is entered
show ip arp	Displays the IP ARP cache

continues

Table 5-45   *EXEC Command Summary for Chapter 5 (Continued)*

Command	Information Supplied
debug ip packet	Issues log messages for each IP packet
terminal ip netmask-format {**bitcount** | **decimal** | **hexadecimal**}	Sets the type of display for subnet masks in **show** commands
ping	Sends and receives ICMP echo messages to verify connectivity
trace	Sends a series of UDP packets with increasing TTL values, to verify the current route to a host
show ipx interface	Provides a detailed view of IPX parameter settings, per interface
show ipx route [*network*]	Shows the entire routing table, or one entry if **network** is entered
show ipx servers	Shows the SAP table
show ipx traffic	Shows IPX traffic statistics
debug ipx routing [*events* | *activity*]	Gives messages describing each routing update
debug ipx sap [*events* | *activity*]	Gives messages describing each SAP update
ping *ipx-address*	Sends IPX packets to verify connectivity

Q&A

As mentioned in Chapter 1, "All About the Cisco Certified Network Associate Certification," the questions and scenarios in this book are more difficult than what you should experience on the actual exam. The questions do not attempt to cover more breadth or depth than the exam; however, they are designed to make sure that you know the answer. Rather than allowing you to derive the answer from clues hidden inside the question itself, the questions challenge your understanding and recall of the subject. Questions from the "Do I Know This Already?" quiz from the beginning of the chapter are repeated here to ensure that you have mastered the chapter's topic areas. Hopefully, these questions will help limit the number of exam questions on which you narrow your choices to two options and then guess.

The answers to these questions can be found in Appendix A, on page 728.

1 What do TCP, UDP, IP, and ICMP stand for? Which protocol is considered to be Layer 3 equivalent when comparing TCP/IP to the OSI protocols?

2 Name the parts of an IP address.

3 Define the term *subnet mask*. What do the bits in the mask whose values are binary 0 tell you about the corresponding IP address(es)?

4 Given the IP address 134.141.7.11 and the mask 255.255.255.0, what is the subnet number?

5 Given the IP address 193.193.7.7 and the mask 255.255.255.0, what is the subnet number?

6 Given the IP address 10.5.118.3 and the mask 255.255.0.0, what is the subnet number?

7 Given the IP address 190.1.42.3 and the mask 255.255.255.0, what is the subnet number?

8 Given the IP address 200.1.1.130 and the mask 255.255.255.224, what is the subnet number?

9 Given the IP address 220.8.7.100 and the mask 255.255.255.240, what is the subnet number?

10 Given the IP address 140.1.1.1 and the mask 255.255.255.248, what is the subnet number?

11 Given the IP address 167.88.99.66 and the mask 255.255.255.192, what is the subnet number?

12 Given the IP address 134.141.7.11 and the mask 255.255.255.0, what is the broadcast address?

13 Given the IP address 193.193.7.7 and the mask 255.255.255.0, what is the broadcast address?

14 Given the IP address 10.5.118.3 and the mask 255.255.0.0, what is the broadcast address?

15 Given the IP address 190.1.42.3 and the mask 255.255.255.0, what is the broadcast address?

16 Given the IP address 200.1.1.130 and the mask 255.255.255.224, what is the broadcast address?

17 Given the IP address 220.8.7.100 and the mask 255.255.255.240, what is the broadcast address?

18 Given the IP address 140.1.1.1 and the mask 255.255.255.248, what is the broadcast address?

19 Given the IP address 167.88.99.66 and the mask 255.255.255.192, what is the broadcast address?

20 Given the IP address 134.141.7.11 and the mask 255.255.255.0, what are the assignable IP addresses in this subnet?

21 Given the IP address 193.193.7.7 and the mask 255.255.255.0, what are the assignable IP addresses in this subnet?

22 Given the IP address 10.5.118.3 and the mask 255.255.0.0, what are the assignable IP addresses in this subnet?

23 Given the IP address 190.1.42.3 and the mask 255.255.255.0, what are the assignable IP addresses in this subnet?

24 Given the IP address 200.1.1.130 and the mask 255.255.255.224, what are the assignable IP addresses in this subnet?

25 Given the IP address 220.8.7.100 and the mask 255.255.255.240, what are the assignable IP addresses in this subnet?

26 Given the IP address 140.1.1.1 and the mask 255.255.255.248, what are the assignable IP addresses in this subnet?

27 Given the IP address 167.88.99.66 and the mask 255.255.255.192, what are the assignable IP addresses in this subnet?

28 Given the IP address 134.141.7.7 and the mask 255.255.255.0, what are all the subnet numbers if the same (static) mask is used for all subnets in this network?

29 Given the IP address 10.5.118.3 and the mask 255.255.255.0, what are all the subnet numbers if the same (static) mask is used for all subnets in this network?

30 Given the IP address 220.8.7.100 and the mask 255.255.255.240, what are all the subnet numbers if the same (static) mask is used for all subnets in this network?

31 Given the IP address 140.1.1.1 and the mask 255.255.255.248, what are all the subnet numbers if the same (static) mask is used for all subnets in this network?

32 How many IP addresses could be assigned in each subnet of 134.141.0.0, assuming that a mask of 255.255.255.0 is used? If the same (static) mask is used for all subnets, how many subnets are there?

33 How many IP addresses could be assigned in each subnet of 10.0.0.0, assuming that a mask of 255.255.255.0 is used? If the same (static) mask is used for all subnets, how many subnets are there?

34 How many IP addresses could be assigned in each subnet of 220.8.7.0, assuming that a mask of 255.255.255.240 is used? If the same (static) mask is used for all subnets, how many subnets are there?

35 How many IP addresses could be assigned in each subnet of 140.1.0.0, assuming a mask of 255.255.255.248 is used? If the same (static) mask is used for all subnets, how many subnets are there?

36 Create a minimal configuration enabling IP on each interface on a 2501 router (two serial, one Ethernet). The NIC assigned you network 8.0.0.0. Your boss says you need at most 200 hosts per subnet. You decide against using VLSM. Your boss also says to plan your subnets so that you can have as many subnets as possible rather than allow for larger subnets later. You decide to start with the lowest numerical values for the subnet number you will use. Assume that point-to-point serial links will be attached to this router and that RIP is the routing protocol.

37 In the previous question, what would be the IP subnet of the link attached to serial 0? If another user wanted to answer the same question but did not have the enable password, what command(s) might provide this router's addresses and subnets?

38 Describe the question and possible responses in setup mode when a router wants to know the mask used on an interface. How can the router derive the correct mask from the information supplied by the user?

39 Name the three classes of unicast IP addresses and list their default masks, respectively. How many of each type could be assigned to companies and organizations by the NIC?

40 Describe how TCP performs error recovery. What role do the routers play?

41 Define the purpose of an ICMP redirect message.

42 Define the purpose of the **trace** command. What type of messages is it sending, and what type of ICMP messages is it receiving?

43 What does IP stand for? What does ICMP stand for? Which protocol is considered to be Layer 3 equivalent when comparing TCP/IP to the OSI protocols?

44 What causes the output from an IOS **ping** command to display "UUUUU?"

45 Describe how to view the IP ARP cache in a Cisco router. Also describe the three key elements of each entry.

46 How many hosts are allowed per subnet if the subnet mask used is 255.255.255.192? How many hosts are allowed for 255.255.255.252?

47 How many subnets could be created if using static length masks in a Class B network when the mask is 255.255.255.224? What about when the mask is 255.255.252.0?

48 How many bytes comprise an IPX address?

49 What do IPX and SPX stand for?

50 Define encapsulation in the context of Cisco routers and Novell IPX.

51 Give an example of an IPX network mask used when subnetting.

52 Describe the headers used for two types of Ethernet encapsulation when using IPX.

53 Name the part of the NetWare protocol specifications that, like TCP, provides end-to-end guaranteed delivery of data.

54 Name the command that lists all the SAP entries in a Cisco router.

55 How many different values are possible for IPX network numbers?

56 Create a configuration enabling IPX on each interface, with RIP and SAP enabled on each as well, for a 2501 (two serial, one Ethernet) router. Use networks 100, 200, and 300 for interfaces S0, S1, and E0, respectively. Choose any node values.

57 In the previous question, what would be the IPX address of the serial 0 interface? If another user wanted to know but did not have the enable password, what command(s) might provide this IPX address?

58 What **show** command lists the IPX address(es) of interfaces in a Cisco router?

59 How many Novell encapsulation types are valid in the IOS for Ethernet interfaces? What about for FDDI and Token Ring?

60 A router is attached to an Ethernet LAN. Some clients on the LAN use Novell's Ethernet_II encapsulation, and some use Ethernet_802.3. If the only subcommand on Ethernet0 reads **ipx network 1**, which of the clients are working? (All, Ethernet_II, or Ethernet_802.3?)

61 A router is attached to an Ethernet LAN. Some clients on the LAN use Novell's Ethernet_802.2 encapsulation, and some use Ethernet_SNAP. Create a configuration that allows both types of clients to send and receive packets through this router.

62 True or false: Up to 64 IPX networks can be used on the same Ethernet by using the IPX secondary address feature. If true, describe the largest number that is practically needed. If false, what is the maximum number that is legal on an Ethernet?

63 In the **ipx network 11** interface subcommand, does the IOS assume that 11 is binary, octal, decimal, or hexadecimal? What is the largest valid value that could be configured instead of 11?

64 What IOS IPX encapsulation keyword implies use of an 802.2 header but no SNAP header? On what types of interfaces is this type of encapsulation valid?

65 Name the two commands typically used to create a default gateway for a router.

66 Assume that subnets of network 10.0.0.0 are in the IP routing table in a router but that no other network and their subnets are known, except that there is also a default route (0.0.0.0) in the routing table. A packet destined for 192.1.1.1 arrives at the router. What configuration command determines whether the default route will be used in this case?

67 Assume that subnets of network 10.0.0.0 are in the IP routing table in a router but that no other network and their subnets are known, except that there is also a default route (0.0.0.0) in the routing table. A packet destined for 10.1.1.1 arrives at the router, but there is no known subnet of network 10 that matches this destination address. What configuration command determines whether the default route will be used in this case?

68 What does the acronym CIDR stand for? What is the original purpose of CIDR?

69 Define the term private addressing as defined in RFC 1918.

70 Define the acronym NAT, and define the basics of its operation.

71 Which requires more lines of source code, FTP or TFTP? Justify your answer.

72 Does FTP or TFTP perform error recovery? If so, describe the basics of how they perform error recovery.

73 Describe the process used by IP routers to perform fragmentation and reassembly of packets.

74 How many TCP segments are exchanged to establish a TCP connection? How many are required to terminate a TCP connection?

75 How many Class B-style networks are reserved by RFC 1918 private addressing?

Scenarios

Scenario 5-1: IP Addressing and Subnet Calculation

Assume that you just took a new job. No one trusts you yet, so they will not give you any passwords to the router. Your mentor at your new company has left you at his desk while he goes to a meeting. He has left a Telnet window up, logged in to one router in user mode. In other words, you can issue only user mode commands.

Assuming that you had issued the following commands (see Example 5-28), draw the most specific network diagram that you can. Write the subnet numbers used on each link onto the diagram.

Example 5-28 *Command Output on Router Fred*

```
fred>show interface
Serial0 is up, line protocol is up
  Hardware is HD64570
  Internet address is 199.1.1.65/27
  MTU 1500 bytes, BW 1544 Kbit, DLY 20000 usec, rely 255/255, load 1/255
  Encapsulation HDLC, loopback not set, keepalive set (10 sec)
  Last input 00:00:07, output 00:00:10, output hang never
  Last clearing of "show interface" counters never
  Input queue: 0/75/0 (size/max/drops); Total output drops: 0
  Queuing strategy: weighted fair
  Output queue: 0/1000/0 (size/max total/drops)
     Conversations  0/1/64 (active/max active/threshold)
     Reserved Conversations 0/0 (allocated/max allocated)
  5 minute input rate 0 bits/sec, 0 packets/sec
  5 minute output rate 0 bits/sec, 0 packets/sec
     27 packets input, 2452 bytes, 0 no buffer
     Received 27 broadcasts, 0 runts, 0 giants, 0 throttles
     0 input errors, 0 CRC, 0 frame, 0 overrun, 0 ignored, 0 abort
     29 packets output, 2044 bytes, 0 underruns
     0 output errors, 0 collisions, 28 interface resets
     0 output buffer failures, 0 output buffers swapped out
     7 carrier transitions
     DCD=up  DSR=up  DTR=up  RTS=up  CTS=up
Serial1 is up, line protocol is up
  Hardware is HD64570
  Internet address is 199.1.1.97/27
  MTU 1500 bytes, BW 1544 Kbit, DLY 20000 usec, rely 255/255, load 1/255
  Encapsulation HDLC, loopback not set, keepalive set (10 sec)
  Last input 00:00:01, output 00:00:01, output hang never
  Last clearing of "show interface" counters never
  Input queue: 0/75/0 (size/max/drops); Total output drops: 0
  Queuing strategy: weighted fair
  Output queue: 0/1000/0 (size/max total/drops)
     Conversations  0/1/64 (active/max active/threshold)
Reserved Conversations 0/0 (allocated/max allocated)
  5 minute input rate 0 bits/sec, 0 packets/sec
```

Example 5-28 *Command Output on Router Fred (Continued)*

```
     5 minute output rate 0 bits/sec, 0 packets/sec
         125 packets input, 7634 bytes, 0 no buffer
         Received 124 broadcasts, 0 runts, 0 giants, 0 throttles
         0 input errors, 0 CRC, 0 frame, 0 overrun, 0 ignored, 0 abort
         161 packets output, 9575 bytes, 0 underruns
         0 output errors, 0 collisions, 1 interface resets
         0 output buffer failures, 0 output buffers swapped out
         4 carrier transitions
         DCD=up  DSR=up  DTR=up  RTS=up  CTS=up
Ethernet0 is up, line protocol is up
Hardware is MCI Ethernet, address is 0000.0c55.AB44 (bia 0000.0c55.AB44)
   Internet address is 199.1.1.33/27
       MTU 1500 bytes, BW 10000 Kbit, DLY 1000 usec, rely 255/255, load 1/255
       Encapsulation ARPA, loopback not set, keepalive set (10 sec)
       ARP type: ARPA, PROBE, ARP Timeout 4:00:00     Last input 0:00:00, output
0:00:00, output hang never
       Output queue 0/40, 0 drops; input queue 0/75, 0 drops
       Five minute input rate 4000 bits/sec, 4 packets/sec
       Five minute output rate 6000 bits/sec, 6 packets/sec
           22197 packets input, 309992 bytes, 0 no buffer
           Received 2343 broadcasts, 0 runts, 0 giants
           0 input errors, 0 CRC, 0 frame, 0 overrun, 0 ignored, 0 abort
           4456 packets output, 145765 bytes, 0 underruns
           3 output errors, 10 collisions, 2 interface resets, 0 restarts


fred>show ip route
Codes: C - connected, S - static, I - IGRP, R - RIP, M - mobile, B - BGP
       D - EIGRP, EX - EIGRP external, O - OSPF, IA - OSPF inter area
       N1 - OSPF NSSA external type 1, N2 - OSPF NSSA external type 2
       E1 - OSPF external type 1, E2 - OSPF external type 2, E - EGP
       i - IS-IS, L1 - IS-IS level-1, L2 - IS-IS level-2, * - candidate default
       U - per-user static route, o - ODR

Gateway of last resort is not set

     199.1.1.0/27 is subnetted, 6 subnets
R       199.1.1.192 [120/1] via 199.1.1.98, 00:00:01, Serial1
R       199.1.1.128 [120/1] via 199.1.1.98, 00:00:01, Serial1
                    [120/1] via 199.1.1.66, 00:00:20, Serial0
R       199.1.1.160 [120/1] via 199.1.1.66, 00:00:20, Serial0
C       199.1.1.64 is directly connected, Serial0
C       199.1.1.96 is directly connected, Serial1
C       199.1.1.32 is directly connected, Ethernet0

fred>show ip protocol
Routing Protocol is "rip"
  Sending updates every 30 seconds, next due in 23 seconds
  Invalid after 180 seconds, hold down 180, flushed after 240
 Outgoing update filter list for all interfaces is not set
  Incoming update filter list for all interfaces is not set
```

continues

Example 5-28 *Command Output on Router Fred (Continued)*

```
 Redistributing: rip
 Default version control: send version 1, receive any version
   Interface       Send  Recv   Key-chain
   Serial0          1    1 2
   Serial1          1    1 2
   Ethernet0        1    1 2
 Routing for Networks:

   199.1.1.0
 Routing Information Sources:
   Gateway         Distance      Last Update
   199.1.1.66          120       00:00:04
   199.1.1.98          120       00:00:14
 Distance: (default is 120)

fred>show cdp neighbor detail
- - - - - - - - - - - - - - - - - - - - - - - -
Device ID: dino
Entry address(es):
  IP address: 199.1.1.66
Platform: Cisco 2500,  Capabilities: Router
Interface: Serial0,  Port ID (outgoing port): Serial0
Holdtime : 148 sec

Version :
Cisco Internetwork Operating System Software
IOS (tm) 2500 Software (C2500-AINR-L), Version 11.2(11), RELEASE SOFTWARE (fc1)
Copyright  1986-1997 by Cisco Systems, Inc.
Compiled Mon 29-Dec-97 18:47 by ckralik


- - - - - - - - - - - - - - - - - - - - - - - -
Device ID: Barney
Entry address(es):
  IP address: 199.1.1.98
Platform: Cisco 2500,  Capabilities: Router
Interface: Serial1,  Port ID (outgoing port): Serial0
Holdtime : 155 sec

Version :
Cisco Internetwork Operating System Software
IOS (tm) 2500 Software (C2500-AINR-L), Version 11.2(11), RELEASE SOFTWARE (fc1)
Copyright  1986-1997 by Cisco Systems, Inc.
Compiled Mon 29-Dec-97 18:47 by ckralik
```

Scenario 5-2: IP Subnet Design with a Class B Network

Your job is to plan a new network. The topology required includes three sites, one Ethernet at each site, and point-to-point serial links for connectivity, as shown in Figure 5-44. The network may grow to need at most 100 subnets, with 200 hosts per subnet maximum. Use network 172.16.0.0. Use Table 5-46 to record your choices, or use a separate piece of paper.

Figure 5-44   *Scenario 5-2 Network Diagram*

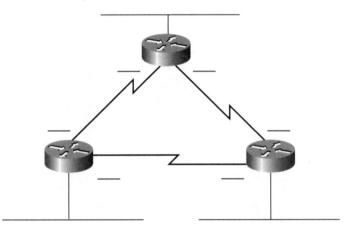

Table 5-46   *Scenario 5-2 Planning Chart*

Location of Subnet Geographically	Subnet Mask	Subnet Number	Router's IP Address
Ethernet off Router A			
Ethernet off Router B			
Ethernet off Router C			
Serial between A and B			
Serial between A and C			
Serial between B and C			

Given the information in Figure 5-44 and Table 5-46, perform the following activities:

1 Determine all subnet masks that meet the criteria in the introduction to this scenario.

2 Choose a mask and pick enough subnets to use for the original topology (refer to Figure 5-44).

3 Create IP-related configuration commands for each router.

Scenario 5-3: IP Subnet Design with a Class C Network

Your job is to plan yet another network. The topology required includes four sites, one Ethernet at each site, and partially meshed Frame Relay for connectivity, as shown in Figure 5-45. The number of subnets will never grow. Choose a mask that will maximize the number of hosts per subnet. Use network 200.1.1.0. Use Table 5-47 to record your choices, or use a separate piece of paper.

Figure 5-45   *Scenario 5-3 Network Diagram*

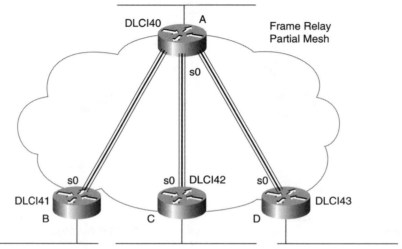

Table 5-47   *Scenario 5-3 Planning Chart*

Location of Subnet	Subnet Mask	Subnet Number	Router's IP Address
Ethernet off Router A			
Ethernet off Router B			
Ethernet off Router C			
Ethernet off Router D			
VC between A and B			
VC between A and C			
VC between A and D			

Given the network setup in Figure 5-45, perform the following activities:

1 Choose the best subnet mask that meets the criteria.

2 Use Table 5-47 to plan which subnet numbers will be used.

3 Create IP-related configuration commands for each router. Use the DLCIs from Figure 5-45.

Scenario 5-4: IPX Examination

Given the network in Figure 5-46 and the command output in Example 5-29, Example 5-30, and Example 5-31, answer the questions and perform the tasks listed after Example 5-31.

Figure 5-46   *Scenario 5-4 Network Diagram*

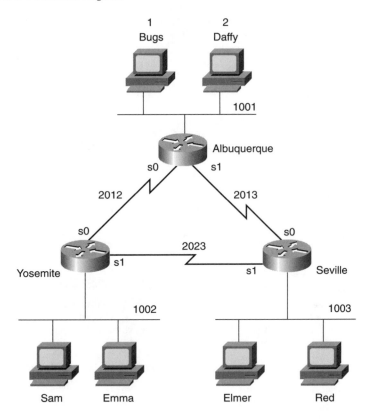

Example 5-29 *Albuquerque Command Output, Scenario 5-4*

```
Albuquerque#show ipx interface brief
Interface           IPX Network Encapsulation Status        IPX State
Serial0             2012        HDLC         up             [up]
Serial1             2013        HDLC         up             [up]
Ethernet0           1001        SAP          up             [up]

Albuquerque#show cdp neighbor detail
-------------------------
Device ID: Yosemite
Entry address(es):
  IP address: 10.1.12.2
  Novell address: 2012.0200.2222.2222
```

continues

Example 5-29 *Albuquerque Command Output, Scenario 5-4 (Continued)*

```
Platform: cisco 2500,  Capabilities: Router
Interface: Serial0,  Port ID (outgoing port): Serial0
Holdtime : 167 sec

Version :
Cisco Internetwork Operating System Software
IOS (tm) 2500 Software (C2500-AINR-L), Version 11.2(11), RELEASE SOFTWARE (fc1)
Copyright  1986-1997 by Cisco Systems, Inc.
Compiled Mon 29-Dec-97 18:47 by ckralik


-----------------------
Device ID: Seville
Entry address(es):
  IP address: 10.1.13.3
  Novell address: 2013.0200.3333.3333
Platform: cisco 2500,  Capabilities: Router
Interface: Serial1,  Port ID (outgoing port): Serial0
Holdtime : 164 sec

Version :
Cisco Internetwork Operating System Software
IOS (tm) 2500 Software (C2500-AINR-L), Version 11.2(11), RELEASE SOFTWARE (fc1)
Copyright  1986-1997 by Cisco Systems, Inc.
Compiled Mon 29-Dec-97 18:47 by ckralik
```

Example 5-30 *Yosemite Command Output, Scenario 5-4*

```
Yosemite#show ipx route
Codes: C - Connected primary network,   c - Connected secondary network
       S - Static, F - Floating static, L - Local (internal), W - IPXWAN
       R - RIP, E - EIGRP, N - NLSP, X - External, A - Aggregate
       s - seconds, u - uses

8 Total IPX routes. Up to 1 parallel paths and 16 hops allowed.

No default route known.

C       1002 (SAP),        E0
C       2012 (HDLC),       Se0
C       2023 (HDLC),       Se1
R          1 [08/03] via   2012.0200.1111.1111,    32s, Se0
R          2 [08/03] via   2012.0200.1111.1111,    33s, Se0
R       1001 [07/01] via   2012.0200.1111.1111,    33s, Se0
R       1003 [07/01] via   2023.0200.3333.3333,    32s, Se1
R       2013 [07/01] via   2012.0200.1111.1111,    33s, Se0

Yosemite#show ipx traffic
System Traffic for 0.0000.0000.0001 System-Name: Yosemite
Rcvd:    169 total, 0 format errors, 0 checksum errors, 0 bad hop count,
         8 packets pitched, 161 local destination, 0 multicast
Bcast:   160 received, 242 sent
Sent:    243 generated, 0 forwarded
```

Example 5-30 *Yosemite Command Output, Scenario 5-4 (Continued)*

```
             0 encapsulation failed, 0 no route
SAP:         2 SAP requests, 0 SAP replies, 2 servers
             0 SAP Nearest Name requests, 0 replies
             0 SAP General Name requests, 0 replies
             60 SAP advertisements received, 57 sent
             6 SAP flash updates sent, 0 SAP format errors
RIP:         1 RIP requests, 0 RIP replies, 9 routes
             98 RIP advertisements received, 120 sent
             45 RIP flash updates sent, 0 RIP format errors
Echo:        Rcvd 0 requests, 0 replies
             Sent 0 requests, 0 replies
             0 unknown: 0 no socket, 0 filtered, 0 no helper
             0 SAPs throttled, freed NDB len 0
Watchdog:
             0 packets received, 0 replies spoofed
Queue lengths:
             IPX input: 0, SAP 0, RIP 0, GNS 0
             SAP throttling length: 0/(no limit), 0 nets pending lost route reply
             Delayed process creation: 0
EIGRP:       Total received 0, sent 0
             Updates received 0, sent 0
             Queries received 0, sent 0
             Replies received 0, sent 0
             SAPs received 0, sent 0
NLSP:        Level-1 Hellos received 0, sent 0
             PTP Hello received 0, sent 0
             Level-1 LSPs received 0, sent 0
             LSP Retransmissions: 0
             LSP checksum errors received: 0
             LSP HT=0 checksum errors received: 0
             Level-1 CSNPs received 0, sent 0
             Level-1 PSNPs received 0, sent 0
             Level-1 DR Elections: 0
             Level-1 SPF Calculations: 0
             Level-1 Partial Route Calculations: 0
```

Example 5-31 *Seville Command Output, Scenario 5-4*

```
Seville#show ipx interface
Serial0 is up, line protocol is up
  IPX address is 2013.0200.3333.3333 [up]
  Delay of this IPX network, in ticks is 6 throughput 0 link delay 0
  IPXWAN processing not enabled on this interface.
  IPX SAP update interval is 1 minute(s)
  IPX type 20 propagation packet forwarding is disabled
  Incoming access list is not set
  Outgoing access list is not set
  IPX helper access list is not set
  SAP GNS processing enabled, delay 0 ms, output filter list is not set
  SAP Input filter list is not set
  SAP Output filter list is not set
```

continues

Example 5-31 *Seville Command Output, Scenario 5-4 (Continued)*

```
    SAP Router filter list is not set
    Input filter list is not set
    Output filter list is not set
    Router filter list is not set
    Netbios Input host access list is not set
    Netbios Input bytes access list is not set
    Netbios Output host access list is not set
    Netbios Output bytes access list is not set
    Updates each 60 seconds, aging multiples RIP: 3 SAP: 3
    SAP interpacket delay is 55 ms, maximum size is 480 bytes
    RIP interpacket delay is 55 ms, maximum size is 432 bytes
    Watchdog processing is disabled, SPX spoofing is disabled, idle time 60
    IPX accounting is disabled
    IPX fast switching is configured (enabled)
    RIP packets received 53, RIP packets sent 55
    SAP packets received 14, SAP packets sent 25
Serial1 is up, line protocol is up
    IPX address is 2023.0200.3333.3333 [up]
    Delay of this IPX network, in ticks is 6 throughput 0 link delay 0
    IPXWAN processing not enabled on this interface.
    IPX SAP update interval is 1 minute(s)
    IPX type 20 propagation packet forwarding is disabled
    Incoming access list is not set
    Outgoing access list is not set
    IPX helper access list is not set
    SAP GNS processing enabled, delay 0 ms, output filter list is not set
    SAP Input filter list is not set
    SAP Output filter list is not set
    SAP Router filter list is not set
    Input filter list is not set
    Output filter list is not set
    Router filter list is not set
    Netbios Input host access list is not set
    Netbios Input bytes access list is not set
    Netbios Output host access list is not set
    Netbios Output bytes access list is not set
    Updates each 60 seconds, aging multiples RIP: 3 SAP: 3
    SAP interpacket delay is 55 ms, maximum size is 480 bytes
    RIP interpacket delay is 55 ms, maximum size is 432 bytes
   Watchdog processing is disabled, SPX spoofing is disabled, idle time 60
    IPX accounting is disabled
    IPX fast switching is configured (enabled)
    RIP packets received 53, RIP packets sent 62
    SAP packets received 13, SAP packets sent 37
Ethernet0 is up, line protocol is up
    IPX address is 1003. 0000.0cac.ab41, SAP [up]
    Delay of this IPX network, in ticks is 1 throughput 0 link delay 0
    IPXWAN processing not enabled on this interface.
    IPX SAP update interval is 1 minute(s)
    IPX type 20 propagation packet forwarding is disabled
    Incoming access list is not set
    Outgoing access list is not set
    IPX helper access list is not set
```

Example 5-31 *Seville Command Output, Scenario 5-4 (Continued)*

```
     SAP GNS processing enabled, delay 0 ms, output filter list is not set
     SAP Input filter list is not set
     SAP Output filter list is not set
     SAP Router filter list is not set
     Input filter list is not set
     Output filter list is not set
     Router filter list is not set
     Netbios Input host access list is not set
     Netbios Input bytes access list is not set
     Netbios Output host access list is not set
     Netbios Output bytes access list is not set
     Updates each 60 seconds, aging multiples RIP: 3 SAP: 3
     SAP interpacket delay is 55 ms, maximum size is 480 bytes
     RIP interpacket delay is 55 ms, maximum size is 432 bytes
     IPX accounting is disabled
     IPX fast switching is configured (enabled)
     RIP packets received 20, RIP packets sent 62
     SAP packets received 18, SAP packets sent 15

Seville#show ipx servers
Codes: S - Static, P - Periodic, E - EIGRP, N - NLSP, H - Holddown, + = detail
2 Total IPX Servers

Table ordering is based on routing and server info

     Type Name                 Net       Address    Port   Route Hops Itf
P    4 Bugs                     1.0000.0000.0001:0451      8/03   3  Se0
P    4 Daffy                    2.0000.0000.0001:0451      8/03   3  Se0
```

Assuming the details established in Figure 5-46 and the command output in Example 5-29, Example 5-30, and Example 5-31 for Scenario 5-4, complete or answer the following:

1 Complete Table 5-48 with all IPX network numbers. List the command(s) you use to find these network numbers.

2 Complete as much of Table 5-49 as possible.

Table 5-48   *IPX Networks in Scenario 5-4*

IPX Network	Location (Such as "Between Albuquerque and Seville")	Command Used to Find This Information

continues

Table 5-48   *IPX Networks in Scenario 5-4 (Continued)*

IPX Network	Location (Such as "Between Albuquerque and Seville")	Command Used to Find This Information

Table 5-49   *IPX Addresses on Routers in Scenario 5-4*

Router	Interface	IPX Network	IPX Node
Albuquerque	E0		
	S0		
	S1		
Yosemite	E0		
	S0		
	S1		
Seville	E0		
	S0		
	S1		

Scenario 5-5: IPX Configuration

Assume the network setup in Figure 5-47.

Figure 5-47   *Scenario 5-5 Network Diagram*

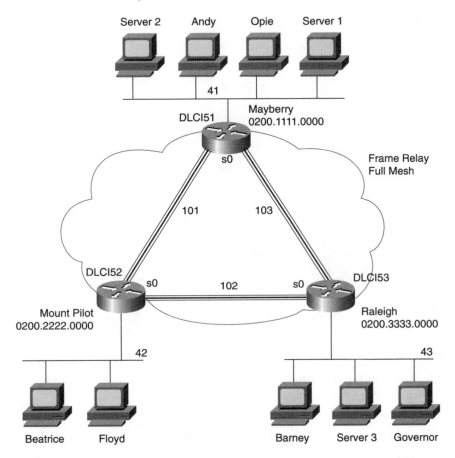

Assuming the details established in Figure 5-47 for Scenario 5-5, complete or answer the following:

1 Configure IPX on all three routers. Use the network numbers listed in the figure. (Do not bother with IP.) Use point-to-point subinterfaces, and use the IPX node addresses shown in the diagram on the serial interfaces.

2 You later find out that Beatrice is using NetWare's Ethernet_II encapsulation, Floyd is using Ethernet_802.3, Barney is using Ethernet_802.2, and Governor is using Ethernet_SNAP. Configure the changes necessary to support each client.

Scenario Answers

Answers to Scenario 5-1: IP Addressing and Subnet Calculation

Assuming that you had issued the commands in Example 5-28, the most specific network diagram would look like Figure 5-48.

Figure 5-48   *Scenario 5-1 Answer—Network with Router Fred*

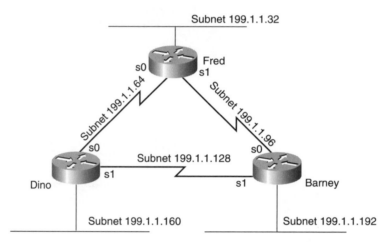

The clues that you should have found in the **show** commands are as follows:

- The types and IP addresses of the interfaces on Fred were in the **show interface** and **show ip interface brief** command output.

- The subnets could be learned from the **show ip route** command or derived from the IP addresses and masks shown in the **show interface** command output.

- The neighboring router's IP addresses could be learned from the **show ip protocol** command.

- The neighboring routers' IP addresses and host names could be learned from the **show cdp neighbor detail** command.

- The metric for subnet 199.1.1.128/27 in RIP updates implies that both neighbors have an equal-cost route to the same subnet. Because two separate but duplicate networks would be a bad design, you can assume that the neighboring routers are attached to the same medium.

- If completely bored, the **telnet 199.1.1.x** command could have been issued for all IP addresses in subnets not directly connected to Fred, hoping to get a router login prompt. That would identify the IP addresses of other router interfaces.

There is no way to know what physical media are beyond the neighboring routers. However, because CDP claims that both routers are 2500 series routers, the possible interfaces on these neighboring routers are limited. Figure 5-48 shows the other subnets as Ethernet segments. Similarly, the figure shows the two neighboring routers attached to the same medium, which is shown as a serial link in Figure 5-48.

Answers to Scenario 5-2: IP Subnet Design with a Class B Network

Figure 5-49 shows one correct answer for the network skeleton presented in Figure 5-44.

Figure 5-49   *Scenario 5-2 Diagram Scratch Pad*

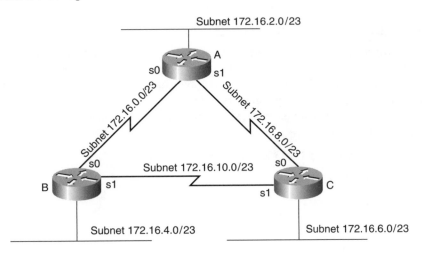

Answers to Task 1 for Scenario 5-2

Given the details in Figure 5-44 and Table 5-46 for Scenario 5-2, the subnet mask criteria are as follows:

- 200 hosts in a subnet, maximum

- 100 subnets, maximum

- Static size masks used all over this network

So, the mask must have at least 8 host bits because $2^7 \times 128$ is not enough and $2^8 \times 256$ is more than enough for numbering 200 hosts in a subnet. The mask must have at least 7 subnet bits, likewise, because 2^7 is the smallest power of 2 that is larger than 100, which is the required number of subnets. The first 16 bits in the mask must be binary 1 because a Class B network (172.16.0.0) is used. Figure 5-50 diagrams the possibilities.

Figure 5-50   *Subnet Mask Options for Scenario 5-2*

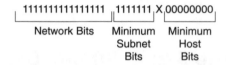

The only bit position in which a decision can be made is the 24th bit, shown with an x in Figure 5-50. That leaves two mask possibilities: 255.255.254.0 and 255.255.255.0. This sample shows the 255.255.254.0 mask because 255.255.255.0 is more intuitive.

Answers to Task 2 for Scenario 5-2

To choose a mask and pick enough subnets to use for the original topology illustrated in Figure 5-44, a review of the longer binary algorithm and shortcut algorithm for deriving subnet numbers is required. To review, subnet numbers have the network number binary value in the network portion of the subnet numbers and have all binary 0s in the host bits. The bits that vary from subnet to subnet are the subnet bits—in other words, you are numbering different subnets in the subnet field.

Valid subnets with mask 255.255.254.0 are as follows:

172.16.0.0 (zero subnet)

172.16.2.0

172.16.4.0

172.16.6.0

.

.

.

172.16.252.0

172.16.254.0 (broadcast subnet)

The first six subnets, including the zero subnet, were chosen for this example, as listed in Table 5-50.

Table 5-50   *Scenario 5-2 Subnets and Addresses*

Location of Subnet Geographically	Subnet Mask	Subnet Number	Router's IP Address
Ethernet off Router A	255.255.254.0	172.16.2.0	172.16.2.1
Ethernet off Router B	255.255.254.0	172.16.4.0	172.16.4.2
Ethernet off Router C	255.255.254.0	172.16.6.0	172.16.6.3
Serial between A and B	255.255.254.0	172.16.0.0	172.16.0.1 (A) and .2 (B)
Serial between A and C	255.255.254.0	172.16.8.0	172.16.8.1 (A) and .3
Serial between B and C	255.255.254.0	172.16.10.0	172.16.10.2 (B) and .3

Answers to Task 3 for Scenario 5-2

Given the details in Figure 5-44 and Table 5-46 for Scenario 5-2, the configurations in Example 5-32, Example 5-33, and Example 5-34 satisfy the exercise of creating IP-related configuration commands for each router. These examples include only the IP-related commands.

Example 5-32 *Router A Configuration, Scenario 5-2*

```
ip subnet-zero
no ip domain-lookup
!
interface serial0
ip address 172.16.0.1 255.255.254.0
interface serial 1
ip address 172.16.8.1 255.255.254.0
interface ethernet 0
ip address 172.16.2.1 255.255.254.0
!
router igrp 6
network 172.16.0.0
```

Example 5-33 *Router B Configuration, Scenario 5-2*

```
ip subnet-zero
no ip domain-lookup
!
interface serial0
ip address 172.16.0.2 255.255.254.0
interface serial 1
ip address 172.16.10.2 255.255.254.0
interface ethernet 0
ip address 172.16.4.2 255.255.254.0
```

continues

Example 5-33 *Router B Configuration, Scenario 5-2 (Continued)*

```
!
router igrp 6
network 172.16.0.0
```

Example 5-34 *Router C Configuration, Scenario 5-2*

```
ip subnet-zero
no ip domain-lookup
!
interface serial0
ip address 172.16.8.3 255.255.254.0
interface serial 1
ip address 172.16.10.3   255.255.254.0
interface ethernet 0
ip address 172.16.6.3 255.255.254.0
!
router igrp 6
network 172.16.0.0
```

Answers to Scenario 5-3: IP Subnet Design with a Class C Network

Planning the network in this scenario requires a topology that includes four sites, one Ethernet at each site, and partially meshed Frame Relay for connectivity, as shown previously in Figure 5-45. The number of subnets will never grow. You must choose a mask that will maximize the number of hosts per subnet, and you must use network 200.1.1.0.

Answers to Task 1 for Scenario 5-3

Given the design criteria and the network setup illustrated in Figure 5-45, this scenario requires tricky subnet masks because a Class C network is used and because subnetting is needed. Using Frame Relay subinterfaces, there will be a need for seven different subnets—one for each Ethernet and one for each Frame Relay VC.

If 3 subnet bits are used, eight mathematical possibilities exist for subnet numbers. However, one is the zero subnet and the other is the broadcast subnet. In this case, use of one or the other is desired because the design called for maximizing the number of hosts per subnet. Deciding against use of the zero and broadcast subnets then would require 4 subnet bits, leaving only 4 host bits, implying 14 hosts per subnet. So, 3 subnet bits and 5 host bits will be used in this solution (mask of 255.255.255.224). Figure 5-51 summarizes the subnets on the network diagram.

Figure 5-51   *Scenario 5-3 Network, with Subnets Written on Diagram*

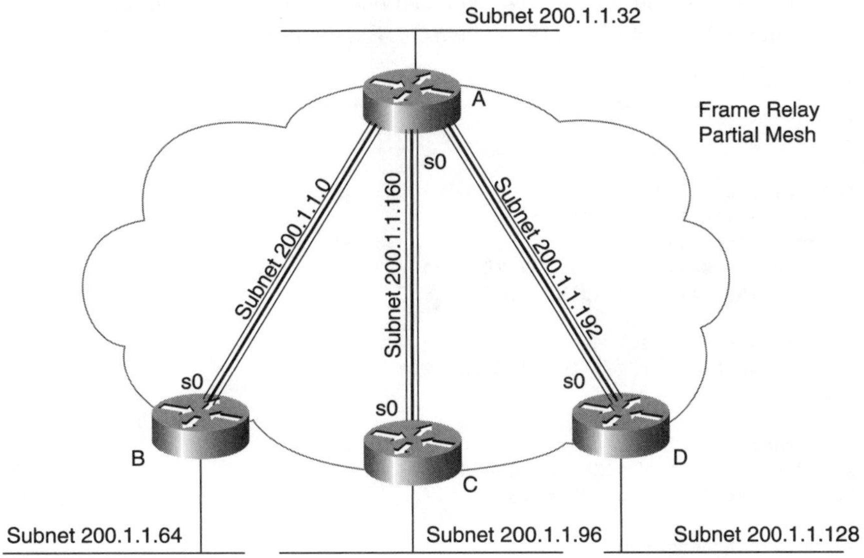

Answers to Task 2 for Scenario 5-3

Given the design criteria and the network setup illustrated in Figure 5-45 for Scenario 5-3, Table 5-51 shows the choices of subnets and addresses in this example. Only one subnet, 200.1.1.224, which is the broadcast subnet, is not used. Of course, you could have chosen a different set of subnets and used them on different links, but the mask you used should have been 255.255.255.224, based on the criteria to maximize the number of hosts per subnet.

Table 5-51   *Scenario 5-3 Addresses and Subnets*

Location of Subnet	Subnet Mask	Subnet Number	Router's IP Address
Ethernet off Router A	255.255.255.224	200.1.1.32	200.1.1.33
Ethernet off Router B	255.255.255.224	200.1.1.64	200.1.1.65
Ethernet off Router C	255.255.255.224	200.1.1.96	200.1.1.97
Ethernet off Router D	255.255.255.224	200.1.1.128	200.1.1.129
VC between A and B	255.255.255.224	200.1.1.0	200.1.1.1 (A) and .2 (B)
VC between A and C	255.255.255.224	200.1.1.160	200.1.1.161 (A) and .162 (B)
VC between A and D	255.255.255.224	200.1.1.192	200.1.1.193 (A) and .194 (B)

Answers to Task 3 for Scenario 5-3

Using the DLCIs from Figure 5-45, you can find the IP-related configuration commands for each router in Example 5-35, Example 5-36, Example 5-37, and Example 5-38.

Example 5-35 *Router A Configuration, Scenario 5-3*

```
ip subnet-zero
no ip domain-lookup
!
interface serial0
encapsulation frame-relay
interface serial 0.1
ip address 200.1.1.1 255.255.255.224
frame-relay interface-dlci 41
!
interface serial 0.2
ip address 200.1.1.161 255.255.255.224
interface-dlci 42
!
interface serial 0.3
ip address 200.1.1.193 255.255.255.224
frame-relay interface-dlci 43
!
interface ethernet 0
ip address 200.1.1.33 255.255.255.224
!
router igrp 6
network 200.1.1.0
```

Example 5-36 *Router B Configuration, Scenario 5-3*

```
ip subnet-zero
no ip domain-lookup
!
interface serial0
encapsulation frame-relay
interface serial 0.1
ip address 200.1.1.2 255.255.255.224
frame-relay interface-dlci 40
!
interface ethernet 0
ip address 200.1.1.65 255.255.255.224
!
router igrp 6
network 200.1.1.0
```

Example 5-37 *Router C Configuration, Scenario 5-3*

```
ip subnet-zero
no ip domain-lookup
!
interface serial0
encapsulation frame-relay
frame-relay interface serial 0.1
ip address 200.1.1.162 255.255.255.224
frame-relay interface-dlci 40
!
interface ethernet 0
ip address 200.1.1.97 255.255.255.224
!
router igrp 6
network 200.1.1.0
```

Example 5-38 *Router D Configuration, Scenario 5-3*

```
ip subnet-zero
no ip domain-lookup
!
interface serial0
encapsulation frame-relay
interface serial 0.1
ip address 200.1.1.194 255.255.255.224
frame-relay interface-dlci 40
!
interface ethernet 0
ip address 200.1.1.129 255.255.255.224
!
router igrp 6
network 200.1.1.0
```

Answers to Scenario 5-4: IPX Examination

Assuming the details established in Figure 5-46 and the command output in Example 5-29, Example 5-30, and Example 5-31 for Scenario 5-4, the **show ipx interface brief** command and **show ipx route** command are the best methods for learning the network numbers in Table 5-52 (Task 1, for this scenario).

Table 5-52   *IPX Networks in Scenario 5-4—Completed Chart*

IPX Network	Location (Such as "Between Albuquerque and Seville")	Command Used to Find This Information
1001	Albuquerque Ethernet0	**show ipx interface brief** on Albuquerque
		show ipx route on Yosemite

continues

Table 5-52 *IPX Networks in Scenario 5-4—Completed Chart (Continued)*

IPX Network	Location (Such as "Between Albuquerque and Seville")	Command Used to Find This Information
1002	Yosemite Ethernet0	**show ipx route** on Yosemite
1003	Seville Ethernet0	**show cdp neighbor detail** on Albuquerque
		show ipx interface on Seville
2012	Albuquerque–Yosemite	**show cdp neighbor detail** on Albuquerque
		show ipx route on Yosemite
		show ipx interface brief on Albuquerque
2013	Albuquerque–Seville	**show cdp neighbor detail** on Albuquerque
		show ipx route on Yosemite
		show ipx interface brief on Albuquerque
		show ipx interface on Seville
2023	Yosemite–Seville	**show ipx route** on Yosemite
		show ipx interface on Seville
1	Bugs' internal network	**show ipx servers** on Seville
		show ipx route on Yosemite
2	Daffy's internal network	**show ipx servers** on Seville
		show ipx route on Yosemite

Assuming the details established in Figure 5-46 and the command output in Example 5-29, Example 5-30, and Example 5-31 for Scenario 5-4, the network numbers are obtained from several sources, as seen in Table 5-52. The additional requirement for Task 2 is to find the node part of the IPX addresses on each interface. The easy way to learn this information is through the **show ipx interface** command. Of course, only one such command was provided in Example 5-29, Example 5-30, and Example 5-31. The answers that could be found in the examples are listed in Table 5-53.

Table 5-53   *IPX Addresses on Routers in Scenario 5-4—Completed Table*

Router	Interface	IPX Network	IPX Node
Albuquerque	E0	1001	
	S0	2012	0200.1111.1111
	S1	2013	
Yosemite	E0	1002	
	S0	2012	0200.2222.2222
	S1	2023	
Seville	E0	1003	0000.0cac.ab41
	S0	2013	0200.3333.3333
	S1	2023	0200.3333.3333

Answers to Scenario 5-5: IPX Configuration

Answers to Task 1 for Scenario 5-5

Assuming the details established in Figure 5-47 for Scenario 5-5, you can find in Example 5-39, Example 5-40, and Example 5-41 the IPX configurations on all three routers: Mayberry, Mount Pilot, and Raleigh, respectively.

Example 5-39 *Mayberry Configuration, Scenario 5-5, Task 1*

```
ipx routing 0200.1111.0000
!
interface serial0
encapsulation frame-relay
!
interface serial 0.2 point-to-point
ipx network 101
frame-relay interface-dlci 52
!
interface serial 0.3 point-to-point
ipx network 103
frame-relay interface-dlci 53

!
interface ethernet 0
ipx network 41
```

Example 5-40 *Mount Pilot Configuration, Scenario 5-5, Task 1*

```
ipx routing 0200.2222.0000
!
interface serial0
encapsulation frame-relay
!
interface serial 0.1 point-to-point
ipx network 101
frame-relay interface-dlci 51
!
interface serial 0.3 point-to-point
ipx network 102
frame-relay interface-dlci 53
!
interface ethernet 0
ipx network 42
```

Example 5-41 *Raleigh Configuration, Scenario 5-5, Task 1*

```
ipx routing 0200.3333.0000
!
interface serial0
encapsulation frame-relay
!
interface serial 0.1 point-to-point
ipx network 103
frame-relay interface-dlci 51
!
interface serial 0.2 point-to-point
ipx network 102
frame-relay interface-dlci 52
!
interface ethernet 0
ipx network 43
```

Your answer should match Examples 5-39 through 5-41, with a few minor exceptions. The book does not specify the serial interface, nor does it restrict the subinterface numbers chosen. Likewise, the Ethernet interface number was not specified. Otherwise, the configuration should identically match these examples.

Answers to Task 2 for Scenario 5-5

Assuming the details established in Figure 5-47 for Scenario 5-5, the second task for Scenario 5-5 calls for additional encapsulations. Beatrice is using NetWare's Ethernet_II encapsulation, Floyd is using Ethernet_802.3, Barney is using Ethernet_802.2, and Governor is using Ethernet_SNAP. Hopefully, you remembered the encapsulation names used in the IOS; the names supplied in the problem statement use the NetWare names. (In real life, a simple question mark when typing the **ipx network** interface subcommand would remind you of the names, but the objective is to memorize things so that you can pass the test. Refer to Table 5-42 for reminders on how to remember the names.) Example 5-42 and Example 5-43 show just the configuration commands used to change the configuration on Mount Pilot and Raleigh to support each client.

Example 5-42 *Mount Pilot Configuration, Scenario 5-5, Task 2—Changes Only*

```
interface ethernet 0
ipx network 42 encapsulation arpa
ipx network 142 secondary
```

Example 5-43 *Raleigh Configuration, Scenario 5-5, Task 2—Changes Only*

```
interface ethernet 0.1
ipx network 43 encapsulation sap
interface ethernet 0.2
ipx network 143 encapsulation snap
```

Two new network numbers are needed: 142 and 143 are used, in this case. Any numbers you use are fine unless they are duplicates of some other network. The **ipx network 142 secondary** command on Mount Pilot has no encapsulation type configured because the default encapsulation type is Novell-ether. The second IPX network command must be configured with the **secondary** keyword, or it will replace the **ipx network** command that was configured first.

This chapter covers the following topics that you will need to master as a CCNA:

- **Distance Vector Routing Protocols**   This section covers the details of distance vector routing protocol logic, including split horizon, holddown timers, and route poisoning. Link-state and balanced hybrid routing protocols are covered briefly.

- **Configuration of RIP and IGRP**   This section covers RIP Versions 1 and 2, plus IGRP configuration details. EXEC commands used to examine the IP routing table are also examined.

- **IPX RIP, SAP, and GNS**   This section covers the concepts and configuration for IPX, with focus on IPX RIP and SAP. Key initialization flows are outlined as well.

- **Tunneling**   This section discusses the use of tunnel interfaces for encapsulating a protocol for transport across an IP network. Configuration for tunnel interfaces is also covered.

- **Integrated Routing Protocols**   This section provides a description of the meaning of the term *integrated routing protocol*.

CHAPTER 6

Routing

Cisco expects CCNAs to demonstrate a comfortable understanding of the logic behind the routing of packets and the logic behind a routing protocol. This chapter focuses on *routing protocols*, the protocols used to discover routes. To fully appreciate the nuances of routing protocols, you need a thorough understanding of routing (the process of forwarding packets). If you have not yet reviewed the section on Layer 3 in Chapter 3, "OSI Reference Model & Layered Communication," and the sections on IP and IPX in Chapter 5, "Network Protocols," then you might want to review those sections before proceeding with this chapter.

The CCNA exam requires you to know the nuances and details of distance vector logic, which is covered in the first section of this chapter. This is the logic used by the Routing Information Protocol (RIP) and Interior Gateway Routing Protocol (IGRP), as well as IP RIP. In fact, some distance vector concepts even are applied to the NetWare Service Advertising Protocol (SAP), even though SAP does not distribute routing information. Along the way, alternative routing protocol algorithms (link-state and Diffusing Update Algorithm [DUAL]) are mentioned briefly.

Implementation details of RIP (Version 1 and Version 2) and IGRP are covered next. Because EIGRP configuration is similar to IGRP, it is also covered briefly. As you'll find on the CCNA exam, knowledge and skills for routing protocol configuration and troubleshooting are topics required of CCNAs.

Implementation of IPX RIP and SAP is another topic for which Cisco expects CCNAs to be prepared. The flows required to connect a client to a server, including the Get Nearest Server (GNS) protocol, also are important when troubleshooting IPX problems. As mentioned in the introduction and Chapter 1, "All About the Cisco Certified Network Associate Certification," Cisco definitely wants to reward CCNA candidates who have good hands-on troubleshooting skills; knowledge of connection sequences for IPX and IP is vital for being ready for any unexpected questions.

How to Best Use This Chapter

By taking the following steps, you can make better use of your study time:

- Keep your notes and the answers for all your work with this book in one place, for easy reference.

- Take the "Do I Know This Already?" quiz, and write down your answers. Studies show that retention is significantly increased through writing down facts and concepts, even if you never look at the information again.

- Use the diagram in Figure 6-1 to guide you to the next step.

Figure 6-1   *How to Use This Chapter*

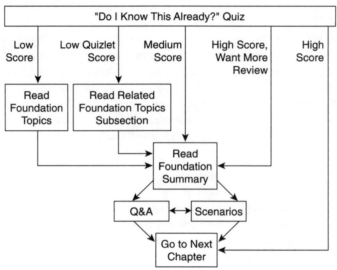

"Do I Know This Already?" Quiz

The purpose of the "Do I Know This Already?" quiz is to help you decide what parts of this chapter to use. If you already intend to read the entire chapter, you do not necessarily need to answer these questions now.

This 16-question quiz helps you choose how to spend your limited study time. The quiz is sectioned into four smaller four-question "quizlets" that are used to help you select the sections of the chapter on which to focus. Figure 6-1 outlines suggestions on how to spend your time in this chapter. Use Table 6-1 to record your score.

Table 6-1 *Scoresheet for Quiz and Quizlets*

Quizlet Number	Foundation Topics Section Covering These Questions	Questions	Score
1	Distance Vector Routing Protocols	1 to 4	
2	Configuration of RIP and IGRP	5 to 8	
3	IPX RIP, SAP, and GNS	9 to 12	
4	Tunneling	13 to 16	
	Integrated Routing Protocols		
All questions		1 to 16	

1 Define what split horizon means to the contents of a routing update. Does this apply to both the distance vector algorithm and the link-state algorithm?

_____

_____

_____

2 Does IPX RIP use Split Horizon?

_____

_____

_____

3 Describe the purpose and meaning of route poisoning.

_____

_____

_____

4 Describe the meaning and purpose of triggered updates.

_____

_____

_____

5   Write down the steps you would take to migrate from RIP to IGRP in a router whose current RIP configuration includes only **router rip**, followed by a **network 10.0.0.0** command.

_____

_____

_____

6   How does the IOS designate a subnet in the routing table as a directly connected network? What about a route learned with IGRP or a route learned with RIP?

_____

_____

_____

7   From a router's user mode, without using debugs or privileged mode, how can you determine what routers are sending you routing updates?

_____

_____

_____

8   If the command **router rip** followed by **network 10.0.0.0**, with no other **network** commands, was configured in a router that has an Ethernet0 interface with IP address 168.10.1.1, would RIP send updates out Ethernet0?

_____

_____

_____

9   Describe the metric(s) used by IPX RIP in a Cisco router.

_____

_____

_____

10   What does GNS stand for? Who creates GNS requests, and who creates GNS replies?

_____

_____

_____

11 If Serial0 has a **bandwidth 1544** interface subcommand and Serial1 has a **bandwidth 56** interface subcommand, what metric will IPX RIP associate with each interface?

_____

_____

_____

12 What **show** commands list IPX RIP metric values in a Cisco router?

_____

_____

_____

13 Define the term integrated multiprotocol routing in the context of the Cisco IOS and Novell IPX.

_____

_____

_____

14 What routing protocols support integrated multiprotocol routing?

_____

_____

_____

15 Identify two reasons for using tunneling.

_____

_____

_____

16 What tunneling transport protocol is used by the IOS?

_____

_____

_____

The answers to the "Do I Know This Already?" quiz are found in Appendix A, "Answers to the 'Do I Know This Already?' Quizzes and Q&A Sections," on page 745. The suggested choices for your next step are as follows:

- **8 or less overall score**—Read the entire chapter. This includes the "Foundation Topics" and "Foundation Summary" sections, the Q&A section, and the scenarios at the end of the chapter.

- **2 or less on any quizlet**—Review the subsection(s) of the "Foundation Topics" part of this chapter, based on Table 6-1. Then move into the "Foundation Summary" section, the quiz, and the scenarios at the end of the chapter.

- **9 to 12 overall score**—Begin with the "Foundation Summary," and then go to the Q&A section and the scenarios at the end of the chapter.

- **13 or more overall score**—If you want more review on these topics, skip to the "Foundation Summary," and then go to the Q&A section and the scenarios at the end of the chapter. Otherwise, move to the next chapter.

Foundation Topics

Distance Vector Routing Protocols

The CCNA exam requires that you be able to describe the logic behind distance vector routing protocols, as well as describe the operation of two distance vector routing protocols, RIP and IGRP. Configuration on a Cisco router is left until the next section.

Terminology relating to routing protocols is often misunderstood; this confusion is a direct result of inconsistent use of terminology by authors. The terminology relating to routing protocols and routing in this book is consistent with the courses in the Cisco CCNA training path, as well as with most Cisco documentation. The first term that needs to be defined is *routing protocol*. This term can be contrasted with *routed protocol*. Chapter 3 provides a silly, but I hope a memorable, story (the "Ted and Ting" story) that can help distinguish between the first two terms. Three definitions follow:

- A *routing protocol* fills the routing table with routing information. Examples include RIP and IGRP.

- A *routed protocol* is a protocol that has an OSI Layer 3 equivalent specification, which defines logical addressing and routing. The packets defined by the network layer (Layer 3) portion of these protocols can be routed. Examples of protocols include IP and IPX.

- The term *routing type* might appear on questions remaining from the older CCNA exam, 640-407. This term refers to the type of routing protocol—for instance, link-state.

IP routing protocols fill the IP routing table with valid, (hopefully) loop-free routes. (As you will see later, distance vector routing protocols have many features that prevent loops, none of which guarantees to prevent loops.) Each route includes a subnet number, the interface out which to forward packets so that they are delivered to that subnet, and the IP address of the next router that should receive packets destined for that subnet (if needed). An analogy to routing is the process a stubborn man might use when taking a trip to somewhere he has never been. He might look for a road sign referring to the destination town and pointing him to the next turn. By repeating the process at each intersection, he should eventually make it to the correct town, at last. Of course, if a routing loop occurs (in other words, he's lost!) and he stubbornly never asks for directions, he could loop forever—or at least until he's out of gas!

Before discussing the underlying logic, the goals of a routing protocol should be considered. The goals documented in the following list are common for any IP routing protocol, regardless of its underlying logic type:

- To dynamically learn and fill the routing table with a route to all subnets in the network.

- If more than one route to a subnet is available, to place the best route in the routing table.

- To notice when routes in the table are no longer valid, and to remove those routes from the routing table.

- If a route is removed from the routing table and another route through another neighboring router is available, to add the route to the routing table. (Many people view this goal and the previous one as a single goal.)

- To add new routes, or to replace lost routes with the best currently available route, as quickly as possible. The time between losing the route and finding a working replacement route is called *convergence* time.

- To prevent routing loops.

Comparing Routing Protocols

Several routing protocols for TCP/IP exist. IP's long history and continued popularity have called for the specification and creation of several different competing options. So, classifying IP routing protocols based on their differences is useful—and also is a fair topic for exam questions.

One major classification of IP routing protocols is whether they are optimized for creating routes inside one organization or routes between two or more interconnected organizations. Exterior routing protocols are optimized for use between routers from different organizations. Border Gateway Protocol (BGP) and Exterior Gateway Protocol (EGP) are the two options for exterior routing protocols; BGP is the most popular and the more recently developed of the two. (EGP is not technically a routing protocol but is a "reachability" protocol; it is obsolete.)

The CCNA exam focuses on interior routing protocols. If you are interested in pursuing CCIE-ISP, CCIE-R/S, or CCNP certification, understanding exterior routing protocols is very important. An excellent learning tool and reference to IP routing and routing protocols is the Cisco Press book *Routing TCP/IP, Volume I*, by Jeff Doyle.

Routing protocol is the term used to describe the programs and processes used to exchange and learn routing information. Other documents call these same programs and processes *routing algorithms*. Personally, I prefer the term *type of routing protocol*, yet a third term for the same concept. Terminology counts; for the CCNA exam, remember all three terms.

One type of routing protocol is the *link-state protocol*. Link-state protocols use a topological database that is created on each router; entries describing each router, each router's attached links, and each router's neighboring routers are included in the database. Each router builds a complete map of the network. The topology database is processed by an algorithm called the *Dijkstra shortest path first (SPF)* algorithm for choosing the best routes to add to the routing table. This detailed topology information along with the Dijkstra algorithm helps link-state protocols avoid loops and converge quickly.

A second type of routing protocol is the *balanced hybrid protocol*. Balanced hybrid is a term created by Cisco to describe the inner workings of EIGRP, which uses the Diffusing Update Algorithm (DUAL) for calculating routes. A balanced hybrid protocol exchanges more topology information than does a distance vector routing protocol, but it does not require full topology and does not require the computationally intensive Dijkstra algorithm for computing loop-free routes.

Distance vector is the other type of routing protocol and will be discussed in much detail in the next subsection.

Several different implementations of distance vector and link-state routing protocols could be covered on the CCNA exam; only RIP Version 1 (RIP-1) and IGRP should be covered in-depth. RIP-1 and IGRP are similar in most details, with the big exception being that IGRP uses a much more robust metric. Both RIP-1 and IGRP are covered in more detail later in this chapter.

Some routing protocols are less likely to be covered on the CCNA exam, including RIP Version 2 (RIP-2). RIP-2 includes many improvements over RIP-1. Most notably, the subnet mask associated with each advertised route is included in the routing update. The mask allows routers to use features such as variable-length subnet masks (VLSMs) and route summarization, both features sure to be covered on the CCNP exams.

Enhanced IGRP (EIGRP) is another balanced hybrid routing protocol, but it uses more advanced features to avoid loops and speed convergence. (EIGRP is also unlikely to be covered on the CCNA exam but is fair game for the CCNP.) The underlying algorithm is called the *Diffusing Update Algorithm (DUAL)*. DUAL defines a method for each router to not only calculate the best current route to each subnet, but to also calculate alternative routes that could be used if the current route fails. An alternate route, using what DUAL defines as a neighboring *feasible successor route*, is guaranteed to be loop-free, so convergence can happen quickly. EIGRP also transmits the subnet mask for each routing entry. Therefore, features such as VLSM and route summarization are easily supported.

Open Shortest Path First (OSPF) is a link-state routing protocol used for IP. Link-state protocols avoid routing loops by transmitting and keeping more detailed topology information, which allows the protocol to use calculations that prevent loops. With OSPF, the subnet mask information is also transmitted, allowing features such as VLSM and route summarization.

Table 6-2 lists interior IP routing protocols and their types. A column referring to whether the routing protocol includes subnet mask information in the routing updates is listed for future reference.

Table 6-2   *Interior IP Routing Protocols and Types*

Routing Protocol	Type	Loop Prevention Mechanisms	Mask Sent in Updates?
RIP-1	Distance vector	Holddown timer, split horizon	No
RIP-2	Distance vector	Holddown timer, split horizon	Yes
IGRP	Distance vector	Holddown timer, split horizon	No
EIGRP	Balanced hybrid	DUAL and feasible successors	Yes
OSPF	Link-state	Dijkstra SPF algorithm and full topology knowledge	Yes

Distance Vector Routing

CCNAs deal with routing problems on a daily basis; some of these problems are a result of the logic behind distance vector routing protocols. To understand what distance vector routing means is to understand how a routing protocol accomplishes the following goals:

- Learning routing information

- Noticing failed routes

- Adding the current best route after one has failed

- Preventing loops

The following list summarizes the behavior of a router that uses the RIP-1 or IGRP distance vector routing protocols:

- *Directly connected* subnets are already known by the router; these routes are advertised to neighboring routers.

- *Routing updates* are broadcast (or multicast, in many cases). This is so that all neighboring routers can learn routes via the single broadcast or multicast update.

- *Routing updates* are listened for so that this router can learn new routes.

- A *metric* describes each route in the update. The metric describes how good the route is; if multiple routes to the same subnet are learned, the lower metric route is used.

- *Topology* information in routing updates includes, at a minimum, the subnet and metric information.

- *Periodic updates* are expected to be received from neighboring routers at a specified interval. Failure to receive updates from a neighbor in a timely manner results in the removal of the routes previously learned from that neighbor.

- A *route* learned from a neighboring router is assumed to be through that router.

- A *failed route* is advertised for a time, with a metric that implies that the network is "infinite" distance. This route is considered unusable. Infinity is defined by each routing protocol to be some very large metric value. For instance, RIP's infinite metric is 16 because RIP's maximum valid hop count is 15.

Figure 6-2 demonstrates how Router A's directly connected subnets are advertised to Router B. In this case, Router A advertises two directly connected routes.

Figure 6-2   *Router A Advertising Directly Connected Routes*

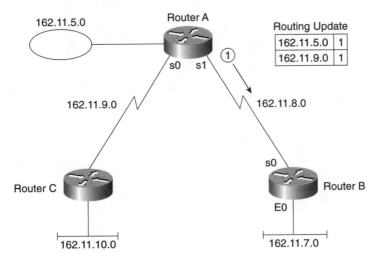

Table 6-3 shows the resulting routing table on Router B.

Table 6-3   *Router B Routing Table, After Receiving Update in Figure 6-2*

Group (Mask Is 255.255.255.0)	Outgoing Interface	Next Router
162.11.5.0	S0	162.11.8.1
162.11.7.0	E0	
162.11.8.0	S0	
162.11.9.0	S0	162.11.8.1

The two directly connected routes on Router B do not have a Next Router field because packets to those subnets can be sent directly to hosts in those subnets. The Next Router field for the routes learned from Router A show Router A's IP address as the next router, as described previously. (A route learned from a neighboring router is assumed to be through that router.) Router B typically learns Router A's IP address for these routes by simply looking at the source IP address of the routing update.

Metric values are cumulative. A subnet learned via an update from a neighbor is advertised, but with a higher metric. For example, an update received on serial 1 lists a subnet with metric 5. Before advertising that subnet in an update sent out some other interface, the router adds to the metric, based on a value associated with serial 1. With RIP, because hop count is the metric, the advertised metric would be 6, in this case. Figure 6-3 and Table 6-4 illustrate the concept.

Figure 6-3   *Router A Advertising Routes Learned from Router C*

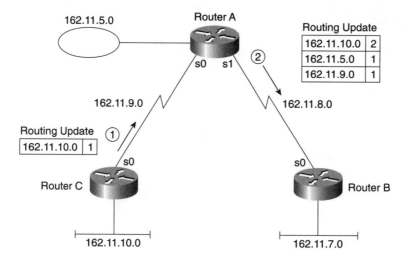

Table 6-4   *Router B Routing Table, After Receiving Update in Figure 6-3*

Group	Outgoing Interface	Next Router
162.11.5.0	S0	162.11.8.1
162.11.7.0	E0	
162.11.8.0	S0	
162.11.9.0	S0	162.11.8.1
162.11.10.0	S0	162.11.8.1

Figure 6-3 demonstrates the seven distance vector routing protocol behaviors previously listed, with the exception of periodic updates and failed routes. The metric describing subnet 162.11.10.0, received from Router C, was incremented by 1 before advertising about that subnet to Router B. This metric value represents hop count, which is used by RIP. (IGRP uses a different metric, which will be discussed later.) The route to 162.11.10.0 that Router B adds to its routing table refers to Router A as the next router because Router B learned the route from Router A; Router B knows nothing about the network topology on the "other side" of Router A.

Distance vector routing protocols doubt the validity of routing information that they learned from a neighboring router if that neighboring router quits sending routing updates. Periodic routing updates are sent by each router. A routing update timer determines how often the updates are sent. The timer should be equal on all routers, although the timers can be configured for different values, causing unpredictable (and bad) results. The absence of routing updates for a preset number of routing timer intervals results in the removal of the routes previously learned from the router that has become silent.

Several issues exist related to loops and convergence required when using distance vector routing protocols. Most of the issues with distance vector routing protocols arise when working with networks with multiple paths because loops are very difficult when there is only one path possible to get to a subnet. Table 6-5 summarizes these issues and lists the names of the solutions, which are explained in the upcoming text.

Table 6-5   *Issues Relating to Distance Vector Routing Protocols in Networks with Multiple Paths*

Issue	Solution
Multiple routes to same subnet, with equal metric	Implementation options involve either using the first route learned or putting multiple routes to the same subnet in the routing table.
Routing loops occurring due to updates passing each other over a single link	**Split horizon**—The routing protocol advertises routes out an interface only if they were not learned from updates entering that interface.
	Split horizon with poison reverse—The routing protocol advertises all routes out an interface, but those learned from earlier updates coming in that interface are marked with infinite distance metrics.
Routing loops occurring due to updates passing each other over alternate paths	**Route poisoning**—When a route to a subnet fails, the subnet is advertised with an infinite distance metric.
Counting to infinity	**Holddown timer**—After knowing that a route to a subnet has failed, a router waits a certain period of time before believing any other routing information about that subnet.
	Triggered updates—An update is sent immediately rather than waiting on the update timer to expire when a route has failed. Used in conjunction with route poisoning, this ensures that all routers know of failed routes before any holddown timers can expire.

Issues When Multiple Routes to the Same Subnet Exist

The first issue is straightforward and is described more easily with the example in Figure 6-4 and Tables 6-6 and 6-7.

Figure 6-4 *Routers A and C Advertising to Router B*

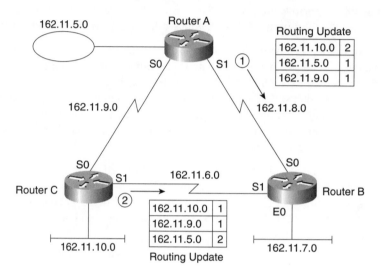

NOTE The routing updates in Figure 6-4 show only the information needed for the point being made in this example; other routes that would normally be in the routing update are omitted.

Table 6-6 *Router B Routing Table, with Two Routes to Same Subnet While Router B Serial 1 Is Down*

Group	Outgoing Interface	Next Router	Metric
162.11.5.0	S0	162.11.8.1	1
162.11.7.0	E0		0
162.11.8.0	S0		0
162.11.9.0	S0	162.11.8.1	1
162.11.10.0	S0	162.11.8.1	2

Table 6-7 *Router B Routing Table, with Two Routes to Same Subnet After Router B Serial 1 Is Up*

Group	Outgoing Interface	Next Router	Metric
162.11.5.0	S0	162.11.8.1	1
162.11.6.0	S1		0
162.11.7.0	E0		0
162.11.8.0	S0		0
162.11.9.0	S0	162.11.8.1	1
162.11.10.0	S1	162.11.6.2	1

Table 6-6 shows B's routing table before B's S1 interface came up; Table 6-7 shows B's routing table after S1 is up. One route was changed, one route was added, and one route that could have been changed was not. The route to 162.11.10.0 was changed because the metric for the route through Router C (metric 1) is smaller than the one from Router A (metric 2). The route to directly connected subnet 162.11.6.0 was added, but not because of this distance vector routing protocol; it was added by Router B because it is a directly connected subnet and because that interface is now up. Finally, the route to subnet 162.11.9.0 is advertised with metric 1 by both Routers A and C. In this case, the route that was already in the table is left in the table, which is a reasonable choice. The choice of just placing one of the two equal metric routes in the table is an implementation decision. Cisco routers can include up to six equal-cost routes in the routing table instead of the choice shown in this example.

Split Horizon, Holddown, and Route Poisoning

Routing loops can occur when using distance vector routing protocols because bad routing information can be propagated. Split horizon is the popular solution to the problem and works very well in most topologies. Figure 6-5 shows an example of this problem.

NOTE   The routing updates in Figure 6-5 show only the information needed for the point being made in this example; other routes that would normally be in the routing update are omitted.

Figure 6-5   *Advertisements Passing on Serial Link for Subnet 162.11.7.0*

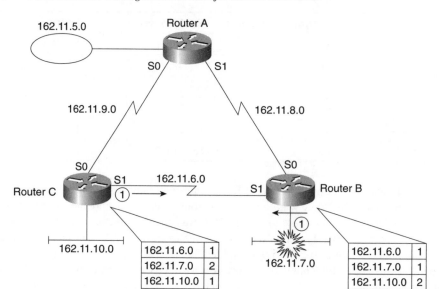

In Figure 6-5, the routing updates are sent periodically. There is no requirement to make the updates flow from C and B at the same time; however, in this case, B and C are sending updates at the same instant in time. This is not a problem until B advertises an infinite-distance (metric) route to 162.11.7.0 because the subnet just failed. However, the update from C passes the update from B on the serial link. Table 6-8 and Table 6-9 show the resulting routing table entries, with a reference to the metric values.

Table 6-8   *Router B Routing Table, After Subnet 162.11.7.0 Failed and Update from Router C Is Received*

Group	Outgoing Interface	Next Router	Metric
162.11.6.0	S1		0
162.11.7.0	S1		2
162.11.10.0	S1	162.11.6.2	1

Table 6-9   *Router C Routing Table, After Subnet 162.11.7.0 Failed and Update from Router B Is Received*

Group	Outgoing Interface	Next Router	Metric
162.11.6.0	S1		0
162.11.7.0	S1		16
162.11.10.0	E0		1

NOTE	In this chapter, the value 16 is used to represent an infinite metric. RIP uses 16 to represent infinite; IGRP uses a delay value of more than 4 billion to imply an infinite distance route.

Now Router C has an infinite distance route, but Router B will send packets to 162.11.7.0 through Router C. Router C claimed to have a metric 2 route to 162.11.7.0 at the same time that Router C was receiving the update that the route to 162.11.7.0 was no longer valid. (*Note*: Infinity is shown as the value 16 in Table 6-9, which is RIP's value for infinity.) So, Router B thinks 162.11.7.0 is reachable through Router C, and Router C thinks 162.11.7.0 is unreachable. The process repeats itself with the next routing update, except Router B advertises metric 3 and Router C advertises an infinite (bad) metric for subnet 162.11.7.0. This will continue until both numbers reach infinity.

For those less patient, each distance vector routing protocol implementation sets a metric value for which the number is considered to be infinite. For example, 16 is infinite for RIP, and 4,294,967,295 is infinite for IGRP.

Split horizon is the solution to the counting to infinity problem, in this case. Split horizon includes two related concepts that affect what routes are included in a routing update:

- An update does not include the subnet of the interface out which the update is sent.

- All routes with *outgoing interface* of interface x are not included in updates sent out that same interface x.

For instance, in Figure 6-6, B's route to subnet 162.11.10.0 points out Serial1, so its update sent out Serial1 does not advertise that subnet. B's update also does not include subnet 162.11.9.0, presumably because B's route to that subnet also points out Serial1. However, because B's route to 162.11.5.0 points out Serial0 to Router A, B advertises about that subnet out Serial1.

The term *split horizon with poison reverse*, or simply *poison reverse*, is a similar feature to split horizon. Instead of not advertising a route out the same interface in which the route was learned, poison reverse means that the routes are advertised but with a poison (infinite) metric. In other words, in Figure 6-6, Router B would also advertise routes to 162.11.6.0, 162.11.9.0, and 162.11.10.0, all with infinite metric.

Split horizon defeats the *counting to infinity* problem over a single link. However, counting to infinity can occur in redundant networks (networks with multiple paths) even with split horizon enabled. The *holddown timer* is part of a solution to the counting to infinity problem when networks have multiple paths to many subnets. Split horizon does not defeat the counting to infinity problem in all topologies. An additional solution is required, which includes a holddown timer and a routing update feature called route poisoning. Figure 6-7 shows an example topology showing counting to infinity.

Figure 6-6   *Split Horizon Enabled, with Poison Reverse*

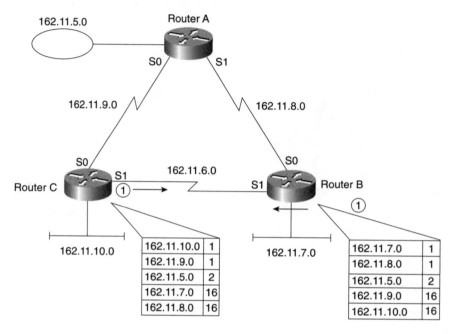

Figure 6-7   *Counting to Infinity*

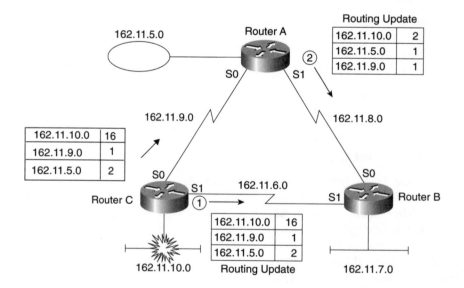

For the scenario in Figure 6-7, subnet 162.11.10.0 fails; Router C sends updates to Router B and Router A, as shown in Step 1 of Figure 6-7. Router A happens to send its next update out its S1 interface to Router B just before it hears the bad news about 162.11.10.0 from Router C, as denoted as Step 2 in Figure 6-7. Table 6-10 shows the result of these two updates entering Router B.

Table 6-10   *Router B Routing Table After Updates in Figure 6-7 Are Received*

Group	Outgoing Interface	Next Router	Metric
162.11.5.0	S0	162.11.8.1	1
162.11.6.0	S1		
162.11.7.0	E0		
162.11.8.0	S0		
162.11.9.0	S0	162.11.8.1	1
162.11.10.0	S0	162.11.8.1	2

Router B now thinks it has a valid route to 162.11.10.0, pointing back to Router A. On B's next update, the router does not advertise subnet 162.11.10.0 out S0 due to split horizon rules, but Router B advertises 162.11.10.0 to Router C out Serial1. Router C incorrectly believes that the route to 162.11.10.0 exists through Router B; Router C also tells Router A that it has a route to 162.11.10.0. So, counting to infinity occurs.

The solution is to enable a holddown timer. In the example in Figure 6-7, Router B's original route to 162.11.10.0 pointed to Router C. It was then changed to point to Router A. Holddown would require Router B to wait for a period to learn new routes after an old one has failed, in this case ignoring the metric 2 route learned from Router A.

NOTE   Holddown is defined as follows: When learning about a failed route, ignore any new information about that subnet for a time equal to the holddown timer.

With holddown enabled, Router B would not believe the metric 2 route learned in Step 1 of Figure 6-7. During the same time, Routers C and A both would be advertising infinite metric routes to 162.11.10.0 to Router B, which also would quickly be receiving only routing updates for 162.11.10.0 with an infinite metric.

(*Infinite* is a term used to signify the concept, not the actual value. Each routing protocol can— and typically does—define a maximum usable metric value, with any number over that being considered infinite.)

Route poisoning is another method to help avoid loops and speed convergence. Route poisoning is different than poison reverse—unfortunately, some well-known TCP/IP references have used these terms in different ways, making things quite a mess. (The typical description in the Cisco context follows.) When a distance vector routing protocol notices that a particular route is no longer valid, it has two choices. One is simply to quit advertising about that subnet; the other is to advertise that route, but with an infinite metric, signifying that the route is bad. Route poisoning calls for the second of these options, which removes any ambiguity about whether the route is still valid. For example, in Figure 6-7 again, a metric of 16 is used to signify infinity. Router C is using route poisoning to ensure that Router A and Router B do not point routes for 162.11.10.0 back through Router C. (The examples in this chapter all used route poisoning— in other words, the bad routes were advertised with an infinite metric.)

One final loop prevention mechanism that also speeds convergence is called *flash updates*, also known as *triggered updates*. When a router notices that a directly connected subnet has changed state, it immediately sends another routing update on its other interfaces rather than waiting on the routing update timer to expire. This causes the information about the route whose status has changed to be forwarded more quickly and starts the holddown timers more quickly as well on the neighboring routers, as seen in Figure 6-8.

Figure 6-8   *Flash Updates*

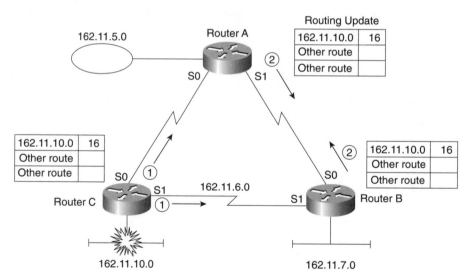

NOTE   The updates are full updates, as is required by distance vector logic. The other routes are not important to the description, so these other routes in the update are not listed.

Router C sends its update immediately after 162.11.10.0 fails. Routers A and B also react immediately, sending updates to their neighbors. Because all the routers will ignore any new information about this subnet for holddown time, fast propagation of the fact that the route failed is not harmful. This mechanism quickly prevents packets from being unnecessarily routed.

Table 6-11 contains a summary of the terms and concepts used by distance vector routing protocols to help avoid loops and speed convergence.

RIP and IGRP

To pass the CCNA exam, you will need to know the particulars of how RIP and IGRP implement distance vector logic. RIP and IGRP both use distance vector logic, so they are very similar in many respects. A couple of major differences exist, however, and will be explained in the upcoming text. Table 6-11 outlines the features of RIP and IGRP.

Table 6-11   *RIP and IGRP Feature Comparison*

Feature	RIP (Defaults)	IGRP (Defaults)
Update timer	30 seconds	90 seconds
Metric	Hop count	Function of bandwidth and delay (default); can include reliability, load, and MTU
Holddown timer	180	280
Flash (triggered) updates	Yes	Yes
Mask sent in update	No for RIP v1; yes for RIP v2	No
Infinity metric value	16	4,294,967,295

The metric with IGRP is more robust than RIP's metric. The metric is calculated using the bandwidth and delay settings on the interface on which the update was received. By using bandwidth and delay, the metric is more meaningful; longer hop routes over faster links can be considered better routes.

The metric used by IP RIP is hop count. When an update is received, the metric for each subnet in the update signifies the number of routers between the router receiving the update and each subnet. Before sending an update, a router increments its metric for routes to each subnet by 1. In other words, a routing update includes metric values that tell the receiving router what its metrics should be.

Finally, the issue of whether the mask is sent is particularly important if VLSMs in the same network are desired. This topic is discussed in the upcoming section "Configuration of RIP and IGRP."

Distance Vector Routing Protocol Summary

Distance vector routing protocols learn and advertise routes. The routes placed in the routing table should be loop-free and should be the best known working route. Metrics are used to choose the best route. Mechanisms such as split horizon and holddown timers are used to prevent routing loops.

Configuration of RIP and IGRP

The CCNA exam requires you to understand RIP and IGRP configuration details. RIP and IGRP configuration requires an understanding of two subtle nuances—namely, what the **network** command really implies and how the router interprets the **network** command. Other than these two details, configuration is relatively easy.

Hands-on experience is the best way to fully learn the details of configuration. In lieu of that, this section lists commands, provides examples, and points out any tricky features. Table 6-12 and Table 6-13 summarize the more popular commands used for RIP and IGRP configuration and verification. Two configuration samples follow. The Cisco IOS documentation is an excellent reference for additional IP commands, and the Cisco Press book *Interconnecting Cisco Network Devices* is an excellent reference, particularly if you are not able to attend the instructor-led version of the class.

Table 6-12   *IP RIP and IGRP Configuration Commands*

Command	Configuration Mode
router rip	Global
router igrp *process-id*	Global
network *net-number*	Router subcommand
passive-interface *type number*	Router subcommand
maximum-paths *x*	Router subcommand
variance *multiplier*	Router subcommand
traffic-share {*balanced*	*min*}	Router subcommand

Table 6-13   *IP RIP and IGRP EXEC*

Command	Function
show ip route [*subnet*]	Shows entire routing table, or one entry if **subnet** is entered
show ip protocol	Shows routing protocol parameters and current timer values
debug ip rip	Issues log messages for each RIP update
debug ip igrp transactions	Issues log messages with details of the IGRP updates
debug ip igrp events	Issues log messages for each IGRP packet

Table 6-13   *IP RIP and IGRP EXEC (Continued)*

Command	Function
ping	Sends and receives ICMP echo messages to verify connectivity
trace	Sends a series of ICMP echoes with increasing TTL values to verify the current route to a host

The network Command

Each **network** command enables RIP or IGRP on a set of interfaces. However, as a CCNA, you must understand the subtleties to what that really means (as explained in the next several paragraphs.) However, what "enables" really means in this case is not obvious from Cisco IOS documentation. Also, the parameters for the **network** command are not intuitive to many people new to Cisco IOS configuration commands; therefore, routing protocol configuration, including the **network** command, is a likely topic for tricky questions on the exam.

The **network** command causes implementation of the following three functions:

- Routing updates are broadcast or multicast out an interface.

- Routing updates are processed if they enter that same interface.

- The subnet directly connected to that interface is advertised.

The **network** command matches some of the interfaces on a router. The interfaces matched by the **network** command have the three functions previously mentioned performed on them. Examples provide a much easier understanding of the **network** command, as demonstrated in Figure 6-9 and Example 6-1.

Figure 6-9   *Sample Router with Five Interfaces*

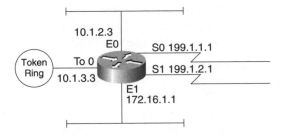

Example 6-1   *Sample Router Configuration with RIP Partially Enabled*

```
interface ethernet 0
ip address 10.1.2.3 255.255.255.0
interface ethernet 1
ip address 172.16.1.1 255.255.255.0
interface tokenring 0
ip address 10.1.3.3 255.255.255.0
interface serial 0
ip address 199.1.1.1 255.255.255.0
interface serial 1
ip address 199.1.2.1 255.255.255.0
!
router rip
network 10.0.0.0
network 199.1.1.0
```

The router matches interfaces with the **network** command by asking this simple question:

> Which of my interfaces have IP addresses in the same network number referenced in this **network** subcommand?

For any interfaces that have IP addresses in the same network number referenced in this **network** subcommand, routing updates are broadcast and listened for, and the connected subnet is advertised. For instance, in the first of the two highlighted **network** commands of Example 6-1, network 10.0.0.0 is configured. Interfaces Ethernet0 and tokenring 0 will be matched. A single **network** command probably will match more than one interface because the parameter to the **network** command is always a Class A, B, or C network number, not a subnet number or IP address. Furthermore, most routers will be attached to multiple subnets of that same Class A, B, or C network. In many smaller networks, subnets of only a single network are used, so a single **network** command could match all interfaces.

In Example 6-1, RIP broadcasts are sent out serial 0, ethernet 0, and tokenring 0. Likewise, RIP updates entering those three interfaces alone are processed. Finally, each RIP update created by this router advertises only directly connected subnets 10.1.2.0, 199.1.1.0, and 10.1.3.0, in addition to any routes learned from other routers using RIP.

A common oversight is to forget to configure a **network** command to match interfaces serial 1 and ethernet 1. Seemingly, if no other routers are attached to that same Ethernet interface, then there is no need to broadcast RIP/IGRP or listen for RIP/IGRP on the interface. However, three functions are enabled by matching an interface with the **network** command, as discussed earlier. With the current configuration in Example 6-1, because no **network** command matches the ethernet 1 and serial 1 interfaces, none of the RIP/IGRP updates from this router will advertise about subnet 172.16.1.0 or network 199.1.2.0.

The passive-interface Command

The **passive-interface** command can be used to cause the router to listen for RIP/IGRP and advertise about the connected subnet, but not to send RIP/IGRP updates on the interface. In Example 6-2, a sample IGRP configuration causes the router to advertise about all connected subnets, to listen on all interfaces for IGRP updates, and to advertise on all interfaces except ethernet 1.

Example 6-2   *Sample IGRP Configuration and* **show ip route** *Output*

```
interface ethernet 0
ip address 10.1.2.3 255.255.255.0
interface ethernet 1
ip address 172.16.1.1 255.255.255.0
interface tokenring 0
ip address 10.1.3.3 255.255.255.0
interface serial 0
ip address 199.1.1.1 255.255.255.0
interface serial 1
ip address 199.1.2.1 255.255.255.0
!
router igrp 1
 network 10.0.0.0
 network 199.1.1.0
 network 199.1.2.0
 network 172.16.0.0
 passive-interface ethernet 1

Mayberry#show ip route
Codes: C - connected, S - static, I - IGRP, R - RIP, M - mobile, B - BGP
       D - EIGRP, EX - EIGRP external, O - OSPF, IA - OSPF inter area
       N1 - OSPF NSSA external type 1, N2 - OSPF NSSA external type 2
       E1 - OSPF external type 1, E2 - OSPF external type 2, E - EGP
       i - IS-IS, L1 - IS-IS level-1, L2 - IS-IS level-2, * - candidate default
       U - per-user static route, o - ODR

Gateway of last resort is not set

     10.0.0.0/24 is subnetted, 3 subnets
C       10.1.2.0 is directly connected, TokenRing0
C       10.1.3.0 is directly connected, Ethernet0
I       10.1.4.0 [100/8539] via 10.1.2.14, 00:00:50, Ethernet0
     172.16.0.0/24 is subnetted, 2 subnets
C       172.16.1.0 is directly connected, Ethernet1
I       172.16.2.0 [100/6244] via 172.16.1.44, 00:00:20, Ethernet1
C     199.1.1.0/24 is directly connected, Serial0
C     199.1.2.0/24 is directly connected, Serial1
```

Notice that the four **network** commands match all five interfaces on the router (refer to Figure 6-9). The **passive-interface** router subcommand causes the router to not send IGRP updates on interface E1. Also, notice the 1 on the **router igrp** command—all other routers using IGRP must use this same process-id, assuming that all routers want to exchange routing information using IGRP.

IGRP Metrics

IGRP uses a composite metric. This metric is calculated as a function of bandwidth, delay, load, and reliability. By default, only the bandwidth and delay are considered; the other parameters are considered only if enabled via configuration. Delay and bandwidth are not measured values but are set via the **delay** and **bandwidth** interface subcommands. (The same formula is used for calculating the metric for EIGRP, but with a scaling factor so that the actual metric values are larger, allowing more granularity in the metric.)

The **show ip route** command in Example 6-2 shows the IGRP metric values in brackets. For example, the route to 10.1.4.0 shows the value [100/8539] beside the subnet number. The metric 8539 is a single value, as calculated based on bandwidth and delay. The metric is calculated (by default) as the sum of the inverse of the minimum bandwidth, plus the cumulative delay on all links in the route. In other words, the higher the bandwidth, the lower the metric; the lower the cumulative delay, the lower the metric.

Split Horizon and Infinity

Split horizon and route poisoning were covered in the section "Distance Vector Routing Protocols." RIP and IGRP are distance vector routing protocols that implement split horizon and route poisoning; these can be better understood by examining **debug** messages. Figure 6-10 and Example 6-3 show a stable network with split horizon rules that affect the RIP updates. Then Ethernet 0 on Yosemite is shut down, and Yosemite advertises an infinite distance route to 10.1.2.0, as seen in Example 6-4.

Figure 6-10   *Split Horizon and Infinite Distance Routes*

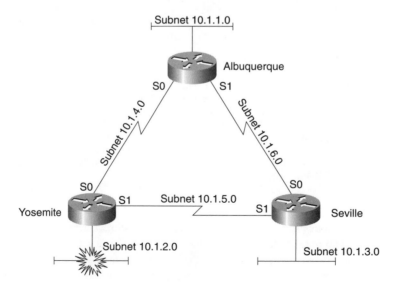

Example 6-3   *RIP Configuration and Debugs on Albuquerque*

```
interface ethernet 0
ip addr 10.1.1.251 255.255.255.0
interface serial 0
ip addr 10.1.4.251 255.255.255.0
interface serial 1
ip addr 10.1.6.251 255.255.255.0
!
router rip
network 10.0.0.0


Albuquerque#debug ip rip
RIP: received v1 update from 10.1.6.253 on Serial1
      10.1.3.0 in 1 hops
      10.1.2.0 in 2 hops
      10.1.5.0 in 1 hops
RIP: sending v1 update to 255.255.255.255 via Serial0 (10.1.4.251)
      subnet  10.1.3.0, metric 2
      subnet  10.1.1.0, metric 1
      subnet  10.1.6.0, metric 1
RIP: sending v1 update to 255.255.255.255 via Serial1 (10.1.6.251)
      subnet  10.1.2.0, metric 2
      subnet  10.1.1.0, metric 1
      subnet  10.1.4.0, metric 1
RIP: sending v1 update to 255.255.255.255 via Ethernet0 (10.1.1.251)
      subnet  10.1.3.0, metric 2
      subnet  10.1.2.0, metric 2
      subnet  10.1.6.0, metric 1
      subnet  10.1.5.0, metric 2
      subnet  10.1.4.0, metric 1
RIP: received v1 update from 10.1.4.252 on Serial0
      10.1.3.0 in 2 hops
      10.1.2.0 in 1 hops
      10.1.5.0 in 1 hops
Albuquerque#
(Yosemite E0 shutdown at this time...)

RIP: received v1 update from 10.1.4.252 on Serial0
      10.1.3.0 in 2 hops
      10.1.2.0 in 16 hops (inaccessible)
      10.1.5.0 in 1 hops
RIP: sending v1 update to 255.255.255.255 via Serial0 (10.1.4.251)
      subnet  10.1.3.0, metric 2
      subnet  10.1.2.0, metric 16
      subnet  10.1.1.0, metric 1
      subnet  10.1.6.0, metric 1
RIP: sending v1 update to 255.255.255.255 via Serial1 (10.1.6.251)
      subnet  10.1.2.0, metric 16
      subnet  10.1.1.0, metric 1
      subnet  10.1.4.0, metric 1
RIP: sending v1 update to 255.255.255.255 via Ethernet0 (10.1.1.251)
      subnet  10.1.3.0, metric 2
```

continues

Example 6-3   *RIP Configuration and Debugs on Albuquerque (Continued)*

```
        subnet  10.1.2.0, metric 16
        subnet  10.1.6.0, metric 1
        subnet  10.1.5.0, metric 2
        subnet  10.1.4.0, metric 1
RIP: received v1 update from 10.1.6.253 on Serial1
        10.1.3.0 in 1 hops
        10.1.2.0 in 16 hops (inaccessible)
        10.1.5.0 in 1 hops
```

Example 6-4   *RIP Configuration on Yosemite*

```
interface ethernet 0
ip addr 10.1.2.252 255.255.255.0
interface serial 0
ip addr 10.1.4.252 255.255.255.0
interface serial 1
ip addr 10.1.5.252 255.255.255.0

router rip
network 10.0.0.0
```

You can see several interesting items in the configuration and debugs as highlighted in Example 6-3 and Example 6-4. RIP is enabled on all interfaces and on all routers in this example. The RIP update sent out Albuquerque's Ethernet0 interface advertises five routes but does not advertise the route to 10.1.1.0 because that is the subnet of that attached Ethernet. Albuquerque's update sent on its Serial1 interface advertises only three routes due to split horizon rules. Finally, notice the update received on Albuquerque, entering Serial0 (from Yosemite) after Yosemite's Ethernet0 interface has failed. Yosemite has described subnet 10.1.2.0 with a metric 16 route, which is considered infinite by RIP.

Example 6-5 shows the configuration added to each of the three routers in Figure 6-10 to migrate to IGRP. The logic of the **network** commands works just like with RIP. The output of the **show** and **debug** commands provides some insights into the differences between RIP and IGRP.

Example 6-5   *Migration to IGRP with Sample **show** and **debug** Commands*

```
(Note: The following commands would be used on all three routers.)
no router rip
router igrp 5
 network 10.0.0.0

Albuquerque#show ip route
Codes: C - connected, S - static, I - IGRP, R - RIP, M - mobile, B - BGP
       D - EIGRP, EX - EIGRP external, O - OSPF, IA - OSPF inter area
       N1 - OSPF NSSA external type 1, N2 - OSPF NSSA external type 2
       E1 - OSPF external type 1, E2 - OSPF external type 2, E - EGP
       i - IS-IS, L1 - IS-IS level-1, L2 - IS-IS level-2, * - candidate default
       U - per-user static route, o - ODR
```

Example 6-5 *Migration to IGRP with Sample **show** and **debug** Commands (Continued)*

```
Gateway of last resort is not set

     10.0.0.0/24 is subnetted, 6 subnets
I       10.1.3.0 [100/8539] via 10.1.6.253, 00:00:28, Serial1
I       10.1.2.0 [100/8539] via 10.1.4.252, 00:00:18, Serial0
C       10.1.1.0 is directly connected, Ethernet0
C       10.1.6.0 is directly connected, Serial1
I       10.1.5.0 [100/10476] via 10.1.4.252, 00:00:18, Serial0
                 [100/10476] via 10.1.6.253, 00:00:29, Serial1
C       10.1.4.0 is directly connected, Serial0
Albuquerque#debug ip igrp transaction
IGRP protocol debugging is on
Albuquerque#
07:43:40: IGRP: sending update to 255.255.255.255 via Serial0 (10.1.4.251)
07:43:40:        subnet 10.1.3.0, metric=8539
07:43:40:        subnet 10.1.1.0, metric=688
07:43:40:        subnet 10.1.6.0, metric=8476
07:43:40: IGRP: sending update to 255.255.255.255 via Serial1 (10.1.6.251)
07:43:40:        subnet 10.1.2.0, metric=8539
07:43:40:        subnet 10.1.1.0, metric=688
07:43:40:        subnet 10.1.4.0, metric=8476
07:43:40: IGRP: sending update to 255.255.255.255 via Ethernet0 (10.1.1.251)
07:43:40:        subnet 10.1.3.0, metric=8539
07:43:40:        subnet 10.1.2.0, metric=8539
07:43:40:        subnet 10.1.6.0, metric=8476
07:43:40:        subnet 10.1.5.0, metric=10476
07:43:40:        subnet 10.1.4.0, metric=8476
07:43:59: IGRP: received update from 10.1.6.253 on Serial1
07:43:59:        subnet 10.1.3.0, metric 8539 (neighbor 688)
07:43:59:        subnet 10.1.5.0, metric 10476 (neighbor 8476)
07:44:18: IGRP: received update from 10.1.4.252 on Serial0
07:44:18:        subnet 10.1.2.0, metric 8539 (neighbor 688)
07:44:18:        subnet 10.1.5.0, metric 10476 (neighbor 8476)
Albuquerque#no debug all
All possible debugging has been turned off
Albuquerque#
Albuquerque#debug ip igrp event
IGRP event debugging is on
Albuquerque#
07:45:00: IGRP: sending update to 255.255.255.255 via Serial0 (10.1.4.251)
07:45:00: IGRP: Update contains 3 interior, 0 system, and 0 exterior routes.
07:45:00: IGRP: Total routes in update: 3
07:45:00: IGRP: sending update to 255.255.255.255 via Serial1 (10.1.6.251)
07:45:00: IGRP: Update contains 3 interior, 0 system, and 0 exterior routes.
07:45:00: IGRP: Total routes in update: 3
07:45:00: IGRP: sending update to 255.255.255.255 via Ethernet0 (10.1.1.251)
07:45:01: IGRP: Update contains 5 interior, 0 system, and 0 exterior routes.
07:45:01: IGRP: Total routes in update: 5
07:45:21: IGRP: received update from 10.1.6.253 on Serial1
07:45:21: IGRP: Update contains 2 interior, 0 system, and 0 exterior routes.
07:45:21: IGRP: Total routes in update: 2
07:45:35: IGRP: received update from 10.1.4.252 on Serial0
```

continues

Example 6-5 *Migration to IGRP with Sample **show** and **debug** Commands (Continued)*

```
07:45:35: IGRP: Update contains 2 interior, 0 system, and 0 exterior routes.
07:45:35: IGRP: Total routes in update: 2
Albuquerque#no debug all
All possible debugging has been turned off
Albuquerque#show ip protocol
Routing Protocol is "igrp 5"
  Sending updates every 90 seconds, next due in 34 seconds
  Invalid after 270 seconds, hold down 280, flushed after 630
  Outgoing update filter list for all interfaces is
  Incoming update filter list for all interfaces is
  Default networks flagged in outgoing updates
  Default networks accepted from incoming updates
  IGRP metric weight K1=1, K2=0, K3=1, K4=0, K5=0
  IGRP maximum hopcount 100
  IGRP maximum metric variance 1
  Redistributing: igrp 5
  Routing for Networks:
    10.0.0.0
  Routing Information Sources:
    Gateway          Distance      Last Update
    10.1.6.253           100       00:00:23
    10.1.4.252           100       00:00:08
  Distance: (default is 100)
```

The configuration at the beginning of Example 6-5 is used to migrate from RIP to IGRP. As highlighted in Example 6-5, the **no router rip** command removes all RIP configuration on the router. The three routers each must use the same IGRP process-id (5, in this case), and because all interfaces on each of the routers are in network 10.0.0.0, only a single **network** subcommand is needed.

The output of the **show ip route** command lists six subnets, just as was the case when RIP was used. The metrics, the second number inside the brackets, are different. In fact, notice the two routes to 10.1.5.0/24—one through Yosemite and one through Seville. Both routes are included because the default setting for **ip maximum-paths** is 4 and because the routes have an equal metric. Looking further into the output of the **debug ip igrp transaction** command, you can see the equal cost routes being advertised. One route is seen in the update received on serial 1; the other route in the update is received on serial 0.

The output of the **debug ip igrp transaction** shows the details of the routing updates, whereas the **debug ip igrp event** command simply mentions that routing updates have been received.

Finally, the **show ip protocol** command lists several important details about the routing protocol. The time remaining until the next routing update is to be sent is mentioned in one of the first messages. Also, the time since an update was received from each neighboring router is listed at the end of the output. Each of the neighbors from which routing information has been received is listed as well. If you are in doubt as to whether updates have been received during the recent past and from what routers, the **show ip protocol** command is the place to find out.

RIP-1 and IGRP—No Subnet Masks

RIP-1 and IGRP do not transmit the subnet mask in the routing updates, as seen in the **debug** output examples in this section. As a CCNA, Cisco expects you to be able to articulate the implications of the missing mask to the function of the routing protocol. Several subtle actions are taken in light of the lack of mask information in the update:

- Updates sent out an interface in network X, when containing routes about subnets of network X, contain the subnet numbers of the subnets of network X but not the corresponding masks.

- Updates sent out an interface in network X, when containing routes about subnets of network Y, are summarized into one route about the entire network Y.

- When receiving a routing update containing routes referencing subnets of network X, the receiving router assumes that the mask in use is the same mask it uses on an interface with an address in network X.

- When receiving an update about network X, if the receiving router has no interfaces in network X, it treats the route as a route to the entire Class A, B, or C network X.

Example 6-6, Example 6-7, and Example 6-8 contain **show** and **debug** command output on Albuquerque, Yosemite, and Seville with the effects described in the preceding list. The network of Figure 6-10 is still in use, but the subnet on Seville's Ethernet has been changed from 10.1.3.0/24 to 10.1.3.192/26. Because RIP-1 does not send the mask in the update, Seville chooses *not* to address 10.1.3.192/26 onto its serial links (which use mask 255.255.255.0), because the update would be ambiguous.

Example 6-6 *Configuration and Debug IP RIP on Albuquerque*

```
interface ethernet 0
ip addr 10.1.1.251 255.255.255.0
interface serial 0
ip addr 10.1.4.251 255.255.255.0
interface serial 1
ip addr 10.1.6.251 255.255.255.0
!
router rip
network 10.0.0.0
```
```
Albuquerque#debug ip rip
RIP protocol debugging is on
Albuquerque#
00:38:23: RIP: received v1 update from 10.1.4.252 on Serial0
00:38:23:       10.1.2.0 in 1 hops
00:38:23:       10.1.5.0 in 1 hops
00:38:33: RIP: sending v1 update to 255.255.255.255 via Serial0 (10.1.4.251)
00:38:33:       subnet  10.1.1.0, metric 1
00:38:33:       subnet  10.1.6.0, metric 1
00:38:33: RIP: sending v1 update to 255.255.255.255 via Serial1 (10.1.6.251)
00:38:33:       subnet  10.1.2.0, metric 2
```

continues

Example 6-6   *Configuration and Debug IP RIP on Albuquerque (Continued)*

```
00:38:33:        subnet  10.1.1.0, metric 1
00:38:33:        subnet  10.1.4.0, metric 1
00:38:33: RIP: sending v1 update to 255.255.255.255 via Ethernet0 (10.1.1.251)
00:38:33:        subnet  10.1.2.0, metric 2
00:38:33:        subnet  10.1.6.0, metric 1
00:38:33:        subnet  10.1.5.0, metric 2
00:38:33:        subnet  10.1.4.0, metric 1
00:38:40: RIP: received v1 update from 10.1.6.253 on Serial1
00:38:40:        10.1.2.0 in 2 hops
00:38:40:        10.1.5.0 in 1 hops
undebug all
All possible debugging has been turned off
Albuquerque#show ip route
Codes: C - connected, S - static, I - IGRP, R - RIP, M - mobile, B - BGP
       D - EIGRP, EX - EIGRP external, O - OSPF, IA - OSPF inter area
       N1 - OSPF NSSA external type 1, N2 - OSPF NSSA external type 2
       E1 - OSPF external type 1, E2 - OSPF external type 2, E - EGP
       i - IS-IS, L1 - IS-IS level-1, L2 - IS-IS level-2, * - candidate default
       U - per-user static route, o - ODR

Gateway of last resort is not set

     10.0.0.0/24 is subnetted, 5 subnets
R        10.1.2.0 [120/1] via 10.1.4.252, 00:00:26, Serial0
C        10.1.1.0 is directly connected, Ethernet0
C        10.1.6.0 is directly connected, Serial1
R        10.1.5.0 [120/1] via 10.1.4.252, 00:00:27, Serial0
                  [120/1] via 10.1.6.253, 00:00:10, Serial1
C        10.1.4.0 is directly connected, Serial0
Albuquerque#
(Suspended telnet resumed to Seville....)

Seville#show ip route
Codes: C - connected, S - static, I - IGRP, R - RIP, M - mobile, B - BGP
       D - EIGRP, EX - EIGRP external, O - OSPF, IA - OSPF inter area
       N1 - OSPF NSSA external type 1, N2 - OSPF NSSA external type 2
       E1 - OSPF external type 1, E2 - OSPF external type 2, E - EGP
       i - IS-IS, L1 - IS-IS level-1, L2 - IS-IS level-2, * - candidate default
       U - per-user static route, o - ODR

Gateway of last resort is not set

     10.0.0.0/8 is variably subnetted, 6 subnets, 2 masks
R        10.1.2.0/24 [120/1] via 10.1.5.252, 00:00:19, Serial1
R        10.1.1.0/24 [120/1] via 10.1.6.251, 00:00:22, Serial0
C        10.1.6.0/24 is directly connected, Serial0
C        10.1.5.0/24 is directly connected, Serial1
R        10.1.4.0/24 [120/1] via 10.1.6.251, 00:00:22, Serial0
                     [120/1] via 10.1.5.252, 00:00:19, Serial1
C        10.1.3.192/26 is directly connected, Ethernet0
Seville#
```

Example 6-7 *Configuration on Yosemite*

```
interface ethernet 0
ip addr 10.1.2.252 255.255.255.0
interface serial 0
ip addr 10.1.4.252 255.255.255.0
interface serial 1
ip address 10.1.2.252 255.255.255.0

router rip
network 10.0.0.0
```

Example 6-8 *Configuration on Seville*

```
interface ethernet 0
ip addr 10.1.3.253   255.255.255.192
interface serial 0
ip addr 10.1.6.253   255.255.255.0
interface serial 1
ip address 10.1.5.253   255.255.255.0
!
router rip
network 10.0.0.0
```

As seen in the highlighted portions of Example 6-6, subnet 10.1.3.192/26 is not advertised by Seville, as seen in its update received into Albuquerque's serial 1 interface. In fact, the **debug** output looks exactly like it would have earlier, when subnet 10.1.3.0/24 was used on Seville's Ethernet, if that Ethernet was down. However, in this case, the Ethernet is up, as shown in the **show ip route** output from Seville at the end of Example 6-6. Essentially, *RIP will not advertise the route with a mask of 255.255.255.192 out an interface that is in the same network but that has a different mask.* If RIP on Seville had advertised the route to 10.1.3.192, Albuquerque and Yosemite would have believed there was a problem because the subnet number is 10.1.3.192, which is not a subnet number with the mask that Albuquerque and Yosemite think is in use (255.255.255.0). So, RIP and IGRP simply do not advertise the route into the same network on an interface that uses a different mask. The use of different masks in parts of the same network is called variable-length subnet masking (VLSM). As seen in this example, VLSM is not supported by RIP (Version 1) or IGRP.

RIP Version 2

RIP Version 2, defined by RFC 1723, is simply an improved version of RIP Version 1. Many features are the same: Hop count is still used for the metric, it is still a distance vector protocol, and it still uses holddown timers and route poisoning. Several features have been added, as listed in Table 6-14.

Table 6-14   *RIP Version 2 Features*

Feature	Description
Transmits subnet mask with route	This feature allows VLSM by passing the mask along with each route so that the subnet is exactly defined.
Provides authentication	Both clear text (RFC-defined) and MD5 encryption (Cisco-added feature) can be used to authenticate the source of a routing update.
Includes a next-hop router IP address in its routing update	A router can advertise a route but direct any listeners to a different router on that same subnet. This is done only when the other router has a better route.
Uses external route tags	RIP can pass information about routes learned from an external source and redistributed into RIP.
Provides multicast routing updates	Instead of sending updates to 255.255.255.255, the destination IP address is 224.0.0.9, an IP multicast address. This reduces the amount of processing required on non-RIP-speaking hosts on a common subnet.

Although all features of RIP-2 are important, certainly the one that allows RIP to continue to be a valid option in modern networks is the support of VLSM by including the subnet mask. For instance, the problem with RIP-1 and IGRP shown in Examples 6-6, 6-7, and 6-8 was caused by the lack of this feature. With RIP-2, the problem is removed. The same network diagram (Figure 6-10) is used in this case. Example 6-9 shows the RIP-2 configuration on each of the three routers, and Example 6-10 shows a sample RIP **debug** on Albuquerque.

Example 6-9   *RIP-2 Sample Configuration for Routers in Figure 6-10*

```
router rip
network 10.0.0.0
version 2
```

Example 6-10 *RIP-2 Routing Updates, No Auto Summary, on Albuquerque*

```
Albuquerque#
debug ip rip
RIP protocol debugging is on
Albuquerque#
00:36:04: RIP: received v2 update from 10.1.4.252 on Serial0
00:36:04:      10.1.2.0/24 -> 0.0.0.0 in 1 hops
00:36:04:      10.1.5.0/24 -> 0.0.0.0 in 1 hops
```

Example 6-10 *RIP-2 Routing Updates, No Auto Summary, on Albuquerque (Continued)*

```
00:36:04:        10.1.3.192/26 -> 0.0.0.0 in 2 hops
00:36:08: RIP: sending v2 update to 224.0.0.9 via Serial0 (10.1.4.251)
00:36:08:        10.1.1.0/24 -> 0.0.0.0, metric 1, tag 0
00:36:08:        10.1.6.0/24 -> 0.0.0.0, metric 1, tag 0
00:36:08:        10.1.3.192/26 -> 0.0.0.0, metric 2, tag 0
00:36:08: RIP: sending v2 update to 224.0.0.9 via Serial1 (10.1.6.251)
00:36:08:        10.1.2.0/24 -> 0.0.0.0, metric 2, tag 0
00:36:08:        10.1.1.0/24 -> 0.0.0.0, metric 1, tag 0
00:36:08:        10.1.4.0/24 -> 0.0.0.0, metric 1, tag 0
00:36:08: RIP: sending v2 update to 224.0.0.9 via Ethernet0 (10.1.1.251)
00:36:08:        10.1.2.0/24 -> 0.0.0.0, metric 2, tag 0
00:36:08:        10.1.6.0/24 -> 0.0.0.0, metric 1, tag 0
00:36:08:        10.1.5.0/24 -> 0.0.0.0, metric 2, tag 0
00:36:08:        10.1.4.0/24 -> 0.0.0.0, metric 1, tag 0
00:36:08:        10.1.3.192/26 -> 0.0.0.0, metric 2, tag 0
00:36:20: RIP: received v2 update from 10.1.6.253 on Serial1
00:36:20:        10.1.2.0/24 -> 0.0.0.0 in 2 hops
00:36:20:        10.1.5.0/24 -> 0.0.0.0 in 1 hops
00:36:20:        10.1.3.192/26 -> 0.0.0.0 in 1 hops
00:36:30: RIP: received v2 update from 10.1.4.252 on Serial0
00:36:30:        10.1.2.0/24 -> 0.0.0.0 in 1 hops
00:36:30:        10.1.5.0/24 -> 0.0.0.0 in 1 hops
00:36:30:        10.1.3.192/26 -> 0.0.0.0 in 2 hops

Albuquerque#no debug all
All possible debugging has been turned off

Albuquerque#show ip route
Codes: C - connected, S - static, I - IGRP, R - RIP, M - mobile, B - BGP
       D - EIGRP, EX - EIGRP external, O - OSPF, IA - OSPF inter area
       N1 - OSPF NSSA external type 1, N2 - OSPF NSSA external type 2
       E1 - OSPF external type 1, E2 - OSPF external type 2, E - EGP
       i - IS-IS, L1 - IS-IS level-1, L2 - IS-IS level-2, * - candidate default
       U - per-user static route, o - ODR

Gateway of last resort is not set

     10.0.0.0/8 is variably subnetted, 6 subnets, 2 masks
R       10.1.2.0/24 [120/1] via 10.1.4.252, 00:00:09, Serial0
C       10.1.1.0/24 is directly connected, Ethernet0
C       10.1.6.0/24 is directly connected, Serial1
R       10.1.5.0/24 [120/1] via 10.1.4.252, 00:00:09, Serial0
                    [120/1] via 10.1.6.253, 00:00:19, Serial1
C       10.1.4.0/24 is directly connected, Serial0
R       10.1.3.192/26 [120/1] via 10.1.6.253, 00:00:19, Serial1
Albuquerque#
```

A couple of important items should be noted in the **debug** output of Example 6-10. (As always, the specific portions of the examples referred to in the text after the example are highlighted.) The updates sent by Albuquerque are sent to multicast IP address 224.0.0.9, as opposed to a broadcast address; this allows the devices that are not using RIP-2 to ignore the updates and not waste processing cycles. The **show ip route** output on Albuquerque lists the previously missing subnet, 10.1.3.192/26; this is expected as highlighted in the **debug ip rip** messages received by Albuquerque from Seville (10.1.6.253). The subnet masks are shown in the prefix style, with /26 representing mask 255.255.255.192. Also, note the **debug** output designating **tag 0**—this means that all the external route tags have value 0, which is the default.

Migration from RIP-1 to RIP-2 requires some planning. RIP-1 sends updates to the broadcast address, whereas RIP-2 uses a multicast. A RIP-1 only router and a RIP-2 only router will not succeed in exchanging routing information. To migrate to RIP-2, one option is to migrate all routers at the same time. This might not be a reasonable political or administrative option, however. If not, then some coexistence between RIP-1 and RIP-2 is required.

The **ip rip send version** command can be used to overcome the problem. Essentially, the configuration tells the router whether to send RIP-1 style updates, RIP-2 style updates, or both for each interface. Consider the familiar Figure 6-10 network, with RIP-1 still configured on all three routers. If two of the routers are migrated—for instance, Albuquerque and Seville—then they can communicate with RIP-2 easily. However, by default these two routers will now send only RIP-2 updates, which Yosemite cannot understand because it is still running RIP-1. The configurations in Examples 6-11, 6-12, and 6-13 overcome the problem by having Albuquerque and Seville send only RIP-1 updates to Yosemite.

Example 6-11 *Configuration on Albuquerque*

```
interface ethernet 0
ip addr 10.1.1.251 255.255.255.0
interface serial 0
ip addr 10.1.4.251 255.255.255.0
ip rip send version 1
ip rip receive version 1
interface serial 1
ip address 10.1.6.251 255.255.255.0
!
router rip
network 10.0.0.0
version 2
```

Example 6-12 *Configuration on Yosemite*

```
interface ethernet 0
ip addr 10.1.2.252 255.255.255.0
interface serial 0
ip addr 10.1.4.252 255.255.255.0
interface serial 1
ip address 10.1.5.252 255.255.255.0
!
router rip
network 10.0.0.0
```

Example 6-13 *Configuration on Seville*

```
interface ethernet 0
ip addr 10.1.2.252 255.255.255.0
interface serial 0
ip addr 10.1.4.252 255.255.255.0
interface serial 1
ip address 10.1.5.252 255.255.255.0
ip rip send version 1
ip rip receive version 1
!
router rip
network 10.0.0.0
version 2
```

As seen in the highlighted lines of the example, with RIP-2 configured, RIP-2 updates are sent and received on each interface that is matched by a **network** command. Because Yosemite will send and receive only RIP-1 updates, the other two routers need the appropriate interface subcommands to tell the router to send and receive RIP-1 updates to and from Yosemite. Both Albuquerque and Seville will continue to send and (hope to) receive RIP-2 updates on all interfaces.

Auto Summary and Route Aggregation

The IOS is optimized to perform routing as fast as possible. Most of the Layer 3 routing performance improvement in the brief history of routers has been through improved algorithms; many times those improved algorithms later have been implemented in hardware to provide additional latency improvements. Although these improvements have been a great benefit, it is typically true that any algorithm that searches a list will run more quickly if the list is short, compared to searching a similar list that is long. Auto summary and route aggregation (also known as route summarization) are two IOS features that reduce the size of the IP routing table.

Auto summarization is a routing protocol feature that operates by this rule:

When advertised on an interface whose IP address is not in network X, routes about subnets in network X will be summarized and advertised as one route. That route will be for the entire Class A, B, or C network X.

Auto summary is a feature of RIP-1 and IGRP that cannot be disabled. For RIP-2 and EIGRP, auto summary can be enabled or disabled. As usual, an example makes the concept much clearer. Consider Figure 6-11, which shows two networks in use: 10.0.0.0 and 172.16.0.0. Seville has four (connected) routes to subnets of network 10.0.0.0. Example 6-14 lists the output of a **show ip route** command on Albuquerque, as well as RIP-2 **debug ip rip** output.

Figure 6-11 *Auto Summarization*

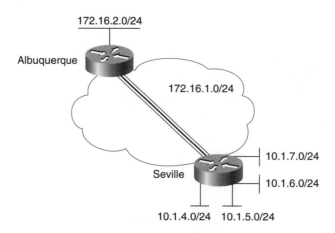

Example 6-14 *Albuquerque's Routing Table When Seville Is Summarizing*

```
Albuquerque#debug ip rip
02:20:42: RIP: sending v2 update to 224.0.0.9 via Serial0.2 (172.16.1.251)
02:20:42:      172.16.2.0/24 -> 0.0.0.0, metric 1, tag 0
02:20:42: RIP: sending v2 update to 224.0.0.9 via Ethernet0 (172.16.2.251)
02:20:42:      172.16.1.0/24 -> 0.0.0.0, metric 1, tag 0
02:20:42:      10.0.0.0/8 -> 0.0.0.0, metric 2, tag 0
02:20:46: RIP: received v2 update from 172.16.1.253 on Serial0.2
02:20:46:      10.0.0.0/8 -> 0.0.0.0 in 1 hops
Albuquerque#
Albuquerque#undebug all
All possible debugging has been turned off
Albuquerque#show ip route
Codes: C - connected, S - static, I - IGRP, R - RIP, M - mobile, B - BGP
       D - EIGRP, EX - EIGRP external, O - OSPF, IA - OSPF inter area
       N1 - OSPF NSSA external type 1, N2 - OSPF NSSA external type 2
       E1 - OSPF external type 1, E2 - OSPF external type 2, E - EGP
       i - IS-IS, L1 - IS-IS level-1, L2 - IS-IS level-2, * - candidate default
       U - per-user static route, o - ODR

Gateway of last resort is not set

     172.16.0.0/24 is subnetted, 2 subnets
C       172.16.1.0 is directly connected, Serial0.2
C       172.16.2.0 is directly connected, Ethernet0
R    10.0.0.0/8 [120/1] via 172.16.1.253, 00:00:09, Serial0.2
```

Notice as highlighted in Example 6-14 that Albuquerque's received update on Serial0.2 from Seville advertises only about the entire Class A network 10.0.0.0/8 because auto summary is enabled on Seville (by default). The IP routing table lists just one route to network 10.0.0.0. This works fine, as long as network 10.0.0.0 is contiguous. Consider Figure 6-12, where

Yosemite also has subnets of network 10.0.0.0 but has no connectivity to Seville other than through Albuquerque.

Figure 6-12   *Auto Summarization Pitfalls*

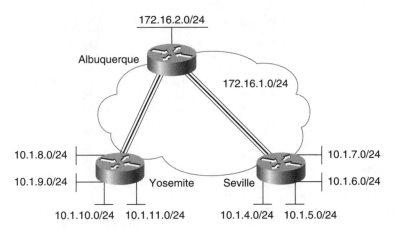

IP subnet design traditionally has not allowed *discontiguous networks*. A *contiguous* network is a single Class A, B, or C network for which all routes to subnets of that network pass through only other subnets of that same single network. *Discontiguous networks* refer to the concept that, in a single Class A, B, or C network, there is at least one case in which the only routes to one subnet pass through subnets of a different network. An easy analogy for residents in the United States is the familiar term *contiguous 48*, referring to the 48 states besides Alaska and Hawaii. To drive to Alaska from the contiguous 48, for example, you must drive through another country (Canada, for the geographically impaired!), so Alaska is not contiguous with the 48 states—in other words, it is discontiguous.

Figure 6-12 breaks that rule. In this figure, there could be a PVC between Yosemite and Seville that uses a subnet of network 10.0.0.0, but that PVC may be down, causing the discontiguous network. The temporarily discontiguous network can be overcome with the use of a routing protocol that transmits masks because the rule of discontiguous subnets can be ignored when using a routing protocol that transmits masks. Consider the routing updates and routing table on Albuquerque in Example 6-15, where auto summarization is disabled on all routers.

Example 6-15 *Albuquerque's Routing Table When Seville is Not Summarizing*

```
debug ip rip
RIP protocol debugging is on
Albuquerque#
02:48:58: RIP: received v2 update from 172.16.1.253 on Serial0.2
02:48:58:        10.1.7.0/24 -> 0.0.0.0 in 1 hops
02:48:58:        10.1.6.0/24 -> 0.0.0.0 in 1 hops
02:48:58:        10.1.5.0/24 -> 0.0.0.0 in 1 hops
02:48:58:        10.1.4.0/24 -> 0.0.0.0 in 1 hops
```

continues

Example 6-15 *Albuquerque's Routing Table When Seville is Not Summarizing (Continued)*

```
02:49:14: RIP: received v2 update from 172.16.3.252 on Serial0.1
02:49:14:      10.1.11.0/24 -> 0.0.0.0 in 1 hops
02:49:14:      10.1.10.0/24 -> 0.0.0.0 in 1 hops
02:49:14:      10.1.9.0/24 -> 0.0.0.0 in 1 hops
02:49:14:      10.1.8.0/24 -> 0.0.0.0 in 1 hops
02:49:16: RIP: sending v2 update to 224.0.0.9 via Serial0.1 (172.16.3.251)
02:49:16:      172.16.1.0/24 -> 0.0.0.0, metric 1, tag 0
02:49:16:      172.16.2.0/24 -> 0.0.0.0, metric 1, tag 0
02:49:16:      10.0.0.0/8 -> 0.0.0.0, metric 2, tag 0
02:49:16: RIP: sending v2 update to 224.0.0.9 via Serial0.2 (172.16.1.251)
02:49:16:      172.16.2.0/24 -> 0.0.0.0, metric 1, tag 0
02:49:16:      172.16.3.0/24 -> 0.0.0.0, metric 1, tag 0
02:49:16:      10.0.0.0/8 -> 0.0.0.0, metric 2, tag 0
02:49:16: RIP: sending v2 update to 224.0.0.9 via Ethernet 0 (172.16.2.251)
02:49:16:      172.16.1.0/24 -> 0.0.0.0, metric 1, tag 0
02:49:16:      172.16.3.0/24 -> 0.0.0.0, metric 1, tag 0
02:49:16:      10.0.0.0/8 -> 0.0.0.0, metric 2, tag 0
Albuquerque#no debug all
All possible debugging has been turned off
Albuquerque#show ip route
Codes: C - connected, S - static, I - IGRP, R - RIP, M - mobile, B - BGP
       D - EIGRP, EX - EIGRP external, O - OSPF, IA - OSPF inter area
       N1 - OSPF NSSA external type 1, N2 - OSPF NSSA external type 2
       E1 - OSPF external type 1, E2 - OSPF external type 2, E - EGP
       i - IS-IS, L1 - IS-IS level-1, L2 - IS-IS level-2, * - candidate default
       U - per-user static route, o - ODR

Gateway of last resort is not set

     172.16.0.0/24 is subnetted, 3 subnets
C       172.16.1.0 is directly connected, Serial0.2
C       172.16.2.0 is directly connected, Ethernet0
C       172.16.3.0 is directly connected, Serial0.1
     10.0.0.0/24 is subnetted, 8 subnets
R       10.1.11.0 [120/1] via 172.16.3.252, 00:00:15, Serial0.1
R       10.1.10.0 [120/1] via 172.16.3.252, 00:00:15, Serial0.1
R       10.1.9.0 [120/1] via 172.16.3.252, 00:00:15, Serial0.1
R       10.1.8.0 [120/1] via 172.16.3.252, 00:00:15, Serial0.1
R       10.1.7.0 [120/1] via 172.16.1.253, 00:00:03, Serial0.2
R       10.1.6.0 [120/1] via 172.16.1.253, 00:00:03, Serial0.2
R       10.1.5.0 [120/1] via 172.16.1.253, 00:00:03, Serial0.2
R       10.1.4.0 [120/1] via 172.16.1.253, 00:00:03, Serial0.2
Albuquerque#
```

Notice as highlighted in Example 6-15 that the routing updates include the individual subnets. Therefore, Albuquerque can see routes to all subnets of network 10 and can route packets to the correct destinations in Seville and Yosemite. With auto summary enabled, Albuquerque would think that both Seville and Yosemite had an equal-metric route to network 10.0.0.0; some packets would be routed incorrectly.

Route summarization (also called route aggregation) works like auto summarization, except that there is no requirement to summarize into a Class A, B, or C network. Consider the same network in Figure 6-12. Albuquerque has eight routes to subnets of network 10.0.0.0; four of those routes are learned from Seville. Consider the subnet, broadcast, and assignable addresses in each of the subnets, as shown in Table 6-15.

Table 6-15   *Route Aggregation Comparison of Subnet Numbers*

Subnet	Mask	Broadcast	Assignable Addresses
10.1.4.0	255.255.255.0	10.1.4.255	10.1.4.1 to 10.1.4.254
10.1.5.0	255.255.255.0	10.1.5.255	10.1.5.1 to 10.1.5.254
10.1.6.0	255.255.255.0	10.1.6.255	10.1.6.1 to 10.1.6.254
10.1.7.0	255.255.255.0	10.1.7.255	10.1.7.1 to 10.1.7.254

Now consider the concept of a subnet 10.1.4.0, with mask 255.255.252.0. In this case, 10.1.4.0/22 (same subnet, written differently) would have a subnet broadcast address of 10.1.7.255 and assignable addresses of 10.1.4.1 to 10.1.7.254. Because 10.1.4.0/22 happens to include all the assignable addresses of the original four subnets, a single route to 10.1.4.0/22 would be just as good as the four separate routes, assuming that the next-hop information would be the same for each of the original four routes.

Route aggregation is simply a tool used to tell a routing protocol to advertise a single, larger subnet rather than the individual smaller subnets. In this case, the routing protocol would advertise 10.1.4.0/22 rather than the four individual subnets. Albuquerque's routing table will then be smaller. EIGRP and OSPF are the only interior IP routing protocols to support route aggregation.

Route summarization of the subnets off Seville is shown in Example 6-16. Still using the network of Figure 6-12, the routers are all migrated to EIGRP. Example 6-16 shows the EIGRP configuration on Albuquerque, EIGRP configuration on Seville, and the resulting IP routing table on Albuquerque. (Yosemite is migrated to EIGRP as well; the configuration is not shown because the example shows only aggregation by Seville.)

Example 6-16 *Route Aggregation Example Using EIGRP*

```
On Seville:

Router eigrp 9
 Network 10.0.0.0
 Network 172.16.0.0
 No auto-summary
!
interface serial 0.1 point-to-point
 ip address 172.16.1.253 255.255.255.0
 frame-relay interface-dlci 901
```

continues

Example 6-16 *Route Aggregation Example Using EIGRP (Continued)*

```
   ip summary-address eigrp 9 10.1.4.0 255.255.252.0
On Albuquerque:
Router eigrp 9
  Network 172.16.0.0
  No auto-summary
Albuquerque#show ip route
Codes: C - connected, S - static, I - IGRP, R - RIP, M - mobile, B - BGP
       D - EIGRP, EX - EIGRP external, O - OSPF, IA - OSPF inter area
       N1 - OSPF NSSA external type 1, N2 - OSPF NSSA external type 2
       E1 - OSPF external type 1, E2 - OSPF external type 2, E - EGP
       i - IS-IS, L1 - IS-IS level-1, L2 - IS-IS level-2, * - candidate default
       U - per-user static route, o - ODR

Gateway of last resort is not set

     172.16.0.0/24 is subnetted, 3 subnets
C       172.16.1.0 is directly connected, Serial0.2
C       172.16.2.0 is directly connected, Ethenet0
C       172.16.3.0 is directly connected, Serial0.1
     10.0.0.0/8 is variably subnetted, 5 subnets, 2 masks
D       10.1.11.0/24 [120/1] via 172.16.3.252, 00:00:15, Serial0.1
D       10.1.10.0/24 [120/1] via 172.16.3.252, 00:00:15, Serial0.1
D       10.1.9.0/24 [120/1] via 172.16.3.252, 00:00:15, Serial0.1
D       10.1.8.0/24 [120/1] via 172.16.3.252, 00:00:15, Serial0.1
D       10.1.4.0/22 [90/2185984] via 172.16.1.253, 00:00:58, Serial0.2
```

The **ip summary-address** interface subcommand on Seville's serial 0.1 interface is used to define the superset of the subnets that should be advertised. Notice the route in Albuquerque's routing table, which indeed shows 10.1.4.0/22, rather than the four individual subnets.

When summarizing, the superset of the original subnets could actually be smaller than the Class A, B, or C network; larger than the network; or exactly matched to a network. For instance, 192.168.4.0, 192.168.5.0, 192.168.6.0, and 192.168.7.0 could be summarized into 192.168.4.0/22, which represents four consecutive Class C networks. Summarization when the summarized group is a set of networks is sometimes called *supernetting*.

Table 6-16 lists the features for summarization of the interior IP routing protocols.

Table 6-16   *Route Aggregation Comparison of Subnet Numbers*

Routing Protocol	Auto Summary Enabled?	Auto Summary Disabled?	Route Aggregation?
RIP Version 1	Yes, by default	Not allowed	No
IGRP	Yes, by default	Not allowed	No
RIP Version 2	Yes, by default	Allowed via configuration	No

Table 6-16   *Route Aggregation Comparison of Subnet Numbers (Continued)*

Routing Protocol	Auto Summary Enabled?	Auto Summary Disabled?	Route Aggregation?
Enhanced IGRP	Yes, by default	Allowed via configuration	Yes
OSPF	No, but can do equivalent with aggregation	Yes	Yes

Multiple Routes to the Same Subnet

By default, the IOS supports four equal-cost routes to the same IP subnet in the routing table at the same time. This number can be changed to between 1 and 6 using the **ip maximum-paths** *x* router configuration subcommand, where *x* is the maximum number of routes to any subnet. As mentioned earlier, the packets are balanced on a per-destination address basis by default; packets also can be balanced on a packet-by-packet basis, but at a performance penalty.

The metric formula used for IGRP (and EIGRP) poses an interesting problem when considering equal-metric routes. IGRP can learn more than one route to the same subnet, with different metrics; however, the metrics are very likely to never be exactly equal. The **variance** router subcommand is used to define how variable the metrics can be for routes to be considered to have equal metrics. The parameter to the command (the multiplier) is multiplied by the lowest of the received metrics for a particular subnet. Any routes with a metric less than the product of "best metric" times the multiplier are considered to be equal.

Some rather interesting twists in logic must be considered when deciding whether to use one or multiple equal-cost routes with IGRP. If **maximum-paths** is set to 1, then the first of these equal-cost routes learned to each subnet is placed into the routing table. However, these could be the routes with the largest metric. To avoid that, **maximum-paths** could be defaulted to 4 or could be coded as some other number; in addition, the **variance** command can be used to define how close the metrics must be in value to be considered equal. However, in that case, some of the traffic will flow over the routes with the best metric, and some will flow over the route with the worst metric. Neither situation seems to be optimal.

A different—and possibly better—alternative is to use the **traffic-share min** router IGRP subcommand in conjunction with **maximum-paths** and **variance**. This command tells the router to add the multiple routes to the routing table, but to send only traffic using the route with the smallest metric. This allows all routes to each subnet to be in the routing table, which is an advantage for faster convergence. However, all traffic goes across the lowest-metric route that is currently in the routing table. The **traffic-share balanced** command, which is the default, tells the router to use all the routes proportionally based on the metrics for each route.

Troubleshooting Routing and Routing Protocols

It is no secret that Cisco would very much like all its certification exams—CCNA included—to be exams that prove that the test taker can build and troubleshoot live networks. Some people work with Cisco routers daily. Others' current job function does not allow frequent access to routers—if this applies to you, you likely are trying to pass this certification so that you can move into jobs that involve routers and switches.

The **show ip route** command has a myriad of options that will be helpful when troubleshooting a large network. The **show ip protocol** command also can provide some very useful information when troubleshooting a routing problem. With a small network, most of the options on the **show ip route** command are unnecessary. However, knowing the options and what each can do will be very useful for your work with larger networks.

Example 6-20 lists the options of the **show ip route** command and gives examples of several of the options. The network is shown in Figure 6-13 and should look familiar from previous examples. In this case, Enhanced IGRP is used between Albuquerque and Seville, and RIP-2 is used between Albuquerque and Yosemite. There is no PVC between Yosemite and Seville. The configurations of the three routers are listed in Examples 6-17, 6-18, and 6-19 first, followed by the example with the **show ip route** options.

Figure 6-13   *Network Environment for Use with show ip route Options*

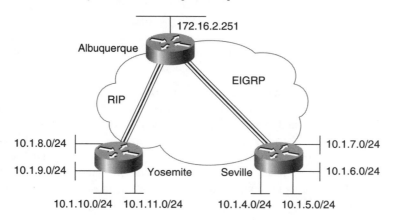

Example 6-17 *Albuquerque Configuration for **show ip route** Example 6-20*

```
Albuquerque#show run
Building configuration...

Current configuration:
!
version 12.0
```

Example 6-17 *Albuquerque Configuration for* **show ip route** *Example 6-20 (Continued)*

```
!
hostname Albuquerque
!
no ip domain-lookup
!
interface Serial0
 no ip address
 no ip directed-broadcast
 encapsulation frame-relay IETF
 clockrate 56000
 frame-relay lmi-type cisco
!
interface Serial0.1 point-to-point
 ip address 172.16.3.251 255.255.255.0
 no ip directed-broadcast
 frame-relay interface-dlci 902
!
interface Serial0.2 point-to-point
 ip address 172.16.1.251 255.255.255.0
 no ip directed-broadcast
 frame-relay interface-dlci 903
!
interface Serial1
 no ip address
 no ip directed-broadcast
 shutdown
!
interface Ethernet0
 ip address 172.16.2.251 255.255.255.0
 no ip directed-broadcast
!
router eigrp 9
 passive-interface Serial0.1
 network 172.16.0.0
 no auto-summary
!
router rip
 version 2
 passive-interface Serial0.2
 network 172.16.0.0
 no auto-summary
!
no ip classless
!
access-list 1 permit 10.0.0.0 0.255.255.255
```

Example 6-18 *Yosemite Configuration for* **show ip route** *Example 6-20*

```
Yosemite#show run
Building configuration...

Current configuration:
!
version 12.0
!
hostname Yosemite
!
no ip domain-lookup
!
interface Serial0
 no ip address
 no ip directed-broadcast
 encapsulation frame-relay IETF
 no fair-queue
 frame-relay lmi-type cisco
!
interface Serial0.1 point-to-point
 ip address 172.16.3.252 255.255.255.0
 no ip directed-broadcast
 frame-relay interface-dlci 901
!
interface Serial1
 no ip address
 no ip directed-broadcast
 shutdown
!
!
interface Ethernet0
 ip address 10.1.8.253 255.255.255.0
!
interface Ethernet1
 ip address 10.1.9.253 255.255.255.0
!
interface Ethernet2
 ip address 10.1.10.253 255.255.255.0
!
interface Ethernet3
 ip address 10.1.11.253 255.255.255.0
!
router rip
 version 2
 network 10.0.0.0
 network 172.16.0.0
 no auto-summary
!
no ip classless
```

Example 6-19 *Seville Configuration for* **show ip route** *Example 6-20*

```
Seville#show run
Building configuration...

Current configuration:
!
version 12.0
!
hostname Seville
!
no ip domain-lookup
!
interface Serial0
 no ip address
 no ip directed-broadcast
 encapsulation frame-relay IETF
 no fair-queue
 frame-relay lmi-type cisco
!
interface Serial0.1 multipoint
 ip address 172.16.1.253 255.255.255.0
 no ip directed-broadcast
 ip summary-address eigrp 9 10.1.4.0 255.255.252.0
 frame-relay interface-dlci 901
!
interface Serial1
 no ip address
 no ip directed-broadcast
 shutdown
!
interface Ethernet0
 ip address 10.1.4.253 255.255.255.0
!
interface Ethernet1
 ip address 10.1.5.253 255.255.255.0
!
interface Ethernet2
 ip address 10.1.6.253 255.255.255.0
!
interface Ethernet3
 ip address 10.1.7.253 255.255.255.0
!
router eigrp 9
 network 10.0.0.0
 network 172.16.0.0
 no auto-summary
!
no ip classless
```

Example 6-20 *show ip route Options—Albuquerque*

```
Albuquerque#show ip route
Codes: C - connected, S - static, I - IGRP, R - RIP, M - mobile, B - BGP
       D - EIGRP, EX - EIGRP external, O - OSPF, IA - OSPF inter area
       N1 - OSPF NSSA external type 1, N2 - OSPF NSSA external type 2
       E1 - OSPF external type 1, E2 - OSPF external type 2, E - EGP
       i - IS-IS, L1 - IS-IS level-1, L2 - IS-IS level-2, * - candidate default
       U - per-user static route, o - ODR

Gateway of last resort is not set

     172.16.0.0/24 is subnetted, 3 subnets
C       172.16.1.0 is directly connected, Serial0.2
C       172.16.2.0 is directly connected, Ethernet0
C       172.16.3.0 is directly connected, Serial0.1
     10.0.0.0/8 is variably subnetted, 5 subnets, 2 masks
R       10.1.11.0/24 [120/1] via 172.16.3.252, 00:00:17, Serial0.1
R       10.1.10.0/24 [120/1] via 172.16.3.252, 00:00:17, Serial0.1
R       10.1.9.0/24 [120/1] via 172.16.3.252, 00:00:17, Serial0.1
R       10.1.8.0/24 [120/1] via 172.16.3.252, 00:00:17, Serial0.1
D       10.1.4.0/22 [90/2185984] via 172.16.1.253, 00:28:01, Serial0.2

Albuquerque#show ip route ?
  Hostname or A.B.C.D  Network to display information about or hostname
  bgp                  Border Gateway Protocol (BGP)
  connected            Connected
  egp                  Exterior Gateway Protocol (EGP)
  eigrp                Enhanced Interior Gateway Routing Protocol (EIGRP)
  igrp                 Interior Gateway Routing Protocol (IGRP)
  isis                 ISO IS-IS
  list                 IP Access list
  odr                  On Demand stub Routes
  ospf                 Open Shortest Path First (OSPF)
  profile              IP routing table profile
  rip                  Routing Information Protocol (RIP)
  static               Static routes
  summary              Summary of all routes
  supernets-only       Show supernet entries only
  traffic-engineering  Traffic engineered routes
  <cr>

Albuquerque#show ip route 10.1.5.8
Routing entry for 10.1.4.0/22
  Known via "eigrp 9", distance 90, metric 2185984, type internal
  Redistributing via eigrp 9
  Last update from 172.16.1.253 on Serial0.2, 00:28:36 ago
  Routing Descriptor Blocks:
  * 172.16.1.253, from 172.16.1.253, 00:28:36 ago, via Serial0.2
      Route metric is 2185984, traffic share count is 1
      Total delay is 20630 microseconds, minimum bandwidth is 1544 Kbit
      Reliability 255/255, minimum MTU 1500 bytes
      Loading 1/255, Hops 1

Albuquerque#show ip route rip
```

Example 6-20 *show ip route* *Options—Albuquerque (Continued)*

```
        10.0.0.0/8 is variably subnetted, 5 subnets, 2 masks
R        10.1.11.0/24 [120/1] via 172.16.3.252, 00:00:22, Serial0.1
R        10.1.10.0/24 [120/1] via 172.16.3.252, 00:00:22, Serial0.1
R        10.1.9.0/24 [120/1] via 172.16.3.252, 00:00:22, Serial0.1
R        10.1.8.0/24 [120/1] via 172.16.3.252, 00:00:22, Serial0.1
Albuquerque#show ip route igrp

Albuquerque#show ip route eigrp
        10.0.0.0/8 is variably subnetted, 5 subnets, 2 masks
D        10.1.4.0/22 [90/2185984] via 172.16.1.253, 00:29:42, Serial0.2

Albuquerque#show ip route connected
        172.16.0.0/24 is subnetted, 3 subnets
C        172.16.1.0 is directly connected, Serial0.2
C        172.16.2.0 is directly connected, Ethernet0
C        172.16.3.0 is directly connected, Serial0.1

Albuquerque#show ip route list 1
        10.0.0.0/8 is variably subnetted, 5 subnets, 2 masks
R        10.1.11.0/24 [120/1] via 172.16.3.252, 00:00:22, Serial0.1
R        10.1.10.0/24 [120/1] via 172.16.3.252, 00:00:22, Serial0.1
R        10.1.9.0/24 [120/1] via 172.16.3.252, 00:00:22, Serial0.1
R        10.1.8.0/24 [120/1] via 172.16.3.252, 00:00:22, Serial0.1
D        10.1.4.0/22 [90/2185984] via 172.16.1.253, 00:29:58, Serial0.2

Albuquerque#show ip route summary
Route Source    Networks    Subnets     Overhead     Memory (bytes)
connected       0           3           156          420
static          0           0           0            0
rip             0           4           208          560
eigrp 9         0           1           52           140
internal        2                                    2320
Total           2           8           416          3440

Albuquerque#show ip route supernet
Codes: C - connected, S - static, I - IGRP, R - RIP, M - mobile, B - BGP
       D - EIGRP, EX - EIGRP external, O - OSPF, IA - OSPF inter area
       N1 - OSPF NSSA external type 1, N2 - OSPF NSSA external type 2
       E1 - OSPF external type 1, E2 - OSPF external type 2, E - EGP
       i - IS-IS, L1 - IS-IS level-1, L2 - IS-IS level-2, * - candidate default
       U - per-user static route, o - ODR

Gateway of last resort is not set
```

The **show ip route** command, with no options, has been seen many times in this book. A review of some of the more important bits of the output is in order; most comments refer to a highlighted portion of an example. First, the legend at the beginning of Example 6-20 defines the letter codes that identify the source of the routing information—for instance, C for connected routes, R for RIP, and I for IGRP. Each of the Class A, B, and C networks is listed, along with each of the subnets of that network. If a static mask is used within that network, then the mask is shown only in the line referring to the network (as is the case in Example 6-20, network 172.16.0.0). If the network uses VLSM, as network 10.0.0.0 appears to do because of the route summarization done by Seville, then the mask information is listed on the lines referring to each of the individual subnets.

Each routing entry lists the subnet number and the outgoing interface. In most cases, the next-hop router's IP address is also listed. The outgoing interface is needed so that the router can choose the type of data link header to use to encapsulate the packet before transmission on that interface. The next-hop router's IP address is needed on interfaces for which the router needs the IP address so that it can find the associated data link address to put in the newly built data link header. For instance, knowing the next-hop IP address of 172.16.3.252, Yosemite's IP address on the Frame Relay VC allows Albuquerque to find the correlated DLCI in the Frame Relay map.

The numbers in brackets in the **show ip route** output for each route are interesting. The second number in brackets represents the metric value for this route. The first number defines the administrative distance.

Administrative distance is important only if multiple IP routing protocols are in use in a single router. When this is true, both routing protocols can learn routes to the same subnets. Because their metric values are different (for example, hop count or a function of bandwidth and delay), there is no way to know which routing protocol's routes are better. So, Cisco supplies a method of defining which routing protocol's routes are better. The IOS implements this concept using something called *administrative distance*.

Administrative distance is an integer value; a value is assigned to each source of routing information. The lower the administrative distance, the better the source of routing information. IGRP's default is 100, OSPF's is 110, RIP's is 120, and Enhanced IGRP's is 90. The value 100 in brackets in the **show ip route** output signifies that the administrative distance used for IGRP routes is 100—in other words, the default value is in use. So, if RIP and IGRP are both used, and if both learn routes to the same subnets, only IGRP's routing information for those subnets will be added to the routing table. If RIP learns about a subnet that IGRP does not know about, that route will be added to the routing table.

Moving down Example 6-20, the **show ip route ?** command lists several options, many of which are shown in the ensuing commands in the example. Limiting the **show ip route** output to the routes learned by a particular routing protocol can be accomplished by referring to that routing protocol. Likewise, the output can be limited to just show connected routes.

One of the more important options for the **show ip route** command is to simply pass an IP address as the last parameter. This tells the router to perform routing table lookup, just as it would for a packet destined to that address. In Example 6-20, the **show ip route 10.1.5.8** returns a set of messages, the first of which identifies the route to 10.1.4.0/22 as the route matched in the routing table. The route that is matched is listed so that you can always know the route that would be used by this router to reach a particular IP address.

Finally, another feature of **show ip route** that is useful in large networks is to filter the output of the command based on an access list. Notice the command **show ip route list 1** in Example 6-20. Access list 1 is configured so that any route about network 10.0.0.0 is matched (permitted by the access list) and all others are denied. By referring to the access list, the **show ip route** output will be filtered, showing only a portion of the routes. This is particularly useful when there are many routes in the routing table.

So, the many options of the **show ip route** command can be particularly useful for troubleshooting in larger networks.

IPX RIP, SAP, and GNS

The CCNA exam requires you not only to know the differences between IPX RIP and IP RIP, but to also know two other NetWare protocols used by the router: Service Advertisement Protocol (SAP) and Get Nearest Server (GNS). Because IPX RIP and IP RIP were originally based on the same protocol (XNS RIP), the two are very similar. SAP and GNS have no equivalent feature in TCP/IP. RIP for IPX works in a similar manner to IP RIP. The most obvious difference is that IPX RIP advertises IPX network numbers, not IP subnet numbers. Table 6-17 lists the similarities and differences.

Table 6-17   *RIP for IPX and IP Compared*

Novell RIP	IP RIP
Uses distance vector	Uses distance vector
Is based on XNS RIP	Is based on XNS RIP
Uses 60-second update timer (default)	Uses 30-second update timer (default)
Uses timer ticks as primary metric, hop count as secondary metric	Uses hop count as only metric

IPX RIP uses two metrics: ticks and hops. Ticks are 1/18 of 1 second; the metric is an integer counter of the number of ticks delay for this route. By default, a Cisco router treats a link as having a certain number of ticks delay. LAN interfaces default to one tick and WAN interfaces default to six ticks. The number of hops is considered only when the number of ticks is a tie. By using ticks as the primary metric, better routes can be chosen instead of just using hop count. For example, a three-hop, three-tick route that uses three Ethernets will be chosen over a two-hop, eight-tick route that uses two Ethernets and a serial link.

Service Advertisement Protocol

Service Advertisement Protocol (SAP) is one of the more important parts of the NetWare protocol specification, but it is also one of the biggest challenges when trying to scale an IPX network. SAP is used by servers to propagate information that describes their services. CCNAs are expected to be very familiar with SAP and the routers' roles in forwarding SAP information.

The SAP process works very much like the process used by a distance vector routing protocol. In fact, SAP uses a concept similar to split horizon to stop a node from advertising SAP information it learned on an interface with updates sent out that same interface. Each server sends SAP updates by default every 60 seconds that include the IPX address, server name, and service type. Every other server and router listens for these updates but does not forward the SAP packet(s). Instead, the SAP information is added to a SAP table in the server or router; then the packets are discarded. When that router or server's SAP timer expires, new SAP broadcasts are sent. As with IPX RIP for routing information, IPX SAP propagates service information until all servers and routers have learned about all servers.

Client initialization flows provide some insight into why routers need to learn SAP information. Consider Figure 6-14, which includes the use of the Get Nearest Server (GNS) request and shows a typical startup with a client configured with a preferred server of Server 2.

The overall goal of Client 1 is to log in to its preferred server, Server 2. The first step is to connect to some server that has a full SAP table so that the client can learn the IPX address of its preferred server. (The preferred server name is configured on the client, not the IPX address of the preferred server.) The router might know the preferred server's name and IPX address in its SAP table, but no IPX message defined allows the client to query the router for name resolution. However, an IPX broadcast message asking for any nearby server is defined by IPX: the GNS request. The router can supply the IPX address of some nearby server (Step 2, in Figure 6-14) because the router has a SAP table.

Next, the client needs to learn which router to use to forward packets to the server discovered by its GNS request. RIP requests and replies are used by the client to learn the route from any router (or server) on the same LAN, as seen in Steps 3 and 4 in Figure 6-14. As a result, Client 1 knows to use the LA router to deliver packets to network 1001.

After connecting to Server 1, the client learns the IPX address of Server 2, its preferred server (Steps 5 and 6, in Figure 6-14). The client needs to know the best route to the preferred server's network; therefore, a RIP request and reply to learn the best next-hop router to network 1002 is shown in Steps 7 and 8, in Figure 6-14. Finally, packets are sent between the client and Server 2 so that the client can log in; the intervening routers are simply routing the packets.

IPX clients create their own IPX address using the network number in the source address field of the GNS reply. The GNS reply is always sent by a router or server on the same network as the client. The client examines the source IPX address of the GNS reply to learn its own IPX network number. The complete client IPX address is formed by putting that network number with the MAC address of the client's LAN interface.

Figure 6-14   *Client Initialization Flows*

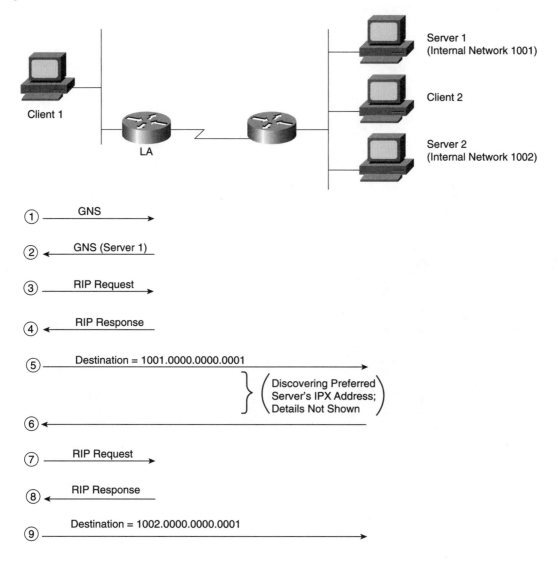

Configuration of IPX

As seen in Chapter 5, enabling RIP and SAP on a router is very straightforward. The **ipx routing** command enables both in a router, and the **ipx network** command on an interface implies that RIP and SAP updates should be sent and listened for on those interfaces. Router Yosemite has been configured for RIP and SAP (see Figure 6-15). The command output in

Example 6-21 shows the result of some RIP and SAP **show** and **debug** commands. (Do not forget—the CCNA exam will ask questions about what commands can be used to view certain details.)

Figure 6-15 *IPX Network with Point-to-Point Serial Links*

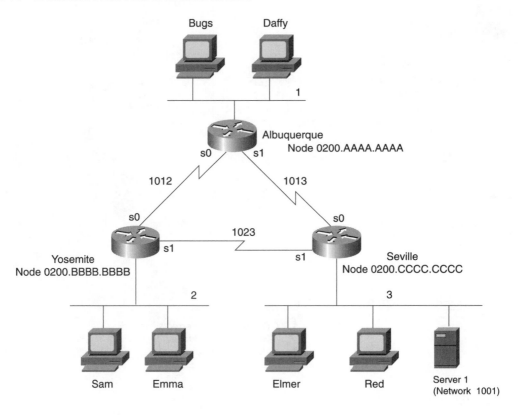

Example 6-21 *Routing and SAP Information on Yosemite*

```
Yosemite#show ipx route
Codes: C - Connected primary network,    c - Connected secondary network
       S - Static, F - Floating static, L - Local (internal), W - IPXWAN
       R - RIP, E - EIGRP, N - NLSP, X - External, A - Aggregate
       s - seconds, u - uses

7 Total IPX routes. Up to 1 parallel paths and 16 hops allowed.

No default route known.

C          2 (SAP),         E0_
C       1012 (HDLC),        Se0
C       1023 (HDLC),        Se1
R          1 [07/01] via    1012.0000.aaaa.aaaa,    14s, Se0
```

Example 6-21 *Routing and SAP Information on Yosemite (Continued)*

```
R           3 [07/01] via      1023.0200.cccc.cccc,    1s, Se1
R        1001 [08/03] via      1023.0200.cccc.cccc,    1s, Se1
R        1013 [12/01] via      1023.0200.cccc.cccc,    1s, Se1
Yosemite#show ipx servers
Codes: S - Static, P - Periodic, E - EIGRP, N - NLSP, H - Holddown, + = detail
1 Total IPX Servers

Table ordering is based on routing and server info

   Type Name                      Net      Address     Port     Route Hops Itf
P     4 Server1                   1001.0000.0000.0001:0451      8/03    3 Se1

Yosemite#debug ipx routing activity
IPX routing debugging is on

Yosemite#
IPXRIP: positing full update to 2.ffff.ffff.ffff via Ethernet0 (broadcast)
IPXRIP: src=2.0200.bbbb.bbbb, dst=2.ffff.ffff.ffff, packet sent
     network 1, hops 2,  delay 8
     network 1001, hops 4,  delay 9
     network 1012, hops 1,  delay 2
     network 3, hops 2,  delay 8
     network 1013, hops 2,  delay 8
     network 1023, hops 1,  delay 2

IPXRIP: positing full update to 1012.ffff.ffff.ffff via Serial0 (broadcast)
IPXRIP: src=1012.0200.bbbb.bbbb, dst=1012.ffff.ffff.ffff, packet sent
     network 1001, hops 4,  delay 14
     network 3, hops 2,  delay 13
     network 1013, hops 2,  delay 13
     network 1023, hops 1,  delay 7
     network 2, hops 1,  delay 7

IPXRIP: update from 1012.0200.aaaa.aaaa
     1013 in 1 hops, delay 7
     1 in 1 hops, delay 7
     1001 in 4 hops, delay 14
     3 in 2 hops, delay 13
IPXRIP: 1023 FFFFFFFF not added, entry in table is static/connected/internal
     1023 in 2 hops, delay 13

IPXRIP: update from 1023.0200.cccc.cccc
     1 in 2 hops, delay 13
     1001 in 3 hops, delay 8
     3 in 1 hops, delay 7
     1013 in 1 hops, delay 7
IPXRIP: positing full update to 1023.ffff.ffff.ffff via Serial1 (broadcast)
IPXRIP: src=1023.0200.bbbb.bbbb, dst=1023.ffff.ffff.ffff, packet sent
     network 1, hops 2,  delay 13
     network 1012, hops 1,  delay 7
     network 2, hops 1,  delay 7
```

continues

Example 6-21 *Routing and SAP Information on Yosemite (Continued)*

```
Yosemite#debug ipx sap activity
IPX service debugging is on

IPXSAP: positing update to 1012.ffff.ffff.ffff via Serial0 (broadcast) (full)
IPXSAP: Update type 0x2 len 96 src:1012.0200.bbbb.bbbb
dest:1012.ffff.ffff.ffff(452)
 type 0x4, "Server1", 1001.0000.0000.0001(451), 4 hops

IPXSAP: Response (in) type 0x2 len 96 src:1012.0200.aaaa.aaaa
dest:1012.ffff.ffff.ffff(452)
 type 0x4, "Server1", 1001.0000.0000.0001(451), 4 hops

IPXSAP: positing update to 1023.ffff.ffff.ffff via Serial1 (broadcast) (full)
IPXSAP: suppressing null update to 1023.ffff.ffff.ffff
IPXSAP: Response (in) type 0x2 len 96 src:1023.0200.cccc.cccc
dest:1023.ffff.ffff.ffff(452)
 type 0x4, "Server1", 1001.0000.0000.0001(451), 3 hops

IPXSAP: positing update to 2.ffff.ffff.ffff via Ethernet0 (broadcast) (full)
IPXSAP: Update type 0x2 len 96 src:2.0000.3089.b170 dest:2.ffff.ffff.ffff(452)
 type 0x4, "Server1", 1001.0000.0000.00011(451), 4 hops
```

Some of the more important portions of the output are highlighted in the example. These features are described in the upcoming paragraphs. The **show ipx route** command lists the metric values in brackets; the number of ticks is listed before the hop count. The number of seconds listed at the end of each line for RIP-derived routes is the time since the routing information was heard; the ticks metric shows only as a number of ticks, never as a number of seconds. For example, in Example 6-21, Yosemite lists a route to network 3, with the numbers [7,1] shown beside the IPX network number. Seven is the number of ticks, which in this case is the sum of six ticks for the serial link to Seville, and one tick for the Ethernet in Seville. The one in brackets represents the hop count.

The **show ipx servers** command purposely was kept small for this example; in many networks, there are thousands of SAP entries. The name of the server and the SAP type are listed; SAP type will be important for SAP filters. The IPX address and socket used by the server for this service also are listed; the socket may be important when filtering IPX packets. The metric values for the route to network 1001 are shown under the word *route*. By having metric information handy, good choices for GNS replies can be made easily. In Example 6-21, Server1 is listed with SAP type 4, which is File Servers; its IPX address is 1001.0000.0000.0001, and it uses IPX port 0451. The route to network 1001 has a metric of eight ticks and three hops; when packets are sent to Server1, they are sent out Yosemite's interface Serial1.

The **debug ipx routing activity** command enables output describing every RIP update sent and received. The number of ticks on LAN interfaces defaults to 1 and on WAN interfaces defaults to 6. Although Albuquerque and Yosemite have coded a bandwidth parameter of 56 on the serial link between them, and the other links default to 1,544, the ticks are not affected. The **ipx delay** *ticks* interface subcommand can be used to change the metric for a particular interface.

Finally, the **debug ipx sap activity** command (highlighted near the end of Example 6-21) enables output describing every SAP update sent and received. Notice the update Yosemite wants to send out network 1023; it is time to send a SAP broadcast, but the SAP update is null. This is because the only SAP in the table (Server1, SAP type 4) was learned from Seville over network 1023, so Yosemite is using split horizon rules to not send information about this SAP back to Seville.

Only one route to each network is allowed in the routing table, by default. Looking back to the beginning of Example 6-20, notice that the route to network 1013, metric [7/1], points to next hop 1023.0200.cccc.cccc (Seville), out Yosemite's Serial 1 interface. However, 1012.0200.aaaa.aaaa (Albuquerque) is sending RIP updates describing a route to network 1013, with seven ticks and one hop into Yosemite's S0 interface (see RIP debug output). Yosemite heard from Seville first; therefore, only that route is included. If the **ipx maximum-paths 2** global command had been configured on Yosemite, both routes would be included. Unlike with IP, when two routes are in the IPX routing table, per-packet load balancing across these paths occurs, even if fast switching is enabled.

NOTE	The default per-packet load balancing used for IPX when multiple routes to the same network are in the routing table may not be desired because packets can arrive out of order. By having the router send all packets to an individual IPX address over the same route every time, those packets should be received in order. The **ipx per-host-load-share** configuration command disables per-packet balancing and enables balancing based on the destination address. Of course, the penalty is that the traffic will not be completely balanced, based on the numbers of packets to each destination.

Tunneling

Tunneling is the process whereby a router encapsulates one Layer 3 protocol inside another protocol (typically IP) for transport across a network to another router. The receiving router de-encapsulates the packet, leaving the original protocol. Each intermediate router that is used between the endpoints of the tunnel is unaware of the protocol being encapsulated. Figure 6-16 shows the basic process and the physical and logical view of an example network.

Although tunneling can encapsulate any Layer 3 protocol, the example in Figure 6-16 shows IPX being encapsulated. The incoming Ethernet frame on the left of the figure is processed as normal, up to a point—the Ethernet header is discarded, and a routing decision is made to forward the packet out *the tunnel interface*. A tunnel interface is created on Router A and Router D to represent the function of tunneling. When the routing logic directs the packet out the tunnel interface, the encapsulation logic described in Figure 6-16 takes over, resulting in an IP packet.

Figure 6-16 *IP Tunneling Concepts*

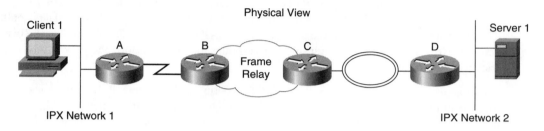

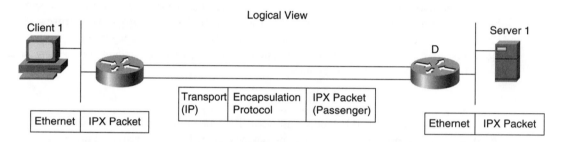

After the IP packet is created, routing logic is repeated by Router A, this time for the new IP packet. Router A routes the IP packet based on the IP routing table, as does Router B and then Router C. Routers B and C have no knowledge that there is an IPX packet inside the IP packet. When the packet arrives at Router D, D notices that the destination address is one of its own addresses, so it examines the data further. Upon finding the *encapsulation protocol header* immediately after the IP header, the router knows that this is a tunneled packet, so Router D strips off the encapsulation header, which leaves the IPX packet, in this case. The IPX packet then is routed, which sends the packet out the Ethernet interface.

Three important terms are used to describe the three parts of the entity that is sent between the two tunneling routers:

- **Passenger protocol**—This is the protocol being encapsulated. In Figure 6-16, IPX is the passenger protocol.

- **Encapsulation protocol**—To identify the passenger protocol, an additional header is used. You can think of this additional header as another place to include a field such as the data link layer's type, DSAP, or protocol field. The IP header defines that one of these encapsulating protocol headers follows IP, and the encapsulation protocol identifies the type of Layer 3 passenger protocol that follows it.

- **Transport protocol**—The transport protocol delivers the passenger protocol across the network. IP is the only choice in the IOS.

For each packet of the encapsulated (passenger) protocol, there is the additional overhead of applying the packet header of the encapsulating (transport) protocol. By adding more bytes of overhead, you certainly reduce the efficiency. So why even use tunneling in the first place? There are several reasons:

- To allow multiple protocols to flow over a single-protocol backbone

- To overcome discontiguous network problems

- To allow virtual private networks (VPNs)

- To overcome the shortcoming of some routing protocols with low maximum metric limitations

- To reduce the amount of overhead of routing protocols

The reduction of overhead and the capability to have an IP-only backbone are the two most compelling reasons to use tunneling. Consider the previous Figure 6-16, which shows a network with a pocket of Novell hosts on each end of the network, but with no Novell hosts in the center of the network. One alternative would have been to configure IPX on all four routers. If tunneling is used in that case, Routers B and C do not need to perform IPX routing. RIP and SAP updates are sent once per timer over the tunnel and are not processed by Routers B and C. The amount of overhead from these protocols is greatly reduced, particularly when non-broadcast multiaccess (NBMA) networks such as Frame Relay are in use. So, the backbone of the WAN network can remain IP only, and when there are only pockets of the different passenger protocols, these protocols can be forwarded using tunnels.

Tunneling for VPNs

As cited in the previous list, one reason for using tunnels is VPNs. Consider Figure 6-17, with the cloud representing a VPN service from a service provider.

Figure 6-17   *Tunneling for VPNs*

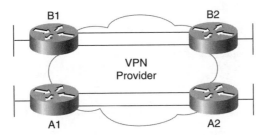

Routers A1 and A2 are owned by Company A, and Routers B1 and B2 are owned by Company B. The two companies do not want their traffic intermingled. If the service provider simply set up routing protocols to each company's sites and advertised all the routes into the service provider network, a couple of undesirable situations will occur. First, route filtering would be required to keep Company A from learning routes to Company B, and vice versa. Also, if either company wanted to use private IP addresses, then the intermingling of IP routes would be disastrous. For instance, if both Company A and Company B decided to use network 10.0.0.0, subnets would overlap and only some of the traffic would be delivered correctly.

The benefit of tunneling for VPNs is that the service provider network does not learn routes about Company A or Company B. The tunnels use addresses in the service provider network. The routing protocol on Routers A1 and A2 send updates to each other over the tunnel, so these two routers think they are logically adjacent. Likewise, Routers B1 and B2 send updates to each other; these updates do not need to be processed by the service provider routers. Also, because the customer routes are not learned by the service provider, there is no need for route redistribution or route filtering.

Configuring Tunneling

Tunneling configuration is not very complicated if you remember the framing with the transport, encapsulation, and passenger protocols. A tunnel interface is created on each router at the ends of the tunnel. To accommodate the transport protocol, an IP address is used at the endpoints of the tunnel; these IP addresses are used as the source and destination IP addresses of the encapsulated packets. The type of encapsulation protocol is configured; there are six alternatives. Finally, the tunnel interface is configured just like any other interface to enable the desired passenger protocols. Examples 6-22 and 6-23 show the configuration of Routers A and D, respectively, from Figure 6-16.

Example 6-22 *Router A Tunnel Configuration*

```
ipx routing
!
interface serial 0
  ip address 10.1.2.1 255.255.255.0
interface ethernet 0
  ip address 10.1.1.1 255.255.255.0
  ipx network 1
!
interface tunnel 0
  tunnel source ethernet 0
  tunnel destination 10.1.5.4
  ipx network 3
!
router igrp 9
network 10.0.0.0
```

Example 6-23 *Router D Tunnel Configuration*

```
ipx routing
!
interface token 0
  ip address 10.1.4.4 255.255.255.0
interface ethernet 0
  ip address 10.1.5.4 255.255.255.0
```

Example 6-23 *Router D Tunnel Configuration (Continued)*

```
  ipx network 2
!
interface tunnel 3
  tunnel source 10.1.5.4
  tunnel destination 10.1.1.1
  ipx network 3
!
router igrp 9
 network 10.0.0.0
```

The configuration is simplified if you concentrate on the transport, encapsulation, and passenger protocols. First, as highlighted in Example 6-22, IP is enabled on all interfaces except the tunnel interface. However, the **tunnel source** command implies the IP address to be used on the interface; this IP address is used as the source for all packets sent out the tunnel interface. Likewise, the **tunnel destination** IP address is used as the destination address for packets sent out each tunnel interface. IP is enabled by default.

The encapsulation protocol in this case has defaulted to generic route encapsulation (GRE). If another protocol were desired, the **tunnel mode** interface subcommand would be used to set the protocol. (While the details of the encapsulation protocols are likely to be beyond the CCNA requirements, the other types are aurp, cayman, dvmrp, eon, ipip, iptalk, and nos.)

The passenger protocol is enabled on the tunnel interface, just as it would be for any other interface. IPX routing is enabled globally, and the **ipx network** command is used on both the Ethernet interface and the tunnel interface. Notice the absence of the **ipx network** command on Router A's serial 0 interface and Router D's Token Ring interface. Because there are no Novell nodes in the center of the network, there is no need to enable IPX on these interfaces.

Integrated Routing Protocols

So far, all the routing protocol functions discussed in this book fall under the classification of *separate multiprotocol routing*. To fully compare and contrast the meaning of this term with the alternative methods of *integrated multiprotocol routing*, a review of multiprotocol routing is in order. Consider Figure 6-18, which should remind you of one such concept.

As discussed in Chapter 3, the router determines what type of Layer 3 packet is inside the received frame. There is a separate routing table for each routable or routed protocol. (If you previously skipped Chapter 3, you may want to review the generalized routing algorithm, or the "Ting and Ted" story.) The routing decision is therefore dependent on a routing table specific for that one Layer 3 protocol. This process is called multiprotocol routing.

Routing protocols fill the routing tables of the various Layer 3 protocols. Although not covered elsewhere in this book, AppleTalk uses yet another derivative of XNS RIP, called the Routing Table Maintenance Protocol (RTMP), as its routing protocol. Consider the simple network in Figure 6-19 and the routing updates that are sent out S0 by Router1.

Figure 6-18 *Multiprotocol Routing*

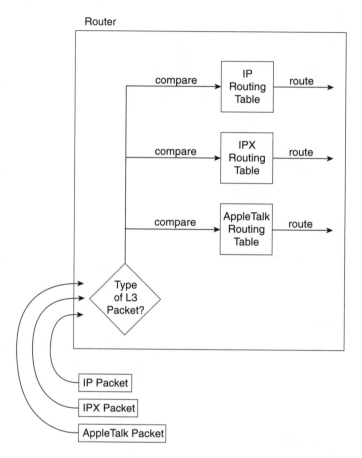

Separate multiprotocol routing is described in Figure 6-19. The word *separate* refers to the separate routing updates sent by the respective routing protocols. Each separate routable protocol (IP, IPX, and AppleTalk) uses a separate routing protocol. (IP uses RIP, IPX uses RIP, and AppleTalk uses RTMP.)

Many similarities exist among IP, IPX, and AppleTalk; these similarities allow integrated multiprotocol routing to exist. In particular, if Router1's E0 interface failed, then IP subnet 10.1.1.0/24, IPX network 1, and AppleTalk Cablerange 1-1 would all be inaccessible. In fact, the key similarity is that all three Layer 3 protocols use the same concept of grouping devices; that is, a group consists of all interfaces attached to the same medium. In fact, the following statement can be made about this similarity:

Events that could cause a router's directly connected IP route to fail will often cause the directly connected IPX and AppleTalk routes associated with that same data link to fail.

Figure 6-19   *IP-RIP, IPX-RIP, and RTMP Updates*

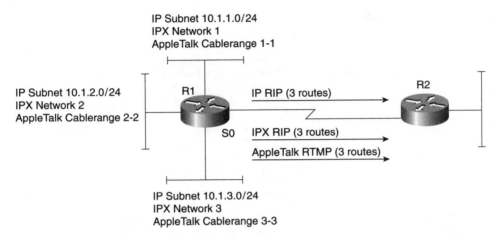

A failure of Router1's E0 interface would cause IP RIP, IPX RIP, and AppleTalk RTMP to advertise that the associated subnet/network/cablerange was not accessible. Each routing protocol would send its own updates, as diagrammed in Figure 6-20.

Figure 6-20   *Multiple Routing Updates—Separate Multiprotocol Routing*

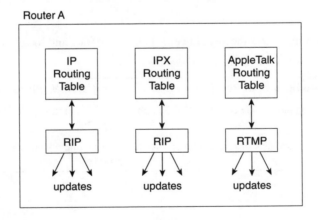

Integrated multiprotocol routing uses a single routing protocol to propagate routing information for multiple routable protocols. EIGRP performs integrated multiprotocol routing for IP, IPX, and AppleTalk. (EIGRP and Integrated IS-IS can also do integrated multiprotocol routing for IP and OSI CLNS.) Figure 6-21 diagrams the basic idea behind integrated multiprotocol routing.

Figure 6-21 *Single Routing Update—Integrated Multiprotocol Routing*

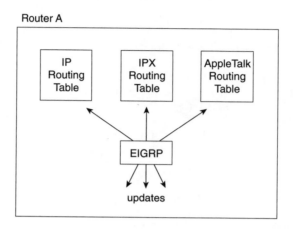

EIGRP happens to have many additional features that are better than IP RIP, IPX RIP, and RTMP. For a full discussion of EIGRP features, refer to the Cisco Press book *Routing TCP/IP, Volume I*, which includes a detailed description of how EIGRP works.

Table 6-18 summarizes the key concepts behind separate and integrated multiprotocol routing.

Table 6-18 *Separate and Integrated Multiprotocol Routing*

Separate Multiprotocol Routing	Integrated Multiprotocol Routing
Multiple routing tables, one each for IP, IPX, and AppleTalk	Multiple routing tables, one each for IP, IPX, and AppleTalk
Multiple routing updates, one per routing protocol	One routing update combined for all three routed protocols

Foundation Summary

Table 6-19 lists the EXEC commands covered in this chapter.

Table 6-19   *EXEC Command Summary for Chapter 6*

Command	Function
show ip protocol	Provides information on IP routing protocols running, IP addresses of neighboring routers using the routing protocol, and timers.
show ip route	Lists IP routes, including subnet, next-hop router, and outgoing interface. Also identifies the source of routing information.
show ipx route	Lists IPX routes, including subnet, next-hop router, and outgoing interface. Also identifies the source of routing information.
show ipx servers	Lists contents of the SAP table, including server name, address, and SAP type.
debug ip rip	Lists detailed contents of both sent and received IP RIP updates.
debug ip igrp transaction	Lists detailed contents of both sent and received IGRP updates.
debug ip igrp event	Lists summary of contents of both sent and received IGRP updates.
debug ipx rip activity	Lists detailed contents of both sent and received IPX RIP updates.
debug ipx sap activity	Lists detailed contents of both sent and received SAP updates.

Table 6-20 lists interior IP routing protocols and their types. A column referring to whether the routing protocol includes subnet mask information in the routing updates is listed for future reference.

Table 6-20   *Interior IP Routing Protocols and Types*

Routing Protocol	Type	Loop Prevention Mechanisms	Mask Sent in Updates?
RIP-1	Distance vector	Holddown timer, split horizon	No
RIP-2	Distance vector	Holddown timer, split horizon	Yes
IGRP	Distance vector	Holddown timer, split horizon	No
EIGRP	Balanced hybrid	DUAL and feasible successors	Yes
OSPF	Link-state	Dijkstra SPF algorithm and full topology knowledge	Yes

Most of the issues with distance vector routing protocols arise when working with networks with multiple paths. Two of these issues are not obvious. Table 6-21 summarizes these issues, and each is explained in succession.

Table 6-21 *Issues Relating to Distance Vector Routing Protocols in Networks with (Multiple Paths)*

Issue	Solution
Multiple routes to same subnet, with equal metric	Implementation options include either using the first route learned or putting multiple routes to the same subnet in the routing table.
Routing loops occurring due to updates passing each other over a single link	**Split horizon**—The routing protocol advertises routes out an interface only if they were not learned from updates entering that interface.
	Split horizon with poison reverse—The routing protocol advertises all routes out an interface, but those learned from earlier updates coming in that interface are marked with infinite distance metrics.
Routing loops occurring due to updates passing each other over alternate paths	**Route poisoning**—When a route to a subnet fails, the subnet is advertised with an infinite distance metric.
Counting to infinity	**Holddown timer**—After knowing that a route to a subnet has failed, a router waits a certain period of time before believing any other routing information about that subnet.
	Triggered updates—The process of immediately sending an update rather than waiting on the update timer to expire when a route has failed. Used in conjunction with route poisoning, this ensures that all routers know of failed routes before any holddown timers can expire.

Table 6-22 outlines the features of RIP and IGRP.

Table 6-22 *RIP and IGRP Feature Comparison*

Feature	RIP (Defaults)	IGRP (Defaults)
Update timer	30 seconds	90 seconds
Metric	Hop count	Function of bandwidth and delay (default); can include reliability, load, and MTU
Holddown timer	180	280
Flash (triggered) updates	Yes	Yes
Mask sent in update	No for RIP-1, yes for RIP-2	No
Infinity metric value	16	4,294,967,295

Table 6-23 and Table 6-24 summarize the more popular commands used for RIP and IGRP configuration and verification.

Table 6-23   *IP RIP and IGRP Configuration Commands*

Command	Configuration Mode
router rip	Global
router igrp *process-id*	Global
network *net-number*	Router subcommand
passive-interface *type number*	Router subcommand
maximum-paths *x*	Router subcommand
variance *multiplier*	Router subcommand
traffic-share {*balanced* / *min*}	Router subcommand

Table 6-24   *IP RIP and IGRP EXEC*

Command	Function
show ip route [*subnet*]	Shows entire routing table, or one entry if **subnet** is entered
show ip protocol	Provides routing protocol parameters and current timer values
debug ip rip	Issues log messages for each RIP update
debug ip igrp transactions	Issues log messages with details of the IGRP updates
debug ip igrp events	Issues log messages for each IGRP packet
ping	Sends and receives ICMP echo messages to verify connectivity
trace	Sends series of ICMP echoes with increasing TTL values to verify the current route to a host

RIP-2, defined by RFC 1723, is simply an improved version of RIP Version 1. Many features are the same: Hop count is still used for the metric, it is still a distance vector protocol, and it still uses holddown timers and route poisoning. Several features have been added; the features are listed in Table 6-25.

Table 6-25   *RIP-2 Features*

Feature	Description
Transmits subnet mask with route	This feature allows VLSM by passing the mask along with each route so that the subnet is exactly defined.

continues

Table 6-25   *RIP-2 Features (Continued)*

Feature	Description
Uses authentication	Both clear text (RFC-defined) and MD5 encryption (Cisco-added feature) can be used to authenticate the source of a routing update.
Uses next-hop router IP address in routing update	A router can advertise a route but direct any listeners to a different router on that same subnet. This is done only when the other router has a better route.
Uses external route tags	RIP can pass information about routes learned from an external source and can be redistributed into RIP.
Provides multicast routing updates	Instead of sending updates to 255.255.255.255, the destination IP address is 224.0.0.9, an IP multicast address. This reduces the amount of processing required on non-RIP-speaking hosts on a common subnet.

Table 6-26 lists the features for summarization of the interior IP routing protocols.

Table 6-26   *Route Aggregation Comparison of Subnet Numbers*

Routing Protocol	Auto Summary Enabled?	Auto Summary Disabled?	Route Aggregation?
RIP Version 1	Yes, by default	Not allowed	No
IGRP	Yes, by default	Not allowed	No
RIP Version 2	Yes, by default	Allowed via configuration	No
EIGRP	Yes, by default	Allowed via configuration	Yes
OSPF	No, but can do equivalent with aggregation	Yes	Yes

Table 6-27 lists the similarities and differences between IP RIP and IPX RIP.

Table 6-27   *RIP for IPX and IP Compared*

Novell RIP	IP RIP
Uses distance vector	Uses distance vector
Is based on XNS RIP	Is based on XNS RIP
Uses 60-second update timer (default)	Uses 30-second update timer (default)
Uses timer ticks as primary metric and hop count as secondary metric	Uses hop count as only metric

Table 6-28 summarizes the key concepts behind separate and integrated multiprotocol routing.

Table 6-28   *Separate and Integrated Multiprotocol Routing*

Separate Multiprotocol Routing	**Integrated Multiprotocol Routing**
Multiple routing tables, one each for IP, IPX, and AppleTalk	Multiple routing tables, one each for IP, IPX, and AppleTalk
Multiple routing updates, one per routing protocol	One routing update combined for all three routed protocols

Figure 6-22 includes the use of the Get Nearest Server (GNS) request and shows a typical startup with a client configured with a preferred server of Server 2.

Figure 6-22   *Client Initialization Flows*

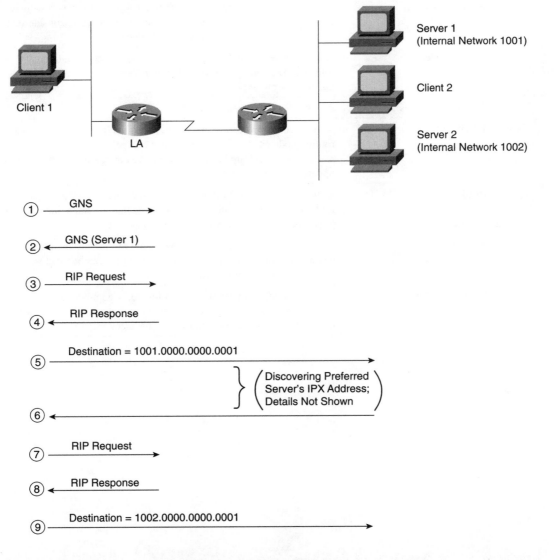

Table 6-29 lists several definitions of terms covered throughout the chapter.

Table 6-29   *Definitions Covered in This Chapter*

Term	Definition
Link-state protocol	A type of logic used by a routing protocol, characterized by exchanges of full topology information, which is processed with the Dijkstra algorithm to form a shortest-path tree to determine routes. OSPF is an example.
Distance vector	A type of logic used by a routing protocol, characterized by exchange of a vector consisting of the destination network and a metric. IP RIP, IPX RIP, and IGRP are examples of distance vector routing protocols.
Route poisoning	A distance vector feature of advertising routes that were previously good but that are now failed, with a metric value that is considered to be infinite. This is a loop-prevention feature.
Flash updates	A distance vector feature of sending new or changed routing information in an update immediately rather than waiting on the next update timer to expire.
Triggered updates	Another term for flash updates.
Update timer	A distance vector feature that defines the interval between sending routing updates. A neighboring router will believe that a neighboring router has failed if updates are not received after some multiple of the update timer (usually 3).
Holddown timer	A distance vector feature that defines how long to wait to update a route for a particular subnet, after hearing that the route that was previously in the routing table has failed.
Split horizon	A distance vector feature that prevents the routing protocol from advertising routes out an interface if the routes were learned from updates entering that interface.
Split horizon with poison reverse	A variation of split horizon. Routes learned via updates entering an interface are advertised in updates sent out that same interface, except that these routes are given an infinite distance metric.

Q&A

As mentioned in Chapter 1, the questions and scenarios in this book are more difficult than what you should experience on the actual exam. The questions do not attempt to cover more breadth or depth than the exam; however, they are designed to make sure that you know the answer. Rather than allowing you to derive the answer from clues hidden inside the question itself, the questions challenge understanding and recall of the subject. Questions from the "Do I Know This Already?" quiz from the beginning of the chapter are repeated here to ensure that you have mastered the chapter's topic areas. Hopefully, these questions will help limit the number of exam questions on which you narrow your choices to two options and then guess.

The answers to these questions can be found in Appendix A, on page 748.

1 What type of routing protocol algorithm uses a holddown timer? What is its purpose?

2 Define what split horizon means to the contents of a routing update. Does this apply to both the distance vector algorithm and the link-state algorithm?

3 Write down the steps you would take to migrate from RIP to IGRP in a router whose current RIP configuration includes only **router rip**, followed by a **network 10.0.0.0** command.

4 How does the IOS designate a subnet in the routing table as a directly connected network? What about a route learned with IGRP and a route learned with RIP?

5 Create a configuration for IGRP on a router with these interfaces and addresses: e0 using 10.1.1.1, e1 using 224.1.2.3, s0 using 10.1.2.1, and s1 using 199.1.1.1. Use process ID 5.

6 Create a configuration for IGRP on a router with these interfaces and addresses: to0 using 200.1.1.1, e0 using 128.1.3.2, s0 using 192.0.1.1, and s1 using 223.254.254.1.

7 From a router's user mode, without using debugs or privileged mode, how can you determine what routers are sending you routing updates?

8 How often does IPX RIP send routing updates, by default?

9 Describe the metric(s) used by IPX RIP in a Cisco router.

10 Does IPX RIP use Split Horizon?

11 True or false: RIP and SAP information is sent in the same packets. If true, can only one of the two be enabled in a router? If false, what commands enable each protocol globally in a router?

12 What does GNS stand for? Who creates GNS requests, and who creates GNS replies?

13 Define the term separate multiprotocol routing in the context of the Cisco IOS and Novell IPX.

14 How often does a router send SAP updates, by default?

15 If Serial0 has a **bandwidth 1544** interface subcommand and Serial1 has a **bandwidth 56** interface subcommand, what metric will IPX RIP associate with each interface?

16 True or false: Routers forward SAP packets as they arrive but broadcast SAP packets on interfaces in which no SAP packets have been received in the last 60 seconds.

17 What **show** commands list IPX RIP metric values in a Cisco router?

18 Define the term integrated multiprotocol routing in the context of the Cisco IOS and Novell IPX.

19 If the commands **router rip** and **network 10.0.0.0**, with no other network commands, were configured in a router that has an Ethernet0 interface with IP address 168.10.1.1, would RIP send updates out Ethernet0?

20 If the commands **router igrp 1** and **network 10.0.0.0** were configured in a router that has an Ethernet0 interface with IP address 168.10.1.1, would IGRP advertise about 168.10.0.0?

21 If the commands **router igrp 1** and **network 10.0.0.0** were configured in a router that has an Ethernet0 interface with IP address 168.10.1.1, mask 255.255.255.0, would this router have a route to 168.10.1.0?

22 What routing protocols support integrated multiprotocol routing?

23 Must IGRP metrics for multiple routes to the same subnet be exactly equal for the multiple routes to be added to the routing table? If not, how close in value do the metrics have to be?

24 When using RIP, what configuration command controls the number of equal-cost routes that can be added to the routing table at the same time? What is the maximum number of equal-cost routes to the same destination that can be included in the IP routing table at once?

25 When using IGRP, what configuration command controls the number of equal-cost routes that can be added to the routing table at the same time? What is the maximum number of equal-cost routes to the same destination that can be included in the IP routing table at once?

26 What feature supported by RIP-2 allows it to support variable-length subnet masks (VLSM)?

27 Name three features of RIP-2 that are not features of RIP-1.

28 What configuration commands are different between a router configured for RIP-1 and a router configured for only support of RIP-2?

29 Identify two reasons for using tunneling.

30 What tunneling transport protocol is used by the IOS?

31 Define the tunneling terms transport protocol, encapsulation protocol, and passenger protocol.

32 List the Interior IP routing protocols that have auto summarization enabled by default. Which of these protocols allows auto summary to be disabled using a configuration command?

33 List the interior IP routing protocols that support route aggregation.

34 Identify the command that would list all IP routes learned via RIP.

35 Identify the command(s) that would list all IP routes in network 172.16.0.0.

36 Assume that several subnets of network 172.16.0.0 exist in a router's routing table. What must be true about those routes so that the output of the **show ip route** command lists mask information only on the line that lists network 172.16.0.0, but not show mask information on each route for each subnet?

37 True or false: Distance vector routing protocols learn routes by transmitting routing updates.

38 Assume that a router is configured to allow only one route in the routing table to each destination network. If more than one route to a particular subnet is learned, and if each route has the same metric value, which route is placed into the routing table if the routing protocol uses distance vector logic?

39 Describe the purpose and meaning of route poisoning.

40 Describe the meaning and purpose of triggered updates.

Scenarios

Scenario 6-1: IP Configuration 1

Your job is to deploy a new network. The network engineering group has provided a list of addresses and a network diagram, as shown in Figure 6-23 and Table 6-30.

Figure 6-23   *Scenario 6-1 Network Diagram*

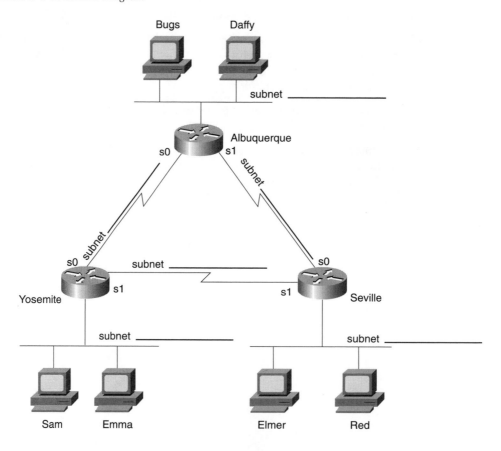

Table 6-30   *Scenario 6-1 IP Addresses*

Location of Subnet Geographically	Subnet Mask	Subnet Number	Subnet Broadcast
Ethernet off router in Albuquerque	255.255.255.0	148.14.1.0	
Ethernet off router in Yosemite	255.255.255.0	148.14.2.0	
Ethernet off router in Seville	255.255.255.0	148.14.3.0	
Serial between Albuquerque and Yosemite	255.255.255.0	148.14.4.0	
Serial between Albuquerque and Seville	255.255.255.0	148.14.5.0	
Serial between Seville and Yosemite	255.255.255.0	148.14.6.0	

Assuming the details established in Figure 6-23 and Table 6-30 for Scenario 6-1, complete or answer the following:

1   Create the configurations to enable IP as described in Table 6-30. Choose IP addresses as appropriate.

2   Describe the contents of the routing table on Seville after the routers are installed and all interfaces are up but no routing protocols or static routes have been configured.

3   Configure static routes for each router so that any host in any subnet could communicate with other hosts in this network.

4   Configure IGRP to replace the static routes in Task 3.

5   Calculate the subnet broadcast address for each subnet.

Scenario 6-2: IP Configuration 2

Your job is to deploy a new network. The network engineering group has provided a list of addresses and a network diagram, with Frame Relay global DLCIs, as shown in Figure 6-24 and Table 6-31.

Figure 6-24 *Scenario 6-2 Network Diagram*

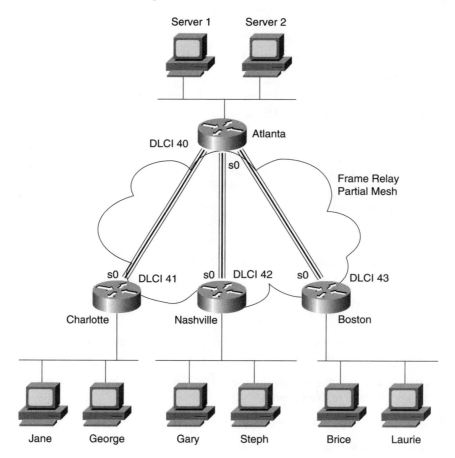

Table 6-31   *Scenario 6-2 IP Addresses*

Location of Subnet Geographically	Subnet Mask	Subnet Number	Subnet Broadcast
Ethernet off router in Atlanta	255.255.255.0	10.1.1.0	
Ethernet off router in Charlotte	255.255.255.0	10.1.2.0	
Ethernet off router in Nashville	255.255.255.0	10.1.3.0	
Ethernet off router in Boston	255.255.255.0	10.1.4.0	
VC between Atlanta and Charlotte	255.255.255.0	10.2.1.0	
VC between Atlanta and Nashville	255.255.255.0	10.2.2.0	
VC between Atlanta and Boston	255.255.255.0	10.2.3.0	

Assuming the details established in Figure 6-24 and Table 6-31 for Scenario 6-2, complete or answer the following:

1 Create the configurations to enable IP as described in Table 6-31. Do not enable a routing protocol.

2 Configure RIP.

3 Calculate the subnet broadcast address for each subnet.

4 Describe the contents of the RIP update from Boston sent to Atlanta; also describe the contents of the RIP update from Atlanta to Charlotte.

Scenario 6-3: IP Addressing and Subnet Derivation

Perform the tasks and answer the questions following the upcoming figures and examples. Figure 6-25 shows the network diagram for Scenario 6-3, and Example 6-24, Example 6-25, and Example 6-26 contain **show** command output from the three routers. Use Table 6-32 to record the subnet numbers and broadcast addresses as directed in the upcoming tasks.

Figure 6-25 *Scenario 6-3 Network Diagram*

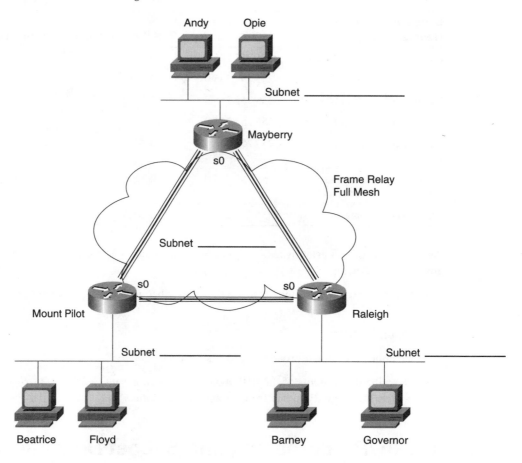

Table 6-32 *Subnets and Broadcast Addresses*

Location of Subnet Geographically	Subnet Mask	Subnet Number	Subnet Broadcast
Ethernet off router in Mayberry	255.255.255.0		
Ethernet off router in Mount Pilot	255.255.255.0		
Ethernet off router in Raleigh	255.255.255.0		
VC between Mayberry and Mount Pilot	255.255.255.0		

Table 6-32   *Subnets and Broadcast Addresses (Continued)*

Location of Subnet Geographically	Subnet Mask	Subnet Number	Subnet Broadcast
VC between Mayberry and Raleigh	255.255.255.0		
VC between Mount Pilot and Raleigh	255.255.255.0		

Example 6-24 *Scenario 6-3,* **show** *Commands on Router Mayberry*

```
Mayberry#show ip route
Codes: C - connected, S - static, I - IGRP, R - RIP, M - mobile, B - BGP
       D - EIGRP, EX - EIGRP external, O - OSPF, IA - OSPF inter area
       N1 - OSPF NSSA external type 1, N2 - OSPF NSSA external type 2
       E1 - OSPF external type 1, E2 - OSPF external type 2, E - EGP
       i - IS-IS, L1 - IS-IS level-1, L2 - IS-IS level-2, * - candidate default
       U - per-user static route, o - ODR

Gateway of last resort is not set

     170.1.0.0/24 is subnetted, 4 subnets
C       170.1.1.0 is directly connected, Serial0
I       170.1.103.0 [100/8539] via 170.1.1.3, 00:00:50, Serial0
I       170.1.102.0 [100/8539] via 170.1.1.2, 00:00:32, Serial0
C       170.1.101.0 is directly connected, Ethernet0

Mayberry#show ip interface brief
Interface           IP-Address      OK? Method Status                Protocol
Serial0             170.1.1.1       YES NVRAM  up                     up
Serial1             10.1.6.251      YES NVRAM  administratively down  down
Ethernet0           170.1.101.1     YES NVRAM  up                     up

Mayberry#debug ip igrp transaction
IGRP protocol debugging is on
Mayberry#debug ip igrp events
IGRP event debugging is on
Mayberry#
IGRP: received update from 170.1.1.3 on Serial0
      subnet 170.1.1.0, metric 10476 (neighbor 8476)
      subnet 170.1.103.0, metric 8539 (neighbor 688)
      subnet 170.1.102.0, metric 10539 (neighbor 8539)
      subnet 170.1.101.0, metric 10539 (neighbor 8539)
IGRP: Update contains 4 interior, 0 system, and 0 exterior routes.
IGRP: Total routes in update: 4
IGRP: received update from 170.1.1.2 on Serial0
      subnet 170.1.1.0, metric 10476 (neighbor 8476)
      subnet 170.1.103.0, metric 10539 (neighbor 8539)
      subnet 170.1.102.0, metric 8539 (neighbor 688)
      subnet 170.1.101.0, metric 10539 (neighbor 8539)
IGRP: Update contains 4 interior, 0 system, and 0 exterior routes.
IGRP: Total routes in update: 4
```

continues

Example 6-24 *Scenario 6-3,* **show** *Commands on Router Mayberry (Continued)*

```
IGRP: sending update to 255.255.255.255 via Serial0 (170.1.1.1)
        subnet 170.1.1.0, metric=8476
        subnet 170.1.103.0, metric=8539
        subnet 170.1.102.0, metric=8539
        subnet 170.1.101.0, metric=688
IGRP: Update contains 4 interior, 0 system, and 0 exterior routes.
IGRP: Total routes in update: 4
IGRP: sending update to 255.255.255.255 via Ethernet0 (170.1.101.1)
        subnet 170.1.1.0, metric=8476
        subnet 170.1.103.0, metric=8539
        subnet 170.1.102.0, metric=8539
IGRP: Update contains 3 interior, 0 system, and 0 exterior routes.
IGRP: Total routes in update:
```

Example 6-25 *Scenario 6-3,* **show** *Commands on Router Mount Pilot*

```
MountPilot#show frame-relay pvc

PVC Statistics for interface Serial0 (Frame Relay DTE)

DLCI = 47, DLCI USAGE = LOCAL, PVC STATUS = ACTIVE, INTERFACE = Serial0

  input pkts 38           output pkts 37          in bytes 3758
  out bytes 3514          dropped pkts 0          in FECN pkts 0
  in BECN pkts 0          out FECN pkts 0         out BECN pkts 0
  in DE pkts 0            out DE pkts 0
  out bcast pkts 36        out bcast bytes 3436
  pvc create time 00:17:39, last time pvc status changed 00:17:39

DLCI = 49, DLCI USAGE = LOCAL, PVC STATUS = ACTIVE, INTERFACE = Serial0

  input pkts 31           output pkts 31          in bytes 3054
  out bytes 3076          dropped pkts 0          in FECN pkts 0
  in BECN pkts 0          out FECN pkts 0         out BECN pkts 0
  in DE pkts 0            out DE pkts 0
  out bcast pkts 31        out bcast bytes 3076
  pvc create time 00:17:40, last time pvc status changed 00:16:40

MountPilot#show frame-relay map

Serial0 (up): ip 170.1.1.1 dlci 47(0x2F,0x8F0), dynamic,
              broadcast,, status defined, active
Serial0 (up): ip 170.1.1.3 dlci 49(0x31,0xC10), dynamic,
              broadcast,, status defined, active

MountPilot#
IGRP: sending update to 255.255.255.255 via Serial0 (170.1.1.2)
        subnet 170.1.1.0, metric=8476
        subnet 170.1.103.0, metric=8539
        subnet 170.1.102.0, metric=688
        subnet 170.1.101.0, metric=8539
IGRP: Update contains 4 interior, 0 system, and 0 exterior routes.
IGRP: Total routes in update: 4
```

Example 6-25 *Scenario 6-3,* **show** *Commands on Router Mount Pilot (Continued)*

```
IGRP: sending update to 255.255.255.255 via Ethernet0 (170.1.102.2)
      subnet 170.1.1.0, metric=8476
      subnet 170.1.103.0, metric=8539
      subnet 170.1.101.0, metric=8539
IGRP: Update contains 3 interior, 0 system, and 0 exterior routes.
IGRP: Total routes in update: 3
IGRP: received update from 170.1.1.1 on Serial0
      subnet 170.1.1.0, metric 10476 (neighbor 8476)
      subnet 170.1.103.0, metric 10539 (neighbor 8539)
      subnet 170.1.102.0, metric 10539 (neighbor 8539)
      subnet 170.1.101.0, metric 8539 (neighbor 688)
IGRP: Update contains 4 interior, 0 system, and 0 exterior routes.
IGRP: Total routes in update: 4
IGRP: received update from 170.1.1.3 on Serial0
      subnet 170.1.1.0, metric 10476 (neighbor 8476)
      subnet 170.1.103.0, metric 8539 (neighbor 688)
      subnet 170.1.102.0, metric 10539 (neighbor 8539)
      subnet 170.1.101.0, metric 10539 (neighbor 8539)
IGRP: Update contains 4 interior, 0 system, and 0 exterior routes.
IGRP: Total routes in update: 4

%FR-5-DLCICHANGE: Interface Serial0 - DLCI 47 state changed to DELETED
MountPilot#

IGRP: received update from 170.1.1.3 on Serial0
      subnet 170.1.1.0, metric 10476 (neighbor 8476)
      subnet 170.1.103.0, metric 8539 (neighbor 688)
      subnet 170.1.102.0, metric 10539 (neighbor 8539)
      subnet 170.1.101.0, metric 10539 (neighbor 8539)
IGRP: Update contains 4 interior, 0 system, and 0 exterior routes.
IGRP: Total routes in update: 4
```

Example 6-26 *Scenario 6-3,* **show** *Commands on Router Raleigh*

```
Raleigh#show ip route
Codes: C - connected, S - static, I - IGRP, R - RIP, M - mobile, B - BGP
       D - EIGRP, EX - EIGRP external, O - OSPF, IA - OSPF inter area
       N1 - OSPF NSSA external type 1, N2 - OSPF NSSA external type 2
       E1 - OSPF external type 1, E2 - OSPF external type 2, E - EGP
       i - IS-IS, L1 - IS-IS level-1, L2 - IS-IS level-2, * - candidate default
       U - per-user static route, o - ODR

Gateway of last resort is not set

     170.1.0.0/24 is subnetted, 4 subnets
C       170.1.1.0 is directly connected, Serial0
C       170.1.103.0 is directly connected, Ethernet0
I       170.1.102.0 [100/8539] via 170.1.1.2, 00:00:09, Serial0
I       170.1.101.0 [100/8539] via 170.1.1.1, 00:00:42, Serial0

Raleigh#show ip interface brief
Interface            IP-Address      OK? Method Status              Protocol
```

continues

Example 6-26 *Scenario 6-3, **show** Commands on Router Raleigh (Continued)*

```
Serial0                 170.1.1.3       YES NVRAM  up                           up
Serial1                 180.1.1.253     YES NVRAM  administratively down down
Ethernet0               170.1.103.3     YES NVRAM  up                           up

Raleigh#show ip protocol
Routing Protocol is "igrp 4"
  Sending updates every 90 seconds, next due in 56 seconds
  Invalid after 270 seconds, hold down 280, flushed after 630
  Outgoing update filter list for all interfaces is not set
  Incoming update filter list for all interfaces is not set
  Default networks flagged in outgoing updates
  Default networks accepted from incoming updates
  IGRP metric weight K1=1, K2=0, K3=1, K4=0, K5=0
  IGRP maximum hopcount 100
  IGRP maximum metric variance 1
  Redistributing: igrp 4
  Routing for Networks:
    170.1.0.0
  Routing Information Sources:
    Gateway         Distance      Last Update
    170.1.1.2           100       00:00:20
    170.1.1.1           100       00:00:53
  Distance: (default is 100)

Raleigh#show frame-relay pvc

PVC Statistics for interface Serial0 (Frame Relay DTE)

DLCI = 47, DLCI USAGE = LOCAL, PVC STATUS = ACTIVE, INTERFACE = Serial0

  input pkts 36            output pkts 35          in bytes 3674
  out bytes 3436           dropped pkts 0          in FECN pkts 0
  in BECN pkts 0           out FECN pkts 0         out BECN pkts 0
  in DE pkts 0             out DE pkts 0
  out bcast pkts 34         out bcast bytes 3358
  pvc create time 00:22:07, last time pvc status changed 00:21:58

DLCI = 48, DLCI USAGE = LOCAL, PVC STATUS = ACTIVE, INTERFACE = Serial0

  input pkts 35            output pkts 35          in bytes 3444
  out bytes 3422           dropped pkts 0          in FECN pkts 0
  in BECN pkts 0           out FECN pkts 0         out BECN pkts 0
  in DE pkts 0             out DE pkts 0
  out bcast pkts 34         out bcast bytes 3358
  pvc create time 00:22:08, last time pvc status changed 00:21:58
```

Assuming the details established in Figure 6-25, Table 6-32, and Example 6-24, Example 6-25, and Example 6-26 for Scenario 6-3, complete or answer the following:

1 Examining the **show** commands on the various routers, complete Table 6-32 with the subnet numbers and broadcast addresses used in this network.

2 Describe the contents of the IGRP update from Raleigh, sent out its virtual circuit to Mount Pilot. How many routes in Raleigh's IGRP update are sent to Mount Pilot? How many routes are there in Raleigh's routing table? Is the number different? Why? (*Hint*: Look at the IGRP debug output in Example 6-25 and the IP routing table in Example 6-26.)

3 If the VC between MountPilot and Mayberry fails and routing protocol convergence completes, will Mayberry have a route to 170.1.1.0/24? Why or why not?

Scenario 6-4: IPX Examination

The CCNA exam includes questions that test your recollection of the details shown in various **show** and **debug** commands. Several tasks and questions are listed after Figure 6-26, Table 6-33, Table 6-34, and Example 6-27, Example 6-28, and Example 6-29; performing these tasks will help you solidify your recollection of what information is available in each command.

Figure 6-26 *Scenario 6-4 Network Diagram*

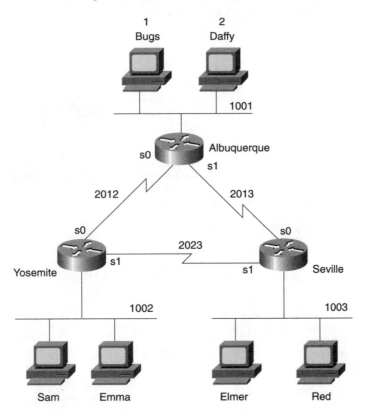

Example 6-27 *Albuquerque Command Output, Scenario 6-4*

```
Albuquerque#show ipx interface brief
Interface          IPX Network Encapsulation Status         IPX State
Serial0            2012        HDLC          up             [up]
Serial1            2013        HDLC          up             [up]
Ethernet0          1001        SAP           up             [up]

Albuquerque#show cdp neighbor detail
-----------------------
Device ID: Yosemite
Entry address(es):
  IP address: 10.1.12.2
  Novell address: 2012.0200.2222.2222
Platform: Cisco 2500,  Capabilities: Router
Interface: Serial0,  Port ID (outgoing port): Serial0
Holdtime : 167 sec

Version :
Cisco Internetwork Operating System Software
IOS (tm) 2500 Software (C2500-AINR-L), Version 11.2(11), RELEASE SOFTWARE (fc1)
Copyright  1986-1997 by Cisco Systems, Inc.
Compiled Mon 29-Dec-97 18:47 by ckralik


-----------------------
Device ID: Seville
Entry address(es):
  IP address: 10.1.13.3
  Novell address: 2013.0200.3333.3333
Platform: Cisco 2500,  Capabilities: Router
Interface: Serial1,  Port ID (outgoing port): Serial0
Holdtime : 164 sec

Version :
Cisco Internetwork Operating System Software
IOS (tm) 2500 Software (C2500-AINR-L), Version 11.2(11), RELEASE SOFTWARE (fc1)
Copyright  1986-1997 by Cisco Systems, Inc.
Compiled Mon 29-Dec-97 18:47 by ckralik

Albuquerque#debug ipx routing activity
IPX routing debugging is on
Albuquerque#
IPXRIP: positing full update to 1001.ffff.ffff.ffff via Ethernet0 (broadcast)
IPXRIP: src=1001.0000.0c35.ab12, dst=1001.ffff.ffff.ffff, packet sent
    network 1003, hops 2,  delay 8
    network 2023, hops 2,  delay 8
    network 1002, hops 2,  delay 8
    network 2013, hops 1,  delay 2
    network 2012, hops 1,  delay 2
IPXRIP: update from 2013.0200.3333.3333
    1002 in 2 hops, delay 13
    2023 in 1 hops, delay 7
    1003 in 1 hops, delay 7
```

Example 6-27 *Albuquerque Command Output, Scenario 6-4 (Continued)*

```
IPXRIP: positing full update to 2012.ffff.ffff.ffff via Serial0 (broadcast)
IPXRIP: src=2012.0200.1111.1111, dst=2012.ffff.ffff.ffff, packet sent
    network 1, hops 3,  delay 8
    network 2, hops 3,  delay 8
    network 1003, hops 2,  delay 13
    network 2013, hops 1,  delay 7
    network 1001, hops 1,  delay 7
IPXRIP: positing full update to 2013.ffff.ffff.ffff via Serial1 (broadcast)
IPXRIP: src=2013.0200.1111.1111, dst=2013.ffff.ffff.ffff, packet sent
    network 1, hops 3,  delay 8
    network 2, hops 3,  delay 8
    network 2023, hops 2,  delay 13
    network 1002, hops 2,  delay 13
    network 2012, hops 1,  delay 7
    network 1001, hops 1,  delay 7
IPXRIP: update from 2012.0200.2222.2222
    1003 in 2 hops, delay 13
    2023 in 1 hops, delay 7
    1002 in 1 hops, delay 7
```

Example 6-28 *Yosemite Command Output, Scenario 6-4*

```
Yosemite#show ipx route
Codes: C - Connected primary network,    c - Connected secondary network
       S - Static, F - Floating static, L - Local (internal), W - IPXWAN
       R - RIP, E - EIGRP, N - NLSP, X - External, A - Aggregate
       s - seconds, u - uses

8 Total IPX routes. Up to 1 parallel paths and 16 hops allowed.

No default route known.

C        1002 (SAP),          To0
C        2012 (HDLC),         Se0
C        2023 (HDLC),         Se1
R           1 [08/03] via     2012.0200.1111.1111,    32s, Se0
R           2 [08/03] via     2012.0200.1111.1111,    33s, Se0
R        1001 [07/01] via     2012.0200.1111.1111,    33s, Se0
R        1003 [07/01] via     2023.0200.3333.3333,    32s, Se1
R        2013 [07/01] via     2012.0200.1111.1111,    33s, Se0


Yosemite#show ipx traffic
System Traffic for 0.0000.0000.0001 System-Name: Yosemite
Rcvd:   169 total, 0 format errors, 0 checksum errors, 0 bad hop count,
        8 packets pitched, 161 local destination, 0 multicast
Bcast:  160 received, 242 sent
Sent:   243 generated, 0 forwarded
        0 encapsulation failed, 0 no route
```

continues

Example 6-28 *Yosemite Command Output, Scenario 6-4 (Continued)*

```
SAP:     2 SAP requests, 0 SAP replies, 2 servers
         0 SAP Nearest Name requests, 0 replies
         0 SAP General Name requests, 0 replies
         60 SAP advertisements received, 57 sent
         6 SAP flash updates sent, 0 SAP format errors
RIP:     1 RIP requests, 0 RIP replies, 9 routes
         98 RIP advertisements received, 120 sent
         45 RIP flash updates sent, 0 RIP format errors
Echo:    Rcvd 0 requests, 0 replies
         Sent 0 requests, 0 replies
         0 unknown: 0 no socket, 0 filtered, 0 no helper
         0 SAPs throttled, freed NDB len 0
Watchdog:
         0 packets received, 0 replies spoofed
Queue lengths:
         IPX input: 0, SAP 0, RIP 0, GNS 0
         SAP throttling length: 0/(no limit), 0 nets pending lost route reply
         Delayed process creation: 0
EIGRP:   Total received 0, sent 0
         Updates received 0, sent 0
         Queries received 0, sent 0
         Replies received 0, sent 0
         SAPs received 0, sent 0
NLSP:    Level-1 Hellos received 0, sent 0
         PTP Hello received 0, sent 0
         Level-1 LSPs received 0, sent 0
         LSP Retransmissions: 0
         LSP checksum errors received: 0
         LSP HT=0 checksum errors received: 0
         Level-1 CSNPs received 0, sent 0
         Level-1 PSNPs received 0, sent 0
         Level-1 DR Elections: 0
         Level-1 SPF Calculations: 0
         Level-1 Partial Route Calculations: 0

Yosemite#debug ipx routing activity
IPX routing debugging is on
Yosemite#
IPXRIP: positing full update to 1002.ffff.ffff.ffff via Ethernet0 (broadcast)
IPXRIP: src=1002.0000.0c24.7841, dst=1002.ffff.ffff.ffff, packet sent
    network 1, hops 4,   delay 9
    network 2, hops 4,   delay 9
    network 1003, hops 2,  delay 8
    network 1001, hops 2,  delay 8
    network 2013, hops 2,  delay 8
    network 2023, hops 1,  delay 2
    network 2012, hops 1,  delay 2
IPXRIP: positing full update to 2012.ffff.ffff.ffff via Serial0 (broadcast)
```

Example 6-28 *Yosemite Command Output, Scenario 6-4 (Continued)*

```
IPXRIP: src=2012.0200.2222.2222, dst=2012.ffff.ffff.ffff, packet sent
    network 1003, hops 2,  delay 13
    network 2023, hops 1,  delay 7
    network 1002, hops 1,  delay 7
IPXRIP: positing full update to 2023.ffff.ffff.ffff via Serial1 (broadcast)
IPXRIP: src=2023.0200.2222.2222, dst=2023.ffff.ffff.ffff, packet sent
    network 1, hops 4,  delay 14
    network 2, hops 4,  delay 14
    network 1001, hops 2,  delay 13
    network 2013, hops 2,  delay 13
    network 2012, hops 1,  delay 7
    network 1002, hops 1,  delay 7
IPXRIP: update from 2012.0200.1111.1111
    1 in 3 hops, delay 8
    2 in 3 hops, delay 8
    1003 in 2 hops, delay 13
    2013 in 1 hops, delay 7
    1001 in 1 hops, delay 7
IPXRIP: update from 2023.0200.3333.3333
    1 in 4 hops, delay 14
    2 in 4 hops, delay 14
    1001 in 2 hops, delay 13
IPXRIP: 2012 FFFFFFFF not added, entry in table is static/connected/internal
    2012 in 2 hops, delay 13
    2013 in 1 hops, delay 7
    1003 in 1 hops, delay 7
```

Example 6-29 *Seville Command Output, Scenario 6-4*

```
Seville#show ipx interface
Serial0 is up, line protocol is up
  IPX address is 2013.0200.3333.3333 [up]
  Delay of this IPX network, in ticks is 6 throughput 0 link delay 0
  IPXWAN processing not enabled on this interface.
  IPX SAP update interval is 1 minute(s)
  IPX type 20 propagation packet forwarding is disabled
  Incoming access list is not set
  Outgoing access list is not set
  IPX helper access list is not set
  SAP GNS processing enabled, delay 0 ms, output filter list is not set
  SAP Input filter list is not set
  SAP Output filter list is not set
  SAP Router filter list is not set
  Input filter list is not set
  Output filter list is not set
  Router filter list is not set
  Netbios Input host access list is not set
  Netbios Input bytes access list is not set
  Netbios Output host access list is not set
```

continues

Example 6-29 *Seville Command Output, Scenario 6-4 (Continued)*

```
   Netbios Output bytes access list is not set
   Updates each 60 seconds, aging multiples RIP: 3 SAP: 3
   SAP interpacket delay is 55 ms, maximum size is 480 bytes
   RIP interpacket delay is 55 ms, maximum size is 432 bytes
   Watchdog processing is disabled, SPX spoofing is disabled, idle time 60
   IPX accounting is disabled
   IPX fast switching is configured (enabled)
   RIP packets received 53, RIP packets sent 55
   SAP packets received 14, SAP packets sent 25
 Serial1 is up, line protocol is up
   IPX address is 2023.0200.3333.3333 [up]
   Delay of this IPX network, in ticks is 6 throughput 0 link delay 0
   IPXWAN processing not enabled on this interface.
 IPX SAP update interval is 1 minute(s)
   IPX type 20 propagation packet forwarding is disabled
   Incoming access list is not set
   Outgoing access list is not set
   IPX helper access list is not set
   SAP GNS processing enabled, delay 0 ms, output filter list is not set
   SAP Input filter list is not set
   SAP Output filter list is not set
   SAP Router filter list is not set
   Input filter list is not set
   Output filter list is not set
   Router filter list is not set
   Netbios Input host access list is not set
   Netbios Input bytes access list is not set
   Netbios Output host access list is not set
   Netbios Output bytes access list is not set
   Updates each 60 seconds, aging multiples RIP: 3 SAP: 3
   SAP interpacket delay is 55 ms, maximum size is 480 bytes
   RIP interpacket delay is 55 ms, maximum size is 432 bytes
   Watchdog processing is disabled, SPX spoofing is disabled, idle time 60
   IPX accounting is disabled
   IPX fast switching is configured (enabled)
   RIP packets received 53, RIP packets sent 62
   SAP packets received 13, SAP packets sent 37
 Ethernet0 is up, line protocol is up
   IPX address is 1003. 0000.0cac.ab41, SAP [up]
   Delay of this IPX network, in ticks is 1 throughput 0 link delay 0
   IPXWAN processing not enabled on this interface.
   IPX SAP update interval is 1 minute(s)
   IPX type 20 propagation packet forwarding is disabled
   Incoming access list is not set
   Outgoing access list is not set
   IPX helper access list is not set
   SAP GNS processing enabled, delay 0 ms, output filter list is not set
   SAP Input filter list is not set
   SAP Output filter list is not set
   SAP Router filter list is not set
   Input filter list is not set
```

Example 6-29 *Seville Command Output, Scenario 6-4 (Continued)*

```
  Output filter list is not set
  Router filter list is not set
  Netbios Input host access list is not set
  Netbios Input bytes access list is not set
  Netbios Output host access list is not set
  Netbios Output bytes access list is not set
  Updates each 60 seconds, aging multiples RIP: 3 SAP: 3
  SAP interpacket delay is 55 ms, maximum size is 480 bytes
  RIP interpacket delay is 55 ms, maximum size is 432 bytes
  IPX accounting is disabled
  IPX fast switching is configured (enabled)
  RIP packets received 20, RIP packets sent 62
  SAP packets received 18, SAP packets sent 15

Seville#show ipx servers
Codes: S - Static, P - Periodic, E - EIGRP, N - NLSP, H - Holddown, + = detail
2 Total IPX Servers

Table ordering is based on routing and server info

    Type Name                     Net     Address     Port    Route Hops Itf
P    4 Bugs                    1.0000.0000.0001:0451   8/03    3  Se0
P    4 Daffy                   2.0000.0000.0001:0451   8/03    3  Se0



Seville#debug ipx sap activity
IPX service debugging is on
Seville#
IPXSAP: Response (in) type 0x2 len 160 src:2023.0200.2222.2222
dest:2023.ffff.ffff.ffff(452)
 type 0x4, "Daffy", 2.0000.0000.0001(451), 4 hops
 type 0x4, "Bugs", 1.0000.0000.0001(451), 4 hops
IPXSAP: positing update to 1003.ffff.ffff.ffff via Ethernet0 (broadcast) (full)
IPXSAP: Update type 0x2 len 160 src:1003.0000.0cac.ab41
dest:1003.ffff.ffff.ffff(452)
 type 0x4, "Daffy", 2.0000.0000.0001(451), 4 hops
 type 0x4, "Bugs", 1.0000.0000.0001(451), 4 hops
IPXSAP: positing update to 2013.ffff.ffff.ffff via Serial0 (broadcast) (full)
IPXSAP: suppressing null update to 2013.ffff.ffff.ffff
IPXSAP: positing update to 2023.ffff.ffff.ffff via Serial1 (broadcast) (full)
IPXSAP: Update type 0x2 len 160 src:2023.0200.3333.3333
dest:2023.ffff.ffff.ffff(452)
 type 0x4, "Daffy", 2.0000.0000.0001(451), 4 hops
 type 0x4, "Bugs", 1.0000.0000.0001(451), 4 hops
IPXSAP: Response (in) type 0x2 len 160 src:2013.0200.1111.1111
dest:2013.ffff.ffff.ffff(452)
 type 0x4, "Bugs", 1.0000.0000.0001(451), 3 hops
 type 0x4, "Daffy", 2.0000.0000.0001(451), 3 hops
```

Given the network in Figure 6-26 and the command output in Example 6-27, Example 6-28, and Example 6-29 for Scenario 6-4, complete or answer the following:

1 Complete Table 6-33 with all IPX network numbers. List the command(s) you use to find these network numbers. List all commands that helped you find the network numbers.

Table 6-33   *IPX Networks in Scenario 6-4*

IPX Network	Location (for example, "Between Albuquerque and Seville")	Command Used to Find This Information

2 Complete Table 6-34 with the IPX addresses of the three routers.

Table 6-34   *IPX Addresses on Routers in Scenario 6-4*

Router	Interface	IPX Network	IPX Node
Albuquerque	E0		
	S0		
	S1		
Yosemite	E0		
	S0		
	S1		
Seville	E0		
	S0		
	S1		

3 Describe the contents of the RIP update from Yosemite sent out its serial 0 interface. Include the numbers of routes and metrics.

4 Examine the **show ipx servers** command from Seville. How many file servers appear to be in the SAP table? What socket is Bugs using? Assuming defaults for ticks on each router, is it possible that more than one serial link exists between Seville and Daffy?

Scenario Answers

Answers to Scenario 6-1: IP Configuration 1

Refer back to the network illustrated in Figure 6-23 and Table 6-30 to establish the Scenario 6-1 design details and the context of the answers to the five tasks for this scenario.

Answers to Task 1 for Scenario 6-1

Task 1 for Scenario 6-1 asks for completed configurations, which are shown in Example 6-30, Example 6-31, and Example 6-32. You could have chosen different IP addresses, but your choices must have had the same first three octets as those shown in Example 6-30.

Example 6-30 *Albuquerque Configuration for Scenario 6-1*

```
hostname Albuquerque
!
enable secret 5 $1$ZvR/$Gpk5a5K5vTVpotd3KUygA1
!
interface Serial0
 ip address 148.14.4.1 255.255.255.0
!
interface Serial1
 ip address 148.14.5.1 255.255.255.0
!
Ethernet0
 ip address 148.14.1.1 255.255.255.0
```

Example 6-31 *Yosemite Configuration for Scenario 6-1*

```
hostname Yosemite
enable secret 5 $1$ZvR/$Gpk5a5K5vTVpotd3KUygA1
!
interface Serial0
 ip address 148.14.4.2 255.255.255.0
!
interface Serial1
 ip address 148.14.6.2 255.255.255.0
!
Ethernet0
 ip address 148.14.2.2 255.255.255.0
```

Example 6-32 *Seville Configuration for Scenario 6-1*

```
hostname Seville
enable secret 5 $1$ZvR/$Gpk5a5K5vTVpotd3KUygA1
!
interface Serial0
 ip address 148.14.5.3 255.255.255.0
```

Example 6-32 *Seville Configuration for Scenario 6-1 (Continued)*

```
!
interface Serial1
 ip address 148.14.6.3 255.255.255.0
!
Ethernet0
 ip address 148.14.3.3 255.255.255.0
```

Answers to Task 2 for Scenario 6-1

Task 2 for Scenario 6-1 asks for a description of the IP routing table on Seville, which is shown in Table 6-35. This table exists before static and dynamic routes are added.

Table 6-35 *Routing Table in Seville*

Group	Outgoing Interface	Next Router
148.14.3.0	e0	
148.14.5.0	s0	
148.14.6.0	s1	

The next-hop router field is always the IP address of another router, or it is null if the route describes a directly connected network.

Answers to Task 3 for Scenario 6-1

Task 3 for Scenario 6-1 asks for static route configuration. The routes to allow users on LANs to reach each other are shown in upcoming examples. However, routes to the subnets on serial links are not shown in these examples for brevity's sake; the users should not need to send packets to IP addresses on the serial links' subnets, but rather to other hosts on the LANs. Example 6-33, Example 6-34, and Example 6-35 show the configurations on the three routers.

Example 6-33 *Albuquerque Configuration, Scenario 6-1*

```
ip route 148.14.2.0 255.255.255.0 148.14.4.2
ip route 148.14.3.0 255.255.255.0 serial1
```

Example 6-34 *Yosemite Configuration, Scenario 6-1*

```
ip route 148.14.1.0 255.255.255.0 148.14.4.1
ip route 148.14.3.0 255.255.255.0 serial1
```

Example 6-35 *Seville Configuration, Scenario 6-1*

```
ip route 148.14.1.0 255.255.255.0 148.14.5.1
ip route 148.14.2.0 255.255.255.0 serial1
```

Both valid styles of static route configuration are shown. In any topological case, the style of static route command using the next router's IP address is valid. If the route points to a subnet that is on the other side of a point-to-point serial link, the static route command can simply refer to the outgoing serial interface.

Answers to Task 4 for Scenario 6-1

Task 4 for Scenario 6-1 asks for IGRP configuration. The same configuration is used on each router and is listed in Example 6-36. The IGRP process-id must be the same number on each router; if an IGRP update is received but lists a different process-id, the update will be ignored.

Example 6-36 *IGRP Configuration, Scenario 6-1*

```
router igrp 1
network 148.14.0.0
```

Answers to Task 5 for Scenario 6-1

Task 5 for Scenario 6-1 asks for the broadcast addresses for each subnet. These are shown in Table 6-36.

Table 6-36 *Scenario 6-1 IP Addresses*

Location of Subnet Geographically	Subnet Mask	Subnet Number	Subnet Broadcast
Ethernet off router in Albuquerque	255.255.255.0	148.14.1.0	148.14.1.255
Ethernet off router in Yosemite	255.255.255.0	148.14.2.0	148.14.2.255
Ethernet off router in Seville	255.255.255.0	148.14.3.0	148.14.3.255
Serial between Albuquerque and Yosemite	255.255.255.0	148.14.4.0	148.14.4.255
Serial between Albuquerque and Seville	255.255.255.0	148.14.5.0	148.14.5.255
Serial between Seville and Yosemite	255.255.255.0	148.14.6.0	148.14.6.255

Answers to Scenario 6-2: IP Configuration 2

Refer back to the network illustrated in Figure 6-24 and Table 6-31 to establish the Scenario 6-2 design details and the context of the answers to the four tasks for this scenario.

Answers to Task 1 for Scenario 6-2

Task 1 for Scenario 6-2 asks for completed configurations, which are shown in Example 6-37, Example 6-38, Example 6-39, and Example 6-40.

Example 6-37 *Atlanta Configuration, Scenario 6-2*

```
Hostname Atlanta
no ip domain-lookup
!
interface serial0
encapsulation frame-relay
interface serial 0.1
ip address 10.2.1.1 255.255.255.0
frame-relay interface-dlci 41
!
interface serial 0.2
ip address 10.2.2.1 255.255.255.0
frame-relay interface-dlci 42
!
interface serial 0.3
ip address 10.2.3.1 255.255.255.0
frame-relay interface-dlci 43
!
interface ethernet 0
ip address 10.1.1.1 255.255.255.0
```

Example 6-38 *Charlotte Configuration, Scenario 6-2*

```
Hostname Charlotte
no ip domain-lookup
!
interface serial0
encapsulation frame-relay
interface serial 0.1
ip address 10.2.1.2 255.255.255.0
frame-relay interface-dlci 40
!
interface ethernet 0
ip address 10.1.2.2 255.255.255.0
```

Example 6-39 *Nashville Configuration, Scenario 6-2*

```
hostname nashville
no ip domain-lookup
!
interface serial0
encapsulation frame-relay
interface serial 0.1
ip address 10.2.2.3 255.255.255.0
frame-relay interface-dlci 40
!
interface ethernet 0
ip address 10.1.3.3 255.255.255.0
```

Example 6-40 *Boston Configuration, Scenario 6-2*

```
hostname boston
no ip domain-lookup
!
interface serial0
encapsulation frame-relay
interface serial 0.1
ip address 10.2.3.4 255.255.255.0
frame-relay interface-dlci 40
!
interface ethernet 0
ip address 10.1.4.4 255.255.255.0
```

Answers to Task 2 for Scenario 6-2

Task 2 for Scenario 6-2 asks for RIP configuration. The same configuration is used on each router and is listed in Example 6-41.

Example 6-41 *RIP Configuration, Scenario 6-2*

```
router rip
network 10.0.0.0
```

Answers to Task 3 for Scenario 6-2

Task 3 for Scenario 6-2 asks for the broadcast addresses for each subnet. These are shown in Table 6-37.

Table 6-37 *Scenario 6-2 IP Addresses*

Location of Subnet Geographically	Subnet Mask	Subnet Number	Subnet Broadcast
Ethernet off router in Atlanta	255.255.255.0	10.1.1.0	10.1.1.255
Ethernet off router in Charlotte	255.255.255.0	10.1.2.0	10.1.2.255
Ethernet off router in Nashville	255.255.255.0	10.1.3.0	10.1.3.255
Ethernet off router in Boston	255.255.255.0	10.1.4.0	10.1.4.255
VC between Atlanta and Charlotte	255.255.255.0	10.2.1.0	10.2.1.255
VC between Atlanta and Nashville	255.255.255.0	10.2.2.0	10.2.2.255
VC between Atlanta and Boston	255.255.255.0	10.2.3.0	10.2.3.255

Answers to Task 4 for Scenario 6-2

Task 4 for Scenario 6-2 requires consideration of the effects of split horizon. Split horizon logic considers subinterfaces to be separate interfaces, in spite of the fact that several subinterfaces share the same physical interface. Boston advertises about 10.1.4.0 in its RIP update only out its subinterface 1. All other routes in Boston's routing table were learned through RIP updates from Atlanta, via updates entering that same subinterface; therefore, Boston will not advertise about those routes in updates it sends on that same subinterface.

The RIP updates from Atlanta to Charlotte, out Atlanta's subinterface 1, advertise about all subnets not learned from RIP updates entering that same subinterface. All subnets except 10.1.2.0 (learned from Charlotte) and 10.2.1.0 (subinterface 1's subnet) will be listed in Atlanta's RIP update to Charlotte. Subnet 10.1.4.0, learned from Boston, will indeed be included in updates to Charlotte; split horizon considers subinterfaces as separate interfaces.

Answers to Scenario 6-3: IP Addressing and Subnet Derivation

Refer back to the network illustrated in Figure 6-25 and Example 6-24, Example 6-25, and Example 6-26 to establish the Scenario 6-3 design details and the context of the answers to the three tasks for this scenario.

Answers to Task 1 for Scenario 6-3

Task 1 for Scenario 6-3 asks you to complete a table with the subnet numbers and broadcast addresses used in this scenario's network after examining the **show** commands on the various routers in Example 6-24, Example 6-25, and Example 6-26. Table 6-38 lists the subnet numbers and broadcast addresses requested in this task.

Table 6-38   *Subnets and Broadcast Addresses*

Location of Subnet Geographically	Subnet Mask	Subnet Number	Subnet Broadcast
Ethernet off router in Mayberry	255.255.255.0	170.1.101.0	170.1.101.255
Ethernet off router in Mount Pilot	255.255.255.0	170.1.102.0	170.1.102.255
Ethernet off router in Raleigh	255.255.255.0	170.1.103.0	170.1.103.255
VC between Mayberry and Mount Pilot	255.255.255.0	170.1.1.0	170.1.1.255

continues

Table 6-38   *Subnets and Broadcast Addresses (Continued)*

Location of Subnet Geographically	Subnet Mask	Subnet Number	Subnet Broadcast
VC between Mayberry and Raleigh	255.255.255.0	170.1.1.0	170.1.1.255
VC between Mount Pilot and Raleigh	255.255.255.0	170.1.1.0	170.1.1.255

Notice that the same subnet was used for all three virtual circuits; a full mesh of virtual circuits was used and a single subnet was chosen rather than one subnet per virtual circuit.

Answers to Task 2 for Scenario 6-3

Task 2 for Scenario 6-3 asks you to describe the contents of the IGRP update from Raleigh, sent out its virtual circuit to Mount Pilot. Notice that there are four routes in the routing table and four routes in the routing update. Split horizon is disabled on serial interfaces using Frame Relay as configured without subinterfaces. Split horizon is disabled by the IOS if using Frame Relay multipoint subinterfaces as well. Therefore, all four routes in the IP routing table are advertised in routing updates sent out Serial0.

Answers to Task 3 for Scenario 6-3

Mayberry still will have a route to 170.1.1.0/24, which is the subnet covering all the Frame Relay interfaces in this scenario. Because only one VC went down and the other VC is still up, it is reasonable to expect that the physical interface is still up. No subinterfaces are configured in this scenario, so Mayberry still will have a connected route for each interface that's currently up, including 170.1.1.0/24 on serial 0.

Answers to Scenario 6-4: IPX Examination

Refer back to the network illustrated in Figure 6-26 and the command output in Example 6-27, Example 6-28, and Example 6-29 to establish the Scenario 6-4 design details and the context of the answers to the four tasks for this scenario.

Answers to Task 1 for Scenario 6-4

Task 1 for Scenario 6-4 asks you to complete a table with all IPX network numbers filled in. In addition, this task asks you to list the command(s) you use to find these network numbers. Table 6-39 provides the IPX network numbers for this scenario. In my opinion, the **show ipx**

interface brief command and **show ipx route** commands are the best methods for learning these network numbers.

Table 6-39   *IPX Networks for Scenario 6-4*

IPX Network	Location (For Example, "Between Albuquerque and Seville")	Command Used to Find This Information
1001	Albuquerque Ethernet0	**show ipx interface brief** on Albuquerque
		debug ipx routing activity on Albuquerque
1002	Yosemite Ethernet0	**show ipx route** on Yosemite
		debug ipx routing activity on Yosemite
1003	Seville Ethernet0	**debug ipx sap** on Seville
		show ipx interface on Seville
2012	Albuquerque-Yosemite	**show ipx interface brief** on Albuquerque
		show cdp neighbor detail on Albuquerque
		debug ipx routing activity on Albuquerque
		show ipx route on Yosemite
		debug ipx routing activity on Yosemite
2013	Albuquerque-Seville	**show cdp neighbor detail** on Albuquerque
		show ipx interface brief on Albuquerque
		debug ipx routing activity on Albuquerque
		show ipx interface on Seville
		debug ipx sap activity on Seville
2023	Yosemite-Seville	**show ipx route** on Yosemite
		debug ipx routing activity on Yosemite
		show ipx interface on Seville

continues

Table 6-39   *IPX Networks for Scenario 6-4 (Continued)*

IPX Network	Location (For Example, "Between Albuquerque and Seville")	Command Used to Find This Information
1	Bugs' internal network	**show ipx servers** on Seville
		show ipx route on Yosemite
2	Daffy's internal network	**show ipx servers** on Seville
		show ipx route on Yosemite

Answers to Task 2 for Scenario 6-4

Task 2 for Scenario 6-4 asks you to complete a table with the IPX addresses of the three routers. The network numbers are obtained from several sources, as seen in Task 1. The additional requirement in Task 2 is to find the node part of the IPX addresses on each interface. The easy way to learn this information is through the **show ipx interface** command. Of course, only one such command was provided in Example 6-27, Example 6-28, and Example 6-29. The output of the RIP and SAP debugs show the source IPX addresses of the updates sent by each router, which supplies the rest of the answers to the question. Table 6-40 provides the completed answers for this task.

Table 6-40   *IPX Addresses on Routers in Scenario 6-4*

Router	Interface	IPX Network	IPX Node
Albuquerque	E0	1001	0000.0c35.ab12
	S0	2012	0200.1111.1111
	S1	2013	0200.1111.1111
Yosemite	E0	1002	0000.0c24.7841
	S0	2012	0200.2222.2222
	S1	2023	0200.2222.2222
Seville	E0	1003	0000.0cac.ab41
	S0	2013	0200.3333.3333
	S1	2023	0200.3333.3333

Answers to Task 3 for Scenario 6-4

Task 3 for Scenario 6-4 asks you to describe the contents of the RIP update from Yosemite sent out its serial 0 interface, including the numbers of routes and metrics. First, just finding the appropriate **debug** messages takes some effort. The needed routing debug message in Example 6-15 begins with the phrase "positing full update to 2012.ffff.ffff.ffff . . . ." Remembering that Yosemite's S0 interface uses IPX network 2012 is a key to knowing to look for that message.

Three networks are advertised: 1003, 2023, and 1002. The hop count and delay are shown in each successive line of **debug** output. More important is what is missing: Networks 1, 2, 1001, and 2013 are left out of the update due to split horizon rules.

Answers to Task 4 for Scenario 6-4

Task 4 for Scenario 6-4 asks you to examine the **show ipx servers** command from Seville. Furthermore, this task asks you to determine how many file servers appear to be in the SAP table, what socket Bugs is using, and, assuming defaults for ticks on each router, whether it is possible that more than one serial link exists in the route between Seville and Daffy. Two file servers are listed in the SAP table: Bugs and Daffy. Both are using socket 451, as shown under the word *port* in the SAP table. (The value is still called a socket; the heading is poorly labeled in the **show ipx servers** command.) Daffy appears to be eight ticks away, and because a serial link defaults to having six ticks, there could only be one serial link between Seville and Daffy.

This chapter covers the following topics that you will need to master as a CCNA:

- **Filtering IP traffic**   This section covers the concepts and configuration needed to filter IP traffic. Both standard and extended access-lists, as well as numbered and named access-lists, are included.

- **Filtering IPX traffic and SAPs**   IPX filtering can be used to filter packets as well as SAP updates. This section covers configuration of both and concentrates on the advantages gained by using SAP filtering.

CHAPTER 7

Understanding Access List Security

When deciding on the name of this chapter, the first title chosen was "Understanding Network Security." Then I thought to myself (that's what you do when you spend weeks on end in your home office writing), "You could easily write a whole book just on this topic!" So, I changed the title to better reflect the scope of this topic in this book, which of course reflects Cisco's expectations of CCNA candidates.

(By the way, someone already wrote the book I imagined—it's called *Designing Network Security*, by Merike Kaeo, ISBN: 1-57870-043-4.)

Cisco expects CCNAs to understand security from the perspective of filtering traffic using access-lists. Cisco also expects CCNAs to master the ideas and configuration behind the Telnet, auxiliary, console, and enable passwords as well; these topics are covered in Chapter 2, "Cisco Internetwork Operating System (IOS) Fundamentals."

The reason that access lists are so important to CCNA candidates is that practically every network uses them; to do more than basic filtering, access lists can be very tricky. In fact, back in 1993, when I was getting certified to teach Cisco classes, the Cisco Worldwide Training folks said that the TAC's most frequent question topic area was how to configure access lists. Access lists are likely to remain a core-competency issue for router support personnel for a long time. Also, several other IOS features call on access list logic to perform packet-matching features.

When studying about access lists in this book or others, keep in mind that there are usually many ways to configure an access list to achieve the same result. Focus on the syntax of the commands and the nuances of the logic. If a particular example (given a set of criteria) is configured differently than you would have configured it, do not be concerned. In this book, I have attempted to point out in the text when a particular list could have been written a different way.

How to Best Use This Chapter

By taking the following steps, you can make better use of your study time:

- Keep your notes and the answers for all your work with this book in one place, for easy reference.

- Take the "Do I Know This Already?" quiz, and write down your answers. Studies show that retention is significantly increased through writing down facts and concepts, even if you never look at the information again.

- Use the diagram in Figure 7-1 to guide you to the next step.

Figure 7-1   *How to Use This Chapter*

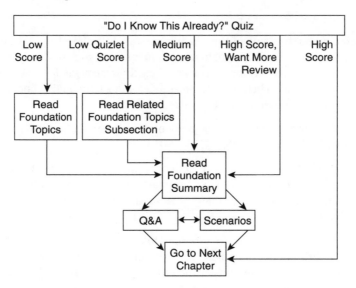

"Do I Know This Already?" Quiz

The purpose of the "Do I Know This Already?" quiz is to help you decide what parts of this chapter to use. If you already intend to read the entire chapter, you do not necessarily need to answer these questions now.

This 12-question quiz helps you determine how to spend your limited study time. The quiz is sectioned into two smaller six-question "quizlets," which correspond to the three major topic headings in the chapter. Figure 7-1 outlines suggestions on how to spend your time in this chapter based on your quiz score. Use Table 7-1 to record your scores.

Table 7-1   *Scoresheet for Quiz and Quizlets*

Quizlet Number	Foundation Topics Section Covering These Questions	Questions	Score
1	Filtering IP Traffic	1 to 6	
2	Filtering IPX Traffic and SAPs	7 to 12	
All questions		1 to 12	

1 Configure a numbered IP access list that would stop packets from subnet 134.141.7.0, 255.255.255.0, from exiting serial 0 on some router. Allow all other packets.

_____

_____

_____

2 How would a user who does not have the enable password find out what access lists have been configured and where they are enabled?

_____

_____

_____

3 How many IP extended **access-list** commands are required to check a particular port number on all IP packets?

_____

_____

_____

4 True or false: If all IP or IPX access list statements in a particular list define the deny action, then the default action is to permit all other packets.

_____

_____

_____

5 How many IP access lists of either type can be active on an interface at the same time?

_____

_____

_____

6 In a standard named IP access list with three statements, a **no** version of the first statement is issued in configuration mode. Immediately following, another access list configuration command is added for the same access list. How many statements are in the list now, and in what position is the newly added statement?

_____

_____

_____

7 In an IPX access list with five statements, a **no** version of the third statement is issued in configuration mode. Immediately following, another access list configuration command is added for the same access list. How many statements are in the list now, and in what position is the newly added statement?

_____

_____

_____

8 Name all the items that a SAP access list can examine to make a match.

_____

_____

_____

9 Name all the items that a standard IPX access list can examine to make a match.

_____

_____

_____

10 Name all the items that a named extended IPX access list can examine to make a match.

_____

_____

_____

11 Configure a SAP numbered access list so that SAPs 4-7 are matched, in network BEEF, with a single command.

_____

_____

_____

12 What command could someone who has only the Telnet password, not the enable password, use to find out what IPX access lists are enabled on which interfaces?

_____

_____

_____

The answers to the "Do I Know This Already?" quiz are found in Appendix A, "Answers to the 'Do I Know This Already?' Quizzes and Q&A Sections," on page 754. The suggested choices for your next step are as follows:

- **6 or less overall score**—Read the entire chapter. This includes the "Foundation Topics" and "Foundation Summary" sections, the Q&A section, and the scenarios at the end of the chapter.

- **3 or less on any quizlet**—Review the subsection(s) of the "Foundation Topics" part of this chapter, based on Table 7-1. Then move into the "Foundation Summary" section, the Q&A section, and the scenarios at the end of the chapter.

- **7, 8, or 9 overall score**—Begin with the "Foundation Summary" section, and then go to the Q&A and the scenarios at the end of the chapter.

- **10 or more overall score**—If you want more review on these topics, skip to the "Foundation Summary" section and then go to the Q&A section and the scenarios at the end of the chapter. Otherwise, move to the next chapter.

Foundation Topics

Filtering IP Traffic

IP access lists perform a variety of functions in a Cisco router. The CCNA exam requires that you know only how to use access lists for filtering; however, access lists can be used to filter routing updates, to match packets for prioritization, and to filter packets. Filtering often is used to make a network more secure, hence the name of this chapter. Table 7-2 and Table 7-3 list the more popular configuration commands and EXEC commands about access lists.

Table 7-2   *IP Access List Configuration Commands*

Command	Configuration Mode and Purpose
access-list {**1-99**} {**permit** | **deny**} *source-addr* [*source-mask*]	Global command for standard numbered access lists
access-list {**100-199**} {**permit** | **deny**} *protocol source-addr* [*source-mask*] [*operator operand*] *destination-addr* [*destination-mask*] [*operator operand*] [**established**]	Global command for extended numbered access lists
ip access-group {*number* | *name* [**in** | **out**] }	Interface subcommand to enable access lists
ip access-list {**standard** | **extended** } *name*	Global command for standard and extended named access lists
deny {*source* [*source-wildcard*] | **any**}[**log**]	Standard named access list subcommand
{**permit** | **deny**} *protocol source-addr* [*source-mask*] [*operator operand*] *destination-addr* [*destination-mask*] [*operator operand*] [**established**]	Extended named access list subcommand
access-class *number* | *name* [**in** | **out**]	Line subcommand for standard or extended access lists

Table 7-3   *IP Access List EXEC Commands*

Command	Function
show ip interface	Includes reference to the access lists enabled on the interface
show access-list	Shows details of configured access lists for all protocols
show ip access-list [*number*]	Shows IP access lists

The logic used for access lists can best be summarized by Figure 7-2.

Figure 7-2   *Locations Where Access List Logic Can Be Applied*

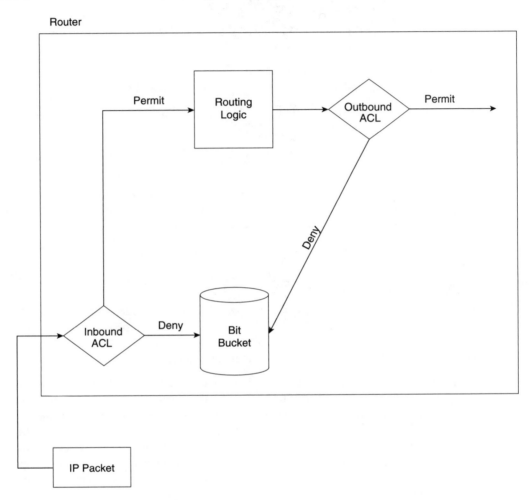

Features of the process described in Figure 7-2 are as follows:

- Packets can be filtered as they enter an interface, before the routing decision.
- Packets can be filtered before they exit an interface, after the routing decision.
- "Deny" is the term used in the IOS to imply that the packet will be filtered.
- "Permit" is the term used in the IOS to imply that the packet will not be filtered.
- The filtering logic is configured in the access list.
- At the end of every access list is an implied "deny all traffic" statement. Therefore, if a packet does not match any of your access list statements, the packet will be blocked.

The two diamond-shaped symbols in Figure 7-2 represent the application of the logic of an access-list. That logic can be summarized as follows:

Step 1   The matching parameters of the first access list statement are compared to the packet.

Step 2   If a match is made, the action defined in this access list statement (permit or deny) is performed, as shown in Figure 7-2.

Step 3   If a match is not made in Step 2, then Steps 1 and 2 are repeated using the next sequential access list statement.

Step 4   If no match is made with an entry in the access list, the deny action is performed.

The logic for access lists is true whether using standard or extended access lists; the only difference between the two types is in what constitutes a match. The following sections on standard IP access lists, extended IP access lists, and named IP access lists outline these differences.

Standard IP Access Lists

Standard access lists can match only by examining the source IP address field in the packet's IP header. Any bit positions in the 32-bit source IP address can be compared to the access list statements; for example, a subnet number can be checked. However, the matching is flexible and does not consider the subnet mask in use; it is just a math problem!

A wildcard mask defines the subset of the 32 bits in the IP address that must be matched. As a CCNA, you will be required to fully understand the use of the wildcard mask to match a subset of an IP address. Matching is performed by comparing an **access-list** command *address* parameter and the packet's source IP address. Mask bits of value binary 0 imply that the same bit positions must be compared in the two IP addresses. Mask bits of value binary 1 are wildcards; the corresponding bit positions in the addresses are considered to match, regardless of values. In other words, binary 1s mean that these bit positions already match—hence the name *wildcard*.

Table 7-4 shows several examples of masks, packet source addresses, and addresses in **access-list** commands.

Table 7-4   *Example Access List Wildcard Masks*

Access List Mask	Source IP Address in Packet	Binary Version of Source IP Addresses	IP Address in access-list Command	Binary Version of IP Address in access-list Command	Explanation
0.0.0.0	1.55.88.111	0000 0001 0011 0111 0101 1000 0110 1111	1.55.88.4	0000 0001 0011 0111 0101 1000 0000 0100	All bits must match, and they do not.
0.0.0.255	1.55.88.111	0000 0001 0011 0111 0101 1000 0110 1111	1.55.88.0	0000 0001 0011 0111 0101 1000 0000 0000	The first 24 bits must match, and they do.
0.0.255.255	1.55.56.7	0000 0001 0011 0111 0011 1000 0000 0111	1.55.0.0	0000 0001 0011 0111 0000 0000 0000 0000	The first 16 bits must match, and they do.
255.255.255.255	5.88.22.5	0000 0101 0101 1000 0001 0110 0000 0101	0.0.0.0	0000 0000 0000 0000 0000 0000 0000 0000	All bits match, regardless of the IP address in the packet.
32.48.0.255	33.1.1.1	0010 0001 0000 0001 0000 0001 0000 0001	1.1.1.0	0000 0001 0000 0001 0000 0001 0000 0000	All bits except the 3rd, 11th, 12th, and last 8 must match. The two numbers match in this case. (This is a rather impractical choice of wildcard mask and is used only to make the point that it is flexible!)

The following example, illustrated by Figure 7-3, Example 7-1, and Example 7-2, shows a basic use of standard IP access lists, with two typical oversights in the first attempt at a complete answer. The criteria for the access list(s) is as follows:

- Sam is not allowed access to Bugs or Daffy.

- Hosts on the Seville Ethernet are not allowed access to hosts on the Yosemite Ethernet.

- All other combinations are allowed.

Figure 7-3   *Network Diagram for Standard Access List Example*

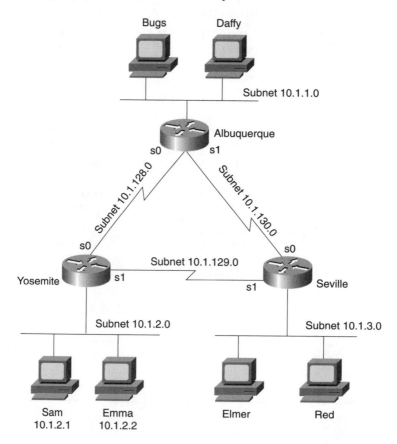

Example 7-1   *Yosemite Configuration for Standard Access List Example*

```
interface serial 0
ip access-group 3
!
access-list 3 deny host 10.1.2.1
access-list 3 permit any
```

Example 7-2   *Seville Configuration for Standard Access List Example*

```
interface serial 1
ip access-group 4
!
access-list 4 deny 10.1.3.0    0.0.0.255
access-list 4 permit any
```

At first glance, these two access lists seem to perform the desired function. In Yosemite, the packets from Sam are filtered before leaving s0; likewise, in Seville, packets from 10.1.3.0/24 are filtered before leaving s1 toward Yosemite. However, if either link into Albuquerque fails, the new route would leave an opening. For example, if the link from Albuquerque to Yosemite fails, Yosemite would learn a route to 10.1.1.0/24 through Seville. Packets from Sam destined for hosts in Albuquerque would leave Yosemite's s1 without being filtered.

An alternative answer to the stated problem is illustrated in Example 7-3. The access list has been removed from Seville, and all filtering is performed on Yosemite.

Example 7-3   *Yosemite Configuration for Standard Access List Example—Alternate Solution Compared to Example 7-1*

```
interface serial 0
ip access-group 3
!
interface serial 1
ip access-group 3
!
interface ethernet 0
ip access-group 4
!
access-list 3 deny host 10.1.2.1
access-list 3 permit any
!
access-list 4 deny 10.1.3.0    0.0.0.255
access-list 4 permit any
```

Example 7-3 denies all traffic that should be denied based on the criteria; however, it denies more traffic than the first of the three criteria says it should! In many cases, the meaning of the criteria for the access lists greatly affects your configuration choices. For example, Example 7-3 solved some of the problems of Example 7-2 by filtering packets from 10.1.2.1 (Sam) and preventing them from exiting both of Yosemite's serial interfaces, keeping Sam from getting to Albuquerque. However, that also prevents Sam from communicating with anyone outside Yosemite. An alternative would be to use the same **access-list 3** logic, but use it as an inbound access-list on Albuquerque's serial interfaces.

As shown in Example 7-3, **access-list 4** does an effective job of meeting the second of the three criteria, however. Because the goal was to stop Seville hosts from communicating with Yosemite's hosts, and because the only LAN hosts off Yosemite are the ones on the local Ethernet, the access list is effective in stopping packets from exiting Ethernet 0.

Extended IP Access Lists

Extended IP access lists are almost identical to standard IP access lists in their use. The key difference between the two types is the variety of fields in the packet that can be compared for matching by extended access lists. To pass the CCNA exam, you must remember all the items that an extended IP access list can check to make a match. As with standard lists, extended access lists are enabled for packets entering or exiting an interface. The list is searched sequentially; the first statement matched stops the search through the list and defines the action to be taken. All these features are true of standard access lists as well. The matching logic, however, is different than that used with standard access lists and makes extended access lists much more complex.

Figure 7-4 shows several of the fields in the packet headers that can be matched. The top set of headers shows the IP protocol type, which identifies what header follows the IP header. The source and destination IP addresses are also shown. In the second set of headers in the figure, an example with a TCP header following the IP header is shown. The TCP source and destination port numbers are listed in the abbreviated TCP header shown in the figure. Table 7-5 provides the complete list of items that can be matched with an IP extended access list.

Figure 7-4   *Extended Access List Matching Options*

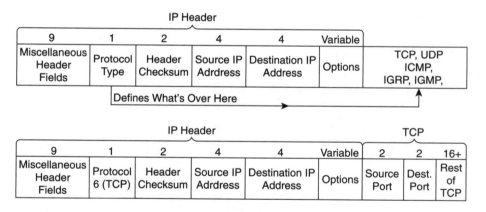

Table 7-5   *IP Standard and Extended Access Lists—Matching*

Type of Access List	What Can Be Matched
IP Standard	Source IP address
	Portions of the source IP address, using a wildcard mask

Table 7-5   *IP Standard and Extended Access Lists—Matching (Continued)*

Type of Access List	What Can Be Matched
IP Extended	Source IP address
	Portions of the source IP address, using a wildcard mask
	Destination IP address
	Portions of the destination IP address, using a wildcard mask
	Protocol type (TCP, UDP, ICMP, IGRP, IGMP, and others)
	Source port
	Destination port
	Established—matches all TCP flows except first flow
	IP TOS
	IP precedence

A statement is considered to match if all options in the statement match. If one option does not match, the statement is skipped, and the next entry in the list is examined. Table 7-6 provides several example access list statements.

Table 7-6   *Sample **access-list** Commands and Logic Explanations*

Access List Statement	Explanation of What Matches
access-list 101 deny tcp any host 10.1.1.1 eq 23	Packet with any source address; destination must be 10.1.1.1, with a TCP header, with destination port 23.
access-list 101 deny tcp any host 10.1.1.1 eq telnet	Same function as last example; **telnet** keyword is used instead of port 23.
access-list 101 deny udp 1.0.0.0 0.255.255.255 lt 1023 any	Packet with source in network 1.0.0.0 to any destination, using UDP with source port less than 1023.
access-list 101 deny udp 1.0.0.0 0.255.255.255 lt 1023 44.1.2.3 0.0.255.255	Packet with source in network 1.0.0.0 to destinations beginning 44.1, using UDP with source port less than 1023.
access-list 101 deny ip 33.1.2.0 0.0.0.255 44.1.2.3 0.0.255.255	Packet with source in 33.1.2.0/24 to destinations beginning 44.1.
access-list 101 deny icmp 33.1.2.0 0.0.0.255 44.1.2.3 0.0.255.255 echo	Packet with source in 33.1.2.0/24 to destinations beginning 44.1, which are ICMP Echo Requests and Replies.

In Table 7-6, the keyword any implies that **any** value is matched. The keyword **host**, followed by an IP address, implies that exactly that IP address is matched. In other words, the **any** keyword implies logic like a wildcard mask of 255.255.255.255, and the **host** keyword implies logic like a wildcard mask of 0.0.0.0.

The sequence of the parameters is very important—and very tricky, in some cases. When checking port numbers, the parameter on the **access-list** command checking the port checks the source port number when placed immediately after the check of the source IP address. Likewise, if the port parameter follows the check of the destination address, the logic matches the destination port. For example, the command **access-list 101 deny tcp any eq telnet any** matches all packets that use TCP and whose source TCP port is 23 (Telnet). Likewise, the **access-list 101 deny tcp any any eq telnet** matches all packets that use TCP and whose destination TCP port is 23 (Telnet).

Extended IP Access Lists, Example 1

The following example, based on the network in Figure 7-3 and configured as in Example 7-4, shows the use of extended IP access lists. The criteria for this first example use the same criteria as in the standard access list example:

1 Sam is not allowed access to Bugs or Daffy.

2 Hosts on the Seville Ethernet are not allowed access to hosts on the Yosemite Ethernet.

3 All other combinations are allowed.

Example 7-4 *Yosemite Configuration for Extended Access List, Example 1*

```
interface serial 0
ip access-group 110
!
interface serial 1
ip access-group 110
!
access-list 110 deny ip host 10.1.2.1 10.1.1.0 0.0.0.255
access-list 110 deny ip 10.1.2.0 0.0.0.255 10.1.3.0 0.0.0.255
access-list 110 permit ip any any
```

Two important side effects occur with the configuration shown in Example 7-4, compared to the standard access list configuration in Examples 7-1 and 7-2. The issue of having packets routed around the access list is already taken care of because the access lists are enabled for output packets on both serial interfaces. Also, most of the packets are filtered at the router nearest the source of the packets, which reduces network overhead. Access lists could have been added at Seville as well, to deny the packets originating from Seville's Ethernet.

Extended IP Access Lists, Example 2

Figure 7-5 presents the network diagram for another example on extended IP access lists.

Figure 7-5   *Network Diagram for Extended Access List, Example 2*

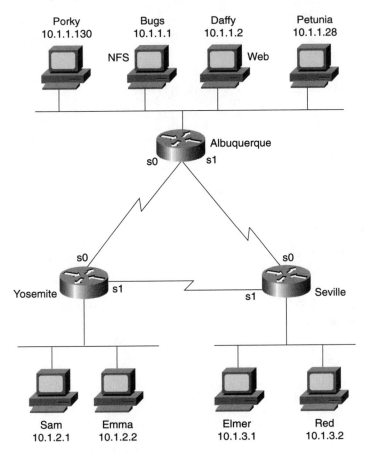

The filtering criteria for this extended access list example is more complicated:

1 The Web server (Daffy) is available to all users.

2 UDP-based clients and servers on Bugs are not available to hosts whose IP addresses are in the upper half of the valid IP addresses in each subnet. (Note: The subnet mask used is 255.255.255.0.)

3 Packets between hosts on the Yosemite Ethernet and the Seville Ethernet are allowed only if packets are routed across the direct serial link.

4 Clients Porky and Petunia can connect to all hosts except Red.

5 Any other connections are permitted.

Example 7-5, Example 7-6, and Example 7-7 show one solution to this second extended access list example.

Example 7-5 *Yosemite Configuration for Extended Access List, Example 2*

```
interface serial 0
ip access-group 110
!
interface serial 1
ip access-group 111
!
! Criterion 1 met with next statement
access-list 110 permit tcp any host 10.1.1.2 eq www
! Criterion 2 met with next statement
access-list 110 deny udp 0.0.0.128  255.255.255.127  host 10.1.1.1
! Criterion 3 met with next statement
access-list 110 deny ip 10.1.2.0 0.0.0.255 10.1.3.0 0.0.0.255
! Criterion 5 met with next statement
access-list 110 permit ip any any
!
! Criterion 1 met with next statement
access-list 111 permit tcp any host 10.1.1.2 eq www
! Criterion 2 met with next statement
access-list 111 deny udp 0.0.0.128  255.255.255.127  host 10.1.1.1
! Criterion 5 met with next statement
access-list 111 permit ip any any
```

Example 7-6 *Seville Configuration for Extended Access List, Example 2*

```
interface serial 0
ip access-group 110
!
interface serial 1
ip access-group 111
!
! Criterion 1 met with next statement
access-list 110 permit tcp any host 10.1.1.2 eq www
! Criterion 2 met with next statement
access-list 110 deny udp 0.0.0.128  255.255.255.127  host 10.1.1.1
! Criterion 3 met with next statement
access-list 110 deny ip 10.1.3.0 0.0.0.255 10.1.2.0 0.0.0.255
! Criterion 5 met with next statement
access-list 110 permit ip any any
!
! Criterion 1 met with next statement
access-list 111 permit tcp any host 10.1.1.2 eq www
! Criterion 2 met with next statement
access-list 111 deny udp 0.0.0.128  255.255.255.127  host 10.1.1.1
! Criterion 5 met with next statement
access-list 111 permit ip any any
```

Example 7-7 *Albuquerque Configuration for Extended Access List, Example 2*

```
interface serial 0
ip access-group 112
!
interface serial 1
ip access-group 112
!
! Criterion 4 met with next four statements
access-list 112 deny ip host 10.1.1.130  host 10.1.3.2
access-list 112 deny ip host 10.1.1.28   host 10.1.3.2
access-list 112 permit ip host 10.1.1.130 any
access-list 112 permit ip host 10.1.1.28 any
! Criterion 5 met with next statement
access-list 112 permit ip any any
```

The access lists on Yosemite and Seville are almost identical; each is focused on the first three criteria. List 110 is used as outbound access-lists on the Yosemite and Seville links connected to Albuquerque. The first three statements in list 110 in each router complete the first three criteria for this example; the only difference is in the source and destination addresses used in the third statement, which checks for the respective subnet numbers at each site.

Both Yosemite and Seville have a list 111 that is used on the link between the two. Each list 111 on Yosemite and Seville is identical to list 110, respectively, except that list 111 is missing one statement. This missing statement (relative to list 110) is the one that meets criterion 3, which states to not filter this traffic from going across the direct serial link; because list 111 is used on that link, there is no need for the extra statement. The final statement in lists 110 and 111 in Seville and Yosemite provide coverage for the fifth point of criteria for this example, allowing all other packets to flow.

The second access list statement in each list 110 and 111 on Seville and Yosemite is trickier than you will see on the CCNA exam. This example is indicative of the types of nuances that you might see on the CCNP and CCIE exams. The mask has only one binary 0 in it, in bit 25 (the first bit in the last byte). The corresponding bit in the address has value 1; in decimal, the address and mask imply addresses whose fourth byte is between 128 and 255, inclusive. Regardless of subnet number, hosts in the upper half of the assignable addresses in each subnet are matched with this combination. (Note: Because the subnet mask is 255.255.255.0, all host addresses in the upper half of the address range are between 128–254 in the last octet.)

Three major problems exist when using extensive detailed criteria for access lists. First, the criteria is open to interpretation. Many people tend to create the lists to match the order in which each point of the criteria are written; no attempt at optimization is made. Finally, the lists are easy to create in such a way that the criteria is not actually accomplished, as in extended IP access list example 2.

Example 7-8 shows an alternative solution to the extended access list example 2 solution, as was shown in Example 7-5, Example 7-6, and Example 7-7. All access lists have been removed from Seville and Yosemite, as compared with that earlier solution.

Example 7-8 *Albuquerque Configuration for Extended Access List Example 2, Second Solution*

```
interface serial 0
ip access-group 112
!
interface serial 1
ip access-group 112
!
! Next statement meets objective 1
access-list 112 permit tcp host 10.1.1.2 eq www any
! Next statement meets objective 2
access-list 112 deny udp  host 10.1.1.1   0.0.0.128   255.255.255.127
! Next statements meet objective 3
access-list 112 deny ip 10.1.3.0 0.0.0.255 10.1.2.0 0.0.0.255
access-list 112 deny ip 10.1.2.0 0.0.0.255 10.1.3.0 0.0.0.255
! Next statement meets objective 4
access-list 112 deny ip host 10.1.1.130  host 10.1.3.2
access-list 112 deny ip host 10.1.1.28   host 10.1.3.2

! Next statement meets objective 5
access-list 112 permit ip any any
```

Several differences exist between the first solution in Examples 7-5, 7-6, and 7-7, and the second solution in Example 7-8. First, all the filtering is performed in Albuquerque. Criterion point 4 is completed more concisely, allowing the **permit all** final statement to allow Porky and Petunia to talk to other hosts besides Red. Packets are sent by Yosemite and Seville to Albuquerque hosts, as well as packets sent back from servers in Albuquerque to the Albuquerque router, before being filtered. However, the number of these packets will be small because the filter prevents the client from sending more than the first packet used to connect to the service.

Named IP Access Lists

Named IP access lists allow the same logic to be configured as with numbered standard and extended access lists. As a CCNA, you will need to remember the differences in syntax of the configuration commands and also be able to create both numbered and named lists with the same logic. The key differences between numbered and named IP access lists are listed here:

- Names are more intuitive reminders of the function of the list.

- Names allow for more access lists than 99 standard and 100 extended, which is the restriction using numbered access lists.

- Named access lists allow individual statements to be deleted. Numbered lists allow for deletion only of the entire list. Insertion of the new statement into a named list requires deletion and re-addition of all statements that should be later in the list than the newly added statement.

- The actual names used must be unique across all named access lists of all protocols and types on an individual router. Names can be duplicated on different routers.

The configuration syntax is very similar between named and numbered IP access lists. The items that can be matched with a numbered standard IP access list are identical to the items that can be matched with a named standard IP access list. Likewise, the items are identical with both numbered and named extended IP access lists.

Two important differences exist between numbered and named access-lists. One key difference is that named access lists use a global command, which moves the user into a named IP access list submode, under which the matching and permit/deny logic is configured. The other key difference is that when a named matching statement is deleted, only that one statement is deleted. With numbered lists, the deletion of any statement in the list deletes all the statements in the list. (This feature will be demonstrated in more detail in an upcoming example.)

Table 7-7 lists the key configuration commands and shows their differences and similarities.

Table 7-7   *Comparison of Named and Numbered IP Access List Configuration Commands*

	Numbered	**Named**
Commands for matching packets: standard IP ACLs	**access-list 1-99 permit | deny . . .**	**ip access-list standard** *name* ***permit | deny . . .**
Commands for matching packets: extended IP ACLs	**access-list 100-199 permit | deny . . .**	**ip access-list extended** *name* ***permit | deny . . .**
Commands for enabling ACLs	**ip access-group 1-99 in | out**	**ip access-group name in | out**
Commands for enabling ACLs	**ip access-group 100-199 in | out**	**ip access-group name in | out**

*   These commands are subcommands of the previous command.

The word *name* represents a name created by the administrator. This name must be unique among all named access lists of all types in this router. Also, note that because the named list does not imply standard or extended by the value of the number of the list, the command explicitly states the type of access list. Also, the . . . represents all the matching parameters, which are identical in meaning and syntax when comparing the respective numbered and named IP access lists. Also note that the same command is used to enable the list on an interface for both numbered and named lists.

One difference between the two types of lists is that individual matching statements can be removed from the named lists. Example 7-9 shows the configuration mode output when entering the access list used on Albuquerque in access list 112 of Example 7-8, but this time as a named access list instead of a numbered access list. One typo is shown in the original creation of the access list in Example 7-9, with changes made to delete and add the statement shown later in this same example. (The statement that is a typo is **deny ip 10.1.2.0 0.0.0.255 10.2.3.0 0.0.0.255**. It is a typo because there is no subnet 10.2.3.0; the intent was to configure 10.1.3.0 instead.)

Example 7-9 *Named Access List Configuration*

```
conf t
Enter configuration commands, one per line.  End with Ctrl-Z.
Router(config)#ip access-list extended barney
Router(config-ext-nacl)#permit tcp host 10.1.1.2 eq www any
Router(config-ext-nacl)#deny udp host 10.1.1.1 0.0.0.128 255.255.255.127
Router(config-ext-nacl)#deny ip 10.1.3.0 0.0.0.255 10.1.2.0 0.0.0.255
! The next statement is purposefully wrong so that the process of changing the list
can be seen.
Router(config-ext-nacl)#deny ip 10.1.2.0 0.0.0.255 10.2.3.0 0.0.0.255

Router(config-ext-nacl)#deny ip host 10.1.1.130 host 10.1.3.2
Router(config-ext-nacl)#deny ip host 10.1.1.28 host 10.1.3.2
Router(config-ext-nacl)#permit ip any any
Router(config-ext-nacl)#^Z
Router#sh run
Building configuration...

Current configuration:

.
. (unimportant statements omitted)
.
!
ip access-list extended barney
 permit tcp host 10.1.1.2 eq www any
 deny    udp host 10.1.1.1 0.0.0.128 255.255.255.127
 deny    ip 10.1.3.0 0.0.0.255 10.1.2.0 0.0.0.255
 deny    ip 10.1.2.0 0.0.0.255 10.2.3.0 0.0.0.255
 deny    ip host 10.1.1.130 host 10.1.3.2
 deny    ip host 10.1.1.28 host 10.1.3.2
 permit ip any any

Router#conf t
Enter configuration commands, one per line.  End with Ctrl-Z.
Router(config)#ip access-list extended barney
Router(config-ext-nacl)#no deny ip 10.1.2.0 0.0.0.255 10.2.3.0 0.0.0.255
Router(config-ext-nacl)#^Z
Router#show access-list

Extended IP access list barney
    permit tcp host 10.1.1.2 eq www any
    deny    udp host 10.1.1.1 0.0.0.128 255.255.255.127
```

Example 7-9 *Named Access List Configuration (Continued)*

```
      deny    ip 10.1.3.0 0.0.0.255 10.1.2.0 0.0.0.255
      deny    ip host 10.1.1.130 host 10.1.3.2
      deny    ip host 10.1.1.28 host 10.1.3.2
      permit ip any any
Router#conf t
Enter configuration commands, one per line.  End with Ctrl-Z.
Router(config)#ip access-list extended barney
Router(config-ext-nacl)#no permit ip any any
Router(config-ext-nacl)#no deny ip host 10.1.1.130 host 10.1.3.2
Router(config-ext-nacl)#no deny ip host 10.1.1.28 host 10.1.3.2
Router(config-ext-nacl)#deny ip 10.1.2.0 0.0.0.255 10.1.3.0 0.0.0.255
Router(config-ext-nacl)#deny ip host 10.1.1.130 host 10.1.3.2
Router(config-ext-nacl)#deny ip host 10.1.1.28 host 10.1.3.2
Router(config-ext-nacl)#permit ip any any
Router(config-ext-nacl)#^Z
Router#sh ip access-list

Extended IP access list barney
    permit tcp host 10.1.1.2 eq www any
    deny    udp host 10.1.1.1 0.0.0.128 255.255.255.127
    deny    ip 10.1.3.0 0.0.0.255 10.1.2.0 0.0.0.255
    deny    ip 10.1.2.0 0.0.0.255 10.1.3.0 0.0.0.255
    deny    ip host 10.1.1.130 host 10.1.3.2
    deny    ip host 10.1.1.28 host 10.1.3.2
    permit ip any any
```

If an access list is not configured but is enabled on an interface with the **ip access-group** command, no packets are filtered due to the **ip access-group** command. After the access list's first command is configured, the IOS implements the access list's logic. This is true of IP standard access lists as well as extended and named access lists. Access lists that filter other types of packets follow this same logic.

Controlling vty Access with IP Access Lists

Access into and out of the virtual terminal line (vty) ports of the IOS can be controlled by IP access lists. (vty is used for Telnet access to and from the IOS.) The inbound case is the more obvious case. For instance, imagine that only hosts in subnet 10.1.1.0/24 were supposed to be capable of telnetting into any of the Cisco routers in a network. In such a case, the configuration in Example 7-10 could be used on each router to deny access from IP addresses not in that one subnet.

Example 7-10 *vty Access Control Using the **access-class** Command*

```
line vty 0 4
 login
 password cisco
 access-class 3 in
!
! Next command is a global command
 access-list 3 permit 10.1.1.0 0.0.0.255
```

The **access-class** command refers to the matching logic in **access-list 3**. The keyword **in** refers to packets that are entering the router when you are trying to Telnet to that router's vtys. The **out** keyword would be used both with outbound Telnet from a router and when using the reverse Telnet feature of the IOS (which is unlikely to be on the exam). The out keyword implies that the packets originated by the Telnet client in the router are checked using the destination address of the packets.

IP Access List Summary

To pass the CCNA exam, you must be proficient in using IP access lists. The most important details to recall are as follows:

- The order of the list is important.

- All matching parameters must be true before a statement is "matched."

- An implied "deny all" is at the end of the list.

The philosophy of choosing the location for access lists is covered in more depth in the CCNP exam than in the CCNA exam. However, filtering packets closer to the source of the packet generally is better because the soon-to-be discarded packets will waste less bandwidth than if the packets were allowed to flow over additional links before being denied.

Be particularly careful of questions relating to existing lists. In particular, if the question suggests that one more **access-list** command should be added, simply adding that command will place the statement at the end of the list, but the statement might need to be earlier in the list to accomplish the goal described in the question. Also focus on the differences between named and numbered IP access lists.

Filtering IPX Traffic and SAPs

IPX access lists can be used to filter IPX packets sent by clients and servers, just as IP access lists are used to filter IP packets. However, similar functions can be performed by using Service Advertising Protocol (SAP) filters, which filter SAP updates sent by servers and routers. SAP filters are more common because they can be used to prevent clients and servers from trying to send packets, as well as to reduce the overhead of SAP updates.

CCNAs deal with SAPs and SAP filtering on a regular basis and with IPX packet filtering a little less often. Both numbered and named IPX access lists are available. The configuration commands used for these filters are listed in Table 7-8; the EXEC commands related to IPX filtering are shown in Table 7-9.

Table 7-8   *IPX Access List Configuration Commands*

Command	Configuration Mode and Purpose
access-list {*800-899*} {**permit** I **deny**} *source-network* [*.source-node* [*source-node-mask*]] [*destination-network* [*.destination-node* [*destination-node-mask*]]]	Global command to create numbered standard IPX access lists
access-list {*900-999*} {**permit** I **deny**} *protocol* [*source-network*] [[[*.source-node* [*source-node-mask*]] I [*.source-node source-network-mask.source-node-mask*]] [*source-socket*] [*destination-network*] [[[*.destination-node* [*destination-node-mask*] I [*.destination-node destination-network-mask. Destination-node-mask*]] [*destination-socket*] **log**	Global command to create numbered extended IPX access lists
access-list {*1000-1099*} {**permit** I **deny**} *network* [*.node*] [*network-mask.node-mask*] [*service-type* [*server-name*]]	Global command to create numbered SAP access lists
ipx access-list {**standard** I **extended** I **sap** } *name*	Global command to begin creation of a named standard, extended, or SAP access list
{**permit** I **deny**} *source-network* [*.source-node* [*source-node-mask*]] [*destination-network* [*.destination-node* [*destination-node-mask*]]]	Named access list subcommand for standard access lists
{**permit** I **deny**} *protocol* [*source-network*] [[[*.source-node* [*source-node-mask*]] I [*.source-node source-network-mask.source-node-mask*]] [*source-socket*] [*destination-network*] [[[*.destination-node* [*destination-node-mask*] I [*.destination-node destination-network-mask. Destination-node-mask*]] [*destination-socket*] **log**	Named access list subcommand for extended access lists
{**permit** I **deny**} *network* [*.node*] [*network-mask.node-mask*] [*service-type* [*server-name*]]	Named access list subcommand for SAP access lists
ipx access-group {*number* I *name* [**in** I **out**] }	Interface subcommand to enable a named or numbered, standard or extended IPX access list
ipx output-sap-filter *list-number*	Interface subcommand to enable SAP access lists used for outbound SAP packets
ipx input-sap-filter *list-number*	Interface subcommand to enable SAP access lists used for inbound SAP packets

Table 7-9   *IPX Access List EXEC Commands*

Command	Function
show ipx interface	Includes reference to the access lists enabled on the interface
show access-list *number*	Shows details of all configured access lists for all protocols
show ipx access-list	Shows details of all IPX access lists

Access lists for filtering packets are covered next; SAP filters are covered in the section "SAP Access Lists."

IPX Packet Filters (Access Lists)

Packet filters in the Cisco IOS use the same general logic for any Layer 3 protocol. Figure 7-6 outlines the path an IPX packet can take through a router. The comments following the figure describe the basic logic behind IPX access lists.

Features of the process described in Figure 7-6 are as follows:

- Packets can be filtered as they enter an interface, before the routing decision.

- Packets can be filtered before they exit an interface, after the routing decision.

- "Deny" is the term used in the IOS to imply that the packet will be filtered.

- "Permit" is the term used in the IOS to imply that the packet will not be filtered.

- The filtering logic is configured in the access list.

The logic created by an access list, as shown in the diamond-shaped symbols in Figure 7-6, is best summarized by the following sequence of events:

Step 1   The matching parameters of the first access list statement are compared to the packet.

Step 2   If a match is made, the action defined in this access list statement (permit or deny) is performed, as shown in Figure 7-6.

Step 3   If a match is not made in Step 2, repeat Steps 1 and 2 using the next sequential access list statement.

Step 4   If no match is made with an entry in the access list, the deny action is performed.

Figure 7-6   *Locations Where Access List Logic Can Be Applied*

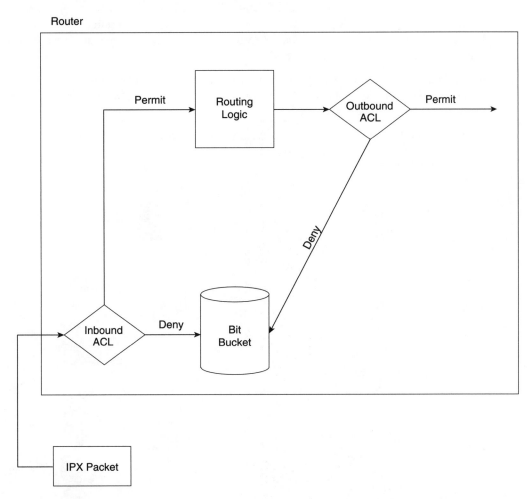

The logic for access lists is true whether using standard or extended access lists. The only difference is that extended access lists include more comparisons to determine a match. These differences are outlined in the next few sections on standard IPX access lists, extended IPX access lists, and SAP access lists.

Standard IPX Access Lists

When deciding what this book should really try to accomplish, I decided that the text of the book should cover the topics in two ways. First, the voluminous details should be summarized in tables and lists whenever possible, to allow easy review for a reader who already knows the topic pretty well. The explanations then should focus on topics that are less obvious from reading the manual; these are the types of tidbits that you get from the instructor in a well-taught class. When discussing IPX packet filters, I will be focusing on these tidbits. If you are new to IPX access lists, you probably will want to read the IOS documentation or the Cisco Press book *Interconnecting Cisco Network Devices*.

Standard IPX access lists can check the source and destination network number. They also can check the node part of the source and destination addresses, and use a wildcard mask to examine the node part of the IPX addresses.

Figure 7-7 and Example 7-11 provide an example network and configuration.

Figure 7-7   *IPX Standard Access List Example*

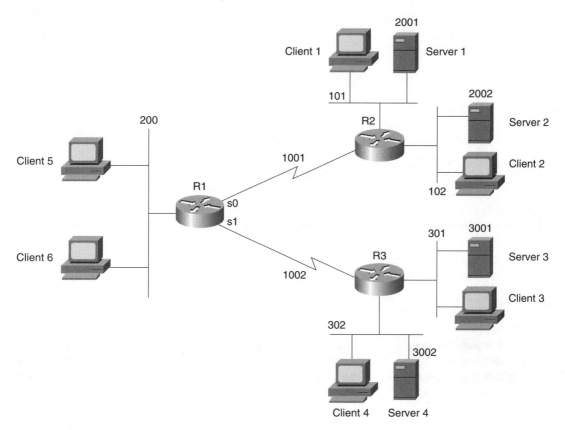

Example 7-11 *R1 Configuration for Standard IPX Access Lists*

```
ipx routing 0200.1111.1111
!
interface serial0
ip address 10.1.1.1 255.255.255.0
ipx network 1001
!
interface serial1
ip address 10.1.2.1 255.255.255.0
ipx network 1002
ipx access-group 820 in
!
interface ethernet 0
ip address 10.1.200.1 255.255.255.0
ipx network 200
ipx access-group 810
!
access-list 810 deny 101
access-list 810 permit -1
!
access-list 820 permit 302

R2#show access-list
IPX access list 810
    deny 101
    permit FFFFFFFF
IPX access list 820
    permit 302

R2#show ipx interface s 1
Serial1 is up, line protocol is up
  IPX address is 1001.0200.1111.1111 [up]
  Delay of this IPX network, in ticks is 6 throughput 0 link delay 0
  IPXWAN processing not enabled on this interface.
  IPX SAP update interval is 1 minute(s)
  IPX type 20 propagation packet forwarding is disabled
  Incoming access list is 820
  Outgoing access list is not set
  IPX helper access list is not set
  SAP GNS processing enabled, delay 0 ms, output filter list is not set
  SAP Input filter list is not set
  SAP Output filter list is not set
  SAP Router filter list is not set
  Input filter list is not set
  Output filter list is not set
  Router filter list is not set
  Netbios Input host access list is not set
  Netbios Input bytes access list is not set

  Netbios Output host access list is not set

  Netbios Output bytes access list is not set
```

The following criteria will be used in this IPX standard access list example established in Figure 7-7 and Example 7-11:

1 Packets from network 101 are not allowed onto network 200.

2 Packets from network 102 are allowed onto network 200.

3 Packets from network 301 are not allowed onto network 200, 101, or 102.

4 Packets from network 302 are allowed to go anywhere.

The example shows one way to accomplish the goals, but other alternatives exist. Access list 810 implements the first two criteria for the example by filtering packets exiting Ethernet 0 on R1. Access list 820 implements the last two criteria for the example by filtering packets entering serial1 on R1.

First, consider the logic in **access-list 810**, which is used to meet the first two criteria. The list denies access from source network 101 and permits all other source network numbers via the explicitly defined "permit all else" as the second statement in the list. If the list had been used as an inbound access-list on serial0 of R1, then packets from network 101 would not be capable of entering R1 for forwarding on to R3. By placing the filter on Ethernet0 as an outbound filter, R1 could forward packets from 101 and 102 on to R3, but only packets from network 102 would make it to network 200.

Next consider the logic in **access-list 820**. This permits only source network 302 and denies all other source networks due to the implied "deny all else" at the end of the list. By applying the list as an inbound list on R1's serial 1, criterion 3 will be met by the default "deny all," and criterion 4 will be met by the explicit "permit" of source network 302.

Several nuances of access list operation are seen (or implied, by omission) in the syntax shown in Example 7-11. **access-list 810** uses the keyword **–1**, which means any and all network numbers. No destination networks were checked with either access list, which is allowed with IPX standard access lists. Also, the optional node mask was not used and is not useful very often. For example, imagine that a requirement was added so that packets from Clients 5 and 6 are not allowed to be sent to network 302. If the IPX addresses for Clients 5 and 6 were 200.0200.1234.0000 and 200.0200.1234.0001, and if no other client's IPX addresses began with 200.0200.1234, then the following **access-list** command could match packets from these two clients:

```
access-list 830 deny 200.0200.1234.0000 0000.0000.ffff
```

The wildcard mask works like the wildcard mask used in IP access lists; the only difference is that it is configured as a hexadecimal number. The final four **f** digits mean that the final four hex digits in the node part of the address are automatically considered to match, but that the first eight digits do need to be checked. However, because almost everyone who uses IPX uses the burned-in MAC address for the node part of the IPX address, the IPX addresses on these clients will almost never have a convenient number to allow packets from both to be matched in the same access list statement. Even if the numbers were convenient for using a wildcard mask, the IPX address would change if the LAN adapter ever was replaced, giving undesired results from the access list. So, unless you are using locally administered MAC addresses on your IPX nodes, the node mask will almost never be useful.

Cisco expects CCNAs to be familiar enough with TCP/IP and IPX protocols to recognize oversights in an access list design before the access-lists are deployed. Such an oversight is true of Example 7-11—or, more accurately, the criteria used for Example 7-11. Note that the criteria all mentioned network numbers, but no servers were mentioned. The oversight is that when clients connect to servers whose code level is NetWare 3.11 and beyond, the address used by the server to communicate with the client uses the server's internal network number. So, in Example 7-11, the effect is an interesting mental exercise. **access-list 810**, with the explicit "permit all," would permit the client-server traffic exiting R1's Ethernet0, while **access-list 820**, with the implied "deny all" would prevent all client-server traffic from entering R1's serial1 interface.

Now thinking in terms of client/server flows with NetWare, consider the following changes in the criteria for these access lists:

1 Packets from Server 1 are not allowed onto network 200.

2 Packets from Server 2 are allowed onto network 200.

3 Packets from Server 3 are not allowed onto network 200, 101, or 102.

4 Packets from Server 4 are allowed to go anywhere.

5 All combinations not mentioned should be permitted.

The new configuration in Example 7-12 successfully focuses on the servers' network numbers, not the network numbers on the LAN segments.

Example 7-12 *R1 Configuration for Standard IPX Access Lists, Modified*

```
ipx routing 0200.1111.1111
!
interface serial0
ip address 10.1.1.1 255.255.255.0
ipx network 1001
!
interface serial1
ip address 10.1.2.1 255.255.255.0
ipx network 1002
ipx access-group 820 in
!
interface ethernet 0
ip address 10.1.200.1 255.255.255.0
ipx network 200
ipx access-group 810
!
access-list 810 deny 2001
access-list 810 permit -1
!
access-list 820 deny 3001
access-list 820 permit -1
```

Extended IPX Access Lists

Extended access lists for IPX can check several additional fields in the IPX packet header, as compared to standard IPX access lists. Cisco expects CCNAs to remember all the items that can be matched using a standard or extended IPX **access-list** command. Table 7-10 summarizes those items, and Figure 7-8 shows the relative location of the fields in the headers.

Figure 7-8   *Header Fields Matchable Using IPX Access Lists*

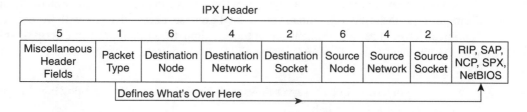

Table 7-10   *IPX Standard and Extended Access Lists—Matching*

Type of Access List	What Can Be Matched
IPX Standard	Source network
	Source IPX address (network and node)
	Source network and portions of the node address, using a node mask
	Destination network
	Destination IPX address (network and node)
	Destination network and portions of the node address, using a node mask
IPX Extended	Same points as with an IPX standard access list in addition to items in the rows that follow
	Portions of entire source IPX address, using a wildcard mask
	Portions of entire destination IPX address, using a wildcard mask
	Protocol type
	Source socket
	Destination socket

The protocol type is a field that is not shown in many examples in other references, such as the Cisco IOS documentation CD. Figure 7-9 shows example packets that would be matched by the various protocol types.

Figure 7-9 *Extended Access List Protocol Types*

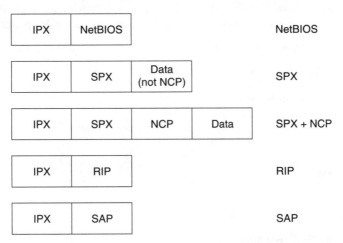

The protocol names can be misleading, particularly the SAP protocol type. Extended access lists can be used to filter entire SAP packets; protocol type SAP would be useful to match those packets. For filtering the content of the SAP updates, which is a hugely popular function, access lists for filtering SAP information would be used. The SAP filters, which use list numbers between 1000 and 1099, are covered in the section "SAP Filters," later in this chapter. SAP filtering does not use extended IPX access lists with a SAP protocol type.

Similarly, extended IPX access lists with protocol type RIP can allow matching of RIP packets, but not the routing information in the RIP update. The most practical use of the *protocol type* parameter is for NetBIOS. If NetBIOS is not an issue, most sites use the **any** keyword for the protocol type.

The *socket* parameter is similar to a TCP or UDP port number. Novell assigns socket values to applications to create the equivalent of a TCP or UDP well-known port. Clients dynamically assign sockets in the range of 4000–7FFF, and Novell assigns sockets to applications in the range of 8000–FFFF. As with IP, there is both a source and destination socket, which is used for multiplexing.

NOTE   Do not confuse SAP type with socket. A file server advertises SAP type 4 but does not use socket number 4 for file services.

The most useful extended access list feature that is not supported by standard access lists is the network wildcard mask. Figure 7-10 and Example 7-13 provide a sample to show when this mask is useful. The access list is configured in R2. The criteria for this packet filter is as follows:

1 Clients in networks 100 and 101 are allowed access to Server 3 and Server 4.

2 Clients in network 300 are not allowed to access Server 1 and Server 2.

Figure 7-10 *IPX Extended Access List Example*

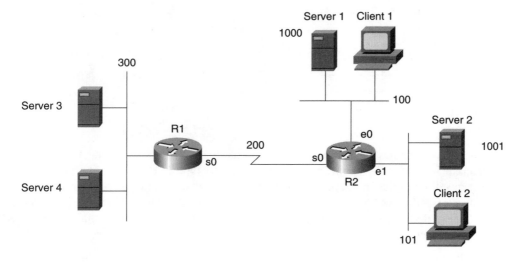

Example 7-13 *R2 Configuration for Extended IPX Access Lists*

```
hostname R2
!
ipx routing 0200.2222.2222
!
interface serial0
ip address 10.1.1.2 255.255.255.0
ipx network 200
ipx access-group 910
!
interface ethernet 0
ip address 10.1.100.2 255.255.255.0
ipx network 100
!
interface ethernet 1
ip address 10.1.101.2 255.255.255.0
ipx network 101
!
access-list 910 deny any 1000 0000000F
access-list 910 permit any -1
```

access-list 910 actually checks for packets sourced from networks 1000 to 100F. The network number is eight hex digits long; the leading 0s are not shown. For the network wildcard mask, all digits are shown in the book, but the leading zeroes are omitted in an actual router configuration. The mask 0000000F means that the first seven hex digits must match 0000100, which are the first seven hex digits of the network number in this case, with leading 0s shown. The last hex digit can be any value. Therefore, networks 1000, 1001, and 14 others are matched.

To exactly match the two networks 1000 and 1001, the mask 00000001 could be used. This mask implies that all bits are checked except the one low-order bit. (Feel free to convert hex 1000 and 1001 to binary to see that only the last bit is different in the two numbers.)

SAP Filters

The key to understanding SAP filters is to understand where SAP packets flow and where they do not. This process is fundamental to the job function of a typical CCNA. The SAP process is very similar to routing updates with a distance vector routing protocol. In fact, SAP uses a split horizon concept as well. The following sequence outlines a day in the life of a SAP packet:

Step 1	A router or server decides it is time to send a SAP broadcast on its attached network, based on the expiration of its SAP timer.
Step 2	That router or server creates enough SAP packets to advertise all its SAP information (up to seven services per packet, by default).
Step 3	That router or server sends the SAP packets out into the attached network.
Step 4	Other routers and servers are attached to the same medium; these routers and servers receive all the SAP packets.
Step 5	The receiving routers and servers examine the information inside the SAP packets and update their SAP tables as necessary.
Step 6	The receiving routers and servers discard the SAP packets.
Step 7	Every server and router uses a SAP timer, which is not synchronized with the other servers and routers. When the timer expires, each server and router performs Steps 1 through 3, and their neighboring servers and routers react and perform Steps 4 through 6.

In other words, the SAP packets are never forwarded by a router or server. This process is effectively the same process used by distance vector routing protocols. So, packet filters filter packets going through a router. Therefore, the IOS uses *distribute lists* (instead of packet filters) to filter routing information. Likewise, IOS uses SAP filters to filter SAP information.

SAP filtering provides two functions: filtering the services listed in outgoing SAP updates, and filtering services listed in received SAP updates. The first function reduces the information sent to the router's neighboring IPX servers and routers. The second function limits what a router adds to its SAP table when an update is received. Unlike packet filters, SAP filters examine the data inside the packet as well. Figure 7-11 outlines the process.

Figure 7-11 *SAP Filter Flow Diagram*

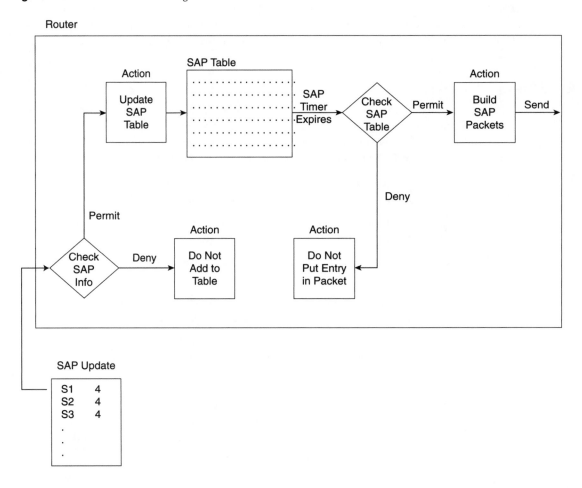

Two main reasons exist for using SAP filters. First, SAP updates can consume a large amount of bandwidth, particularly in nonbroadcast multiaccess (NBMA) networks. If clients in one division never need services from servers in another division, there is no need to waste bandwidth advertising the services. The second reason for SAP filters is that they can accomplish the same task as most IPX packet filters, but with less overhead. (This second reason will be outlined in the SAP filtering sample in Example 7-14.) SAP filters will be used to accomplish the same set of criteria that was mentioned with Example 7-13 and Figure 7-10. As a reminder, the criteria for that filter is as follows:

1 Clients in networks 100 and 101 are allowed to access Server 3 and Server 4.

2 Clients in network 300 are not allowed to access Server 1 and Server 2.

Example 7-14 *R1 Configuration for SAP Filters*

```
Hostname  R1
!
ipx routing 0200.1111.111
!
interface serial0
ip address 10.1.1.1 255.255.255.0
ipx network 200
ipx input-sap-filter 1005
!
interface ethernet 0
ip address 10.1.30.1 255.255.255.0
ipx network 300
!
access-list 1005 deny 1000 0000000F
access-list 1005 permit -1
```

The effect of the SAP filter on R1 is somewhat obvious. How the filter stops clients in network 300 from reaching Server 1 and Server 2 is not as obvious. The filter examines inbound SAP updates from R2. Services in networks 1000 to 100F are filtered. All other services are not filtered; the **–1** keyword signifies all networks. (Extended IPX access lists can use the keyword **any**. SAP filters do not currently use that keyword.) So, there will never be an entry in R1's SAP table for networks 1000 to 100F.

The key to understanding what stops clients from reaching Server 1 and Server 2 is to recall the GNS process and its purpose. (Figure 6-14, in Chapter 6, "Routing," outlined the process.) Either Server 3 or Server 4 will be used as the GNS server for clients in network 300. (The router will not reply to GNS requests if a real server exists on the LAN at some later IOS releases; before that, the router delayed replying so that any local servers would send the first reply.) Neither Server 3 nor Server 4 will know of Server 1 or Server 2 because they are relying on R1 to advertise SAP information, and R1 has filtered SAPs about networks 1000 to 100F. Therefore, network 300 clients will not be capable of logging in to Server 1 or Server 2 because *clients can connect only to servers in the SAP table of their GNS server.*

SAP filtering to disallow certain clients from using certain servers is more efficient than IPX packet filters. SAPs are sent once every 60 seconds, whereas packet filters cause the IOS to examine every IPX packet, a much more frequent task. So, you are more likely to use SAP filers in real networks, and you also are more likely to see SAP filters on the exam, as compared with IPX packet filters.

The following list shows the fields that can be matched for each service advertised, or to be advertised, in a SAP update.

- Source network

- Source IPX address (network and node)

- Portions of the source address, using a wildcard mask

- Destination network

- Destination IPX address (network and node)

- Portions of the destination address, using a wildcard mask

- Service type

- Server name

Named IPX Access Lists

Named IPX access lists allow the same logic to be configured as with numbered standard, extended, and SAP access lists. As a CCNA, you will need to remember the differences in syntax of the configuration commands and be able to create both numbered and named lists with the same logic. The key differences between numbered and named IP access lists are listed here:

- Names are more intuitive reminders of the function of the list.

- Names allow more access lists than 100 standard, extended, and SAP access lists, which is the restriction using numbered access lists.

- Named access lists allow individual statements to be deleted. Numbered lists allow for deletion only of the entire list. Insertion of the new statement into a named list requires deletion and re-addition of all statements that should follow the newly added statement.

- The actual names used must be unique across all named access lists of all protocols and types on an individual router. Names can be duplicated on different routers.

The configuration syntax is very similar between named and numbered IPX access lists. The items that can be matched with a numbered standard IPX access list are identical to the items that can be matched with a named standard IPX access list. Likewise, the items are identical with both numbered and named extended IPX access lists, as well as with numbered and named SAP access lists.

One key difference is that named access lists use a global command, which moves the user into a named IPX access list submode, under which the matching and permit/deny logic is configured. The other key difference is that when a named matching statement is deleted, only that specific statement is deleted. With numbered lists, the deletion of any statement in the list deletes all the statements in the list. (This feature will be demonstrated in more detail in an upcoming example.)

Table 7-11 lists the key IPX access list configuration commands and shows their differences and similarities.

Table 7-11   *Comparison of Named and Numbered IPX Access List Configuration Commands*

	Numbered	**Named**
Standard matching command	**access-list 800-899 permit | deny . . .**	*__ipx access-list standard__ *name* **permit | deny . . .**
Extended matching command	**access-list 900-999 permit | deny . . .**	*__ipx access-list extended__ *name* **permit | deny . . .**
SAP matching command	**access-list 1000-1099 permit | deny . . .**	*__ipx access-list sap__ *name* **permit | deny . . .**
Standard access list enabling command	**ipx access-group 800-899 in | out**	**ipx access-group** *name* **in | out**
Extended access list enabling command	**ipx access-group 900-999 in | out**	**ipx access-group** *name* **in | out**
SAP filter enabling command	**ipx output-sap-filter 1000-1099** **ipx input-sap-filter 1000-1099**	**ipx output-sap-filter** *name* **ipx input-sap-filter** *name*

*   The **permit** and **deny** commands are subcommands to the **ipx access-list** command.

The word *name* represents a name created by the administrator. This name must be unique among all named access lists of all types in this router. Also, note that because the named list does not imply standard, extended, or SAP by the value of the number of the list, the command explicitly states the type of access list. Also, the . . . represent all the matching parameters, which are identical in meaning and syntax when comparing the respective numbered and named IPX access lists. Also note that the same command is used to enable the list on an interface for both numbered and named lists.

One difference between the two types of lists is that individual matching statements can be removed from the named lists. Example 7-15 shows the configuration mode output when entering a named SAP access list on R1. The key to this example is to notice the changes. One statement is deleted and then re-added to the list, but this changes the order of the list. Example 7-15 shows the details.

Example 7-15 *Named IPX SAP Access List Configuration*

```
configure terminal
Enter configuration commands, one per line.  End with CNTL/Z.
R1(config)#ipx access-list sap fred
R1(config-ipx-sap-nacl)#deny 2 7
R1(config-ipx-sap-nacl)#deny 3
R1(config-ipx-sap-nacl)#deny 4 7
R1(config-ipx-sap-nacl)#permit -1
R1(config-ipx-sap-nacl)#^Z

R1#show ipx access-lists
IPX sap access list fred
    deny 2 7
    deny 3
    deny 4 7
    permit FFFFFFFF
R1#config t
Enter configuration commands, one per line.  End with CNTL/Z.
R1(config)#ipx access-list sap fred
R1(config-ipx-sap-nacl)#no deny 4 7
R1(config-ipx-sap-nacl)#^Z

R1#show ipx access-lists
IPX sap access list fred
    deny 2 7
    deny 3
    permit FFFFFFFF

R1#config t
Enter configuration commands, one per line.  End with CNTL/Z.
R1(config)#ipx access-list sap fred
R1(config-ipx-sap-nacl)#deny 4 7
R1(config-ipx-sap-nacl)#^Z

R1#show ipx access-lists
IPX sap access list fred
    deny 2 7
    deny 3
    permit FFFFFFFF
    deny 4 7

R1#config t
Enter configuration commands, one per line.  End with CNTL/Z.
R1(config)#ipx access-list sap fred
R1(config-ipx-sap-nacl)#no permit -1
R1(config-ipx-sap-nacl)#permit -1
R1(config-ipx-sap-nacl)#^Z

R1#show ipx access-lists
IPX sap access list fred
    deny 2 7
    deny 3
    deny 4 7
    permit FFFFFFFF
```

Example 7-15 *Named IPX SAP Access List Configuration (Continued)*

```
R1#configure t
Enter configuration commands, one per line.  End with CNTL/Z.
R1(config)#interface s 0.1
R1(config-subif)#ipx output-sap-filter fred
R1(config-subif)#^Z

R1#show running
Building configuration...

Current configuration:
!
version 12.0
service timestamps debug uptime
service timestamps log uptime
no service password-encryption
!
hostname R1
!
enable secret 5 $1$chuM$zon5bAnWNCu38hzCmAr.k.
!
ip subnet-zero
no ip domain-lookup
ipx routing 0000.3089.b170
!
!
!
interface Serial0
 no ip address
 no ip directed-broadcast
 encapsulation frame-relay IETF
 clockrate 56000
 frame-relay lmi-type cisco
!
interface Serial0.1 multipoint
 ip address 168.13.100.1 255.255.255.0
 no ip directed-broadcast
 ipx network 100
 ipx output-sap-filter fred
 frame-relay interface-dlci 902
 frame-relay interface-dlci 903
!
! Additional configuration not shown...
```

Foundation Summary

The Foundation Summary is a collection of tables and figures that provide a convenient review of many key concepts in this chapter. For those of you who already feel comfortable with the topics in this chapter, this summary could help you recall a few details. For those of you who just read this chapter, this review should help solidify some key facts. For any of you doing your final prep before the exam, these tables and figures will be a convenient way to review the day before the exam.

Table 7-12 and Table 7-13 list the more popular configuration commands and EXEC commands about access lists.

Table 7-12   *IP Access List Configuration Commands*

Command	Configuration Mode and Purpose
access-list {**1-99**} {**permit** I **deny**} *source-addr* [*source-mask*]	Global command for standard numbered access lists
access-list {**100-199**} {**permit** I **deny**} *protocol source-addr* [*source-mask*] [*operator operand*] *destination-addr* [*destination-mask*] [*operator operand*] [**established**]	Global command for extended numbered access lists
ip access-group {number I *name* [**in** I **out**] }	Interface subcommand to enable access lists
ip access-list {**standard** I **extended** } *name*	Global command for standard and extended named access lists
deny {*source* [*source-wildcard*] I **any**}[**log**]	Standard named access list subcommand
{**permit** I **deny**} *protocol source-addr* [*source-mask*] [*operator operand*] *destination-addr* [*destination-mask*] [*operator operand*] [**established**]	Extended named access list subcommand
access-class *number* I *name* [**in** I **out**]	Line subcommand for standard or extended access lists

Table 7-13   *IP Access List EXEC commands*

Command	Function
show ip interface	Includes reference to the access lists enabled on the interface
show access-list	Shows details of configured access lists for all protocols
show ip access-list [*number*]	Shows IP access lists

Table 7-14 provides the complete list of items that can be matched with an IP extended access list.

Table 7-14   *IP Standard and Extended Access Lists—Matching*

Type of Access List	What Can Be Matched
IP Standard	Source IP address
	Portions of the source IP address, using a wildcard mask
IP Extended	Source IP address
	Portions of the source IP address, using a wildcard mask
	Destination IP address
	Portions of the destination IP address, using a wildcard mask
	Protocol type (TCP, UDP, ICMP, IGRP, IGMP, and others)
	Source port
	Destination port
	Established—matches all TCP flows except the first flow
	IP TOS
	IP precedence

Table 7-15 provides several example **access-list** statements.

Table 7-15   *Sample **access-list** Commands and Logic Explanations*

Access List Statement	Explanation of What Matches
ip access-list 101 deny tcp any host 10.1.1.1 eq 23	Packet with any source address; destination must be 10.1.1.1, with a TCP header, with destination port 23.
ip access-list 101 deny tcp any host 10.1.1.1 eq telnet	Same function as last example; **telnet** keyword used instead of port 23.
ip access-list 101 deny udp 1.0.0.0 0.255.255.255 lt 1023 any	Packet with source in network 1.0.0.0 to any destination, using UDP with source port less than 1023.
ip access-list 101 deny udp 1.0.0.0 0.255.255.255 lt 1023 44.1.2.3 0.0.255.255	Packet with source in network 1.0.0.0 to destinations beginning 44.1, using UDP with source port less than 1023.
ip access-list 101 deny ip 33.1.2.0 0.0.0.255 44.1.2.3 0.0.255.255	Packet with source in 33.1.2.0/24 to destinations beginning 44.1.
ip access-list 101 deny icmp 33.1.2.0 0.0.0.255 44.1.2.3 0.0.255.255 echo	Packet with source in 33.1.2.0/24 to destinations beginning 44.1, which are ICMP Echo Requests and Replies.

The configuration commands used for IPX-related filters are listed in Table 7-16; the EXEC commands related to IPX filtering are shown in Table 7-17.

Table 7-16   *IPX Access List Configuration Commands*

Command	Configuration Mode and Purpose
access-list {*800-899*} {**permit** I **deny**} *source-network* [*.source-node* [*source-node-mask*]] [*destination-network* [*.destination-node* [*destination-node-mask*]]]	Global command to create numbered standard IPX access lists
access-list {*900-999*} {**permit** I **deny**} *protocol* [*source-network*] [[[*.source-node* [*source-node-mask*]] I [*.source-node source-network-mask.source-node-mask*]] [*source-socket*] [*destination-network*] [[[*.destination-node* [*destination-node-mask*] I [*.destination-node destination-network-mask. Destination-node-mask*]] [*destination-socket*] **log**	Global command to create numbered extended IPX access lists
access-list {*1000-1099*} {**permit** I **deny**} *network* [*.node*] [*network-mask.node-mask*] [*service-type* [*server-name*]]	Global command to create numbered SAP access lists
ipx access-list {**standard** I **extended** I **sap** } *name*	Global command to begin creation of a named standard, extended, or SAP access list
{**permit** I **deny**} *source-network* [*.source-node* [*source-node-mask*]] [*destination-network* [*.destination-node* [*destination-node-mask*]]]	Named access list subcommand for standard access lists
{**permit** I **deny**} *protocol* [*source-network*] [[[*.source-node* [*source-node-mask*]] I [*.source-node source-network-mask.source-node-mask*]] [*source-socket*] [*destination-network*] [[[*.destination-node* [*destination-node-mask*] I [*.destination-node destination-network-mask. Destination-node-mask*]] [*destination-socket*] **log**	Named access list subcommand for extended access lists
{**permit** I **deny**} *network* [*.node*] [*network-mask.node-mask*] [*service-type* [*server-name*]]	Named access list subcommand for SAP access lists
ipx access-group {*number* I *name* [**in** I **out**] }	Interface subcommand to enable a named or numbered, standard or extended IPX access list
ipx output-sap-filter *list-number*	Interface subcommand to enable SAP access lists used for outbound SAP packets
ipx input-sap-filter *list-number*	Interface subcommand to enable SAP access lists used for inbound SAP packets

Table 7-17   *Access List EXEC Commands*

Command	Function
show ipx interface	Includes reference to the access lists enabled on the interface
show access-list *number*	Shows details of all configured access lists for all protocols
show ipx access-list	Shows details of all IPX access lists

Table 7-18 summarizes the items that can be matched by extended and standard IPX access lists.

Table 7-18   *IPX Standard and Extended Access Lists—Matching*

Type of Access List	What Can Be Matched
IPX Standard	Source network
	Source IPX address (network and node)
	Source network and portions of the node address, using a node mask
	Destination network
	Destination IPX address (network and node)
	Destination network and portions of the node address, using a node mask
IPX Extended	Same points as with an IPX standard access list, as well as the following points
	Portions of source IPX address, using a wildcard mask
	Portions of destination IPX address, using a wildcard mask
	Protocol type
	Source socket
	Destination socket

The following list shows the fields that can be matched for each service advertised, or to be advertised, in a SAP update.

- Source network

- Source IPX address (network and node)

- Portions of the source address, using a wildcard mask

- Destination network

- Destination IPX address (network and node)

- Portions of the destination address, using a wildcard mask

- Service type

- Server name

Q&A

As mentioned in Chapter 1, "All About the Cisco Certified Network Associate Certification," the questions and scenarios in this book are more difficult than what you should experience on the actual exam. The questions do not attempt to cover more breadth or depth than the exam; however, they are designed to make sure that you know the answer. Rather than allowing you to derive the answer from clues hidden inside the question itself, the questions challenge your understanding and recall of the subject. Questions from the "Do I Know This Already?" quiz from the beginning of the chapter are repeated here to ensure that you have mastered the chapter's topic areas. Hopefully, these questions will help limit the number of exam questions on which you narrow your choices to two options and then guess.

The answers to these questions can be found in Appendix A, on page 754.

1 Configure a numbered IP access list that would stop packets from subnet 134.141.7.0, 255.255.255.0, from exiting serial 0 on some router. Allow all other packets.

2 Configure an IP access list that allows only packets from subnet 193.7.6.0, 255.255.255.0, going to hosts in network 128.1.0.0 and using a Web server in 128.1.0.0, to enter serial 0 on some router.

3 How would a user who does not have the enable password find out what access lists have been configured and where they are enabled?

4 Configure and enable an IP access list that would stop packets from subnet 10.3.4.0/24 from getting out serial interface S0 and that would stop packets from 134.141.5.4 from entering S0. Permit all other traffic.

5 Configure and enable an IP access list that would allow packets from subnet 10.3.4.0/24, to any Web server, to get out serial interface S0. Also, allow packets from 134.141.5.4 going to all TCP-based servers using a well-known port to enter serial 0. Deny all other traffic.

6 Create an IPX packet filter to prevent packets from entering Serial0, except for packets from address 500.0000.0000.0001 destined for any node in network 4.

7 What services use IPX socket 4? What about Socket 7?

8 Create a configuration to add a SAP access list to filter all print services (SAP 7) from being advertised out a router's serial 0 and serial1 interfaces.

9 Name all the items that a SAP access list can examine to make a match.

10 Can standard IP access lists be used to check the source IP address when enabled with the **ip access-group 1 in** command, and can they check the destination IP addresses when using the **ip access-group 1 out** command?

11 How many IP extended **access-list** commands are required to check a particular port number on all IP packets?

12 True or false: If all IP or IPX access list statements in a particular list define the deny action, then the default action is to permit all other packets.

13 In an IPX access list with five statements, a **no** version of the third statement is issued in configuration mode. Immediately following, another access list configuration command is added for the same access list. How many statements are in the list now, and in what position is the newly added statement?

14 How many IP access lists of either type can be active on an interface at the same time?

For questions 16 through 18, assume that all parts of the network in Figure 7-12 are up and working. IGRP is the IP routing protocol in use. Answer the questions following Example 7-16, which contains an additional configuration in the Mayberry router.

15 Describe the types of packets that this filter would discard, and tell at what point they would be discarded.

16 Does the access list in Example 7-16 stop packets from getting to Web server Governor? Why or why not?

17 Referring to Figure 7-12, create and enable access lists so that access to Web server Governor is allowed from hosts at any site, but so that no other access to hosts in Raleigh is allowed.

18 Name all the items that a standard IPX access list can examine to make a match.

19 Name all the items that an extended IPX access list can examine to make a match.

20 Name all the items that a standard IP access list can examine to make a match.

21 Name all the items that an extended IP access list can examine to make a match.

22 True or false: When using extended IP access lists for restricting vty access, the matching logic is a best match of the list, rather than a first match in the list.

23 In a standard numbered IP access list with three statements, a **no** version of the first statement is issued in configuration mode. Immediately following, another access list configuration command is added for the same access list. How many statements are in the list now, and in what position is the newly added statement?

24 In a standard named IP access list with three statements, a **no** version of the first statement is issued in configuration mode. Immediately following, another access list configuration command is added for the same access list. How many statements are in the list now, and in what position is the newly added statement?

Figure 7-12   *Network Diagram for Questions 16 Through 18*

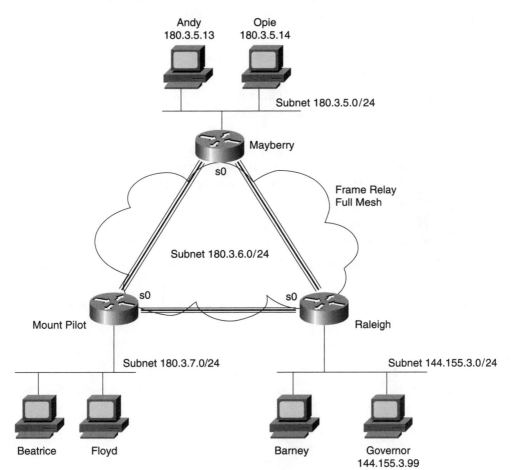

Example 7-16 *Access List at Mayberry*

```
access-list 44 permit 180.3.5.13 0.0.0.0
!
interface serial 0
ip access-group 44
```

25 In an extended named IPX access list with five statements, a **no** version of the second statement is issued in configuration mode. Immediately following, another access list configuration command is added for the same access list. How many statements are in the list now, and in what position is the newly added statement?

26 Name all the items that a named extended IPX access list can examine to make a match.

27 Name all the items that a named standard IP access list can examine to make a match.

28 Configure a SAP numbered access list so that SAPs 4 through 7 are matched in network BEEF with a single command.

29 Configure a named IP access list that would stop packets from subnet 134.141.7.0, 255.255.255.0, from exiting serial 0 on some router. Allow all other packets.

30 Configure a named IP access list that allows only packets from subnet 193.7.6.0, 255.255.255.0, going to hosts in network 128.1.0.0 and using a Web server in 128.1.0.0, to enter serial 0 on some router.

31 List the types of IP access lists (numbered standard, numbered extended, named standard, named extended) that can be enabled to prevent Telnet access into a router. What commands would be used to enable this function, assuming that **access-list 2** was already configured to match the right packets?

32 What command could someone who has only the telnet password, not the enable password, use to find out what IPX access lists were enabled on which interfaces?

33 What command would display the contents of IPX **access-list 904**, and that access list alone?

34 What command lists the IP extended access lists enabled on serial 1 without showing other interfaces?

Scenarios

Scenario 7-1: IP Filtering Sample 1

Scenarios 7-1 through 7-3 all use Figure 7-13, each with a different set of requirements for filtering. In each case, configure a correct access list for the routers and enable the access list. Place the access list in the router that filters the unneeded packets as quickly as possible—that is, before the packets have been sent far away from the originator.

Figure 7-13   *Network Diagram for IP Filtering Scenarios 7-1, 7-2, and 7-3*

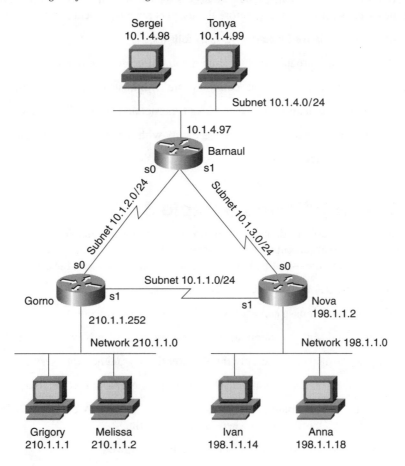

The filtering criteria for Scenario 7-1 is as follows:

1 Grigory can use the hosts on Nova's Ethernet.

2 All other hosts in Gorno (besides Grigory) cannot use the hosts on Nova's Ethernet.

3 All other communications are allowed.

Scenario 7-2: IP Filtering Sample 2

Again using the network diagram in Figure 7-13, create and enable access lists for a totally different set of requirements. Place the access list in the routers to filter the unneeded packets as quickly as possible—that is, before the packets have been sent far away from the originator.

The filtering criteria for Scenario 7-2 is as follows:

1 Hosts on the Barnaul Ethernet cannot communicate with hosts in the Gorno Ethernet.

2 Grigory and Melissa cannot communicate with hosts on the Nova Ethernet.

3 Other communications between Nova Ethernet and Gorno Ethernet are allowed.

4 Sergei (in Barnaul) can communicate only with other hosts in Barnaul.

5 Any communication paths not specified are allowed.

Scenario 7-3: IP Filtering Sample 3

Again using the network diagram in Figure 7-13, create and enable access lists for a totally different set of requirements. Place the access list in the router that filters the unneeded packets as quickly as possible—that is, before the packets have been sent far away from the originator.

The filtering criteria for Scenario 7-3 is as follows:

1 Grigory and Melissa can access any Web server in Nova.

2 Grigory and Melissa cannot access any other servers in Nova using TCP.

3 Sergei (Barnaul) can use only the Web services—and no other services—in Nova.

4 Hosts in Gorno can communicate with hosts in Nova, unless otherwise stated.

5 Web clients in Barnaul are not allowed to connect to the Web server in Nova unless specifically mentioned elsewhere in these criteria.

6 Any unspecified communication should be disallowed.

Scenario 7-4: IPX Filtering

IPX packet and SAP filtering concepts and configuration are reviewed in this scenario. Sample configurations are supplied first. Your job is to interpret the current access lists and then create new packet access lists and SAP access lists to meet some additional criteria. The details are listed after Figure 7-14 and Examples 7-17 through 7-20.

Figure 7-14   *Network Diagram for Scenario 7-4*

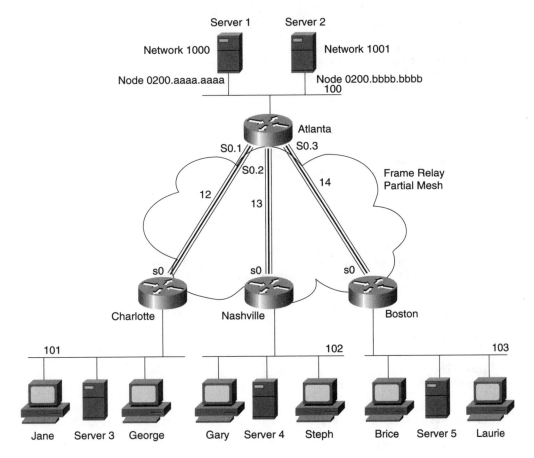

Example 7-17 *Atlanta Configuration*

```
ipx routing 0200.1111.1111
!
interface serial0
encapsulation frame-relay
!
interface serial 0.1 point-to-point
ip address 168.10.12.1  255.255.255.0
ipx network 12
ipx access-group 801 in
frame-relay interface-dlci 52
!
interface serial 0.2 point-to-point
ip address 168.10.13.1 255.255.255.0
ipx network 13
ipx access-group 903 in
frame-relay interface-dlci 53
!
interface serial 0.3 point-to-point
ip address 168.10.14.1 255.255.255.0
ipx network 14
ipx access-group 903 in
frame-relay interface-dlci 54
!
interface ethernet 0
ip address 168.10.100.1 255.255.255.0
ipx network 100
!
access-list 903 deny any 102.0000.0000.0000 1.ffff.ffff.ffff all 100
access-list 903 permit any any
access-list 801 deny 101 100.0200.bbbb.bbbb
access-list 801 permit -1
```

Example 7-18 *Charlotte Configuration*

```
ipx routing 0200.2222.2222
!
interface serial0
encapsulation frame-relay
!
interface serial 0.1 point-to-point
ip address 168.10.12.2 255.255.255.0
ipx network 12
frame-relay interface-dlci 51
!
interface ethernet 0
ip address 168.10.101.2 255.255.255.0
ipx network 101
```

Example 7-19 *Nashville Configuration*

```
ipx routing 0200.3333.3333
!
interface serial0
encapsulation frame-relay
!
interface serial 0.2 point-to-point
ip address 168.10.13.3 255.255.255.0
ipx network 13
frame-relay interface-dlci 51
!
interface ethernet 0
ip address 168.10.102.3 255.255.255.0
ipx network 102
```

Example 7-20 *Boston Configuration*

```
ipx routing 0200.4444.4444
!
interface serial0
encapsulation frame-relay
!
interface serial 0.3 point-to-point
ip address 168.10.14.4 255.255.255.0
ipx network 14
frame-relay interface-dlci 51
!
interface ethernet 0
ip address 168.10.103.4 255.255.255.0
ipx network 103
```

Given the network in Figure 7-14 and the configurations in Example 7-17 through 7-20, answer the questions and perform the tasks that follow.

1 Characterize the traffic that is discarded due to the access lists used on Atlanta. Can clients in the remote sites access the servers in Atlanta?

2 Create IPX packet filters to meet the following criteria:

— Clients in Nashville and Boston are not allowed access to Server 1.

— Clients in Charlotte are not allowed access to Server 2.

— Use standard access lists, if possible.

— Place the access lists close to the source of the packets.

— Assume that all access lists from Task 1 have been disabled and deleted.

3 Create SAP filters that perform the same function as described in Task 2.

Scenario Answers

Answers to Scenario 7-1: IP Filtering Sample 1

The solution to fulfilling the criteria stipulated for this access list is straightforward. Simply matching Grigory to permit his traffic and denying packets from 210.1.1.0 is all that is needed for the first two criteria. A "permit all" needs to be explicitly configured at the end of the list.

Example 7-21 provides the solution for this scenario. The access list will be enabled on Nova. The problem with list 43 is that if the link from Barnaul to Gorno goes down, and if Gorno learns a route to Barnaul's subnets via Nova, Nova will be filtering all inbound packets from (non-Grigory) Gorno hosts. A better list would be to use an extended access-list, matching both the source and the destination addresses. **access-list 143** also is shown in Example 7-21, which would avoid the problem seen in **access-list 43**. (**access-list 43** is enabled in the example.)

Example 7-21 *Solution to Scenario 7-1—Nova*

```
access-list 43 permit host 210.1.1.1
access-list 43 deny 210.1.1.0 0.0.0.255
access-list 43 permit any
!
access-list 143 permit ip host 210.1.1.1 198.1.1.0 0.0.0.255
access-list 143 deny ip 210.1.1.0 0.0.0.255 198.1.1.0 0.0.0.255
access-list 143 permit ip any any
!
interface serial 0
ip access-group 43 in
!
interface serial 1
ip access-group 43 in
```

Answers to Scenario 7-2: IP Filtering Sample 2

Many solutions could fulfill the criteria stipulated for this scenario. The solutions provided in Examples 7-22 and 7-23 attempt to filter packets as close to the source of the packet as possible. It is impossible to determine whether your correct solution is better than the one given here, or vice versa, without more information about traffic loads and business needs in the network. Comments shown inside the configurations in Example 7-22 and Example 7-23 provide most of the detailed commentary.

Example 7-22 *Scenario 7-2 Answer—Barnaul Access List*

```
! Next statement meets Criterion 1
access-list 101 deny ip 10.1.4.0 0.0.0.255 210.1.1.0 0.0.0.255
! next statement meets criteria 4
access-list 101 deny ip host 10.1.4.98 any
! Criterion 5 met in the next statement
access-list 101 permit ip any any
```

Example 7-22 *Scenario 7-2 Answer—Barnaul Access List (Continued)*

```
interface serial 0
ip access-group 101
!
interface serial 1
ip access-group 101
```

Example 7-23 *Scenario 7-2 Answer—Gorno Access List*

```
! Next statements meet Criterion 2
access-list 101 deny ip host 210.1.1.1 198.1.1.0 0.0.0.255
access-list 101 deny ip host 210.1.1.2 198.1.1.0 0.0.0.255
! Next statement meets Criterion 3, but it's not required, due to the final
statement
access-list 101 permit ip 210.1.1.0 0.0.0.255 198.1.1.0 0.0.0.255
access-list 101 permit ip any any
!
interface serial 0
ip access-group 101
!
interface serial 1
ip access-group 101
```

Answers to Scenario 7-3: IP Filtering Sample 3

Many solutions could fulfill the criteria stipulated for this scenario. The solutions provided in Examples 7-24 and 7-25 attempt to filter packets as close to the source of the packet as possible. It is impossible to determine whether your correct solution is better than the one given here, or vice versa, without more information about traffic loads and business needs in the network. Comments shown inside the configurations in Example 7-24 and Example 7-25 provide most of the detailed commentary.

Example 7-24 *Scenario 7-3 Answer—Barnaul Access List*

```
! Next statements meet Criterion 3
access-list 101 permit tcp host 10.1.4.98 198.1.1.0 0.0.0.255 eq www
access-list 101 deny tcp host 10.1.4.98 198.1.1.0.0.0.0.25 lt 1023
! Next statement meets Criterion 5, but it's not really needed
access-list 101 deny ip 10.1.4.0 0.0.0.255 198.1.1.0 0.0.0.255 eq www
! Criterion 6 is met in the default
!
interface serial 0
ip access-group 101
!
interface serial 1
ip access-group 101
```

Example 7-25 *Scenario 7-3 Answer—Gorno Access List*

```
! Next statements meet Criterion 1
access-list 101 permit tcp host 210.1.1.1 198.1.1.0 0.0.0.255 eq www
access-list 101 permit tcp host 210.1.1.2 198.1.1.0 0.0.0.255 eq www
! Next statements meet Criterion 2
access-list 101 deny tcp host 210.1.1.1 198.1.1.0 0.0.0.255 lt 1023
access-list 101 deny tcp host 210.1.1.2 198.1.1.0 0.0.0.255 lt 1023
! Next statement meets criterion 4
access-list 101 permit ip 210.1.1.0 0.0.0.255 198.1.1.0 0.0.0.255
!Default meets Criterion 6
!
interface serial 0
ip access-group 101
!
interface serial 1
ip access-group 101
```

The default action can be used to shorten the list. For example, in Example 7-24 the commands **access-list 101 deny tcp host 10.1.4.98 198.1.1.0 0.0.0.255 lt 1023** and **access-list 101 deny ip 10.1.4.0 0.0.0.255 198.1.1.0 0.0.0.255 eq www** in access list 101 are not really needed because the default is to deny these anyway. So, list 101 would perform the same function if it had only one statement in it (**access-list 101 permit tcp host 10.1.4.98 198.1.1.0 0.0.0.255 eq www**).

Answers to Scenario 7-4: IPX Filtering

Refer to the network illustrated in Figure 7-14 and Examples 7-17 through 7-20 to establish the Scenario 7-4 design details and the context of the answers to the three tasks for this scenario.

Answers to Task 1 for Scenario 7-4

Task 1 for Scenario 7-4 asks you to characterize the traffic that is discarded due to the access lists used on Atlanta. Furthermore, you need to determine whether clients in the remote sites can access the servers in Atlanta. The answer is not obvious in this case. The extended access list is particularly confusing, given all the options. The parameters coded in the first entry in list 903 in Example 7-17 are as follows:

- **Deny**—Direction to throw away packets that match.

- **Any**—Any protocol type.

- **102.0000.0000.0000**—Source IPX address. The node part of the address will be masked, so all 0s are coded in the node part of the address. The node part of the address must be configured; otherwise, the syntax does not allow the right to use the network wildcard mask.

- **1.ffff.ffff.ffff**—Source network and node wildcard mask. With leading zeroes written in, the mask would be 00000001.ffff.ffff.ffff. This mask matches networks 102 and 103, which are identical except for the final bit in the network part of the address. The mask means, "all bits in the network must match network 102, except for the last bit in the network number." (All Fs for the node mean that any node number will match.)

- **All**—All sockets.

- **100**—Destination network.

So, the first entry in list 903 matches packets from network 102 and 103, destined for network 100, any protocol, any socket. These packets are denied. The second entry in 903 permits all protocols, all source networks, and, by implication, all destination networks; in other words, this statement changes the default to be "permit all else."

By enabling list 903 for inbound packets on Atlanta's serial 0.2 and serial 0.3 interfaces, clients in Nashville and Boston cannot reach network 100.

Access list 801 stops all packets from network 101 from reaching Server 2's Ethernet IPX address. It also has a "permit everything else" statement at the end of the list, but because standard IPX access lists do not use the any keyword, **–1** is used to signify **any**.

Neither list stops access to Server 1 or Server 2 because the destination of packets to these servers will be the internal IPX addresses (1000.0000.0000.0001 and 1001.0000.0000.0001). Packets sent to networks 1000 and 1001 will not be matched until the "permit all" at the end of the lists.

Answers to Task 2 for Scenario 7-4

Task 2 for Scenario 7-4 asks you to create IPX packet filters to meet the following criteria:

- Clients in Nashville and Boston are not allowed access to Server 1.

- Clients in Charlotte are not allowed access to Server 2.

- Use standard access lists, if possible.

- Place the access lists close to the source of the packets.

- Assume that all access lists from Task 1 have been disabled and deleted.

This can be accomplished by configuring standard IPX access lists. Because the goal is to filter packets close to the source, and because the client initiates the process of connecting to a server, the filters all were placed at the remote routers and not in Atlanta. Each filter matches packets sourced in their local IPX networks and destined for network 1000 (if filtering packets destined for Server 1), or destined for network 1001 (if filtering packets destined for Server 2). Examples 7-26 through 7-28 show the configurations necessary to create IPX packet filters to satisfy the criteria.

Example 7-26 *Charlotte with Access List Configured, Scenario 7-4, Task 2*

```
access-list 800 deny 101 1001
access-list 800 permit -1
!
interface serial 0.1 point-to-point
ipx access-group 800
```

Example 7-27 *Nashville with Access List Configured, Scenario 7-4, Task 2*

```
access-list 800 deny 102 1000
access-list 800 permit -1
!
interface serial 0.2 point-to-point
ipx access-group 800
```

Example 7-28 *Boston with Access List Configured, Scenario 7-4, Task 2*

```
access-list 800 deny 103 1000
access-list 800 permit -1
!
interface serial 0.3 point-to-point
ipx access-group 800
```

Answers to Task 3 for Scenario 7-4

Task 3 for Scenario 7-4 asks you to create SAP filters that perform the same function as described in Task 2. Task 3 suggests a very simple solution, but the simple solution works only because there are local servers in Charlotte, Nashville, and Boston. First, take a look at the solution; then read over some comments.

Because the local server in each case will be the GNS server for the local clients, respectively, all that is needed is to stop Server 1 and Server 2 SAP information from being advertised into the remote sites. In an effort to reduce overhead, the SAP filters will be placed in Atlanta because SAP information originates in the servers. Example 7-29 provides the solution.

Example 7-29 *Atlanta with SAP Filter Configured, Scenario 7-4, Task 3*

```
access-list 1050 deny 1000
access-list 1050 permit -1
!
access-list 1051 deny 1001
access-list 1051 permit -1
!
interface serial 0.1 point-to-point
ipx output-sap-filter 1051
!
interface serial 0.2 point-to-point
ipx output-sap-filter 1050
!
interface serial 0.3 point-to-point
ipx output-sap-filter 1050
```

SAPs about Server 1 (network 1000) are filtered from being sent out serial 0.2 and serial 0.3 to Nashville and Boston, respectively. Likewise, SAPs about Server 2 (network 1001) are filtered from being sent out serial 0.1 to Charlotte. Server 3 will not know about Server 2, so it cannot tell Charlotte clients about Server 2. Likewise, Server 4 and Server 5 will not know about Server 1, so they cannot tell Nashville clients and Boston clients about Server 1.

SAP filters are also great for reducing traffic, of course. However, when using them for stopping particular clients and servers from communicating, there are some caveats. If no servers were in place in Charlotte, Nashville, or Boston, the remote clients would have used Server 1 or Server 2 as their GNS server. Server 1 and Server 2 have full knowledge of each other's SAP information because they are on the same Ethernet. Therefore, clients would be capable of connecting to the servers, in spite of efforts to prevent the connections using SAP filtering.

This chapter covers the following topics that you will need to master as a CCNA:

- **Point-to-Point Leased Lines**   This section covers basic operation and terminology used with point-to-point leased lines. Configuration and debugging of PPP, HDLC, and LAPB are shown as well.

- **Frame Relay Protocols**   Frame Relay is one of the most popular WAN services today. The concepts and terminology used with Frame Relay are discussed in detail, including the use of Frame Relay DLCIs.

- **Frame Relay Configuration**   Several variations for Frame Relay configuration exist. This section covers the default style of configuration and then discusses the various options. The text also details design choices of how to assign IP subnet and IPX network numbers.

- **ISDN Protocols and Design**   As with Frame Relay, ISDN has its own set of concepts, terms, and acronyms. This section covers the protocol basics.

- **Dial-on-Demand Routing and ISDN Configuration**   Dial-on-demand routing (DDR) is the name for the IOS features that relate to dialing other routers to add new links for routing packets. This section covers DDR concepts and configuration, with ISDN configuration information interspersed.

- **A Comparison of WAN Options**   This section gives a brief summary of the WAN options covered in this chapter.

CHAPTER 8

WAN Protocols and Design

CCNAs deal with both permanent and dialed WAN connections on routers on a regular basis. In fact, with the pervasiveness of LAN switches in modern buildings, more frequently the issues relating to router installation and troubleshooting are about WAN connections.

This chapter is rather long; if you plan to read the entire chapter, you might want to treat it as three separate sections. These three major sections are outlined in Table 8-1. The first of these topical areas discusses point-to-point leased lines. The second covers Frame Relay, and the last details DDR and ISDN.

Cisco expects CCNAs to be able to configure, verify, and troubleshoot WAN connections. The conceptual material in this chapter is important, but it is Cisco's desire that the exam serve as proof that you are able to make this stuff work. Focusing on the command examples and scenarios will help.

How to Best Use This Chapter

By taking the following steps, you can make better use of your study time:

- Keep your notes and the answers for all your work with this book in one place, for easy reference.

- Take the "Do I Know This Already?" quiz, and write down your answers. Studies show that retention is significantly increased through writing down facts and concepts, even if you never look at the information again.

- Use the diagram in Figure 8-1 to guide you to the next step.

Figure 8-1   *How to Use This Chapter*

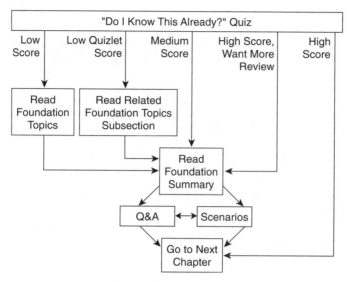

"Do I Know This Already?" Quiz

The purpose of the "Do I Know This Already?" quiz is to help you decide what parts of this chapter to use. If you already intend to read the entire chapter, you do not necessarily need to answer these questions now.

This 12-question quiz helps you choose how to spend your limited study time. The quiz is sectioned into three smaller four-question "quizlets," which correspond to the three major headings in the chapter. Figure 8-1 outlines suggestions on how to spend your time in this chapter. Use Table 8-1 to record your score.

Table 8-1   *Scoresheet for Quiz and Quizlets*

Quizlet Number	Foundation Topics Sections Covering These Questions	Questions	Score
1	Point-to-Point Leased Lines	1 to 4	
2	Frame Relay Protocols Frame Relay Configuration	5 to 8	
3	ISDN Protocols and Design Dial-on-Demand Routing and ISDN Configuration	9 to 12	
All questions		1 to 12	

1 Can PPP perform dynamic assignment of IP addresses? If so, is the feature always enabled?

_____

_____

_____

2 Create a configuration to enable PPP on serial 0 for IP and IPX. Make up IP and IPX Layer 3 addresses as needed.

_____

_____

_____

3 CHAP configuration uses names and passwords. Given Routers A and B, describe what names and passwords must match in the respective CHAP configurations.

_____

_____

_____

4 What field has Cisco added to the HDLC header, making it proprietary?

_____

_____

_____

5 Explain the purpose of Inverse ARP. Explain how Inverse ARP uses Frame Relay broadcasts.

_____

_____

_____

6 Would a Frame Relay switch connected to a router behave differently if the IETF option were deleted from the encapsulation **frame-relay ietf** command on that attached router? Would a router on the other end of the VC behave any differently if the same change were made?

_____

_____

_____

7 What **show** command will tell you the time that a PVC became active? How does the router know what time the PVC came active?

_____

_____

_____

8 What **debug** options will show Inverse ARP messages?

_____

_____

_____

9 What does the acronym LAPD stand for? Is it used as the Layer 2 protocol on dialed ISDN bearer channels? If not, what is used?

_____

_____

_____

10 Define the term _reference point_. List two examples of reference points.

_____

_____

_____

11 Describe the decision process performed by the IOS to attempt to dial a connection using legacy DDR.

_____

_____

_____

12 If packets from 10.1.1.0/24 were "interesting" in relation to DDR configuration such that packets from 10.1.1.0/24 would cause a DDR connection out an interface BRI0, list the configuration commands that would make the IOS think that those packets were interesting on BRI0.

_____

_____

_____

The answers to the quiz are found in Appendix A, "Answers to the 'Do I Know This Already?' Quizzes and Q&A Sections," on page 768. The suggested choices for your next step are as follows:

- **6 or less overall score**—Read the entire chapter. This includes the "Foundation Topics" and "Foundation Summary" sections, the Q&A section, and the scenarios at the end of the chapter.

- **2 or less on any quizlet**—Review the subsection(s) of the "Foundation Topics" part of this chapter, based on the following list. Then move into the "Foundation Summary" section, the quiz, and the scenarios at the end of the chapter.

- **7, 8, or 9 overall score**—Begin with the "Foundation Summary" section, and then go to the Q&A section and the scenarios at the end of the chapter.

- **10 or more overall score**—If you want more review on these topics, skip to the "Foundation Summary" section and then go to the Q&A section and the scenarios at the end of the chapter. Otherwise, move to the next chapter.

Foundation Topics

Point-to-Point Leased Lines

WAN protocols used on point-to-point serial links provide the basic function of delivery of data across that one link. As a CCNA, you will be required to understand and configure a variety of protocols used on point-to-point links, including Link Access Procedure Balanced (LAPB), High-Level Data Link Control (HDLC), and Point-to-Point Protocol (PPP). Each of these WAN protocols has the following functions in common:

- LAPB, HDLC, and PPP provide for delivery of data across a single point-to-point serial link.

- LAPB, HDLC, and PPP deliver data on synchronous serial links. (PPP supports asynchronous functions as well.)

Framing is one core feature of any synchronous serial data link protocol. Each of these protocols defines framing so that receiving stations know where the beginning of the frame is, what address is in the header, and the point at which the packet begins. By doing so, the router receiving data can distinguish between idle frames and data frames. Synchronous links, rather than asynchronous links, are typically used between routers.

Synchronous simply means that there is an imposed time ordering at the sending and receiving ends of the link. Essentially, the sides agree to a certain speed, but because it is very expensive to build devices that can truly operate at exactly the same speed, the devices adjust their rates to match a clock source. The process works almost like the scenes in spy novels, when the spies synchronize their watches; in this case, the watches or clocks are synchronized automatically multiple times per minute. Unlike asynchronous links, in which no bits are sent during idle times, synchronous data links define idle frames. These frames do nothing more than provide plenty of signal transitions so that clocks can be adjusted on the receiving end, consequently maintaining synchronization.

Before describing the features of these data link protocols, a brief reference to some popularly used WAN terminology is useful. Table 8-2 lists the terms.

Table 8-2   *WAN Terminology*

Term	Definition
Synchronous	The imposition of time ordering on a bit stream. More practically speaking, a device will try to use the same speed as another on the other end of a serial link. However, by examining transitions between voltage states on the link, the device can notice slight variations in the speed on each end so that it can adjust its speed.

Table 8-2   *WAN Terminology (Continued)*

Term	Definition
Asynchronous	The lack of an imposed time ordering on a bit stream. More practically speaking, both sides agree to the same speed, but there is no check or adjustment of the rates if they are slightly different. However, because only 1 byte per transfer is sent, slight differences in clock speed are not an issue. A start bit is used to signal the beginning of a byte.
Clock source	The device to which the other devices on the link adjust their speed when using synchronous links.
DSU/CSU	Data Services Unit and Channel Services Unit. This is used on digital links as an interface to the telephone company in the United States. Routers typically use a short cable from a serial interface to a DSU/CSU, which is attached to the line from the telco with a similar configuration at the other router on the other end of the link. The routers use their attached DSU/CSU as the clock source.
Telco	Telephone company.
4-wire circuit	A line from the telco with four wires, comprised of two twisted-pair wires. Each pair is used to send in one direction, so a 4-wire circuit allows full-duplex communication.
2-wire circuit	A line from the telco with two wires, comprised of one twisted-pair wire. The pair is used to send in only one direction at a time, so a 2-wire circuit allows only half-duplex communication.
T/1	A line from the telco that allows transmission of data at 1.544Mbps. This can be used with a T/1 multiplexor.
T/1 mux	A multiplexor that separates the T/1 into 24 different 64kbps channels. In the United States, one of every 8 bits in each channel can be used by the telco so that the channels are effectively 56kbps channels.
E/1	Like a T/1, but in Europe. It uses a rate of 2.048Mbps and 32 64kbps channels.

Three key attributes help to differentiate among these synchronous serial data link protocols (LAPB, HDLC, and PPP):

- Whether the protocol supports synchronous communications, asynchronous communications, or both.

- Whether the protocol provides error recovery. (The LAPB, HDLC, and PPP protocols all provide error detection.)

- Whether an architected Protocol Type field exists. In other words, the protocol specifications define a field in the header that identifies the type of packet contained in the data portion of the frame.

First, a few words about the criteria used to compare these WAN protocols might prove helpful. Synchronous protocols allow more throughput over a serial link than asynchronous protocols do. However, asynchronous protocols require less expensive hardware because there is no need to watch transitions and adjust the clock rate. For links between routers, synchronous links are typically desired and used. All the protocols covered in this section support synchronous links.

Another comparison criteria is error recovery. Error recovery is covered in detail in Chapter 3, "OSI Reference Model & Layered Communication," but a brief review is in order here. All the data link protocols described here use a field in the trailer, usually called the frame check sequence (FCS), that is used to verify whether bit errors occurred during transmission of the frame. If so, the frame is discarded. Error recovery is the process that causes retransmission of the lost frame(s); error recovery may be performed by the data link protocol or a higher-layer protocol, or error recovery may not be performed at all. Regardless, all WAN data link protocols perform error detection, which involves noticing the error and discarding the frame.

Finally, the definition and use of an architected Protocol Type field is the final criteria for comparison. As described in more detail in Chapter 3, each data link protocol that supports multiple network layer protocols needs a method of defining the type of packet encapsulated inside the WAN data link frame. If such a field is part of the protocol specification, it is considered "architected"—in other words, specified in the protocol. If Cisco must add some other header information to create a Protocol Type field, then that type field is not considered to be architected.

Table 8-3 lists these point-to-point data link protocols and their attributes. (For a review of the Protocol Type field, refer to Chapter 3.)

Table 8-3   *Point-to-Point Data Link Protocol Attributes*

Protocol	Error Correction?	Architected Type Field?	Other Attributes
Synchronous Data Link Control (SDLC)	Yes	None	SDLC supports multipoint links; it assumes that the SNA header occurs after the SDLC header.
Link Access Procedure Balanced (LAPB)	Yes	None	Spec assumes a single configurable protocol after LAPB. LAPB is used mainly with X.25. Cisco uses a proprietary type field to support multiprotocol traffic.
Link Access Procedure on the D channel (LAPD)	No	No	LAPD is not used between routers, but is used on the D channel from router to ISDN switch for signaling.

Table 8-3   *Point-to-Point Data Link Protocol Attributes (Continued)*

Protocol	Error Correction?	Architected Type Field?	Other Attributes
High-Level Data Link Control (HDLC)	No	No	HDLC serves as Cisco's default on serial links. Cisco uses a proprietary type field to support multiprotocol traffic.
Point-to-Point Protocol (PPP)	Enables the user to choose whether error correction is performed; correction uses LAPB	Yes	PPP was meant for multiprotocol interoperability from its inception, unlike all the others. PPP also supports asynchronous communication.

Note: Be careful not to confuse LAPB and LAPD. The D can help remind you that it is for an ISDN D channel, but don't let that make you think that the B is for an ISDN B channel.

HDLC and PPP Configuration

One common task for CCNAs is to enable an appropriate point-to-point data link protocol. The configuration is straightforward, with LAPB being the exception. (Be sure to configure the same WAN data link protocol on each end of the serial link. Otherwise, the routers will misinterpret the incoming frames, and the link will not work.) Tables 8-4 and 8-5 summarize the configuration commands and the **show** and **debug** commands used for HDLC and PPP configuration.

Table 8-4   *PPP and HDLC Configuration Commands*

Command	Configuration Mode
encapsulation {hdlc | ppp | lapb}	Interface subcommand
compress [Predictor | stac | mppc [ignore-pfc]]	Interface subcommand

Table 8-5   *Point-to-Point Related show and debug Commands*

Command	Function
show interface	Lists statistics and details of interface configuration, including the encapsulation type.
show compress	Lists compression ratios.
show process	Lists processor and task utilization. Is useful in watching for increased utilization due to compression.

Example 8-1 lists configuration for PPP, followed by the changed configuration for a migration to HDLC. Assume that Router A and Router B have a serial link attached to their serial 0 ports, respectively.

Example 8-1 *Configuration for PPP and HDLC*

```
Router A                          Router B

Interface serial 0                Interface serial 0
encapsulation ppp                 encapsulation ppp
.                                 .
. later, changed to...            . later, changed to...
.                                 .
interface serial 0                interface serial 0
encapsulation hdlc                encapsulation hdlc
```

Changing serial encapsulations in configuration mode is tricky compared to some other configuration commands in a Cisco router. In Example 8-1, converting back to HDLC (the default) is done with the **encapsulation hdlc** command, not by using a command such as **no encapsulation ppp**. Additionally, any other interface subcommands that are pertinent only to PPP are also removed when the **encapsulation hdlc** command is used.

PPP provides several other features in addition to synchronization and framing. The features fall into two categories: those needed regardless of the Layer 3 protocol sent across the link, and those particular to each Layer 3 protocol.

The PPP Link Control Protocol (LCP) provides the base features needed regardless of the Layer 3 protocol sent across the link. A series of PPP control protocols, such as IP Control Protocol (IPCP), provide features for a particular Layer 3 protocol to function well across the link. For example, IPCP provides for IP address assignment; this feature is used extensively with Internet dialup connections today.

Only one LCP is needed per link, but multiple control protocols are needed. If a router is configured for IPX, AppleTalk, and IP on a PPP serial link, the router configured for PPP encapsulation automatically tries to bring up the appropriate control protocols for each Layer 3 protocol. Table 8-6 summarizes the features of LCP, which performs functions not specific to a particular Layer 3 protocol.

Table 8-6 *PPP LCP Features*

Function	Name of LCP Feature	Description
Error detection	Link Quality Monitoring (LQM)	PPP can take down a link based on the percentage of errors on the link. LQM exchanges statistics about lost packets versus sent packets in each direction; when compared to packets and bytes sent, this yields a percentage of errored traffic. The percentage of loss that causes a link to be taken down is enabled and defined by a configuration setting.

Table 8-6   *PPP LCP Features (Continued)*

Function	Name of LCP Feature	Description
Looped link detection	Magic number	Using a magic number, routers send messages to each other with a different magic number. If you ever receive your own magic number, the link is looped. A configuration setting determines whether the link should be taken down when looped.
Authentication	PAP and CHAP	Mostly used on dial links, PAP and CHAP can be used to authenticate the device on the other end of the link.
Compression	STAC and Predictor	This is software compression.
Multilink support	Multilink PPP	Fragments of packets are load-balanced across multiple links. This feature is more often used with dial. The section "Multilink PPP," later in the chapter, covers this concept in greater detail.

Error Detection and Looped Link Detection

Error detection and looped link detection are two key features of PPP. Looped link detection allows for faster convergence when a link fails because it is looped. (Links are typically looped for testing purposes.) When this occurs, a router continues to receive the looped Cisco proprietary keepalive messages, so the router might not think that the link has failed. For instance, the absence of routing updates from a neighbor for a certain length of time is used to drive convergence. Waiting on such an event when the link is looped increases convergence time.

Looped link detection defeats this problem using a PPP feature called *magic numbers*. The router sends PPP messages instead of keepalives; these messages include a magic number, which is different on each router. If a line is looped, the router receives a message with its own magic number instead of getting a message with the magic number identifying the router on the other end of the link. A router receiving its own magic number knows that the frame it sent has been looped back. If configured to do so, the router can take down the interface, which speeds convergence.

Error detection (not error recovery) is accomplished by a PPP feature called *Link Quality Monitoring (LQM)*. PPP at each end of the link sends messages describing the number of correctly received packets and bytes. This is compared to the number of packets and bytes sent to calculate a percentage loss. The router can be configured to take down the link after a configured error rate has been exceeded so that future packets are sent over a longer—but hopefully better—path.

Compression

Compression can be performed on LAPB, HDLC, and PPP point-to-point serial links. The goal of compression is to reduce the number of bytes sent across the link. However, there is a price to pay for compression—CPU cycles and possibly increased latency for the packets. The following list summarizes the trade-offs when considering whether to use compression:

- More processing is required on the router to compress each frame, as compared with no compression.

- Latency per frame will increase because of the processing required.

- Latency per frame will decrease in cases when the uncompressed packets have waited in the output queue due to link congestion. With the compressed frames, however, the queue is shorter.

- Link utilization will decrease.

So, in cases in which the leased lines are expensive or a faster line cannot be justified, then compression can be desirable. However, care must be taken to avoid excessive CPU utilization. Cisco recommends avoiding sustained CPU utilization exceeding between 40 and 65 percent, depending on the platform.

Compression can be performed in software or in hardware. Any IOS router can perform LAPB, HDLC, and PPP link compression in software; when software compression is used, CPU utilization is impacted. For hardware compression, either a VIP2 card or a Compression Service Adapter (CSA) on a 72xx or 75xx series router is required. When hardware compression is performed, the CPU is not affected.

Several compression algorithms are available in the IOS to perform PPP compression: the *STAC*, *Predictor*, and *Microsoft Point-to-Point Compression* algorithm (MPPC). The details of the algorithms are beyond the scope of the CCNA exam. However, the MPPC algorithm and protocols can be used between a router and a PC on a dial connection when compression is desired.

HDLC supports compression only with the STAC algorithm. LAPB supports STAC and Predictor algorithms. Only PPP supports the MPPC algorithm. Table 8-7 summarizes the support for each type.

Table 8-7   *Compression Types for Serial Encapsulations*

Encapsulation Type	Type of Compression Supported in IOS
PPP	STAC, Predictor, MPPC
LAPB	STAC, Predictor
HDLC	STAC

Configuration for PPP and HDLC compression is very straightforward. Consider Figure 8-2 and Example 8-2. A pair of routers is using a serial link and is configured for PPP STAC compression.

Figure 8-2   *Serial Link Configured for Compression*

Example 8-2   *PPP Compression Configuration and Verification*

```
! Seville's Pertinent configuration:
!
interface Serial1
 ip address 10.1.11.253 255.255.255.0
 encapsulation ppp
 compress stac

! Mars's Pertinent configuration:
!
interface Serial1
 ip address 10.1.11.1 255.255.255.0
 encapsulation ppp
 compress stac
!

Seville#show compress
 Serial1
        Software compression enabled
uncompressed bytes xmt/rcv 10710562/11376835
1  min avg ratio xmt/rcv 2.773/2.474
5  min avg ratio xmt/rcv 4.084/3.793
10 min avg ratio xmt/rcv 4.125/3.873
no bufs xmt 0 no bufs rcv 0
resets 0

Seville#show process
CPU utilization for five seconds: 15%/15%; one minute: 27%; five minutes: 26%
 PID QTy      PC Runtime (ms)    Invoked   uSecs    Stacks TTY Process
   1 Csp  31C084C         4024      13359     301  720/1000   0 Load Meter
```

The configuration in Example 8-2, compared to a scenario without using compression, simply requires that the interfaces on each end of the link have the same compression algorithm enabled with the **compress** command. The **show compress** command in the example does not have any particularly interesting numbers, mainly because of the lack of traffic in the network. The 1-, 5-, and 10-minute averages are the transmit and receive compression ratios, which are particularly useful for discovering whether the compression is effective. In fact, if most of the traffic being sent has been compressed already, then the compression ratios probably will be low; Cisco recommends not using compression if this is the case.

The **show process** output, which is abbreviated, shows the CPU utilization. The numbers seem to be in a reasonable range; for perspective, however, I simply let a **ping** command run on the Seville router for a few minutes to create the output. No true user traffic was generated for Example 8-2. Watching for compression driving the CPU utilization too high will be important.

WAN Cabling Standards

Cisco expects CCNAs to have an understanding of the cabling options for LAN and WAN interfaces. For any of the point-to-point serial links or Frame Relay links in this chapter, all that is needed on the router is a synchronous serial interface. Traditionally, this interface is a 60-pin D-shell connector. This interface must then be cabled to a DSU/CSU, which in turn is connected to the cable supplied by the service provider. Figure 8-3 shows a typical connection, with the serial cabling options listed.

Figure 8-3 *Serial Cable Options*

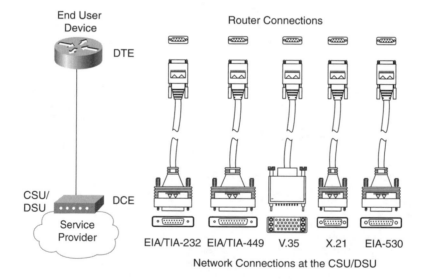

Table 8-8 summarizes the variety of standards that define the types of connectors and physical signaling protocols used on WAN interfaces.

Table 8-8   *WAN Interface Standards*

Standard	Standards Body	Number of Pins on Interface
EIA/TIA 232	Telecommunications Industry Association	25
EIA/TIA 449	Telecommunications Industry Association	37
EIA/TIA 530	Telecommunications Industry Association	25
V.35	International Telecommunications Union	34
X.21	International Telecommunications Union	15

These cables provide connectivity to the external DSU/CSU, as seen in Figure 8-3. The interface to the service provider is dependent on the type of connection; the connector could be RJ-11, RJ-48, RJ-45, or possibly coax.

Some serial interfaces have an integrated DSU/CSU and do not require a cable of the types shown in the figure. Depending on the expected type of line, a variety of physical interfaces are used. These interfaces are the same as those used for external CSU/DSU devices.

The TIA is accredited by ANSI for development of telecommunications standards. Also, the TIA works with the ITU on international standards. For more information on these standards bodies, and for the opportunity to spend money to get copies of the standards, you can refer to the Web sites www.tiaonline.org or www.itu.int.

Frame Relay Protocols

Frame Relay provides delivery of variable-sized data frames to multiple WAN-connected sites. Other than point-to-point links, Frame Relay is the WAN protocol most typically seen by CCNAs. This section reviews the details of how Frame Relay accomplishes its goal of delivery of frames to multiple WAN-connected sites.

Frame Relay is a well-chosen name for reminding you that it most closely relates to OSI Layer 2. The term *frame* is generally associated with a collection of data bits that includes an OSI Layer 2 equivalent header. For example, an Ethernet frame includes the Ethernet header/trailer. Frame Relay uses addresses, but that addressing does not attempt to create a logical address structure that could be used over a variety of media; therefore, Frame Relay addressing is closer to OSI Layer 2 addressing standards and is considered to be a Layer 2 protocol. (Refer to Chapter 3 for a review of OSI layers.)

The remainder of this section summarizes the Frame Relay protocol details expected to be on the exam.

Frame Relay Features and Terminology

Frame Relay is a multiaccess network, which actually means that more than two devices can attach to the medium. Multiaccess is the first and most obvious difference between Frame Relay and leased lines. However, leased lines are used as the access link component of Frame Relay networks. Consider Figure 8-4, which is a valuable resource for reviewing Frame Relay concepts.

Figure 8-4   *Frame Relay Components*

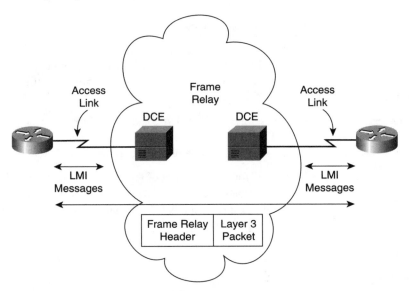

The access link between the router and the Frame Relay switch is a leased line. Both sites represented in Figure 8-4 are connected to some nearby switch via a leased line. The service provider interconnects their switches to provide connectivity.

Table 8-9 lists the components in Figure 8-4 and some associated terms.

Table 8-9   *Frame Relay Terms and Concepts*

Virtual circuit (VC)	A VC is a logical concept that represents the path that frames travel between DTEs. VCs are particularly useful when comparing Frame Relay to leased physical circuits.
Permanent virtual circuit (PVC)	A PVC is a VC that is predefined. A PVC can be equated to a leased line in concept.
Switched virtual circuit (SVC)	An SVC is a VC that is set up dynamically. An SVC can be equated to a dial connection in concept.

Table 8-9   *Frame Relay Terms and Concepts (Continued)*

Data terminal equipment (DTE)	DTEs are also known as data-circuit termination equipment. For example, routers are DTEs when connected to a Frame Relay service from a telecommunication company.
Data communications equipment (DCE)	Frame Relay switches are DCE devices.
Access link	The access link is the leased line between DTE and DCE.
Access rate (AR)	The access rate is the speed at which the access link is clocked. This choice affects the price of the connection.
Committed information rate (CIR)	The CIR is the rate at which the DTE can send data for an individual VC, for which the provider commits to deliver that amount of data. The provider will send any data in excess of this rate for this VC if its network has capacity at the time. This choice typically affects the price of each VC.
Burst rate	The burst rate is the rate and length of time for which, for a particular VC, the DTE can send faster than the CIR, and the provider agrees to forward the data. This choice typically affects the price of each VC.
Data link connection identifier (DLCI)	A DLCI is a Frame Relay address and is used in Frame Relay headers to identify the virtual circuit.
Forward explicit congestion notification (FECN)	The FECN is the bit in the Frame Relay header that signals to anyone receiving the frame (switches and DTEs) that congestion is occurring in the same direction as the frame. Switches and DTEs can react by slowing the rate by which data is sent in that direction.
Backward explicit congestion notification (BECN)	The BECN is the bit in the Frame Relay header that signals to anyone receiving the frame (switches and DTEs) that congestion is occurring in the opposite (backward) direction as the frame. Switches and DTEs can react by slowing the rate by which data is sent in that direction.
Discard eligibility (DE)	The DE is the bit in the Frame Relay header that signals to a switch to, if frames must be discarded, please choose this frame to discard instead of another frame without the DE bit set.
Nonbroadcast multiaccess (NBMA)	NBMA refers to a network in which broadcasts are not supported, but more than two devices can be connected.
Local Management Interface (LMI)	LMI is the protocol used between a DCE and DTE to manage the connection. Signaling messages for SVCs, PVC status messages, and keepalives are all LMI messages.
Link access procedure—frame mode bearer services (LAPF)	LAPF is the basic Frame Relay header and trailer; it includes DLCI, FECN, BECN, and DE bits.

The definitions for Frame Relay are contained in documents from the ITU and from ANSI. The Frame Relay Forum, a vendor consortium, also defines several Frame Relay specifications, many of which have been added to the standards body's documents. Table 8-10 lists the most important of these specifications.

Table 8-10 *Frame Relay Protocol Specifications*

What the Specification Defines	ITU Document	ANSI Document
Data link specifications, including LAPF header/trailer	Q.922 Annex A	T1.618
PVC management, LMI	Q.933 Annex A	T1.617 Annex D
SVC signaling	Q.933	T1.617
Multiprotocol encapsulation (originated in RFC 1490/2427)	Q.933 Annex E	T1.617 Annex F

LMI and Encapsulation Types

When first learning about Frame Relay, it's often easy to confuse the LMI and encapsulation used with Frame Relay; Cisco expects CCNAs to master the differences. The LMI is a definition of the messages used between the DTE (for example, a router) and the DCE (for example, the Frame Relay switch owned by the service provider). The encapsulation defines the headers used, in addition to the basic Frame Relay header, for transporting the frame from DTE to DTE. The switch and its connected router care about using the same LMI; the switch does not care about the encapsulation.

The three LMI protocols available in the IOS are defined by Cisco, the ITU, and ANSI, and each is slightly different and therefore not compatible with the other two. For instance, the Cisco and ANSI Q.933-A LMIs call for use of DLCI 1023 for LMI messages, whereas T1.617-D calls for DLCI 0. Some of the messages have different fields in their information elements. The DTE simply needs to know which of the two (DLCI 1023 or DLCI 0) to use; it must match the one used by the switch.

Using the same LMI type on a DTE and its connected DCE is required. LMI autosense is supported by the IOS in version 11.2, so there is no need to code the LMI type. If desired, the LMI type can be configured, but this disables the autosense feature. One LMI type exists per serial interface because the LMI controls the single physical access link, which is connected to a single switch.

The most important LMI message relating to topics on the exam is the LMI *status enquiry* message, which signals whether a PVC is up or down. Even though each PVC is predefined, its status can change. As with all LMI messages, status enquiry messages flow between the switch (DCE) and the DTE. For instance, a routing protocol reacts when a PVC is down, signaling that routes over that PVC are lost.

Table 8-11 outlines the three LMI types, their origin, and the keyword used in the Cisco **frame-relay lmi-type** interface subcommand.

Table 8-11   *Frame Relay LMI Types*

Name	Document	IOS LMI-Type Parameter
Cisco	Proprietary	cisco
ANSI	T1.617 Annex D	ansi
ITU	Q.933 Annex A	q933a

As with other data link protocols, Frame Relay defines a header and a trailer, with fields in each that allow the switches and DTEs to successfully deliver the frame across the network. Encapsulation refers to the process of using such headers and trailers to contain data supplied by a higher layer. (Refer to Chapter 3 for additional concepts about encapsulation.)

Frame Relay uses a link access procedure—frame bearer services (LAPF) header, defined by Q.922-A. The sparse LAPF framing provides error detection with an FCS in the trailer, as well as the DLCI, DE, FECN, and BECN fields. Figure 8-5 diagrams the frame.

Figure 8-5   *LAPF Header*

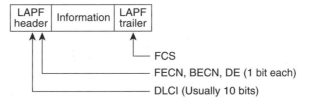

Figure 8-5 does not show the presence of a Protocol Type field. As discussed in Chapter 3, a field in the header must define the type of header that begins the Information field. If Frame Relay is using only the LAPF header, then DTEs (including routers) cannot support multi-protocol traffic because there is no way to identify the type of protocol in the Information field. (For more information about the concept of a Protocol Type field in data link headers, refer to Chapter 3.)

Two solutions were created to compensate for the lack of a Protocol Type field. Cisco and three other companies created an additional header, which comes first in the Information field shown in Figure 8-5. It includes a 2-byte-long Protocol Type field, with values matching the same field used for HDLC by Cisco. The second solution was defined in RFC 1490, "Multiprotocol Interconnect over Frame Relay," which was written to ensure multivendor interoperability between Frame Relay DTEs. This solution includes use of a Protocol Type field and adds many options, including support for bridged frames. ITU and ANSI later incorporated RFC 1490 headers into specs Q.933 Annex E and T.617 Annex F, respectively.

RFC 1490 has been superceded by RFC 2427. You probably will want to remember both numbers, particularly the older 1490 because it is referred to often in documentation from Cisco and other vendors.

Figure 8-6 provides a conceptual diagram of the two forms of encapsulation. *Because the frames flow from DTE to DTE, both DTEs must agree to the encapsulation used.* However, each VC can use a different encapsulation.

Figure 8-6   *Cisco and RFC 1490/2427 Encapsulations*

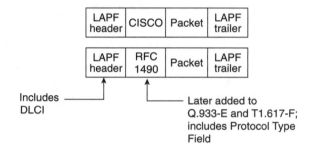

DLCI Addressing and Frame Relay Switching

The data link connection identifier (DLCI) is the Frame Relay address. DLCIs, not DTEs, are used to address virtual circuits. The logic and use of these addresses is very different from the addresses seen for other protocols covered in this book. This difference is mainly due to the use of the DLCI and the fact that *there is a single DLCI field in the header—there is not a source and destination DLCI.*

DLCIs are used to address the virtual circuit (VC); the logic behind the way routers use DLCI values is subtle. For example, in Figure 8-7, Router A has a VC to both Router B and Router C; Router A will need to use a different DLCI for each VC. The Frame Relay switches swap the DLCI in transit. For example, Router A sends a frame with DLCI 41, expecting that it will be delivered to Router B. Likewise, Router A sends frames with DLCI 42 when it wants the frame to be delivered to Router C.

Figure 8-7   *Frame Relay Addressing*

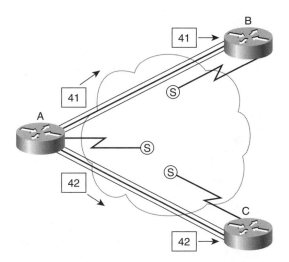

Frame Relay DLCIs are locally significant; this means that the addresses need to be unique only on the local access link. A popular analogy that explains local addressing is that there can be only a single street address of 2000 Pennsylvania Avenue, Washington, D.C., but there can be a 2000 Pennsylvania Avenue in every town in the United States. Likewise, DLCIs must be unique on each access link.

In Figure 8-7, as frames traverse Router A's access link, they have either DLCI 41 or 42 in the header, which meets the requirement that the addresses be unique on that access link. Likewise, for all VCs terminating at Router B, unique DLCI values must be used for each one. Because there is only one VC to Router B in Figure 8-7, there is no possibility of an overlap.

DLCIs are usually changed as the frames traverse the Frame Relay network. Consider the revised network of Figure 8-8, in which DLCI 41 and 42 are still used by Router A on the access link. Before the frames are forwarded on the access links to Router B and Router C, the Frame Relay switches convert the DLCI to a value of 40 in each case. The DLCI values are chosen by the service provider; the only requirement of local addressing can be summarized as follows:

> **DLCIs must be unique on each access link. The DLCI used to identify an individual VC on one access link has no bearing on the value that is chosen to identify the VC on the access link at the other end of the VC.**

Figure 8-8 *Frame Relay Local Addressing, with Different DLCIs on Each End*

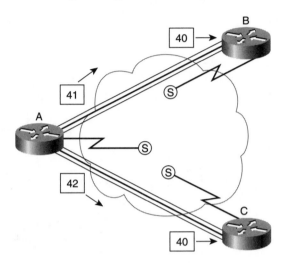

With the convention shown in Figure 8-8, the DLCI values are different on each end of the VC. However, the values shown in Figure 8-7 are also valid. In practice, the style shown in Figure 8-8 is the typical choice, but it seems to be a bit more confusing. But why? The answer lies in a term called *global addressing*

The concept of global addressing is the reason that typical Frame Relay networks use a different DLCI value on each end of the VC. Global addressing allows you to think of the Frame Relay network like a LAN in terms of addressing concepts. Consider Figure 8-9, with the DLCI values shown. In this figure, think of the DLCI values as an address for the DTE, which is similar to how a unicast MAC address represents a LAN card.

On a LAN, if Host B wants to send a frame to Host A, Host B sends a frame with Host A's MAC address as the destination. Similarly, if Router B wants to send a frame to Router A, then Router B (by the convention of global addressing) sends a frame with Router A's global DLCI value in the header. Likewise, Router C sends frames with DLCI 40 to reach Router A, by convention. Router A sends frames with DLCI 41 to reach Router B, and with DLCI 42 to reach Router C, again, by the convention of global addressing. Figure 8-9 shows the DLCIs used for global addressing and the actual values placed into the Frame Relay headers for correct delivery across the network. Table 8-12 summarizes the DLCIs used in the figure.

Figure 8-9   *Frame Relay Global Addressing Convention, with Reality of Local Addressing*

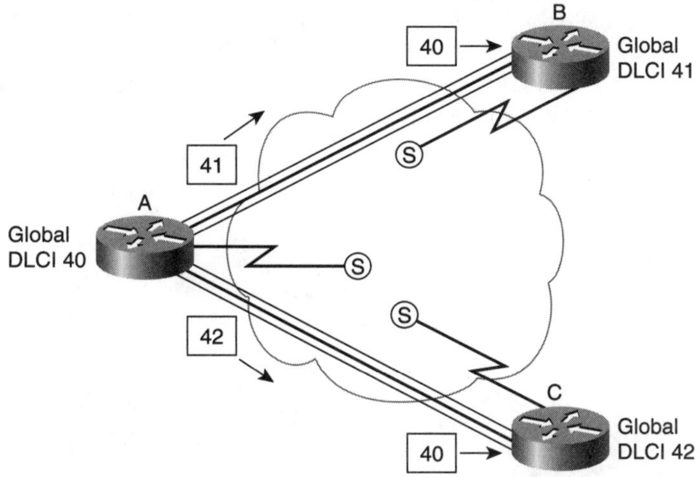

Table 8-12   *DLCI Swapping in Frame Relay Cloud*

Frame Sent by Router . . .	With DLCI Field	Is Delivered to Router . . .	With DLCI Field
A	41	B	40
A	42	C	40
B	40	A	41
C	40	A	42

Figure 8-9 shows a frame being sent from Router A to Router B in one case, and to Router C in the other case. As Router A sends a frame with DLCI 41, the Frame Relay switches send the frame toward Router B. Before being sent on the access link to Router B, the final switch changes the DLCI to 40 so that Router B knows who sent the frame. Similarly, Router A sends a frame with DLCI 42, and it is received by Router C with DLCI 40.

In fact, the DLCIs used match the sample network with local addressing of Figure 8-8. In essence:

- Local addressing is how Frame Relay addressing works. However, by following the convention of global addressing, planning is easier because the addressing appears similar to LAN addressing.

- A global address for one DTE simply means that all other DTEs with a VC to this one DTE use its global address on their local access links.

One particularly convenient benefit of global addressing is that new sites can be added with more convenience. Examine Figure 8-10, with Routers D and E added. The service provider simply states that global DLCI 43 and 44 will be used for these two routers. If these two routers also have only one PVC to Router A, all the DLCI planning is complete. You know that Router D and Router E will use DLCI 40 to reach Router A, and that Router A will use DLCI 43 to reach Router D and DLCI 44 to reach Router E.

Figure 8-10   *Adding Frame Relay Sites: Global Addressing*

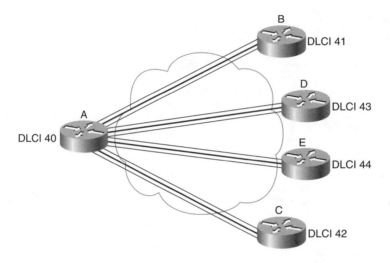

The remaining samples in this chapter use global addressing in any planning diagrams, unless otherwise stated. One practical way to determine whether the diagram lists the local DLCIs or the global DLCI convention is this: If two VCs terminate at a DTE and a single DLCI is shown, then it probably represents the global DLCI convention. If one DLCI is shown per VC, then it is depicting local DLCI addressing.

Network Layer Concerns with Frame Relay

As a CCNA, you will need to concern yourself with three key issues relating to Layer 3 flows over Frame Relay:

* Choices for Layer 3 addresses on Frame Relay interfaces

* Broadcast handling

* Split horizon

The sections that follow cover these issues in depth.

Layer 3 Addressing

This section examines three cases of Layer 3 addressing when using Frame Relay. Figure 8-11 starts the first case with an illustration of a fully meshed Frame Relay network. In a full mesh, each router has a direct connection to every other router, allowing the Frame Relay cloud to be treated as one Layer 3 network. Figure 8-11 also shows IPX and IP addresses. The IPX and IP addresses would be configured as subcommands on the serial interface. Table 8-13 summarizes the addresses used in Figure 8-11.

Figure 8-11 *Full Mesh with IP and IPX Addresses*

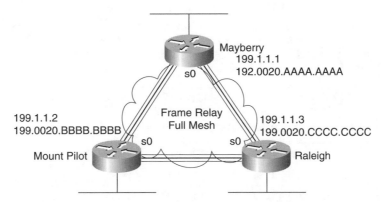

Table 8-13 *IP and IPX Addresses, with No Subinterfaces*

Router	IP Address of Frame Relay Interface	IPX Network of Frame Relay Interface	IPX Address
Mayberry	199.1.1.1	199	199.0200.aaaa.aaaa
Mount Pilot	199.1.1.2	199	199.0200.bbbb.bbbb
Raleigh	199.1.1.3	199	199.0200.cccc.cccc

The second case is a partially meshed Frame Relay network (see Figure 8-12). Because all four routers do not have VCs to each other, each VC uses a different set of Layer 3 groups. Table 8-14 shows the IPX and IP addresses for the partially meshed Frame Relay network illustrated in Figure 8-12. The addresses would be configured as subcommands on the serial interface. (*Note:* The notation /24 signifies a subnet mask with 24 binary 1s—in other words, 255.255.255.0.)

Figure 8-12   *Partial Mesh with IP and IPX Addresses*

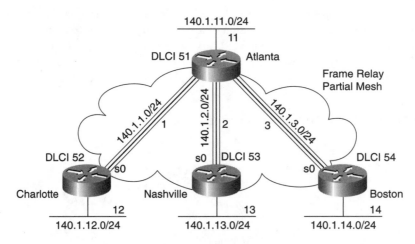

Table 8-14   *IP and IPX Addresses, with Point-to-Point Subinterfaces*

Router	Subnet	IP Address	IPX Network	IPX Address
Atlanta	140.1.1.0/24	140.1.1.1	1	1.0200.aaaa.aaaa
Charlotte	140.1.1.0/24	140.1.1.2	1	1.0200.bbbb.bbbb
Atlanta	140.1.2.0/24	140.1.2.1	2	2.0200.aaaa.aaaa
Nashville	140.1.2.0/24	140.1.2.3	2	2.0200.cccc.cccc
Atlanta	140.1.3.0/24	140.1.3.1	3	3.0200.aaaa.aaaa
Boston	140.1.3.0/24	140.1.3.4	3	3.0200.dddd.dddd

Subinterfaces allow the Atlanta router to have three IP addresses and three IPX addresses associated with its serial 0 interface. Subinterfaces can treat each VC as though it were a point-to-point serial link. Each of the three subinterfaces of serial 0 on Atlanta would be assigned a different IP address and IPX address from the list in Table 8-14. Example configurations follow in the next section of this chapter.

The third case of Layer 3 addressing is a hybrid between the first two illustrated in Figure 8-11 and Figure 8-12. Consider Figure 8-13, which shows a trio of routers with VCs between each of them, as well as two other VCs to remote sites.

Figure 8-13   *Hybrid of Full and Partial Mesh*

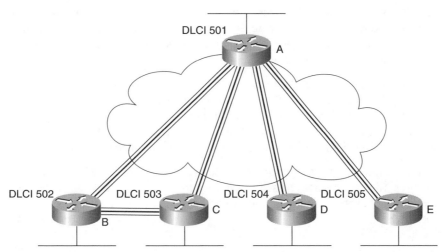

Two options exist for Layer 3 addressing in this case. The first is to treat each VC as a separate Layer 3 group; five subnets and five IPX networks would be needed for the Frame Relay network. However, if Routers A, B, and C are considered alone, they meet the criteria that each can send packets directly to each other, like a full mesh. This would allow Routers A, B, and C to use one subnet and IPX network. The other two VCs—between A and D, and between A and E—are treated as two separate Layer 3 groups. The result is a total of three subnets and three IPX network numbers.

To accomplish either style of Layer 3 addressing in this third and final case, subinterfaces are used. Point-to-point subinterfaces are used when a single VC is considered to be all that is in the group. Multipoint subinterfaces are used among Routers A, B, and C in Figure 8-13. The section "Frame Relay Configuration," later in the chapter, provides full configurations for all three cases illustrated in Figure 8-11, Figure 8-12, and Figure 8-13. Table 8-15 summarizes the addresses and subinterfaces used.

Table 8-15   *IP and IPX Addresses, and Point-to-Point and Multipoint Subinterfaces*

Router	Subnet	IP Address	IPX Network	IPX Address	Subinterface Type
A	140.1.1.0/24	140.1.1.1	1	1.0200.aaaa.aaaa	Multipoint
B	140.1.1.0/24	140.1.1.2	1	1.0200.bbbb.bbbb	Multipoint
C	140.1.1.0/24	140.1.1.3	1	1.0200.cccc.cccc	Multipoint
A	140.1.2.0/24	140.1.2.1	2	2.0200.aaaa.aaaa	Point-to-point
D	140.1.2.0/24	140.1.2.4	2	2.0200.dddd.dddd	Point-to-point
A	140.1.3.0/24	140.1.3.1	3	3.0200.aaaa.aaaa	Point-to-point
E	140.1.3.0/24	140.1.3.5	3	3.0200.eeee.eeee	Point-to-point

Broadcast Handling

Broadcasts are not supported over a Frame Relay network. In other words, no capability exists for a DTE to send a frame that is replicated and delivered across more than one VC. However, routers need to send broadcasts for several features to work. In particular, routing protocol updates and SAP updates are broadcasts.

The solution to the broadcast dilemma for Frame Relay has two parts. First, the IOS sends copies of the broadcasts across each VC that you instruct it to. Of course, if there are only a few VCs, this is not a big problem. However, if hundreds of VCs terminate in one router, then for each broadcast, hundreds of copies could be sent. The IOS can be configured to limit the amount of bandwidth that is used for these replicated broadcasts.

As the second part of the solution, the router tries to minimize the impact of the first part of the solution. The router places these broadcasts into a different queue than user traffic so that the user does not experience a large spike in delay each time some broadcast is replicated and sent over each VC.

NOTE   Although the CCNP exam, not the CCNA exam, covers such issues about dealing with overhead, a short example can show the significance of this overhead. For example, if a router knows 1000 routes, uses RIP, and has 50 VCs, then 1.072MB of RIP updates are sent every 30 seconds. That averages to 285kbps. (Math: 536-byte RIP packets, with 25 routes in each packet, for 40 packets per update, with copies sent over 50 VCs: $536 \times 40 \times 50 = 1.072$ megabytes per update interval. $1.072 \times 8 / 30$ seconds = 285kbps).

Knowing how to tell the router to forward these broadcasts out to each VC will be important on the CCNA exam and is covered in the "Frame Relay Configuration" section later in this chapter. The issues that relate to dealing with the volume of these updates is more likely a topic for the CCNP and CCIE exams.

Split Horizon

Split horizon is useful for preventing routing loops by preventing a router from advertising a route onto the same interface in which the route was learned. (Refer to Chapter 6, "Routing Protocols," for a full explanation.) However, split horizon could cause some problems with Frame Relay. Thankfully, several configuration options help you deal with this issue. But first, refer back to Figure 8-12. If split horizon was enabled on Atlanta, then Atlanta would learn about 140.1.12.0/24 from Charlotte but would not advertise the route to 140.1.12.0/24 in its updates to Nashville or Boston.

Split horizon logic applies to subinterfaces if they are configured. In other words, Atlanta uses a different subinterface for each VC to the three remote sites. Split horizon is enabled on each subinterface. However, because the routing updates from Charlotte are considered to enter Atlanta via one subinterface, and because routing updates to Nashville and Boston exit two other subinterfaces, then advertising 140.1.12.0/24 to Nashville and Boston is allowed.

Split horizon would be a problem in Figure 8-11, however. When all three VCs are up, no problem exists. However, if the VC from Mount Pilot to Raleigh went down, then split horizon on Mayberry would be harmful. Mount Pilot will advertise routes to 199.1.11.0, and Mayberry will receive that information in a routing update. However, because no subinterfaces are used, Mayberry would not advertise 199.1.11.0 to Raleigh with split horizon enabled.

The multipoint subinterfaces in Figure 8-13 would experience the same problems for the same reasons described for Figure 8-11.

The solution to the problem is to disable split horizon when not using subinterfaces or when using multipoint subinterfaces. The IOS defaults to disable split horizon on Frame Relay interfaces in all cases except for point-to-point subinterfaces. Table 8-16 summarizes these settings and shows that the current default settings work around the split horizon issues described in the last few paragraphs.

Table 8-16   *Split Horizon and Frame Relay Interfaces*

Type of Configuration	Split Horizon Is ...
No subinterfaces	Disabled
Point-to-point subinterfaces	Enabled
Multipoint subinterfaces	Disabled

If the default value for split horizon is not desired, then the **ip split horizon** interface configuration command can be used to enable split horizon. Similarly, the **no ip split horizon** interface configuration command disables split horizon on that interface.

How Address Mapping Works

Frame Relay mapping is a topic you could ignore and still make Frame Relay work in a Cisco router. However, Cisco requires that CCNAs understand Frame Relay address mapping, for two main reasons. First, static mapping is just the kind of nasty question that is likely to crop up on the exam. Second, understanding mapping offers a good opportunity to review the concepts behind routing. As with most features implemented dynamically and by default, you can ignore mapping most of the time.

Mapping is required when using some other data links, but not all. For example, with IP, the ARP process dynamically builds a mapping between an IP address and a LAN address. This section discusses the basics behind why mapping is needed for LAN connections and Frame Relay, with a focus on Frame Relay.

Consider Figure 8-14 and the routing table that follows (Table 8-17).

Figure 8-14 *Basic Point-to-Point Network*

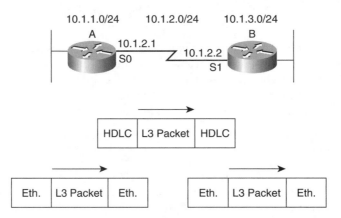

Table 8-17 *Partial Routing Table on Router A for Figure 8-14*

Subnet	Outgoing Interface	Next Router
10.1.3.0	serial 0	10.1.2.2

The core routing logic must be considered to fully appreciate mapping. Router A receives an Ethernet frame from some host and strips the Ethernet header (and trailer). The destination IP address of the packet is compared to the IP routing table, and an entry is matched. The matched routing table entry tells the router to route the packet out serial 0 to 10.1.2.2 next (Router B's S1 IP address). Router A builds the HDLC header/trailer and sends the frame.

The fact that Router B's IP address on the common serial link is 10.1.2.2 has nothing to do with the contents of the HDLC header and trailer; Router B's IP address is immaterial in this case. If Router A can get the frame across the link, there is only one possible recipient—Router B. So, no mapping is needed between the Layer 3 address and the HDLC address on a point-to-point link.

Now consider a diagram with Ethernet between the routers (see Figure 8-15) and the routing table that follows (see Table 8-18).

Figure 8-15   *Basic Ethernet Network*

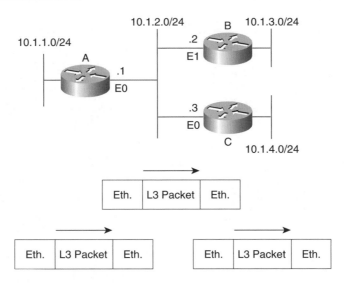

Table 8-18   *Partial Routing Table on Router A for Figure 8-15*

Subnet	Outgoing Interface	Next Router
10.1.3.0	Ethernet 0	10.1.2.2

Again consider the core routing logic. Router A receives an Ethernet frame from some host and strips the Ethernet header (and trailer). Router A decides to route the packet out Ethernet 0 to the next router, 10.1.2.2 (Router B's E1 IP address). Router A builds the new Ethernet header/trailer and sends the frame.

Router A builds the Ethernet header based on the next-hop router's IP address—namely, 10.1.2.2 (Router B's E1 IP address). The destination Ethernet address in the header built by Router A is Router B's E1 address. Router A learns this information dynamically using the IP ARP protocol. Similarly, with IPX routing, the next-hop router's IPX address has the corresponding LAN address embedded in the IPX address. (With other Layer 3 protocols, there are other processes on LANs for learning the corresponding LAN address.) The information learned by IP ARP in this case is the information that maps the next-hop IP address to the LAN address used to reach it; this is called *mapping*. A more general definition for mapping follows:

> **The information that correlates to the next-hop router's Layer 3 address, and the Layer 2 address used to reach it, is called mapping. Mapping is needed on multiaccess networks.**

Now consider the Frame Relay network in Figure 8-16, along with the routing table in Table 8-19.

Figure 8-16   *Basic Frame Relay Network*

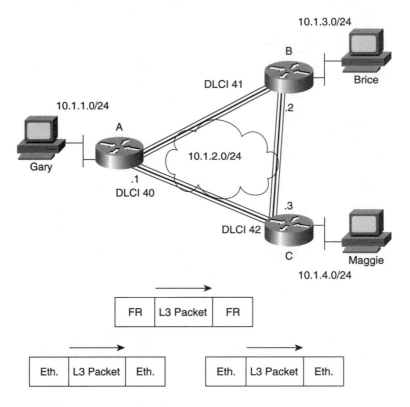

Table 8-19   *Partial Routing Table on Router A for Figure 8-16*

Subnet	Outgoing Interface	Next Router
10.1.3.0	Serial 0	10.1.2.2

Again consider the core routing logic. Router A receives an Ethernet frame from some host and strips the Ethernet header (and trailer). It decides to route the packet out serial 0 to the next router, 10.1.2.2 (Router B's S0 IP address). Router A builds the Frame Relay header/trailer and sends the frame.

Although Router A knows the serial interfaces out which to forward the frame, Router A does not know the correct DLCI yet. A mapping is needed in Router A to correlate 10.1.2.2 (Router B) and the DLCI Router A used to reach Router B. However, the same IP ARP used on LANs will not work on Frame Relay because there is no support for broadcasts. Therefore, ARP cannot be used to discover that DLCI.

Two solutions exist by which Router A can learn the mapping between Router B's IP address and DLCI. One uses a statically configured mapping, and the other uses a dynamic process called *Inverse ARP.*

Table 8-20 lists the IP and IPX addresses of the three routers in Figure 8-16.

Table 8-20   *Layer 3 Addresses and DLCIs Used with Figure 8-16*

Router	Global DLCI	IP Address	IPX Address
A	40	10.1.2.1	2.0200.aaaa.aaaa
B	41	10.1.2.2	2.0200.bbbb.bbbb
C	42	10.1.2.3	2.0200.cccc.cccc

Example 8-3 lists the static Frame Relay map for the three routers in Figure 8-16. The DLCIs in Table 8-20 are the same as those used in Figure 8-16.

Example 8-3   *frame-relay map Commands*

```
Router A:

interface serial 0
frame-relay map ip 10.1.2.2 41 broadcast
frame-relay map ipx 2.0200.bbbb.bbbb 41 broadcast
frame-relay map ip 10.1.2.3 42 broadcast
frame-relay map ipx 2.0200.cccc.cccc 42 broadcast

Router B:

interface serial 0
frame-relay map ip 10.1.2.1 40 broadcast
frame-relay map ipx 2.0200.aaaa.aaaa 40 broadcast
frame-relay map ip 10.1.2.3 42 broadcast
frame-relay map ipx 2.0200.cccc.cccc 42 broadcast

Router C:

interface serial 0
frame-relay map ip 10.1.2.1 40 broadcast
frame-relay map ipx 2.0200.aaaa.aaaa 40 broadcast
frame-relay map ip 10.1.2.2 41 broadcast
frame-relay map ipx 2.0200.bbbb.bbbb 41 broadcast
```

Consider the case in which Gary makes an FTP connection to Brice. The **frame-relay map** command for Router A referencing 10.1.2.2 would be used for packets originating from Gary and going to Brice. Conversely, a packet sent back from Brice to Gary would cause Router B to use its map statement referring to Router A's IP address of 10.1.2.1. Mapping is needed for each next-hop Layer 3 address for each Layer 3 protocol being routed. Even with a network this small, the configuration process can be laborious. A better solution is a dynamic protocol called Inverse ARP.

Inverse ARP acquires mapping information in a manner opposite of IP ARP, but the information that maps the Layer 3 and Layer 2 addresses is still found. Inverse ARP is basic; after the VC is up, each DTE announces its network layer address to the DTE on the other end of the VC. (Inverse ARP is enabled by default at IOS 11.2 and beyond, unless point-to-point subinterfaces are used.) Table 8-21 summarizes what would occur in the network in Figure 8-16.

Table 8-21 *Inverse ARP Messages for Figure 8-16*

Sending Router	DLCI in Header of I-ARP Frame When Sent	Receiving Router	DLCI in Header of I-ARP Frame When Received	Information in Inverse ARP
A	41	B	40	I am 10.1.2.1.
A	41	B	40	I am 2.0200.aaaa.aaaa.
A	42	C	40	I am 10.1.2.1.
A	42	C	40	I am 2.0200.aaaa.aaaa.
B	40	A	41	I am 10.1.2.2.
B	40	A	41	I am 2.0200.bbbb.bbbb.
B	42	C	41	I am 10.1.2.2.
B	42	C	41	I am 2.0200.bbbb.bbbb.
C	40	A	42	I am 10.1.2.3.
C	40	A	42	I am 2.0200.cccc.cccc.
C	41	B	42	I am 10.1.2.3.
C	41	B	42	I am 2.0200.cccc.cccc.

Although Table 8-21 lists a seemingly large number of messages, no static **frame-relay map** commands are needed. All the necessary mapping information is learned dynamically.

Inverse ARP is enabled by default if no subinterfaces are in use. Inverse ARP is also on by default for multipoint subinterfaces. However, Inverse ARP is not enabled on point-to-point subinterfaces because point-to-point subinterfaces behave like a true point-to-point line in regard to routing; if the packet needs to be sent out a point-to-point subinterface, then there is only one possible next router and only one DLCI in use. So, Inverse ARP is not needed with point-to-point subinterfaces.

Review: Basic Frame Relay Initialization

Now that the text has covered all the pertinent concepts, it's time to review the basic initialization process on a Frame Relay network. First, the LMI sends a status enquiry notifying the DTE when the VC is up. After this process, Inverse ARP frames are sent by the routers in each direction for each Layer 3 protocol configured for the VC. Packets can be forwarded at this point. Of course, routing protocols will send their initial updates, routes will be learned, and only then will end-user traffic be able to flow. Figure 8-17 outlines the process.

Figure 8-17   *Frame Relay Initialization*

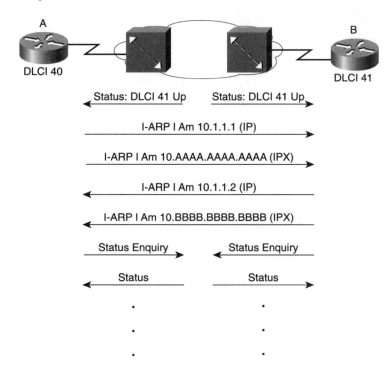

LMI status messages inform the routers when the PVC first comes up. Because Inverse ARP frames could not be delivered until the VC was up but can be delivered now, the Inverse ARP announcements declare the Layer 3 addresses. Unless keepalives have been turned off, both the switch and the router expect to send and receive periodic status and status enquiry messages, respectively.

Compression

Compression can be performed on frames sent out a Frame Relay interface. Two general types of compression are allowed: payload compression and TCP header compression. With TCP header compression, only the TCP header is compressed; all other headers and data remain uncompressed. As its name suggests, payload compression compresses the payload of the Frame Relay frame.

Regardless of which type of compression is used, the Frame Relay header itself cannot be compressed. If the Frame Relay header were compressed, the intermediate Frame Relay switches would not be capable of forwarding the frames.

Payload Compression

Figure 8-18 provides the basic concept behind payload compression and shows what is compressed:

Figure 8-18   *Frame Relay Payload Compression*

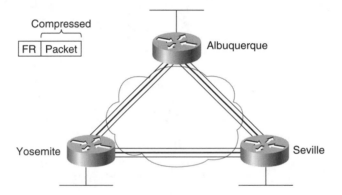

If payload compression was used on the VC between Albuquerque and Yosemite, the Frame Relay header would remain intact, but the packet (the payload) would be compressed before transmission and uncompressed upon reception.

Two types of payload compression are available. The first historically used the STAC algorithm, which predicts the values that follow the earlier bytes in the compressed payload. The algorithm did not follow any standard. That process works fine, but it can run only in software—no support for this algorithm exists for Frame Relay on the Versatile Interface Processor (VIP) or the Compression Service Adapter (CSA).

The second payload compression option is to use the Frame Relay Forum standard compression. The FRF.9 Implementation Agreement (IA) defines the details and is available free from the Frame Relay Forum if you would like to see more details (http://www.frforum.com). The FRF.9 document calls for the use of the STAC algorithm as well, but with some details that differ from the original Cisco protocol. Cisco has added support for the FRF.9 payload compression into the CSA and the VIP2. Even if compressing in software, Cisco recommends using the FRF.9 payload compression over the original Cisco implementation of STAC.

TCP Header Compression

TCP header compression is seemingly unnecessary, given that payload compression is available. Why bother just compressing the TCP header? Well, compression algorithms can be optimized if the data to be compressed has a known format and a tendency toward using particular values. The 40-byte TCP header can be reduced to an average of 10 bytes. One of the biggest reasons that TCP header compression can be beneficial is that it takes little processing because of the efficient compression algorithm. Also, if a large amount of traffic is made up of small IP packets with TCP, then the compression ratio can be more than 2-to-1. For instance, in the "old" days when Telnet was used on a frequent basis by end users, many IP packets were sent with the IP header, the TCP header, and just a few bytes of data typed by the user. So, efficient compression with the possibility of more than 2-to-1 compression ratio is a very reasonable option. If most of the IP packets using TCP in a network are large, then the compression ratio will not be very high, making TCP header compression a less-attractive option.

Frame Relay Configuration

Configuration of Frame Relay in a Cisco router is relatively straightforward if all the defaults are taken. Cisco expects CCNAs to know several of the optional parameters that are shown in this section as well.

Hands-on experience is the best way to fully learn the details of configuration. In lieu of that, this section lists commands, provides examples, and points out tricky features. Table 8-22 and Table 8-23 summarize the more popular commands used for Frame Relay configuration and verification. Two configuration samples follow. The Cisco IOS documentation is an excellent reference for additional IP commands, and the Cisco Press book *Interconnecting Cisco Network Devices* is an excellent reference, particularly if you are not able to attend the instructor-led version of the class.

Table 8-22 *Frame Relay Configuration Commands*

Command	Configuration Mode	Purpose
encapsulation frame-relay [**ietf** | **cisco**]	Interface	Defines Frame Relay encapsulation that is used rather than HDLC, PPP, and so on.
frame-relay lmi-type {**ansi** | **q933a** | **cisco**}	Interface	Defines the type of LMI messages sent to the switch.
bandwidth *num*	Interface	Sets the route's perceived speed of the interface. Bandwidth is used by some routing protocols to influence the metric.

continues

Table 8-22 *Frame Relay Configuration Commands (Continued)*

Command	Configuration Mode	Purpose
frame-relay map *protocol protocol-address dlci* [**payload-compress** {**packet-by-packet** | **frf9 stac**}] [**broadcast**] [**ietf** | **cisco**]	Interface	Statically defines a mapping between a network layer address and a DLCI.
keepalive *sec*	Interface	Defines whether and how often LMI status enquiry messages are sent and expected.
interface serial *num.sub* [*point-to-point* | *multipoint*]	Global	Creates a subinterface, or references a previously created subinterface.
frame-relay interface-dlci *dlci* [**ietf** | **cisco**]	Interface	Defines a DLCI used for a VC to another DTE.
frame-relay payload-compress {**packet-by-packet** | **frf9 stac**}	Interface subcommand	Defines payload compression on point-to-point subinterfaces.

Table 8-23 *Frame Relay Related EXEC Commands*

Command	Function
show interface	Shows physical interface status.
show frame-relay {**pvc** | **map** | **lmi** }	Shows PVC status, mapping (dynamic and static), and LMI status.
debug frame-relay {**lmi** | **events**}	Lists messages describing LMI flows (LMI option). The **events** option lists inverse ARP information. Other options include **lapf**, **informationelements**, **ppp**, and **packet**.

Determining when and how to use subinterfaces for Frame Relay configuration is the most difficult part of the configuration. Subinterfaces are never required; subinterfaces can be used in any Frame Relay configuration, and most sites tend to use them. Some general guidelines when using subinterfaces include the following:

- When the network is partially meshed, using point-to-point subinterfaces overcomes split horizon issues by treating each subinterface as a separate interface.

- When the network is partially meshed, using a multipoint subinterface will work.

- When the network is truly fully meshed, a multipoint subinterface can be used to reduce the number of network-layer groups (for example, IP subnets) that are used.

- When the network is truly fully meshed, point-to-point subinterfaces can be used. This is typically chosen to maintain consistency with other Frame Relay networks elsewhere in the network that are not fully meshed. This choice requires a larger number of IP subnets to be used.

- When the network contains some fully meshed portions (for example, when 3 sites have VCs between each other but the other 10 do not), a multipoint subinterface can be used for the fully meshed portion and point-to-point subinterfaces can be used for the rest.

- When the network contains some fully meshed portions (for example, when 3 sites have VCs between each other but the other 10 do not), using only point-to-point subinterfaces is another option. This requires more IP subnets and IPX networks than when using a multipoint subinterface for the fully meshed portion of the network.

- Many sites avoid confusion by always using point-to-point subinterfaces to maintain consistency.

Correlating the DLCI(s) to their subinterfaces is required when using either type of subinterface. LMI enquiry messages notify the router that PVCs are active; the router then needs to know which subinterface uses the DLCI. An individual DLCI is used by only one subinterface. For a point-to-point subinterface, only one DLCI is used; for multipoint, many DLCIs are used.

Three samples of Layer 3 addressing were used earlier in the chapter, with the networks diagrammed in Figure 8-11, Figure 8-12, and Figure 8-13. The configurations matching those networks and addresses are shown next.

Configuring Networks Without Subinterfaces

The first sample network (based on the environment depicted in Figure 8-11) does not use subinterfaces. Example 8-4, Example 8-5, and Example 8-6 show the configuration for this network.

Example 8-4 *Mayberry Configuration*

```
ipx routing 0200.aaaa.aaaa
!
interface serial0
encapsulation frame-relay
ip address  199.1.1.1  255.255.255.0
ipx network  199
!
interface ethernet 0
ip address  199.1.10.1  255.255.255.0
ipx network  1
!
router igrp 1
network  199.1.1.0
network 199.1.10.0
```

Example 8-5 *Mount Pilot Configuration*

```
ipx routing 0200.bbbb.bbbb
!
interface serial0
encapsulation frame-relay
ip address  199.1.1.2  255.255.255.0
ipx network  199
!
interface ethernet 0
ip address  199.1.11.2   255.255.255.0
ipx network  2
!
router igrp 1
network  199.1.1.0
network 199.1.11.0
```

Example 8-6 *Raleigh Configuration*

```
ipx routing 0200.cccc.cccc
!
interface serial0
encapsulation frame-relay
ip address  199.1.1.3  255.255.255.0
ipx network  199
!
interface ethernet 0
ip address  199.1.12.3   255.255.255.0
ipx network  3
!
router igrp 1
network  199.1.1.0
network 199.1.12.0
```

The configuration is simple in comparison with the protocol concepts. All default settings (IOS version 12.0) were used and are as follows:

- The LMI type is automatically sensed.

- The encapsulation is Cisco instead of IETF.

- PVC DLCIs are learned via LMI status messages.

- Inverse ARP is enabled (by default) and is triggered when the status message declaring that the VCs are up has been received.

In some cases, the default values will not be appropriate. For instance, if one router was not a Cisco router and did not support Cisco encapsulation, then IETF encapsulation would be required. For the purpose of showing an alternate configuration, suppose that the following requirements were added:

- The Raleigh router requires IETF encapsulation on both VCs.

- Mayberry's LMI type should be ANSI; LMI autosense should not be used.

Example 8-7 and Example 8-8 show the changes that would be made to Mayberry and Raleigh.

Example 8-7 *Mayberry Configuration with New Requirements*

```
ipx routing 0200.aaaa.aaaa
!
interface serial0
encapsulation frame-relay
frame-relay lmi-type ansi
frame-relay interface-dlci 42 ietf
ip address  199.1.1.1  255.255.255.0
ipx network  199
! rest of configuration unchanged from Example 8-4.
```

Example 8-8 *Raleigh Configuration with New Requirements*

```
ipx routing 0200.cccc.cccc
!
interface serial0
encapsulation frame-relay ietf
ip address  199.1.1.3  255.255.255.0
ipx network  199
!
! rest of configuration unchanged from example 8-6.
```

The encapsulation was changed in two different ways. Raleigh changed its encapsulation for both its PVCs with the **ietf** keyword on the **encapsulation** command. Mayberry could not change because only one of the two VCs to Mayberry was directed to use IETF encapsulation. So, Mayberry was forced to code the **frame-relay interface-dlci** command, coding the DLCI for the VC to Raleigh. The **ietf** keyword was needed to change from the default encapsulation of cisco.

The LMI configuration in Mayberry would have been fine without any changes because autosense would have recognized ANSI. However, by coding the **frame-relay lmi-type ansi**, Mayberry is forced to use ANSI because this command disables autonegotiation of the LMI type.

Mount Pilot's **frame-relay interface-dlci** configuration would need to be modified like Mayberry's for the VC from Mount Pilot to Raleigh so that VC will use IETF encapsulation. This change is not shown in an example.

Configuring Networks with Point-to-Point Subinterfaces

The second sample network (based on the environment depicted in Figure 8-12) uses point-to-point subinterfaces. Example 8-9, Example 8-10, Example 8-11, and Example 8-12 show the configuration for this network.

Example 8-9 *Atlanta Configuration*

```
ipx routing 0200.aaaa.aaaa
!
interface serial0
encapsulation frame-relay
!
interface serial 0.1 point-to-point
ip address 140.1.1.1   255.255.255.0
ipx network 1
frame-relay interface-dlci 52
!
interface serial 0.2 point-to-point
ip address 140.1.2.1 255.255.255.0
ipx network 2
frame-relay interface-dlci 53
!
interface serial 0.3 point-to-point
ip address 140.1.3.1 255.255.255.0
ipx network 3
frame-relay interface-dlci 54
!
interface ethernet 0
ip address 140.1.11.1 255.255.255.0
ipx network 11
```

Example 8-10 *Charlotte Configuration*

```
ipx routing 0200.bbbb.bbbb
!
interface serial0
encapsulation frame-relay
!
interface serial 0.1 point-to-point
ip address 140.1.1.2   255.255.255.0
ipx network 1
frame-relay interface-dlci 51
!
interface ethernet 0
ip address 140.1.12.2 255.255.255.0
ipx network 12
```

Example 8-11 *Nashville Configuration*

```
ipx routing 0200.cccc.cccc
!
interface serial0
encapsulation frame-relay
!
interface serial 0.2 point-to-point
ip address 140.1.2.3 255.255.255.0
ipx network 2
frame-relay interface-dlci 51
!
```

Example 8-11 *Nashville Configuration (Continued)*

```
interface ethernet 0
ip address 140.1.13.3 255.255.255.0
ipx network 13
```

Example 8-12 *Boston Configuration*

```
ipx routing 0200.dddd.dddd
!
interface serial0
encapsulation frame-relay
!
interface serial 0.3 point-to-point
ip address 140.1.3.4 255.255.255.0
ipx network 3
frame-relay interface-dlci 51
!
interface ethernet 0
ip address 140.1.14.4  255.255.255.0
ipx network 14
```

Point-to-point subinterfaces were used in this configuration because the network is not fully meshed. The **frame-relay interface-dlci** command is needed when using subinterfaces. This is because the status messages come into the physical interface stating that a VC with a particular DLCI is up; the IOS then needs to associate that VC with a subinterface.

The subinterface numbers in the example configuration happen to match on either end of the VCs. For example, subinterface 2 was used in Atlanta for the PVC to Nashville; Nashville also uses subinterface 2. There is no requirement that the subinterface numbers be the same.

Example 8-13 shows the output from the most popular IOS Frame Relay EXEC commands for monitoring Frame Relay, as issued on router Atlanta.

Example 8-13 *Output from EXEC Commands on Atlanta*

```
Atlanta#show frame-relay pvc

PVC Statistics for interface Serial0 (Frame Relay DTE)

DLCI = 52, DLCI USAGE = LOCAL, PVC STATUS = ACTIVE, INTERFACE = Serial0.1

  input pkts 843         output pkts 876        in bytes 122723
  out bytes 134431       dropped pkts 0         in FECN pkts 0
  in BECN pkts 0         out FECN pkts 0        out BECN pkts 0
  in DE pkts 0           out DE pkts 0
  out bcast pkts 876      out bcast bytes 134431
  pvc create time 05:20:10, last time pvc status changed 05:19:31
  --More--
DLCI = 53, DLCI USAGE = LOCAL, PVC STATUS = ACTIVE, INTERFACE = Serial0.2

  input pkts 0          output pkts 875        in bytes 0
  out bytes 142417      dropped pkts 0         in FECN pkts 0
```

continues

Example 8-13 *Output from EXEC Commands on Atlanta (Continued)*

```
  in BECN pkts 0           out FECN pkts 0          out BECN pkts 0
  in DE pkts 0             out DE pkts 0
  out bcast pkts 875       out bcast bytes 142417
  pvc create time 05:19:51, last time pvc status changed 04:55:41
  --More--
DLCI = 54, DLCI USAGE = LOCAL, PVC STATUS = ACTIVE, INTERFACE = Serial0.3

  input pkts 10            output pkts 877          in bytes 1274
  out bytes 142069         dropped pkts 0           in FECN pkts 0
  in BECN pkts 0           out FECN pkts 0          out BECN pkts 0
  in DE pkts 0             out DE pkts 0
  out bcast pkts 877       out bcast bytes 142069
  pvc create time 05:19:52, last time pvc status changed 05:17:42

Atlanta#show frame-relay map
Serial0.3 (up): point-to-point dlci, dlci 54(0x36,0xC60), broadcast
          status defined, active
Serial0.2 (up): point-to-point dlci, dlci 53(0x35,0xC50), broadcast
          status defined, active
Serial0.1 (up): point-to-point dlci, dlci 52(0x34,0xC40), broadcast
          status defined, active

Atlanta#debug frame-relay lmi
Frame Relay LMI debugging is on
Displaying all Frame Relay LMI data

Serial0(out): StEnq, myseq 163, yourseen 161, DTE up
datagramstart = 0x45AED8, datagramsize = 13
FR encap = 0xFCF10309
00 75 01 01 01 03 02 A3 A1

Serial0(in): Status, myseq 163
RT IE 1, length 1, type 1
KA IE 3, length 2, yourseq 162, myseq 163
```

Useful management information is held in the output of the **show frame-relay pvc** command. The counters for each VC, including increments in the FECN and BECN counters, can be particularly useful. Likewise, comparing the packets/bytes sent versus what is received on the other end of the VC is also quite useful because it reflects the number of packets/bytes lost inside the Frame Relay cloud. Also, seeing a PVC as active means that it is usable (as opposed to inactive), which is a great place to start when troubleshooting. All this information can be better gathered by an SNMP manager.

The output of the **show frame-relay map** command is surprising after the discourse about mapping. A DLCI is listed in each entry, but no mention of corresponding Layer 3 addresses is made. However, because the subinterfaces are point-to-point, this omission by IOS is intended—the subinterface acts like a point-to-point link, with two participants. Mapping is needed only when more than two devices are attached to the link. (See the section "How Address Mapping Works," earlier in this chapter, for more information.)

The **debug frame-relay lmi** output shows an indication of both sending and receiving LMI enquiries. The status message is sent by the switch, whereas the status enquiry is sent by the DTE (router). The IOS **keepalive** setting does not cause packets to flow between routers, but rather it causes the router to send LMI messages to the switch. It also causes the router to expect LMI messages from the switch.

Configuring Networks with Coexisting Point-to-Point and Multipoint Subinterfaces

The Frame Relay networks built by CCNAs most likely will include both point-to-point and multipoint subinterfaces. This last sample network (based on the environment depicted in Figure 8-13) uses both types of subinterfaces. Example 8-14, Example 8-15, Example 8-16, Example 8-17, and Example 8-18 show the configuration for this network.

Example 8-14 *Router A Configuration*

```
hostname RouterA
!
ipx routing 0200.aaaa.aaaa
!
interface serial0
encapsulation frame-relay
!
interface serial 0.1 multipoint
ip address 140.1.1.1  255.255.255.0
ipx network 1
frame-relay interface-dlci 502
frame-relay interface-dlci 503
!
interface serial 0.2 point-to-point
ip address 140.1.2.1 255.255.255.0
ipx network 2
frame-relay interface-dlci 504
!
interface serial 0.3 point-to-point
ip address 140.1.3.1 255.255.255.0
ipx network 3
frame-relay interface-dlci 505
!
interface ethernet 0
ip address 140.1.11.1 255.255.255.0
ipx network 11
```

Example 8-15 *Router B Configuration*

```
hostname RouterB
!
ipx routing 0200.bbbb.bbbb
!
interface serial0
encapsulation frame-relay
```

continues

Example 8-15 *Router B Configuration (Continued)*

```
!
interface serial 0.1 multipoint
ip address 140.1.1.2   255.255.255.0
ipx network 1
frame-relay interface-dlci 501
frame-relay interface-dlci 503
!
interface ethernet 0
ip address 140.1.12.2 255.255.255.0
ipx network 12
```

Example 8-16 *Router C Configuration*

```
hostname RouterC
!
ipx routing 0200.cccc.cccc
!
interface serial0
encapsulation frame-relay
!
interface serial 0.1 multipoint
ip address 140.1.1.3   255.255.255.0
ipx network 1
frame-relay interface-dlci 501
frame-relay interface-dlci 502
!
interface ethernet 0
ip address 140.1.13.3 255.255.255.0
ipx network 13
```

Example 8-17 *Router D Configuration*

```
hostname RouterD
!
ipx routing 0200.dddd.dddd
!
interface serial0
encapsulation frame-relay
!
interface serial 0.1 point-to-point
ip address 140.1.2.4   255.255.255.0
ipx network 2
frame-relay interface-dlci 501
!
interface ethernet 0
ip address 140.1.14.4 255.255.255.0
ipx network 14
```

Example 8-18 *Router E Configuration*

```
hostname RouterE
!
ipx routing 0200.eeee.eeee
!
interface serial0
encapsulation frame-relay
!
interface serial 0.1 point-to-point
ip address 140.1.3.5 255.255.255.0
ipx network 3
frame-relay interface-dlci 501
!
interface ethernet 0
ip address 140.1.15.5 255.255.255.0
ipx network 15
```

No mapping statements were required for the configuration in Example 8-14 through Example 8-18 because Inverse ARP is enabled on the multipoint subinterfaces by default. The point-to-point subinterfaces do not require mapping statements because after the outgoing subinterface is identified, there is only one possible router to which to forward the frame.

Router A is the only router using both multipoint and point-to-point subinterfaces. On Router A's serial 0.1 interface, multipoint is in use, with DLCIs for Router B and Router C listed. On Router A's other two subinterfaces, which are point-to-point, only a single DLCI needs to be listed. In fact, only one **frame-relay interface-dlci** command is allowed on a point-to-point subinterface because only one VC is allowed. Otherwise, the configurations between the two types are similar.

Example 8-19 shows the results of the Inverse ARP and a copy of the **debug frame-relay events** showing the contents of the Inverse ARP. The **debug** on Example 8-19 provides some insight into Inverse ARP operation.

Example 8-19 *Frame Relay Maps and Inverse ARP on Router C*

```
RouterC#show frame-relay map
Serial0.10 (up): ip 140.1.1.1 dlci 501(0x1F5,0x7C50), dynamic,
               broadcast,, status defined, active
Serial0.10 (up): ip 140.1.1.2 dlci 502(0x1F6,0x7C60), dynamic,
               broadcast,, status defined, active
Serial0.10 (up): ipx 1.0200.aaaa.aaaa dlci 501(0x1F5,0x7C50), dynamic,
               broadcast,, status defined, active
Serial0.10 (up): ipx 1.0200.bbbb.bbbb dlci 502(0x1F6,0x7C60), dynamic,
               broadcast,, status defined, active

RouterC#debug frame-relay events
Frame Relay events debugging is on

RouterC#configure terminal
Enter configuration commands, one per line.  End with Ctrl-Z.
RouterC(config)#interface serial 0.1
```

continues

Example 8-19 *Frame Relay Maps and Inverse ARP on Router C (Continued)*

```
RouterC(config-subif)#no shutdown
RouterC(config-subif)#^Z
RouterC#

Serial0.1: FR ARP input
Serial0.1: FR ARP input
Serial0.1: FR ARP input
datagramstart = 0xE42E58, datagramsize = 30
FR encap = 0x7C510300
80 00 00 00 08 06 00 0F 08 00 02 04 00 09 00 00
8C 01 01 01 7C 51 8C 01 01 03

datagramstart = 0xE427A0, datagramsize = 46
FR encap = 0x7C510300
80 00 00 00 08 06 00 0F 81 37 02 0A 00 09 00 00
00 00 00 01 02 00 AA AA AA AA 7C 51 00 00 00 01
02 00 CC CC CC CC 1B 99 D0 CC

datagramstart = 0xE420E8, datagramsize = 30
FR encap = 0x7C610300
80 00 00 00 08 06 00 0F 08 00 02 04 00 09 00 00
8C 01 01 02 7C 61 8C 01 01 03

Serial0.1: FR ARP input
datagramstart = 0xE47188, datagramsize = 46
FR encap = 0x7C610300
80 00 00 00 08 06 00 0F 81 37 02 0A 00 09 00 00
00 00 00 01 02 00 BB BB BB BB 7C 61 00 00 00 01
02 00 CC CC CC CC 1B 99 D0 CC
```

The **show frame-relay map** command provides a full insight into mapping. The neighboring routers' IP and IPX addresses correlate to the DLCIs. This is possible because the Inverse ARP messages flow over a VC; the Inverse ARP contains a Layer 3 protocol type and address. The DLCI correlates to a subinterface based on configuration.

The messages about Inverse ARP in the **debug frame-relay events** output is not so obvious. One easy exercise is to search for the hex version of the IP and IPX addresses in the output. These addresses have been highlighted in Example 8-19. For example, the first 3 bytes of 140.1.1.0 are 8C 01 01 in hexadecimal; this field happens to start on the left side of the output, so it is easy to recognize visually. The IPX address should be much easier to recognize because it is already in hexadecimal format in the configuration.

NOTE   Enabling **debug** options increases the CPU utilization of the router. Depending on how much
processing is required and how many messages are generated, it is possible to significantly
degrade performance and possibly crash the router. This is a result of memory and processing
used to look for the requested information and to process the messages. You might want to first
type the command **no debug all** and then type your debug command. If your debug creates too
much output, the **no debug all** command can be easily retrieved (press Ctrl+P twice).

If Inverse ARP was not used at all on any of the three routers, the following **frame-relay map**
statements would have been required on Router A (see Example 8-20). Similar commands
would have been required on Routers B and C.

Example 8-20 *frame-relay map Commands*

```
frame-relay map ip 140.1.1.2 502 broadcast
frame-relay map ip 140.1.1.3 503 broadcast
frame-relay map ipx 1.0200.bbbb.bbbb 502 broadcast
frame-relay map ipx 1.0200.cccc.cccc 503 broadcast
```

Payload Compression Configuration

The configuration of the two styles of Frame Relay payload compression are very similar. The
details of the configuration are different, however, when using a point-to-point subinterface as
opposed to a multipoint subinterface. Examine the configuration on the Albuquerque and
Yosemite routers, which each use a point-to-point subinterface for the PVC between the two.
Figure 8-19 and Examples 8-21 and 8-22 display the network and the configuration.

Figure 8-19   *Network with Frame Relay Payload Compression*

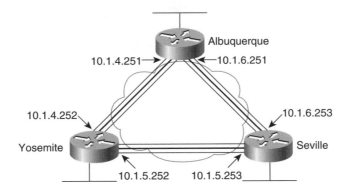

Example 8-21 *Payload Compression Configuration, Albuquerque*

```
hostname Albuquerque
!
no ip domain-lookup
ipx routing 0200.aaaa.aaaa
!
interface Serial0
 no ip address
 encapsulation frame-relay IETF
 frame-relay lmi-type cisco
!
interface Serial0.1 point-to-point
 ip address 10.1.4.251 255.255.255.0
 no ip directed-broadcast
 ipx network 4
 frame-relay interface-dlci 902 IETF
 frame-relay payload-compression packet-by-packet
!
interface Serial0.2 point-to-point
 ip address 10.1.6.251 255.255.255.0
 no ip directed-broadcast
 ipx network 6
 frame-relay interface-dlci 903
!
interface Serial1
 no ip address
 no ip directed-broadcast
 shutdown
!
interface Ethernet0
 ip address 10.1.1.251 255.255.255.0
 ipx network 1
!
router igrp 5
 network 10.0.0.0
```

Example 8-22 *Payload Compression Configuration, Yosemite*

```
hostname Yosemite
!
no ip domain-lookup
ipx routing 0200.bbbb.bbbb
!
interface Serial0
 no ip address
 encapsulation frame-relay IETF
 frame-relay lmi-type cisco
!
interface Serial0.1 point-to-point
 ip address 10.1.4.252 255.255.255.0
 no ip directed-broadcast
 ipx network 4
 frame-relay interface-dlci 901 IETF
```

Example 8-22 *Payload Compression Configuration, Yosemite (Continued)*

```
 frame-relay payload-compression packet-by-packet
!
interface Serial0.2 point-to-point
 ip address 10.1.5.252 255.255.255.0

 ipx network 5
 frame-relay interface-dlci 903
!
interface Serial1
 no ip address

 shutdown
!
interface Ethernet0
 ip address 10.1.2.252 255.255.255.0
 ipx network 2
!
router igrp 5
 network 10.0.0.0
```

All that is necessary on the point-to-point subinterfaces to enable the Cisco STAC payload compression is the **frame-relay payload-compression packet-by-packet** interface subcommand on the subinterface on each end of the VC. Payload compression is enabled on a per-VC basis, but because the subinterface is a point-to-point subinterface, only one VC is allowed on the interface—that VC is implied as the one on which to perform compression.

If FRF.9 compression was desired instead, the **frame-relay payload-compression frf9 stac** interface subcommand would have been used. Using **frf9 stac** as two separate keywords might seem to imply that other options besides stac are available, but there are no other options. In addition, you might think that the **stac** keyword can be omitted, but it is required. You can think of **packet-by-packet** as referring to the Cisco standard stac algorithm, and **frf9 stac** as referring to the FRF.9 standard.

The configuration when using a multipoint subinterface requires the use of the **frame-relay map** command, even if Inverse ARP is used to automatically map the DLCIs to the Layer 3 addresses. Examples 8-23 and 8-24 show a similar configuration for the network in Figure 8-20, except that the routers are now using multipoint subinterfaces. (Some unrelated configuration details are not shown in these examples.)

Figure 8-20 *Multipoint Network with Payload Compression*

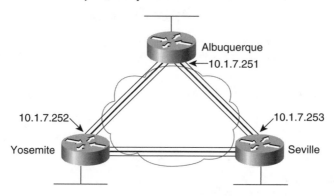

Example 8-23 *Payload Compression Configuration, Albuquerque, Multipoint Subinterfaces*

```
hostname Albuquerque
!
interface Serial0
 no ip address
 encapsulation frame-relay IETF
 frame-relay lmi-type cisco
!
interface Serial0.1 multipoint
 ip address 10.1.7.251 255.255.255.0
 no ip directed-broadcast
 ipx network 7
 frame-relay interface-dlci 902 IETF
 frame-relay interface-dlci 903 IETF
 frame-relay map ip 10.1.7.252 902 payload-compress frf9 stac
```

Example 8-24 *Payload Compression Configuration, Yosemite, Multipoint Subinterfaces*

```
hostname Yosemite
!
interface Serial0
 no ip address
 encapsulation frame-relay IETF
 frame-relay lmi-type cisco
!
interface Serial0.1 multipoint
 ip address 10.1.7.252 255.255.255.0
 no ip directed-broadcast
 ipx network 7
 frame-relay interface-dlci 901 IETF
 frame-relay interface-dlci 903 IETF
 frame-relay map ip 10.1.7.251 901 payload-compress frf9 stac
```

All that is necessary on the multipoint subinterfaces on Yosemite to enable FRF.9 compression on just the VC to Albuquerque is one interface subcommand on each of the two routers. The **frame-relay map ip 10.1.7.251 901 payload-compress frf9 stac** interface subcommand on Yosemite tells the IOS for IP packets header out DLCI 901 to enable payload compression and use the FRF.9 style of configuration. A similar command is used on Albuquerque—if compression is disabled on only one end of the VC, or if a different type of compression is enabled, then no packets will flow across the link.

If the Cisco STAC payload compression was desired instead, the **frf9 stac** keywords would need to be replaced by the **packet-by-packet** keyword.

ISDN Protocols and Design

The goal of this section is to summarize the details and to clarify complex features of ISDN and related IOS functions. The CCNA exam focuses on Basic Rate Interface (BRI) functions, and the CCNP and CCIE cover all of ISDN, including PRI.

ISDN Channels

Two types of ISDN interfaces are focused on in IOS documentation: Basic Rate Interface (BRI) and Primary Rate Interface (PRI). Both BRI and PRI provide multiple digital bearer channels over which temporary connections can be made and data can be sent. The result is digital dial access to multiple sites concurrently. Table 8-24 summarizes the features of BRI and PRI.

Table 8-24   *BRI and PRI Features*

Type of Interface	Number of Bearer Channels (B Channels)	Number of Signaling Channels (D Channels)
BRI	2	1 (16kbps)
PRI (T/1)	23	1 (64kbps)
PRI (E/1)	30	1 (64kbps)

Bearer channels (B channels) are used to transport data. B channels are called bearer channels because they bear the burden of transporting the data. B channels operate at up to 64kbps, although the speed might be lower depending on the service provider. The section "ISDN Configuration," later in the chapter, discusses how to configure the correct speed for the bearer channels. D channels are used for signaling.

ISDN Protocols

Coverage of ISDN protocols and their specifications on the CCNA exam poses a particularly difficult problem for the CCNA candidate. The International Telecommunications Union (ITU) defines the most well-known specifications for ISDN, but there are far more specifications than anyone would want to try to memorize. The problem is choosing what to memorize and what to ignore. My personal philosophy is that standards information is best kept in a book rather than in my own memory. With Cisco's emphasis on proving your hands-on skills using the CCNA and CCNP exams, hopefully a de-emphasis on memorizing standards will be a convenient side effect. However, these standards are fair game for the exam.

The characterizations of several key protocols made by the Cisco ICND course are important for the exam. Table 8-25 is directly quoted from the ICND course. Take care to learn the information in the Issue column—knowing what each series of specifications is about will be useful.

Table 8-25   *ISDN Protocol Table*

Issue	Protocols	Key Examples
Telephone network and ISDN	E-series	E.163: international telephone numbering plan
		E.164: international ISDN addressing
ISDN concepts, aspects, and interfaces	I-series	I.100 series: concepts, structures, terminology
		I.400 series: User-Network Interfaces (UNI)
Switching and signaling	Q-series	Q.921: LAPD
		Q.931: ISDN network layer

The OSI layers correlating to the different ISDN specifications are also mentioned in both the ITM and the ICND CCNA prerequisite courses. Memorizing the specifications in Table 8-26 and the OSI layer each specification matches is also useful.

Table 8-26   *ISDN I-Series and Q-Series Mentioned in ICND and ITM: OSI Layer Comparison*

Layer, as Compared to OSI	I-Series	Equivalent Q-Series Specification	General Purpose
1	ITU-T I.430		Defines connectors, encoding, framing, and reference points
	ITU-T I.431		
2	ITU-T I.440	ITU-T Q.920	Defines the LAPD protocol used on the D channel to encapsulate signaling requests
	ITU-T I.4411	ITU-T Q.921	

Table 8-26   *ISDN I-Series and Q-Series Mentioned in ICND and ITM: OSI Layer Comparison (Continued)*

Layer, as Compared to OSI	I-Series	Equivalent Q-Series Specification	General Purpose
3	ITU-T I.450	ITU-T Q.930	Defines signaling messages—for example, call setup and takedown messages
	ITU-T I.451	ITU-T Q.931	

A tool to help you remember the specifications and layers is that the second digit in the Q-series matches the OSI layer. For example, in ITU-T Q.920, the second digit, 2, corresponds to OSI Layer 2. In the I-series, the second digit of the specification numbers is two more than the corresponding OSI layer. For example, I.430, with the second digit of value 3, defines OSI Layer 1 equivalent functions.

LAPD is used to deliver signaling messages to the ISDN switch—for example, a call setup message. Figure 8-21 shows the use of LAPD versus PPP on B channels.

Figure 8-21   *LAPD and PPP on D and B Channels*

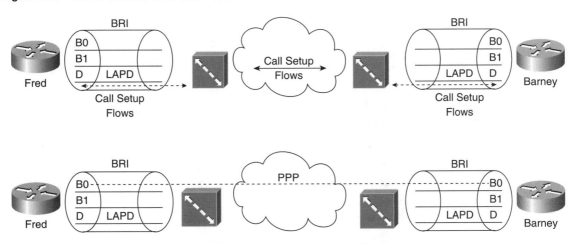

The call is established through the service provider network; PPP is used as the data link protocol on the B channel from end to end. LAPD is used between the router and the ISDN switch at each local central office (CO) and remains up so that new signaling messages can be sent and received. Because the signals are sent outside the channel used for data, this is called *out-of-band signaling*.

The BRI encodes bits at 192 kbps, with most of the bandwidth (144 kbps) being used for the two B channels and the D channel. The additional bits are used for framing.

NOTE | For further reading, refer to the ITM course, available from Cisco for a nominal fee. (The ITM Version 2 CD is based on Cisco Press's *Internetwork Technology Handbook, 2nd Edition*, ISBN: 1-57870-102-3.)

The service profile identifier (SPID) used in signaling is important to the configuration of ISDN and is likely to be mentioned on the exam. The SPID works like an ISDN phone number—in fact, if buying ISDN for home use, the service provider personnel probably will call it the *ISDN phone number* instead of SPID. Call setup messages refer to both the called and the calling SPIDs. If a router wants to call another router, a SPID is used for call setup.

ISDN Function Groups and Reference Points

Many people are confused about the terms ISDN *reference point* and ISDN *function group*. One key reason for the confusion is that only some function groups—and therefore some reference points—are used in a single topology. Cisco expects CCNAs to be familiar with all function groups and reference points. In an effort to clear up these two topics, consider the following inexact but more familiar definitions of the two:

- **Function groups**—A set of functions implemented by a device and software.

- **Reference points**—The interface between two function groups; this includes cabling details.

Most people understand concepts better if they can visualize a network or actually implement the network. However, for a good understanding of function groups and reference points, keep the following facts in mind:

- Not all reference points are used in any one topology; in fact, one or two might never be used in a particular part of the world.

- After the equipment is ordered and working, there is no need to think about function groups and reference points.

- The router configuration does not refer to reference points and function groups, so many people ignore these details.

A cabling diagram is helpful for examining the reference points and the function groups. Figure 8-22 shows the cabling diagram for several examples.

Figure 8-22   *ISDN Function Groups and Reference Points*

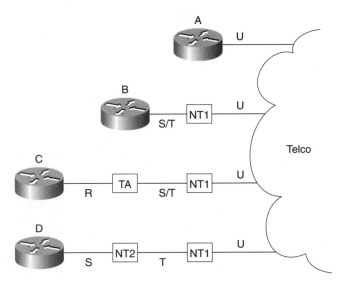

Router A was ordered with an ISDN BRI U reference point, referring to the I.430 reference point defining the interface between the customer premise and the telco in North America. Router B was bought with an ISDN BRI S/T interface, implying that it must be cabled to a function group NT1 device in North America. An NT1 function group device must be connected to the telco line through a U reference point in North America; the S/T interface defines the connection to Router B. Router B is called a TE1 (Terminal Equipment 1) function group device. Finally, non-ISDN equipment is called a TE2 (Terminal Equipment 2) device and is attached using the R reference point to a terminal adapter (TA) function group device. Alternately, a TE1 can connect using an S reference point to an NT2 function group, as shown in case D of Figure 8-15.

Table 8-27 summarizes the types from Figure 8-22. Table 8-28 and Table 8-29 provide a summary of formal definitions.

Table 8-27   *Figure 8-22 Function Groups and Reference Point Summary*

Router	Function Group(s)	Connected to Reference Point(s)
A	TE1, NT1	U
B	TE1	S/T (combined S and T)
C	TE2	R
D	TE1	S

Table 8-28 *Definitions for Function Groups in Figure 8-22*

Function Group	Acronym Stands for	Description
TE1	Terminal Equipment 1	ISDN-capable four-wire cable. Understands signaling, 2B+D. Uses S reference point.
TE2	Terminal Equipment 2	Equipment that does not understand ISDN protocols and specifications (no ISDN awareness). Uses R reference point, typically an RS-232 or V.35 cable, to connect to a TA.
TA	Terminal adapter	Equipment that uses R and S reference points. Can be thought of as the TE1 function group on behalf of a TE2.
NT1	Network Termination Type 1	CPE equipment in North America. Connects with U reference point (two-wire) to telco. Connects with T or S reference points to other customer premise equipment.
NT2	Network Termination Type 2	Equipment that uses a T reference point to the telco outside North America, or to an NT1 inside North America. Uses an S reference point to connect to other customer premise equipment.
NT1/NT2		A combined NT1 and NT2 in the same device. This is relatively common in North America.

Table 8-29 *Definitions for Reference Points in Figure 8-22*

Reference Point	Connection Between
R	TE2 and TA.
S	TE1 or TA and NT2.
T	NT2 and NT1.
U	NT1 and telco.
S/T	TE1 or TA, connected to an NT1, when no NT2 is used. Alternately, the connection from a TE1 or TA to a combined NT1/NT2.

Jargon definitely confuses the issue with home ISDN services. Figure 8-23 outlines the problem.

Figure 8-23   *Home ISDN User and Reference Points*

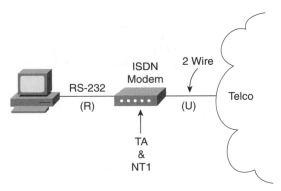

Popularly used, ISDN terminology for home-based consumers sometimes muddles the terminology from the ISDN specifications. The home user orders the service, and the telco offers to sell the user one of several "ISDN modems." What is actually received is a TA and NT1 in one device. A PC uses a serial port to connect to the TA, which uses reference point R. However, the terms reference point, TA, and NT1 are almost never used by providers, hence the confusion.

One other detail of the ISDN protocols that might be on the exam is the ISDN SBus. The ISDN SBus allows multiple devices to share the same BRI by sharing the S reference point. SBus is a great idea, but it has not been deployed extensively. SBus takes the S reference point and allows multiple TE1s to connect to the same NT1. This enables multiple TE1s to use the same BRI. If all the TE1s were data devices, then instead of using an SBus, a better solution would be to place all TE1s on a LAN and use an ISDN-capable router. To support ISDN phones, fax, video, and data TE1 devices, however, the SBus can be used. Figure 8-24 shows a basic SBus topology.

Figure 8-24   *ISDN SBus*

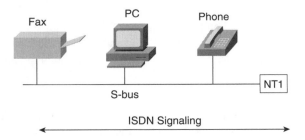

ISDN signaling can be created by the TE1s and responded to by TE1s. However, because the BRI is shared among the TE1s, the SPID received in a call setup request no longer uniquely identifies the TE1. Therefore, a suffix called a *subaddress* is added to the SPID. Each TE1 on the SBus uses a different subaddress. The service provider connected to this NT1 and to any other NT1 from which calls are set up must support subaddressing before the user can use SBus.

Typical Use of ISDN

ISDN typically is used for temporary dial connections. Attractive pricing has also caused some companies to use permanently dialed ("nailed-up") ISDN connections instead of leased lines. ISDN lines can provide access at 128kbps, using both B channels. Compression can increase throughput, potentially getting 500kbps of throughput through the line. xDSL technology is an emerging competitor to ISDN for dial-in ISPs.

Temporary connections between routers are another typical use of ISDN, both for backup and for occasional connection. Backup is self-explanatory. Occasional connections would include traffic for sites that do not use online applications or video conferencing, and cases in which additional bandwidth between sites is desired. Most of the configuration needed for these occasional connections is related to a topic called *dial-on-demand routing (DDR)*, which is covered in a later section of this chapter. Figure 8-25 shows some of the typical network topologies when using ISDN.

The scenarios in Figure 8-25 can be described as follows:

- Case 1 shows dial-on-demand routing. Logic is configured in the routers to trigger the dial when the traffic that needs to get to another site is sent by the user.

- Case 2 shows a typical telecommuting environment.

- Case 3 shows the typical dial-backup topology. The leased line fails, so an ISDN call is established between the same two routers.

- Case 4 shows a case in which an ISDN BRI could be used to dial directly to another router to replace a Frame Relay access link or a failed VC.

- Case 5 depicts an ISDN line that could be used to dial into the Frame Relay provider's network, replacing a failed VC or access link with a VC running over an ISDN connection to the Frame Relay switch.

PAP and CHAP

PPP and HDLC can be used on B channels, but PPP provides several features that make it the preferred choice in a dial environment. HDLC and PPP overhead per-data frame is identical; however, PPP provides LQM, as well as CHAP and PAP authentication and Layer 3 address assignment through several of the control protocols. Each of these features is particularly important in a dial environment.

Password Authentication Protocol (PAP) and Challenge Handshake Authentication Protocol (CHAP) are used to authenticate (verify) that the endpoints on a dial connection are allowed to connect. CHAP is the preferred method today because the identifying codes flowing over the link are created using a Message Digest 5 (MD5) one-way hash, which is more secure than the clear-text passwords sent by PAP.

Figure 8-25   *Typical Occasional Connections Between Routers*

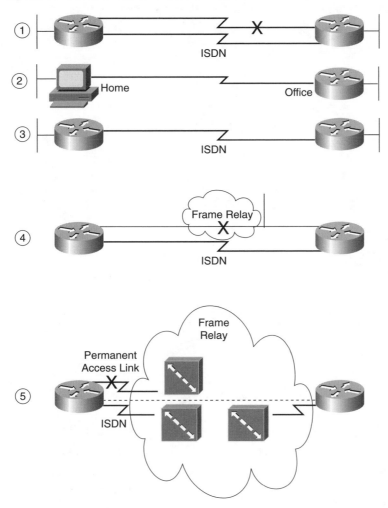

Both PAP and CHAP require the exchange of messages between devices. The dialed-to router expects to receive a user name and password from the dialing router with both PAP and CHAP. With PAP, the user name and password are sent by the dialing router. With CHAP, the dialed-to router sends a message (called a challenge) that asks the dialing router to send its user name and password. The challenge includes a random number, which is part of the input into the MD5 hash algorithm. The dialing router replies with the MD5 hash value, which is a function of its ID (host name), its password, and the random number supplied in the challenge. The dialed-to router repeats the same hash algorithm; if the received value matches the computed value, the

CHAP authentication is passed. Figure 8-26 illustrates the message flow in PAP and CHAP environments. Example 8-25 shows the CHAP configuration for Figure 8-26.

Figure 8-26 *PAP and CHAP Messages*

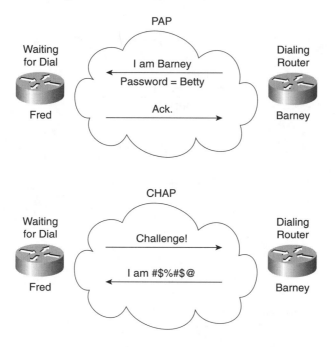

Example 8-25 *CHAP Configuration Sample*

```
Router Fred                              Router Barney

username Barney password Bedrock         username Fred password Bedrock
!                                        !
Interface serial 0                       Interface serial 0
encapsulation ppp                        encapsulation ppp
ppp authentication chap                  ppp authentication chap
.                                        .
```

Notice that each router refers to the other router's host name; each router uses its own host name in CHAP flows, unless overridden by configuration. Each codes the same password. When Router Barney receives a challenge from Router Fred, Router Barney sends an encrypted value, which is the value Fred should compute given the name Barney, the password Bedrock, and the original random number. CHAP authentication is completed if the two values match.

Multilink PPP

Multilink PPP is a function that allows multiple links between a router and some other device over which traffic is balanced. The need for this function is straightforward; some other considerations about when to use it are subtle. Figure 8-27 illustrates the most obvious need for Multilink PPP.

Figure 8-27   *Multilink PPP for Dial-In Device*

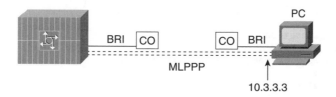

For faster service, the PC that has dialed in would want to use both B channels efficiently. Figure 8-27 shows two dotted lines between the PC and the access server, signifying that two B channels are in use between the devices. Multilink PPP breaks a packet into fragments, sends some fragments across each of the two links, and reassembles them at the other end of the link. The net result is that the links are utilized approximately the same amount.

Multilink PPP is also useful between routers. For example, in Figure 8-28, videoconferencing between Atlanta and Nashville uses six B channels between two routers.

Figure 8-28   *Multiple B Channels Between Routers*

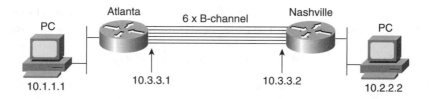

In this example, if multilink PPP is used, the links have almost identical utilization. The negative is that the routers must fragment and reassemble every packet. However, the 384Kb needed for the video conference is available.

Now consider the alternative—without multilink PPP, but simply with PPP on each of the six links. Six routes to subnet 10.2.2.0/24 would exist in Router A's routing table. With any of the faster internal switching methods in a Cisco router (fast switching, optimum switching, NetFlow switching), the balancing effect is that *all packets to the same IP address use the same link*. The result is that router Atlanta sends some packets over one link and some over the other, but the balancing is unpredictable. More importantly, all packets to the videoconference system's single IP address in Nashville will use the same link, effectively limiting the videoconference to 64 kbps. An alternative is to disable the faster switching methods in the router so that multiple routes to the same subnet are used in a round-robin fashion. However, that is not recommended because it significantly slows the internal processing on the router. For that reason, multilink PPP is a better choice in this case.

Example 8-26 shows a sample multilink PPP configuration. The Atlanta and Nashville routers will use two B channels of the same BRI.

Example 8-26 *Multilink PPP Configuration for Atlanta*

```
username Nashville password Robert
interface bri 0
ip addr 10.3.3.1 255.255.255.0
encapsulation ppp
dialer idle-timeout 300
dialer load-threshold 25 either
dialer map 10.3.3.2 name Nashville 16155551234
dialer-group 1
ppp authentication chap
ppp multilink
```

The two key commands are the **ppp multilink** and the **dialer load-threshold** commands. **ppp multilink** enables multilink PPP; **dialer load-threshold** tells the router to dial another B channel if the utilization average on the currently used links is more than 25 percent for either inbound or outbound utilization.

Dial-on-Demand Routing and ISDN Configuration

As a CCNA, you'll need to understand both ISDN configuration and the related DDR configuration that causes the IOS to use the BRI interface. Dial-on-demand routing (DDR) configuration and concepts must be understood before the ISDN configuration topics will make complete sense. In fact, ISDN configuration can be very brief, whereas DDR can become quite involved. In this section, DDR is explained first, with ISDN configuration included later.

DDR defines the logic behind when a router chooses to dial another site, whether ISDN, synchronous serial, or asynchronous serial interfaces are used. In this chapter, the examples reflect ISDN; the DDR logic is the same for any of the three types of dial interfaces. DDR includes several variations; the variation called DDR legacy is covered in this chapter. Those of you who want to pursue CCNP and CCIE certification should expand your knowledge of DDR concerning DDR dialer profiles in particular.

Little additional ISDN configuration is required in addition to the core DDR configuration. In fact, one detail that is covered deeply in the earlier ISDN concepts section is the use of certain reference points by Cisco's products; there is no need to configure the IOS to know which interface is used. Cisco's BRI implementation includes a choice of an S/T interface or a U interface. In either case, BRI configuration in the router is identical.

Hands-on experience is the best way to fully learn the details of configuration. In lieu of that, this section lists commands, provides examples, and points out tricky features. Table 8-30 and

Table 8-31 summarize the more popular commands used for ISDN configuration and verification. The Cisco IOS documentation is an excellent reference for additional IP commands, and the Cisco Press book *Interconnecting Cisco Network Devices* is another good reference, particularly if you are not able to attend the instructor-led version of the class.

Table 8-30   *ISDN Configuration Commands*

Command	Configuration Mode	Purpose
isdn switch-type *switch-type*	Global or interface	Defines to the router the type of ISDN switch to which the ISDN line is connected at the central office.
isdn spid1 *spid*	Interface	Defines the first SPID.
isdn spid2 *spid*	Interface	Defines the second SPID.
isdn caller *number*	Interface	Defines a valid number for incoming calls when using call screening.
isdn answer1 [*called-party-number*][*:subaddress*]	Interface	Specifies the ISDN number or subaddress that must be used on incoming calls for this router to answer.
isdn answer2 [*called-party-number*][*:subaddress*]	Interface	Specifies a second ISDN number or subaddress that must be used on incoming calls for this router to answer.
dialer-list [*list nnn*] **protocol** [*protocol-type*] **permit I deny**	Global	Defines types of traffic considered interesting.
dialer-group *n*	Interface	Enables dialer list on this interface.
dialer in-band	Interface	Enables dial out and dial in on this interface. This command is used only for serial lines that connect to a TA, not for native ISDN interfaces that use the out-of-band D channel.
dialer string *string*	Interface	Is the dial string used when dialing only one site.
dialer map *protocol next-hop address* [name *hostname*] [speed 56 I 64] [broadcast] *dial-string*	Interface	Is the dial string to reach the next hop. However, the **map** command is used when dialing more than one site. This also is the name used for authentication. Broadcast ensures that copies of broadcasts go to this next-hop address.

Table 8-31   *ISDN-Related EXEC Commands*

Command	Function
show interfaces bri *number*[*:b-channel*]	Includes reference to the access lists enabled on the interface.
show controllers bri *number*	Shows Layer 1 statistics and status for B and D channels.
show isdn {**active** | **history** | **memory** | **status** | **timers**}	Shows various ISDN status information.
show interfaces bri *number*[[*:bchannel*] | [*first*] [*last*]] [**accounting**]	Displays interface information about the D channel or the B channel(s).
show dialer interface bri *number*	Lists DDR parameters on the BRI interface. Shows whether currently dialed by indicating current status. Also shows previous attempts to dial and whether they were successful.
debug isdn q921	Lists ISDN Layer 2 messages.
debug isdn q931	Lists ISDN Layer 3 messages (call setup/teardown).
debug dialer {**events** | **packets**}	Lists information when a packet is directed out a dial interface, telling whether the packet is interesting.

DDR Legacy Concepts and Configuration

Two ways exist by which to configure DDR. The two styles of DDR configuration are called *DDR legacy* and *DDR dialer profiles*. The main difference between the two is that DDR legacy associates dial details with a physical interface, but DDR dialer profiles-style configuration disassociates the dial configuration from a physical interface, allowing a great deal of flexibility. The concepts behind legacy DDR apply to DDR dialer profiles as well, but DDR legacy is a little less detailed. Although not overly stated in the course, the DDR coverage in the ICND class is for DDR legacy.

DDR can be used to cause the router to dial or to receive a dial on asynchronous serial interfaces, synchronous serial interfaces, and ISDN BRI and PRI interfaces. All examples in this chapter use ISDN BRI.

The following list identifies the four key concepts behind DDR configuration. The first two concepts are not actually related to the dial process, but relate to the process of choosing when to dial and when not to dial. The other two concepts relate to dialing, or signaling. The term *signaling* is used in ISDN to describe the processes of call setup and takedown, and it is used synonymously with the term *dialing* here. The four key concepts are as follows:

> **Step 1**   Routing packets out of the to-be-dialed interface
>
> **Step 2**   Determining the subset of these packets that trigger the dialing process

Step 3   Dialing (signaling)

Step 4   Determining when the connection is terminated

Each of these is addressed in succession, followed by a discussion of DDR legacy configuration. After learning about the basic DDR concepts and configuration procedures, you will learn about ISDN-specific configuration. Finally, this section concludes with a complete DDR and ISDN example.

DDR Step 1: Routing Packets out the Interface to Be Dialed

Figure 8-29 provides the backdrop for these discussions. In these discussions, the SanFrancisco router will be dialing into the main site in LosAngeles.

Figure 8-29   *Sample DDR Network*

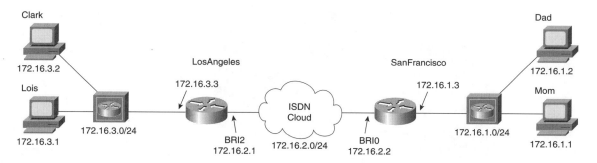

The router must choose when to dial. The first step in this process relates to the following fact:

DDR will not dial until some traffic is directed (routed) out the dial interface.

The router needs to route packets so that they are queued to go out the dial interface. Cisco's design for DDR defines that the router receives some user-generated traffic and, through normal routing processes, decides to route the traffic out the interface to be dialed. The router (SanFrancisco) can receive a packet that must be routed out BRI0; routing the packet out BRI0 triggers the IOS, causing the dial to occur.

Of course, routes are not learned over a dial link while the dial link is down. In Figure 8-29, for instance, SanFrancisco will have no routes to 172.16.3.0/24 learned via a routing protocol. Therefore, static routes are configured on SanFrancisco. This can be done for any protocol that is supported by DDR for the purpose of triggering the dial. All routable protocols can be configured to trigger the dial; IP will be used in the upcoming examples. Any traffic that could be routed or bridged across a leased link is supported after the link is up.

To begin the process of building a DDR configuration, IP routes are added to the configuration so that packets can be directed out BRI0 on SanFrancisco:

```
! SanFrancisco Static routes.
ip route 172.16.3.0 255.255.255.0 172.16.2.1
```

DDR Step 2: Determining the Subset of The Packets That Trigger the Dialing Process

Together, Steps 1 and 2 of legacy DDR logic determine when the dial is attempted. These combined steps are typically called *triggering the dial*. In Step 1, a packet is routed out an interface to be dialed, but that packet alone does not necessarily cause the dial to occur. The IOS allows the second step to define a subset of the packets routed in Step 1 to actually cause the route to dial. The logic flow works as shown in Figure 8-30.

Figure 8-30 *DDR Logic for Triggering the Dial*

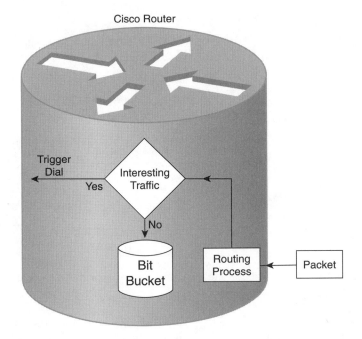

The choice in Step 2 is simply put like this: "Is this packet, which is being routed out this dial interface, worthy of causing the dial to occur?" The packets that are worthy of causing the device to dial are called *interesting packets* by Cisco. Cisco does not categorize those packets that are not worthy of causing the dial; in effect, they are "boring." The capability to exactly determine the interesting packets grants the router administrator control over when the dial is made. This is particularly important if the dialed connection is incrementally charged by the minute.

Two different methods can be used to define the interesting packets. *Interesting* can be defined as all packets of one or more Layer 3 protocols (for example, all IP packets). In that case, any user in SanFrancisco can send a packet to any host in 172.16.3.0/24 and trigger the dial connection. That might be exactly what is desired, or it might not be. The second method is that *interesting* can be defined as packets permitted by an access list. In this case, if the access list permits the packet, it is considered interesting.

Example 8-27 shows additional configuration on SanFrancisco, in two cases. One shows all IP packets being considered as interesting, and the other shows all packets to the Web server Lois (refer to Figure 8-29) considered as interesting.

Example 8-27 *Defining Interesting Packets to Activate the Circuit from SanFrancisco to LosAngeles*

```
ip route 172.16.3.0 255.255.255.0 172.16.2.1
access-list 101 permit tcp any host 172.16.3.1 eq 80
dialer-list 1 protocol ip permit
dialer-list 2 protocol ip list 101
interface bri 0
encapsulation ppp
ip address 172.16.2.2 255.255.255.0
!Use this one if all IP is considered interesting ...
dialer-group 1
! OR Use next statement to trigger for Web to Server Lois
dialer-group 2
```

The **dialer-group** interface subcommand enables the logic that determines what is interesting. It refers to a dialer list, which can refer either to an entire protocol suite or to an access list, as shown. (After the link is up, packets are not filtered using list 101—the logic is used just for determining what is interesting and what is boring.)

DDR Step 3: Dialing (Signaling)

The dialing router needs additional information before the dial can occur. First, for non-ISDN interfaces, it is necessary to communicate the dial string to the external dialing device. In-band signaling (dialing) must be enabled on these interfaces using the command **dialer in-band**. This is not necessary on a BRI interface because it uses the out-of-band D channel for signaling. Table 8-32 summarizes what the command implies on different interfaces.

Table 8-32 *Effect of the **dialer in-band** Command*

Type of Interface	Type of Signaling Used
Async	AT command set (in-band)
Sync	V.25 bis (in-band)
ISDN	ISDN D channel with Q.921/Q.931 (out-of-band)

The second piece of information needed before dialing is the phone number. With the network in Figure 8-29, the configuration is straightforward. The command is **dialer string** *string*, where *string* is the phone number. Example 8-28 completes the DDR configuration associated with Figure 8-29 that allows the dial to occur.

Example 8-28 *SanFrancisco Configuration—Dial Now Can Occur*

```
ip route 172.16.3.0 255.255.255.0 172.16.2.1
!
access-list 101 permit tcp any host 172.16.3.1 eq 80
!
dialer-list 2 protocol ip list 101
!
interface bri 0
 ip address 172.16.2.2 255.255.255.0
 encapsulation ppp
 dialer string 14045551234
 dialer-group 2
```

The **dialer in-band** command is omitted because an ISDN BRI is used in this case. The only new command added here is the **dialer string** command, which shows the phone number that is to be used for signaling a connection. The signaling occurs on the D channel of the BRI.

When more than one site is dialed from the same interface, several dial strings are needed. For example, Figure 8-31 adds a third site, GothamCity, to the network. The client's FTP connections to the FTP server running on Commissioner will be considered interesting traffic for causing dial connections to GothamCity.

Figure 8-31 *Mapping Between Next Hop and Dial String*

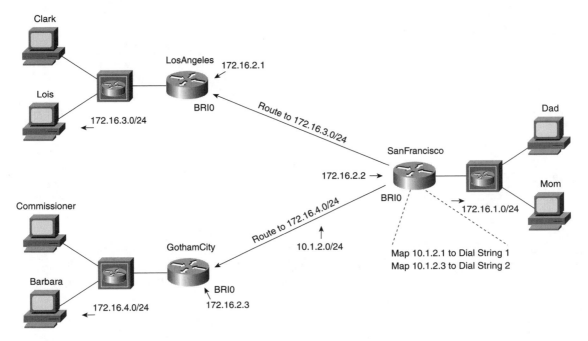

The dilemma for SanFrancisco will now be how to determine which ISDN telephone number to signal. The key is in the **ip route** commands and the new **dialer map** command. Of course, there are unique ISDN telephone numbers for both LosAngeles and GothamCity. Because the static routes will direct the router to send the packet to either 172.16.2.1 or 172.16.2.3, all that is needed is a mapping between these next-hop addresses and their respective ISDN telephone numbers. The **dialer map** command does exactly that. Example 8-29 shows the mostly complete configuration.

Example 8-29 *SanFrancisco Configuration—Two Dial-to Sites,* **dialer map** *in Use*

```
ip route 172.16.3.0 255.255.255.0 172.16.2.1
ip route 172.16.4.0 255.255.255.0 172.16.2.3
! Added usernames for CHAP support!
username LosAngeles password Clark
username GothamCity password Bruce
access-list 101 permit tcp any host 172.16.3.1 eq 80
! Added next statement to make The Client's FTP connection interesting!
access-list 101 permit tcp any host 172.16.4.1 eq 21
!
dialer-list 2 protocol ip list 101
!
interface bri 0
 ip address 172.16.2.2 255.255.255.0
 encapsulation ppp
 ppp authentication chap
 dialer map ip 172.16.2.1 broadcast name  LosAngeles 14045551234
 dialer map ip 172.16.2.3 broadcast name GothamCity 1999999999901
 dialer-group 2
!
router igrp 6
network 172.16.0.0
```

The **dialer map** commands imply that if the interesting packet were routed to 172.16.2.1, the dial to LosAngeles would occur. Conversely, if the interesting packet were routed to 172.16.2.3, the dial to GothamCity would occur. The definition of *interesting* is expanded to include packets to the FTP server in GothamCity.

Two other important configuration elements are included in Example 8-29. First, CHAP authentication was configured. PAP or CHAP is required if dialing to more than one site with ISDN—and PAP and CHAP require PPP. The user name expected from the other router is coded in the corresponding **dialer map** command.

Broadcast handling is the final configuration element that must be addressed. Just as with any other point-to-point serial link, there is no true data link broadcast. If a broadcast must be sent on the interface, however, it is necessary to issue the **broadcast** command to tell the interface to forward the packet across the link.

DDR Step 4: Determining When the Connection Is Terminated

The dialed link acts just like a leased line while it is up. If a particular Layer 3 protocol is enabled on the link, it can be routed across the link. Transparent (encapsulated) bridging can be used just like any other point-to-point link. Routing updates, IPX SAPs, AppleTalk ZIP, and other broadcasts are sent across the link if the **broadcast** keyword is coded. Most importantly, any access list used to define which packets are interesting does not filter the traffic on the interface. If packet filters are desired, an access list must be enabled on the interface.

Additional parallel links can be dialed if more capacity is desired. To do so, dialer profiles must be configured. Additionally, the **dialer load-threshold** *load* command is used to define the link utilization that must be exceeded for another link to be dialed.

The decision to take the link down is the most intriguing part about what happens while the link is up. Although any type of packets can be routed across the link, only interesting packets are considered worthy of keeping the link up. An idle timer counts the time since the last interesting packet went across the link. If that time expires, the link is brought down.

Two idle timers can be set. With the **dialer idle-timeout** *seconds* command, the idle time as previously described is set. If interesting traffic that needs to flow to another dial site is occurring, however, another shorter idle timer can be used. The **dialer fast-idle** *seconds* command enables you to configure a typically lower number than the idle timer so that when other sites need to be dialed, the link that is currently up but can be brought down earlier in the process of idling out as per the **dialer idle-timeout** command.

ISDN Configuration

Example 8-30 and Example 8-31 show the DDR configuration for the network in Figure 8-31. ISDN configuration details have been added; the text following these two examples describes the ISDN commands shown.

Example 8-30 *SanFrancisco Configuration—Complete*

```
ip route 172.16.3.0 255.255.255.0 172.16.2.1
ip route 172.16.4.0 255.255.255.0 172.16.2.3
! Added usernames for CHAP support!
username LosAngeles password Clark
username GothamCity password Bruce
!
access-list 101 permit tcp any host 172.16.3.1 eq 80
access-list 101 permit tcp any host 172.16.4.1 eq 21
!
dialer-list 2 protocol ip list 101
!
interface bri 0
  encapsulation ppp
  ppp authentication chap
  isdn spid1 555555111101
  isdn spid2 555555222202
  dialer idle-timeout 300
```

Example 8-30 *SanFrancisco Configuration—Complete (Continued)*

```
dialer fast-idle 120
 dialer map ip 172.16.2.1 broadcast name LosAngeles 14045551234
 dialer map ip 172.16.2.3 broadcast speed 56 name GothamCity 1999999999901
 dialer-group 2
!
router igrp 6
network 172.16.0.0
```

Example 8-31 *LosAngeles Configuration—Receive Only*

```
username SanFrancisco password Clark
!
interface bri 0
 encapsulation ppp
 ppp authentication chap
 isdn switch-type basic-ni1
!
router igrp 6
network 172.16.0.0
```

The ISDN configuration commands are delineated in the examples via highlighted text; those commands are described in the upcoming text. For example, the switch types are a required parameter for connection to DMS-100 or National ISDN switches; ask your service provider for the type of switch at each site. The LosAngeles BRI is attached to a National ISDN switch in this case. The switch type can be configured with the **isdn switch-type** command, which can be used as a global command, or with an interface subcommand if the router is connected to multiple different types of ISDN switches. The SPIDs might not be required; they are used as a form of authentication by the switch. The SPIDs are configured with BRI interface subcommands on SanFrancisco. Also, hidden in part of the DDR configuration, the speed of the B channel from SanFrancisco to GothamCity will be 56kbps, according to the speed parameter in the **dialer map** command on SanFrancisco.

PAP or CHAP authentication is required for ISDN BRI dial connections. PAP and CHAP configuration is covered earlier in this chapter, in the section "PAP and CHAP."

As seen in Example 8-32, a DDR dial connection over BRI0 has occurred from SanFrancisco to LosAngeles:

Example 8-32 *SanFrancisco DDR commands*

```
SanFrancisco# show interfaces bri 0:1

BRI0:1 is down, line protocol is down
  Hardware is BRI
  MTU 1500 bytes, BW 64 Kbit, DLY 20000 usec, rely 255/255, load 1/255
  Encapsulation PPP, loopback not set, keepalive set (10 sec)
  LCP Open
  Open: IPCP, CDPCP
  Last input 00:00:05, output 00:00:05, output hang never
```

continues

Example 8-32 *SanFrancisco DDR commands (Continued)*

```
     Last clearing of "show interface" counters never
     Input queue: 0/75/0 (size/max/drops); Total output drops: 0
     Queuing strategy: weighted fair
     Output queue: 0/1000/64/0 (size/max total/threshold/drops)
        Conversations  0/1/256 (active/max active/max total)
        Reserved Conversations 0/0 (allocated/max allocated)
     5 minute input rate 0 bits/sec, 0 packets/sec
     5 minute output rate 0 bits/sec, 0 packets/sec
        44 packets input, 1986 bytes, 0 no buffer
        Received 0 broadcasts, 0 runts, 0 giants, 0 throttles
        0 input errors, 0 CRC, 0 frame, 0 overrun, 0 ignored, 0 abort
        49 packets output, 2359 bytes, 0 underruns
        0 output errors, 0 collisions, 7 interface resets
        0 output buffer failures, 0 output buffers swapped out
        11 carrier transitions
        DCD=up  DSR=up  DTR=up  RTS=up  CTS=up


SanFrancisco# show dialer interface bri 0

BRI0 - dialer type = ISDN

Dial String      Successes   Failures    Last called   Last status

0 incoming call(s) have been screened.

BRI0: B-Channel 1
Idle timer (300 secs), Fast idle timer (120 secs)
Wait for carrier (30 secs), Re-enable (15 secs)

Dialer state is data link layer up

Dial reason: ip (s=172.16.1.1, d=172.16.3.1)


Time until disconnect 18 secs
Current call connected 00:14:00
Connected to 14045551234 (LosAngeles)

BRI0: B-Channel 2
Idle timer (300 secs), Fast idle timer (120 secs)
Wait for carrier (30 secs), Re-enable (15 secs)
Dialer state is idle

 SanFrancisco# show isdn active
 ------------------------------------------------------------------------
                         ISDN ACTIVE CALLS
 ------------------------------------------------------------------------
History Table MaxLength = 320 entries
History Retain Timer = 15 Minutes
 ------------------------------------------------------------------------
 Call Calling    Called       Duration  Remote   Time until   Recorded Charges
```

Example 8-32 *SanFrancisco DDR commands (Continued)*

```
Type Number      Number         Seconds   Name      Disconnect   Units/Currency
- - - - - - - - - - - - - - - - - - - - - - - - - - - - - - - - - - - - - - - - - - - -
Out              14045551234    Active(847) LosAngeles   11       u
- - - - - - - - - - - - - - - - - - - - - - - - - - - - - - - - - - - - - - - - - - - -


SanFrancisco# show isdn status
The current ISDN Switchtype = ntt
ISDN BRI0 interface
    Layer 1 Status:
        ACTIVE
    Layer 2 Status:
        TEI = 64, State = MULTIPLE_FRAME_ESTABLISHED
    Layer 3 Status:
        1 Active Layer 3 Call(s)
    Activated dsl 0 CCBs = 1
        CCB:callid=8003, callref=0, sapi=0, ces=1, B-chan=1
    Number of active calls = 1
    Number of available B-channels = 1
    Total Allocated ISDN CCBs = 1


SanFrancisco# debug isdn q931
ISDN q931 protocol debugging is on
TX -> SETUP pd = 8 callref = 0x04
 Bearer Capability i = 0x8890
 Channel ID i = 0x83
 Called Party Number i = 0x80, `14045551234'
SanFrancisco#no debug all
All possible debugging has been turned off

SanFrancisco# debug dialer events
Dialer event debugging is on
Dialing cause: BRI0: ip (s=172.16.1.1, d=172.16.3.1)
SanFrancisco#no debug all
All possible debugging has been turned off

SanFrancisco# debug dialer packets
Dialer packet debugging is on
BRI0: ip (s=172.16.1.1, d=172.16.3.1) 444 bytes, interesting (ip PERMIT)
```

The current timer values and call setup reason are listed by the first command in Example 8-32, **show dialer interface bri 0**. The call has been up for 14 minutes, and 18 seconds are left before the 300-second inactivity timer will expire and take the connection down. The **show isdn active** command lists the fact that a single active call exists to LosAngeles, with now only 11 seconds left until disconnect. The **show isdn status** command lists the switch type (ntt) and lists the fact that one call is active, which leaves one inactive B channel.

Remembering the general idea behind the debug command output is also useful for CCNAs so that the right options can be enabled quickly. The **debug isdn q921** command (not shown) lists details of the LAPD protocol between the router and the ISDN switch. The **debug isdn q931** command lists output for call setup and disconnect; the output in the example shows output typical of what happened on SanFrancisco when the call to LosAngeles was made. The **debug dialer events** and **debug dialer packets** commands provide similar information when a packet is a candidate for causing the dial to occur—in other words, when a packet is routed out the dial interface.

A Comparison of WAN Options

Networking professionals need to know about many WAN options when designing networks. Certainly, Cisco requires CCNAs to have a solid foundation of the WAN technologies in this chapter. Cisco also expects CCNAs to be able to compare and contrast these different WAN technologies. This section summarizes many of the concepts found earlier in this chapter, with a focus on comparison.

The permanent WAN connectivity options can be categorized into two main groups: synchronous serial leased lines and packet switching services. PPP, HDLC, and LAPB are the three data link protocols most typical on leased lines, with Frame Relay being the most pervasive packet-switched service. In fact, Frame Relay is better named a *frame switching* service to imply that the protocol is a Layer 2 protocol, but when talking similar services as a group, *packet switching* is the typical term used. X.25 and ATM services also fall into the packet switching category.

X.25 and ATM are not discussed in this exam guide in any depth. (For more information, refer to the documents referenced in Appendix B, "Decimal to Hexadecimal and Binary Conversion Table.") X.25 is very similar to Frame Relay because it uses VCs and has error-recovery built in to each link and each end-to-end VC. ATM is similar in its use of virtual connections, which are conceptually equivalent to VCs. However, ATM includes the concept of segmentation and reassembly (SAR), in which the device at the edge of the ATM network breaks the frames to be sent into smaller cells (53 bytes) that are reassembled at the other end of the VC. The details of how each of these three packet-switching protocols are implemented is different; however, each creates a multiaccess network, with direct packet forwarding allowed only between pairs of devices that have a VC between them.

Table 8-33 summarizes these types of permanent connections and lists some of the strengths and weaknesses.

Table 8-33   *Comparison of Leased Versus Packet Switching*

Type of WAN Service	Data Link Protocols	Strengths and Weaknesses
Leased		Delivers pervasive availability. Can be expensive for long circuits. Is more expensive for providers to engineer than are packet services.
	PPP	Can improve speed of routing protocol convergence. Allows multivendor interoperability. Has available error recovery option.
	HDLC	Is the IOS default. Requires Cisco router on each end.
	LAPB	Provides error recovery, but this also can result in throttling (slowing) the data rate.
Packet-switched		Allows addition of new sites to be made quickly. Typically involves a lower cost.
	Frame Relay	Allows bursting past CIR, giving perception of "free" capacity. Is pervasive in the United States.
	ATM	As a WAN technology, is not as pervasively available as Frame Relay. Has an attractive built-in Quality of Service feature.
	X.25	Is available pervasively in some parts of the world. Offers beneficial error-recovery features when links have higher error rates. Typically is the third choice of these three if all are available to all connected sites.

The product selection phase on any design project can and should necessarily include key individuals from the organization that will be purchasing or leasing the hardware, Cisco (or the reseller), and any contracted service companies participating in the future deployment of the new equipment. (Some of you probably fall into each of those categories, and possibly into several.) When choosing products, having the vendor or reseller involved can help avoid the problem of trying to be aware of all possible products and options, particularly for new or impending products.

To combat some of the challenges of choosing products from a widely varied product line, Cisco developed the use of three key words to describe the type of product deployed in a typical enterprise network: Core, Distribution, and Access. Figure 8-32 provides a basic network, and Table 8-34 summarizes the meaning behind these three categorizations.

Figure 8-32 *Core, Distribution, and Access Layers*

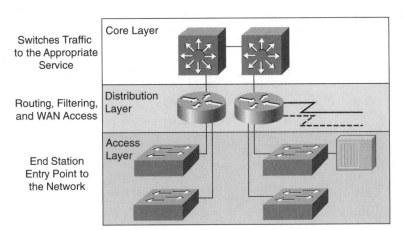

Table 8-34 *Comparison of Core, Distribution, and Access Layers*

Layer	Features	Desired Device Characteristics
Core	Fast transport, often at the topological center of the network. Packet manipulation is not performed here.	Highest forwarding speed
Distribution	Aggregation of access points. Any media translation or security (for instance, access lists) is performed here.	High interface density, high processing capacity per interface for packet manipulation
Access	Entry point for end-user devices, both LAN and dial.	High variety of interface types, less processing capacity required (versus distribution)

Cisco expects CCNAs to understand the needs of each of these layers in a typical network. Conveniently, if router product numbers are listed from low numbers to high, the products that tend to be listed first are access routers, then distribution, and then core, for the most part. For instance, Figure 8-33 comes directly from the ICND course, which is one of the two suggested prerequisites for the CCNA exam. The figure lists the main product families.

Figure 8-33   *Router Product Families*

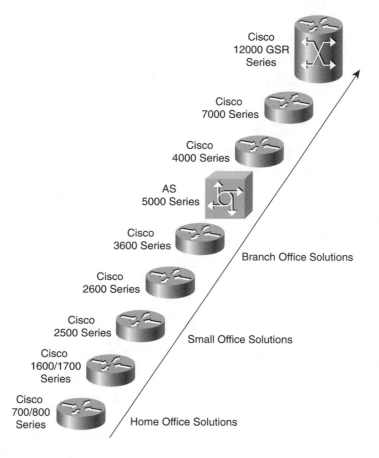

Many of the lower-end routers have both BRI interfaces and asynchronous support (1700, 2600, and 3600), so these would make excellent access routers. The 3600 and 4000 series have more port density than the smaller routers and have RISC processors for better performance on packet manipulation. Finally, the 7000 series, which includes the 7200 and 7500 routers, and the Gigabit Switch Router (GSR) provide the highest forwarding capacity.

All these routers support synchronous serial interface, which can be configured for PPP, HDLC, LAPB, Frame Relay, and X.25. ATM requires a specific interface due to the SAR function. For instance, the 3600 series supports ATM support at OC-3 speeds and higher; some slower ATM interfaces are supported on access routers.

Foundation Summary

The Foundation Summary is a collection of tables and figures that provide a convenient review of many of the key concepts in this chapter. For those of you already comfortable with the topics in this chapter, this summary could help you recall a few details. For those of you who just read this chapter, this review should help solidify some key facts. For any of you doing your final prep before the exam, these tables and figures will hopefully be a convenient way to review the day before the exam.

Table 8-35 summarizes the configuration commands used for HDLC and PPP configuration:

Table 8-35   *PPP and HDLC Configuration Commands*

Command	Configuration Mode
encapsulation {hdlc	ppp	lapb}	Interface subcommand
compress [predictor	stac	mppc [ignore-pfc]]	Interface subcommand

Table 8-36 summarizes the more popular commands used for Frame Relay configuration.

Table 8-36   *Frame Relay Configuration Commands*

Command	Configuration Mode	Purpose
encapsulation frame-relay [ietf	cisco]	Interface	Defines Frame Relay encapsulation; is used rather than HDLC, PPP, and so on.
frame-relay lmi-type {ansi	q933a	cisco}	Interface	Defines the type of LMI messages sent to the switch.
bandwidth *num*	Interface	Sets the route's perceived speed of the interface. Bandwidth is used by some routing protocols to influence the metric.
frame-relay map *protocol protocol-address dlci* [payload-compress {packet-by-packet	frf9 stac}] [broadcast] [ietf	cisco]	Interface	Statically defines a mapping between a network layer address and a DLCI.
keepalive *sec*	Interface	Defines whether and how often LMI status enquiry messages are sent and expected.
interface serial *num.sub* [*point-to-point*	*multipoint*]	Global	Creates a subinterface, or references a previously created subinterface.

Table 8-36   *Frame Relay Configuration Commands (Continued)*

Command	Configuration Mode	Purpose
frame-relay interface-dlci *dlci* [**ietf** I **cisco**]	Interface	Defines a DLCI used for a VC to another DTE.
frame-relay payload-compress {**packet-by-packet** I **frf9 stac**}	Interface subcommand	Defines payload compression on point-to-point subinterfaces.

Table 8-37 summarizes the more popular commands used for ISDN configuration and verification.

Table 8-37   *ISDN Configuration Commands*

Command	Configuration Mode	Purpose
isdn switch-type *switch-type*	Global or interface	Defines to the router the type of ISDN switch to which the ISDN line is connected at the central office.
isdn spid1 *spid*	Interface	Defines the first SPID.
isdn spid2 *spid*	Interface	Defines the second SPID.
isdn caller *number*	Interface	Defines a valid number for incoming calls when using call screening.
isdn answer1 [*called-party-number*][*:subaddress*]	Interface	Specifies the ISDN number or subaddress that must be used on incoming calls for this router to answer.
isdn answer2 [*called-party-number*][*:subaddress*]	Interface	Specifies a second ISDN number or subaddress that must be used on incoming calls for this router to answer.
dialer-list [*list nnn*] **protocol** [*protocol-type*] **permit** I **deny**	Global	Defines types of traffic considered interesting.
dialer-group *n*	Interface	Enables a dialer list on this interface.
dialer in-band	Interface	Enables dial out and dial in on this interface. This command is used only for serial lines that connect to a TA, not for native ISDN interfaces that use the out-of-band D channel.
dialer string *string*	Interface	Is a dial string used when dialing only one site.

continues

Table 8-37   *ISDN Configuration Commands (Continued)*

Command	Configuration Mode	Purpose
dialer map *protocol next-hop address* [**name** *hostname*] [**speed** **56** | **64**] [**broadcast**] *dial-string*	Interface	Is a dial string to reach the next hop. However, the **map** command is used when dialing more than one site. This also is the name used for authentication. Broadcast ensures that copies of broadcasts go to this next-hop address.

Table 8-38 summarizes the **show** and **debug** commands in this chapter.

Table 8-38   *show/debug Command Summary for Chapter 8*

Command	Information Supplied
show interface	Lists statistics and details of interface configuration, including the encapsulation type.
show compress	Lists compression ratios.
show process	Lists processor and task utilization; is useful in watching for increased utilization due to compression.
show interface	Shows physical interface status.
show frame-relay {**pvc** | **map** | **lmi**}	Shows PVC status, mapping (dynamic and static), and LMI status.
show interfaces bri *number[:b-channel]*	Includes a reference to the access lists enabled on the interface.
show isdn {**active** | **history** | **memory** | **status** | **timers**}	Shows various ISDN status information.
show interfaces bri *number*[[**:**bchannel*] | [*first*] [*last*]] [**accounting**]	Displays interface information about the D channel or the B channel(s).
show dialer interface bri *number*	Lists DDR parameters on the BRI interface. Shows whether currently dialed, by indicating current status. Also shows previous attempts to dial and tells whether they were successful.
debug isdn q921	Lists ISDN Layer 2 messages.
debug isdn q931	Lists ISDN Layer 3 messages (call setup/teardown).
debug dialer {**events** | **packets**}	Lists information when a packet is directed out a dial interface, telling if the packet is interesting.

Table 8-38   *show/debug Command Summary for Chapter 8 (Continued)*

Command	Information Supplied
debug frame-relay {**lmi** l **events**}	Lists messages describing LMI flows (LMI option). The **events** option lists inverse ARP information. Other options include **lapf**, **informationelements**, **PPP**, and **packet**.
debug ppp { **authentication** l **bap** l **cbcp** l **compression** l **error** l **multilink** l **negotiation** l **packet** l **tasks**}	Uses the following most important options for CCNAs: negotiation, which shows the control protocol initialization, and authentication, which shows PAP and CHAP flows.
debug lapb	Lists information for LAPB frames.

Table 8-39 lists a brief reference to some popularly used WAN terminology.

Table 8-39   *WAN Terminology*

Term	Definition
Synchronous	The imposition of time ordering on a bit stream. More practically speaking, a device will try to use the same speed as another on the other end of a serial link. However, by examining transitions between voltage states on the link, the device can notice slight variations in the speed on each end so that it can adjust its speed.
Asynchronous	The lack of an imposed time ordering on a bit stream. More practically speaking, both sides agree to the same speed, but there is no check or adjustment of the rates if they are slightly different. However, because only 1 byte per transfer is sent, slight differences in clock speed are not an issue. A start bit is used to signal the beginning of a byte.
Clock source	The device to which the other devices on the link adjust their speed when using synchronous links.
DSU/CSU	Data Services Unit and Channel Services Unit. This is used on digital links as an interface to the telephone company in the United States. Routers typically use a short cable from a serial interface to a DSU/CSU, which is attached to the line from the telco with a similar configuration at the other router on the other end of the link. The routers use their attached DSU/CSU as the clock source.
Telco	Telephone company.
4-wire circuit	A line from the telco with four wires, comprised of two twisted-pair wires. Each pair is used to send in one direction, so a 4-wire circuit allows full-duplex communication.
2-wire circuit	A line from the telco with two wires, comprised of one twisted-pair wire. The pair is used to send in only one direction at a time, so a 2-wire circuit allows only half-duplex communication.

continues

Table 8-39   *WAN Terminology (Continued)*

Term	Definition
T/1	A line from the telco that allows transmission of data at 1.544Mbps. This can be used with a T/1 multiplexor.
T/1 mux	A multiplexor that separates the T/1 into 24 different 64kbps channels. In the United States, one of every 8 bits in each channel can be used by the telco so that the channels are effectively 56kbps channels.
E/1	Like a T/1, but in Europe. It uses a rate of 2.048Mbps and 32 64kbps channels.

Table 8-40 lists the point-to-point data link protocols and their attributes.

Table 8-40   *Point-to-Point Data Link Protocol Attributes*

Protocol	Error Correction?	Architected Type Field?	Other Attributes
Synchronous Data Link Control (SDLC)	Yes	None	SDLC supports multipoint links; it assumes that an SNA header occurs after the SDLC header.
Link Access Procedure Balanced (LAPB)	Yes	None	Spec assumes a single configurable protocol after LAPB. This is used mainly with X.25. Cisco uses a proprietary type field to support multiprotocol traffic.
Link Access Procedure on the D channel (LAPD)	No	No	LAPD is not used between routers. It is used on a D channel from the router to the ISDN switch for signaling.
High-Level Data Link Control (HDLC)	No	No	HDLC is Cisco's default on serial links. Cisco uses a proprietary type field to support multiprotocol traffic.
Point-to-Point Protocol (PPP)	Allows user to choose whether error correction is performed; correction uses LAPB	Yes	PPP was meant for multiprotocol interoperability from its inception, unlike all the others. PPP also supports asynchronous communication.

Note: Be careful about confusing LAPB and LAPD. The D can help remind you that it is for an ISDN D channel, but don't let that make you think that the B is for an ISDN B channel.

A variety of standards define the types of connectors and physical signaling protocols used on the interfaces. Table 8-41 summarizes these standards:

Table 8-41 *WAN Interface Standards*

Standard	Standards Body	Number of Pins on Interface
EIA/TIA 232	Telecommunications Industry Association	25
EIA/TIA 449	Telecommunications Industry Association	37
EIA/TIA 530	Telecommunications Industry Association	25
V.35	International Telecommunications Union	34
X.21	International Telecommunications Union	15

Table 8-42 lists a variety of terms associated with Frame Relay.

Table 8-42 *Frame Relay Terms and Concepts*

Virtual circuit (VC)	A VC is a logical concept that represents the path that frames travel between DTEs. VCs are particularly useful when comparing Frame Relay to leased physical circuits.
Permanent virtual circuit (PVC)	A PVC is a VC that is predefined. A PVC can be equated to a leased line in concept.
Switched virtual circuit (SVC)	An SVC is a VC that is set up dynamically. An SVC can be equated to a dial connection in concept.
Data terminal equipment (DTE)	DTEs are also known as data-circuit termination equipment. For example, routers are DTEs when connected to a Frame Relay service from a telecommunication company.
Data communications equipment (DCE)	Frame Relay switches are DCE devices.
Access link	The access link is the leased line between DTE and DCE.
Access rate (AR)	The access rate is the speed at which the access link is clocked. This choice affects the price of the connection.
Committed information rate (CIR)	The CIR is the rate at which the DTE can send data for an individual VC, for which the provider commits to deliver that amount of data. The provider will send any data in excess of this rate for this VC if its network has capacity at the time. This choice typically affects the price of each VC.
Burst rate	The burst rate is the rate and length of time for which, for a particular VC, the DTE can send faster than the CIR, and the provider agrees to forward the data. This choice affects the price of each VC typically.

continues

Table 8-42   *Frame Relay Terms and Concepts (Continued)*

Data link connection identifier (DLCI)	A DLCI is a Frame Relay address and is used in Frame Relay headers to identify the virtual circuit.
Forward explicit congestion notification (FECN)	The FECN is the bit in the Frame Relay header that signals to anyone receiving the frame (switches and DTEs) that congestion is occurring in the same direction as the frame. Switches and DTEs can react by slowing the rate by which data is sent in that direction.
Backward explicit congestion notification (BECN)	The BECN is the bit in the Frame Relay header that signals to anyone receiving the frame (switches and DTEs) that congestion is occurring in the opposite (backward) direction as the frame. Switches and DTEs can react by slowing the rate by which data is sent in that direction.
Discard eligibility (DE)	The DE is the bit in the Frame Relay header that signals to a switch that, if frames must be discarded, please choose this frame to discard instead of another frame without the DE bit set.
Nonbroadcast multiaccess (NBMA)	NBMA refers to a network in which broadcasts are not supported but more than two devices can be connected.
Local Management Interface (LMI)	LMI is the protocol used between a DCE and a DTE to manage the connection. Signaling messages for SVCs, PVC status messages, and keepalives are all LMI messages.
Link access procedure—frame mode bearer services (LAPF)	LAPF is the basic Frame Relay header and trailer, which includes DLCI, FECN, BECN, and DE bits.

Table 8-43 outlines the three Frame Relay LMI types, their origin, and the keyword used in the Cisco **frame-relay lmi-type** interface subcommand:

Table 8-43   *Frame Relay LMI Types*

Name	Document	IOS LMI-Type Parameter
Cisco	Proprietary	cisco
ANSI	T1.617 Annex D	ansi
ITU	Q.933 Annex A	q933a

Figure 8-34 shows several examples of ISDN BRI topology, with function groups and reference points.

Figure 8-34   *ISDN Function Groups and Reference Points*

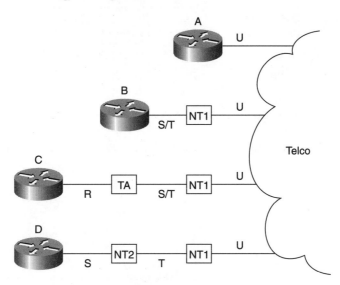

Table 8-44 lists the function groups and reference points shown in Figure 8-34.

Table 8-44   *Figure 8-34 Function Groups and Reference Point Summary*

Router	Function Group(s)	Connected to Reference Point(s)
A	TE1, NT1	U
B	TE1	S/T (combined S and T)
C	TE2	R
D	TE1	S

Table 8-45 summarizes these types of permanent connections and lists some of the strengths and weaknesses.

Table 8-45   *Comparison of Leased Versus Packet Switching*

Type of WAN Service	Data Link Protocols	Strengths and Weaknesses
Leased		Offers pervasive availability. Can be expensive for long circuits. Is more expensive for providers to engineer than are packet services.
	PPP	Can improve speed of routing protocol convergence. Allows multivendor interoperability. Offers error recovery option.

continues

Table 8-45 *Comparison of Leased Versus Packet Switching (Continued)*

Type of WAN Service	Data Link Protocols	Strengths and Weaknesses
	HDLC	Is the IOS default. Requires a Cisco router on each end.
	LAPB	Provides error recovery, but this also can result in throttling (slowing) the data rate.
Packet Switched		Allows addition of new sites to be made quickly. Typically involves a lower cost.
	Frame Relay	Allows bursting past CIR, giving perception of free capacity. Is pervasive in the United States.
	ATM	As a WAN technology, is not as pervasively available as Frame Relay. Offers built-in Quality of Service as its most attractive feature.
	X.25	Is available pervasively in some parts of the world. Error recovery features are beneficial when links have higher error rates. Typically is the third choice of these three if all are available to all connected sites.

Figure 8-35 outlines the process of Frame Relay initialization.

Figure 8-35 *Frame Relay Initialization*

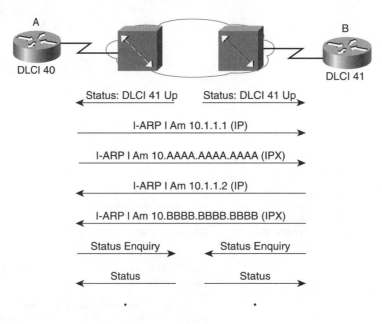

Figure 8-36 lists the main Cisco router product families.

Figure 8-36   *Router Product Families*

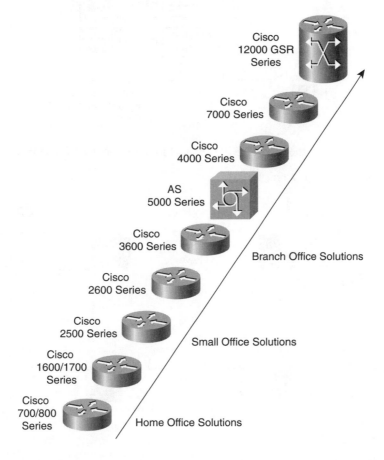

Figure 8-37 provides a conceptual diagram of the two forms of Frame Relay encapsulation.
Because the frames flow from DTE to DTE, both DTEs must agree to the encapsulation used.
However, each VC can use a different encapsulation.

Figure 8-37 *Cisco and RFC 1490/2427 Encapsulations*

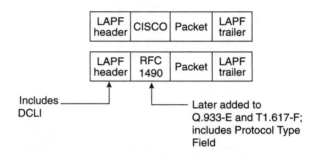

Figure 8-38 shows the use of LAPD versus PPP on ISDN BRI B channels.

Figure 8-38 *LAPD and PPP on D and B Channels*

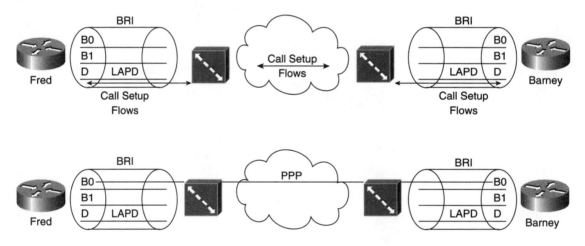

Q&A

As mentioned in Chapter 1, "All About the Cisco Certified Network Associate Certification," the questions and scenarios in this book are more difficult than what you should experience on the actual exam. The questions do not attempt to cover more breadth or depth than the exam; however, they are designed to make sure that you know the answer. Rather than allowing you to derive the answer from clues hidden inside the question itself, the questions challenge your understanding and recall of the subject. Questions from the "Do I Know This Already?" quiz from the beginning of the chapter are repeated here to ensure that you have mastered the chapter's topic areas. Hopefully, these questions will help limit the number of exam questions on which you narrow your choices to two options and then guess.

The answers to these questions can be found in Appendix A, on page 768.

 1 Name two WAN data link protocols for which the standards define a protocol type field, which is used to define the type of header that follows the WAN data link header.

 2 Name two WAN data link protocols that define a method of announcing the Layer 3 addresses of the interface to other devices attached to the WAN.

 3 What does the acronym LAPD stand for? Is it used as the Layer 2 protocol on dialed ISDN bearer channels? If not, what is used?

 4 "Frame Relay uses source and destination DLCIs in the Frame Relay header, with length 10, 11, or 12 bits." Which parts of this statement do you agree with? Which parts do you disagree with? Why?

 5 Explain the purpose of Inverse ARP. Explain how Inverse ARP uses Frame Relay broadcasts.

 6 Would a Frame Relay switch connected to a router behave differently if the IETF option were deleted from the **encapsulation frame-relay ietf** command on that attached router? Would a router on the other end of the VC behave any differently if the same change were made?

 7 What does NBMA stand for? Does it apply to PPP links? What about X.25 networks or Frame Relay networks?

 8 Define the terms DCE and DTE in the context of the physical layer and a point-to-point serial link.

 9 What layer of OSI is most closely related to the functions of Frame Relay? Why?

 10 When Inverse ARP is used by default, what additional configuration is needed to get IGRP routing updates to flow over each VC?

 11 Define the attributes of a partial-mesh and full-mesh Frame Relay network.

 12 What key pieces of information are required in the **frame-relay map** statement?

13 When creating a partial-mesh Frame Relay network, are you required to use subinterfaces?

14 What benefit related to routing protocols can be gained by using subinterfaces with a partial mesh?

15 Can PPP perform dynamic assignment of IP addresses? If so, is the feature always enabled?

16 Create a configuration to enable PPP on serial 0 for IP and IPX. Make up IP and IPX Layer 3 addresses as needed.

17 Create a configuration for Router1 that has Frame Relay VCs to Router2 and Router3 (DLCIs 202 and 203, respectively) for Frame Relay on Router1's serial 1 interface. Use any IP and IPX addresses you like. Assume that the network is not fully meshed.

18 What **show** command will tell you the time that a PVC became active? How does the router know what time the PVC became active?

19 What **show** commands list Frame Relay information about mapping? In what instances will the information displayed include the Layer 3 addresses of other routers?

20 True or false: The **no keepalive** command on a Frame Relay serial interface causes no further Cisco proprietary keepalive messages to be sent to the Frame Relay switch.

21 What **debug** options will show Inverse ARP messages?

22 True or false: The Frame Relay **map** configuration command allows more than one Layer 3 protocol address mapping on the same configuration command.

23 What do the letters in ISDN represent? What about BRI and PRI?

24 Define the term function group. List two examples of function groups.

25 Define the term reference point. List two examples of reference points.

26 How many bearer channels are in a BRI? What about a PRI in North America? What about a PRI in Europe?

27 True or false: ISDN defines protocols that can be functionally equivalent to OSI Layers 1, 2, and 3. Defend your answer.

28 What reference points are used by ISDN BRI interfaces on Cisco routers?

29 What do the letters LAPD represent? Is LAPD used on ISDN channels? If so, which ones?

30 Name the standards body that defines ISDN protocols.

31 What ISDN functions do standards ITU-T Q.920 and Q.930 define? Does either standard correlate to an OSI layer?

32 What ISDN functions does standard ITU-T I.430 define? Does it correlate to an OSI layer?

33 What do the letters SPID represent, and what does the term mean?

34 Define the terms TE1, TE2, and TA. Which term(s) imply that one of the other two must be in use?

35 What reference point is used between the customer premise and the phone company in North America? What about in Europe?

36 Define the term SBus, and give one example of when it would be useful.

37 What data link (OSI Layer 2) protocols are valid on an ISDN B channel?

38 Define the terms PAP and CHAP. Which one(s) send the passwords in clear text format?

39 Define MLPPP. Describe the typical home or small office use of MLPPP.

40 CHAP configuration uses names and passwords. Given Routers A and B, describe what names and passwords must match in the respective CHAP configurations.

41 Configure ISDN interface BRI1, assuming that it is attached to a DMS-100 ISDN switch, that it uses only one SPID of 404555121201, and that you want to screen calls so that only calls from 404555999901 are accepted.

42 Name the configuration command used to enable FRF.9 compression on a point-to-point Frame Relay subinterface.

43 List the types of compression that are available on PPP links.

44 Describe the decision process performed by the IOS to attempt to dial a connection using legacy DDR.

45 If packets from 10.1.1.0/24 were "interesting" in relation to DDR configuration, such that packets from 10.1.1.0/24 caused a DDR connection out an interface BRI0, list the configuration commands that would make the IOS think that those packets were interesting on BRI0.

46 List the typical EIA/TIA standard interfaces used for serial cables with a Cisco router.

47 What field has Cisco added to the HDLC header, making it proprietary?

Scenarios

Scenario 8-1: Point-to-Point Verification

Use Example 8-33, Example 8-34, and Example 8-35 when completing the exercises and answering the questions that follow.

Example 8-33 *Albuquerque Command Output, Scenario 8-1*

```
Albuquerque#show ip interface brief
Interface          IP-Address      OK? Method Status          Protocol
Serial0            199.1.1.129     YES NVRAM  up              up
Serial1            199.1.1.193     YES NVRAM  up              up
Ethernet0          199.1.1.33      YES NVRAM  up              up

Albuquerque#show ip route
Codes: C - connected, S - static, I - IGRP, R - RIP, M - mobile, B - BGP
       D - EIGRP, EX - EIGRP external, O - OSPF, IA - OSPF inter area
N1 - OSPF NSSA external type 1, N2 - OSPF NSSA external type 2
       E1 - OSPF external type 1, E2 - OSPF external type 2, E - EGP
       i - IS-IS, L1 - IS-IS level-1, L2 - IS-IS level-2, * - candidate default
       U - per-user static route, o - ODR

Gateway of last resort is not set

     199.1.1.0/24 is variably subnetted, 7 subnets, 2 masks
C       199.1.1.192/27 is directly connected, Serial1
C       199.1.1.130/32 is directly connected, Serial0
C       199.1.1.128/27 is directly connected, Serial0
I       199.1.1.160/27 [100/10476] via 199.1.1.130, 00:00:01, Serial0
                        [100/10476] via 199.1.1.194, 00:00:54, Serial1
I       199.1.1.64/27 [100/8539] via 199.1.1.130, 00:00:01, Serial0
I       199.1.1.96/27 [100/8539] via 199.1.1.194, 00:00:54, Serial1
C       199.1.1.32/27 is directly connected, Ethernet0

Albuquerque#show ipx route
Codes: C - Connected primary network,    c - Connected secondary network
       S - Static, F - Floating static, L - Local (internal), W - IPXWAN
       R - RIP, E - EIGRP, N - NLSP, X - External, A - Aggregate
       s - seconds, u - uses

6 Total IPX routes. Up to 1 parallel paths and 16 hops allowed.

No default route known.

C       1001 (SAP),        E0
C       2001 (PPP),        Se0
C       2003 (HDLC),       Se1
R       1002 [07/01] via   2001.0200.bbbb.bbbb,   50s, Se0
R       1003 [07/01] via   2003.0200.cccc.cccc,   57s, Se1
R       2002 [07/01] via   2001.0200.bbbb.bbbb,   51s, Se0
```

Example 8-33 *Albuquerque Command Output, Scenario 8-1 (Continued)*

```
Albuquerque#debug ppp negotiation
PPP protocol negotiation debugging is on

%LINK-3-UPDOWN: Interface Serial0, changed state to up

Se0 PPP: Treating connection as a dedicated line
Se0 PPP: Phase is ESTABLISHING, Active Open
Se0 LCP: O CONFREQ [Closed] id 15 len 10
Se0 LCP:    MagicNumber 0x003C2A1F (0x0506003C2A1F)
Se0 LCP: I CONFREQ [REQsent] id 34 len 10
Se0 LCP:    MagicNumber 0x0648CFD3 (0x05060648CFD3)
Se0 LCP: O CONFACK [REQsent] id 34 len 10
Se0 LCP:    MagicNumber 0x0648CFD3 (0x05060648CFD3)
Se0 LCP: TIMEout: Time = 0xBA0E0 State = ACKsent
Se0 LCP: O CONFREQ [ACKsent] id 16 len 10
Se0 LCP:    MagicNumber 0x003C2A1F (0x0506003C2A1F)
Se0 LCP: I CONFACK [ACKsent] id 16 len 10
Se0 LCP:    MagicNumber 0x003C2A1F (0x0506003C2A1F)
Se0 LCP: State is Open
Se0 PPP: Phase is UP
Se0 IPCP: O CONFREQ [Closed] id 3 len 10
Se0 IPCP:    Address 199.1.1.129 (0x0306C7010181)
Se0 CDPCP: O CONFREQ [Closed] id 3 len 4
Se0 LLC2CP: O CONFREQ [Closed] id 3 len 4
Se0 IPXCP: O CONFREQ [Closed] id 3 len 18
Se0 IPXCP:    Network 0x00002001 (0x010600002001)
Se0 IPXCP:    Node 0200.aaaa.aaaa (0x02080200AAAAAAAA)
Se0 IPCP: I CONFREQ [REQsent] id 4 len 10
Se0 IPCP:    Address 199.1.1.130 (0x0306C7010182)
Se0 IPCP: O CONFACK [REQsent] id 4 len 10
Se0 IPCP:    Address 199.1.1.130 (0x0306C7010182)
Se0 CDPCP: I CONFREQ [REQsent] id 6 len 4
Se0 CDPCP: O CONFACK [REQsent] id 6 len 4
Se0 LLC2CP: I CONFREQ [REQsent] id 6 len 4
Se0 LLC2CP: O CONFACK [REQsent] id 6 len 4
Se0 IPXCP: I CONFREQ [REQsent] id 4 len 18
Se0 IPXCP:    Network 0x00002001 (0x010600002001)
Se0 IPXCP:    Node 0200.bbbb.bbbb (0x02080200BBBBBBBB)
Se0 IPXCP: O CONFACK [REQsent] id 4 len 18
Se0 IPXCP:    Network 0x00002001 (0x010600002001)
Se0 IPXCP:    Node 0200.bbbb.bbbb (0x02080200BBBBBBBB)
```

Example 8-34 *Yosemite Command Output, Scenario 8-1*

```
Yosemite#show ipx interface brief
Interface       IPX Network Encapsulation Status            IPX State
Serial0         2001        PPP           up                [up]
Serial1         2002        LAPB          up                [up]
Ethernet0       1002        SAP           up                [up]

Yosemite#show ipx route
Codes: C - Connected primary network,    c - Connected secondary network
```

continues

Example 8-34 *Yosemite Command Output, Scenario 8-1 (Continued)*

```
         S - Static, F - Floating static, L - Local (internal), W - IPXWAN
         R - RIP, E - EIGRP, N - NLSP, X - External, A - Aggregate
         s - seconds, u - uses

6 Total IPX routes. Up to 1 parallel paths and 16 hops allowed.

No default route known.

C       1002 (SAP),        E0
C       2001 (PPP),        Se0
C       2002 (LAPB),       Se1
R       1001 [07/01] via   2001.0200.aaaa.aaaa,    46s, Se0
R       1003 [13/02] via   2001.0200.aaaa.aaaa,    47s, Se0
R       2003 [07/01] via   2001.0200.aaaa.aaaa,    47s, Se0

Yosemite#show interface serial 1 accounting
Serial1
                    Protocol   Pkts In   Chars In   Pkts Out   Chars Out
                          IP        37       2798         41        3106

Yosemite#ping ipx 2002.0200.cccc.cccc

Type escape sequence to abort.
Sending 5, 100-byte IPX Cisco Echoes to 2002.0200.cccc.cccc, timeout is 2 seconds:
.....
Success rate is 0 percent (0/5)

Yosemite#ping 199.1.1.162

Type escape sequence to abort.
Sending 5, 100-byte ICMP Echos to 199.1.1.162, timeout is 2 seconds:
!!!!!
Success rate is 100 percent (5/5), round-trip min/avg/max = 8/8/8 ms

Yosemite#ping ipx 1003.0000.30ac.70ef

Type escape sequence to abort.
Sending 5, 100-byte IPX Cisco Echoes to 1003.0000.30ac.70ef, timeout is 2 seconds:
!!!!!
Success rate is 100 percent (5/5), round-trip min/avg/max = 8/8/12 ms
```

Example 8-35 *Seville Command Output, Scenario 8-1*

```
Seville#show ip route
Codes: C - connected, S - static, I - IGRP, R - RIP, M - mobile, B - BGP
       D - EIGRP, EX - EIGRP external, O - OSPF, IA - OSPF inter area
       N1 - OSPF NSSA external type 1, N2 - OSPF NSSA external type 2
       E1 - OSPF external type 1, E2 - OSPF external type 2, E - EGP
       i - IS-IS, L1 - IS-IS level-1, L2 - IS-IS level-2, * - candidate default
       U - per-user static route, o - ODR

Gateway of last resort is not set
```

Example 8-35 *Seville Command Output, Scenario 8-1 (Continued)*

```
        199.1.1.0/27 is subnetted, 6 subnets
C       199.1.1.192 is directly connected, Serial0
I       199.1.1.128 [100/10476] via 199.1.1.161, 00:00:36, Serial1
                    [100/10476] via 199.1.1.193, 00:01:09, Serial0
C       199.1.1.160 is directly connected, Serial1
I       199.1.1.64 [100/8539] via 199.1.1.161, 00:00:36, Serial1
C       199.1.1.96 is directly connected, Ethernet0
I       199.1.1.32 [100/8539] via 199.1.1.193, 00:01:09, Serial0

Seville#show ipx route
Codes: C - Connected primary network,    c - Connected secondary network
       S - Static, F - Floating static, L - Local (internal), W - IPXWAN
       R - RIP, E - EIGRP, N - NLSP, X - External, A - Aggregate
       s - seconds, u - uses

6 Total IPX routes. Up to 1 parallel paths and 16 hops allowed.

No default route known.

C       1003 (SAP),         E0
C       2002 (LAPB),        Se1
C       2003 (HDLC),        Se0
R       1001 [07/01] via    2003.0200.aaaa.aaaa,    2s, Se0
R       1002 [13/02] via    2003.0200.aaaa.aaaa,    2s, Se0
R       2001 [07/01] via    2003.0200.aaaa.aaaa,    2s, Se0

Seville#show interface serial 0 accounting
Serial0
                  Protocol   Pkts In   Chars In   Pkts Out   Chars Out
                        IP        44       3482         40        3512
                       IPX        46       3478         44        2710
                       CDP        21       6531         26        7694

Seville#debug lapb
LAPB link debugging is on

%LINK-3-UPDOWN: Interface Serial1, changed state to up

Serial1: LAPB O SABMSENT (2) SABM P
Serial1: LAPB I SABMSENT (2) UA F
Serial1: LAPB I CONNECT (104) IFRAME 0 0
Serial1: LAPB O CONNECT (76) IFRAME 0 1Serial1: LAPB I CONNECT (76) IFRAME 1 1
Serial1: LAPB O CONNECT (2) RR (R) 2
Seville#
Seville#ping 199.1.1.161


Type escape sequence to abort.
Sending 5, 100-byte ICMP Echos to 199.1.1.161, timeout is 2 seconds:
!!!!!
Success rate is 100 percent (5/5), round-trip min/avg/max = 8/8/12 ms
Seville#
```

continues

Example 8-35 *Seville Command Output, Scenario 8-1 (Continued)*

```
Serial1: LAPB O CONNECT (102) IFRAME 1 3
Serial1: LAPB I CONNECT (102) IFRAME 3 2
Serial1: LAPB O CONNECT (2) RR (R) 4
Serial1: LAPB O CONNECT (102) IFRAME 2 4
Serial1: LAPB I CONNECT (102) IFRAME 4 3
Serial1: LAPB O CONNECT (2) RR (R) 5
Serial1: LAPB O CONNECT (102) IFRAME 3 5
Serial1: LAPB I CONNECT (2) RR (R) 4
Serial1: LAPB I CONNECT (102) IFRAME 5 4
Serial1: LAPB O CONNECT (2) RR (R) 6
Serial1: LAPB O CONNECT (102) IFRAME 4 6
Serial1: LAPB I CONNECT (102) IFRAME 6 5
Serial1: LAPB O CONNECT (2) RR (R) 7
Serial1: LAPB O CONNECT (102) IFRAME 5 7
Serial1: LAPB I CONNECT (102) IFRAME 7 6
Serial1: LAPB O CONNECT (2) RR (R) 0
```

Assuming the details established in Example 8-33 through Example 8-35 for Scenario 8-1, complete or answer the following:

1 Create a diagram for the network.

2 Complete Table 8-47.

Table 8-47 *Layer 3 Addresses on the PPP Serial Links*

Router	Serial Port	Encapsulation	IP Address	IPX Address
Albuquerque	s0			
Albuquerque	s1			
Yosemite	s0			
Yosemite	s1			
Seville	s0			
Seville	s1			

3 Why are there seven IP routes in Albuquerque and Yosemite, and only six in Seville?

Scenario 8-2: Frame Relay Verification

Use Example 8-36, Example 8-37, Example 8-38, and Example 8-39 when completing the exercises and answering the questions that follow.

Example 8-36 *Atlanta Command Output, Scenario 8-2*

```
Atlanta#show interface s 0
Serial0 is up, line protocol is up
  Hardware is HD64570
  MTU 1500 bytes, BW 1544 Kbit, DLY 20000 usec, rely 255/255, load 1/255
  Encapsulation FRAME-RELAY, loopback not set, keepalive set (10 sec)
  LMI enq sent  32, LMI stat recvd 32, LMI upd recvd 0, DTE LMI up
  LMI enq recvd 0, LMI stat sent  0, LMI upd sent  0
  LMI DLCI 1023  LMI type is CISCO  frame relay DTE
  Broadcast queue 0/64, broadcasts sent/dropped 75/0, interface broadcasts 59
  Last input 00:00:00, output 00:00:07, output hang never
  Last clearing of "show interface" counters never
  Queuing strategy: fifo
  Output queue 0/40, 0 drops; input queue 0/75, 0 drops
  5 minute input rate 0 bits/sec, 0 packets/sec
  5 minute output rate 0 bits/sec, 0 packets/sec
     74 packets input, 5697 bytes, 0 no buffer
     Received 32 broadcasts, 0 runts, 0 giants, 0 throttles
     0 input errors, 0 CRC, 0 frame, 0 overrun, 0 ignored, 0 abort
     110 packets output, 9438 bytes, 0 underruns
     0 output errors, 0 collisions, 2 interface resets
     0 output buffer failures, 0 output buffers swapped out
     0 carrier transitions
     DCD=up  DSR=up  DTR=up  RTS=up  CTS=up

Atlanta#show interface s 0.1
Serial0.1 is up, line protocol is up
  Hardware is HD64570
  Internet address is 168.10.202.1/24
  MTU 1500 bytes, BW 1544 Kbit, DLY 20000 usec, rely 255/255, load 1/255
  Encapsulation FRAME-RELAY

Atlanta#show interface s 0.2
Serial0.2 is up, line protocol is up
  Hardware is HD64570
  Internet address is 168.10.203.1/24
  MTU 1500 bytes, BW 1544 Kbit, DLY 20000 usec, rely 255/255, load 1/255
  Encapsulation FRAME-RELAY

Atlanta#show interface s 0.3
Serial0.3 is up, line protocol is up
  Hardware is HD64570
  Internet address is 168.10.204.1/24
  MTU 1500 bytes, BW 1544 Kbit, DLY 20000 usec, rely 255/255, load 1/255
Encapsulation FRAME-RELAY

Atlanta#show frame-relay map
Serial0.3 (up): point-to-point dlci, dlci 54(0x36,0xC60), broadcast, IETF
          status defined, active
Serial0.2 (up): point-to-point dlci, dlci 53(0x35,0xC50), broadcast
          status defined, active
Serial0.1 (up): point-to-point dlci, dlci 52(0x34,0xC40), broadcast
          status defined, active
```

continues

Example 8-36 *Atlanta Command Output, Scenario 8-2 (Continued)*

```
Atlanta#show frame-relay lmi

LMI Statistics for interface Serial0 (Frame Relay DTE) LMI TYPE = CISCO
  Invalid Unnumbered info 0        Invalid Prot Disc 0
  Invalid dummy Call Ref 0         Invalid Msg Type 0
  Invalid Status Message 0         Invalid Lock Shift 0
  Invalid Information ID 0         Invalid Report IE Len 0
  Invalid Report Request 0         Invalid Keep IE Len 0
  Num Status Enq. Sent 43          Num Status msgs Rcvd 43
  Num Update Status Rcvd 0         Num Status Timeouts 0

Atlanta#debug frame-relay events
Frame Relay events debugging is on

Atlanta#configure terminal
Enter configuration commands, one per line.  End with Ctrl-Z.
Atlanta(config)#interface serial 0
Atlanta(config-if)#shutdown

%LINEPROTO-5-UPDOWN: Line protocol on Interface Serial0.1, changed state to down
%LINEPROTO-5-UPDOWN: Line protocol on Interface Serial0.2, changed state to down
%LINEPROTO-5-UPDOWN: Line protocol on Interface Serial0.3, changed state to down
%LINEPROTO-5-UPDOWN: Line protocol on Interface Serial0, changed state to down
%LINK-5-CHANGED: Interface Serial0, changed state to administratively down
%FR-5-DLCICHANGE: Interface Serial0 - DLCI 54 state changed to DELETED
%FR-5-DLCICHANGE: Interface Serial0 - DLCI 53 state changed to DELETED
%FR-5-DLCICHANGE: Interface Serial0 - DLCI 52 state changed to DELETED

Atlanta(config-if)#no shutdown
Atlanta(config-if)#^Z

%LINEPROTO-5-UPDOWN: Line protocol on Interface Serial0.1, changed state to up
%FR-5-DLCICHANGE: Interface Serial0 - DLCI 52 state changed to ACTIVE
%LINEPROTO-5-UPDOWN: Line protocol on Interface Serial0.2, changed state to up
%FR-5-DLCICHANGE: Interface Serial0 - DLCI 53 state changed to ACTIVE
%LINEPROTO-5-UPDOWN: Line protocol on Interface Serial0.3, changed state to up
%FR-5-DLCICHANGE: Interface Serial0 - DLCI 54 state changed to ACTIVE
%SYS-5-CONFIG_I: Configured from console by console
%LINEPROTO-5-UPDOWN: Line protocol on Interface Serial0, changed state to up
%LINK-3-UPDOWN: Interface Serial0, changed state to up

Atlanta#show frame map
Serial0.3 (up): point-to-point dlci, dlci 54(0x36,0xC60), broadcast, IETF
          status defined, active
Serial0.2 (up): point-to-point dlci, dlci 53(0x35,0xC50), broadcast
          status defined, active
Serial0.1 (up): point-to-point dlci, dlci 52(0x34,0xC40), broadcast
          status defined, active

Atlanta#debug frame-relay lmi
Frame Relay LMI debugging is on
Displaying all Frame Relay LMI data
Atlanta#
```

Example 8-36 *Atlanta Command Output, Scenario 8-2 (Continued)*

```
Serial0(out): StEnq, myseq 6, yourseen 5, DTE up
datagramstart = 0x45B25C, datagramsize = 13
FR encap = 0xFCF10309
00 75 01 01 01 03 02 06 05

Serial0(in): Status, myseq 6
RT IE 1, length 1, type 1
KA IE 3, length 2, yourseq 6 , myseq 6
```

Example 8-37 *Charlotte Command Output, Scenario 8-2*

```
Charlotte#show interface s 0.1
Serial0.1 is up, line protocol is up
  Hardware is HD64570
  Internet address is 168.10.202.2/24
  MTU 1500 bytes, BW 1544 Kbit, DLY 20000 usec, rely 255/255, load 1/255
  Encapsulation FRAME-RELAY

Charlotte#show cdp neighbor detail
-------------------------
Device ID: Atlanta
Entry address(es):
  IP address: 168.10.202.1
  Novell address: 202.0200.aaaa.aaaa
Platform: Cisco 2500,  Capabilities: Router
Interface: Serial0.1,  Port ID (outgoing port): Serial0.1
Holdtime : 164 sec

Version :
Cisco Internetwork Operating System Software
IOS (tm) 2500 Software (C2500-AINR-L), Version 11.2(11), RELEASE SOFTWARE (fc1)
Copyright  1986-1997 by Cisco Systems, Inc.
Compiled Mon 29-Dec-97 18:47 by ckralik

Charlotte#show frame-relay map
Serial0.1 (up): point-to-point dlci, dlci 51(0x33,0xC30), broadcast
          status defined, active
Charlotte#show frame-relay pvc

PVC Statistics for interface Serial0 (Frame Relay DTE)

DLCI = 51, DLCI USAGE = LOCAL, PVC STATUS = ACTIVE, INTERFACE = Serial0.1

  input pkts 36           output pkts 28          in bytes 4506
  out bytes 2862          dropped pkts 1          in FECN pkts 0
  in BECN pkts 0          out FECN pkts 0         out BECN pkts 0
  in DE pkts 0            out DE pkts 0
  out bcast pkts 26        out bcast bytes 2774
  pvc create time 00:08:54, last time pvc status changed 00:01:26

Charlotte#show frame-relay lmi
```

continues

Example 8-37 *Charlotte Command Output, Scenario 8-2 (Continued)*

```
LMI Statistics for interface Serial0 (Frame Relay DTE) LMI TYPE = CCITT
  Invalid Unnumbered info 0      Invalid Prot Disc 0
  Invalid dummy Call Ref 0       Invalid Msg Type 0
  Invalid Status Message 0       Invalid Lock Shift 0
  Invalid Information ID 0        Invalid Report IE Len 0
  Invalid Report Request 0       Invalid Keep IE Len 0
  Num Status Enq. Sent 54        Num Status msgs Rcvd 37
  Num Update Status Rcvd 0       Num Status Timeouts 17
```

Example 8-38 *Nashville Command Output, Scenario 8-2*

```
Nashville#show cdp neighbor detail
-------------------------
Device ID: Atlanta
Entry address(es):
  IP address: 168.10.203.1
  Novell address: 203.0200.aaaa.aaaa
Platform: Cisco 2500,  Capabilities: Router
Interface: Serial0.1,  Port ID (outgoing port): Serial0.2
Holdtime : 139 sec

Version :
Cisco Internetwork Operating System Software
IOS (tm) 2500 Software (C2500-AINR-L), Version 11.2(11), RELEASE SOFTWARE (fc1)
Copyright  1986-1997 by Cisco Systems, Inc.
Compiled Mon 29-Dec-97 18:47 by ckralik

Nashville#show frame-relay pvc

PVC Statistics for interface Serial0 (Frame Relay DTE)

DLCI = 51, DLCI USAGE = LOCAL, PVC STATUS = ACTIVE, INTERFACE = Serial0.1

  input pkts 52          output pkts 47         in bytes 6784
  out bytes 6143         dropped pkts 0         in FECN pkts 0
  in BECN pkts 0         out FECN pkts 0        out BECN pkts 0
  in DE pkts 0           out DE pkts 0
  out bcast pkts 46       out bcast bytes 6099
  pvc create time 00:13:50, last time pvc status changed 00:06:51

Nashville#show frame-relay traffic
Frame Relay statistics:
    ARP requests sent 0, ARP replies sent 0
    ARP requests recvd 0, ARP replies recvd 0

Nashville#show frame-relay lmi

LMI Statistics for interface Serial0 (Frame Relay DTE) LMI TYPE = CISCO
  Invalid Unnumbered info 0      Invalid Prot Disc 0
  Invalid dummy Call Ref 0       Invalid Msg Type 0
  Invalid Status Message 0       Invalid Lock Shift 0
```

Example 8-38 *Nashville Command Output, Scenario 8-2 (Continued)*

```
Invalid Information ID 0        Invalid Report IE Len 0
Invalid Report Request 0       Invalid Keep IE Len 0
Num Status Enq. Sent 84        Num Status msgs Rcvd 84
Num Update Status Rcvd 0       Num Status Timeouts 0
```

Example 8-39 *Boston Command Output, Scenario 8-2*

```
Boston#show interface s 0.1
Serial0.1 is up, line protocol is up
  Hardware is HD64570
  Internet address is 168.10.204.4/24
  MTU 1500 bytes, BW 1544 Kbit, DLY 20000 usec, rely 255/255, load 1/255
  Encapsulation FRAME-RELAY

Boston#show cdp neighbor detail
-------------------------
Device ID: Atlanta
Entry address(es):
  IP address: 168.10.204.1
  Novell address: 204.0200.aaaa.aaaa
Platform: Cisco 2500,  Capabilities: Router
Interface: Serial0.1,  Port ID (outgoing port): Serial0.3
Holdtime : 125 sec

Version :
Cisco Internetwork Operating System Software
IOS (tm) 2500 Software (C2500-AINR-L), Version 11.2(11), RELEASE SOFTWARE (fc1)
Copyright  1986-1997 by Cisco Systems, Inc.
Compiled Mon 29-Dec-97 18:47 by ckralik

Boston#show frame-relay map
Serial0.1 (up): point-to-point dlci, dlci 51(0x33,0xC30), broadcast, IETF
          status defined, active

Boston#show frame-relay pvc

PVC Statistics for interface Serial0 (Frame Relay DTE)

DLCI = 51, DLCI USAGE = LOCAL, PVC STATUS = ACTIVE, INTERFACE = Serial0.1

  input pkts 65           output pkts 54         in bytes 8475
  out bytes 6906          dropped pkts 1         in FECN pkts 0
  in BECN pkts 0          out FECN pkts 0        out BECN pkts 0
  in DE pkts 0            out DE pkts 0
  out bcast pkts 52       out bcast bytes 6792
  pvc create time 00:15:43, last time pvc status changed 00:07:54
Num Update Status Rcvd 0    Num Status Timeouts 0
```

Assuming the details established in Example 8-36 through Example 8-39 for Scenario 8-2, complete or answer the following:

1 Create a diagram for the network based on the command output in Example 8-36 through Example 8-39.

2 Complete Table 8-48 with the Layer 3 addresses on the serial links.

Table 8-48 *Layer 3 Addresses in Scenario 8-2*

Router	Port	Subinterface	IP Address	IPX Address
Atlanta	s0			
Atlanta	s0			
Atlanta	s0			
Atlanta	s0			
Charlotte	s0			
Charlotte	s0			
Nashville	s0			
Nashville	s0			
Boston	s0			
Boston	s0			

3 Complete Table 8-49 with LMI types and encapsulations used.

Table 8-49 *LMI and Encapsulations Used in Scenario 8-2*

Router	Port	Subinterface	LMI Type	Encapsulation
Atlanta	s0			
Atlanta	s0			
Atlanta	s0			
Atlanta	s0			
Charlotte	s0			
Charlotte	s0			
Nashville	s0			
Nashville	s0			
Boston	s0			
Boston	s0			

Scenario 8-3: Point-to-Point Configuration

Your job is to deploy a new network for an environmental research firm. Two main research sites are in Boston and Atlanta; a T/1 line has been ordered between those two sites. The field site in Alaska will need occasional access; ISDN BRI will be used. Another field site in the rain forest of Podunk has a digital 56kbps link, but it has bursts of errors because parts of the line are microwave.

The design criteria are listed following Figure 8-39, which shows the routers and links. Note that some design criteria are contrived to force you to configure different features; these are designated with an asterisk (*).

Figure 8-39   *Scenario 8-3 Environmental Research Network*

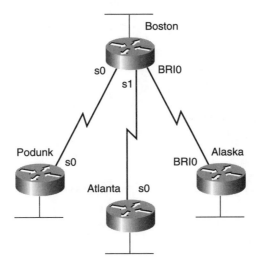

The design criteria are as follows:

- Use three different WAN data link protocols.*

- ISDN BRI will be used between Boston and Alaska. Boston's phone number is 1115551111; Alaska's is 2225552222.

- Both ISDN BRIs are attached to DMS-100 switches.

- Use IP subnets and IPX networks in Table 8-50. Allocate addresses as needed.

- All IP user traffic is considered interesting for DDR.

- IPX RIP and IP IGRP are the routing protocols of choice.

Table 8-50 *Scenario 8-3 Chart of Layer 3 Groups for the Network in Figure 8-23*

Data Link	IP Subnet	IPX Network
Boston Ethernet	200.1.1.0/24	101
Podunk Ethernet	200.1.2.0/24	102
Atlanta Ethernet	200.1.3.0/24	103
Alaska Ethernet	200.1.4.0/24	104
Boston-Podunk	200.1.5.4/30	202
Boston-Atlanta	200.1.5.8/30	203
Boston-Alaska	200.1.5.12/30	204

Assuming the design criteria previously listed and the information in Table 8-50 for Scenario 8-3, complete or answer the following:

1 Create configurations for all four routers.

2 Defend your choices for the different data link protocols.

3 Name all methods that Boston is using in your configuration to learn the Layer 3 addresses on the other end of each link.

Scenario 8-4: Frame Relay Configuration

Your job is to deploy a new network. Site A is the main site, with PVC connections to the other four sites. Sites D and E also have a PVC between them. Examine Figure 8-40 and perform the activities that follow.

Figure 8-40   *Scenario 8-4 Frame Relay Network*

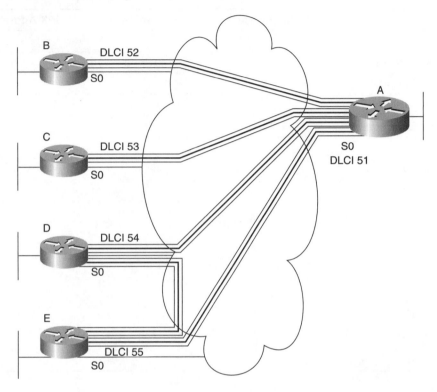

1 Plan the IP and IPX addresses to be used. Use Table 8-51 if helpful. Use IP network 168.15.0.0.

2 Using the DLCIs in Figure 8-40, create configurations for Routers A, B, and E. Use multipoint subinterfaces for the VCs between A, D, and E.

3 Create alternate configurations for Router A and Router E using point-to-point subinterfaces instead of multipoint.

4 Describe the contents of the IP and IPX routing tables on Router A, assuming that the network created from the preceding task is working properly. Only LAN-based IP subnets and IPX networks need to be listed for this exercise. Use Table 8-51 and Table 8-52 if useful.

Table 8-51   *Scenario 8-4 Layer 3 Address Planning Chart*

Interface	Subinterface	IP Address	IPX Address
A's Ethernet			
B's Ethernet			
C's Ethernet			
D's Ethernet			
E's Ethernet			
A's S0			
A's S0			
A's S0			
A's S0			
A's S0			
B's S0			
C's S0			
D's S0			
D's S0			
E's S0			
E's S0			

Table 8-52   *Scenario 8-4: IP and IPX Routing Table Contents*

Layer 3 Group	Outgoing Interface	Next-Hop IP Address, or Connected	Next-Hop IPX Address, or Connected

Scenario 8-5: Frame Relay Configuration Dissection

A four-router Frame Relay network has been configured. Consider the configurations in Example 8-40, Example 8-41, Example 8-42, and Example 8-43, and answer the questions that follow.

Example 8-40 *Scenario 8-5, Router 1 Configuration*

```
Hostname Router1
!
ipx routing 0200.1111.1111
!
interface serial0
encapsulation frame-relay
!
interface serial 0.1
ip address 180.1.1.1 255.255.255.0
ipx network AAA1801
frame-relay interface-dlci 501
!
interface serial 0.2
ip address 180.1.2.1 255.255.255.0
ipx network AAA1802
frame-relay interface-dlci 502
!
interface serial 0.1
ip address 180.1.3.1 255.255.255.0
ipx network AAA1803
frame-relay interface-dlci 503
!
interface ethernet 0
ip address 180.1.10.1 255.255.255.0
ipx network AAA18010
!
router igrp 1
network 180.1.0.0
```

Example 8-41 *Scenario 8-5, Router 2 Configuration*

```
Hostname Router2
!
ipx routing 0200.2222.2222
!
interface serial0
encapsulation frame-relay
!
interface serial 0.1
ip address 180.1.1.2 255.255.255.0
ipx network AAA1801
frame-relay interface-dlci 500
!
interface ethernet 0
```

continues

Example 8-41 *Scenario 8-5, Router 2 Configuration (Continued)*

```
ip address 180.1.11.2 255.255.255.0
ipx network AAA18011
!
router igrp 1
network 180.1.0.0
```

Example 8-42 *Scenario 8-5, Router 3 Configuration*

```
Hostname Router3
!
ipx routing 0200.3333.3333
!
interface serial0
encapsulation frame-relay
!
interface serial 0.1
ip address 180.1.2.3 255.255.255.0
ipx network AAA1802
frame-relay interface-dlci 500
!
interface ethernet 0
ip address 180.1.12.3 255.255.255.0
ipx network AAA18012
!
router igrp 1
network 180.1.0.0
```

Example 8-43 *Scenario 8-5, Router 4 Configuration*

```
Hostname router4
!
ipx routing 0200.4444.4444
!
interface serial0
encapsulation frame-relay
!
interface serial 0.1
ip address 180.1.3.4 255.255.255.0
ipx network AAA1803
frame-relay interface-dlci 500
!
interface ethernet 0
ip address 180.1.13.4 255.255.255.0
ipx network AAA18013
!
router igrp 1
network 180.1.0.0
```

Assuming the details established in Example 8-40 through Example 8-43 for Scenario 8-5, complete or answer the following:

1 Draw a diagram of the network.

2 Is IGRP split horizon on or off? How can you tell?

3 What type of Frame Relay encapsulation is used?

4 Create the commands on Router 1 and Router 2 to disable Inverse ARP and instead use static mapping.

Answers to Scenarios

Answers to Scenario 8-1: Point-to-Point Verification

Figure 8-41 is a diagram that matches the configuration.

Figure 8-41 *Sample Cartoon Network*

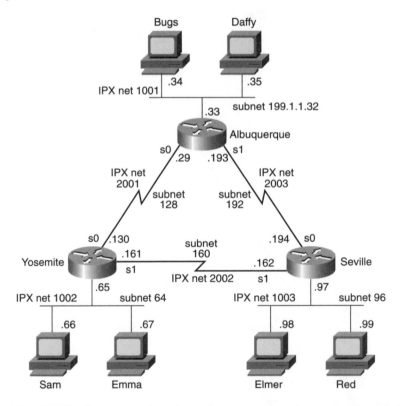

The IP and IPX addresses used on the various router interfaces were one of the tasks for this scenario. Table 8-53 is a completed version of Table 8-47, which was the blank table in which you recorded your answers for this task. Finding all the IP and IPX addresses in Examples 8-33, 8-34, and 8-35 requires some persistence. The best plan of attack is to find all IP addresses and masks that you can, then find all IPX network numbers, and finally decide which addresses are in the same IP subnet and IPX network.

The full IPX addresses are a little more difficult to find. The best method with the commands shown is via the **show ipx interface brief** command and the **show ipx route** command. In particular, the routing table lists the full IPX addresses, not just the network numbers.

The encapsulations are not easy to notice from the commands listed. The **show interface** command would have simply listed the answer. However, in this case, a few subtle reminders were included. The **debug** output on Albuquerque and Seville shows PPP output on Albuquerque's S0 interface and LAPB output for Seville's S1 interface. The **show ipx route** commands also happen to list the encapsulation for connected networks. Table 8-53 summarizes the details.

Table 8-53   *Scenario 8-1 Layer 3 Addresses on the Point-to-Point Serial Links—Completed Table*

Router	Serial Port	Encapsulation	IP Address	IPX Address
Albuquerque	s0	PPP	199.1.1.129	2001.0200.aaaa.aaaa
Albuquerque	s1	HDLC	199.1.1.193	2003.0200.aaaa.aaaa
Yosemite	s0	PPP	199.1.1.130	2001.0200.bbbb.bbbb
Yosemite	s1	LAPB	199.1.1.161	2002.0200.bbbb.bbbb
Seville	s0	HDLC	199.1.1.194	2003.0200.cccc.cccc
Seville	s1	LAPB	199.1.1.162	2002.0200.cccc.cccc

An extra IP route is included in the routing tables on the PPP-connected routers. When the IPCP announces the IP addresses on each end of the link, the IOS decides to add a host route specifically to that IP address. For example, Albuquerque has a route to 199.1.1.128/27 (subnet on serial link to Yosemite) and to 199.1.1.130/32 (Yosemite's address on that same link). The /32 signifies that the route is a host route.

Answers to Scenario 8-2: Frame Relay Verification

Figure 8-42 is a diagram that matches the configuration.

Discovering the IP addresses and subinterfaces is relatively straightforward. The **show** commands for most subinterfaces are provided, and these list the IP address and mask used. The **show cdp neighbor detail** commands also mentioned the IP address of the connected routers.

The full IPX addresses were more challenging to deduce. The only command that listed the IPX addresses was the **show cdp neighbor detail** command, which was used in Examples 8-37, 8-38, and 8-39. The **show frame-relay map** command should seemingly have provided that information, but because all the subinterfaces are point-to-point, no true mapping is needed. The subinterface acts like a point-to-point link, so the neighboring router's IPX address is not shown in the **show frame-relay map** command output. A **debug frame-relay events** command, which shows output for Inverse ARP flows, could have identified the IPX addresses, but Inverse ARP is not enabled on point-to-point subinterfaces because it is not needed.

In short, there was no way to deduce all IPX addresses from the scenario.

Figure 8-42 *Scenario 8-2 Network Derived from **show** and **debug** Commands*

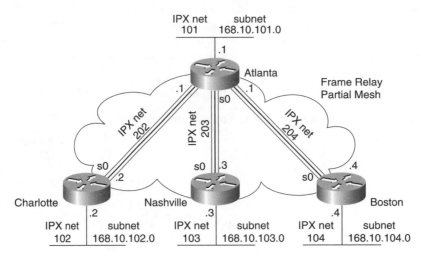

Table 8-54 lists the answers for Layer 3 addresses and subinterface numbers (Table 8-48, in the scenario description).

Table 8-54 *Layer 3 Addresses in Scenario 8-2—Completed Table*

Router	Port	Subinterface	IP Address	IPX Address
Atlanta	s0	1	168.10.202.1	202.0200.AAAA.AAAA
Atlanta	s0	2	168.10.203.1	203.0200.AAAA.AAAA
Atlanta	s0	3	168.10.204.1	204.0200.AAAA.AAAA
Atlanta	s0			
Charlotte	s0	1	168.10.202.2	202.????.????.????
Charlotte	s0			
Nashville	s0	1	168.10.203.3	203. ????.????.????
Nashville	s0			
Boston	s0	1	168.10.204.4	204. ????.????.????
Boston	s0			

Note: There was not enough information to derive the IPX addresses for Charlotte, Nashville, and Boston. The IPX network numbers are implied by the **show cdp neighbor detail** command output.

The LMI type was discovered only by examining the output of the **show frame-relay lmi** command. However, this command does not list whether the LMI type was learned via autosensing or whether it was configured.

The encapsulation type is much more obscure. The **show frame-relay map** command output holds the answer. Table 8-55 summarizes those answers (Table 8-49, in the scenario description).

Table 8-55   *Scenario 8-2 LMI and Encapsulations Used—Completed Table*

Router	Port	Subinterface	LMI Type	Encapsulation
Atlanta	s0	—	Cisco	
Atlanta	s0	1		cisco
Atlanta	s0	2		cisco
Atlanta	s0	3		ietf
Charlotte	s0	—	Q933A	
Charlotte	s0	1		cisco
Nashville	s0	—	Cisco	
Nashville	s0	1		cisco
Boston	s0	—	Cisco	
Boston	s0	1		ietf

Answers to Scenario 8-3: Point-to-Point Configuration

Example 8-44, Example 8-45, Example 8-46, and Example 8-47 show the configurations.

Example 8-44 *Boston Configuration for Scenario 8-3, Point-to-Point Configuration*

```
hostname Boston
ipx routing 0200.aaaa.aaaa
no ip domain-lookup
username Alaska password Larry
isdn switch-type basic-dms100
!
interface serial0
encapsulation multi-lapb-dce
ip address 200.1.5.5 255.255.255.252
ipx network 202
!
interface serial1
encapsulation hdlc
ip address 200.1.5.9 255.255.255.252
ipx network 203
!
```

continues

Example 8-44 *Boston Configuration for Scenario 8-3, Point-to-Point Configuration (Continued)*

```
interface bri0
encapsulation ppp
isdn spid1 1115551111
ip address 200.1.5.13 255.255.255.252
ipx network 204
ppp authentication chap
!
interface ethernet 0
ip address 200.1.1.1 255.255.255.0
ipx network 101
!
router igrp 1
network 200.1.1.0
network 200.1.5.0
```

Example 8-45 *Podunk Configuration for Scenario 8-3, Point-to-Point Configuration*

```
hostname Podunk
ipx routing 0200.bbbb.bbbb
no ip domain-lookup
!
interface serial0
encapsulation multi-lapb
ip address 200.1.5.6 255.255.255.252
ipx network 202
!
interface ethernet 0
ip address 200.1.2.1 255.255.255.0
ipx network 102
!
router igrp 1
network 200.1.2.0
network 200.1.5.0
```

Example 8-46 *Atlanta Configuration for Scenario 8-3, Point-to-Point Configuration*

```
hostname Atlanta
ipx routing 0200.cccc.cccc
no ip domain-lookup
!
interface serial0
encapsulation hdlc
ip address 200.1.5.10 255.255.255.252
ipx network 203
!
interface ethernet 0
ip address 200.1.3.1 255.255.255.0
ipx network 103
!
router igrp 1
network 200.1.3.0
network 200.1.5.0
```

Example 8-47 *Alaska Configuration for Scenario 8-3, Frame Relay Configuration*

```
hostname Alaska
no ip domain-lookup
ipx routing 0200.dddd.dddd
!
isdn switch-type basic-dms100
username Boston password Larry
!
interface BRI 0
encapsulation ppp
ip address 200.1.5.14 255.255.255.252
ipx network 204
isdn spid1 22255522220
ppp authentication chap
!
dialer-group 1
dialer idle-timeout 120
dialer map ip 200.1.5.13  name Boston 11115551111
!
interface ethernet 0
ip address 200.1.4.1 255.255.255.0
ipx network 104
!
router igrp 1
network 200.1.4.0
network 200.1.5.0
!
dialer-list 1 protocol ip permit
```

The choices for serial encapsulation in this solution are HDLC, PPP, and LAPB. PPP was chosen on the ISDN B channel because it provides CHAP authentication. LAPB is used on the link with known continuing high error rates so that LAPB can recover data lost going across the link. Because the problem statement also requests three different encapsulations, HDLC was chosen.

As you progress through your certifications, Cisco will try to ask questions that force you to deduce a fact from a limited amount of information. The final question in this scenario requires that you think beyond the topic of serial encapsulations. PPP control protocols are used by Boston on the PPP link to discern the Layer 3 addresses on the other end of the link. However, LAPB and HDLC do not perform this function. CDP is enabled on each of these links by default and is sending messages to discover information about Boston's neighbors. Also, Boston examines the source address of routing updates to learn the Layer 3 addresses of its neighbors.

Answers to Scenario 8-4: Frame Relay Configuration

Check your IP and IPX address design against the ones chosen in Table 8-56. Of course, your choices most likely are different. However, you should have one subnet per VC when using only point-to-point subinterfaces. With the original criteria of Routers A, D, and E each using multipoint subinterfaces, those three subinterfaces should have been in the same IP subnet and IPX network. Table 8-35 gives the planned Layer 3 addresses for the configurations using multipoint among those three routers.

Table 8-56   *Scenario 8-4 Layer 3 Address Planning Chart, Multipoint A-D-E*

Interface	Subinterface	IP Address	IPX Address
A's Ethernet		168.15.101.1	101.0200.AAAA.AAAA
B's Ethernet		168.15.102.1	102.0200.BBBB.BBBB
C's Ethernet		168.15.103.1	103.0200.CCCC.CCCC
D's Ethernet		168.15.104.1	104.0200.DDDD.DDDD
E's Ethernet		168.15.105.1	105.0200.EEEE.EEEE
A's S0	2	168.15.202.1	202.0200.AAAA.AAAA
A's S0	3	168.15.203.1	203.0200.AAAA.AAAA
A's S0	1	168.15.200.1	200.0200.AAAA.AAAA
B's S0	2	168.15.202.2	202.0200.BBBB.BBBB
C's S0	3	168.15.203.3	203.0200.CCCC.CCCC
D's S0	1	168.15.200.4	200.0200.DDDD.DDDD
E's S0	1	168.15.200.5	200.0200.EEEE.EEEE

Assuming the DLCIs in Figure 8-40, Example 8-48, Example 8-49, and Example 8-50, show the configurations for Routers A, B, and E, respectively, using multipoint subinterfaces for the VCs between A, D, and E.

Example 8-48 *Router A Configuration, Scenario 8-4*

```
ipx routing 0200.aaaa.aaaa
!
interface serial0
encapsulation frame-relay
!
interface serial 0.1 multipoint
ip address 168.15.200.1  255.255.255.0
ipx network 200
frame-relay interface-dlci 54
frame-relay interface-dlci 55
!
interface serial 0.2 point-to-point
ip address 168.15.202.1  255.255.255.0
ipx network 202
interface-dlci 52
!
interface serial 0.3 point-to-point
ip address 168.15.203.1  255.255.255.0
ipx network 203
```

Example 8-48 *Router A Configuration, Scenario 8-4 (Continued)*

```
interface-dlci 53
!

!
interface ethernet 0
ip address 168.15.101.1 255.255.255.0
ipx network 101
!
router igrp 1
network 168.15.0.0
```

Example 8-49 *Router B Configuration, Scenario 8-4*

```
ipx routing 0200.bbbb.bbbb
!
interface serial0
encapsulation frame-relay
!
interface serial 0.2 point-to-point
ip address 168.15.202.2  255.255.255.0
ipx network 202
frame-relay interface-dlci 51
!
interface ethernet 0
ip address 168.15.102.1 255.255.255.0
ipx network 102
!
router igrp 1
network 168.15.0.0
```

Example 8-50 *Router E Configuration, Scenario 8-4*

```
ipx routing 0200.eeee.eeee
!
interface serial0
encapsulation frame-relay
!
interface serial 0.1 multipoint
ip address 168.15.200.5  255.255.255.0
ipx network 200
frame-relay interface-dlci 51
frame-relay interface-dlci 54
!
interface ethernet 0
ip address 168.15.105.1 255.255.255.0
ipx network 105
!
router igrp 1
network 168.15.0.0
```

Multipoint subinterfaces will work perfectly well in this topology. Using multipoint also conserves IP subnets, as seen in the next task in this scenario. When changing strategy to use only point-to-point subinterfaces, each of the three VCs in the triangle of Routers A, D, and E will require a different subnet and IPX network number. Table 8-57 shows the choices made here. Example 8-51 and Example 8-52 show alternate configurations for Router A and Router E using point-to-point instead of multipoint subinterfaces.

Table 8-57 *Scenario 8-4 Layer 3 Address Planning Chart, All Point-to-Point Subinterfaces*

Interface	Subinterface	IP Address	IPX Address
A's Ethernet		168.15.101.1	101.0200.AAAA.AAAA
B's Ethernet		168.15.102.1	102.0200.BBBB.BBBB
C's Ethernet		168.15.103.1	103.0200.CCCC.CCCC
D's Ethernet		168.15.104.1	104.0200.DDDD.DDDD
E's Ethernet		168.15.105.1	105.0200.EEEE.EEEE
A's S0	2	168.15.202.1	202.0200.AAAA.AAAA
A's S0	3	168.15.203.1	203.0200.AAAA.AAAA
A's S0	4	168.15.204.1	204.0200.AAAA.AAAA
A's S0	5	168.15.205.1	205.0200.AAAA.AAAA
B's S0	2	168.15.202.2	202.0200.BBBB.BBBB
C's S0	3	168.15.203.3	203.0200.CCCC.CCCC
D's S0	4	168.15.204.4	204.0200.DDDD.DDDD
D's S0	1	168.15.190.4	190.0200.DDDD.DDDD
E's S0	5	168.15.205.5	205.0200.EEEE.EEEE
E's S0	1	168.15.190.5	190.0200.EEEE.EEEE

Example 8-51 *Router A Configuration, Scenario 8-4, All Point-to-Point Subinterfaces*

```
ipx routing 0200.aaaa.aaaa
!
interface serial0
encapsulation frame-relay
!
interface serial 0.2 point-to-point
ip address 168.15.202.1  255.255.255.0
ipx network 202
frame-relay interface-dlci 52
!
interface serial 0.3 point-to-point
ip address 168.15.203.1  255.255.255.0
ipx network 203
frame-relay interface-dlci 53
```

Example 8-51 *Router A Configuration, Scenario 8-4, All Point-to-Point Subinterfaces (Continued)*

```
!
interface serial 0.4 point-to-point
ip address 168.15.204.1  255.255.255.0
ipx network 204
frame-relay interface-dlci 54
!
interface serial 0.5 point-to-point
ip address 168.15.205.1  255.255.255.0
ipx network 205
frame-relay interface-dlci 55
!
interface ethernet 0
ip address 168.15.101.1 255.255.255.0
ipx network 101
!
router igrp 1
network 168.15.0.0
```

Example 8-52 *Router E Configuration, Scenario 8-4, Subinterfaces*

```
ipx routing 0200.eeee.eeee
!
interface serial0
encapsulation frame-relay
!
interface serial 0.1 point-to-point
ip address 168.15.190.5  255.255.255.0
ipx network 190
interface-dlci 54
!
interface serial 0.5 point-to-point
ip address 168.15.200.5  255.255.255.0
ipx network 200
interface-dlci 51
!
interface ethernet 0
ip address 168.15.105.1 255.255.255.0
ipx network 105
!
router igrp 1
network 168.15.0.0
```

The contents of the IP and IPX routing tables asked for in Step 4 of this scenario will be provided in shorthand in Table 8-58. The third byte of the IP address is shown in the Layer 3 group column because the third byte (octet) fully comprises the subnet field. Not coincidentally, the IPX network number was chosen as the same number, mainly to make network operation easier.

Table 8-58   *Scenario 8-4 IP and IPX Routing Table Contents, Router A*

Layer 3 Group	Outgoing Interface	Next-Hop IP Address, or Connected	Next-Hop IPX Address, or Connected
101	E0	Connected	Connected
102	S0.2	168.15.202.2	202.0200.bbbb.bbbb
103	S0.3	168.15.203.3	203.0200.cccc.cccc
104	S0.4	168.15.204.4	204.0200.dddd.dddd
105	S0.5	168.15.205.5	205.0200.eeee.eeee

Answers to Scenario 8-5: Frame Relay Configuration Dissection

Figure 8-43 supplies the network diagram described in Scenario 8-5. The subinterfaces are all point-to-point, which is a clue that each VC has a subnet and IPX network associated with it. An examination of the IP addresses or IPX network numbers should have been enough to deduce which routers are attached to each end of each VC.

Figure 8-43   *Diagram to Scenario 8-5 Frame Relay Network*

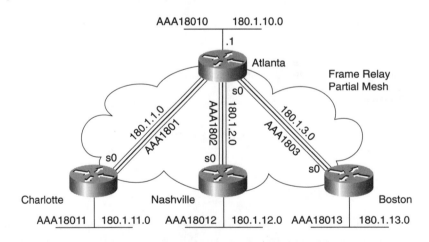

Split horizon is turned off on all interfaces because that is the default with point-to-point subinterfaces and because no command has been configured to turn it on.

Cisco encapsulation was used in each case. The **encapsulation frame-relay** command defaults to the use of Cisco encapsulation.

Disabling Inverse ARP is unlikely in real networks. However, this exercise was added so that you can be ready for the exam. Example 8-53 and Example 8-54 show the commands used to migrate to not using Inverse ARP. The maps are necessary for both IP and IPX because both need to be routed across the Frame Relay network.

Example 8-53 *Scenario 8-5, Atlanta Router—Changes for Static Mapping*

```
Atlanta(config)# interface serial 0.1
Atlanta(config-subif)#no frame-relay interface-dlci 501
Atlanta(config-subif)#frame-relay map ip 180.1.1.2 501 broadcast
Atlanta(config-subif)#frame-relay map ipx aaa1801.0200.2222.2222 501 broadcast
Atlanta(config-subif)# interface serial 0.2
Atlanta(config-subif)#no frame-relay interface-dlci 502
Atlanta(config-subif)#frame-relay map ip 180.1.2.3 502 broadcast
Atlanta(config-subif)#frame-relay map ipx aaa1802.0200.3333.3333 502 broadcast
Atlanta(config-subif)# interface serial 0.3
Atlanta(config-subif)#no frame-relay interface-dlci 503
Atlanta(config-subif)#frame-relay map ip 180.1.3.4 503 broadcast
Atlanta(config-subif)#frame-relay map ipx aaa1803.0200.4444.4444 503 broadcast
```

Example 8-54 *Scenario 8-5, Charlotte Router—Changes for Static Mapping*

```
Charlotte(config)# interface serial 0.1
Charlotte(config-subif)#no frame-relay interface-dlci 500
Charlotte(config-subif)#frame-relay map ip 180.1.1.1 500 broadcast
Charlotte(config-subif)#frame-relay map ipx aaa1801.0200.1111.1111 500 broadcast
```

The **interface-dlci** settings are no longer needed because the IOS can deduce which DLCI is used by the subinterface based on the **map** command.

CHAPTER 9

Scenarios for Final Preparation

This chapter is designed to assist you in final preparation for the CCNA exam by providing additional practice with the core coverage of the exam. These exercises and tasks require a broad perspective, which means that you will need to draw on knowledge you acquired in each of Chapters 2 through 8. This chapter also focuses on configuration and verification commands in ways that will help you learn and review much better than another set of questions could. These scenarios are designed with the following assumptions in mind:

- You might forget many details by the time you have completed your study of the other chapters. These scenarios cover the entire breadth of topics to remind you about many of these details.

- Your understanding of the concepts at this point in your study is complete; practice and repetition is useful so that you can answer quickly and confidently on the exam.

This chapter is not the only chapter you should use when doing your final preparation for the CCNA exam. The concepts in Chapter 3, "OSI Reference Model & Layered Communication," are not covered in this chapter, mainly because Chapter 3 deals with concepts and theory; however, Chapter 3 concepts are a very important part of the CCNA exam. Review the questions at the end of that chapter, and look at the tables that detail the functions of each OSI layer and the example protocols at each layer, as a final review of OSI.

The "Foundation Summary" section in each chapter is another great way to review the topics as your exam date approaches. Figure 9-1 describes your final preparation options with this book.

As shown, if you want even more final preparation, many practice questions are located in each chapter and on the CD. All prechapter quizzes and chapter-ending questions, with answers, are listed in Appendix A, "Answers to the 'Do I Know This Already?' Quizzes and Q&A Sections." You can quickly read and review these conveniently located questions and go over the answers and explanations. In addition, the CD includes testing software and many other additional questions in the format of the CCNA exam (multiple-choice questions). These questions should be a valuable resource when you are performing final preparations.

Figure 9-1 *Final CCNA Exam Preparation Study Strategy*

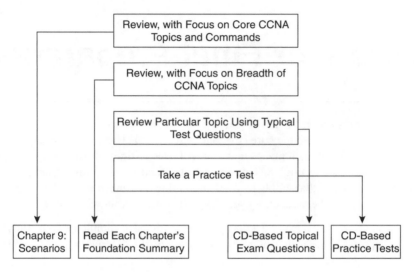

How to Best Use This Chapter

The focus of these scenarios is on easily forgotten items. The first such items are the **show** and **debug** commands. Their options are often ignored, mainly because you can get online help about the correct option easily when using the Cisco CLI. However, questions about the exact command options used to see a particular piece of information are scattered throughout the exam. Take care to review the output of the commands in these scenarios.

NOTE   You should not count on the CCNA exam to have only multiple-choice questions—it also can have fill-in-the blank questions, with particular emphasis on commands and command options.

Another focus of this chapter is a review of command-line tricks and acronym trivia. Like it or not, part of the preparation involves memorization; hopefully, these reminders will help you answer a question or two on the exam.

Additional examples for IP and IPX addressing are included with each scenario. You can be sure that IP addressing, subnetting, and broadcast addresses will be on the exam. Also, take care to recall the Novell encapsulation options, which are also reviewed in these scenarios.

Finally, this chapter contains more configurations for almost all options already covered in the book. If you can configure these options without online help, you should feel confident that you can choose the correct command from a list of five options in a multiple-choice question.

If you have enough time, review all parts of each scenario. However, if you have limited time, you can review only part of a scenario. For example, the solutions to Part A of each scenario are the background information for Part B; the solutions to Part B of each scenario are the background information for Part C. So, if you read Part A or B, decide you already know those details, and don't want to take the time to wade through your own answer, just look at the answer in the book; it will lead you into the next part of the scenario.

If you are reading this chapter as your final review before taking the exam, let me take this opportunity to wish you success. Hopefully you will be relaxed and confident for your exam—and hopefully this book has helped you build your knowledge and confidence.

Scenario 9-1

Part A of Scenario 9-1 begins with some planning guidelines that include planning IP addresses, IPX network numbers, the location of SAP filters, and the location of IP standard access lists. After you complete Part A, Part B of the scenario asks you to configure the three routers to implement the planned design and a few other features. Finally, Part C asks you to examine router command output to discover details about the current operation. Part C also lists some questions related to the user interface and protocol specifications.

Scenario 9-1, Part A—Planning

Your job is to deploy a new network with three sites, as shown in Figure 9-2.

The decision to use point-to-point serial links, as well as the product choices, has already been made. For Part A of this scenario, perform the following tasks:

1 Plan the IP addressing and subnets used in this network. Class B network 163.1.0.0 has been assigned by the NIC. The maximum number of hosts per subnet is 100. Assign IP addresses to the PCs as well.

2 Plan the IPX network numbers to be used. You can choose the internal network numbers of the servers as well.

3 Plan the location and logic of IP access lists to filter for the following criteria: Hosts on the Ethernet attached to R1 are not allowed to send or receive IP traffic to or from hosts on the Ethernet attached to R3. (Do not code the access lists; just code the location and logic for the access lists. Part B will ask for configuration, and because the answer to Part B will be based on where the access lists are placed, you probably will want to see the answer in Part A before configuring.)

Figure 9-2 *Scenario 9-1 Network Diagram*

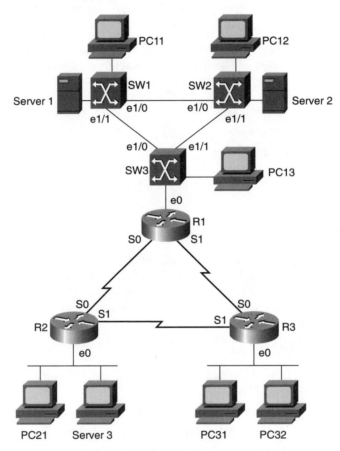

4 Plan the location and logic of SAP filters to prevent clients on the Ethernet off R2 from logging in to Server 2. Again, do not create the configuration, but simply make notes about the logic and location of the access lists.

Assume that a single VLAN is used on the switches near Router 1 (R1).

Table 9-1 and Table 9-2 are provided as a convenient place to record your IP subnets, IPX networks, and IP addresses when performing the planning tasks for this scenario.

Table 9-1   *Scenario 9-1, Part A—IP Subnet and IPX Network Planning Chart*

Location of Subnet/ Network Geographically	Subnet Mask	Subnet Number	IPX Network
R1 Ethernet			
R2 Ethernet			
R3 Ethernet			
Serial between R1 and R2			
Serial between R1 and R3			
Serial between R2 and R3			
Server 1 internal			
Server 2 internal			
Server 3 internal			

Table 9-2   *Scenario 9-1, Part A—IP Address Planning Chart*

Host	Address
PC11	
PC12	
PC13	
PC21	
PC31	
PC32	
R1-E0	
R1-S0	
R1-S1	
R2-E0	
R2-S0	
R2-S1	
R3-E0	
R3-S0	
R3-S1	

Solutions to Scenario 9-1, Part A—Planning

Keeping the design as simple as possible, yet without making it too simple so as not to be useful as the network evolves, is a good practice. In these suggested answers, the numbering scheme is chosen to help those of us with fading memories.

1 The IP subnet design includes the use of mask 255.255.255.128. The design criteria leaves enough ambiguity that you could argue that any mask with at least 7 host bits was valid; therefore, the much easier mask of 255.255.255.0 would be valid. However, I chose a more challenging mask, just to give you more difficult practice.

2 The IPX network number assignment is simply a matter of choosing numbers; these are recorded, along with the IP addresses, in Table 9-3. The IP addresses are assigned in Table 9-4.

Table 9-3   *Scenario 9-1, Part A—IP Subnet and IPX Network Planning Chart Completed*

Location of Subnet/ Network Geographically	Subnet Mask	Subnet Number	IPX Network
R1 Ethernet	255.255.255.128	163.1.1.128	1
R2 Ethernet	255.255.255.128	163.1.2.128	2
R3 Ethernet	255.255.255.128	163.1.3.128	3
Serial between R1 and R2	255.255.255.128	163.1.12.128	12
Serial between R1 and R3	255.255.255.128	163.1.13.128	13
Serial between R2 and R3	255.255.255.128	163.1.23.128	23
Server 1 internal	—	—	101
Server 2 internal	—	—	102
Server 3 internal	—	—	103

Table 9-4   *Scenario 9-1, Part A—IP Address Planning Chart Completed*

Host	Address
PC11	163.1.1.211
PC12	163.1.1.212
PC13	163.1.1.213
PC21	163.1.2.221
PC31	163.1.3.231
PC32	163.1.3.232
R1-E0	163.1.1.201
R1-S0	163.1.12.201

Table 9-4   *Scenario 9-1, Part A—IP Address Planning Chart Completed (Continued)*

Host	Address
R1-S1	163.1.13.201
R2-E0	163.1.2.202
R2-S0	163.1.12.202
R2-S1	163.1.23.202
R3-E0	163.1.3.203
R3-S0	163.1.13.203
R3-S1	163.1.23.203

3 As usual, the access lists can be placed in several areas to achieve the desired function. Also as usual, the criteria for the access list is subject to interpretation. One solution is to filter packets sent from hosts on the Ethernet off R3, filtering them as they enter R1, on either of R1's serial interfaces. By filtering packets in only one direction, applications that require a two-way flow will not successfully communicate. By filtering on both of R1's serial interfaces for inbound traffic, any valid route for the incoming packets will be checked.

4 For the SAP filter, several options also exist; one is shown here. By stopping R2 from adding the SAP for Server 2 to its SAP table, R2 will never advertise that server in a GNS request, nor will Server 3 learn about Server 2's SAPs from R2's SAP updates. So, the plan is to place incoming SAP filters on both serial interfaces on R2, to filter Server 2 from being added to R2's SAP table.

Scenario 9-1, Part B—Configuration

The next step in your job is to deploy the network designed in Scenario 9-1, Part A. Use the solutions for Part A of Scenario 9-1 to direct you in identifying IP and IPX addresses and determining the logic behind the access lists. For Scenario 9-1, Part B, perform the following tasks:

1 Configure IP, IPX, and IP access lists and IPX SAP filters based on Scenario 9-1, Part A's design.

2 Use RIP as the IP routing protocol.

3 Use PPP as the data link protocol on the link between R2 and R3. Use the default serial encapsulation elsewhere.

Solutions to Scenario 9-1, Part B—Configuration

Example 9-1, Example 9-2, and Example 9-3 show the configurations for Scenario 9-1, Part B, given the criteria in Tasks 1, 2, and 3.

Example 9-1 *R1 Configuration*

```
hostname R1
!
ipx routing 0200.1111.1111
!
interface Serial0
 ip address 163.1.12.201 255.255.255.128
 ipx network 12
 ip access-group 83 in
!
interface Serial1
 ip address 163.1.13.201 255.255.255.128
 ipx network 13
 ip access-group 83 in
!
Ethernet0
 ip address 163.1.1.201 255.255.255.128
ipx network 1
!
router rip
network 163.1.0.0
!
access-list 83 deny 163.1.3.128 0.0.0.127
access-list 83 permit any
```

Example 9-2 *R2 Configuration*

```
hostname R2
!
ipx routing 0200.2222.2222
!
interface Serial0
 ip address 163.1.12.202 255.255.255.128
 ipx network 12
 ipx input-sap-filter 1010
!
interface Serial1
 encapsulation ppp
 ip address 163.1.23.202 255.255.255.128
 ipx network 23
 ipx input-sap-filter 1010
!
Ethernet0
 ip address 163.1.2.202 255.255.255.128
 ipx network 2
!
router rip
network 163.1.0.0
```

Example 9-2   *R2 Configuration (Continued)*

```
!
access-list 1010 deny 102
access-list 1010 permit -1
```

Example 9-3   *R3 Configuration*

```
hostname R3
!
ipx routing 0200.3333.3333
!
interface Serial0
 ip address 163.1.13.203 255.255.255.128
 ipx network 13
!
interface Serial1
 encapsulation ppp
 ip address 163.1.23.203 255.255.255.128
 ipx network 23
!
Ethernet0
 ip address 163.1.3.203 255.255.255.128
ipx network 3
!
router rip
network 163.1.0.0
```

Scenario 9-1 Part C—Verification and Questions

The CCNA exam tests you on your memory of the kinds of information you can find in the output of various **show** commands. Using Example 9-4, Example 9-5, and Example 9-6 as references, answer the questions following the examples.

NOTE   In the network from which these commands were captured, several administrative settings not mentioned in the scenario were configured. For instance, the enable password was configured. Any **show running-config** commands in the examples in this chapter might have other unrelated configurations.

Example 9-4   *Scenario 9-1, Part C—R1 **show** and **debug** Output*

```
R1#show ip interface brief
Interface              IP-Address        OK? Method Status              Protocol
Serial0                163.1.12.201      YES NVRAM  up                  up
Serial1                163.1.13.201      YES NVRAM  up                  up
Ethernet0              163.1.1.201       YES NVRAM  up                  up
R1#show access-lists
```

continues

Example 9-4 *Scenario 9-1, Part C—R1 **show** and **debug** Output (Continued)*

```
Standard IP access list 83
    deny    163.1.3.0, wildcard bits 0.0.0.127
    permit any
R1#
R1#debug ipx sap event
IPX service events debugging is on
R1#
IPXSAP: positing update to 1.ffff.ffff.ffff via Ethernet0 (broadcast) (full)
IPXSAP: positing update to 13.ffff.ffff.ffff via Serial1 (broadcast) (full)
IPXSAP: positing update to 12.ffff.ffff.ffff via Serial0 (broadcast) (full)
IPXSAP: positing update to 1.ffff.ffff.ffff via Ethernet0 (broadcast) (full)
R1#undebug all
All possible debugging has been turned off
R1#
R1#debug ipx sap activity
IPX service debugging is on
R1#
IPXSAP: positing update to 13.ffff.ffff.ffff via Serial1 (broadcast) (full)
IPXSAP: Update type 0x2 len 224 src:13.0200.1111.1111 dest:13.ffff.ffff.ffff(452)
 type 0x4, "Server3", 103.0000.0000.0001(451), 4 hops
 type 0x4, "Server1", 101.0000.0000.0001(451), 3 hops
 type 0x4, "Server2", 102.0000.0000.0001(451), 3 hops
IPXSAP: positing update to 12.ffff.ffff.ffff via Serial0 (broadcast) (full)
IPXSAP: Update type 0x2 len 160 src:12.0200.1111.1111 dest:12.ffff.ffff.ffff(452)
 type 0x4, "Server1", 101.0000.0000.0001(451), 3 hops
 type 0x4, "Server2", 102.0000.0000.0001(451), 3 hops
R1#undebug all
All possible debugging has been turned off
R1#
R1#
R1#debug ipx routing event
IPX routing events debugging is on
R1#
IPXRIP: positing full update to 1.ffff.ffff.ffff via Ethernet0 (broadcast)
IPXRIP: positing full update to 13.ffff.ffff.ffff via Serial1 (broadcast)
IPXRIP: positing full update to 12.ffff.ffff.ffff via Serial0 (broadcast)
IPXRIP: 13 FFFFFFFF not added, entry in table is static/connected/internal
IPXRIP: 12 FFFFFFFF not added, entry in table is static/connected/internal
IPXRIP: positing full update to 1.ffff.ffff.ffff via Ethernet0 (broadcast)
R1#undebug all
All possible debugging has been turned off
R1#
R1#debug ipx routing activity
IPX routing debugging is on
R1#
IPXRIP: update from 1.0000.0c89.b130
    102 in 2 hops, delay 2
    101 in 2 hops, delay 2
```

Example 9-4 *Scenario 9-1, Part C—R1 **show** and **debug** Output (Continued)*

```
IPXRIP: positing full update to 13.ffff.ffff.ffff via Serial1 (broadcast)
IPXRIP: src=13.0200.1111.1111, dst=13.ffff.ffff.ffff, packet sent
    network 103, hops 4,   delay 14
    network 23, hops 2,   delay 13
    network 2, hops 3,   delay 8
    network 101, hops 3,   delay 8
    network 102, hops 3,   delay 8
    network 1, hops 1,   delay 7
    network 12, hops 1,   delay 7
IPXRIP: positing full update to 12.ffff.ffff.ffff via Serial0 (broadcast)
IPXRIP: src=12.0200.1111.1111, dst=12.ffff.ffff.ffff, packet sent
    network 3, hops 2,   delay 13
    network 2, hops 3,   delay 8
  network 101, hops 3,   delay 8
network 102, hops 3,   delay 8
    network 1, hops 1,   delay 7
    network 13, hops 1,   delay 7
IPXRIP: update from 12.0200.2222.2222
    103 in 3 hops, delay 8
IPXRIP: 13 FFFFFFFF not added, entry in table is static/connected/internal
    13 in 2 hops, delay 13
    3 in 2 hops, delay 13
    23 in 1 hops, delay 7
    2 in 1 hops, delay 7
IPXRIP: update from 13.0200.3333.3333
    103 in 4 hops, delay 14
IPXRIP: 12 FFFFFFFF not added, entry in table is static/connected/internal
    12 in 2 hops, delay 13
    3 in 1 hops, delay 7
    2 in 2 hops, delay 13
    23 in 1 hops, delay 7
IPXRIP: positing full update to 1.ffff.ffff.ffff via Ethernet0 (broadcast)
IPXRIP: src=1.0000.0ccf.21cd, dst=1.ffff.ffff.ffff, packet sent
    network 103, hops 4,   delay 9
    network 3, hops 2,   delay 8
    network 23, hops 2,   delay 8
    network 13, hops 1,   delay 2
    network 12, hops 1,   delay 2
IPXRIP: update from 1.0000.0c89.b130
    102 in 2 hops, delay 2
    101 in 2 hops, delay 2
    2 in 2 hops, delay 2

R1#undebug all
All possible debugging has been turned off
R1#
R1#debug ip rip events
RIP event debugging is on
R1#
RIP: received v1 update from 163.1.13.203 on Serial1
RIP: Update contains 4 routes
```

continues

Example 9-4 *Scenario 9-1, Part C—R1* ***show*** *and* ***debug*** *Output (Continued)*

```
RIP: sending v1 update to 255.255.255.255 via Serial0 (163.1.12.201)
RIP: Update contains 4 routes
RIP: Update queued
RIP: Update sent via Serial0
RIP: sending v1 update to 255.255.255.255 via Serial1 (163.1.13.201)
RIP: Update contains 4 routes
RIP: Update queued
RIP: Update sent via Serial1
RIP: sending v1 update to 255.255.255.255 via Ethernet0 (163.1.1.201)
RIP: Update contains 7 routes
RIP: Update queued
RIP: Update sent via Ethernet0

RIP: received v1 update from 163.1.12.202 on Serial0
RIP: Update contains 4 routes
R1#undebug all
All possible debugging has been turned off
R1#
R1#debug ip rip
RIP protocol debugging is on
R1#
RIP: received v1 update from 163.1.12.202 on Serial0
      163.1.2.128 in 1 hops
      163.1.3.128 in 2 hops
      163.1.23.128 in 1 hops
      163.1.23.203 in 1 hops
RIP: received v1 update from 163.1.13.203 on Serial1
      163.1.2.128 in 2 hops
      163.1.3.128 in 1 hops
      163.1.23.128 in 1 hops
      163.1.23.202 in 1 hops
RIP: sending v1 update to 255.255.255.255 via Serial0 (163.1.12.201)
      subnet  163.1.3.128, metric 2
      subnet  163.1.1.128, metric 1
      subnet  163.1.13.128, metric 1
      host    163.1.23.202, metric 2
RIP: sending v1 update to 255.255.255.255 via Serial1 (163.1.13.201)
      subnet  163.1.2.128, metric 2
      subnet  163.1.1.128, metric 1
      subnet  163.1.12.128, metric 1
      host    163.1.23.203, metric 2
RIP: sending v1 update to 255.255.255.255 via Ethernet0 (163.1.1.201)
      subnet  163.1.2.128, metric 2
      subnet  163.1.3.128, metric 2
      subnet  163.1.12.128, metric 1
      subnet  163.1.13.128, metric 1
      subnet  163.1.23.128, metric 2
      host    163.1.23.203, metric 2
      host    163.1.23.202, metric 2

R1#undebug all
All possible debugging has been turned off
R1#
```

Example 9-5 *Scenario 9-1, Part C—R2 **show** and **debug** Output*

```
R2#show interface
Serial0 is up, line protocol is up
  Hardware is HD64570
  Internet address is 163.1.12.202/25
  MTU 1500 bytes, BW 56 Kbit, DLY 20000 usec, rely 255/255, load 1/255
  Encapsulation HDLC, loopback not set, keepalive set (10 sec)
  Last input 00:00:04, output 00:00:00, output hang never
  Last clearing of "show interface" counters never
  Queuing strategy: fifo
  Output queue 0/40, 0 drops; input queue 0/75, 0 drops
  5 minute input rate 0 bits/sec, 0 packets/sec
  5 minute output rate 0 bits/sec, 0 packets/sec
     1242 packets input, 98477 bytes, 0 no buffer
     Received 898 broadcasts, 0 runts, 0 giants, 0 throttles
     0 input errors, 0 CRC, 0 frame, 0 overrun, 0 ignored, 0 abort
     1249 packets output, 91395 bytes, 0 underruns
     0 output errors, 0 collisions, 2 interface resets
     0 output buffer failures, 0 output buffers swapped out
     12 carrier transitions
     DCD=up  DSR=up  DTR=up  RTS=up  CTS=up
Serial1 is up, line protocol is up
  Hardware is HD64570
  Internet address is 163.1.23.202/25
  MTU 1500 bytes, BW 1544 Kbit, DLY 20000 usec, rely 255/255, load 1/255
  Encapsulation PPP, loopback not set, keepalive set (10 sec)
  LCP Open
  Open: IPCP, CDPCP, LLC2, IPXCP
  Last input 00:00:02, output 00:00:02, output hang never
  Last clearing of "show interface" counters never
  Input queue: 0/75/0 (size/max/drops); Total output drops: 0
  Queuing strategy: weighted fair
  Output queue: 0/1000/0 (size/max total/drops)
     Conversations  0/1/64 (active/max active/threshold)
     Reserved Conversations 0/0 (allocated/max allocated)
  5 minute input rate 0 bits/sec, 0 packets/sec
  5 minute output rate 0 bits/sec, 0 packets/sec
     1654 packets input, 90385 bytes, 0 no buffer
     Received 1644 broadcasts, 0 runts, 0 giants, 0 throttles
     0 input errors, 0 CRC, 0 frame, 0 overrun, 0 ignored, 0 abort
     1674 packets output, 96130 bytes, 0 underruns
     0 output errors, 0 collisions, 8 interface resets
     0 output buffer failures, 0 output buffers swapped out
     13 carrier transitions
     DCD=up  DSR=up  DTR=up  RTS=up  CTS=up
Ethernet0 is up, line protocol is up
  Hardware is MCI Ethernet, address is 0000.0c89.b170 (bia 0000.0c89.b170)
  Internet address is 163.1.2.202, subnet mask is 255.255.255.128
  MTU 1500 bytes, BW 10000 Kbit, DLY 100000 usec, rely 255/255, load 1/255
  Encapsulation ARPA, loopback not set, keepalive set (10 sec)
  ARP type: ARPA, ARP Timeout 4:00:00
```

continues

Example 9-5 *Scenario 9-1, Part C—R2* **show** *and* **debug** *Output (Continued)*

```
Last input 00:00:00, output 00:00:04, output hang never
  Last clearing of "show interface" counters never
  Queuing strategy: fifo
  Output queue 0/40, 0 drops; input queue 0/75, 0 drops
  5 minute input rate 0 bits/sec, 0 packets/sec
  5 minute output rate 0 bits/sec, 0 packets/sec
     2274 packets input, 112381 bytes, 0 no buffer
     Received 1913 broadcasts, 0 runts, 0 giants, 0 throttles
     0 input errors, 0 CRC, 0 frame, 0 overrun, 0 ignored, 0 abort
     863 packets output, 110146 bytes, 0 underruns
     0 output errors, 0 collisions, 2 interface resets
     0 output buffer failures, 0 output buffers swapped out
     6 transitions

R2#show ipx interface brief
Interface            IPX Network Encapsulation Status         IPX State
Serial0              12          HDLC         up              [up]
Serial1              23          PPP          up              [up]
Ethernet0            2           SAP          up              [up]

R2#show ipx route
Codes: C - Connected primary network,    c - Connected secondary network
       S - Static, F - Floating static, L - Local (internal), W - IPXWAN
       R - RIP, E - EIGRP, N - NLSP, X - External, A - Aggregate
       s - seconds, u - uses

9 Total IPX routes. Up to 1 parallel paths and 16 hops allowed.

No default route known.

C         2 (SAP),         E0
C        12 (HDLC),        Se0
C        23 (PPP),         Se1
R         1 [07/01] via    12.0200.1111.1111,    59s, Se0
R         3 [07/01] via    23.0200.3333.3333,     5s, Se1
R        13 [07/01] via    23.0200.3333.3333,     5s, Se1
R       101 [08/03] via    12.0200.1111.1111,     0s, Se0
R       102 [08/03] via    12.0200.1111.1111,     0s, Se0
R       103 [02/02] via     2.0000.0cac.70ef,    21s, E0

R2#show ip protocol
Routing Protocol is "rip"
  Sending updates every 30 seconds, next due in 6 seconds
  Invalid after 180 seconds, hold down 180, flushed after 240
  Outgoing update filter list for all interfaces is not set
  Incoming update filter list for all interfaces is not set
  Redistributing: rip
   Default version control: send version 1, receive any version
    Interface       Send  Recv  Key-chain
    Serial0           1    1 2
    Serial1           1    1 2
    Ethernet0         1    1 2
```

Example 9-5 *Scenario 9-1, Part C—R2 **show** and **debug** Output (Continued)*

```
    Routing for Networks:
      163.1.0.0
    Routing Information Sources:
      Gateway          Distance      Last Update
      163.1.13.201          120      00:00:02
      163.1.23.202          120      00:00:09
    Distance: (default is 120)

R2#show ipx servers
Codes: S - Static, P - Periodic, E - EIGRP, N - NLSP, H - Holddown, + = detail
3 Total IPX Servers

Table ordering is based on routing and server info

    Type Name                       Net      Address      Port     Route Hops Itf
P      4 Server3                    103.0000.0000.0001:0451     2/02    2  E0
P      4 Server1                    101.0000.0000.0001:0451     8/03    3  Se0
P      4 Server2                    102.0000.0000.0001:0451     8/03    3  Se0
```

Example 9-6 *Scenario 9-1, Part C—R3 **show** and **debug** Output*

```
R3#show running-config
Building configuration...

Current configuration:
!
version 11.2
no service password-encryption
no service udp-small-servers
no service tcp-small-servers
!
hostname R3
!
enable secret 5 $1$kI1V$NkybGlP9tzP7BYvAKYT.c1
!
no ip domain-lookup
ipx routing 0200.3333.3333
!
interface Serial0
 ip address 163.1.13.203 255.255.255.128
 ipx network 13
 no fair-queue
!
interface Serial1
 ip address 163.1.23.203 255.255.255.128
 encapsulation ppp
 ipx network 23
!
interface Ethernet0
 ip address 163.1.3.203 255.255.255.128
 ipx network 3
```

continues

Example 9-6 *Scenario 9-1, Part C—R3* **show** *and* **debug** *Output (Continued)*

```
!
router rip
 network 163.1.0.0
!
no ip classless
!
!
!
!
line con 0
 password cisco
 login
line aux 0
line vty 0 4
 password cisco
 login
!
end

R3#show ip arp
Protocol  Address             Age (min)  Hardware Addr   Type    Interface
Internet  163.1.3.203              -     0000.0c89.b1b0  SNAP    Ethernet0

R3#show ip route
Codes: C - connected, S - static, I - IGRP, R - RIP, M - mobile, B - BGP
       D - EIGRP, EX - EIGRP external, O - OSPF, IA - OSPF inter area
       N1 - OSPF NSSA external type 1, N2 - OSPF NSSA external type 2
       E1 - OSPF external type 1, E2 - OSPF external type 2, E - EGP
       i - IS-IS, L1 - IS-IS level-1, L2 - IS-IS level-2, * - candidate default
       U - per-user static route, o - ODR

Gateway of last resort is not set

     163.1.0.0/16 is variably subnetted, 7 subnets, 2 masks
R       163.1.2.128/25 [120/1] via 163.1.23.202, 00:00:22, Serial1
C       163.1.3.128/25 is directly connected, Ethernet0
R       163.1.1.128/25 [120/1] via 163.1.13.201, 00:00:28, Serial0
R       163.1.12.128/25 [120/1] via 163.1.13.201, 00:00:28, Serial0
                        [120/1] via 163.1.23.202, 00:00:22, Serial1
C       163.1.13.128/25 is directly connected, Serial0
C       163.1.23.128/25 is directly connected, Serial1
C       163.1.23.202/32 is directly connected, Serial1

R3#trace 163.1.13.203


Type escape sequence to abort.
Tracing the route to 163.1.13.203

  1 163.1.13.201 16 msec 16 msec 16 msec
  2 163.1.13.203 44 msec *  32 msec
```

Example 9-6   *Scenario 9-1, Part C—R3* **show** *and* **debug** *Output (Continued)*

```
R3#ping 163.1.13.203

Type escape sequence to abort.
Sending 5, 100-byte ICMP Echos to 163.1.13.203, timeout is 2 seconds:
!!!!!
Success rate is 100 percent (5/5), round-trip min/avg/max = 64/66/68 ms

R3#ping 13.0200.3333.3333

Type escape sequence
 to abort.
Sending 5, 100-byte IPX Cisco Echoes to 13.0200.3333.3333, timeout is 2 seconds:
!!!!!
Success rate is 100 percent (5/5), round-trip min/avg/max = 68/69/72 ms
```

Answer the following questions. Use Example 9-4, Example 9-5, and Example 9-6 as references when the question refers directly to this scenario.

   1   Describe how the switches choose the root of the spanning tree.

   2   If Switch1 becomes the root, and if all interface costs are equal on all interfaces on all switches, which ports will be considered to be root ports?

   3   If Switch3 blocks on port E1 and then later Switch2's E0 port fails, what notifies Switch3 so that it can forward on its E1 port? In what interim Spanning Tree states will E1 be before it forwards?

   4   Describe the contents of an IP RIP update from R1 to R3. What **debug** command options provide the details of what is in the RIP update?

   5   Describe the contents of an IPX RIP update from R1 to R2. What **debug** command options provide the details of what is in the IPX RIP update?

   6   What command tells you the contents of the ARP cache? Does it contain IP as well as IPX addresses?

   7   What commands list the routing metrics used for IP subnets? What about for IPX networks?

   8   What command would be used to find the path a packet would take from R3 to 163.1.1.1?

   9   What **show** command identifies which routes were learned with IP RIP? What about with IPX RIP? What in the command identifies these routing protocols?

   10   What **show** command lists SAP information in the router?

   11   What **debug** command options create debug messages with the details of the SAP updates? Which options just provide messages referring to the fact that an update is sent, without listing the details?

12 What **debug** command options provide IP RIP update details?

13 Imagine that R3's E0 interface needed to use a new IP address and mask (10.1.1.1, 255.255.255.0). If the user was in user mode, what steps would be necessary to change the IP address?

14 With the user in privileged mode, the user remembers that the IP RIP configuration should be updated, based on the change in the previous question. List the steps necessary to make this change.

15 If an EXEC command you cannot recall begins with the letter C, how can you get help to list all commands that start with C? List the steps; assume that you are in privileged mode.

16 Name the two commands to list the currently used configuration in a router.

17 Name the two commands to list the configuration that will be used the next time the router is reloaded.

18 What does CDP stand for?

19 Define the metric used by IPX RIP.

20 What does GNS stand for? What role does R2 play in the GNS process? What about R3?

Solutions to Scenario 9-1, Part C—Verification and Questions

The answers to the questions for Scenario 9-1, Part C are as follows:

1 Each bridge and switch sends a CBPDU claiming to be the root. The bridge or switch with the lowest bridge priority—or, if a tie occurs, the bridge or switch with the lowest value for root bridge ID—is considered to be the root.

2 Because all port costs are equal, Switch2 will be getting CBPDUs with a lower cost in E1/0. Likewise, Switch3 will be receiving CBPDUs with a lower cost on its E1/0 port. So, each switch will consider its E1/0 port to be its root port; this port is placed in a forwarding state.

3 Switch3 reacts after Switch2's MaxAge time expires and Switch2 stops sending CBPDU messages onto its E1 (the Ethernet segment that Switch2 and Switch3 have in common). Switch3 then transitions its E1 port to listening state, then to learning state, and finally to forwarding state.

4 The **debug ip rip** command provides the detailed RIP debug output. The **debug ip rip event** shows summary information about the same updates. An example of each is shown in Example 9-4. This example shows four routes being described in the update to R3. One of the routes (appropriately) missing in the update is 163.1.13.128, which is the subnet on the serial link between R1 and R3. The other (appropriately) missing route is the route to 163.1.3.128—thus, R1's best route to that subnet is through R3. Split-horizon rules prevent either route from being advertised.

5   The command **debug ipx routing activity** is used to provide the detailed IPX RIP debug output. This output is also shown in Example 9-4. Two routes from R1's routing table are not included in the update: namely, networks 12 and 2. Network 12 is on the common serial link, and R1's route to network 2 points through R2. Both networks are not included due to split-horizon rules.

6   The **show ip arp** command (refer to Example 9-6) contains only MAC and IP addresses, not IPX addresses, because IPX does not use a concept like ARP on LANs.

7   The **show ip route** and **show ipx route** commands list the metric values (refer to Examples 9-5 and 9-6). The metric value for each IP subnet is the second of the two numbers inside brackets. Two IPX metrics are located between brackets for IPX routes: the number of timer ticks and the number of hops.

8   The **trace 163.1.1.1** command (refer to Example 9-6) would be used.

9   The **show ip route** and **show ipx route** commands identify the source of the routing information (refer to Examples 9-5 and 9-6). The source of the routing information is coded in a field on the left side of the output line and is based on the legend of such codes that appear at the beginning of the command output before the actual routing table entries are listed.

10 The **show ipx servers** command lists the SAP table (refer to Example 9-5).

11 The **debug ipx sap events** command just displays a message when an update is sent, with no details about the contents of the update. The **debug ipx sap activity** command displays the details of what is sent in the update (refer to Example 9-4).

12 The **debug ip rip** command displays the details of what is sent in the update (refer to Example 9-4).

13 Use the following steps:

```
R3> enable
password: password
R3#configure terminal
R3(config)#interface ethernet 0
R3(config-if)#ip address 10.1.1.1 255.255.255.0
R3(config)#Ctrl-Z
R3#
```

14 Use the following steps:

```
R3#configure terminal
R3(config)#router rip
R3(config-router)#network 10.0.0.0
R3(config)#Ctrl-Z
R3#
```

15 Use the following steps:

```
R3#c?
clear  clock  configure  connect  copy

R3#c
```

16 **show running-config** and **write terminal** would be used.

17 **show startup-config** and **show config** would be used.

18 CDP stands for Cisco Discovery Protocol.

19 The primary metric is a counter of timer ticks. If two routes to the same network tie with the ticks metric, the hop count is considered.

20 GNS stands for Get Nearest Server. Any router can respond to GNS requests, which are issued by clients. Both R2 and R3 will reply by default; R2's response is unlikely to be used because its GNS delay will ensure that its reply is slower than the server on the same Ethernet.

Scenario 9-2

This scenario uses the familiar Frame Relay network with three routers and a full mesh of virtual circuits. Some planning exercises begin the scenario (Scenario 9-2, Part A), followed by configuration (Scenario 9-2, Part B). Finally, a series of questions, some based on **show** and **debug** command output, finish the scenario (Scenario 9-2, Part C).

Scenario 9-2, Part A—Planning

Your job is to deploy a new network with three sites, as shown in Figure 9-3. The choice to use Frame Relay, as well as the product choices, have already been made. For Part A of this scenario, perform the following tasks:

1 Subnet planning has been completed. Before implementation, you are responsible for providing a list for the local LAN administrators defining the IP addresses that they can assign to hosts. Using Table 9-5, derive the subnet numbers and broadcast addresses, and define the range of valid IP addresses. A static mask of 255.255.255.192 is used on all subnets.

2 PC11 and PC12 use different IPX encapsulations, as do PC21 and PC22. Figure 9-4 shows the types of headers used by each PC. Plan the encapsulation types to be used, including the correct keywords used in the IOS.

3 Plan the IPX network numbers to be used. Use Table 9-6 to record the information.

Figure 9-3   *Scenario 9-2 Network Diagram*

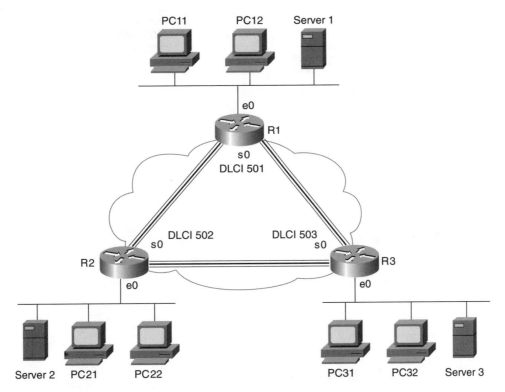

Figure 9-4   *Scenario 9-2, Part A—IPX Encapsulations*

PC11	Eth.	IPX	Data	
PC12	802.3	IPX	Data	
PC21	802.3	802.2	IPX	Data
PC22	802.3	802.2	SNAP	IPX	Data

Table 9-5   *Scenario 9-2, Part A—IP Subnet Planning Chart; Mask 255.255.255.192*

Router Interface	IP Address	Subnet Number	Subnet Broadcast Address	Range of Valid Addresses
R1 E0	168.11.11.101			
R2 E0	168.11.12.102			
R3 E0	168.11.13.103			
R1 S0	168.11.123.201			
R2 S0	168.11.123.202			
R3 S0	168.11.123.203			

Table 9-6   *Scenario 9-2, Part A—IPX Network Number Planning Chart*

Location of Network	IPX Network
Attached to R1 E0	
Attached to R2 E0	
Attached to R3 E0	
Frame Relay	
Server 1 Internal	
Server 2 Internal	
Server 3 Internal	

Solutions to Scenario 9-2, Part A—Planning

1 The first task was to derive the subnet numbers and broadcast addresses, so the assignable addresses in each subnet become obvious. One important item to note is that the three Frame Relay interfaces are in the same subnet, which is a clue that subinterfaces will not be used and that the Frame Relay interfaces will be treated as a single network. Table 9-7 provides the answers to this question.

Table 9-7   *Scenario 9-2, Part A—IP Subnet and IPX Network Planning Chart Completed*

Router Interface	IP Address	Subnet Number	Subnet Broadcast Address	Range of Valid Addresses
R1 E0	168.11.11.101	168.11.11.64	168.11.11.127	65 to 126 in last octet
R2 E0	168.11.12.102	168.11.12.64	168.11.12.127	65 to 126 in last octet
R3 E0	168.11.13.103	168.11.13.64	168.11.13.127	65 to 126 in last octet

Table 9-7   *Scenario 9-2, Part A—IP Subnet and IPX Network Planning Chart Completed (Continued)*

Router Interface	IP Address	Subnet Number	Subnet Broadcast Address	Range of Valid Addresses
R1 S0	168.11.123.201	168.11.123.192	168.11.123.255	193 to 254 in last octet
R2 S0	168.11.123.202	168.11.123.192	168.11.123.255	193 to 254 in last octet
R3 S0	168.11.123.203	168.11.123.192	168.11.123.255	193 to 254 in last octet

2 The second planning item requires remembering the four encapsulations for IPX on Ethernet. The important item here is to correlate the headers used by the devices to the correct name used by Cisco in the encapsulation command. Table 9-8 summarizes the encapsulations for the four PCs.

Table 9-8   *Scenario 9-2, Part A—IPX Encapsulations*

PC	Cisco IOS's Encapsulation
PC11	ARPA
PC12	Novell-ether
PC21	SAP
PC22	SNAP

3 Choosing IPX network numbers does not pose a particularly challenging task. However, realizing that two network numbers are needed on R1's E0 and on R2's E0 is the hidden part of the objective. As long as your network numbers are not duplicated, and as long as you planned for two IPX networks for the two aforementioned Ethernet interfaces, any network numbers are fine. Table 9-9 lists the network numbers that will be used as the basis of the configuration in Scenario 9-2, Part B.

Table 9-9   *Scenario 9-2, Part A—IPX Network Number Planning Chart Completed*

Host	Address
R1 E0	110 (ARPA)
R1 E0	111 (Novell-ether)
R2 E0	120 (SAP)
R2 E0	121 (SNAP)
R3 E0	130
Frame Relay	123
Server 1 internal	101
Server 2 internal	102
Server 3 internal	103

Scenario 9-2, Part B—Configuration

The next step in your job is to deploy the network designed in Scenario 9-2, Part A. Use the solutions to Scenario 9-2, Part A to direct you in identifying IP and IPX addresses and the encapsulations to be used. For Scenario 9-2, Part B, perform the following tasks:

1   Configure IP and IPX to be routed. Use IP IGRP and IPX RIP as routing protocols. Use IGRP process-id 1.

2   Use secondary IPX addresses to accommodate the multiple IPX encapsulation types described in Scenario 9-2, Part A.

3   Configure Frame Relay without the use of subinterfaces. R1's attached switch uses LMI type ANSI. Cisco encapsulation should be used for all routers.

4   Assume that after you installed the network, you were forced to disable IP IGRP on R2. Define the required IP static routes to allow hosts on all three Ethernets to communicate. (This is unlikely in real life; it's just an excuse to review IP static routes!)

5   Assume that after you installed the network, you were forced to disable Inverse ARP on R2. Define static mappings as necessary for all hosts to communicate.

Solutions to Scenario 9-2, Part B—Configuration

Example 9-7, Example 9-8, and Example 9-9 show the configurations for Tasks 1, 2, and 3.

Example 9-7   *R1 Configuration*

```
ipx routing 0200.aaaa.aaaa
!
interface serial0
encapsulation frame-relay
ip address  168.11.123.201  255.255.255.192
ipx network  123
frame-relay interface-dlci 502
frame-relay interface-dlci 503
!
interface ethernet 0
ip address  168.11.11.101  255.255.255.192
!
ipx network  110 encapsulation arpa
ipx network  111 encapsulation novell-ether secondary
!
router igrp 1
network 168.11.0.0
```

Example 9-8 *R2 Configuration*

```
ipx routing 0200.bbbb.bbbb
!
interface serial0
encapsulation frame-relay
ip address  168.11.123.202  255.255.255.192
ipx network  123
frame-relay interface-dlci 501
frame-relay interface-dlci 503
!
interface ethernet 0
ip address  168.11.12.102  255.255.255.192
ipx network  120 encapsulation sap
ipx network  121 encapsulation snap secondary
!
router igrp 1
network 168.11.0.0
```

Example 9-9 *R3 Configuration*

```
ipx routing 0200.cccc.cccc
!
interface serial0
encapsulation frame-relay
ip address  168.11.123.203  255.255.255.192
ipx network  123
frame-relay interface-dlci 501
frame-relay interface-dlci 502
!
interface ethernet 0
ip address  168.11.13.103  255.255.255.192
ipx network  130
!
router igrp 1
network 168.11.0.0
```

For Task 4 in Scenario 9-2, Part B, static routes need to be defined in all three routers. R2 will need routes to the two LAN-based subnets at the other sites. Likewise, R1 and R3 will need routes to 168.11.12.64 (Ethernet off R2). Example 9-10 lists the routes in all three routers.

Example 9-10 *Static Routes*

```
R1(config)#ip route 168.11.12.64 255.255.255.192 168.11.123.202

R2(config)#ip route 168.11.11.64 255.255.255.192 168.11.123.201
R2(config)#ip route 168.11.13.64 255.255.255.192 168.11.123.203

R3(config)#ip route 168.11.12.64 255.255.255.192 168.11.123.202
```

Finally, Task 5 requests that static **frame-relay map** commands be configured. The **map** commands are necessary for each routed protocol. Also, the **broadcast** keyword is needed so that packets that would normally be broadcast, such as routing updates, will be sent as unicasts across each VC for each protocol. Example 9-11 lists the additional commands.

Example 9-11 *frame-relay map Commands*

```
R1(config)#frame-relay map ip 168.11.123.202 502 broadcast
R1(config)#frame-relay map ipx 123.0200.bbbb.bbbb 502 broadcast

R2(config)#frame-relay map ip 168.11.123.201 501 broadcast
R2(config)#frame-relay map ip 168.11.123.203 503 broadcast
R2(config)#frame-relay map ipx 123.0200.aaaa.aaaa 501 broadcast
R2(config)#frame-relay map ipx 123.0200.cccc.cccc 503 broadcast

R3(config)#frame-relay map ip 168.11.123.202 502 broadcast
R3(config)#frame-relay map ipx 123.0200.bbbb.bbbb 502 broadcast
```

Scenario 9-2, Part C—Verification and Questions

The CCNA exam tests your memory of the kinds of information you can find in the output of various **show** commands. Using Example 9-12, Example 9-13, and Example 9-14 as references, answer the questions following the examples.

NOTE   In the network from which these commands were captured, several administrative settings not mentioned in the scenario were configured. For instance, the enable password was configured. Any **show running-config** commands in the examples in this chapter might have other unrelated configuration.

Example 9-12 *Scenario 9-2, Part C—R1 show and debug Output*

```
R1#show ipx interface brief
Interface         IPX Network Encapsulation Status                 IPX State
Serial0           123         FRAME-RELAY  up                      [up]
Serial1           unassigned  not config'd administratively down   n/a
Ethernet0         110         ARPA         up                      [up]
Ethernet0         111         Novell-ether up                      [up]

R1#show ip interface brief
Interface         IP-Address      OK? Method Status                Protocol
Serial0           168.11.123.201  YES NVRAM  up                    up
Serial1           unassigned      YES unset  administratively down down
Ethernet0         168.11.11.101   YES NVRAM  up                    up

R1#debug ipx sap activity
IPX service debugging is on
R1#
IPXSAP: positing update to 110.ffff.ffff.ffff via Ethernet0 (broadcast) (full)
```

Example 9-12 *Scenario 9-2, Part C—R1* **show** *and* **debug** *Output (Continued)*

```
IPXSAP: Update type 0x2 len 96 src:110.0000.0ccf.21cd dest:110.ffff.ffff.ffff(452)
 type 0x4, "Server3", 103.0000.0000.0001(451), 4 hops
IPXSAP: positing update to 111.ffff.ffff.ffff via Ethernet0 (broadcast) (full)
IPXSAP: Update type 0x2 len 224 src:111.0000.0ccf.21cd
dest:111.ffff.ffff.ffff(452)
 type 0x4, "Server3", 103.0000.0000.0001(451), 4 hops
 type 0x4, "Server1", 101.0000.0000.0001(451), 3 hops
 type 0x4, "Server2", 102.0000.0000.0001(451), 3 hops
IPXSAP: Response (in) type 0x2 len 160 src:110.0000.0c89.b130
dest:110.ffff.ffff.ffff(452)
 type 0x4, "Server2", 102.0000.0000.0001(451), 2 hops
 type 0x4, "Server1", 101.0000.0000.0001(451), 2 hops
IPXSAP: positing update to 123.ffff.ffff.ffff via Serial0 (broadcast) (full)
IPXSAP: Update type 0x2 len 160 src:123.0200.aaaa.aaaa
dest:123.ffff.ffff.ffff(452)
 type 0x4, "Server1", 101.0000.0000.0001(451), 3 hops
 type 0x4, "Server2", 102.0000.0000.0001(451), 3 hops
IPXSAP: Response (in) type 0x2 len 96 src:123.0200.bbbb.bbbb
dest:123.ffff.ffff.ffff(452)
 type 0x4, "Server3", 103.0000.0000.0001(451), 3 hops
R1#undebug all
All possible debugging has been turned off
R1#
R1#debug ipx routing activity
IPX routing debugging is on
R1#
IPXRIP: positing full update to 123.ffff.ffff.ffff via Serial0 (broadcast)
IPXRIP: src=123.0200.aaaa.aaaa, dst=123.ffff.ffff.ffff, packet sent
    network 555, hops 2,  delay 8
    network 101, hops 3,  delay 8
    network 102, hops 3,  delay 8
    network 111, hops 1,  delay 7
    network 110, hops 1,  delay 7
IPXRIP: update from 123.0200.3333.3333
    130 in 1 hops, delay 7
IPXRIP: update from 123.0200.bbbb.bbbb
    444 in 2 hops, delay 8
    103 in 3 hops, delay 8
    121 in 1 hops, delay 7
    120 in 1 hops, delay 7
IPXRIP: positing full update to 110.ffff.ffff.ffff via Ethernet0 (broadcast)
IPXRIP: src=110.0000.0ccf.21cd, dst=110.ffff.ffff.ffff, packet sent
    network 120, hops 2,  delay 8
    network 121, hops 2,  delay 8
    network 103, hops 4,  delay 9
    network 444, hops 3,  delay 9
    network 130, hops 2,  delay 8
    network 111, hops 1,  delay 2
    network 123, hops 1,  delay 2
IPXRIP: positing full update to 111.ffff.ffff.ffff via Ethernet0 (broadcast)
IPXRIP: src=111.0000.0ccf.21cd, dst=111.ffff.ffff.ffff, packet sent
```

continues

Example 9-12 *Scenario 9-2, Part C—R1* ***show*** *and* ***debug*** *Output (Continued)*

```
        network 120, hops 2,  delay 8
        network 121, hops 2,  delay 8
        network 103, hops 4,  delay 9
        network 444, hops 3,  delay 9
        network 130, hops 2,  delay 8
        network 555, hops 2,  delay 3
        network 101, hops 3,  delay 3
        network 102, hops 3,  delay 3
        network 110, hops 1,  delay 2
        network 123, hops 1,  delay 2
IPXRIP: update from 110.0000.0c89.b130
        102 in 2 hops, delay 2
        101 in 2 hops, delay 2
        555 in 1 hops, delay 2
R1#
R1#undebug all
All possible debugging has been turned off
R1#
R1#debug ip igrp transactions
IGRP protocol debugging is on
R1#
IGRP: sending update to 255.255.255.255 via Serial0 (168.11.123.201)
        subnet 168.11.123.192, metric=180571
        subnet 168.11.11.64, metric=688
        subnet 168.11.13.64, metric=180634
        subnet 168.11.12.64, metric=180634
IGRP: sending update to 255.255.255.255 via Ethernet0 (168.11.11.101)
        subnet 168.11.123.192, metric=180571
        subnet 168.11.13.64, metric=180634
        subnet 168.11.12.64, metric=180634
IGRP: received update from 168.11.123.202 on Serial0
        subnet 168.11.123.192, metric 182571 (neighbor 180571)
        subnet 168.11.11.64, metric 182634 (neighbor 180634)
        subnet 168.11.13. 64, metric 182634 (neighbor 180634)
        subnet 168.11.12. 64, metric 180634 (neighbor 688)
IGRP: received update from 168.11.123.203 on Serial0
        subnet 168.11.123.192, metric 182571 (neighbor 8476)
        subnet 168.11.11. 64, metric 182634 (neighbor 8539)
        subnet 168.11.13. 64, metric 180634 (neighbor 688)
        subnet 168.11.12. 64, metric 182634 (neighbor 8539)
IGRP: sending update to 255.255.255.255 via Serial0 (168.11.123.201)
        subnet 168.11.123.192, metric=180571
        subnet 168.11.11. 64, metric=688
        subnet 168.11.13. 64, metric=180634
        subnet 168.11.12. 64, metric=180634
IGRP: sending update to 255.255.255.255 via Ethernet0 (168.11.11.101)
        subnet 168.11.123.192, metric=180571
        subnet 168.11.13. 64, metric=180634
        subnet 168.11.12. 64, metric=180634
R1#undebug all
All possible debugging has been turned off
```

Example 9-13 *Scenario 9-2, Part C—R2 **show** and **debug** Output*

```
R2#show interface
Serial0 is up, line protocol is up
  Hardware is HD64570
  Internet address is 168.11.123.202/26
  MTU 1500 bytes, BW 56 Kbit, DLY 20000 usec, rely 255/255, load 1/255
  Encapsulation FRAME-RELAY, loopback not set, keepalive set (10 sec)
  LMI enq sent  1657, LMI stat recvd 1651, LMI upd recvd 0, DTE LMI up
  LMI enq recvd 0, LMI stat sent  0, LMI upd sent  0
  LMI DLCI 0  LMI type is ANSI Annex D  frame relay DTE
  Broadcast queue 0/64, broadcasts sent/dropped 979/0, interface broadcasts 490
  Last input 00:00:01, output 00:00:01, output hang never
  Last clearing of "show interface" counters never
  Queuing strategy: fifo
  Output queue 0/40, 0 drops; input queue 0/75, 0 drops
  5 minute input rate 0 bits/sec, 0 packets/sec
  5 minute output rate 0 bits/sec, 0 packets/sec
     4479 packets input, 165584 bytes, 0 no buffer
     Received 1 broadcasts, 0 runts, 0 giants, 0 throttles
     0 input errors, 0 CRC, 0 frame, 0 overrun, 0 ignored, 0 abort
     4304 packets output, 154785 bytes, 0 underruns
     0 output errors, 0 collisions, 4 interface resets
     0 output buffer failures, 0 output buffers swapped out
     12 carrier transitions
     DCD=up  DSR=up  DTR=up  RTS=up  CTS=up
Serial1 is administratively down, line protocol is down
  Hardware is HD64570
  MTU 1500 bytes, BW 1544 Kbit, DLY 20000 usec, rely 255/255, load 1/255
  Encapsulation PPP, loopback not set, keepalive set (10 sec)
  LCP Closed
  Closed: CDPCP, LLC2
  Last input never, output never, output hang never
  Last clearing of "show interface" counters never
  Input queue: 0/75/0 (size/max/drops); Total output drops: 0
  Queuing strategy: weighted fair
  Output queue: 0/1000/0 (size/max total/drops)
     Conversations  0/0/64 (active/max active/threshold)
     Reserved Conversations 0/0 (allocated/max allocated)
  5 minute input rate 0 bits/sec, 0 packets/sec
  5 minute output rate 0 bits/sec, 0 packets/sec
     0 packets input, 0 bytes, 0 no buffer
     Received 0 broadcasts, 0 runts, 0 giants, 0 throttles
     0 input errors, 0 CRC, 0 frame, 0 overrun, 0 ignored, 0 abort
     0 packets output, 0 bytes, 0 underruns
     0 output errors, 0 collisions, 5 interface resets
     0 output buffer failures, 0 output buffers swapped out
     0 carrier transitions
     DCD=down  DSR=down  DTR=down  RTS=down  CTS=down
Ethernet0 is up, line protocol is up
  Hardware is MCI Ethernet, address is 0000.0c89.b170 (bia 0000.0c89.b170)
  Internet address is 168.11.12.102/26, subnet mask is 255.255.255.192
```

continues

Example 9-13 *Scenario 9-2, Part C—R2* ***show*** *and* ***debug*** *Output (Continued)*

```
   MTU 1500 bytes, BW 10000 Kbit, DLY 100000 usec, rely 255/255, load 1/255
   Encapsulation ARPA, loopback not set, keepalive set (10 sec)
   ARP type: ARPA, ARP Timeout 4:00:00
   Last input 00:00:04, output 00:00:04, output hang never
   Last clearing of "show interface" counters never
   Queuing strategy: fifo
   Output queue 0/40, 0 drops; input queue 0/75, 0 drops
   5 minute input rate 0 bits/sec, 0 packets/sec
   5 minute output rate 0 bits/sec, 0 packets/sec
      6519 packets input, 319041 bytes, 0 no buffer
      Received 5544 broadcasts, 0 runts, 0 giants, 0 throttles
      0 input errors, 0 CRC, 0 frame, 0 overrun, 0 ignored, 0 abort
      2055 packets output, 192707 bytes, 0 underruns
      0 output errors, 0 collisions, 2 interface resets
      0 output buffer failures, 0 output buffers swapped out
      6 transitions

R2#show ipx interface brief
Interface           IPX Network Encapsulation Status                IPX State
Serial0             123         FRAME-RELAY   up                    [up]
Serial1             unassigned  not config'd  administratively down n/a
Ethernet0           120         SAP           up                    [up]
Ethernet0           121         SNAP          up                    [up]

R2#show ip protocol
Routing Protocol is "igrp 1"
  Sending updates every 90 seconds, next due in 6 seconds
  Invalid after 270 seconds, hold down 280, flushed after 630
  Outgoing update filter list for all interfaces is not set
  Incoming update filter list for all interfaces is not set
  Default networks flagged in outgoing updates
  Default networks accepted from incoming updates
  IGRP metric weight K1=1, K2=0, K3=1, K4=0, K5=0
  IGRP maximum hopcount 100
  IGRP maximum metric variance 1
  Redistributing: igrp 1
  Routing for Networks:
    168.11.0.0
  Routing Information Sources:
    Gateway         Distance      Last Update
    168.11.123.201       100      00:00:02
    168.11.123.203       100      00:00:09
  Distance: (default is 100)

R2#show ipx route
Codes: C - Connected primary network,    c - Connected secondary network
       S - Static, F - Floating static, L - Local (internal), W - IPXWAN
       R - RIP, E - EIGRP, N - NLSP, X - External, A - Aggregate
       s - seconds, u - uses

9 Total IPX routes. Up to 1 parallel paths and 16 hops allowed.

No default route known.
```

Example 9-13 *Scenario 9-2, Part C—R2 **show** and **debug** Output (Continued)*

```
C       120 (SAP),          E0
c       121 (SNAP),         E0
C       123 (FRAME-RELAY),  Se0
R       101 [08/03] via     123.0200.aaaa.aaaa,    21s, Se0
R       102 [02/02] via     123.0200.0cac.70ef,    22s, E0
R       103 [08/03] via     120.0000.aaaa.aaaa,    29s, Se0
R       110 [07/01] via     123.0200.aaaa.aaaa,    22s, Se0
R       111 [07/01] via     123.0200.aaaa.aaaa,    22s, Se0
R       130 [07/01] via     123.0200.cccc.cccc,    19s, Se0

R2#show ipx servers
Codes: S - Static, P - Periodic, E - EIGRP, N - NLSP, H - Holddown, + = detail
2 Total IPX Servers

Table ordering is based on routing and server info

    Type Name                     Net     Address       Port     Route Hops Itf
P    4 Server3                 103.0000.0000.0001:0451    8/03    3  Se0
P    4 Server1                 101.0000.0000.0001:0451    8/03    3  Se0
P    4 Server2                 102.0000.0000.0001:0451    2/02    2  E0

R2#show frame-relay pvc

PVC Statistics for interface Serial0 (Frame Relay DTE)

DLCI = 501, DLCI USAGE = LOCAL, PVC STATUS = ACTIVE, INTERFACE = Serial0

  input pkts 780          output pkts 529        in bytes 39602
  out bytes 29260         dropped pkts 0         in FECN pkts 0
  in BECN pkts 0          out FECN pkts 0        out BECN pkts 0
  in DE pkts 0            out DE pkts 0
  out bcast pkts 525      out bcast bytes 28924
  pvc create time 04:36:40, last time pvc status changed 04:34:54
DLCI = 503, DLCI USAGE = LOCAL, PVC STATUS = ACTIVE, INTERFACE = Serial0

  input pkts 481          output pkts 493        in bytes 30896
  out bytes 34392         dropped pkts 0         in FECN pkts 0
  in BECN pkts 0          out FECN pkts 0        out BECN pkts 0
  in DE pkts 0            out DE pkts 0
  out bcast pkts 493      out bcast bytes 34392
  pvc create time 04:36:41, last time pvc status changed 04:34:55

R2#show frame-relay map
Serial0 (up): ipx 123.0200.aaaa.aaaa dlci 501(0x1F5,0x7C50), dynamic,
              broadcast,, status defined, active
Serial0 (up): ipx 123.0200.cccc.cccc dlci 503(0x1F7,0x7C70), dynamic,
              broadcast,, status defined, active
Serial0 (up): ip 168.11.123.201 dlci 501(0x1F5,0x7C50), dynamic,
              broadcast,, status defined, active
Serial0 (up): ip 168.11.123.203 dlci 503(0x1F7,0x7C70), dynamic,
              broadcast,, status defined, active
```

Example 9-14 *Scenario 9-2, Part C—R3* **show** *and* **debug** *Output*

```
R3#show running-config
Building configuration...

Current configuration:
!
version 11.2
no service password-encryption
no service udp-small-servers
no service tcp-small-servers
!
hostname R3
!
enable secret 5 $1$kI1V$NkybGlP9tzP7BYvAKYT.c1
!
no ip domain-lookup
ipx routing 0200.cccc.cccc
!
interface Serial0
 ip address 168.11.123.203 255.255.255.192
 encapsulation frame-relay
 ipx network 123
 no fair-queue
 frame-relay interface-dlci 501
 frame-relay interface-dlci 502
!
interface Serial1
 no ip address
 encapsulation ppp
 shutdown
 clockrate 56000
!
interface Ethernet0
 ip address 168.11.13.103 255.255.255.192
 ipx network 130
 ring-speed 16
!
router igrp 1
 network 168.11.0.0
!
no ip classless
!
!
!
!
line con 0
 password cisco
 login
line aux 0
line vty 0 4
 password cisco
 login
!
end
```

Example 9-14 *Scenario 9-2, Part C—R3* ***show*** *and* ***debug*** *Output (Continued)*

```
R3#show ip arp
Protocol  Address           Age (min)  Hardware Addr   Type   Interface
Internet  168.11.13.103        -       0000.0c89.b1b0  SNAP   Ethernet0

R3#show ip route
Codes: C - connected, S - static, I - IGRP, R - RIP, M - mobile, B - BGP
       D - EIGRP, EX - EIGRP external, O - OSPF, IA - OSPF inter area
       N1 - OSPF NSSA external type 1, N2 - OSPF NSSA external type 2
       E1 - OSPF external type 1, E2 - OSPF external type 2, E - EGP
       i - IS-IS, L1 - IS-IS level-1, L2 - IS-IS level-2, * - candidate default
       U - per-user static route, o - ODR

Gateway of last resort is not set

     168.11.0.0/26 is subnetted, 4 subnets
C       168.11.123.192 is directly connected, Serial0
I       168.11.11.64 [100/8539] via 168.11.123.201, 00:00:06, Serial0
C       168.11.13. 64 is directly connected, Ethernet0
I       168.11.12. 64 [100/8539] via 168.11.123.202, 00:00:46, Serial0

R3#ping 168.11.11.80

Type escape sequence to abort.
Sending 5, 100-byte ICMP Echos to 168.11.11.80, timeout is 2 seconds:
!!!!!
Success rate is 100 percent (5/5), round-trip min/avg/max = 76/76/76 ms

R3#trace 168.11.11.80

Type escape sequence to abort.
Tracing the route to 168.11.11.80

  1 168.11.123.201 44 msec 44 msec 44 msec
  2 168.11.11.250 44 msec *   40 msec

R3#show ipx servers
Codes: S - Static, P - Periodic, E - EIGRP, N - NLSP, H - Holddown, + = detail
3 Total IPX Servers

Table ordering is based on routing and server info

    Type Name                  Net      Address    Port    Route Hops Itf
P     4 Server1                101.0000.0000.0001:0451     8/03   3  Se0
P     4 Server2                102.0000.0000.0001:0451     8/03   3  Se0
P     4 Server3                103.0000.0000.0001:0451     2/02   2  E0

R3#show frame-relay map
Serial0 (up): ipx 123.0200.aaaa.aaaa dlci 501(0x1F5,0x7C50), dynamic,
              broadcast,, status defined, active
Serial0 (up): ipx 123.0200.bbbb.bbbb dlci 502(0x1F6,0x7C60), dynamic,
              broadcast,, status defined, active
```

continues

Example 9-14 *Scenario 9-2, Part C—R3 **show** and **debug** Output (Continued)*

```
Serial0 (up): ip 168.11.123.201 dlci 501(0x1F5,0x7C50), dynamic,
               broadcast,, status defined, active
Serial0 (up): ip 168.11.123.202 dlci 502(0x1F6,0x7C60), dynamic,
               broadcast,, status defined, active

R3#show frame-relay lmi

LMI Statistics for interface Serial0 (Frame Relay DTE) LMI TYPE = CISCO
  Invalid Unnumbered info 0         Invalid Prot Disc 0
  Invalid dummy Call Ref 0          Invalid Msg Type 0
  Invalid Status Message 0          Invalid Lock Shift 0
  Invalid Information ID 0          Invalid Report IE Len 0
  Invalid Report Request 0          Invalid Keep IE Len 0
  Num Status Enq. Sent 1677         Num Status msgs Rcvd 1677
  Num Update Status Rcvd 0          Num Status Timeouts 0
```

Using Example 9-12, Example 9-13, and Example 9-14 as references, answer the following questions:

1 What command tells you how much time must elapse before the next IP IGRP update is sent by a router?

2 What command shows you a summary of the IP addresses on that router?

3 What **show** command identifies which routes were learned with IP IGRP? What about with IPX RIP? What in the command output identifies these routing protocols?

4 What **show** command lists SAP information in the router?

5 Describe the contents of an IP IGRP update from R1 to R3. What **debug** command options provide the details of what is in the IGRP update?

6 What password is required to move from user mode to privileged mode? What configuration command(s) can be used to set the password that is required?

7 If a serial interface configuration subcommand you cannot recall starts with the letter D, how can you get help to list all commands that start with D? List all steps; assume that you are in privileged mode.

8 After changing the configuration and moving back to privileged mode, you want to save your configuration. Name the two commands that can be used.

9 List all characters displayed onscreen during the process of getting into configuration mode from privileged mode, changing the host name from R1 to R2, and then getting back to privileged mode.

10 In this network, if setup mode were used to configure the IP addresses on the interface, how would the subnet mask information be entered?

11 If a routing loop occurred so that IP packets destined to 168.11.12.66 were routed between routers continually, what stops the packet from rotating forever? Are any notification messages sent when the routers notice what is happening? If so, what is the message(s)?

12 Describe the role of R1 relating to TCP error recovery for an FTP connection between PC11 and PC21.

13 Define integrated multiprotocol routing.

14 Describe how R2 learns that R1's IP address is 168.11.123.201.

15 What does NBMA stand for?

16 When does IGRP use split-horizon rules on interfaces with Frame Relay encapsulation?

17 What effect does the **no keepalive** interface subcommand have on Frame Relay interfaces?

18 If just the VC between R1 and R3 needed to use encapsulation of **ietf**, what configuration changes would be needed?

19 What command lists the total number of Status Enquiry messages received on a Frame Relay interface?

20 List examples of two ISDN function groups.

21 What type of ISDN channel is used for signaling?

Solutions to Scenario 9-2, Part C—Verification and Questions

The answers to the questions for Scenario 9-2, Part C are as follows:

1 The **show ip protocol** command (refer to Example 9-13) gives this information.

2 The **show ip interface brief** command (refer to Example 9-12) gives this information.

3 The **show ip route** and **show ipx route** commands list the metric values (refer to Examples 9-5 and 9-6). The metric value for each IP subnet is the second of the two numbers inside brackets. Two IPX metrics are located between brackets for IPX routes: the number of timer ticks and the number of hops.

4 The **show ipx servers** command (refer to Example 9-14) lists this information.

5 The **debug ip igrp transaction** command provides **debug** output with details of the IGRP updates. The output immediately follows the **IGRP: sending update to 255.255.255.255 via Serial0 (168.11.123.201)** message in Example 9-12. Notice that all four routes are advertised because split horizon is disabled on the serial interface when no subinterfaces are used.

6 The enable password is the required password; the user is prompted after typing the **enable** EXEC command. The **enable** and **enable secret** commands define the password; if both are configured, the **enable secret** password is used.

7 The steps are as follows:

```
R3#configure terminal
R3(config)#interface serial 0
R3(config-if)#D?

dce-terminal-timing-enable  default           delay  description  dialer
dialer-group                down-when-looped  dspu   dxi
R3(config-if)#d#Ctrl-Z
R3#
```

8 **write memory** and **copy running-config startup-config** are the two commands that could be used.

9 The onscreen code is as follows:

```
R1#configure terminal
R1(config)#hostname R2
R2(config)Ctrl-Z
R2#
```

The most important part of this question is to realize that configuration changes are immediate. Notice that the prompt is changed immediately after the **hostname** command.

10 Enter the mask information as the number of subnet bits rather than simply typing the mask. In this network, mask 255.255.255.192 implies 6 host bits. A Class B network is used, which implies 16 network bits, leaving 10 subnet bits.

11 The Time To Live field in the IP header is decremented by each router. After the number is decremented to 0, the router discards the packet. That router also sends an ICMP TTL-exceeded message to the host that originally sent the packet.

12 The router plays no role in TCP error recovery in this case. The endpoint hosts are responsible for the TCP processing.

13 Integrated multiprotocol routing means that routed protocols IP, IPX, and AppleTalk use a common routing protocol, which consolidates routing updates.

14 Inverse ARP is used by R1 to announce its IP and IPX addresses on the serial interface used for Frame Relay. The Inverse ARP message is sent over the VC between the two routers. R2 learns based on receiving the message.

15 NBMA stands for nonbroadcast multiaccess.

16 IGRP uses split horizon on point-to-point subinterfaces only. If multipoint subinterfaces are used, or if no subinterfaces are used, split horizon is off by default.

17 LMI keepalive messages, which flow between the router and the switch, are no longer sent. No keepalive messages pass from router to router.

18 The **frame-relay interface-dlci** command could be changed on Router1 and Router3 to include the keyword **ietf** at the end of the command—for example, **frame-relay interface-dlci 501 ietf** on R3.

19 The **show frame-relay lmi** command (refer to Example 9-14) lists this information.

20 NT1, NT2, TE1, TE2, and TA are all function groups.

21 D channels are used for signaling.

Scenario 9-3

Part A of the final review scenario begins with some planning guidelines that include planning IP addresses, IPX network numbers, the location of SAP filters, and the location of IP standard access lists. After you complete Part A, Part B of Scenario 9-3 asks you to configure the three routers to implement the planned design and a few other features. Finally, in Part C of Scenario 9-3, some errors have been introduced into the network, and you are asked to examine router command output to find the errors. Part C of Scenario 9-3 also lists some questions relating to the user interface and protocol specifications.

Scenario 9-3, Part A—Planning

Your job is to deploy a new network with three sites, as shown in Figure 9-5. The decision to use Frame Relay, as well as the product choices, has already been made. To complete Scenario 9-3, Part A, perform the following tasks:

1 Plan the IP addressing and subnets used in this network. Class B network 170.1.0.0 has been assigned by the NIC. The maximum number of hosts per subnet is 300. Assign IP addresses to the PCs as well. Use Table 9-10 and Table 9-11 to record your answers.

2 Plan the IPX network numbers to be used. You can choose the internal network numbers of the servers as well. Each LAN should support both SAP and SNAP encapsulations.

3 Plan the location and logic of IP access lists to filter for the following criteria:

   — Access to servers in PC11 and PC12 is allowed for Web and FTP clients from anywhere else.

   — All other traffic to or from PC11 and PC12 is not allowed.

   — No IP traffic between the Ethernets off R2 and R3 is allowed.

   — All other IP traffic between any sites is allowed.

4 Plan the location and logic of SAP filters. Ensure that Server 3 is accessed only by clients on the Ethernet off R2.

5 After your subnet numbers are chosen, calculate the broadcast addresses and the range of valid IP addresses in each subnet. Use Table 9-12, if convenient.

Figure 9-5   *Scenario 9-3 Network Diagram*

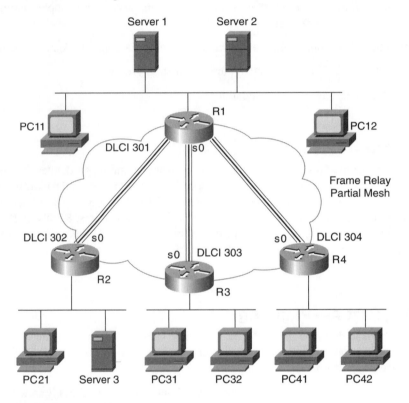

Table 9-10   *Scenario 9-3, Part A—IP Subnet and IPX Network Planning Chart*

Location of Subnet/ Network Geographically	Subnet Mask	Subnet Number	IPX Network
Ethernet off R1			
Ethernet off R2			
Ethernet off R3			
Ethernet off R4			
Virtual circuit between R1 and R2			

Table 9-10   *Scenario 9-3, Part A—IP Subnet and IPX Network Planning Chart (Continued)*

Location of Subnet/ Network Geographically	Subnet Mask	Subnet Number	IPX Network
Virtual circuit between R1 and R3			
Virtual circuit between R1 and R4			
Server 1 internal			
Server 2 internal			
Server 3 internal			

Table 9-11   *Scenario 9-3, Part A—IP Address Planning Chart*

Host	Address
PC11	
PC12	
PC21	
PC31	
PC32	
PC41	
PC42	
R1-E0	
R1-S0-sub _____	
R1-S0-sub _____	
R1-S0-sub _____	
R2-E0	
R2-S0-sub _____	
R3-E0	
R3-S0-sub _____	
R4-E0	
R4-S0-sub _____	
Server 1	
Server 2	
Server 3	

Table 9-12   *Scenario 9-3, Part A—IP Subnet Planning Chart*

Subnet Number	Subnet Broadcast Address	Range of Valid Addresses

Solutions to Scenario 9-3, Part A—Planning Answers

The IP subnet design includes the use of mask 255.255.254.0. The same mask is used throughout the network, therefore at least 9 host bits are needed because at least one subnet contains 300 hosts.

The IPX network number assignment process is straightforward when using multiple encapsulations on the same Ethernet—you simply have to chose two different network numbers, one per encapsulation type. Each encapsulation type on the router requires the use of a separate IPX network. The subnets, networks, and IP addresses are recorded in Table 9-13 and Table 9-14.

Table 9-13   *Scenario 9-3, Part A—IP Subnet and IPX Network Planning Chart Completed*

Location of Subnet/ Network Geographically	Subnet Mask	Subnet Number	IPX Network
Ethernet off R1	255.255.254.0	170.1.2.0	2, 3
Ethernet off R2	255.255.254.0	170.1.4.0	4, 5
Ethernet off R3	255.255.254.0	170.1.6.0	6, 7
Ethernet off R4	255.255.254.0	170.1.8.0	8, 9
Virtual circuit between R1 and R2	255.255.254.0	170.1.10.0	10
Virtual circuit between R1 and R3	255.255.254.0	170.1.12.0	12
Virtual circuit between R1 and R4	255.255.254.0	170.1.14.0	14
Server 1 internal	—	—	101

Table 9-13   *Scenario 9-3, Part A—IP Subnet and IPX Network Planning Chart Completed (Continued)*

Location of Subnet/ Network Geographically	Subnet Mask	Subnet Number	IPX Network
Server 2 internal	—	—	102
Server 3 internal	—	—	103

The choice of IP addresses can conform to any standard you like, as long as the addresses are in the correct subnets. Refer to Table 9-15 for the list of valid addresses for the subnets chosen. In Table 9-14, a convention is used such that the numbers reflect the number of the PC. For the routers, the convention uses addresses in the second half of the range of addresses in each subnet; this convention is used simply as a reminder of the addresses that are valid in this subnetting scheme.

Table 9-14   *Scenario 9-3, Part A—IP Address Planning Chart Completed*

Host	Address
PC11	170.1.2.11
PC12	170.1.2.12
PC21	170.1.4.21
PC31	170.1.6.31
PC32	170.1.6.32
PC41	170.1.8.41
PC42	170.1.8.42
R1-E0	170.1.3.1
R1-S0-sub __2__	170.1.10.1
R1-S0-sub __3__	170.1.12.1
R1-S0-sub __4__	170.1.14.1
R2-E0	170.1.5.2
R2-S0-sub __2__	170.1.10.2
R3-E0	170.1.7.3
R3-S0-sub __3__	170.1.12.3
R4-E0	170.1.9.4
R4-S0-sub __4__	170.1.14.4
Server 1	170.1.2.101
Server 2	170.1.2.102
Server 3	170.1.4.103

The IP access lists can be placed in several places effectively. Stopping packets in one of the two directions will succeed in stopping users from actually connecting to the servers. For the first set of criteria, an access list stopping packets from entering the serial interface of R1, thus stopping packets destined to PC11 and PC12, will suffice. For the second criteria to disallow traffic between Site 2 and Site 3, the access lists are also placed in R1. The access lists will stop the packets earlier in their life if they are placed in R2 and R3, but the traffic will be minimal because no true application traffic will ever successfully be generated between IP hosts at Sites 2 and 3.

So, the design shown here calls for all filtered packets to be filtered via access lists enabled on subinterfaces on R1's S0 interface. Other options are valid as well.

The SAP filter can be placed in several places, but there is one very obvious location. A SAP filter is added on R2 to filter Server 3 from the SAP table. The filter could filter incoming SAPs on R2's E0 or filter outgoing SAP updates out R2's S0 port. In this case, anticipating the day that a second Ethernet port is used on R2, and anticipating the fact that the objective probably meant that local clients should have access to Server 3, the plan in this case is to filter outbound SAPs on R2's S0 interface.

Finally, the broadcast addresses for each subnet are shown in Table 9-15. As a reminder, to calculate the broadcast address, you should write down the subnet number in binary. Then copy down the network and subnet portions of the subnet number directly below it, leaving the host bit positions empty. Then write all binary 1s in the host bit positions. Finally, convert the number back to decimal, 8 bits at a time. The result is the subnet broadcast address and is the high end of the range of assignable addresses in that subnet.

Table 9-15 shows the answers, which include the subnet numbers, their corresponding broadcast addresses, and the range of valid assignable IP addresses.

Table 9-15 *Scenario 9-3, Part A—IP Subnet Planning Chart*

Subnet Number	Subnet Broadcast Address	Range of Valid Addresses (Last 2 Bytes)
170.1.2.0	170.1.3.255	2.1 through 3.254
170.1.4.0	170.1.5.255	4.1 through 5.254
170.1.6.0	170.1.7.255	6.1 through 7.254
170.1.8.0	170.1.9.255	8.1 through 9.254
170.1.10.0	170.1.11.255	10.1 through 11.254
170.1.12.0	170.1.13.255	12.1 through 13.254
170.1.14.0	170.1.15.255	14.1 through 15.254

Scenario 9-3, Part B—Configuration

The next step in your job is to deploy the network designed in Scenario 9-3, Part A. Use the solutions to Scenario 9-3, Part A to direct you in identifying IP and IPX addresses, access lists, and the encapsulations to be used. For Scenario 9-3, Part B, perform the following tasks:

1 Configure IP and IPX to be routed. Use IP IGRP and IPX RIP as routing protocols. Use IGRP process-id 1.

2 Use secondary IPX addresses to accommodate the multiple IPX encapsulation types described in Scenario 9-3, Part A.

3 Configure Frame Relay using point-to-point subinterfaces. R1's attached Frame Relay switch uses LMI type ANSI. Cisco encapsulation should be used for all routers, except for the VC between R1 and R4.

Solutions to Scenario 9-3, Part B—Configuration

Examples 9-15 through 9-18 show the configurations for Tasks 1, 2, and 3 for Part B of Scenario 3.

Example 9-15 *R1 Configuration*

```
ipx routing 0200.aaaa.aaaa
!
interface serial0
encapsulation frame-relay
interface serial 0.2 point-to-point
 ip address  170.1.10.1  255.255.254.0
 ipx network  10
 frame-relay interface-dlci 302
 ip access-group 102 in
!
interface serial 0.3 point-to-point
 ip address  170.1.12.1  255.255.254.0
 ipx network  12
 frame-relay interface-dlci 303
 ip access-group 103 in
!
interface serial 0.4 point-to-point
 ip address  170.1.14.1  255.255.254.0
 ipx network  14
 frame-relay interface-dlci 304 ietf
 ip access-group 104 in
!
interface ethernet 0
ip address  170.1.3.1  255.255.254.0
ipx network  2 encapsulation sap
ipx network  3 encapsulation snap secondary
!
router igrp 1
```

continues

Example 9-15 *R1 Configuration (Continued)*

```
network 170.1.0.0

!
access-list 102 permit tcp any host 170.1.2.11 eq ftp
access-list 102 permit tcp any host 170.1.2.11 eq www
access-list 102 permit tcp any host 170.1.2.12 eq ftp
access-list 102 permit tcp any host 170.1.2.12 eq www
access-list 102 deny ip any host 170.1.2.11
access-list 102 deny ip any host 170.1.2.12
access-list 102 deny ip 170.1.4.0 0.0.1.255 170.1.6.0 0.0.1.255
access-list 102 permit ip any any

access-list 103 permit tcp any host 170.1.2.11 eq ftp
access-list 103 permit tcp any host 170.1.2.11 eq www
access-list 103 permit tcp any host 170.1.2.12 eq ftp
access-list 103 permit tcp any host 170.1.2.12 eq www
access-list 103 deny ip any host 170.1.2.11
access-list 103 deny ip any host 170.1.2.12
access-list 103 deny ip 170.1.6.0 0.0.1.255 170.1.4.0 0.0.1.255
access-list 103 permit ip any any

access-list 104 permit tcp any host 170.1.2.11 eq ftp
access-list 104 permit tcp any host 170.1.2.11 eq www
access-list 104 permit tcp any host 170.1.2.12 eq ftp
access-list 104 permit tcp any host 170.1.2.12 eq www
access-list 104 deny ip any host 170.1.2.11
access-list 104 deny ip any host 170.1.2.12
access-list 104 permit ip any any
```

Example 9-16 *R2 Configuration*

```
ipx routing 0200.bbbb.bbbb
!
interface serial0
encapsulation frame-relay
interface serial 0.1 point-to-point
 ip address  170.1.10.2  255.255.254.0
 ipx network  10
 frame-relay interface-dlci 301
 ipx output-sap-filter 1001
!
interface ethernet 0
ip address  170.1.5.2  255.255.254.0
ipx network  4 encapsulation sap
ipx network  5 encapsulation snap secondary
!
router igrp 1
network 170.1.0.0
!
access-list 1001 deny 103
access-list 1001 permit -1
```

Example 9-17 *R3 Configuration*

```
ipx routing 0200.cccc.cccc
!
interface serial0
encapsulation frame-relay
interface serial 0.1 point-to-point
 ip address  170.1.12.3  255.255.254.0
 ipx network  12
 frame-relay interface-dlci 301
!
interface ethernet 0
ip address  170.1.7.3  255.255.254.0
ipx network  6 encapsulation sap
ipx network  7 encapsulation snap secondary
!
router igrp 1
network 170.1.0.0
```

Example 9-18 *R4 Configuration*

```
ipx routing 0200.dddd.dddd
!
interface serial0
encapsulation frame-relay ietf
interface serial 0.1 point-to-point
 ip address  170.1.14.4  255.255.254.0
 ipx network  14
 frame-relay interface-dlci 301
!
interface ethernet 0
ip address  170.1.9.4  255.255.254.0
ipx network  8 encapsulation sap
ipx network  9 encapsulation snap secondary
!
router igrp 1
network 170.1.0.0
```

Three different access lists are shown on R1. List 102 is used for packets entering subinterface 2. List 103 is used for packets entering subinterface 3, and list 104 is used for packets entering subinterface 4. Lists 102 and 103 check for packets between sites 2 and 3, and they also check for packets to PC11 and PC12. The mask used to check all hosts in subnets 170.1.4.0 and 170.1.6.0 is rather tricky. The mask represents 23 binary 0s and 9 binary 1s, meaning that the first 23 bits of the number in the access list must match the first 23 bits in the source or destination address in the packet. This matches all hosts in each subnet because there are 23 combined network and subnet bits.

Two IPX networks are used on each Ethernet because two encapsulations are used.

The Frame Relay configuration was relatively straightforward. The LMI type is autosensed. The encapsulation of **ietf** between R1 and R4 is configured in two ways. First, R1 uses the **ietf** keyword on the **frame-relay interface-dlci** command. On R4, the **encapsulation** command lists the **ietf** option, implying **ietf** encapsulation for all VCs on this serial interface.

Scenario 9-3, Part C—Verification and Questions

The CCNA exam tests your memory of the kinds of information you can find in the output of various **show** commands. Using Examples 9-19 through 9-22 as references, answer the questions following the examples.

Example 9-19 *Scenario 9-3, Part C—R1* **show** *and* **debug** *Output*

```
R1#show ip interface brief
Interface          IP-Address      OK? Method Status                Protocol
Serial0            unassigned      YES unset  up                    up
Serial0.2          170.1.10.1      YES NVRAM  up                    up
Serial0.3          170.1.12.1      YES NVRAM  up                    up
Serial0.4          170.1.14.1      YES NVRAM  up                    up
Serial1            unassigned      YES unset  administratively down down
Ethernet0          170.1.3.1       YES NVRAM  up                    up


R1#show cdp neighbor detail
-------------------------
Device ID: R2
Entry address(es):
  IP address: 170.1.10.2
  Novell address: 10.0200.bbbb.bbbb
Platform: cisco 2500,  Capabilities: Router
Interface: Serial0.2,  Port ID (outgoing port): Serial0.1
Holdtime : 132 sec
Version :
Cisco Internetwork Operating System Software
IOS (tm) 2500 Software (C2500-AINR-L), Version 11.2(11), RELEASE SOFTWARE (fc1)
Copyright  1986-1997 by Cisco Systems, Inc.
Compiled Mon 29-Dec-97 18:47 by ckralik


-------------------------
Device ID: R3
Entry address(es):
  IP address: 170.1.12.3
  Novell address: 12.0200.cccc.cccc
Platform: Cisco 2500,  Capabilities: Router
Interface: Serial0.3,  Port ID (outgoing port): Serial0.1
Holdtime : 148 sec

Version :
Cisco Internetwork Operating System Software
IOS (tm) 2500 Software (C2500-AINR-L), Version 11.2(11), RELEASE SOFTWARE (fc1)
Copyright  1986-1997 by Cisco Systems, Inc.
Compiled Mon 29-Dec-97 18:47 by ckralik
```

Example 9-19 *Scenario 9-3, Part C—R1* **show** *and* **debug** *Output (Continued)*

```
- - - - - - - - - - - - - - - - - - - - - - - -
Device ID: R4
Entry address(es):
  IP address: 170.1.14.4
  Novell address: 14.0200.dddd.dddd
Platform: Cisco 2500,  Capabilities: Router
Interface: Serial0.4,  Port ID (outgoing port): Serial0.1
Holdtime : 149 sec

Version :
Cisco Internetwork Operating System Software
IOS (tm) 2500 Software (C2500-AINR-L), Version 11.2(11), RELEASE SOFTWARE (fc1)
Copyright  1986-1997 by Cisco Systems, Inc.
Compiled Mon 29-Dec-97 18:47 by ckralik

R1#show ipx servers
Codes: S - Static, P - Periodic, E - EIGRP, N - NLSP, H - Holddown, + = detail
2 Total IPX Servers

Table ordering is based on routing and server info

    Type Name                       Net     Address   Port    Route Hops Itf
P     4 Server1                     101.0000.0000.0001:0451    2/02   2  E0
P     4 Server2                     102.0000.0000.0001:0451    2/02   2  E0
R1#
R1#debug ipx sap activity
IPX service debugging is on

R1#
IPXSAP: positing update to 2.ffff.ffff.ffff via Ethernet0 (broadcast) (full)
IPXSAP: suppressing null update to 2.ffff.ffff.ffff
IPXSAP: positing update to 3.ffff.ffff.ffff via Ethernet0 (broadcast) (full)
IPXSAP: Update type 0x2 len 160 src:3.0000.0ccf.21cd dest:3.ffff.ffff.ffff(452)
 type 0x4, "Server2", 102.0000.0000.0001(451), 3 hops
 type 0x4, "Server1", 101.0000.0000.0001(451), 3 hops
IPXSAP: Response (in) type 0x2 len 160 src:2.0000.0c89.b130
dest:2.ffff.ffff.ffff(452)
 type 0x4, "Server1", 101.0000.0000.0001(451), 2 hops
 type 0x4, "Server2", 102.0000.0000.0001(451), 2 hops
IPXSAP: positing update to 10.ffff.ffff.ffff via Serial0.2 (broadcast) (full)
IPXSAP: Update type 0x2 len 160 src:10.0200.aaaa.aaaa dest:10.ffff.ffff.ffff(452)
 type 0x4, "Server2", 102.0000.0000.0001(451), 3 hops
 type 0x4, "Server1", 101.0000.0000.0001(451), 3 hops
IPXSAP: positing update to 14.ffff.ffff.ffff via Serial0.4 (broadcast) (full)
IPXSAP: Update type 0x2 len 160 src:14.0200.aaaa.aaaa dest:14.ffff.ffff.ffff(452)
 type 0x4, "Server2", 102.0000.0000.0001(451), 3 hops
 type 0x4, "Server1", 101.0000.0000.0001(451), 3 hops
IPXSAP: positing update to 12.ffff.ffff.ffff via Serial0.3 (broadcast) (full)
IPXSAP: Update type 0x2 len 160 src:12.0200.aaaa.aaaa dest:12.ffff.ffff.ffff(452)
 type 0x4, "Server2", 102.0000.0000.0001(451), 3 hops
 type 0x4, "Server1", 101.0000.0000.0001(451), 3 hops
```

continues

Example 9-19 *Scenario 9-3, Part C—R1* **show** *and* **debug** *Output (Continued)*

```
R1#undebug all
All possible debugging has been turned off
R1#
R1#debug ipx routing activity

IPX routing debugging is on
R1#
IPXRIP: update from 12.0200.cccc.cccc
    7 in 1 hops, delay 7
    6 in 1 hops, delay 7
IPXRIP: positing full update to 14.ffff.ffff.ffff via Serial0.4 (broadcast)
IPXRIP: src=14.0200.aaaa.aaaa, dst=14.ffff.ffff.ffff, packet sent
    network 4, hops 2,  delay 13
    network 5, hops 2,  delay 13
    network 103, hops 4,  delay 14
    network 10, hops 1,  delay 7
    network 6, hops 2,  delay 13
    network 7, hops 2,  delay 13
    network 3, hops 1,  delay 7
    network 2, hops 1,  delay 7
    network 101, hops 3,  delay 8
    network 102, hops 3,  delay 8
    network 12, hops 1,  delay 7
IPXRIP: positing full update to 12.ffff.ffff.ffff via Serial0.3 (broadcast)
IPXRIP: src=12.0200.aaaa.aaaa, dst=12.ffff.ffff.ffff, packet sent
    network 8, hops 2,  delay 13
    network 9, hops 2,  delay 13
    network 14, hops 1,  delay 7
    network 4, hops 2,  delay 13
    network 5, hops 2,  delay 13
    network 103, hops 4,  delay 14
    network 10, hops 1,  delay 7
    network 3, hops 1,  delay 7
    network 2, hops 1,  delay 7
    network 101, hops 3,  delay 8
    network 102, hops 3,  delay 8
IPXRIP: update from 14.0200.dddd.dddd
    9 in 1 hops, delay 7
    8 in 1 hops, delay 7
IPXRIP: update from 10.0200.bbbb.bbbb
    444 in 2 hops, delay 8
    103 in 3 hops, delay 8
    5 in 1 hops, delay 7
    4 in 1 hops, delay 7
IPXRIP: positing full update to 3.ffff.ffff.ffff via Ethernet0 (broadcast)
IPXRIP: src=3.0000.0ccf.21cd, dst=3.ffff.ffff.ffff, packet sent
    network 8, hops 2,  delay 8
    network 9, hops 2,  delay 8
    network 14, hops 1,  delay 2
    network 4, hops 2,  delay 8
    network 5, hops 2,  delay 8
    network 103, hops 4,  delay 9
```

Example 9-19 *Scenario 9-3, Part C—R1* **show** *and* **debug** *Output (Continued)*

```
            network 10, hops 1,  delay 2
            network 6, hops 2,  delay 8
            network 7, hops 2,  delay 8
            network 2, hops 1,  delay 2
            network 101, hops 3,  delay 3
            network 102, hops 3,  delay 3
            network 12, hops 1,  delay 2
IPXRIP: update from 2.0000.0c89.b130
      102 in 2 hops, delay 2
      101 in 2 hops, delay 2
IPXRIP: positing full update to 2.ffff.ffff.ffff via Ethernet0 (broadcast)
IPXRIP: src=2.0000.0ccf.21cd, dst=2.ffff.ffff.ffff, packet sent
            network 8, hops 2,  delay 8
            network 9, hops 2,  delay 8
            network 14, hops 1,  delay 2
            network 4, hops 2,  delay 8
            network 5, hops 2,  delay 8
            network 103, hops 4,  delay 9
            network 10, hops 1,  delay 2
            network 6, hops 2,  delay 8
            network 7, hops 2,  delay 8
            network 3, hops 1,  delay 2
            network 12, hops 1,  delay 2
IPXRIP: positing full update to 10.ffff.ffff.ffff via Serial0.2 (broadcast)
IPXRIP: src=10.0200.aaaa.aaaa, dst=10.ffff.ffff.ffff, packet sent
            network 8, hops 2,  delay 13
            network 9, hops 2,  delay 13
            network 14, hops 1,  delay 7
            network 6, hops 2,  delay 13
            network 7, hops 2,  delay 13
            network 3, hops 1,  delay 7
            network 2, hops 1,  delay 7
            network 101, hops 3,  delay 8
            network 102, hops 3,  delay 8
            network 12, hops 1,  delay 7
R1#
R1#undebug all
All possible debugging has been turned off
R1#
R1#debug ip igrp transactions
IGRP protocol debugging is on
R1#
IGRP: received update from 170.1.14.4 on Serial0.4
        subnet 170.1.8.0, metric 8539 (neighbor 688)
IGRP: sending update to 255.255.255.255 via Serial0.2 (170.1.10.1)
        subnet 170.1.8.0, metric=8539
        subnet 170.1.14.0, metric=8476
        subnet 170.1.12.0, metric=8476
        subnet 170.1.2.0, metric=688
        subnet 170.1.6.0, metric=8539
IGRP: sending update to 255.255.255.255 via Serial0.3 (170.1.12.1)
        subnet 170.1.10.0, metric=8476
```

continues

Example 9-19 *Scenario 9-3, Part C—R1* **show** *and* **debug** *Output (Continued)*

```
          subnet 170.1.8.0, metric=8539
          subnet 170.1.14.0, metric=8476
          subnet 170.1.2.0, metric=688
          subnet 170.1.4.0, metric=8539
IGRP: sending update to 255.255.255.255 via Serial0.4 (170.1.14.1)
          subnet 170.1.10.0, metric=8476
          subnet 170.1.12.0, metric=8476
          subnet 170.1.2.0, metric=688
          subnet 170.1.6.0, metric=8539
          subnet 170.1.4.0, metric=8539
IGRP: sending update to 255.255.255.255 via Ethernet0 (170.1.3.1)
          subnet 170.1.10.0, metric=8476
          subnet 170.1.8.0, metric=8539
          subnet 170.1.14.0, metric=8476
          subnet 170.1.12.0, metric=8476
          subnet 170.1.6.0, metric=8539
          subnet 170.1.4.0, metric=8539
IGRP: received update from 170.1.10.2 on Serial0.2
          subnet 170.1.4.0, metric 8539 (neighbor 688)
IGRP: received update from 170.1.12.3 on Serial0.3
          subnet 170.1.6.0, metric 8539 (neighbor 688)
R1#
R1#undebug all
All possible debugging has been turned off
```

Example 9-20 *Scenario 9-3, Part C—R2* **show** *and* **debug** *Output*

```
R2#show interface
Serial0 is up, line protocol is up
  Hardware is HD64570
  MTU 1500 bytes, BW 56 Kbit, DLY 20000 usec, rely 255/255, load 1/255
  Encapsulation FRAME-RELAY, loopback not set, keepalive set (10 sec)
  LMI enq sent  144, LMI stat recvd 138, LMI upd recvd 0, DTE LMI up
  LMI enq recvd 0, LMI stat sent  0, LMI upd sent  0
  LMI DLCI 0  LMI type is ANSI Annex D  frame relay DTE
  Broadcast queue 0/64, broadcasts sent/dropped 73/0, interface broadcasts 48
  Last input 00:00:04, output 00:00:04, output hang never
  Last clearing of "show interface" counters never
  Input queue: 0/75/0 (size/max/drops); Total output drops: 0
  Queuing strategy: weighted fair
  Output queue: 0/1000/0 (size/max total/drops)
     Conversations  0/1/64 (active/max active/threshold)
     Reserved Conversations 0/0 (allocated/max allocated)
  5 minute input rate 0 bits/sec, 0 packets/sec
  5 minute output rate 0 bits/sec, 0 packets/sec
     232 packets input, 17750 bytes, 0 no buffer
     Received 1 broadcasts, 0 runts, 0 giants, 0 throttles
     0 input errors, 0 CRC, 0 frame, 0 overrun, 0 ignored, 0 abort
     225 packets output, 12563 bytes, 0 underruns
     0 output errors, 0 collisions, 4 interface resets
     0 output buffer failures, 0 output buffers swapped out
```

Example 9-20 *Scenario 9-3, Part C—R2* **show** *and* **debug** *Output (Continued)*

```
         12 carrier transitions
         DCD=up  DSR=up  DTR=up  RTS=up  CTS=up
   --More--
 Serial0.1 is up, line protocol is up
   Hardware is HD64570
   Internet address is 170.1.10.2/23
   MTU 1500 bytes, BW 56 Kbit, DLY 20000 usec, rely 255/255, load 1/255
   Encapsulation FRAME-RELAY
   --More--
 Serial1 is administratively down, line protocol is down
   Hardware is HD64570
   MTU 1500 bytes, BW 1544 Kbit, DLY 20000 usec, rely 255/255, load 1/255
   Encapsulation PPP, loopback not set, keepalive set (10 sec)
   LCP Closed
   Closed: CDPCP, LLC2
   Last input never, output never, output hang never
   Last clearing of "show interface" counters never
   Input queue: 0/75/0 (size/max/drops); Total output drops: 0
   Queuing strategy: weighted fair
 Output queue: 0/1000/0 (size/max total/drops)
      Conversations  0/0/64 (active/max active/threshold)
      Reserved Conversations 0/0 (allocated/max allocated)
   5 minute input rate 0 bits/sec, 0 packets/sec
   5 minute output rate 0 bits/sec, 0 packets/sec
      0 packets input, 0 bytes, 0 no buffer
      Received 0 broadcasts, 0 runts, 0 giants, 0 throttles
      0 input errors, 0 CRC, 0 frame, 0 overrun, 0 ignored, 0 abort
      0 packets output, 0 bytes, 0 underruns
      0 output errors, 0 collisions, 5 interface resets
      0 output buffer failures, 0 output buffers swapped out
      0 carrier transitions
      DCD=down  DSR=down  DTR=down  RTS=down  CTS=down
   --More--
 Ethernet0 is up, line protocol is up
   Hardware is TMS380, address is 0000.0c89.b170 (bia 0000.0c89.b170)
   Internet address is 170.1.5.2/23
   MTU 1500 bytes, BW 10000 Kbit, DLY 100000 usec, rely 255/255, load 1/255
   Encapsulation ARPA, loopback not set, keepalive set (10 sec)
   ARP type: ARPA, ARP Timeout 4:00:00
   Last input 00:00:00, output 00:00:01, output hang never
   Last clearing of "show interface" counters never
   Queuing strategy: fifo
 Output queue 0/40, 0 drops; input queue 0/75, 0 drops
   5 minute input rate 0 bits/sec, 0 packets/sec
   5 minute output rate 0 bits/sec, 0 packets/sec
      583 packets input, 28577 bytes, 0 no buffer
      Received 486 broadcasts, 0 runts, 0 giants, 0 throttles
      0 input errors, 0 CRC, 0 frame, 0 overrun, 0 ignored, 0 abort
      260 packets output, 31560 bytes, 0 underruns
      0 output errors, 0 collisions, 2 interface resets
      0 output buffer failures, 0 output buffers swapped out
      6 transitions
```

continues

Example 9-20 *Scenario 9-3, Part C—R2 **show** and **debug** Output (Continued)*

```
R2#show ipx interface brief
Interface          IPX Network Encapsulation Status                  IPX State
Serial0            unassigned  not config'd up                       n/a
Serial0.1          10          FRAME-RELAY  up                       [up]
Serial1            unassigned  not config'd administratively down    n/a
Ethernet0          4           SAP          up                       [up]
Ethernet0          5           SNAP         up                       [up]
R2#
R2#show ipx route
Codes: C - Connected primary network,    c - Connected secondary network
       S - Static, F - Floating static, L - Local (internal), W - IPXWAN
       R - RIP, E - EIGRP, N - NLSP, X - External, A - Aggregate
       s - seconds, u - uses

14 Total IPX routes. Up to 1 parallel paths and 16 hops allowed.

No default route known.

C         4 (SAP),          E0
c         5 (SNAP),         E0
C        10 (FRAME-RELAY),  Se0.1
R         2 [07/01] via      10.0200.aaaa.aaaa,    47s, Se0.1
R         3 [07/01] via      10.0200.aaaa.aaaa,    48s, Se0.1
R         6 [13/02] via      10.0200.aaaa.aaaa,    48s, Se0.1
R         7 [13/02] via      10.0200.aaaa.aaaa,    48s, Se0.1
R         8 [13/02] via      10.0200.aaaa.aaaa,    48s, Se0.1
R         9 [13/02] via      10.0200.aaaa.aaaa,    48s, Se0.1
R        12 [07/01] via      10.0200.aaaa.aaaa,    48s, Se0.1
R        14 [07/01] via      10.0200.aaaa.aaaa,    48s, Se0.1
R       101 [08/03] via      10.0200.aaaa.aaaa,    48s, Se0.1
R       102 [08/03] via      10.0200.aaaa.aaaa,    48s, Se0.1
R       103 [02/02] via       4.0000.0cac.70ef,    42s, E0

R2#ping 14.0200.dddd.dddd
Translating "14.0200.dddd.dddd"

Type escape sequence to abort.
Sending 5, 100-byte IPX Cisco Echoes to 14.0200.dddd.dddd, timeout is 2 seconds:
!!!!!
Success rate is 100 percent (5/5), round-trip min/avg/max = 140/144/148 ms

R2#show ipx servers
Codes: S - Static, P - Periodic, E - EIGRP, N - NLSP, H - Holddown, + = detail
3 Total IPX Servers

Table ordering is based on routing and server info

   Type Name                      Net     Address     Port    Route Hops Itf
P     4 Server3                   103.0000.0000.0001:0451     2/02   2   E0
P     4 Server1                   101.0000.0000.0001:0451     8/03   3   Se0.1
P     4 Server2                   102.0000.0000.0001:0451     8/03   3   Se0.1

R2#show frame-relay pvc
```

Example 9-20 *Scenario 9-3, Part C—R2* **show** *and* **debug** *Output (Continued)*

```
PVC Statistics for interface Serial0 (Frame Relay DTE)

DLCI = 301, DLCI USAGE = LOCAL, PVC STATUS = ACTIVE, INTERFACE = Serial0.1

  input pkts 102          output pkts 82          in bytes 16624
  out bytes 11394         dropped pkts 0          in FECN pkts 0
  in BECN pkts 0          out FECN pkts 0         out BECN pkts 0
  in DE pkts 0            out DE pkts 0
  out bcast pkts 76        out bcast bytes 10806
  pvc create time 00:25:09, last time pvc status changed 00:23:15

R2#show frame-relay lmi

LMI Statistics for interface Serial0 (Frame Relay DTE) LMI TYPE = ANSI
  Invalid Unnumbered info 0      Invalid Prot Disc 0
  Invalid dummy Call Ref 0       Invalid Msg Type 0
  Invalid Status Message 0       Invalid Lock Shift 0
  Invalid Information ID 0        Invalid Report IE Len 0
  Invalid Report Request 0       Invalid Keep IE Len 0
  Num Status Enq. Sent 151       Num Status msgs Rcvd 145
  Num Update Status Rcvd 0       Num Status Timeouts 7
R2#
```

Example 9-21 *Scenario 9-3c—R3* **show** *and* **debug** *Output*

```
R3#show ipx servers
Codes: S - Static, P - Periodic, E - EIGRP, N - NLSP, H - Holddown, + = detail
2 Total IPX Servers

Table ordering is based on routing and server info

    Type Name                    Net      Address      Port     Route Hops Itf
P    4 Server1                   101.0000.0000.0001:0451       8/03   3  Se0.1
P    4 Server2                   102.0000.0000.0001:0451       8/03   3  Se0.1

R3#show ip arp
Protocol  Address              Age (min)  Hardware Addr   Type   Interface
Internet  170.1.7.3               -        0000.0c89.b1b0  SNAP   Ethernet0

R3#show ip route
Codes: C - connected, S - static, I - IGRP, R - RIP, M - mobile, B - BGP
       D - EIGRP, EX - EIGRP external, O - OSPF, IA - OSPF inter area
       N1 - OSPF NSSA external type 1, N2 - OSPF NSSA external type 2
       E1 - OSPF external type 1, E2 - OSPF external type 2, E - EGP
       i - IS-IS, L1 - IS-IS level-1, L2 - IS-IS level-2, * - candidate default
       U - per-user static route, o - ODR

Gateway of last resort is not set

     170.1.0.0/23 is subnetted, 7 subnets
I       170.1.10.0 [100/10476] via 170.1.12.1, 00:00:57, Serial0.1
```

continues

Example 9-21 *Scenario 9-3c—R3 **show** and **debug** Output (Continued)*

```
I       170.1.8.0 [100/10539] via 170.1.12.1, 00:00:57, Serial0.1
I       170.1.14.0 [100/10476] via 170.1.12.1, 00:00:57, Serial0.1
C       170.1.12.0 is directly connected, Serial0.1
I       170.1.2.0 [100/8539] via 170.1.12.1, 00:00:57, Serial0.1
C       170.1.6.0 is directly connected, Ethernet0
I       170.1.4.0 [100/10539] via 170.1.12.1, 00:00:57, Serial0.1

R3#trace 170.1.9.4

Type escape sequence to abort.
Tracing the route to 170.1.9.4

  1 170.1.12.1 40 msec 40 msec 44 msec
  2 170.1.14.4 80 msec *  80 msec

R3#trace 170.1.5.2

Type escape sequence to abort.
Tracing the route to 170.1.5.2

  1 170.1.12.1 40 msec 40 msec 40 msec
  2 170.1.10.2 72 msec *  72 msec

R3#ping 170.1.5.2

Type escape sequence to abort.
Sending 5, 100-byte ICMP Echos to 170.1.5.2, timeout is 2 seconds:
!!!!!
Success rate is 100 percent (5/5), round-trip min/avg/max = 136/136/140 ms

R3#ping
Protocol [ip]:
Target IP address: 170.1.5.2
Repeat count [5]:
Datagram size [100]:
Timeout in seconds [2]:
Extended commands [n]: y
Source address or interface: 170.1.7.3
Type of service [0]:
Set DF bit in IP header? [no]:
Validate reply data? [no]:
Data pattern [0xABCD]:
Loose, Strict, Record, Timestamp, Verbose[none]:
Sweep range of sizes [n]:
Type escape sequence to abort.
Sending 5, 100-byte ICMP Echos to 170.1.5.2, timeout is 2 seconds:
UUUUU
Success rate is 0 percent (0/5)

R3#show frame-relay lmi

LMI Statistics for interface Serial0 (Frame Relay DTE) LMI TYPE = CISCO
  Invalid Unnumbered info 0          Invalid Prot Disc 0
```

Example 9-21 *Scenario 9-3c—R3* ***show*** *and* ***debug*** *Output (Continued)*

```
         Invalid dummy Call Ref 0        Invalid Msg Type 0
         Invalid Status Message 0        Invalid Lock Shift 0
         Invalid Information ID 0         Invalid Report IE Len 0
         Invalid Report Request 0        Invalid Keep IE Len 0
         Num Status Enq. Sent 172        Num Status msgs Rcvd 172
         Num Update Status Rcvd 0        Num Status Timeouts 0

R3#show frame-relay map
Serial0.1 (up): point-to-point dlci, dlci 301(0x12D,0x48D0), broadcast
          status defined, active
```

Example 9-22 *Scenario 9-3, Part C—R4* ***show*** *and* ***debug*** *Output*

```
R4#show ip interface brief
Interface               IP-Address      OK? Method Status                 Protocol
Serial0                 unassigned      YES unset  up                     up
Serial0.1               170.1.14.4      YES NVRAM  up                     up
Serial1                 unassigned      YES unset  administratively down  down
Ethernet0               170.1.9.4       YES NVRAM  up                     up

R4#show ipx interface brief
Interface           IPX Network Encapsulation Status               IPX State
Serial0             unassigned  not config'd  up                   n/a
Serial0.1           14          FRAME-RELAY   up                   [up]
Serial1             unassigned  not config'd  administratively down n/a
Ethernet0           8           SAP           up                   [up]
Ethernet0           9           SNAP          up                   [up]

R4#show ipx servers
Codes: S - Static, P - Periodic, E - EIGRP, N - NLSP, H - Holddown, + = detail
2 Total IPX Servers

Table ordering is based on routing and server info

   Type Name                       Net      Address      Port    Route Hops Itf
P     4 Server1                    101.0000.0000.0001:0451      8/03   3  Se0.1
P     4 Server2                    102.0000.0000.0001:0451      8/03   3  Se0.1

R4#show ipx route
Codes: C - Connected primary network,    c - Connected secondary network
       S - Static, F - Floating static, L - Local (internal), W - IPXWAN
       R - RIP, E - EIGRP, N - NLSP, X - External, A - Aggregate
       s - seconds, u - uses

14 Total IPX routes. Up to 1 parallel paths and 16 hops allowed.

No default route known.

C          8 (SAP),        E0
c          9 (SNAP),       E0
C         14 (FRAME-RELAY), Se0.1
R          2 [07/01] via      14.0200.aaaa.aaaa,    33s, Se0.1
```

continues

Example 9-22 *Scenario 9-3, Part C—R4 **show** and **debug** Output (Continued)*

```
R           3 [07/01] via      14.0200.aaaa.aaaa,  34s, Se0.1
R           4 [13/02] via      14.0200.aaaa.aaaa,  34s, Se0.1
R           5 [13/02] via      14.0200.aaaa.aaaa,  34s, Se0.1
R           6 [13/02] via      14.0200.aaaa.aaaa,  34s, Se0.1
R           7 [13/02] via      14.0200.aaaa.aaaa,  34s, Se0.1
R          10 [07/01] via      14.0200.aaaa.aaaa,  34s, Se0.1
R          12 [07/01] via      14.0200.aaaa.aaaa,  34s, Se0.1
R         101 [08/03] via      14.0200.aaaa.aaaa,  34s, Se0.1
R         102 [08/03] via      14.0200.aaaa.aaaa,  34s, Se0.1
R         103 [14/04] via      14.0200.aaaa.aaaa,  34s, Se0.1

R4#show cdp neighbor detail
-----------------------
Device ID: R1
Entry address(es):
  IP address: 170.1.14.1
  Novell address: 14.0200.aaaa.aaaa
Platform: Cisco 2500,  Capabilities: Router
Interface: Serial0.1,  Port ID (outgoing port): Serial0.4
Holdtime : 178 sec

Version :
Cisco Internetwork Operating System Software
IOS (tm) 2500 Software (C2500-AINR-L), Version 11.2(11), RELEASE SOFTWARE (fc1)
Copyright 1986-1997 by Cisco Systems, Inc.
Compiled Mon 29-Dec-97 18:47 by ckralik

R4#show frame-relay pvc

PVC Statistics for interface Serial0 (Frame Relay DTE)

DLCI = 301, DLCI USAGE = LOCAL, PVC STATUS = ACTIVE, INTERFACE = Serial0.1

  input pkts 85           output pkts 63          in bytes 14086
  out bytes 8464          dropped pkts 0          in FECN pkts 0
  in BECN pkts 0          out FECN pkts 0         out BECN pkts 0
  in DE pkts 0            out DE pkts 0
  out bcast pkts 53        out bcast bytes 7614
  pvc create time 00:18:40, last time pvc status changed 00:18:40
```

Using Examples 9-19 through 9-22 as references, answer the following questions:

1 The ping of 170.1.5.2 (R2's E0 interface) from R3 was successful (refer to Example 9-21). Why was it successful if the access lists in R1 are enabled as shown in its configuration?

2 Describe the SAP update entering R1 over its S0.2 subinterface. How many services are described?

3 What **show** commands could be executed on R4 to display the IP and IPX addresses of R1?

4 What command lists the IP subnet numbers to which R2 is connected?

5 What commands list the routing metrics used for IP subnets? What about for IPX networks?

6 What command is used to verify that IPX packets can be delivered and returned to another router?

7 If you do not know the enable password, how can you see what access lists are used?

8 You are not physically close to R2 or R3. What two methods can be used to gain access to the user mode command prompt?

9 After typing **show ip route**, you want to type **show ip route 168.11.12.64**. Describe the steps to do so, taking the least amount of keystrokes.

10 After typing **show ip route**, you want to type **show ip arp**. Describe the steps to do so, taking the least amount of keystrokes.

11 Name the editing commands (keyboard key sequences) to do the following:

— Move to the beginning of the command line

— Move to the end of the command line

— Move to the beginning of the previous word

— Move to the beginning of the next word

— Move backward one character

— Move forward one character

12 Describe the process of upgrading to a new version of IOS. What memory in the router is affected?

13 What do TCP and UDP stand for? Which provides error recovery?

14 What does ICMP stand for?

15 Describe how R2 learns that R1's IP address is 170.1.10.1.

16 What does DLCI stand for? How big can a DLCI be?

17 What additional configuration is needed on R3 to get routing updates to flow over the VC to R1?

18 What **show** command will list Frame Relay PVCs and the IP and IPX addresses on the other end of the PVC in this network?

19 What **show** command lists the status of the VC between R1 and R2?

20 What do ISDN, BRI, and PRI stand for?

21 List examples of two ISDN reference points.

22 What layers in the OSI model do the ISDN specifications Q.920 and Q.930 most closely match?

23 What ISDN reference points are supported by Cisco routers?

24 What command(s) can be used to discover details about a neighboring router without logging in to that router?

Solutions to Scenario 9-3, Part C—Verification and Questions

The answers to the questions for Scenario 9-3, Part C are as follows:

1 The **ping** command uses the outgoing interface's IP address as the source address in the packet, which in this case would be 170.1.12.3. Access lists 102 and 103 check the source and destination IP addresses, looking for the subnets on the Ethernet segments. Therefore, the packet is not matched. Look further in Example 9-21 to see an extended **ping**, with source IP address 170.1.7.3 (R3's E0 IP address), and see that it fails. That's because the extended **ping** calls for the use of 170.1.7.3 as the source IP address.

2 Two services are in the update instead of the three services listed in R2's SAP table. These messages are displayed after the **debug ipx sap activity** command in Example 9-19. This simply shows that the SAP filter on R2 is working properly.

3 The **show ip route** (Example 9-21) and **show ipx route** (Example 9-20) commands list the IP and IPX addresses of the neighboring routers. Because only point-to-point subinterfaces are in use, the **show frame-relay map** command (refer to Example 9-21) does not show details of the neighboring routers' Layer 3 addresses. The **show cdp neighbor detail** command (refer to Example 9-22) also shows information about IP and IPX addresses.

4 The **show ip route** command (refer to Example 9-21) lists these numbers. The routes with a C in the left column signify connected subnets.

5 The **show ip route** and **show ipx route** commands list the metric values (refer to Examples 9-21 and 9-20, respectively). The metric value for each IP subnet is the second of the two numbers inside brackets. Two IPX metrics are located between brackets for IPX routes: the number of timer ticks and the number of hops.

6 The **ping** command can be used to verify IPX and IP connectivity, as well as several other network layer (Layer 3) protocols (refer to Example 9-21).

7 Use the **show access-lists** command.

8 You can dial into a modem attached to the auxiliary port, or you can Telnet.

9 Press the up-arrow key, or press Ctrl+p to retrieve the last command. Then type the subnet number, which leaves **show ip route 168.11.12.64** on the command line. Press Enter.

10 Press the up-arrow key, or press Ctrl+p to retrieve the last command. Then press the Backspace key until the word "route" is erased. Then type **arp**, which leaves **show ip arp** on the command line. Press Enter.

11 The answers are as follows:

— Beginning of command line: **Ctrl+a**

— End of command line: **Ctrl+e**

— Beginning of previous word: **Esc+b**

— Beginning of next word: **Esc+f**

— Backward one character: **Ctrl+b**

— Forward one character: **Ctrl+f**

12 A file is obtained from Cisco via disk or FTP download over the Internet; this file is the IOS. The file is placed into the default directory on some TFTP server accessible to the router. The **copy tftp flash** command is issued on the router, and the user answers questions to tell the router the name and location of the new IOS. Flash memory is updated as a result of this process. The new IOS is not used until the router is reloaded.

13 TCP stands for Transmission Control Protocol; UDP stands for User Datagram Protocol. TCP provides error recovery.

14 ICMP stands for Internet Control Message Protocol.

15 The Inverse ARP process is not used when the subinterface is a point-to-point subinterface; therefore, R2 can learn of R1's IP and IPX addresses only with CDP, or by looking at the source addresses of the IPX RIP and IP IGRP routing updates.

16 DLCI stands for data link connection identifier. Lengths between 10 and 14 bits are defined, with a 10-bit number being the most typically implemented size.

17 No other configuration is necessary; this question is a trick question. This is the kind of misdirection that you might expect to see on some of the exam questions. Read the questions slowly, and read them twice.

18 The **show frame-relay pvc** command will list the PVCs. When multipoint subinterfaces are used, or when no subinterfaces are used for Frame Relay configuration, then the **show frame-relay map** command will list the IP and IPX addresses. The **show ip route** and **show ipx route** commands, or the **show cdp neighbor detail** command, can be used to see the addresses in either case.

19 The **show frame-relay pvc** command displays the status.

20 ISDN stands for Integrated Services Digital Network. BRI stands for Basic Rate Interface. PRI stands for Primary Rate Interface.

21 A reference point is an interface between function groups. R, S, T, and U are the reference points. S and T are combined in many cases and together are called the S/T reference point.

22 Q.920 performs functions similar to OSI Layer 2, and Q.930 performs functions similar to OSI Layer 3.

23 Cisco routers' ISDN interfaces are either S/T or U interfaces.

24 The **show cdp neighbor detail** command gives these details.

Answers to the "Do I Know This Already?" Quizzes and Q&A Sections

Answers to the Chapter 2 "Do I Know This Already?" Quiz

1 *What are the two different names for the router's mode of operation that, when accessed, enables you to issue commands that could be disruptive to router operations?*

Enable and privileged mode. Both are commonly used and found in Cisco documentation.

2 *What command would you use to receive command help if you knew that a **show** command option begins with a **c**, but you cannot recall the option?*

You would use **show c?**. Help would appear immediately after you typed the **?** symbol. You would not need to press Enter afterward; if you did so, the router would try to execute the command with only the parameters you had typed after the **?**.

3 *After typing **show ip route**, which is the only command you issued since logging in to the router, you now want to issue the **show ip arp** command. What steps would you take to execute this command by using command recall keystrokes?*

Press the Up-arrow key, Backspace five times, and then type **arp**. The Up-arrow key retrieves the **show ip route** command. The Backspace key moves the cursor backward and erases the character. Typing inserts the characters into the line.

4 *What is the name of the user interface mode of operation used when you cannot issue disruptive commands?*

User mode.

5 *What configuration command causes the router to require a password from a user at the console? What configuration mode context must you be in—that is, what command(s) must be typed before this command after entering configuration mode? List the commands in the order in which they must be typed while in config mode.*

```
line console 0
login
```

The **line console 0** command is a context-setting command; it adds no information to the configuration by itself. The command can be typed from any part of configuration mode. The **login** command, which follows the **line console 0** command, tells the IOS that a password prompt is desired at the console.

6 *What does CDP stand for?*

Cisco Discovery Protocol. CDP is Cisco proprietary and is not dependent on a particular Layer 3 protocol to be configured and working.

7 *What does the NV stand for in NVRAM?*

Nonvolatile. NVRAM is used for storing the startup configuration file used when the router is brought up. NVRAM is battery-powered if it is really RAM. In some routers, Cisco has (sneakily) used a small portion of Flash memory for the purpose of NVRAM, but Cisco would not ask such trivia on the test.

8 *Name two commands used to view the configuration that is currently used in a router. Which one is a more recent addition to the IOS?*

write terminal and **show running-config**. The newer command is **show running-config** and, hopefully, is easier to remember.

9 *What two methods could a router administrator use to cause a router to load the IOS stored in ROM?*

Setting the configuration register boot field to binary 0001, or adding **boot system rom** to the configuration file and copying it to the startup configuration file. To set the configuration register to hex 2101, which would yield binary 0001 in the boot field, the **config-register 0x2101** global configuration command would be used.

10 *What is the process used to update the contents of Flash memory so that a new IOS in a file called c4500-d-mz.120-5.bin, on TFTP server 128.1.1.1, is copied into Flash memory?*

copy tftp flash. The other details, namely the IP address of the TFTP server and the file name, are requested via prompts to the user.

11 *Two different IOS files are in a router's Flash memory: one called c2500-j-l.111-3.bin and one called c2500-j-l.112-14.bin. Which one does the router use when it boots up? How could you force the other IOS file to be used? Without looking at the router configuration, what command could be used to discover which file was used for the latest boot of the router?*

The first IOS file listed in the **show flash** command is the one used at reload time, unless a boot system command is configured. The configuration command **boot system flash xyz123.bin** would override the order of the files in Flash memory. The **show version** command displays the file name of the IOS for the latest reload of a router. The **show version** output tells you the version as well as the name of the file that was used at the last reload. This information is particularly difficult to find in the output of the command; watch for three lines, separated by empty lines above and below. The IOS file loaded is in one of those messages.

12 *What are the primary purposes of Flash memory in a Cisco router?*

To store IOS and microcode files and to allow remote loading of new versions of these files. In most routers, only an IOS is found. If microcode is upgraded, these files also reside in Flash memory.

Answers to the Chapter 2 Q&A Section

1 *What are the two names for the router's mode of operation that, when accessed, enables you to issue commands that could be disruptive to router operations?*

Enable mode and privileged mode. Both modes are commonly used and found in Cisco documentation.

2 *What are three methods of logging on to a router?*

Console, auxiliary port, and Telnet. All three cause the user to enter user EXEC mode.

3 *What is the name of the user interface mode of operation used when you cannot issue disruptive commands?*

User EXEC mode.

4 *Can the auxiliary port be used for anything besides remote modem user access to a router? If so, what other purpose can it serve?*

Yes: For direct attachment of a terminal, and dial for the purpose of routing packets. Although originally created to support remote administration access, many customers use an auxiliary port for dial backup, particularly when analog lines are desired or when that is all that is available.

5 *How many console ports can be installed on a Cisco 7500 router?*

One. This is a purposefully strange question. You do not order the console port; every router comes with one and only one. So, technically, you do not even order one because it is implied by ordering the router.

6 *What command would you use to receive command help if you knew that a **show** command option begins with a c, but you cannot recall the option?*

show c?. Help would appear immediately after you typed the **?** symbol. You would not need to press Enter after the **?**. If you did so, the router would try to execute the command with only the parameters you had typed after the **?**.

7 *While you are logged in to a router, you issue the command* **copy ?** *and get a response of "Unknown command, computer name, or host." Offer an explanation as to why this error message appears.*

The user was in user mode. The user must be in enable/privileged mode to use the **copy** command. When in user mode, the router does not provide help for privileged commands and treats the request for help as if there is no such command.

8 *Is the number of retrievable commands based on the number of characters in each command, or is it simply a number of commands, regardless of their size?*

Number of commands. The length (that is, number of characters) of each command does not affect the command history buffer.

9 *How can you retrieve a previously used command? (Name two ways.)*

Ctrl+p and Up-arrow. Up-arrow refers literally to the Up arrow key on the keyboard. Not all terminal emulators support **Ctrl+p** or Up-arrow, so recalling both methods is useful.

10 *After typing* **show ip route**, *which is the only command you typed since logging in to the router, you now want to issue the* **show ip arp** *command. What steps would you take to execute this command by using command recall keystrokes?*

Press Up-arrow, Backspace five times, and type **arp**. The Up-arrow key retrieves the **show ip route** command. Backspace moves the cursor backward and erases the character. Typing inserts the characters into the line.

11 *After typing* **show ip route 128.1.1.0**, *you now want to issue the command* **show ip route 128.1.4.0**. *What steps would you take to do so, using command recall and command editing keystrokes?*

Press Up-arrow, **Ctrl+b** (or Left-arrow) twice, and Backspace once, and then type 4. The **Ctrl+b** and Left-arrow keys back up one character in the line, without deleting the character. Backspace deletes the 1, in this case. Typing inserts into the line.

12 *What configuration command causes the router to require a password from a user at the console? What configuration mode context must you be in—that is, what command(s) must be typed before this command after entering configuration mode? List the commands in the order in which they must be typed while in config mode.*

```
line console 0
login
```

The **line console 0** command is a context-setting command; it adds no information to the configuration. The command can be typed from any part of configuration mode. The **login** command, which follows the **line console 0** command, tells IOS that a password prompt is desired at the console.

13 *What configuration command is used to tell the router the password that is required at the console? What configuration mode context must you be in—that is, what command(s) must you type before this command after entering configuration mode? List the commands in the order in which they must be typed while in config mode.*

```
line console 0
password xxxxxxx
```

The **password** command tells the IOS the value that should be typed when a user wants access from the console. This value is requested by the IOS because of the login command. The password xxxxxxx must be typed while in console configuration mode, which is reached by typing line console 0.

14 *What are the primary purposes of Flash memory in a Cisco router?*

To store IOS and microcode files and to allow remote loading of new versions of these files. In most routers, only an IOS is found. If microcode is upgraded, the files also reside in Flash memory.

15 *What is the intended purpose of NVRAM memory in a Cisco router?*

To store a single configuration file, used at router load time. NVRAM does not support multiple files.

16 *What does the NV stand for in NVRAM?*

Nonvolatile. NVRAM is battery powered if it is really RAM. In some routers, Cisco has (sneakily) used a small portion of Flash memory for the purpose of NVRAM, but Cisco would not ask such trivia on the test.

17 *What is the intended purpose of RAM in a Cisco router?*

RAM is used as IOS working memory (storing such things as routing tables or packets) and for IOS code storage. (In some router models, not all the IOS is copied into RAM. Some of the IOS is left in Flash memory so that more RAM is available for working memory.)

18 *What is the main purpose of ROM in a Cisco router?*

To store a small limited-function IOS and to store bootstrap code. Typically, this IOS is used only during maintenance or emergencies.

19 *What configuration command would be needed to cause a router to use an IOS image named c2500-j-l.112-14.bin on TFTP server 128.1.1.1 when the router is reloaded? If you forgot the first parameter of this command, what steps must you take to learn the correct parameters and add the command to the configuration? (Assume that you are not logged in to the router when you start.)*

```
boot system tftp 128.1.1.1 c2500-j-l.112-14.bin
```

As for the second part of the question: Log in from con/aux/telnet, type the **enable** command, type the enable password, type the **configure terminal** command, and type **boot ?**. Help appears for the first parameter of the **boot** command.

20 *What command sets the password that would be required after typing the* **enable** *command? Is that password encrypted by default?*

enable password or **enable secret**. The password in the **enable** command is not encrypted by default. The enable secret password is encrypted using MD5.

21 *To have the correct syntax, what must you add to the following configuration command:*

```
banner This is Ivan Denisovich's Gorno Router--Do Not Use
```

A delimiter character that is not part of the banner is the first parameter, which is followed by the banner text, which is followed by the delimiter character. For example, the "#" is the delimiter in the following command:

```
banner # This is Ivan.... Do Not Use #
```

22 *Name two commands that affect the text used as the command prompt.*

hostname and **prompt**.

23 *When using setup mode, you are prompted at the end of the process as to whether you want to use the configuration parameters you just typed in. Which type of memory is this configuration stored in if you type yes?*

Both NVRAM and RAM. Setup is the only IOS feature that modifies both the active and the startup configuration files as the result of one action by the user.

24 *What two methods could a router administrator use to cause a router to load the IOS stored in ROM?*

Setting the configuration register boot field to binary 0001, or adding **boot system rom** to the configuration file and copying it to the startup configuration file. To set the configuration register to hex 2101, which would yield binary 0001 in the boot field, the **config-register 0x2101** global configuration command would be used.

25 *What could a router administrator do to cause a router to load file xyz123.bin from TFTP server 128.1.1.1 upon the next reload? Is there more than one way to accomplish this?*

```
boot system tftp xyz123.bin 128.1.1.1
```

This is the only way to make the router load this file from the TFTP server.

26 *What is the process used to update the contents of Flash memory so that a new IOS in a file called c4500-d-mz.120-5.bin on TFTP server 128.1.1.1 is copied into Flash memory?*

copy tftp flash. The other details, namely the IP address of the TFTP server and the file name, are requested via prompts to the user.

27 *Name three possible problems that could prevent the command **boot system tftp c2500-j-l.112-14.bin 128.1.1.1** from succeeding.*

The possible reasons include: 128.1.1.1 is not accessible through the network; there is no TFTP server on 128.1.1.1; the file is not in the TFTP default directory; the file is corrupted; a **boot** command could precede this **boot** command in the configuration file; and the IOS referenced in the first **boot** command would be used instead.

28 *Two different IOS files are in a router's Flash memory: one called c2500-j-l.111-3.bin and one called c2500-j-l.112-14.bin. Which one does the router use when it boots up? How could you force the other IOS file to be used? Without looking at the router configuration, what command could be used to discover which file was used for the latest boot of the router?*

The first IOS file listed in the **show flash** command is the one used at reload time, unless a **boot system** command is configured. The configuration command **boot system flash xyz123.bin** would override the order in Flash memory. **show version** is the command used to display the file name of the IOS for the latest reload of a router. The **show version** output tells you the version, as well as the name of the file that was used at last reload time. It is particularly difficult to find in the output of the command.

29 *What does CDP stand for?*

Cisco Discovery Protocol. CDP is proprietary and is not dependent on a particular Layer 3 protocol to be configured and working.

30 *On what type of interfaces is CDP enabled by default? (Assume IOS versions 11.0 and later.)*

On all interfaces that support SNAP headers. These include LANs, Frame Relay, and ATM.

31 *What command can be used to provide as much detailed information as possible with CDP?*

show cdp neighbor detail.

32 *Is the password required at the console the same one that is required when Telnet is used to access a router?*

No. The Telnet ("virtual terminal") password is not the same password, although many installations use the same value.

33 *How could a router administrator disable CDP?*

The **no cdp run** command disables CDP for the entire router. The **no cdp enable** interface subcommand disables it for just that interface.

34 *Which IP routing protocols could be enabled using setup?*

RIP and IGRP.

35 *Name two commands used to view the configuration to be used at the next reload of the router. Which one is a more recent addition to the IOS?*

show config and **show startup-config**. **show startup-config** is the newer one and, hopefully, is easier to remember.

36 *Name two commands used to view the configuration that is currently used in a router. Which one is a more recent addition to the IOS?*

write terminal and **show running-config**. **show running-config** is the newer command and, hopefully, is easier to remember.

37 *True or False: The **copy startup-config running-config** command always changes the currently used configuration for this router to exactly match what is in the startup configuration file. Explain.*

False. Some configuration commands do not replace an existing command but are simply added to a list of related commands. If such a list exists, the **copy startup-config running-config** command simply adds those to the end of the list. Many of these lists in a router configuration are order-dependent.

Answers to the Chapter 3 "Do I Know This Already?" Quiz

1 *Name the seven layers of the OSI model.*

Application (Layer 7), presentation (Layer 6), session (Layer 5), transport (Layer 4), network (Layer 3), data link (Layer 2), and physical (Layer 1).

2 *What is the main purpose(s) of Layer 3?*

The network layer defines logical addressing and routing as a means to deliver data across an entire network. IP and IPX are two examples of Layer 3 equivalent protocols.

3 *What is the main purpose(s) of Layer 2?*

The data link layer defines addressing specific to a particular medium as part of the means to provide delivery of data across that medium. It also includes the protocols used to determine what device(s) access the media at any point in time.

4 *What OSI layer typically encapsulates using both a header and a trailer?*

The data link layer. The trailer typically includes a frame check sequence (FCS), which is used to perform error detection.

5 *Describe the features required for a protocol to be considered connectionless.*

Unordered low-overhead delivery of data from one host to another is the service provided in most connectionless protocol services.

6 *Describe the features required for a protocol to be considered connection-oriented.*

The protocol must either exchange messages with another device before data is allowed to be sent, or some pre-established correlation between the two endpoints must be defined. TCP is an example of a connection-oriented protocol that exchanges messages before data may be sent; Frame Relay is a connection-oriented protocol for which pre-established correlation between endpoints is defined.

7 *In a particular error-recovering (reliable) protocol, the sender sends three frames, labeled 2, 3, and 4. On its next sent frame, the receiver of these frames sets an acknowledgment field to 4. What does this typically imply?*

Setting the acknowledgment field to 4 implies that frames through number 3 were received successfully. Most windowing, error-recovery (reliable) protocols use forward acknowledgment.

8 *Name three connection-oriented protocols.*

TCP, SPX, LLC Type 2, and X.25 are some examples of connection-oriented protocols that happen to provide error recovery. ATM and Frame Relay are also connection-oriented, but without error recovery.

9 *Name three terms popularly used as synonyms for MAC address.*

NIC address, card address, LAN address, hardware address, Ethernet address, Token Ring address, FDDI address, and burned-in address are used synonymously with MAC address. All of these names are used casually and in formal documents, and they refer to the same 6-byte MAC address concept as defined by IEEE.

10 *What portion of a MAC address encodes an identifier representing the manufacturer of the card?*

The first 3 bytes. For instance, Cisco is assigned 0000.0C as one of its Organizationally Unique Identifiers (OUIs). Many Cisco router Ethernet interfaces have MAC addresses beginning with that value. The output of the **show interface** command for a LAN interface lists the burned in address after the acronym BIA.

11 *Are DLCI addresses defined by a Layer 2 or a Layer 3 protocol?*

Layer 2. While not specifically covered in this chapter, Frame Relay protocols do not define a logical addressing structure that can usefully exist outside a Frame Relay network; by definition, the addresses would be OSI Layer 2 equivalent.

12 *How many bits are present in a MAC address?*

MAC addresses comprise 48 bits. The first 24 bits for burned-in addresses represent a code that identifies the manufacturer.

13 *How many bits are present in an IPX address?*

IPX addresses comprise 80 bits—32 bits in the network portion and 48 bits in the node portion.

14 *Name the two main parts of an IP address. Which part identifies the "group" of which this address is a member?*

Network and host are the two main parts of an IP address. As described in Chapter 5, "Network Protocols," technically there are three portions of the IP address: network, subnet, and host. However, because most people think of the network and subnet portions as one portion, another correct answer to this question, using popular terminology, would be subnet and host.

15 *Describe the differences between a routed protocol and a routing protocol.*

The routed protocol defines the addressing and Layer 3 header in the packet that is actually forwarded by a router. The routing protocol defines the process of routers exchanging topology data such that the routers know how to forward the data. A router uses the routing table created by the routing protocol to choose how to forward a routed protocol packet.

16 *Name at least three routed protocols.*

TCP/IP (IP), Novell (IPX), OSI (CLNP), DECNET (CLNP), AppleTalk (DDP), and VINES are some examples of routed protocols.

Answers to the Chapter 3 Q&A Section

1 *Name the seven layers of the OSI model.*

Application (Layer 7), presentation (Layer 6), session (Layer 5), transport (Layer 4), network (Layer 3), data link (Layer 2), and physical (Layer 1). Some mnemonics to help you recall the names of the layers are: All People Seem To Need Data Processing (Layer 7 to 1), Please Do Not Take Sausage Pizzas Away (Layer 1 to 7), and the ever-popular Pew! Dead Ninja Turtles Smell Particularly Awful (Layer 1 to 7).

2 *What is the main purpose(s) of Layer 7?*

Layer 7 (application layer) provides standardized services to applications. The definition for this layer is typically ambiguous because it varies. The key is that it does not define a user interface, but instead is a sort of toolbox used by application developers. For example, a Web browser is an application that uses HTML format text, as defined by the TCP/IP application layer, to describe the graphics to be displayed onscreen.

3 *What is the main purpose(s) of Layer 6?*

Layer 6 (presentation layer) defines data formats, compression, and possibly encryption.

4 *What is the main purpose(s) of Layer 5?*

Layer 5 (session layer) controls the conversation between two endpoints. Although the term used is session, the term conversation more accurately describes what is accomplished. The session layer ensures that not only communication but also useful sets of communication between endpoints is accomplished.

5 *What is the main purpose(s) of Layer 4?*

Layer 4 (transport layer) provides end-to-end error recovery, if requested.

6 *What is the main purpose(s) of Layer 3?*

Layer 3 (network layer) defines logical addressing and routing as a means to deliver data across an entire network. IP and IPX are two examples of Layer 3 equivalent protocols.

7 *What is the main purpose(s) of Layer 2?*

The data link layer defines addressing specific to a particular medium as part of the means to provide delivery of data across that medium. It also includes the protocols used to determine what device(s) accesses the media at any point in time.

8 *What is the main purpose(s) of Layer 1?*

Layer 1 (physical layer) is responsible for encoding energy signals onto the medium and interpreting a received energy signal. Layer 1 also defines the connector and cabling details.

9 *Describe the process of data encapsulation as data is processed from creation until it exits a physical interface to a network. Use the OSI model as an example.*

Data encapsulation represents the process of a layer adding a header (and possibly a trailer) to the data as it is processed by progressively lower layers in the protocol specification. In the context of OSI, each layer could add a header so that—other than the true application data—there would be six other headers (Layers 2 to 7) and a trailer for Layer 2, with this L2-PDU being encoded by the physical layer onto the network media.

10 *Describe the features required for a protocol to be considered connectionless.*

Unordered low-overhead delivery of data from one host to another is the service provided in most connectionless protocol services.

11 *Name at least three connectionless protocols.*

LLC type 1, UDP, IPX, IP, and PPP are some examples of connectionless protocols. Remember, Frame Relay, X.25, and ATM are connection-oriented, regardless of whether they define error recovery.

12 *Describe the features required for a protocol to be considered connection-oriented.*

The protocol must either exchange messages with another device before data is allowed to be sent, or some pre-established correlation between the two endpoints must be defined. TCP is an example of a connection-oriented protocol that exchanges messages before data may be sent; Frame Relay is a connection-oriented protocol for which pre-established correlation between endpoints is defined.

13 *In a particular error-recovering protocol, the sender sends three frames, labeled 2, 3, and 4. On its next sent frame, the receiver of these frames sets an acknowledgment field to 4. What does this typically imply?*

Frames up through number 3 were received successfully. Most windowing, error-recovery protocols use forward acknowledgment.

14 *Name three connection-oriented protocols.*

TCP, SPX, LLC Type 2, and X.25 are some examples of connection-oriented protocols that provide error recovery. ATM and Frame Relay are also connection-oriented, but without error recovery.

15 *What does MAC stand for?*

MAC stands for Media Access Control.

16 *Name three terms popularly used as a synonym for MAC address.*

NIC address, card address, LAN address, hardware address, Ethernet address, Token Ring address, FDDI address, and burned-in address are all synonymous with MAC address. All of these names are used casually and in formal documents, and refer to the same 6-byte MAC address concept as defined by IEEE.

17 *Are IP addresses defined by a Layer 2 or Layer 3 protocol?*

IP addresses are defined by the IP part of TCP/IP, which is the second layer of TCP/IP. However, compared to OSI, IP most closely matches OSI Layer 3 in function, so the popular (and CCNA exam) answer is Layer 3.

18 *Are IPX addresses defined by a Layer 2 or Layer 3 protocol?*

IP addresses are defined by a Layer 3 protocol.

19 *Are OSI NSAP addresses defined by a Layer 2 or Layer 3 protocol?*

OSI NSAP addresses are defined by a Layer 3 protocol. Of course, they are truly Layer 3 because they are defined by OSI. The number of bits in the address is variable. However, it is highly unlikely that questions about NSAPs would be on the exam because they are not mentioned in any objective and are not covered in any class.

20 *What portion of a MAC address encodes an identifier representing the manufacturer of the card?*

The first 3 bytes comprise the portion of a MAC address that encodes an identifier representing the manufacturer of the card.

21 *Are MAC addresses defined by a Layer 2 or Layer 3 protocol?*

MAC addresses are defined by a Layer 2 protocol. Ethernet and Token Ring MAC addresses are defined in the 802.3 and 802.5 specifications.

22 *Are DLCI addresses defined by a Layer 2 or Layer 3 protocol?*

DLCI addresses are defined by a Layer 2 protocol. Although they are not specifically covered in this chapter, Frame Relay protocols do not define a logical addressing structure that can usefully exist outside a Frame Relay network; by definition, the addresses would be OSI Layer 2 equivalent.

23 *Name two differences between Layer 3 addresses and Layer 2 addresses.*

Layer 3 addresses can be used regardless of media type, whereas Layer 2 addresses are useful only on a particular medium. Layer 3 addresses are designed with a minimum of two parts, the first of which creates a grouping concept. Layer 2 addresses do not have a grouping concept that allows the setup interfaces on the same medium to share the same value in a portion of the data link address, which is how Layer 3 addresses are structured.

24 *How many bits are present in an IP address?*

IP addresses have 32 bits: a variable number in the network portion, and the rest of the 32 in the host portion. IP Version 6 uses a much larger address. Stay tuned!

25 *How many bits are present in an IPX address?*

IPX addresses have 80 bits: 32 bits in the network portion and 48 bits in the node portion.

26 *How many bits are present in a MAC address?*

MAC addresses have 48 bits. The first 24 bits for burned-in addresses represent a code that identifies the manufacturer.

27 *Name the two main parts of an IPX address. Which part identifies which "group" this address is a member of?*

Network number and node number are the two main parts of an IPX address. Addresses with the same network number are in the same group. On LAN interfaces, the node number is made to have the same value as the LAN MAC address.

28 *Name the two main parts of an IP address. Which part identifies which "group" this address is a member of?*

Network and host are the two main parts of an IP address. As described in Chapter 5, technically there are three portions of the IP address: network, subnet, and host. However, because most people think of the network and subnet portions as one portion, another correct answer to this question, using popular terminology, would be subnet and host.

29 *Name the two main parts of a MAC address. Which part identifies which "group" this address is a member of?*

There are no parts, and nothing defines a grouping concept in a MAC address. This is a trick question. Although you might have guessed that the MAC address has two parts—the first part dictated to the manufacturer, and the second part made up by the manufacturer—there is no grouping concept.

30 *Name three benefits to layering networking protocol specifications.*

Some examples of benefits to layering networking protocol specifications include reduced complexity, standardized interfaces, modular engineering, interoperable technology, accelerated evolution, and simplified teaching and learning. Questions such as this on the exam will require some subjective interpretation of the wording on your part. The wording in this answer is consistent with the outdated CCNA exam 640-407, but some questions on the current exam remain from the old one, so the wording in this answer might be helpful.

31 *What header and/or trailer does a router discard as a side effect of routing?*

A router discards the data link header and trailer as a side effect of routing. This is because the network layer, where routing is defined, is interested in delivering the network layer (Layer 3) PDU from end to end. Routing uses intermediate data links (Layer 2) to transport the data to the next routers and eventually to the true destination. The data link header and trailer are useful only to deliver the data to the next router or host, so the header and trailer are discarded by each router.

32 *Describe the differences between a routed protocol and a routing protocol.*

The routed protocol defines the addressing and Layer 3 header in the packet that is actually forwarded by a router. The routing protocol defines the process of routers exchanging topology data so that the routers know how to forward the data. A router uses the routing table created by the routing protocol to choose how to forward a routed protocol packet.

33 *Name at least three routed protocols.*

TCP/IP (IP), Novell (IPX), OSI (CLNP), DECNET (CLNP), AppleTalk (DDP), and VINES are some examples of routed protocols.

34 *Name at least three routing protocols.*

IP RIP, IP IGRP, IP/IPX/AppleTalk EIGRP, IP OSPF, OSI NLSP, AppleTalk RTMP, Vines VTP, OSI IS-IS are some examples of routing protocols

35 *How does an IP host know what router to send a packet to? In which cases does an IP host choose to send a packet to this router instead of directly to the destination host?*

Typically an IP host knows to what router to send a packet based on its configured default router. If the destination of the packet is in another subnet, the host sends the packet to the default router. Otherwise, the host sends the packet directly to the destination host because it is in the same subnet and, by definition, must be on the same data link.

36 *How does an IPX host know which router to send a packet to? In which case does an IPX host choose to send a packet to this router instead of directly to the destination host?*

An IPX host knows which router to send a packet to by broadcasting a RIP request to locate any servers or routers on the attached IPX network that have a route to the destination network. If the destination is an IPX address on the attached network, a router is not needed and the node forwards the packet directly instead of sending a RIP request.

37 *Name three items in an entry in any routing table.*

The group identifier, the interface by which to forward the packet, and the Layer 3 address of the next router to send this packet to are three items that you will always find in a routing table entry.

38 *What OSI layer typically encapsulates using both a header and a trailer?*

The data link layer typically encapsulates using both a header and a trailer. The trailer typically includes a frame check sequence (FCS), which is used to perform error detection.

Answers to the Chapter 4 "Do I Know This Already?" Quiz

1 *What do the letters MAC stand for? What other terms have you heard to describe the same or similar concept?*

Media Access Control (MAC). Many terms are used to describe a MAC address: NIC, LAN, hardware, burned-in, Universally Administered Address (UAA), Locally Administered Address (LAA), Ethernet, Token Ring, FDDI, card, wire, and real are all terms used to describe this same address in different instances.

2 *What standards body owns the process of ensuring unique MAC addresses worldwide?*

IEEE. The first half of the burned-in MAC address is a value assigned to the manufacturer by the IEEE. As long as the manufacturer uses that prefix and doesn't duplicate values it assigns in the last 3 bytes, global uniqueness is attained.

3 *What is the distance limitation of 10BaseT? 100BaseTX?*

10BaseT allows 100 meters between the device and the hub or switch, as does 100BaseTX. Table 4-5 on page 144 summarizes the lengths for all Ethernet LAN types.

4 *How fast is Fast Ethernet?*

100 million bits per second (100 Mbps).

5 *What routing protocol does a transparent bridge use to learn about Layer 3 addressing groupings?*

None. Bridges do not use routing protocols. Transparent bridges do not care about Layer 3 address groupings. Devices on either side of a transparent bridge are in the same Layer 3 group—in other words, the same IP subnet or IPX network.

6 *Name two of the methods of internal switching on typical switches today. Which provides less latency for an individual frame?*

Store-and-forward, cut-through, and fragment-free. Cut-through has less latency per frame but does not check for bit errors in the frame, including errors caused by collisions. Store-and-forward stores the entire received frame, verifies that the FCS is correct, and then sends the frame. Cut-through sends the first bytes of the frame out before the last bytes of the incoming frame have been received. Fragment-free is like cut-through, in that the frame can be sent before the incoming frame is totally received; however, fragment-free processing waits to receive the first 64 bytes, to ensure no collisions, before beginning to forward the frame.

7 *If a switch hears three different configuration BPDUs from three different neighbors on three different interfaces, and if all three specify that Bridge 1 is the root, how does it choose which interface is its root port?*

The root port is the port in which the CBPDU with the lowest-cost value is received. The root port is placed into a forwarding state on each bridge and switch.

8 *Assume that a building has 100 devices attached to the same Ethernet. These users then are migrated onto two separate shared Ethernet segments, each with 50 devices, with a transparent bridge in between. List two benefits that would be derived for a typical user.*

Fewer collisions and less waiting should occur because twice as much capacity exists. Also, if the placement of devices causes a small percentage of traffic to be forwarded by the bridge, fewer collisions and less waiting should occur.

9 *Define the term broadcast domain.*

A set of Ethernet devices for which a broadcast sent by any one of them should be received by all others in the group. Unlike routers, bridges and switches do not stop the flow of broadcasts. Two segments separated by a router would each be in a different broadcast domain. A switch can create multiple broadcast domains by creation of multiple VLANs, but a router must be used to route packets between the VLANs.

10 *Describe the benefits of creating three VLANs of 25 ports each, versus a single VLAN of 75 ports, in each case using a single switch. Assume that all ports are switched ports (each port is a different collision domain).*

Three different broadcast domains are created with three VLANs, so the devices' CPU utilization should decrease due to decreased broadcast traffic. Traffic between devices in different VLANs will pass through some routing function, which can add some latency for those packets. Better management and control are gained by including a router in the path for those packets.

11 *If two Cisco LAN switches are connected using Fast Ethernet, what VLAN trunking protocols could be used? If only one VLAN spanned both switches, is a VLAN trunking protocol needed?*

ISL and 802.1Q are the trunking protocols used by Cisco over Fast Ethernet. If only one VLAN spans the two switches, a trunking protocol is not needed. Trunking or tagging protocols are used to tag a frame as being in a particular VLAN; if only one VLAN is used, tagging is unnecessary.

12 *Define the term VLAN.*

Virtual LAN (VLAN) refers to the process of treating one subset of a switch's interfaces as one broadcast domain. Broadcasts from one VLAN are not forwarded to other VLANs; unicasts between VLANs must use a router. Advanced methods, such as Layer 3 switching in a NetFlow feature card in a Catalyst 5000 switch, can be used to allow the LAN switch to forward traffic between VLANs without each individual frame being routed by a router. However, for the depth of CCNA, such detail is not needed.

13 *How many IP addresses must be configured for network management on a Cisco Catalyst 1900 switch if eight ports are to be used with three VLANs?*

A single IP address is needed. There is no need for an IP address per port because the switch is not a router. The management IP address is considered to be in VLAN1.

14 *What Catalyst 1900 switch command displays the version of IOS running in the switch?*

This is a trick question. The **show version** command shows the level of switch software, but because the switch does not run IOS, no command will display the level of IOS in the switch.

15 *Configuration is added to the running configuration in RAM when commands are typed in Catalyst 1900 configuration mode. What causes these commands to be saved into NVRAM?*

Unlike the router IOS, commands are saved in both running config and in NVRAM as the user enters the configuration commands. No separate command, such as **copy running-config startup-config** in the router IOS, is needed.

16   *Name the three VTP modes. Which of these does not allow VLANs to be added or modified?*

Server and client modes are used to actively participate in VTP, and transparent mode is used to simply stay out of the way of servers and clients while not participating in VTP. Switches in client mode cannot change or add VLANs.

Answers to the Chapter 4 Q&A Section

1   *What do the letters MAC stand for? What other terms have you heard to describe the same or similar concept?*

Media Access Control (MAC). Many terms are used to describe a MAC address: NIC, LAN, hardware, burned-in, UAA (Universally Administered Address), LAA (Locally Administered Address), Ethernet, Token Ring, FDDI, card, wire, and real are all terms used to describe this same address in different instances.

2   *Name two benefits of LAN segmentation using transparent bridges.*

The main benefits are reduced collisions and more bandwidth. Multiple 10- or 100-Mbps Ethernet segments are created, and unicasts between devices on the same segment are not forwarded by the bridge, which reduces overhead.

3   *What routing protocol does a transparent bridge use to learn about Layer 3 addressing groupings?*

None. Bridges do not use routing protocols. Transparent bridges do not care about Layer 3 address groupings. Devices on either side of a transparent bridge are in the same Layer 3 group—in other words, the same IP subnet or IPX network.

4   *What settings are examined by a bridge or switch to determine which should be elected as root of the Spanning Tree?*

The bridge priority is first examined (the lowest wins). In case of a tie, the lowest bridge ID wins. The priority is prepended to the bridge ID in the actual CBPDU message so that the combined fields can be easily compared.

5   *Define the term VLAN.*

Virtual LAN (VLAN) refers to the process of treating one subset of a switch's interfaces as one broadcast domain. Broadcasts from one VLAN are not forwarded to other VLANs; unicasts between VLANs must use a router. Advanced methods, such as Layer 3 switching in a NetFlow feature card in a Catalyst 5000 switch, can be used to allow the LAN switch to forward traffic between VLANs without each individual frame being routed by a router. However, for the depth of CCNA, such detail is not needed.

6 *Assume that a building has 100 devices attached to the same Ethernet. These users then are migrated onto two separate shared Ethernet segments, each with 50 devices, with a transparent bridge in between. List two benefits that would be derived for a typical user.*

Fewer collisions and less waiting should occur because twice as much capacity exists. Also, if the placement of devices causes a small percentage of traffic to be forwarded by the bridge, fewer collisions and less waiting should occur.

7 *What standards body owns the process of ensuring unique MAC addresses worldwide?*

IEEE. The first half of the burned-in MAC address is a value assigned to the manufacturer by the IEEE. As long as the manufacturer uses that prefix and doesn't duplicate values it assigns in the last 3 bytes, global uniqueness is attained.

8 *Assume that a building has 100 devices attached to the same Ethernet. These devices are migrated to two different shared Ethernet segments, each with 50 devices. The two segments are connected to a Cisco LAN switch to allow communication between the two sets of users. List two benefits that would be derived for a typical user.*

Two switch ports are used, which reduces the possibility of collisions. Also, each segment has its own 10- or 100-Mbps capacity, allowing more throughput and reducing the likelihood of collisions. Furthermore, although unlikely to be on the CCNA exam, some Cisco switches can reduce the flow of multicasts using the Cisco Group Message Protocol (CGMP).

9 *Name two of the methods of internal switching on typical switches today. Which provides less latency for an individual frame?*

Store-and-forward, cut-through, and FragmentFree. Cut-through has less latency per frame but does not check for bit errors in the frame, including errors caused by collisions. Store-and-forward stores the entire received frame, verifies that the FCS is correct, and then sends the frame. Cut-through sends the first bytes of the frame out before the last bytes of the incoming frame have been received. Fragment free is similar to cut-through in that the frame can be sent before the incoming frame is totally received; however, fragment-free processing waits to receive the first 64 bytes, to ensure no collisions, before beginning to forward the frame.

10 *What is the distance limitation of 10BaseT? 100BaseTX?*

10BaseT allows 100 meters between the device and the hub or switch, as does 100BaseTX. Table 4-5 on page 144 summarizes the lengths for all Ethernet LAN types.

11 *Describe how a transparent bridge decides whether it should forward a frame, and tell how it chooses the interface out which to forward the frame.*

The bridge examines the destination MAC address of a frame and looks for the address in its bridge (or address) table. If found, the matching entry tells the bridge which output interface to use to forward the frame. If not found, the bridge forwards the frame out all other interfaces (except for interfaces blocked by Spanning Tree and the interface in which the frame was received). The bridge table is built by examining incoming frames' source MAC addresses.

12 *How fast is Fast Ethernet?*

100 million bits per second (100 Mbps).

13 *Describe the benefit of the Spanning-Tree Protocol as used by transparent bridges and switches.*

Physically redundant paths in the network are allowed to exist and be used when other paths fail. Also, loops in the bridged network are avoided. Loops are particularly bad because bridging uses LAN headers, which do not provide a mechanism to mark a frame so that its lifetime can be limited; in other words, the frame can loop forever.

14 *If a switch hears three different configuration BPDUs from three different neighbors on three different interfaces, and if all three specify that Bridge 1 is the root, how does the switch choose which interface is its root port?*

The root port is the port in which the CBPDU with the lowest-cost value is received. The root port is placed in forwarding state on each bridge and switch.

15 *How does a transparent bridge build its address table?*

The bridge listens for incoming frames and examines the source MAC address. If not in the table, the source address is added, along with the port (interface) by which the frame entered the bridge. The bridge also marks an entry for freshness so that entries can be removed after a period of disuse. This reduces table size and allows for easier table changes in case a Spanning Tree change forces more significant changes in the bridge (address) table.

16 *How many bytes long is a MAC address?*

6 bytes long, or 48 bits.

17 *Assume that a building has 100 devices attached to the same Ethernet. These users then are migrated onto two separate Ethernet segments, each with 50 devices and separated by a router. List two benefits that would be derived for a typical user.*

Collisions are reduced by creating two collision domains. Broadcasts also are reduced because the router does not forward broadcasts. Routers provide greater control and administration as well.

18 *Does a bridge/switch examine just the incoming frame's source MAC, destination MAC, or both? Why does it examine the one(s) it examines?*

The bridge/switch examines both MAC addresses. The source is examined so that entries can be added to the bridge/address table. The destination address is examined to determine the interface out which to forward the frame. Table lookup is required for both addresses for any frame that enters an interface. That is one of the reasons that LAN switches, which have a much larger number of interfaces than traditional bridges, need to have optimized hardware and logic to perform table lookup quickly.

19 *Define the term collision domain.*

A collision domain is a set of Ethernet devices for which concurrent transmission of a frame by any two of them will result in a collision. Bridges, switches, and routers separate LAN segments into different collision domains. Repeaters and shared hubs do not separate segments into different collision domains.

20 *When a bridge or switch using Spanning-Tree Protocol first initializes, who does it assert should be the root of the tree?*

Each bridge/switch begins by sending CBPDUs claiming itself as the root bridge.

21 *Name the three reasons why a port is placed in forwarding state as a result of Spanning Tree.*

First, all ports on the root bridge are placed in forwarding state. Second, one port on each bridge is considered its root port, which is placed in forwarding state. Finally, on each LAN segment, one bridge is considered to be the designated bridge on that LAN; that designated bridge's interface on the LAN is placed in forwarding state.

22 *Define the difference between broadcast and multicast MAC addresses.*

Both identify more than one device on the LAN. Broadcast always implies all devices on the LAN, whereas multicast implies some subset of all devices. Multicast is not allowed on Token Ring; broadcast is allowed on all LAN types. Devices that intend to receive frames addressed to a particular multicast address must be aware of the particular multicast address(es) they should process. These addresses are dependent on the applications used. Read RFC 1112, the Internet Group Message Protocol (IGMP), for related information about the use of Ethernet multicast in conjunction with IP multicast. For example, the broadcast address is FFFF.FFFF.FFFF, and one sample multicast address is 1000.5e00.0001.

23 *Excluding the preamble and starting delimiter fields, but including all other Ethernet headers and trailers, what is the maximum number of bytes in an Ethernet frame?*

1518 bytes. See Figure 4-5 on page 141 for more detail.

24 *Define the term broadcast domain.*

A broadcast domain is a set of Ethernet devices for which a broadcast sent by any one of them should be received by all others in the group. Unlike routers, bridges and switches do not stop the flow of broadcasts. Two segments separated by a router would each be in a different broadcast domain. A switch can create multiple broadcast domains by creating multiple VLANs, but a router must be used to route packets between the VLANs.

25 *Describe the benefits of creating three VLANs of 25 ports each, versus a single VLAN of 75 ports, in each case using a single switch. Assume that all ports are switched ports (each port is a different collision domain).*

Three different broadcast domains are created with three VLANs, so the devices' CPU utilization should decrease due to decreased broadcast traffic. Traffic between devices in different VLANs will pass through some routing function, which can add some latency for those packets. Better management and control are gained by including a router in the path for those packets.

26 *If two Cisco LAN switches are connected using Fast Ethernet, what VLAN trunking protocols could be used? If only one VLAN spanned both switches, is a VLAN trunking protocol needed?*

ISL and 802.1Q are the trunking protocols used by Cisco over Fast Ethernet. If only one VLAN spans the two switches, a trunking protocol is not needed. Trunking or tagging protocols are used to tag a frame as being in a particular VLAN; if only one VLAN is used, tagging is unnecessary.

27 *Explain the function of the loopback and collision detection features of an Ethernet NIC in relation to half-duplex and full-duplex operations.*

The loopback feature copies the transmitted frame back onto the receive pin on the NIC interface. The collision detection logic compares the received frame to the transmitted frame during transmission; if the signals do not match, then a collision is occurring. This logic implies that half duplex is being used because if collisions can occur, only one transmitter at a time is allowed. With full duplex, collisions cannot occur, so the loopback and collision detection features are not needed, and concurrent transmission and reception is allowed.

28 *Name the three interface states that the Spanning-Tree Protocol uses, other than forwarding. Which of these states is transitory?*

Blocking, listening, and learning. Blocking is the only stable state; the other two are transitory between blocking and forwarding. Table 4-13 on page 170 summarizes the states and their features.

29 *What are the two reasons that a nonroot bridge/switch places a port in forwarding state?*

If the port is the designated bridge on its LAN segment, the port is placed in forwarding state. Also, if the port is the root port, it is placed in forwarding state. Otherwise, the port is placed in blocking state.

30 *Can the root bridge/switch ports be placed in blocking state?*

The root bridge's ports are always in a forwarding state because they always have cost 0 to the root, which ensures that they are always the designated bridges on their respective LAN segments.

31 *How many IP addresses must be configured for network management on a Cisco Catalyst 1900 switch if eight ports are to be used and with three VLANs?*

A single IP address is needed. No need exists for an IP address per port because the switch is not a router. The management IP address is considered to be in VLAN1.

32 *What command on a 1900 series switch would cause the switch to block frames destined to 0200.7777.7777, entering interface 0/5, from going out port 0/6?*

The **mac-address-table restricted static 0200.7777.7777 0/6 0/5** global configuration command would block the frames. This also makes address 0200.7777.7777 permanently held in the MAC address table for port 0/6.

33 *What Catalyst 1900 switch command displays the version of IOS running in the switch?*

This is a trick question. The **show version** command shows the level of switch software, but because the switch does not run IOS, no command will display the level of IOS in the switch.

34 *What does the Catalyst 1900 switch command **address violation disable** do?*

This global configuration command tells the switch what action to take when the maximum number of addresses on a port has been exceeded. If a new dynamically learned MAC address on some port had caused the maximum (as defined by the port secure command) to be exceeded, the port would have been disabled.

35 *What command erases the startup config in a Catalyst 1900 switch?*

The **delete nvram** EXEC command erases the configuration file in NVRAM. In fact, although it is easy to call it the startup-config, commands instead refer to this configuration file as NVRAM.

36 *Configuration is added to the running configuration in RAM when commands are typed in Catalyst 1900 configuration mode. What causes these commands to be saved into NVRAM?*

Unlike the router IOS, commands are saved in both running config and in NVRAM as the user enters the configuration commands. No separate command, such as **copy running-config startup-config** in the router IOS, is needed.

37 *How do EXEC and configuration commands refer to the two Fast Ethernet ports on a Catalyst 1912 switch?*

These two ports are known as fastethernet 0/26 and 0/27. 0/25 is always reserved for the AUI port, and 0/1 through 0/24 are always reserved for the (up to) first 24 Ethernet ports.

38 *What Catalyst 1900 switch command displays the switching table?*

The **show mac-address-table** command displays the table the switch uses to make switching decisions.

39 *What does VTP do, and what does the abbreviation stand for?*

VLAN Trunking Protocol is a protocol used to transmit configuration information about VLANs between interconnected switches. VTP helps prevent misconfiguration, eases administration of the switches, and also reduces broadcast overhead by the use of VTP pruning.

40 *Name the three VTP modes. Which of these does not allow VLANs to be added or modified?*

Server and client modes are used to actively participate in VTP; transparent mode is used to simply stay out of the way of servers and clients while not participating in VTP. Switches in client mode cannot change or add VLANs.

41 *What Catalyst 1900 switch command assigns a port to a particular VLAN?*

The **vlan-membership static** *x* interface subcommand assigns the port to VLAN number *x*.

42 *What Catalyst 1900 switch command creates vlan 10 and assigns it a name of bigbadvlan?*

The **vlan 10 name bigbadvlan** global configuration command creates the VLAN.

43 *What Catalyst 1900 switch command lists the details about VLAN number 10?*

The **show vlan 10** command displays VLAN information about VLAN number 10.

44 *What Catalyst 1900 switch command configures ISL trunking on fastethernet port 26 so that as long as the switch port on the other end of the trunk is not disabled (off) or configured to not negotiate to become a trunk, the trunk will definitely be placed in trunking mode?*

The **trunk desirable** interface subcommand tells this switch to be in trunking mode (in other words, to use ISL) as long as the switch in the other end of the trunk is configured for on, autonegotiate, or desirable. If the other switch has configured the trunk as off or nonegotiate, trunking will not be enabled.

45 *What type of VTP mode allows a switch to create VTP advertisements?*

Only VTP servers generate VTP advertisements.

Answers to the Chapter 5 "Do I Know This Already?" Quiz

1 *What do TCP, UDP, IP, and ICMP stand for? Which protocol is considered to be Layer 3 equivalent when comparing TCP/IP to the OSI protocols?*

Transmission Control Protocol, User Datagram Protocol, Internet Protocol, and Internet Control Message Protocol. Both TCP and UDP are Layer 4 protocols. ICMP is considered a Layer 3 protocol because it is used for control and management of IP. IP is the core part of the network layer of TCP/IP, so it is also considered to be a Layer 3 protocol.

2 *Describe how TCP performs error recovery. What role do the routers play?*

TCP numbers the first byte in each segment with a sequence number. The receiving host uses the acknowledgment field in segments it sends back to acknowledge receipt of the data. If the receiver sends an acknowledgment number that is a smaller number than the sender expected, the sender believes the intervening bytes were lost, so the sender resends them. The router plays no role unless the TCP connection ends in the router—for example, a Telnet into a router.

3 *Does FTP or TFTP perform error recovery? If so, describe the basics of how error recovery is performed.*

Both FTP and TFTP perform error recovery. FTP relies on TCP, whereas TFTP performs application layer recovery one block of data at a time.

4 *How many TCP segments are exchanged to establish a TCP connection? How many are required to terminate a TCP connection?*

A three-way connection establishment sequence is performed, and a four-flow connection termination sequence is used.

5 *Given the IP address 134.141.7.11 and the mask 255.255.255.0, what is the subnet number?*

The subnet is 134.141.7.0. The binary algorithm is shown in the following table.

Address	134.141.7.11	1000 0110 1000 1101 **0000 0111** 0000 1011
Mask	255.255.255.0	1111 1111 1111 1111 **1111 1111** 0000 0000
Result	134.141.7.0	1000 0110 1000 1101 **0000 0111** 0000 0000

6 *Given the IP address 134.141.7.11 and the mask 255.255.255.0, what is the subnet broadcast address?*

The broadcast address is 134.141.7.255. The binary algorithm is shown in the following table.

Address	134.141.7.11	1000 0110 1000 1101 **0000 0111** 0000 1011
Mask	255.255.255.0	1111 1111 1111 1111 **1111 1111** 0000 0000
Result	134.141.7.0	1000 0110 1000 1101 **0000 0111** 0000 0000
Broadcast Address	134.141.7.255	1000 0110 1000 1101 0000 0111 **1111 1111**

7 *Given the IP address 200.1.1.130 and the mask 255.255.255.224, what are the assignable IP addresses in this subnet?*

The subnet number is 200.1.1.128, and the subnet broadcast address is 200.1.1.159. The assignable addresses are all the addresses between the subnet and broadcast addresses, namely 200.1.1.129 to 200.1.1.158.

8 *Given the IP address 220.8.7.100 and the mask 255.255.255.240, what are all the subnet numbers if the same (static) mask is used for all subnets in this network?*

The Class C network number is 220.8.7.0. The mask implies that the bits 25 through 28, which are the first 4 bits in the fourth octet, comprise the subnet field. Essentially, the subnet numbers have the same numbers in the network portion and the same (all binary 0) value in the host portion of the number. Each individual subnet number has a unique value in the subnet portion of the number.

The binary algorithm is shown in the following table. Refer to the section "Given a Network Number and a Static Subnet Mask, What Are the Valid Subnet Numbers?" in Chapter 5 for a review of the algorithm.

First three octets in binary	1101 1100 0000 1000 0000 0111		
Host field with all zeros added	1101 1100 0000 1000 0000 0111	0000	
All binary 0 subnet field added, completing the first subnet number	1101 1100 0000 1000 0000 0111 **0000** 0000		220.8.7.0
Added binary 1 to subnet field, giving second subnet number	1101 1100 0000 1000 0000 0111 **0001** 0000		220.8.7.16
Added binary 1 to subnet field, giving third subnet number	1101 1100 0000 1000 0000 0111 **0010** 0000		220.8.7.32
Added binary 1 to subnet field, giving fourth subnet number	1101 1100 0000 1000 0000 0111 **0011** 0000		220.8.7.48
Added binary 1 to subnet field, giving fifth subnet number	1101 1100 0000 1000 0000 0111 **0100** 0000		220.8.7.64
Added binary 1 to subnet field, giving sixth subnet number	1101 1100 0000 1000 0000 0111 **0101** 0000		220.8.7.80
	Skipped a few for brevity		
Last subnet number	1101 1100 0000 1000 0000 0111 **1111** 0000		220.8.7.240

9 *Create a minimal configuration enabling IP on each interface on a 2501 router (two serial, one Ethernet). The NIC assigned you network 8.0.0.0. Your boss says that you need, at most, 200 hosts per subnet. You decide against using VLSM. Your boss says to plan your subnets so that you can have as many subnets as possible, rather than allow for larger* *subnets later. You decide to start with the lowest numerical values for the subnet number you will use. Assume that point-to-point serial links will be attached to this router and that RIP is the routing protocol.*

```
router rip
network 8.0.0.0
interface ethernet 0
ip address 8.0.1.1 255.255.255.0
interface serial 0
ip address 8.0.2.1 255.255.255.0
interface serial 1
ip address 8.0.3.1 255.255.255.0
```

The zero subnet was not used in this solution. If desired, the **ip subnet-zero** global command could have been used, enabling subnet 8.0.0.0 as well as the subnets 8.0.1.0, 8.0.2.0, and 8.0.3.0 to be used in the configuration.

10 *Describe the question and possible responses in setup mode when a router wants to know the mask used on an interface. How can the router derive the correct mask from the information supplied by the user?*

When using versions of the IOS before version 12.0, the question asks for the number of subnet bits. The router creates a subnet mask with *x* more binary 1s than the default mask for the class of network of which the interface's IP address is a member. (*x* is the number in the response.) "Number of subnet bits" from the setup question uses the definition that there are three parts to an address—network, subnet, and host. The size of the network field is based on the class of address; the interface's address was typed in response to an earlier setup question. The mask simply has binary 1s in the network and subnet fields, and binary 0s in the host field.

With version 12.0 and beyond, setup prompts for the subnet mask in canonical decimal format—for example, 255.255.255.0.

11 *Define the purpose of the **trace** command. What type of messages does it send, and what type of ICMP messages does it receive?*

The **trace** command learns the current route to a destination address. It uses IP packets with UDP as the transport layer protocol, with TTL values beginning at 1 and then incrementing by 1 in successive messages. The result is that intervening routers find that the TTL is exceeded and send ICMP "TTL exceeded" messages back to the originator of the packet, which is the router where the **trace** command is being executed. The source addresses of the "TTL exceeded" packets identify each router. By sending other packets with TTL=2, then 3, and so on, eventually the packet is received by the host. The host returns a "port unreachable" ICMP message, which lets the **trace** command know that the endpoint host has been reached.

12 *What causes the output from an IOS **ping** command to display "UUUUU"?*

U is an indication that an unreachable message was received. The type of unreachable message is not implied by the "U".

13 *How many bytes comprise an IPX address?*

Ten bytes. The network portion is 32 bits, and the node portion is 48 bits. The node part conveniently is the same size as a LAN MAC address.

14 *Give an example of an IPX network mask used when subnetting.*

There is no such thing as subnetting with IPX. This is an example of a question meant to shake your confidence on the exam. Thoughts like, "I never read about subnetting IPX!" can destroy your concentration. Be prepared for unusual questions or answers like this on the exam.

15 *Create a configuration enabling IPX on each interface, with RIP and SAP enabled on each as well, for a 2501 (two serial, one Ethernet) router. Use networks 100, 200, and 300 for interfaces S0, S1, and E0, respectively. Choose any node values.*

```
ipx routing 0200.1111.1111
interface serial 0
ipx network 100
interface serial 1
ipx network 200
interface ethernet 0
ipx network 300
```

The node part of the address was supplied in the **ipx routing** command so that the IPX addresses are easily recognizable on the serial interfaces. This helps with troubleshooting because it will be easier to remember the IPX addresses used when pinging.

16 *What **show** command lists the IPX address(es) of interfaces in a Cisco router?*

show ipx interface. The other **show** commands list only the IPX network numbers, not the entire IPX addresses.

Answers to the Chapter 5 Q&A Section

1 *What do TCP, UDP, IP, and ICMP stand for? Which protocol is considered to be Layer 3 equivalent when comparing TCP/IP to the OSI protocols?*

Transmission Control Protocol, User Datagram Protocol, Internet Protocol, and Internet Control Message Protocol. Both TCP and UDP are Layer 4 protocols. ICMP is considered a Layer 3 protocol because it is used for control and management of IP. IP is the core part of the network layer of TCP/IP.

2 *Name the parts of an IP address.*

Network, subnet, and host are the three parts of an IP address. However, many people commonly treat the network and subnet parts of an address as a single part, leaving only two parts, the subnet and host parts. On the exam, the multiple-choice format should provide extra clues as to which terminology is used.

3 *Define the term subnet mask. What do the bits in the mask whose values are binary 0 tell you about the corresponding IP address(es)?*

A subnet mask defines the number of host bits in an address. The bits of value 0 define which bits in the address are host bits. The mask is an important ingredient in the formula to dissect an IP address; along with knowledge of the number of network bits implied for Class A, B, and C networks, the mask provides a clear definition of the size of the network, subnet, and host parts of an address.

4 *Given the IP address 134.141.7.11 and the mask 255.255.255.0, what is the subnet number?*

The subnet is 134.141.7.0. The binary algorithm is shown in the table that follows.

Address	134.141.7.11	1000 0110 1000 1101 **0000 0111** 0000 1011
Mask	255.255.255.0	1111 1111 1111 1111 **1111 1111** 0000 0000
Result	134.141.7.0	1000 0110 1000 1101 **0000 0111** 0000 0000

5 *Given the IP address 193.193.7.7 and the mask 255.255.255.0, what is the subnet number?*

The network number is 193.193.7.0. Because this is a Class C address and the mask used is 255.255.255.0 (the default), there is no subnetting in use. The binary algorithm is shown in the table that follows.

Address	193.193.7.7	1100 0001 1100 0001 0000 0111 0000 0111
Mask	255.255.255.0	1111 1111 1111 1111 1111 1111 0000 0000
Result	193.193.7.0	1100 0001 1100 0001 0000 0111 0000 0000

6 *Given the IP address 10.5.118.3 and the mask 255.255.0.0, what is the subnet number?*

The subnet is 10.5.0.0. The binary algorithm math is shown in the table that follows.

Address	10.5.118.3	0000 1010 **0000 0101** 0111 0110 0000 0011
Mask	255.255.0.0	1111 1111 **1111 1111** 0000 0000 0000 0000
Result	10.5.0.0	0000 1010 **0000 0101** 0000 0000 0000 0000

7 *Given the IP address 190.1.42.3 and the mask 255.255.255.0, what is the subnet number?*

The subnet is 190.1.42.0. The binary algorithm math is shown in the table that follows.

Address	190.1.42.3	1011 1110 0000 0001 **0010 1010** 0000 0011
Mask	255.255.255.0	1111 1111 1111 1111 **1111 1111** 0000 0000
Result	190.1.42.0	1011 1110 0000 0001 **0010 1010** 0000 0000

8 *Given the IP address 200.1.1.130 and the mask 255.255.255.224, what is the subnet number?*

The subnet is 200.1.1.128. The binary algorithm math is shown in the table that follows.

Address	200.1.1.130	1100 1000 0000 0001 0000 0001 **1000** 0010
Mask	255.255.255.224	1111 1111 1111 1111 1111 1111 **1110** 0000
Result	200.1.1.128	1100 1000 0000 0001 0000 0001 **1000** 0000

9 *Given the IP address 220.8.7.100 and the mask 255.255.255.240, what is the subnet number?*

The subnet is 220.8.7.96. The binary algorithm math is shown in the table that follows.

Address	220.8.7.100	1101 1100 0000 1000 0000 0111 **0110** 0100
Mask	255.255.255.240	1111 1111 1111 1111 1111 1111 **1111** 0000
Result	220.8.7.96	1101 1100 0000 1000 0000 0111 **0110** 0000

10 *Given the IP address 140.1.1.1 and the mask 255.255.255.248, what is the subnet number?*

The subnet is 140.1.1.0. The binary algorithm math is shown in the table that follows.

Address	140.1.1.1	1000 1100 0000 0001 **0000 0001 0000 0**001
Mask	255.255.255.248	1111 1111 1111 1111 **1111 1111 1111 1**000
Result	140.1.1.0	1000 1100 0000 0001 **0000 0001 0000 0**000

11 *Given the IP address 167.88.99.66 and the mask 255.255.255.192, what is the subnet number?*

The subnet is 167.88.99.64. The binary algorithm math is shown in the table that follows.

Address	167.88.99.66	1010 0111 0101 1000 **0110 0011 01**00 0010
Mask	255.255.255.192	1111 1111 1111 1111 **1111 1111 11**00 0000
Result	167.88.99.64	1010 0111 0101 1000 **0110 0011 01**00 0000

12 *Given the IP address 134.141.7.11 and the mask 255.255.255.0, what is the subnet broadcast address?*

The broadcast address is 134.141.7.255. The binary algorithm is shown in the table that follows.

Address	134.141.7.11	1000 0110 1000 1101 **0000 0111** 0000 1011
Mask	255.255.255.0	1111 1111 1111 1111 **1111 1111** 0000 0000
Result	134.141.7.0	1000 0110 1000 1101 **0000 0111** 0000 0000
Broadcast Address	134.141.7.255	1000 0110 1000 1101 0000 0111 **1111 1111**

13 *Given the IP address 193.193.7.7 and the mask 255.255.255.0, what is the broadcast address?*

The broadcast address is 193.193.7.255. Because this is a Class C address and the mask used is 255.255.255.0 (the default), there is no subnetting in use. The binary algorithm is shown in the table that follows.

Address	193.193.7.7	1100 0001 1100 0001 0000 0111 0000 0111
Mask	255.255.255.0	1111 1111 1111 1111 1111 1111 0000 0000
Result	193.193.7.0	1100 0001 1100 0001 0000 0111 0000 0000
Broadcast Address	193.193.7.255	1100 0001 1100 0001 0000 0111 **1111 1111**

14 *Given the IP address 10.5.118.3 and the mask 255.255.0.0, what is the broadcast address?*

The subnet is 10.5.0.0. The binary algorithm math is shown in the table that follows.

Address	10.5.118.3	0000 1010 **0000 0101** 0111 0110 0000 0011
Mask	255.255.0.0	1111 1111 **1111 1111** 0000 0000 0000 0000
Result	10.5.0.0	0000 1010 **0000 0101** 0000 0000 0000 0000
Broadcast Address	10.5.255.255	0000 1010 0000 0101 **1111 1111 1111 1111**

15 *Given the IP address 190.1.42.3 and the mask 255.255.255.0, what is the broadcast address?*

The broadcast address is 190.1.42.255. The binary algorithm math is shown in the table that follows.

Address	190.1.42.3	1011 1110 0000 0001 **0010 1010** 0000 0011
Mask	255.255.255.0	1111 1111 1111 1111 **1111 1111** 0000 0000
Result	190.1.42.0	1011 1110 0000 0001 **0010 1010** 0000 0000
Broadcast Address	190.1.42.255	1011 1110 0000 0001 0010 1010 **1111 1111**

16 *Given the IP address 200.1.1.130 and the mask 255.255.255.224, what is the broadcast address?*

The broadcast address is 200.1.1.159. The binary algorithm math is shown in the table that follows.

Address	200.1.1.130	1100 1000 0000 0001 0000 0001 **1000** 0010
Mask	255.255.255.224	1111 1111 1111 1111 1111 1111 **1110** 0000
Result	200.1.1.128	1100 1000 0000 0001 0000 0001 **1000** 0000
Broadcast Address	200.1.1.159	1100 1000 0000 0001 0000 0001 100**1 1111**

17 *Given the IP address 220.8.7.100 and the mask 255.255.255.240, what is the broadcast address?*

The broadcast address is 220.8.7.111. The binary algorithm is shown in the table that follows.

Address	220.8.7.100	1101 1100 0000 1000 0000 0111 **0110** 0100
Mask	255.255.255.240	1111 1111 1111 1111 1111 1111 **1111** 0000
Result	220.8.7.96	1101 1100 0000 1000 0000 0111 **0110** 0000
Broadcast Address	220.8.7.111	1101 1100 0000 1000 0000 0111 0110 **1111**

18 *Given the IP address 140.1.1.1 and the mask 255.255.255.248, what is the broadcast address?*

The broadcast address is 140.1.1.7. The binary algorithm math is shown in the table that follows.

Address	140.1.1.1	1000 1100 0000 0001 **0000 0001 0000 0**001
Mask	255.255.255.248	1111 1111 1111 1111 **1111 1111 1111 1**000
Result	140.1.1.0	1000 1100 0000 0001 **0000 0001 0000 0**000
Broadcast Address	140.1.1.7	1000 1100 0000 0001 0000 0001 0000 0**111**

19 *Given the IP address 167.88.99.66 and the mask 255.255.255.192, what is the broadcast address?*

The broadcast address is 167.88.99.127. The binary algorithm math is shown in the table that follows.

Address	167.88.99.66	1010 0111 0101 1000 **0110 0011 01**00 0010
Mask	255.255.255.192	1111 1111 1111 1111 **1111 1111 11**00 0000
Result	167.88.99.64	1010 0111 0101 1000 **0110 0011 01**00 0000
Broadcast Address	167.88.99.127	1010 0111 0101 1000 0110 0011 01**11 1111**

20 *Given the IP address 134.141.7.11 and the mask 255.255.255.0, what are the assignable IP addresses in this subnet?*

The subnet number is 134.141.7.0, and the subnet broadcast address is 134.141.7.255. The assignable addresses are all the addresses between the subnet and broadcast addresses, namely 134.141.7.1 to 134.141.7.254.

21 *Given the IP address 193.193.7.7 and the mask 255.255.255.0, what are the assignable IP addresses in this subnet?*

The subnet number is 193.193.7.0, and the subnet broadcast address is 193.193.7.255. The assignable addresses are all the addresses between the subnet and broadcast addresses, namely 193.193.7.1 to 193.193.7.254.

22 *Given the IP address 10.5.118.3 and the mask 255.255.0.0, what are the assignable IP addresses in this subnet?*

The subnet number is 10.5.0.0, and the subnet broadcast address is 10.5.255.255. The assignable addresses are all the addresses between the subnet and broadcast addresses, namely 10.5.0.1 to 10.5.255.254.

23 *Given the IP address 190.1.42.3 and the mask 255.255.255.0, what are the assignable IP addresses in this subnet?*

The subnet number is 190.1.42.0, and the subnet broadcast address is 190.1.42.255. The assignable addresses are all the addresses between the subnet and broadcast addresses, namely 190.1.42.1 to 190.1.42.254.

24 *Given the IP address 200.1.1.130 and the mask 255.255.255.224, what are the assignable IP addresses in this subnet?*

The subnet number is 200.1.1.128, and the subnet broadcast address is 200.1.1.159. The assignable addresses are all the addresses between the subnet and broadcast addresses, namely 200.1.1.129 to 200.1.1.158.

25 *Given the IP address 220.8.7.100 and the mask 255.255.255.240, what are the assignable IP addresses in this subnet?*

The subnet number is 220.8.7.96, and the subnet broadcast address is 220.8.7.111. The assignable addresses are all the addresses between the subnet and broadcast addresses, namely 220.8.7.97 to 220.8.7.110.

26 *Given the IP address 140.1.1.1 and the mask 255.255.255.248, what are the assignable IP addresses in this subnet?*

The subnet number is 140.1.1.0, and the subnet broadcast address is 140.1.1.7. The assignable addresses are all the addresses between the subnet and broadcast addresses, namely 140.1.1.1 to 140.1.1.6.

27 *Given the IP address 167.88.99.66 and the mask 255.255.255.192, what are the assignable IP addresses in this subnet?*

The subnet number is 167.88.99.64, and the subnet broadcast address is 167.88.99.127. The assignable addresses are all the addresses between the subnet and broadcast addresses, namely 167.88.99.65 to 167.88.99.126.

28 *Given the IP address 134.141.7.7 and the mask 255.255.255.0, what are all the subnet numbers if the same (static) mask is used for all subnets in this network?*

The Class B network number is 134.141.0.0. The mask implies that the entire third octet, and only that octet, comprises the subnet field. Essentially, the subnet numbers have the same numbers in the network portion and the same (all binary 0) value in the host portion of the number. Each individual subnet number has a unique value in the subnet portion of the number.

The binary algorithm is shown in the table that follows. Refer to the section "Given a Network Number and a Static Subnet Mask, What Are the Valid Subnet Numbers?" in Chapter 5 for a review of the algorithm.

Step 2 (only one line shown)	1000 0110 1000 1101		
Step 3 (only one line shown)	1000 0110 1000 1101	0000 0000	
Step 4	1000 0110 1000 1101 **0000 0000** 0000 0000		134.141.0.0
Step 5	1000 0110 1000 1101 **0000 0001** 0000 0000		134.141.1.0
Step 6	1000 0110 1000 1101 **0000 0010** 0000 0000		134.141.2.0
Step 6	1000 0110 1000 1101 **0000 0011** 0000 0000		134.141.3.0
Step 6	1000 0110 1000 1101 **0000 0100** 0000 0000		134.141.4.0
Step 6	1000 0110 1000 1101 **0000 0101** 0000 0000		134.141.5.0
	Skipped a few for brevity		
Step 6	1000 0110 1000 1101 **1111 1111** 0000 0000		134.141.255.0

29 *Given the IP address 10.5.118.3 and the mask 255.255.255.0, what are all the subnet numbers if the same (static) mask is used for all subnets in this network?*

The Class A network number is 10.0.0.0. The mask implies that the entire second and third octets, and only those octets, comprise the subnet field. Essentially, the subnet numbers have the same numbers in the network portion and the same (all binary 0) value in the host portion of the number. Each individual subnet number has a unique value in the subnet portion of the number.

The binary algorithm is shown in the table that follows. Refer to the section "Given a Network Number and a Static Subnet Mask, What Are the Valid Subnet Numbers?" in Chapter 5 for a review of the algorithm.

Step 2 (only one line shown)	0000 1010		
Step 3 (only one line shown)	0000 1010	0000 0000	
Step 4	0000 1010 **0000 0000 0000 0000** 0000 0000		10.0.0.0
Step 5	0000 1010 **0000 0000 0000 0001** 0000 0000		10.0.1.0
Step 6	0000 1010 **0000 0000 0000 0010** 0000 0000		10.0.2.0
Step 6	0000 1010 **0000 0000 0000 0011** 0000 0000		10.0.3.0
Step 6	0000 1010 **0000 0000 0000 0100** 0000 0000		10.0.4.0
Step 6	0000 1010 **0000 0000 0000 0101** 0000 0000		10.0.5.0
	Skipped a few for brevity		
Step 6	0000 1010 **1111 1111 1111 1111** 0000 0000		10.255.255.0

30 *Given the IP address 220.8.7.100 and the mask 255.255.255.240, what are all the subnet numbers if the same (static) mask is used for all subnets in this network?*

The Class C network number is 220.8.7.0. The mask implies that the bits 25 to 28, which are the first 4 bits in the fourth octet, comprise the subnet field. Essentially, the subnet numbers have the same numbers in the network portion and the same (all binary 0) value in the host portion of the number. Each individual subnet number has a unique value in the subnet portion of the number.

Refer to the section "Given a Network Number and a Static Subnet Mask, What Are the Valid Subnet Numbers?" in Chapter 5 for a review of the algorithm.

Step 2 (only one line shown)	1101 1100 0000 1000 0000 0111		
Step 3 (only one line shown)	1101 1100 0000 1000 0000 0111	0000	
Step 4	1101 1100 0000 1000 0000 0111 **0000** 0000		220.8.7.0
Step 5	1101 1100 0000 1000 0000 0111 **0001** 0000		220.8.7.16
Step 6	1101 1100 0000 1000 0000 0111 **0010** 0000		220.8.7.32
Step 6	1101 1100 0000 1000 0000 0111 **0011** 0000		220.8.7.48
Step 6	1101 1100 0000 1000 0000 0111 **0100** 0000		220.8.7.64
Step 6	1101 1100 0000 1000 0000 0111 **0101** 0000		220.8.7.80
	Skipped a few for brevity		
Step 6	1101 1100 0000 1000 0000 0111 **1111** 0000		220.8.7.240

31 *Given the IP address 140.1.1.1 and the mask 255.255.255.248, what are all the subnet numbers if the same (static) mask is used for all subnets in this network?*

The Class B network number is 140.1.0.0. The mask implies that the bits 17 to 29, which are all the bits in the third octet and the first 5 bits in the fourth octet, comprise the subnet field. Essentially, the subnet numbers have the same numbers in the network portion and the same (all binary 0) value in the host portion of the number. Each individual subnet number has a unique value in the subnet portion of the number.

The binary algorithm is shown in the table that follows. Refer to the section "Given a Network Number and a Static Subnet Mask, What Are the Valid Subnet Numbers?" in Chapter 5 for a review of the algorithm.

Step 2 (only one line shown)	1000 1100 0000 0001	
Step 3 (only one line shown)	1000 1100 0000 0001 **0000 0000 0000 0000**	
Step 4	1000 1100 0000 0001 **0000 0000 0000 1000**	140.1.0.0
Step 5	1000 1100 0000 0001 **0000 0000 0001 1000**	140.1.0.8
Step 6	1000 1100 0000 0001 **0000 0000 0010 0000**	140.1.0.16

Step 6	1000 1100 0000 0001 **0000 0000 0010 1**000	140.1.0.24
Step 6	1000 1100 0000 0001 **0000 0000 0011 0**000	140.1.0.32
Step 6	1000 1100 0000 0001 **0000 0000 0011 1**000	140.1.0.40
	Skipped a few for brevity	
Step 6	1000 1100 0000 0001 **1111 1111 1111 1**000	140.1.255.248

32 *How many IP addresses could be assigned in each subnet of 134.141.0.0, assuming that a mask of 255.255.255.0 is used? If the same (static) mask is used for all subnets, how many subnets are there?*

There will be $2^{hostbits}$, or 2^8 hosts per subnet, minus two special cases. The number of subnets will be $2^{subnetbits}$, or 2^8, in this case. The chart that follows summarizes the related information in the same manner as the "Foundation Topics" section of Chapter 5 described the binary algorithm to solve this type of problem.

Network and Mask	Number of Network Bits	Number of Host Bits	Number of Subnet Bits	Number of Hosts per Subnet	Number of Subnets
134.141.0.0, 255.255.255.0	16	8	8	254	256

33 *How many IP addresses could be assigned in each subnet of 10.0.0.0, assuming that a mask of 255.255.255.0 is used? If the same (static) mask is used for all subnets, how many subnets are there?*

There will be $2^{hostbits}$, or 2^8 hosts per subnet, minus two special cases. The number of subnets will be $2^{subnetbits}$, or 2^{16}, in this case. The chart that follows summarizes the related information in the same manner as the "Foundation Topics" section of Chapter 5 described the binary algorithm to solve this type of problem.

Network and Mask	Number of Network Bits	Number of Host Bits	Number of Subnet Bits	Number of Hosts per Subnet	Number of Subnets
10.0.0.0, 255.255.255.0	8	8	16	254	65,536

34 *How many IP addresses could be assigned in each subnet of 220.8.7.0, assuming that a mask of 255.255.255.240 is used? If the same (static) mask is used for all subnets, how many subnets are there?*

There will be 2^{hostbits}, or 2^4 hosts per subnet, minus two special cases. The number of subnets will be $2^{\text{subnetbits}}$, or 2^4, in this case. The chart that follows summarizes the related information in the same manner as the "Foundation Topics" section of Chapter 5 described the binary algorithm to solve this type of problem.

Network and Mask	Number of Network Bits	Number of Host Bits	Number of Subnet Bits	Number of Hosts per Subnet	Number of Subnets
220.8.7.0, 255.255.255. 240	24	4	4	14	16

35 *How many IP addresses could be assigned in each subnet of 140.1.0.0, assuming a mask of 255.255.255.248 is used? If the same (static) mask is used for all subnets, how many subnets are there?*

There will be 2^{hostbits}, or 2^3 hosts per subnet, minus two special cases. The number of subnets will be $2^{\text{subnetbits}}$, or 2^{13}, in this case. The chart that follows summarizes the related information in the same manner as the "Foundation Topics" section of Chapter 5 described the binary algorithm to solve this type of problem.

Network and Mask	Number of Network Bits	Number of Host Bits	Number of Subnet Bits	Number of Hosts per Subnet	Number of Subnets
140.1.0.0	16	3	13	6	8096

36 *Create a minimal configuration enabling IP on each interface on a 2501 router (two serial, one Ethernet). The NIC assigned you network 8.0.0.0. Your boss says you need at most 200 hosts per subnet. You decide against using VLSM. Your boss also says to plan your subnets so that you can have as many subnets as possible rather than allow for larger subnets later. You decide to start with the lowest numerical values for the subnet number you will use. Assume that point-to-point serial links will be attached to this router and that RIP is the routing protocol.*

```
router rip
network 8.0.0.0
interface ethernet 0
ip address 8.0.1.1 255.255.255.0
interface serial 0
ip address 8.0.2.1 255.255.255.0
interface serial 1
ip address 8.0.3.1 255.255.255.0
```

The zero subnet was not used in this solution. If desired, the **ip subnet-zero** global command could have been used, enabling subnet 8.0.0.0 as well as the subnets 8.0.1.0, 8.0.2.0, and 8.0.3.0 to be used in the configuration.

37 *In the previous question, what would be the IP subnet of the link attached to serial 0? If another user wanted to answer the same question but did not have the enable password, what command(s) might provide this router's addresses and subnets?*

The attached subnet is 8.0.2.0, 255.255.255.0. The **show interface**, **show ip interface**, and **show ip interface brief** commands would supply this information, as would **show ip route**. The **show ip route** command would show the actual subnet number instead of the address of the interface.

38 *Describe the question and possible responses in setup mode when a router wants to know the mask used on an interface. How can the router derive the correct mask from the information supplied by the user?*

When using versions of the IOS before version 12.0, the question asks for the number of subnet bits. The router creates a subnet mask with x more binary 1s than the default mask for the class of network of which the interface's IP address is a member. (x is the number in the response.) "Number of subnet bits" from the setup question uses the definition that there are three parts to an address—network, subnet, and host. The size of the network field is based on the class of address; the interface's address was typed in response to an earlier setup question. The mask simply has binary 1s in the network and subnet fields, and binary 0s in the host field.

With version 12.0 and beyond, setup prompts for the subnet mask in canonical decimal format—for example, 255.255.255.0.

39 *Name the three classes of unicast IP addresses and list their default masks, respectively. How many of each type could be assigned to companies and organizations by the NIC?*

Class A, B, and C, with default masks 255.0.0.0, 255.255.0.0, and 255.255.255.0, respectively. 2^7 Class A networks are mathematically possible; 2^{14} Class Bs are possible; and 2^{21} Class C networks are possible. There are two reserved network numbers in each range.

40 *Describe how TCP performs error recovery. What role do the routers play?*

TCP numbers the first byte in each segment with a sequence number. The receiving host uses the acknowledgment field in segments it sends back to acknowledge receipt of the data. If the receiver sends an acknowledgment number that is a smaller number than the sender expected, the sender believes that the intervening bytes were lost, so the sender resends them. The router plays no role unless the TCP connection ends in the router—for example, a telnet into a router. A full explanation is provided in the section, "Error Recovery (Reliability)" in Chapter 5.

41 *Define the purpose of an ICMP redirect message.*

The ICMP redirect message enables a router to tell a host to use a different router than itself because that other router has a better route to the subnet to which the host sent a packet. The redirect also implies that the router sending the redirect, the host sending the original packet, and the better router all have interfaces attached to this same subnet.

42 *Define the purpose of the **trace** command. What type of messages is it sending, and what type of ICMP messages is it receiving?*

The **trace** command learns the current route to a destination address. It uses IP packets with UDP as the transport layer protocol, with TTL values beginning at 1 and then incrementing by 1 in successive messages. The result is that intervening routers will find that the TTL is exceeded and will send ICMP "TTL exceeded" messages back to the originator of the packet, which is the router where the **trace** command is being executed. The source addresses of the "TTL exceeded" packets identify each router. By sending other packets with TTL=2, then 3, and so on, eventually the packet is received by the host. The host returns a "port unreachable" ICMP message, which lets the **trace** command know that the endpoint host has been reached.

43 *What does IP stand for? What does ICMP stand for? Which protocol is considered to be Layer 3 equivalent when comparing TCP/IP to the OSI protocols?*

Internet Protocol and Internet Control Message Protocol. Both protocols are considered to be part of TCP/IP's protocols equivalent to OSI Layer 3. ICMP is also considered a Layer 3 protocol because it is used for control and management of IP. However, an IP header precedes an ICMP header, so it is common to treat ICMP as another Layer 4 protocol, like TCP and UDP. ICMP does not provide services to a higher layer, so it is really an adjunct part of Layer 3.

44 *What causes the output from an IOS **ping** command to display "UUUUU?"*

U is an indication that an unreachable message was received. The type of unreachable message is not implied by the "U".

45 *Describe how to view the IP ARP cache in a Cisco router. Also describe the three key elements of each entry.*

show ip arp displays the IP ARP cache in a Cisco router. Each entry contains the IP address, the MAC address, and the interface from which the information was learned. The encapsulation type is also in the table entry.

46 *How many hosts are allowed per subnet if the subnet mask used is 255.255.255.192? How many hosts are allowed for 255.255.255.252?*

255.255.255.192 has 6 bits of value 0, giving 2^6 hosts, minus the two reserved numbers, for 62. The 255.255.255.252 mask leaves 2^2 hosts, minus the two reserved numbers, for two hosts. 255.255.255.252 is often used on serial links when using VLSM; point-to-point links need only two IP addresses.

47 *How many subnets could be created if using static length masks in a Class B network when the mask is 255.255.255.224? What about when the mask is 255.255.252.0?*

With a Class B network, the first 16 bits are network bits. With mask 255.255.255.224, there are 5 host bits, leaving 11 subnet bits. 2^{11} is 2048. If the zero and broadcast subnets are avoided, 2046 are left. For the mask 255.255.252.0, there are 10 host bits, leaving 6 subnet bits. 2^6 is 64; if avoiding the two special cases, that leaves 62 possible subnets.

48 *How many bytes comprise an IPX address?*

Ten bytes. The network portion is 32 bits, and the node portion is 48 bits. The node part conveniently is the same size as a LAN MAC address.

49 *What do IPX and SPX stand for?*

Internetwork Packet Exchange and Sequenced Packet Exchange.

50 *Define encapsulation in the context of Cisco routers and Novell IPX.*

Data link encapsulation describes the details of the data link header and trailer created by a router as the result of routing a packet out an interface. Novell allows several options on LANs. Encapsulation is used for any routed protocol on every router interface. Novell just happens to have many options that are still in use, particularly on Ethernet.

51 *Give an example of an IPX network mask used when subnetting.*

There is no such thing as subnetting with IPX. This is an example of a question meant to shake your confidence on the exam. Thoughts like, "I never read about subnetting IPX!" can destroy your concentration. Be prepared for unusual questions or answers like this on the exam.

52 *Describe the headers used for two types of Ethernet encapsulation when using IPX.*

Ethernet_II uses Ethernet version 2 headers (destination and source address, and type field). Ethernet_802.3 uses an 802.3 header (destination and source address, and length field). Ethernet_802.2 uses an 802.3 header and an 802.2 header (802.2 adds DSAP, SSAP, and Control fields). Ethernet_SNAP uses an 802.3 header, an 802.2 header, and then a SNAP header (SNAP adds OUI and protocol fields). The names in this answer use Novell's names. The corresponding keywords in the IOS are arpa, novell-ether, SAP, and SNAP, respectively. The Novell names refer to the last header before the IPX header. See Table 5-32 and Table 5-33, on pages 301 and 302, for a reference for all LAN encapsulations.

53 *Name the part of the NetWare protocol specifications that, like TCP, provides end-to-end guaranteed delivery of data.*

SPX (Sequenced Packet Exchange).

54 *Name the command that lists all the SAP entries in a Cisco router.*

show ipx servers. Many people remember that the command uses either the **servers**, or **server**, or **service**, or **sap** keyword. The exam is likely to list those four keywords as the four answers; spend a little time memorizing the commands summarized at the beginning of each configuration section in most chapters of this book.

55 *How many different values are possible for IPX network numbers?*

2^{32}, or around four billion. Networks 0 and FFFFFFFF are reserved. The size of the network number is one big reason why there is no need for subnetting IPX networks.

56 *Create a configuration enabling IPX on each interface, with RIP and SAP enabled on each as well, for a 2501 (two serial, one Ethernet) router. Use networks 100, 200, and 300 for interfaces S0, S1, and E0, respectively. Choose any node values.*

```
ipx routing 0200.1111.1111
interface serial 0
ipx network 100
interface serial 1
ipx network 200
interface ethernet 0
ipx network 300
```

The node part of the address was supplied in the IPX routing command so that the IPX addresses are easily recognizable on the serial interfaces. This helps troubleshooting because it will be easier to remember the IPX addresses used when pinging.

57 *In the previous question, what would be the IPX address of the serial 0 interface? If another user wanted to know but did not have the enable password, what command(s) might provide this IPX address?*

```
100.0200.1111.1111
show ipx interface
```

If you left off the node parameter on the IPX routing command in the previous question, the IPX address would have a node number equal to the MAC address used on the Ethernet interface.

58 *What **show** command lists the IPX address(es) of interfaces in a Cisco router?*

show ipx interface. The other **show** commands list only the IPX network numbers, not the entire IPX addresses.

59 *How many Novell encapsulation types are valid in the IOS for Ethernet interfaces? What about for FDDI and Token Ring?*

There are four encapsulations for Ethernet, three encapsulations for FDDI, and two encapsulations for Token Ring. Table 5-32 and Table 5-33, on pages 301 and 302, list the different encapsulations.

60 *A router is attached to an Ethernet LAN. Some clients on the LAN use Novell's Ethernet_II encapsulation, and some use Ethernet_802.3. If the only subcommand on Ethernet0 reads* **ipx network 1**, *which of the clients are working? (All, Ethernet_II, or Ethernet_802.3?)*

Just those with Ethernet_802.3 are working. The associated IOS keyword is **novell-ether**, and this is the default IPX encapsulation. This question is just trying to test your recall of the default encapsulation for Ethernet.

61 *A router is attached to an Ethernet LAN. Some clients on the LAN use Novell's Ethernet_802.2 encapsulation, and some use Ethernet_SNAP. Create a configuration that allows both types of clients to send and receive packets through this router.*

```
interface ethernet 0
ipx network 1 encapsulation sap
ipx network 2 encapsulation snap secondary
```

Subinterfaces could also have been used instead of secondary IPX networks.

62 *True or false: Up to 64 IPX networks can be used on the same Ethernet by using the IPX secondary address feature. If true, describe the largest number that is practically needed. If false, what is the maximum number that is legal on an Ethernet?*

False. Only one network per encapsulation is allowed. Because four Ethernet encapsulations can be used with IPX, four IPX networks are supported. Using the same logic, only three networks are allowed on FDDI, and two on Token Ring.

63 *In the* **ipx network 11** *interface subcommand, does the IOS assume that 11 is binary, octal, decimal, or hexadecimal? What is the largest valid value that could be configured instead of 11?*

All IPX network numbers are considered to be hexadecimal by the IOS. The largest value is FFFFFFFE, with FFFFFFFF being reserved as the broadcast network.

64 *What IOS IPX encapsulation keyword implies use of an 802.2 header but no SNAP header? On what types of interfaces is this type of encapsulation valid?*

SAP encapsulation on the IOS implies use of the 802.2 header immediately before the IPX packet. SAP and SNAP are valid on Ethernet, FDDI, and Token Ring. SAP also refers to the field in the 802.2 header that is used to identify IPX as the type of packet that follows the 802.2 header.

65 *Name the two commands typically used to create a default gateway for a router.*

The **ip default-gateway** command and the **ip route 0.0.0.0 0.0.0.0** command. Both accomplish the goal of having the router use a known route as the default for packets that are not matched in the routing table. The **ip route 0.0.0.0 0.0.0.0** uses the fact that network 0.0.0.0 is used by the IOS to represent the default network.

66 *Assume that subnets of network 10.0.0.0 are in the IP routing table in a router but that no other network and their subnets are known, except that there is also a default route (0.0.0.0) in the routing table. A packet destined for 192.1.1.1 arrives at the router. What configuration command determines whether the default route will be used in this case?*

If the command **ip classless** is configured, the packet is routed using the default route. If **no ip classless** is configured, then the packet will be discarded.

67 *Assume that subnets of network 10.0.0.0 are in the IP routing table in a router but that no other network and their subnets are known, except that there is also a default route (0.0.0.0) in the routing table. A packet destined for 10.1.1.1 arrives at the router, but there is no known subnet of network 10 that matches this destination address. What configuration command determines whether the default route will be used in this case?*

The packet will be routed using the default route, regardless of other configuration commands. In this particular scenario, where the Class A, B, or C network is known, there is no match for the destination in the known subnets, and a default exists, the default must be used.

68 *What does the acronym CIDR stand for? What is the original purpose of CIDR?*

Classless Interdomain Routing is the concept of grouping multiple sequential network numbers into a single routing table entry, for the purpose of improving scalability of Internet routers by reducing the size of the IP routing table.

69 *Define the term private addressing as defined in RFC 1918.*

Some hosts will never need to communicate with other hosts across the Internet. For such hosts, assignment of IP addresses from registered networks wastes IP addresses. To conserve IP addresses, a set of network numbers, called *private addresses*, has been reserved and can be used in these cases to help conserve IP addresses for use over the Internet.

70 *Define the acronym NAT and the basics of its operation.*

Network Address Translation is a mechanism for allowing hosts with private addresses or addresses that conflict with IP addresses from a registered network to communicate with hosts over the Internet. The basic operation involves the NAT router changing the IP addresses in packets to and from these hosts so that the only type of IP address used in flows through the Internet uses addresses that are legitimately registered.

71 *Which requires more lines of source code, FTP or TFTP? Justify your answer.*

TFTP requires less code. It was designed to be simple (that is, trivial), with the small amount of memory needed to load the code ranking as an advantage to using TFTP. FTP is much more robust, with many more features and more code.

72 *Does FTP or TFTP perform error recovery? If so, describe the basics of how they perform error recovery.*

Both FTP and TFTP perform error recovery. FTP relies on TCP, whereas TFTP performs application layer recovery one block of data at a time.

73 *Describe the process used by IP routers to perform fragmentation and reassembly of packets.*

When a packet must be forwarded but the packet is larger than the maximum transmission unit (MTU) size for the outgoing interface, the router fragments the packet, as long as the Don't Fragment bit is not set. No IP router reassembles the fragments; fragments are reassembled at the final destination host.

74 *How many TCP segments are exchanged to establish a TCP connection? How many are required to terminate a TCP connection?*

A three-way connection establishment sequence is used, and a four-flow connection termination sequence is used.

75 *How many Class B-style networks are reserved by RFC 1918 private addressing?*

Sixteen Class B networks are reserved for use as private networks in RFC 1918, networks 172.16.0.0 to 172.31.0.0.

Answers to the Chapter 6 "Do I Know This Already?" Quiz

1 *Define what split horizon means to the contents of a routing update. Does this apply to both the distance vector algorithm and the link-state algorithm?*

Routing updates sent out an interface do not contain routing information about subnets learned from updates entering the same interface. Split horizon is used only by distance vector routing protocols.

2 *Does IPX RIP use Split Horizon?*

Split horizon means that routes learned by receiving updates on interface x will not be advertised in the routing updates sent out interface x. IPX RIP uses split horizon by default. SAP also uses split horizon concepts.

3 *Describe the purpose and meaning of route poisoning.*

Route poisoning is the distance vector routing protocol feature in which a newly bad route is advertised with an infinite metric. Routers receiving this routing information then can mark the route as a bad route immediately. The purpose is to prevent routing loops.

4 *Describe the meaning and purpose of triggered updates.*

A triggered update is the routing protocol feature in which an update is sent immediately when new routing information is learned rather than waiting on a timer to complete before sending another routing update.

5 *Write down the steps you would take to migrate from RIP to IGRP in a router whose current RIP configuration includes only **router rip**, followed by a **network 10.0.0.0** command.*

Issue the following commands in configuration mode:

```
router igrp 5
network 10.0.0.0
no router rip
```

If RIP still was configured, IGRP's routes would be chosen over RIP. The IOS considers IGRP to be a better source of routing information, by default, as defined in the administrative distance setting (default 120 for RIP, 100 for IGRP).

6 *How does the IOS designate a subnet in the routing table as a directly connected network? What about a route learned with IGRP or a route learned with RIP?*

The **show ip route** command lists routes with a designator in the left side of the command output. **C** represents connected routes, **I** is used for IGRP, and **R** represents routes derived from RIP.

7 *From a router's user mode, without using debugs or privileged mode, how can you determine what routers are sending you routing updates?*

The **show ip protocol** command output lists the routing sources—the IP addresses of routers sending updates to this router. Knowing how to determine a fact without looking at the configuration will better prepare you for the exam. Also, the **show ip route** command lists next-hop router IP addresses. The next-hop routers listed identify the routers that are sending routing updates.

8 *If the command **router rip** followed by **network 10.0.0.0**, with no other **network** commands, was configured in a router that has an Ethernet0 interface with IP address 168.10.1.1, would RIP send updates out Ethernet0?*

No. There must be a network statement for network 168.10.0.0 before RIP will advertise out that interface.

9 *Describe the metric(s) used by IPX RIP in a Cisco router.*

The primary metric is a counter of timer ticks. If two routes to the same network tie with the ticks metric, the hop count is considered. Ticks are increments of 1/18ths of a second. The number of ticks is not measured but is set with defaults of 1 on LAN interfaces and 6 on WAN interfaces. The IPX delay interface subcommand overrides the defaults.

10 *What does GNS stand for? Who creates GNS requests, and who creates GNS replies?*

GNS stands for Get Nearest Server. Clients create the request, which is a broadcast looking for a nearby server. Servers and routers reply, based on their SAP table, with the IPX address of a server whose RIP metric is low.

11 *If Serial0 has a **bandwidth 1544** interface subcommand and Serial1 has a **bandwidth 56** interface subcommand, what metric will IPX RIP associate with each interface?*

The IOS is unaffected by an interface's bandwidth when considering IPX RIP metrics; ticks will default to 6 for any serial interface, regardless of bandwidth setting.

12 *What **show** commands list IPX RIP metric values in a Cisco router?*

```
show ipx route
show ipx servers
```

This is a trick question. The services listed by the **show ipx servers** command also contain a reference to the RIP metrics; the information is handy when looking for good servers for a GNS reply.

13 *Define the term integrated multiprotocol routing in the context of the Cisco IOS and Novell IPX.*

Integrated multiprotocol routing means that multiple routed protocols use a common routing protocol, which consolidates routing updates. EIGRP is the only such routing protocol covered in the recommended training path for CCNAs; EIGRP exchanges routing information for IP, IPX, and AppleTalk. IGRP and Integrated IS-IS support both IP and OSI CLNS routable protocols.

14 *What routing protocols support integrated multiprotocol routing?*

EIGRP supports integrated multiprotocol routing for IP, IPX, and AppleTalk. IGRP and Integrated IS-IS support integrated multiprotocol routing for IP and OSI CLNS.

15 *Identify reasons for using tunneling.*

The four reasons outlined in this text are these:

- To allow multiprotocol traffic to flow over an IP backbone

- To support VPNs

- To overcome discontiguous network problems

- To overcome the shortcoming of some routing protocols with low maximum metric limitations

Other reasons may also be valid because this question is somewhat subjective.

16 *What tunneling transport protocol is used by the IOS?*

To answer this question, you must understand the term *transport protocol. Transport protocol* refers to the protocol that encapsulates the data and transports the data to the other side of the tunnel. There is only one transport protocol in the IOS: IP.

Answers to the Chapter 6 Q&A Section

1 *What type of routing protocol algorithm uses a holddown timer? What is its purpose?*

Distance vector. Holddown helps prevent counting to infinity problems. Holddown is explained in detail in the section "Distance Vector Routing Protocols" in Chapter 6. After hearing that a route has failed, a router waits for holddown time before believing any new information about the route.

2 *Define what split horizon means to the contents of a routing update. Does this apply to both the distance vector algorithm and the link state algorithm?*

Routing updates sent out an interface do not contain routing information about subnets learned from updates entering the same interface. Split horizon is used only by distance vector routing protocols.

3 *Write down the steps you would take to migrate from RIP to IGRP in a router whose current RIP configuration includes only **router rip**, followed by a **network 10.0.0.0** command.*

Issue the following commands in configuration mode:

```
router igrp 5
network 10.0.0.0
no router rip
```

If RIP still were configured, IGRP's routes would be chosen over RIP. The IOS considers IGRP to be a better source of routing information by default, as defined in the administrative distance setting (default 120 for RIP, 100 for IGRP).

4 *How does the IOS designate a subnet in the routing table as a directly connected network? What about a route learned with IGRP and a route learned with RIP?*

The **show ip route** command lists routes with a designator in the left side of the command output. **C** represents connected routes, **I** is used for IGRP, and **R** represents RIP-derived routes.

5 *Create a configuration for IGRP on a router with these interfaces and addresses: e0 using 10.1.1.1, e1 using 224.1.2.3, s0 using 10.1.2.1, and s1 using 199.1.1.1. Use process ID 5.*

```
router igrp 5
network 10.0.0.0
network 199.1.1.0
```

If you noticed that 224.1.2.3 is not a valid Class A, B, or C address, you get full credit. A new address will be needed for Ethernet 1, with a matching network command.

6 *Create a configuration for IGRP on a router with these interfaces and addresses: to0 using 200.1.1.1, e0 using 128.1.3.2, s0 using 192.0.1.1, and s1 using 223.254.254.1.*

```
router igrp 1
network 200.1.1.0
network 128.1.0.0
network 192.0.1.0
network 223.254.254.0
```

Because four different networks are used, four network commands are required. If you noticed that the question did not specify the process ID (1, in this sample) but configured one, you get full credit. A few of these network numbers are used in examples; memorize the range of valid A, B, and C network numbers.

7 *From a router's user mode, without using debugs or privileged mode, how can you determine what routers are sending you routing updates?*

The **show ip protocol** command output lists the routing sources, the IP addresses of routers sending updates to this router. Knowing how to determine a fact without looking at the configuration will better prepare you for the exam. Also, the **show ip route** command lists next-hop router IP addresses. The next-hop routers listed identify the routers that are sending routing updates.

8 *How often does IPX RIP send routing updates, by default?*

Every 60 seconds.

9 *Describe the metric(s) used by IPX RIP in a Cisco router.*

The primary metric is a counter of timer ticks. If two routes to the same network tie with the ticks metric, the hop count is considered. Ticks are increments of 1/18ths of a second. The number of ticks is not measured but is set with defaults of 1 on LAN interfaces and 6 on WAN interfaces. The IPX delay interface subcommand overrides the defaults.

10 *Does IPX RIP use Split Horizon?*

Split horizon means that routes learned via updates received on interface *x* will not be advertised in routing updates sent out interface *x*. IPX RIP uses split horizon by default. SAP also uses split horizon concepts.

11 *True or false: RIP and SAP information is sent in the same packets. If true, can only one of the two be enabled in a router? If false, what commands enable each protocol globally in a router?*

False. Only one command is used, and it enables both: **ipx routing**. Neither type of update is sent unless IPX is also enabled on the interface with the **ipx network** interface subcommand.

12 *What does GNS stand for? Who creates GNS requests, and who creates GNS replies?*

GNS stands for Get Nearest Server. Clients create the request, which is a broadcast looking for a nearby server. Servers and routers reply, based on their SAP table, with the IPX address of a server whose RIP metric is low.

13 *Define the term separate multiprotocol routing in the context of the Cisco IOS and Novell IPX.*

Separate multiprotocol routing means that each routed protocol, such as IP, IPX, or AppleTalk, uses a separate set of routing protocols, which each send separate routing updates to advertise routing information.

14 *How often does a router send SAP updates, by default?*

Every 60 seconds.

15 *If Serial0 has a **bandwidth 1544** interface subcommand and Serial1 has a **bandwidth 56** interface subcommand, what metric will IPX RIP associate with each interface?*

The IOS is unaffected by an interface's bandwidth when considering IPX RIP metrics; ticks will default to 6 for any serial interface, regardless of bandwidth setting.

16 *True or false: Routers forward SAP packets as they arrive but broadcast SAP packets on interfaces in which no SAP packets have been received in the last 60 seconds.*

False. Routers never forward SAP packets, but they instead read the information in the updates, update their own SAP tables, and then discard the packets. Routers also send SAP updates every update timer (default 60 seconds), regardless of what other routers may do.

This sample question is another case of tricky wording that may be used to make sure you know the topic.

17 *What **show** commands list IPX RIP metric values in a Cisco router?*

```
show ipx route
show ipx servers
```

This is a trick question. The services listed by the **show ipx servers** command also contain a reference to the RIP metrics; the information is handy when looking for good servers for a GNS reply.

18 *Define the term integrated multiprotocol routing in the context of the Cisco IOS and Novell IPX.*

Integrated multiprotocol routing means that multiple routed protocols use a common routing protocol, which consolidates routing updates. EIGRP is the only such routing protocol covered in the recommended training path for CCNAs; EIGRP exchanges routing information for IP, IPX, and AppleTalk. IGRP and Integrated IS-IS support both IP and OSI CLNS routable protocols.

19 *If the commands **router rip** and **network 10.0.0.0**, with no other network commands, were configured in a router that has an Ethernet0 interface with IP address 168.10.1.1, would RIP send updates out Ethernet0?*

No. There must be a network statement for network 168.10.0.0 before RIP will advertise out that interface. The **network** command simply selects the connected interfaces on which to send and receive updates.

20 *If the commands **router igrp 1** and **network 10.0.0.0** were configured in a router that has an Ethernet0 interface with IP address 168.10.1.1, would IGRP advertise about 168.10.0.0?*

No. There must be a network statement for network 168.10.0.0 before IGRP will advertise about that directly connected subnet.

21 *If the commands **router igrp 1** and **network 10.0.0.0** were configured in a router that has an Ethernet0 interface with IP address 168.10.1.1, mask 255.255.255.0, would this router have a route to 168.10.1.0?*

Yes. The route will be in the routing table because it is a directly connected subnet, not because of any action by IGRP.

22 *What routing protocols support integrated multiprotocol routing?*

EIGRP supports integrated multiprotocol routing for IP, IPX, and AppleTalk. IGRP and Integrated IS-IS support integrated multiprotocol routing for IP and OSI CLNS.

23 *Must IGRP metrics for multiple routes to the same subnet be exactly equal for the multiple routes to be added to the routing table? If not, how close in value do the metrics have to be?*

IGRP (and EIGRP) use a concept called variance, which represents how close the metrics to the same subnet must be before the metrics are considered equal. The **variance** router subcommand is used to set the value.

24 *When using RIP, what configuration command controls the number of equal-cost routes that can be added to the routing table at the same time? What is the maximum number of equal-cost routes to the same destination that can be included in the IP routing table at once?*

The **ip maximum-paths** *x* router subcommand is used in RIP configuration mode to set the number. The maximum is 6, and the default is 4.

25 *When using IGRP, what configuration command controls the number of equal-cost routes that can be added to the routing table at the same time? What is the maximum number of equal-cost routes to the same destination that can be included in the IP routing table at once?*

The **ip maximum-paths** *x* router subcommand is used in IGRP configuration mode to set the number. The maximum is 6, and the default is 4.

26 *What feature supported by RIP-2 allows it to support variable-length subnet masks (VLSM)?*

The association and transmission of mask information with each route allows VLSM support with any routing protocol, RIP-2 included.

27 *Name three features of RIP-2 that are not features of RIP-1.*

The features included in RIP-2 but not in RIP-1 include: transmission of subnet mask with routes, authentication, next-hop router IP address in routing update, external route tags, and multicast routing updates.

28 *What configuration commands are different between a router configured for RIP-1 and a router configured for only support of RIP-2?*

The **router rip** and **network** commands would be identical. The RIP-2 router would require a version 2 router subcommand to enable RIP-2.

29 *Identify reasons for using tunneling.*

The four reasons outlined in this text are: to allow multiprotocol traffic to flow over an IP backbone, to support VPNs, to overcome discontiguous network problems, and to overcome the shortcoming of some routing protocols with low maximum metric limitations. Other reasons also might be valid because this question is somewhat subjective.

30 *What tunneling transport protocol is used by the IOS?*

To answer this question, you must know what the term transport protocol refers to. Transport protocol refers to the protocol that both encapsulates the data and transports the data to the other side of the tunnel. This is a trick question—there is only one transport protocol in the IOS: IP.

31 *Define the tunneling terms transport protocol, encapsulation protocol, and passenger protocol.*

The term *transport protocol* refers to the protocol that both encapsulates the data and transports the data to the other side of the tunnel. The *encapsulation protocol* follows the transport protocol; its main purpose is to have a type field to identify the type of packet that is encapsulated. This encapsulated protocol is called the *passenger protocol* because it is being carried to the other end of the tunnel.

32 *List the Interior IP routing protocols that have auto summarization enabled by default. Which of these protocols allows auto summary to be disabled using a configuration command?*

RIP-1, IGRP, EIGRP, and RIP-2 all have auto summarization enabled by default. EIGRP and RIP-2 can disable this feature.

33 *List the interior IP routing protocols that support route aggregation.*

EIGRP and OSPF support route aggregation.

34 *Identify the command that would list all IP routes learned via RIP.*

The **show ip route rip** command would list only RIP-learned routes.

35 *Identify the command(s) that would list all IP routes in network 172.16.0.0.*

show ip route 172.16.0.0 lists all the routes in 172.16.0.0. Also, the **show ip route list 1** command would list routes in network 172.16.0.0, assuming that the following configuration command also existed: **access-list 1 permit 172.16.0.0 0.0.255.255**.

36 *Assume that several subnets of network 172.16.0.0 exist in a router's routing table. What must be true about those routes so that the output of the **show ip route** command lists mask information only on the line that lists network 172.16.0.0, but not show mask information on each route for each subnet?*

If all the subnets of 172.16.0.0 use the same mask, the output of the **show ip route** command lists only the mask in the heading line for the network. If VLSM were in use, then each route for each subnet would reflect the mask used in that case.

37 *True or false: Distance vector routing protocols learn routes by transmitting routing updates.*

False. Routes are learned by receiving routing updates from neighboring routers.

38 *Assume that a router is configured to allow only one route in the routing table to each destination network. If more than one route to a particular subnet is learned, and if each route has the same metric value, which route is placed into the routing table if the routing protocol uses distance vector logic?*

In this scenario, the first route learned is placed into the table. If that route is removed at a later time, the next routing update received after the original route has been removed is added to the routing table.

39 *Describe the purpose and meaning of route poisoning.*

Route poisoning is the distance vector routing protocol feature in which a newly bad route is advertised with an infinite metric. Routers receiving this routing information then can mark the route as a bad route immediately. The purpose is to prevent routing loops.

40 *Describe the meaning and purpose of triggered updates.*

A triggered update is the routing protocol feature in which an update is sent immediately when new routing information is learned rather than waiting on a timer to complete before sending another routing update.

Answers to the Chapter 7 "Do I Know This Already?" Quiz

1 *Configure a numbered IP access list that would stop packets from subnet 134.141.7.0, 255.255.255.0, from exiting serial 0 on some router. Allow all other packets.*

```
access-list 4 deny 134.141.7.0 0.0.0.255
access-list 4 permit any
interface serial 0
ip access-group 4
```

The first access list statement denied packets from that subnet. The other statement is needed because of the default action to deny packets not explicitly matched in an access list statement.

2 *How would a user who does not have the enable password find out what access lists have been configured and where they are enabled?*

The **show access-list** command lists all access lists. The **show ip interfaces** and **show ipx interfaces** commands identify interfaces on which the access lists are enabled.

3 *How many IP extended access-list commands are required to check a particular port number on all IP packets?*

Two statements are required. If the protocol type IP is configured, the port number is not allowed to be checked. So, the TCP or UDP protocol type must be used to check the port numbers. Therefore, if port 25 needs to be checked for both TCP and UDP, two statements are needed: one for TCP and one for UDP.

4 *True or false: If all IP or IPX access list statements in a particular list define the deny action, then the default action is to permit all other packets.*

False. The default action at the end of any IP or IPX access list is to deny all other packets.

5 *How many IP access lists of either type can be active on an interface at the same time?*

Only one IP access list per interface, per direction. In other words, one inbound and one outbound are allowed, but no more.

6 *In a standard named IP access list with three statements, a **no** version of the first statement is issued in configuration mode. Immediately following, another access list configuration command is added for the same access list. How many statements are in the list now, and in what position is the newly added statement?*

Three statements will remain in the list, with the newly added statement at the end of the list. The **no deny | permit. . .** command deletes only that single named access list subcommand in named lists. However, when the command is added again, it cannot be placed anywhere except at the end of the list.

7 *In an IPX access list with five statements, a **no** version of the third statement is issued in configuration mode. Immediately following, another access list configuration command is added for the same access list. How many statements are in the list now, and in what position is the newly added statement?*

Only one statement will remain in the list: the newly added statement. The **no access-list** *x* command deletes the entire access list, even if all the parameters in an individual command are typed in when issuing the **no** version of the command.

8 *Name all the items that a SAP access list can examine to make a match.*

- Network
- IPX address (network and node)
- Subsets of the first two using a wildcard
- Service type
- Server name

Many people would consider checking the network number and checking a full IPX address as the same item. These functions are listed separately here only to make sure you recall that both variations are possible.

9 *Name all the items that a standard IPX access list can examine to make a match.*

- Source network
- Source IPX address (network and node)
- Subset of node part of address (using mask)

- Destination network
- Destination IPX address (network and node)
- Subset of node part of IPX address (using mask)

Many people would consider checking the network number and checking a full IPX address as the same item. These functions are listed separately here only to make sure you recall that both variations are possible. Also, the mask can be used only if the full IPX address is specified and masks out only parts of the node part of the address.

10 *Name all the items that a named extended IPX access list can examine to make a match.*

- Protocol
- Source socket
- Source network
- Source IPX address (network and node)
- Subset of entire address (using mask)
- Destination socket
- Destination network
- Destination IPX address (network and node)
- Subset of entire IPX address (using mask)

The same matching criteria are used for numbered extended IPX access lists as that used for named extended IPX access lists.

11 *Configure a SAP numbered access list so that SAPs 4 to 7 are matched, in network BEEF, with a single command.*

You cannot match more than one SAP with a single access list statement. To match four separate SAP values, four separate access list statements are required.

12 *What command could someone who has only the Telnet password, not the enable password, use to find out what IPX access lists are enabled on which interfaces?*

The **show ipx interfaces** command lists all interfaces and details about each interface, including the name and number of all standard, extended, and SAP access lists enabled on each interface.

Answers to the Chapter 7 Q&A Section

1 *Configure a numbered IP access list that would stop packets from subnet 134.141.7.0, 255.255.255.0, from exiting serial 0 on some router. Allow all other packets.*

```
access-list 4 deny 134.141.7.0 0.0.0.255
access-list 4 permit any
interface serial 0
ip access-group 4
```

The first access list statement denied packets from that subnet. The other statement is needed because the default action to deny packets is not explicitly matched in an access list statement.

2 *Configure an IP access list that allows only packets from subnet 193.7.6.0, 255.255.255.0, going to hosts in network 128.1.0.0 and using a Web server in 128.1.0.0, to enter serial 0 on some router.*

```
access-list 105 permit tcp 193.7.6.0 0.0.0.255
128.1.0.0 0.0.255.255 eq www
!
interface serial 0
ip access-group 105 in
```

A "deny all" is implied at the end of the list.

3 *How would a user who does not have the enable password find out what access lists have been configured and where they are enabled?*

The **show access-list** command lists all access lists. The **show ip interfaces** and **show ipx interfaces** commands identify interfaces on which the access lists are enabled.

4 *Configure and enable an IP access list that would stop packets from subnet 10.3.4.0/24 from getting out serial interface S0 and that would stop packets from 134.141.5.4 from entering S0. Permit all other traffic.*

```
access-list 1 deny 10.3.4.0 0.0.0.255
access-list 1 permit any
access-list 2 deny 134.141.5.4
access-list 2 permit any
interface serial 0
ip access-group 1
ip access-group 2 in
```

5 *Configure and enable an IP access list that would allow packets from subnet 10.3.4.0/24, to any Web server, to get out serial interface S0. Also, allow packets from 134.141.5.4 going to all TCP-based servers using a well-known port to enter serial 0. Deny all other traffic.*

```
access-list 101 permit tcp 10.3.4.0 0.0.0.255 any eq www
access-list 102 permit tcp host 134.141.5.4 any lt 1023
interface serial 0
ip access-group 101 out
ip access-group 102 in
```

Two extended access lists are required. List 101 permits packets in the first of the two criteria, in which packets exiting S0 are examined. List 102 permits packets for the second criterion, in which packets entering S0 are examined.

6 *Create an IPX packet filter to prevent packets from entering Serial0, except for packets from address 500.0000.0000.0001 destined for any node in network 4.*

```
access-list 800 permit 500.0000.0000.0001 4
interface serial0
ipx access-group 800 in
```

A "deny all else" is implied at the end of the list.

7 *What services use IPX socket 4? What about Socket 7?*

None. This is a trick question. SAP types 4 and 7 represent file and print services, respectively. However, sockets are different, and there is no correlation between SAP service types and sockets. The message: Read all the words in the question! Some questions are purposefully designed to ensure that you know what each term means.

8 *Create a configuration to add a SAP access list to filter all print services (SAP 7) from being advertised out a router's serial 0 and serial1 interfaces.*

```
access-list 1000 deny -1 7
access-list 1000 permit -1
interface serial 0
ipx output-sap-filter 1000
interface serial1
ipx output-sap-filter 1000
```

In the two **access-list 1000** commands, the **–1** represents the wildcard meaning "any network." SAP type **7** is for print services; the first statement matches those services and denies those services. However, other proprietary print solutions could use a different SAP type. This access list matches only for the standard SAP type for printers.

9 *Name all the items that a SAP access list can examine to make a match.*

- Network
- IPX address (network and node)
- Subnets of the first two using a wildcard
- Service type
- Server name

Many people would consider checking the network number and checking a full IPX address as the same item. These functions are listed separately here only to make sure you recall that both variations are possible.

10 *Can standard IP access lists be used to check the source IP address when enabled with the **ip access-group 1 in** command, and can they check the destination IP addresses when using the **ip access-group 1 out** command?*

No. Standard IP access lists check only the source IP address, regardless of whether the packets are checked when inbound or outbound.

11 *How many IP extended **access-list** commands are required to check a particular port number on all IP packets?*

Two statements are required. If the protocol type IP is configured, the port number is not allowed to be checked. So, the TCP or UDP protocol type must be used to check the port numbers. Therefore, if port 25 needs to be checked for both TCP and UDP, two statements are needed: one for TCP and one for UDP.

12 *True or false: If all IP or IPX access list statements in a particular list define the deny action, then the default action is to permit all other packets.*

False. The default action at the end of any IP or IPX access list is to deny all other packets.

13 *In an IPX access list with five statements, a **no** version of the third statement is issued in configuration mode. Immediately following, another access list configuration command is added for the same access list. How many statements are in the list now, and in what position is the newly added statement?*

Only one statement will remain in the list: the newly added statement. The **no access-list** *x* command deletes the entire access list, even if all the parameters in an individual command are typed in when issuing the **no** version of the command.

14 *How many IP access lists of either type can be active on an interface at the same time?*

Only one IP access list per interface, per direction. In other words, one inbound and one outbound are allowed, but no more.

For questions 16 through 18, assume that all parts of the network in Figure A-1 are up and working. IGRP is the IP routing protocol in use. Answer the questions following Example A-1, which contains an additional configuration in the Mayberry router.

Figure A-1   *Network Diagram for Questions 16 Through 18*

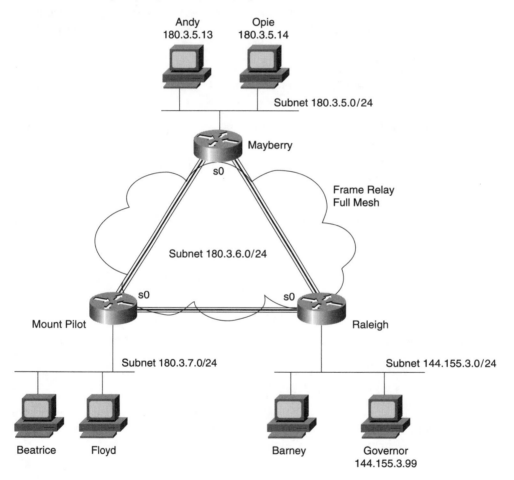

Example A-1 *Access List at Mayberry*

```
access-list 44 permit 180.3.5.13 0.0.0.0
!
interface serial 0
ip access-group 44
```

15 *Describe the types of packets that this filter would discard, and tell at what point they would be discarded.*

Only packets coming from Andy exit Mayberry's Serial 0 interface. Packets originating inside the Mayberry router—for example, a **ping** command issued from Mayberry, will work because the IOS will not filter packets originating in that router. Opie is still out of luck—he'll never get (a packet) out of Mayberry!

16 *Does the access list in Example A-1 stop packets from getting to Web server Governor? Why or why not?*

Packets from Andy can get to Web server Governor; packets from Mount Pilot can be delivered to Governor if the route points directly from Mount Pilot to Raleigh so that the packets do not pass through Mayberry. Therefore, the access list, as coded, stops only hosts other than Andy on the Mayberry Ethernet from reaching Web server Governor.

17 *Referring to Figure A-1, create and enable access lists so that access to Web server Governor is allowed from hosts at any site, but so that no other access to hosts in Raleigh is allowed.*

```
! this access-list is enabled on the Raleigh router
access-list 130 permit tcp 180.3.5.0  0.0.0.255 host 144.155.3.99 eq www
access-list 130 permit tcp 180.3.7.0  0.0.0.255 host 144.155.3.99 eq www
!
interface serial 0
ip access-group 130 in
```

This access list performs the function, but it also filters IGRP updates as well. That is part of the danger with inbound access lists; with outbound lists, the router will not filter packets originating in that router. With inbound access lists, all packets entering the interface are examined and could be filtered. An IGRP protocol type is allowed in the extended **access-list** command; therefore, IGRP updates easily can be matched. The command **access-list 130 permit igrp any** performs the needed matching of IGRP updates, permitting those packets. (This command would need to appear before any statements in list 130 that might match IGRP updates.)

18 *Name all the items that a standard IPX access list can examine to make a match.*

- Source network

- Source IPX address (network and node)

- Subset of node part of address (using mask)

- Destination network

- Destination IPX address (network and node)

- Subset of node part of IPX address (using mask)

Many people would consider checking the network number and checking a full IPX address as the same item. These functions are listed separately here only to make sure you recall that both variations are possible. Also, the mask can be used only if the full IPX address is specified and masks out only parts of the node part of the address.

19 *Name all the items that an extended IPX access list can examine to make a match.*

- Protocol

- Source socket

- Source network

- Source IPX address (network and node)

- Subset of entire address (using mask)

- Destination socket

- Destination network

- Destination IPX address (network and node)

- Subset of entire IPX address (using mask)

Many people would consider checking the network number and checking a full IPX address as the same item. These functions are listed separately here only to make sure you recall that both variations are possible. Also, the mask can be used only if the full IPX address is specified and masks out only parts of the node part of the address.

20 *Name all the items that a standard IP access list can examine to make a match.*

- Source IP address

- Subset of entire source address (using mask)

21 *Name all the items that an extended IP access list can examine to make a match.*

- Protocol type

- Source port

- Source IP address

- Subset of entire source address (using mask)

- Destination port

- Destination IP address

- Subset of entire destination address (using mask)

22 *True or false: When using extended IP access lists for restricting VTY access, the matching logic is a best match of the list, rather than a first match in the list.*

False. Access list logic is always first match for any application of the list.

23 *In a standard numbered IP access list with three statements, a **no** version of the first statement is issued in configuration mode. Immediately following, another access list configuration command is added for the same access list. How many statements are in the list now, and in what position is the newly added statement?*

Only one statement will remain in the list: the newly added statement. The **no access-list** *x* command deletes the entire access list, even if all the parameters in an individual command are typed in when issuing the no version of the command.

24 *In a standard named IP access list with three statements, a **no** version of the first statement is issued in configuration mode. Immediately following, another access list configuration command is added for the same access list. How many statements are in the list now, and in what position is the newly added statement?*

Three statements will remain in the list, with the newly added statement at the end of the list. The **no deny | permit. . .** command deletes only that single named access list subcommand in named lists. However, when the command is added again, it cannot be placed anywhere except at the end of the list.

25 *In an extended named IPX access list with five statements, a **no** version of the second statement is issued in configuration mode. Immediately following, another access list configuration command is added for the same access list. How many statements are in the list now, and in what position is the newly added statement?*

Five statements will remain in the list, with the newly added statement at the end of the list. The **no deny | permit. . .** command deletes only that single named access list subcommand in named lists. However, when the command is added again, it cannot be placed anywhere except at the end of the list.

26 *Name all the items that a named extended IPX access list can examine to make a match.*

- Protocol
- Source socket
- Source network
- Source IPX address (network and node)
- Subset of entire address (using mask)
- Destination socket
- Destination network
- Destination IPX address (network and node)
- Subset of entire IPX address (using mask)

The same matching criteria are used for numbered extended IPX access lists as are used for named extended IPX access lists.

27 *Name all the items that a named standard IP access list can **examine to make a match.***

- Source IP address
- Subset of entire source address (using mask)

Named standard IP access lists match the same items that numbered IP access lists match.

28 *Configure a SAP numbered access list so that SAPs 4 through 7 are matched in network BEEF with a single command.*

You cannot match more than one SAP with a single access list statement. To match four separate SAP values, four separate access list statements are required.

29 *Configure a named IP access list that would stop packets from subnet 134.141.7.0, 255.255.255.0, from exiting serial 0 on some router. Allow all other packets.*

```
ip access-list standard fred
 deny 134.141.7.0 0.0.0.255
 permit any
!
interface serial 0
ip access-group fred
```

The first access list statement denies packets from that subnet. The other statement is needed because the default action to deny packets is not explicitly matched in an access list statement.

30 *Configure a named IP access list that allows only packets from subnet 193.7.6.0, 255.255.255.0, going to hosts in network 128.1.0.0 and using a Web server in 128.1.0.0, to enter serial 0 on some router.*

```
ip access-list extended barney
 permit tcp 193.7.6.0 0.0.0.255 128.1.0.0 0.0.255.255 eq www
 !
interface serial 0
ip access-group barney in
```

A "deny all" is implied at the end of the list.

31 *List the types of IP access lists (numbered standard, numbered extended, named standard, named extended) that can be enabled to prevent Telnet access into a router. What commands would be used to enable this function, assuming that **access-list 2** was already configured to match the right packets?*

Any type of IP access list can be enabled for preventing VTY access. The command **line vty 0 4**, followed by **ip access-group 2 in**, would enable the feature using access-list 2.

32 *What command could someone who has only the telnet password, not the enable password, use to find out what IPX access lists were enabled on which interfaces?*

The **show ipx interfaces** command lists all interfaces and details about each interface, including the name and number of all standard, extended, and SAP access lists enabled on each interface.

33 *What command would display the contents of IPX **access-list 904**, and that access list alone?*

Both the **show access-list 904** and the **show ipx access-list 904** commands would show the same contents. Both actually show the information in the same format.

34 *What command lists the IP extended access lists enabled on serial 1 without showing other interfaces?*

The **show ip interface serial 1** command lists the names and numbers of the IP access lists enabled on serial 1.

Answers to the Chapter 8 "Do I Know This Already?" Quiz

1 *Can PPP perform dynamic assignment of IP addresses? If so, is the feature always enabled?*

PPP's IPCP protocol can assign an IP address to the device on the other end of the link. This process is not required and is not performed by default. PPP usually does address assignment for dial access, such as when a user dials an Internet service provider.

2 *Create a configuration to enable PPP on serial 0 for IP and IPX. Make up IP and IPX Layer 3 addresses as needed.*

```
interface serial 0
ip addr 1.1.1.1 255.255.255.0
ipx network 1
encapsulation ppp
```

encapsulation ppp is all that is needed for PPP. Having IP and IPX enabled causes PPP to enable the control protocols for each.

3 *CHAP configuration uses names and passwords. Given Routers A and B, describe what names and passwords must match in the respective CHAP configurations.*

Router A has name B and a corresponding password configured. Router B has name A and the same password configured. The names used are the host names of the routers unless the CHAP name is configured.

4 *What field has Cisco added to the HDLC header, making it proprietary?*

A Protocol Type field has been added to allow support for multiprotocol traffic. HDLC was not architected to allow for multiprotocol support originally.

5 *Explain the purpose of Inverse ARP. Explain how Inverse ARP uses Frame Relay broadcasts.*

A router discovers the Layer 3 address(es) of a router on the other end of a VC when that other router sends an Inverse ARP message. The message is not a broadcast. Broadcasts are not supported over Frame Relay.

6 *Would a Frame Relay switch connected to a router behave differently if the IETF option were deleted from the encapsulation **frame-relay ietf** command on that attached router? Would a router on the other end of the VC behave any differently if the same change were made?*

The switch does not behave differently. The other router, however, must also use IETF encapsulation; otherwise, the routers will not be looking at the correct fields to learn the packet type. The IETF-defined headers include the Protocol Type field options.

7 *What **show** command will tell you the time that a PVC became active? How does the router know what time the PVC became active?*

The **show frame-relay pvc** command lists the time since the PVC came up, so you can subtract this time from the current time of day to derive the time at which the VC came up. The router learns this from an LMI message.

8 *What **debug** options will show Inverse ARP messages?*

debug frame-relay events, as shown in Example 8-19 on page 561.

9 *What does the acronym LAPD stand for? Is it used as the Layer 2 protocol on dialed ISDN bearer channels? If not, what is used?*

Link Access Procedure, D-channel. LAPD is not used on bearer channels, but instead on the signaling channel. PPP is typically used on bearer channels.

10 *Define the term reference point. List two examples of reference points.*

A reference point is an interface between function groups. R, S, T, and U are the reference points. S and T are combined in many cases and then called the S/T reference point. Reference points refer to cabling, which implies the number of wires used. In particular, the S and T points use a four-wire interface; the U interface uses a two-wire cable.

11 *Describe the decision process performed by the IOS to attempt to dial a connection using legacy DDR.*

First, some traffic must be routed out the interface to be dialed; this is typically accomplished by adding static routes pointing out the interface. Then, "interesting" must be defined; any packets routed out the interface that are considered interesting will cause the interface to be dialed.

12 *If packets from 10.1.1.0/24 were "interesting" in relation to DDR configuration such that packets from 10.1.1.0/24 would cause a DDR connection out an interface BRI0, list the configuration commands that would make the IOS think that those packets were interesting on BRI0.*

The access list that follows defines the packets from 10.1.1.0/24. The **dialer-list** defines the use of **access-list 1** for deciding what is interesting. The **dialer-group** command enables that logic on interface BRI0.

```
access-list 1 permit 10.1.1.0 0.0.0.255
!
dialer-list 2 protocol ip list 1
!
interface bri 0
 dialer-group 2
```

Answers to the Chapter 8 Q&A Section

1 *Name two WAN data link protocols for which the standards define a protocol type field, which is used to define the type of header that follows the WAN data-link header.*

PPP and Frame Relay. The Frame Relay protocol field was added to the standard based on efforts from the IETF.

2 *Name two WAN data link protocols that define a method of announcing the Layer 3 addresses of the interface to other devices attached to the WAN.*

PPP and Frame Relay. PPP uses control protocols specific to each Layer 3 protocol supported. Frame Relay uses Inverse ARP.

3 *What does the acronym LAPD stand for? Is it used as the Layer 2 protocol on dialed ISDN bearer channels? If not, what is used?*

Link Access Procedure, D-channel. It is not used on bearer channels, but instead is used on the signaling channel. PPP is typically used on bearer channels.

4 *"Frame Relay uses source and destination DLCIs in the Frame Relay header, with length 10, 11, or 12 bits." Which parts of this statement do you agree with? Which parts do you disagree with? Why?*

There is only one DLCI field in the Frame Relay header, but it can be 10, 11, or 12 bits in length. For further information, refer to the section "Frame Relay Protocols."

5 *Explain the purpose of Inverse ARP. Explain how Inverse ARP uses Frame Relay broadcasts.*

A router discovers the Layer 3 address(es) of a router on the other end of a VC when that other router sends an Inverse ARP message. The message is not a broadcast. Broadcasts are not supported over Frame Relay.

6 *Would a Frame Relay switch connected to a router behave differently if the IETF option were deleted from the **encapsulation frame-relay ietf** command on that attached router? Would a router on the other end of the VC behave any differently if the same change were made?*

The switch does not behave differently. The other router, however, must also use IETF encapsulation; otherwise, the routers will not be looking at the correct fields to learn the packet type. The IETF-defined headers include the Protocol Type field options.

7 *What does NBMA stand for? Does it apply to PPP links? What about X.25 networks or Frame Relay networks?*

Nonbroadcast multiaccess. PPP is nonbroadcast, but not multiaccess. X.25 and Frame Relay are NBMA networks. Multiaccess really means more than two devices connected to the data link; therefore, when one device sends data, the intended receiver is not obvious.

8 *Define the terms DCE and DTE in the context of the physical layer and a point-to-point serial link.*

DTE refers to the device that looks for clocking from the device on the other end of the cable on a synchronous link. The DCE supplies that clocking. An X.25 switch is a DCE in the X.25 use of the word but probably is a DTE receiving clock from a DSU/CSU or Mux from the physical layer perspective.

9 *What layer of OSI is most closely related to the functions of Frame Relay? Why?*

OSI Layers 1 and 2. As usual, Frame Relay refers to well-known physical layer specifications. Frame Relay does define headers for delivery across the Frame Relay cloud, but it provides no addressing structure to allow VCs among multiple different Frame Relay networks; thus, it is not considered to match OSI Layer 3 functions. With the advent of Frame Relay SVCs, it could be argued that Frame Relay performs some Layer 3–like functions.

10 *When Inverse ARP is used by default, what additional configuration is needed to get IGRP routing updates to flow over each VC?*

No additional configuration is required. The forwarding of broadcasts as unicasts is enabled on each VC and protocol for which an Inverse ARP is received.

11 *Define the attributes of a partial mesh and full mesh Frame Relay network.*

In a partial mesh network, not all DTEs are connected with a VC. In a full mesh network, all DTEs are connected with a VC.

12 *What key pieces of information are required in the **frame-relay map** statement?*

Layer 3 protocol, next-hop router's Layer 3 address, DLCI to reach that router, and whether to forward broadcasts. Frame Relay maps are not required if Inverse ARP is in use.

13 *When creating a partial mesh Frame Relay network, are you required to use subinterfaces?*

No. Subinterfaces can be used and are preferred with a partial mesh because this removes split horizon issues by treating each VC as its own interface. Likewise, subinterfaces are optional when the network is a full mesh. Most people tend to use subinterfaces today.

14 *What benefit related to routing protocols can be gained by using subinterfaces with a partial mesh?*

Split horizon issues are avoided by treating each VC as a separate interface. Split horizon is still enabled; routing loops are not a risk, but all routes are learned.

15 *Can PPP perform dynamic assignment of IP addresses? If so, is the feature always enabled?*

PPP's IPCP protocol can assign an IP address to the device on the other end of the link. This process is not required. PPP usually does address assignment for dial access, for example, when a user dials an Internet service provider.

16 *Create a configuration to enable PPP on serial 0 for IP and IPX. Make up IP and IPX Layer 3 addresses as needed.*

```
interface serial 0
ip addr 1.1.1.1 255.255.255.0
ipx network 1
encapsulation ppp
```

encapsulation ppp is all that is needed for PPP. Having IP and IPX enabled causes PPP to enable the control protocols for each.

17 *Create a configuration for Router1 that has Frame Relay VCs to Router2 and Router3 (DLCIs 202 and 203, respectively) for Frame Relay on Router1's serial 1 interface. Use any IP and IPX addresses you like. Assume that the network is not fully-meshed.*

```
interface serial 1
encapsulation frame-relay
interface serial 1.1 point-to-point
ip address 168.10.1.1 255.255.255.0
ipx network 1
frame-relay interface-dlci 202
interface serial 1.2 point-to-point
ip address 168.10.2.1 255.255.255.0
ipx network 2
frame-relay interface-dlci 203
```

This is not the only valid configuration given the problem statement. However, because there is not a full mesh, then point-to-point subinterfaces are the best choice. Cisco encapsulation is used by default. The LMI type is autosensed.

18 *What **show** command will tell you the time that a PVC became active? How does the router know what time the PVC became active?*

The **show frame-relay pvc** command lists the time since the PVC came up. The router learns this from an LMI message.

19 *What **show** commands list Frame Relay information about mapping? In what instances will the information displayed include the Layer 3 addresses of other routers?*

show frame-relay map. The mapping information includes Layer 3 addresses when multipoint subinterfaces are used or when no subinterfaces are used. The two cases in which the neighboring routers' Layer 3 addresses are shown are the two cases in which Frame Relay acts like a multiaccess network. With point-to-point subinterfaces, the logic works like a point-to-point link, where the next router's Layer 3 address is not important to the routing process.

20 *True or false: The **no keepalive** command on a Frame Relay serial interface causes no further Cisco proprietary keepalive messages to be sent to the Frame Relay switch.*

False. This command stops LMI status inquiry messages from being sent. If the switch is expecting these, the switch could take down the PVCs to this DTE. Be careful—this is exactly the type of tricky wording on the exam. The messages do not go between the two routers over Frame Relay, but the Cisco keepalive message is not sent on true point-to-point links.

21 *What **debug** options will show Inverse ARP messages?*

debug frame-relay events, as shown in Example 8-19 on page 561.

22 *True or false: The Frame Relay **map** configuration command allows more than one Layer 3 protocol address mapping on the same configuration command.*

False. The syntax allows only a single network layer protocol and address to be configured.

23 *What do the letters in ISDN represent? What about BRI and PRI?*

Integrated Services Digital Network. Basic Rate Interface. Primary Rate Interface. BRI is the most likely to be on the exam.

24 *Define the term function group. List two examples of function groups.*

A function group is a set of ISDN functions that need to be implemented by a device. NT1, NT2, TE1, TE2, and TA are all function groups.

25 *Define the term reference point. List two examples of reference points.*

A reference point is an interface between function groups. R, S, T, and U are reference points. S and T are combined in many cases and then called the S/T reference point. Reference points refer to cabling, which implies the number of wires used. In particular, the S and T points use a four-wire interface; the U interface uses a two-wire cable.

26 *How many bearer channels are in a BRI? What about a PRI in North America? What about a PRI in Europe?*

BRI uses two bearer channels and one signaling channel (2B+D). PRI uses 23B+D in North America and 30B+D in Europe. The signaling channel on BRI is a 16-kbps channel; on PRI, it is a 64-kbps channel.

27 *True or false: ISDN defines protocols that can be functionally equivalent to OSI Layers 1, 2, and 3. Defend your answer.*

True. Reference points in part define the physical interfaces. Used on the signaling channel, LAPD is a data link protocol. SPIDs define a logical addressing structure and are roughly equivalent to OSI Layer 3. Table 8-26 on page 568 summarizes ISDN protocols as compared with the OSI model.

28 *What reference points are used by ISDN BRI interfaces on Cisco routers?*

A BRI interface with an S/T reference point, or a BRI with a U reference point, can be bought from Cisco. With an S/T interface, an external NT1, NT2, or NT1/NT2 device is required. With the U interface, no external device is required.

29 *What do the letters LAPD represent? Is LAPD used on ISDN channels? If so, which ones?*

Link Access Procedure, D-channel. LAPD is used only on ISDN D channels to deliver signaling messages to the local ISDN switch. Many people don't understand the function of LAPD, thinking it is used on the B channels after the dial is complete. The encapsulation chosen in the router configuration determines the data link protocol on the bearer channels. There is no option on Cisco routers to turn off LAPD on the signaling channel.

30 *Name the standards body that defines ISDN protocols.*

International Telecommunications Union (ITU). This group was formerly the CCITT. The ITU is governed by the United Nations.

31 *What ISDN functions do standards ITU-T Q.920 and Q.930 define? Does either standard correlate to an OSI layer?*

Q.920 defines the ISDN data link specifications, such as LAPD; Q.930 defines Layer 3 functions, such as call setup messages. I.440 and I.450 are equivalent to Q.920 and Q.930, respectively.

32 *What ISDN functions does standard ITU-T I.430 define? Does it correlate to an OSI layer?*

I.430 defines ISDN BRI physical layer specifications. It is similar to OSI Layer 1. There is no Q-series equivalent specification to I.430.

33 *What do the letters SPID represent, and what does the term mean?*

Service profile identifier. This is the ISDN phone number used in signaling.

34 *Define the terms TE1, TE2, and TA. Which term(s) imply that one of the other two must be in use?*

Terminal Equipment 1, Terminal Equipment 2, and terminal adapter. A TE2 device requires a TA. A TE2 uses the R reference point. An S reference point is needed to perform ISDN signaling; it is provided in that case by the TA.

35 *What reference point is used between the customer premise and the phone company in North America? What about in Europe?*

The U interface is used in North America. Elsewhere, the T interface is used. The NT1 function, the dividing point between the T and U reference points, is implemented in telco equipment outside North America.

36 *Define the term SBus, and give one example of when it would be useful.*

SBus is a bus with many devices sharing the S reference point. ISDN-capable phones, faxes, and computers that wish to share the same BRI connect to the same NT1 using an SBus. The SPIDs include subaddresses to distinguish among the multiple devices when using an SBus.

37 *What data link (OSI Layer 2) protocols are valid on an ISDN B channel?*

HDLC, PPP, and LAPB are all valid options. PPP is the preferred choice, however. If using DDR to more than one site, PAP or CHAP authentication is required. If used, PPP must be used. PPP also provides automatic IP address assignment, which is convenient for PC dial-in.

38 *Define the terms PAP and CHAP. Which one(s) send the passwords in clear text format?*

Password Authentication Protocol, Challenge Handshake Authentication Protocol. PAP sends the passwords as simple text, whereas CHAP uses MD5 hashing to protect the password contents.

39 *Define MLPPP. Describe the typical home or small office use of MLPPP.*

Multilink Point-to-Point Protocol. MLPPP is used to treat multiple B channels as a single link because MLPPP fragments packets and sends different fragments across the multiple links to balance the traffic. MLPPP is very useful for sharing two B channels in home or small office use. It is not restricted to home use.

40 *CHAP configuration uses names and passwords. Given Routers A and B, describe what names and passwords must match in the respective CHAP configurations.*

Router A has name B and a corresponding password configured. Router B has name A and the same password configured. The names used are the host names of the routers unless the CHAP name is configured.

41 *Configure ISDN interface BRI1, assuming that it is attached to a DMS-100 ISDN switch, that it uses only one SPID of 404555121201, and that you want to screen calls so that only calls from 404555999901 are accepted.*

```
isdn switch-type basic-dms100
interface bri1
  isdn spid1 404555121201
  isdn caller 404555999901
```

The **switch-type** command is required. The SPID(s) is required only with some switches. The **isdn caller** command is needed only for call screening.

42 *Name the configuration command used to enable FRF.9 compression on a point-to-point Frame Relay subinterface.*

The **frame-relay payload-compress frf9 stac** command enables FRF.9 compression on a Frame Relay subinterface.

43 *List the types of compression that are available on PPP links.*

The STAC, Predictor, and MPPC compression types are available on PPP interfaces in the IOS.

44 *Describe the decision process performed by the IOS to attempt to dial a connection using legacy DDR.*

First, some traffic must be routed out the interface to be dialed; this is typically accomplished by adding static routes pointing out the interface. Then, interesting must be defined; any packets routed out the interface that are considered interesting will cause the interface to be dialed.

45 *If packets from 10.1.1.0/24 were "interesting" in relation to DDR configuration, such that packets from 10.1.1.0/24 caused a DDR connection out an interface BRI0, list the configuration commands that would make the IOS think that those packets were interesting on BRI0.*

The access list that follows defines the packets from 10.1.1.0/24. The **dialer-list** defines the use of **access-list 1** for deciding what is interesting. The **dialer-group** command enables that logic on interface BRI0.

```
access-list 1 permit 10.1.1.0 0.0.0.255
!
dialer-list 2 protocol ip list 1
!
interface bri 0
 dialer-group 2
```

46 *List the typical EIA/TIA standard interfaces used for serial cables with a Cisco router.*

EIA/TIA-232, EIA/TIA-449, and EIA/TIA-530 are typical. V.35 and X.21, which are ITU standards, are also typical. Be careful on the exam—this question asked for EIA/TIA standards, so V.35 and X.21 would not be correct.

47 *What field has Cisco added to the HDLC header, making it proprietary?*

A Protocol Type field has been added to allow support for multiprotocol traffic. HDLC was not architected to allow for multiprotocol support originally.

APPENDIX B

Decimal to Hexadecimal and Binary Conversion Table

Decimal Value	Hexadecimal Value	Binary Value
0	00	0000 0000
1	01	0000 0001
2	02	0000 0010
3	03	0000 0011
4	04	0000 0100
5	05	0000 0101
6	06	0000 0110
7	07	0000 0111
8	08	0000 1000
9	09	0000 1001
10	0A	0000 1010
11	0B	0000 1011
12	0C	0000 1100
13	0D	0000 1101
14	0E	0000 1110
15	0F	0000 1111
16	10	0001 0000
17	11	0001 0001
18	12	0001 0010
19	13	0001 0011
20	14	0001 0100
21	15	0001 0101
22	16	0001 0110
23	17	0001 0111
24	18	0001 1000

continues

Decimal Value	Hexadecimal Value	Binary Value
25	19	0001 1001
26	1A	0001 1010
27	1B	0001 1011
28	1C	0001 1100
29	1D	0001 1101
30	1E	0001 1110
31	1F	0001 1111
32	20	0010 0000
33	21	0010 0001
34	22	0010 0010
35	23	0010 0011
36	24	0010 0100
37	25	0010 0101
38	26	0010 0110
39	27	0010 0111
40	28	0010 1000
41	29	0010 1001
42	2A	0010 1010
43	2B	0010 1011
44	2C	0010 1100
45	2D	0010 1101
46	2E	0010 1110
47	2F	0010 1111
48	30	0011 0000
49	31	0011 0001
50	32	0011 0010
51	33	0011 0011
52	34	0011 0100
53	35	0011 0101
54	36	0011 0110
55	37	0011 0111

Decimal Value	Hexadecimal Value	Binary Value
56	38	0011 1000
57	39	0011 1001
58	3A	0011 1010
59	3B	0011 1011
60	3C	0011 1100
61	3D	0011 1101
62	3E	0011 1110
63	3F	0011 1111
64	40	0100 0000
65	41	0100 0001
66	42	0100 0010
67	43	0100 0011
68	44	0100 0100
69	45	0100 0101
70	46	0100 0110
71	47	0100 0111
72	48	0100 1000
73	49	0100 1001
74	4A	0100 1010
75	4B	0100 1011
76	4C	0100 1100
77	4D	0100 1101
78	4E	0100 1110
79	4F	0100 1111
80	50	0101 0000
81	51	0101 0001
82	52	0101 0010
83	53	0101 0011
84	54	0101 0100
85	55	0101 0101
86	56	0101 0110

continues

Decimal Value	Hexadecimal Value	Binary Value
87	57	0101 0111
88	58	0101 1000
89	59	0101 1001
90	5A	0101 1010
91	5B	0101 1011
92	5C	0101 1100
93	5D	0101 1101
94	5E	0101 1110
95	5F	0101 1111
96	60	0110 0000
97	61	0110 0001
98	62	0110 0010
99	63	0110 0011
100	64	0110 0100
101	65	0110 0101
102	66	0110 0110
103	67	0110 0111
104	68	0110 1000
105	69	0110 1001
106	6A	0110 1010
107	6B	0110 1011
108	6C	0110 1100
109	6D	0110 1101
110	6E	0110 1110
111	6F	0110 1111
112	70	0111 0000
113	71	0111 0001
114	72	0111 0010
115	73	0111 0011
116	74	0111 0100
117	75	0111 0101

Decimal Value	Hexadecimal Value	Binary Value
118	76	0111 0110
119	77	0111 0111
120	78	0111 1000
121	79	0111 1001
122	7A	0111 1010
123	7B	0111 1011
124	7C	0111 1100
125	7D	0111 1101
126	7E	0111 1110
127	7F	0111 1111
128	80	1000 0000
129	81	1000 0001
130	82	1000 0010
131	83	1000 0011
132	84	1000 0100
133	85	1000 0101
134	86	1000 0110
135	87	1000 0111
136	88	1000 1000
137	89	1000 1001
138	8A	1000 1010
139	8B	1000 1011
140	8C	1000 1100
141	8D	1000 1101
142	8E	1000 1110
143	8F	1000 1111
144	90	1001 0000
145	91	1001 0001
146	92	1001 0010
147	93	1001 0011
148	94	1001 0100

continues

Decimal Value	Hexadecimal Value	Binary Value
149	95	1001 0101
150	96	1001 0110
151	97	1001 0111
152	98	1001 1000
153	99	1001 1001
154	9A	1001 1010
155	9B	1001 1011
156	9C	1001 1100
157	9D	1001 1101
158	9E	1001 1110
159	9F	1001 1111
160	A0	1010 0000
161	A1	1010 0001
162	A2	1010 0010
163	A3	1010 0011
164	A4	1010 0100
165	A5	1010 0101
166	A6	1010 0110
167	A7	1010 0111
168	A8	1010 1000
169	A9	1010 1001
170	AA	1010 1010
171	AB	1010 1011
172	AC	1010 1100
173	AD	1010 1101
174	AE	1010 1110
175	AF	1010 1111
176	B0	1011 0000
177	B1	1011 0001
178	B2	1011 0010
179	B3	1011 0011

Decimal Value	Hexadecimal Value	Binary Value
180	B4	1011 0100
181	B5	1011 0101
182	B6	1011 0110
183	B7	1011 0111
184	B8	1011 1000
185	B9	1011 1001
186	BA	1011 1010
187	BB	1011 1011
188	BC	1011 1100
189	BD	1011 1101
190	BE	1011 1110
191	BF	1011 1111
192	C0	1100 0000
193	C1	1100 0001
194	C2	1100 0010
195	C3	1100 0011
196	C4	1100 0100
197	C5	1100 0101
198	C6	1100 0110
199	C7	1100 0111
200	C8	1100 1000
201	C9	1100 1001
202	CA	1100 1010
203	CB	1100 1011
204	CC	1100 1100
205	CD	1100 1101
206	CE	1100 1110
207	CF	1100 1111
208	D0	1101 0000
209	D1	1101 0001
210	D2	1101 0010

continues

Decimal Value	Hexadecimal Value	Binary Value
211	D3	1101 0011
212	D4	1101 0100
213	D5	1101 0101
214	D6	1101 0110
215	D7	1101 0111
216	D8	1101 1000
217	D9	1101 1001
218	DA	1101 1010
219	DB	1101 1011
220	DC	1101 1100
221	DD	1101 1101
222	DE	1101 1110
223	DF	1101 1111
224	E0	1110 0000
225	E1	1110 0001
226	E2	1110 0010
227	E3	1110 0011
228	E4	1110 0100
229	E5	1110 0101
230	E6	1110 0110
231	E7	1110 0111
232	E8	1110 1000
233	E9	1110 1001
234	EA	1110 1010
235	EB	1110 1011
236	EC	1110 1100
237	ED	1110 1101
238	EE	1110 1110
239	EF	1110 1111
240	F0	1111 0000
241	F1	1111 0001

Decimal Value	Hexadecimal Value	Binary Value
242	F2	1111 0010
243	F3	1111 0011
244	F4	1111 0100
245	F5	1111 0101
246	F6	1111 0110
247	F7	1111 0111
248	F8	1111 1000
249	F9	1111 1001
250	FA	1111 1010
251	FB	1111 1011
252	FC	1111 1100
253	FD	1111 1101
254	FE	1111 1110
255	FF	1111 1111

E

I

T

W

X

Y-Z

CCIE Professional Development

Cisco LAN Switching

Kennedy Clark, CCIE; Kevin Hamilton, CCIE

1-57870-094-9 • AVAILABLE NOW

This volume provides an in-depth analysis of Cisco LAN switching technologies, architectures, and deployments, including unique coverage of Catalyst network design essentials. Network designs and configuration examples are incorporated throughout to demonstrate the principles and enable easy translation of the material into practice in production networks.

Advanced IP Network Design

Alvaro Retana, CCIE; Don Slice, CCIE; and Russ White, CCIE

1-57870-097-3 • AVAILABLE NOW

Network engineers and managers can use these case studies, which highlight various network design goals, to explore issues including protocol choice, network stability, and growth. This book also includes theoretical discussion on advanced design topics.

Large-Scale IP Network Solutions

Khalid Raza, CCIE; and Mark Turner

1-57870-084-1 • AVAILABLE NOW

Network engineers can find solutions as their IP networks grow in size and complexity. Examine all the major IP protocols in-depth and learn about scalability, migration planning, network management, and security for large-scale networks.

Routing TCP/IP, Volume I

Jeff Doyle, CCIE

1-57870-041-8 • AVAILABLE NOW

This book takes the reader from a basic understanding of routers and routing protocols through a detailed examination of each of the IP interior routing protocols. Learn techniques for designing networks that maximize the efficiency of the protocol being used. Exercises and review questions provide core study for the CCIE Routing and Switching exam.

www.ciscopress.com

Cisco Career Certifications

CCDA Exam Certification Guide

Anthony Bruno, CCIE & Jacqueline Kim

0-7357-0074-5 • AVAILABLE NOW

CCDA Exam Certification Guide is a comprehensive study tool for DCN Exam #640-441. Written by a CCIE and a CCDA, and reviewed by Cisco technical experts, *CCDA Exam Certification Guide* will help you understand and master the exam objectives. In this solid review on the design areas of the DCN exam, you'll learn to design a network that meets a customer's requirements for performance, security, capacity, and scalability.

Designing Cisco Networks

Edited by Diane Teare

1-57870-105-8 • AVAILABLE NOW

Based on the Cisco Systems instructor-led and self-study course available worldwide, *Designing Cisco Networks* will help you understand how to analyze and solve existing network problems while building a framework that supports the functionality, performance, and scalability required from any given environment. Self-assessment through exercises and chapter-ending tests starts you down the path for attaining your CCDA certification.

Interconnecting Cisco Network Devices

Edited by Steve McQuerry

1-57870-111-2 • AVAILABLE NOW

Based on the Cisco course taught worldwide, *Interconnecting Cisco Network Devices* teaches you how to configure Cisco switches and routers in multiprotocol internetworks. ICND is the primary course recommended by Cisco Systems for CCNA #640-507 preparation. If you are pursuing CCNA certification, this book is an excellent starting point for your study.

Building Cisco Remote Access Networks

Catherine Paquet

1-57870-091-4 • AVAILABLE NOW

Based on the actual Cisco BCRAN course, this book teaches you how to design, configure, maintain, and scale a remote access network using Cisco products. *Building Cisco Remote Access Networks* helps you enable and enhance the on-demand connectivity of a small office, home office, or telecommuter site to a Central site. Prepare for CCNP and CCDP certification while learning the fundamentals of remote access networks.

Cisco Press Solutions

Enhanced IP Services for Cisco Networks
Donald C. Lee, CCIE

1-57870-106-6 • AVAILABLE NOW

This is a guide to improving your network's capabilities by understanding the new enabling and advanced Cisco IOS services that build more scalable, intelligent, and secure networks. Learn the technical details necessary to deploy Quality of Service, VPN technologies, IPsec, the IOS firewall and IOS Intrusion Detection. These services will allow you to extend the network to new frontiers securely, protect your network from attacks, and increase the sophistication of network services.

Developing IP Multicast Networks, Volume I
Beau Williamson, CCIE

1-57870-077-9 • AVAILABLE NOW

This book provides a solid foundation of IP multicast concepts and explains how to design and deploy the networks that will support appplications such as audio and video conferencing, distance-learning, and data replication. Includes an in-depth discussion of the PIM protocol used in Cisco routers and detailed coverage of the rules that control the creation and maintenance of Cisco mroute state entries.

Designing Network Security
Merike Kaeo

1-57870-043-4 • AVAILABLE NOW

Designing Network Security is a practical guide designed to help you understand the fundamentals of securing your corporate infrastructure. This book takes a comprehensive look at underlying security technologies, the process of creating a security policy, and the practical requirements necessary to implement a corporate security policy.

Internetworking Routing Architectures
Bassam Halabi

1-56205-652-2 • AVAILABLE NOW

The BGP Bible! Explore the ins and outs of interdomain routing network designs. Learn to integrate your network into the global Internet, become an expert in data routing manipulation, build large-scale autonomous systems, and configure the required policies using the Cisco IOS language.

CISCO SYSTEMS

CISCO PRESS

www.ciscopress.com

Cisco Press Solutions

EIGRP Network Design Solutions
Ivan Pepelnjak, CCIE
1-57870-165-1 • AVAILABLE NOW

EIGRP Network Design Solutions uses case studies and real-world configuration examples to help you gain an in-depth understanding of the issues involved in designing, deploying, and managing EIGRP-based networks. This book details proper designs that can be used to build large and scalable EIGRP-based networks and documents possible ways each EIGRP feature can be used in network design, implmentation, troubleshooting, and monitoring.

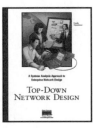

Top-Down Network Design
Priscilla Oppenheimer
1-57870-069-8 • AVAILABLE NOW

Building reliable, secure, and manageable networks is every network professional's goal. This practical guide teaches you a systematic method for network design that can be applied to campus LANs, remote-access networks, WAN links, and large-scale internetworks. Learn how to analyze business and technical requirements, examine traffic flow and Quality of Service requirements, and select protocols and technologies based on performance goals.

Cisco IOS Releases: The Complete Reference
Mack M. Coulibaly
1-57870-179-1 • AVAILABLE NOW

Cisco IOS Releases: The Complete Reference is the first comprehensive guide to the more than three dozen types of Cisco IOS releases being used today on enterprise and service provider networks. It details the release process and its numbering and naming conventions, as well as when, where, and how to use the various releases. A complete map of Cisco IOS software releases and their relationships to one another, in addition to insights into decoding information contained within the software, make this book an indispensable resource for any network professional.

CISCO SYSTEMS

CISCO PRESS

www.ciscopress.com

Cisco Press Solutions

Residential Broadband, Second Edition
George Abe
1-57870-177-5 • AVAILABLE NOW

This book will answer basic questions of residential broadband networks such as: Why do we need high speed networks at home? How will high speed residential services be delivered to the home? How do regulatory or commercial factors affect this technology? Explore such networking topics as xDSL, cable, and wireless.

Internetworking Technologies Handbook, Second Edition
Kevin Downes, CCIE, Merilee Ford, H. Kim Lew, Steve Spanier, Tim Stevenson
1-57870-102-3 • AVAILABLE NOW

This comprehensive reference provides a foundation for understanding and implementing contemporary internetworking technologies, providing you with the necessary information needed to make rational networking decisions. Master terms, concepts, technologies, and devices that are used in the internetworking industry today. You also learn how to incorporate networking technologies into a LAN/WAN environment, as well as how to apply the OSI reference model to categorize protocols, technologies, and devices.

OpenCable Architecture
Michael Adams
1-57870-135-X • AVAILABLE NOW

Whether you're a television, data communications, or telecommunications professional, or simply an interested business person, this book will help you understand the technical and business issues surrounding interactive television services. It will also provide you with an inside look at the combined efforts of the cable, data, and consumer electronics industries' efforts to develop those new services.

Cisco Press Fundamentals

IP Routing Primer
Robert Wright, CCIE
1-57870-108-2 • **AVAILABLE NOW**

Learn how IP routing behaves in a Cisco router environment. In addition to teaching the core fundamentals, this book enhances your ability to troubleshoot IP routing problems yourself, often eliminating the need to call for additional technical support. The information is presented in an approachable, workbook-type format with dozens of detailed illustrations and real-life scenarios integrated throughout.

Cisco Router Configuration
Allan Leinwand, Bruce Pinsky, Mark Culpepper
1-57870-022-1 • **AVAILABLE NOW**

An example-oriented and chronological approach helps you implement and administer your internetworking devices. Starting with the configuration devices "out of the box;" this book moves to configuring Cisco IOS for the three most popular networking protocols today: TCP/IP, AppleTalk, and Novell Interwork Packet Exchange (IPX). You also learn basic administrative and management configuration, including access control with TACACS+ and RADIUS, network management with SNMP, logging of messages, and time control with NTP.

IP Routing Fundamentals
Mark A. Sportack
1-57870-071-x • **AVAILABLE NOW**

This comprehensive guide provides essential background information on routing in IP networks for network professionals who are deploying and maintaining LANs and WANs daily. Explore the mechanics of routers, routing protocols, network interfaces, and operating systems.

For the latest on Cisco Press resources and Certification and

Training guides, or for information on publishing opportunities, visit

www.ciscopress.com

Cisco Press books are available at your local bookstore, computer store, and online booksellers.